Work Engendered

Toward a New History
of American Labor

Edited by

Ava Baron

Cornell University Press

Ithaca and London

First published 1991 by Cornell University Press.
First printing, Cornell Paperbacks, 1991.

International Standard Book Number 0-8014-2256-6 (cloth)
International Standard Book Number 0-8014-9543-1 (paper)
Library of Congress Catalog Card Number 91-2281
Printed in the United States of America
*Librarians: Library of Congress cataloging information
appears on the last page of the book.*

Cornell University Press strives to utilize environmentally responsible suppliers and materials to the fullest extent possible in the publishing of its books. Such materials include vegetable-based, low-VOC inks and acid-free papers that are also either recycled, totally chlorine-free, or partly composed of nonwood fibers.

Cloth printing   10 9 8 7 6 5 4 3 2 1
Paperback printing   10 9 8 7 6 5 4 3

WORK ENGENDERED

FOR NOAH

Contents

Acknowledgments

I am grateful to the contributors for their encouragement in the development of this book. Peter Agree of Cornell University Press believed in this project from the start. I also thank Richard Butsch for his help at every stage. Rider College provided partial support for this work.

A. B.

WORK ENGENDERED

CHAPTER ONE

Gender and Labor History: Learning from the Past, Looking to the Future

Ava Baron

This books brings together essays that look at labor history through the lens of gender. It is not a book about women workers, although women and women's work are central subjects in some of its chapters. Rather, this book shows that gender colors a myriad of relations of power and hierarchy, including those between employers and workers, men and boys, and whites and blacks, as well as those between men and women. Gender is continually reconstituted as various groups politically contest multiple notions of masculinity and femininity.

Building on recent developments in history and theory, these essays suggest new ways to think about and study the history of work and the working class. They examine some of the processes by which the gender constructions of American social institutions were realigned in the nineteenth and twentieth centuries, and show how such constructions shaped the experiences of working-class people within these newly constituted institutions. This volume does not purport to answer or resolve the many questions and dilemmas that confront labor historians and feminist thinkers today. By demonstrating the significance of gender for understanding work, economy, and class, as well as relations between men and women workers, it places the challenge of constructing a gendered labor history before us.

Before we can integrate gender into labor history, we need first to assess the progress already made. Though the new labor historians and women's labor historians have made valuable contributions to this effort, conceptual roadblocks remain.

I am grateful to Mary Blewett, Eileen Boris, Richard Butsch, Dorothy Sue Cobble, Patricia Cooper, Jacquelyn Dowd Hall, Nancy Hewitt, Joan Scott, Philip Scranton, and Elliot Shore for their thoughtful comments and criticisms.

2   *Ava Baron*

Developments in the "New Labor History"

The 1970s was an exciting decade in labor history. Labor history was transformed from the study of labor organizations and their leaders to the study of workers, their work, their communities, and their everyday lives. By the 1980s, however, labor history was in crisis. There have been repeated calls for synthesis of the massive research created by the new labor history.[1] Yet historians have been unable to agree on a new theoretical framework or even on the possibility or desirability of a synthesis.[2]

Until the 1960s American labor historians followed the institutional tradition established by John R. Commons and focused on the labor movement and collective bargaining, producing studies of union leaders, interunion rivalries over jurisdiction, and battles over union organization and power. This research made labor history a legitimate area of inquiry. But the old labor history's focus on formal institutions of power, on male leaders and their organizations, virtually excluded women from consideration.[3]

Influenced by the development of social history and the research of such scholars as E. P. Thompson and Herbert Gutman, labor history shifted from the study of men who held formal positions of power in trade unions to the study of ordinary union members and unorganized workers. Labor history became working-class history, focused on work-

[1] See David Montgomery, "To Study the People: The American Working Class," *Labor History*, 21 (Fall 1980), 485–512; David Brody, "Labor History in the 1970s: Toward a History of the American Worker," in *The Past Before Us: Contemporary Historical Writing in the United States,* ed. Michael Kammen (Ithaca: Cornell University Press, 1980), and "The Old Labor History and the New: In Search of an American Working Class," *Labor History*, 20 (Winter 1979), 123–26; Herbert Gutman, "The Missing Synthesis: Whatever Happened to History?" *The Nation,* Nov. 21, 1981, 521, 553–54; "Interview with Herbert Gutman," *Radical History Review,* 27 (May 1983), 217–18; Ronald W. Schatz, "Labor Historians, Labor Economics, and the Question of Synthesis: Review Essay," *Journal of American History,* 71 (June 1984), 93–100.

[2] On the problems of creating a synthesis, see Alan Dawley, "A Preface to Synthesis," *Labor History,* 29 (Summer 1988), 363–77. In 1984 Northern Illinois University sponsored a conference intended to help produce this synthesis, but the lack of foundation for a new theoretical synthesis became apparent. See Eric Foner, "Labor Historians Seek Useful Past," *In These Times,* Dec. 12–16, 1984, 11; Mari Jo Buhle, "The Future of American Labor History: Toward a Synthesis?" *Radical Historians' Newsletter,* no. 44 (November 1984), 1–2. Essays based on the conference are published in *Perspectives on American Labor History: The Problem of Synthesis,* ed. J. Carroll Moody and Alice Kessler-Harris (De Kalb: Northern Illinois University Press, 1989).

[3] See John R. Commons, *A History of Labor in the United States,* 4 vols. (New York: Macmillan, 1918–1935); Selig Perlman, *A Theory of the Labour Movement* (New York: Macmillan, 1928); Philip Taft, *The A.F. of L. in the Time of Gompers* (New York: Harper & Row, 1957) and *The A.F. of L. from the Death of Gompers to the Merger* (New York: Harper & Row, 1959). The "old" labor history is alternatively known as the institutional approach, the Commons school, and the Wisconsin school.

ers, their work, values, and everyday lives. The community study approach adopted by many new labor historians allowed in-depth exploration of workers' culture, including religion, politics, family, labor associations, and leisure activities.[4] Historians quickly began to realize that if they were to understand the role of culture and community in the making of the American working class, they would have to know how ethnicity shaped working-class experience and influenced labor solidarity. Gutman led the way with his study of the workplace and community cultures of immigrant groups.[5]

Another dimension of the new labor history was its focus on the workplace. In response to Harry Braverman's influential study of the capitalist labor process, labor historians began to explore workers' responses to management's attempts to deskill work. David Montgomery, for example, analyzed workers' resistance at "the point of production," illustrating ways male workers maintained control over production despite management's efforts. Such work provided a valuable corrective to research that emphasized capitalists' control of the labor process by identifying the ways craftworkers fought to maintain their status and privileges. As a result of such research, struggles between workers and capitalists over control of the work process are now seen as part of the way work is transformed.[6]

Recently labor historians have indicated renewed interest in trade unions but from an "un-Commons" perspective. These "new institutionalists," as Philip Scranton has labeled them, combine community-centered analyses with studies of workers' movements, look at unions in the context of a larger political economy and in relation to other institutions, and explore the connections between unions and the legal system, the workplace, and politics.[7]

---

[4]See, e.g., John Bodnar, *Workers' World: Kinship, Community, and Protest in an Industrial Society* (Baltimore: Johns Hopkins University Press, 1982); John Cumbler, *Working Class Community in Industrial America: Work, Leisure, and Struggle in Two Industrial Cities, 1880–1930* (Westport, Conn.: Greenwood, 1979); Alan Dawley, *Class and Community: The Industrial Revolution in Lynn* (Cambridge: Harvard University Press, 1976); Paul Faler, *Mechanics and Manufacturers in the Early Industrial Revolution: Lynn, Massachusetts, 1780–1860* (Albany: SUNY Press, 1981); Daniel Walkowitz, *Worker City, Company Town: Iron and Cotton Worker Protest in Troy and Cohoes, New York, 1855–84* (Urbana: University of Illinois Press, 1978).

[5]Herbert G. Gutman, *Work, Culture, and Society in Industrializing America: Essays in American Working-Class History* (New York: Knopf, 1976). For a discussion of the ways American labor historians have incorporated ethnic history, see Brody, "Labor History of the 1970s," 257–58.

[6]Harry Braverman, *Labor and Monopoly Capital* (New York: Monthly Review Press, 1974); David Montgomery, *Workers' Control in America: Studies in the History of Work, Technology and Labor Struggles* (New York: Cambridge University Press, 1979).

[7]Philip Scranton, "None Too Porous Boundaries: Labor History and the History of Technology," *Technology and Culture*, 29 (October 1988), 722–43. This new approach can be found in, e.g., Brian Greenberg, *Worker and Community: Responses to Industrialization*

The new labor history also opened up possibilities for the study of women workers. It is no coincidence that as the new labor history developed alongside women's history, research on women workers and women's work burgeoned. The new labor history, through its emphasis on workers without formal positions of power and its study of working people within the context of community, encouraged the study of women as family members and as workers and contributed to the development and legitimation of women's labor history as an area of study. Methodological developments in social history (such as quantitative and interdisciplinary studies) and the use of nontraditional sources of evidence (such as folklore and birth, property, and tax records) further facilitated research on women.[8]

Working-class historians' interest in culture and community led to an incorporation of some of the interests of and concepts used by women's historians. Today more working-class historians discuss male workers as family members and the influence of their family responsibilities on their organizations and labor struggles.[9] Women's historians' research on the importance of kin networks for obtaining employment and the significance of an "informal economy" that included boarding and scavenging have been used to good effect in some studies of men's labor history.[10]

Yet as men's working-class historians have applauded the development of women's labor history, accorded respect to its creators, and recognized its valuable insights for and even criticisms of labor history, working-class history has remained a preserve of male workers. New labor historians often still refer to "workers" and "the working class" when they are writing only about male workers.[11] The terms *labor history* and

in a Nineteenth-Century American City, Albany, New York, 1850–1884 (Albany: SUNY Press, 1985); Christopher L. Tomlins, *The State and the Unions: Labor Relations, Law, and the Organized Labor Movement in America, 1880–1960* (New York: Cambridge University Press, 1985); David Montgomery, *The Fall of the House of Labor: The Workplace, the State, and American Labor Activism, 1865–1925* (New York: Cambridge University Press, 1987); Leon Fink, *Workingmen's Democracy: The Knights of Labor and American Politics* (Urbana: University of Illinois Press, 1983).

[8] For a discussion of some of the ways women's history benefited from the insights of E. P. Thompson and Herbert Gutman, see Mari Jo Buhle, "Recent Contributions to Women's History," *Radical History Review*, 11 (1975), 4–11.

[9] See, e.g., Bodnar, *Workers' World*; Greenberg, *Worker and Community*.

[10] On kinship and ethnic ties as a means of occupational entry, see, e.g., Bodnar, *Workers' World*; on the importance of an informal economy, see, e.g., James Barrett, *Work and Community in the Jungle: Chicago's Packinghouse Workers, 1894–1922* (Urbana: University of Illinois Press, 1987).

[11] This tendency is pervasive in labor history. I am providing a few examples but do not mean to single them out as unusual. See David Bensman, *The Practice of Solidarity; American Hat Finishers in the Nineteenth Century* (Urbana: University of Illinois Press, 1985); Richard Oestreicher, "Urban Working Class Political Behavior and Theories of American Electoral Politics, 1870–1940," *Journal of American History*, 74 (March 1988), 1257–86,

working-class history typically refer to the history of workingmen and their work. The dangers of synthesizing a history that has yet to integrate gender fully are clear. The periodization used by labor historians to study the working class, for example, relies on male experience and changes in men's status despite women's historians' persuasive arguments that traditional periodization has been gender-biased.[12] David Montgomery, for instance, in his work on the American working class during the 1920s, bases his periodization on a series of androcentric assumptions: he focuses on militancy in industries dominated by male workers and on participation in trade unions rather than on forms of labor activism in which women were more likely to have been involved. As Susan Benson has pointed out, his analysis would look different had he taken gender into account and explored how women's experiences differed from men's.[13]

and his *Solidarity and Fragmentation: Working People and Class Consciousness in Detroit, 1875–1900* (Urbana: University of Illinois Press, 1986); Brian Greenberg, "Worker and Community: Fraternal Orders in Albany, New York, 1845–1885," in *Life and Labor: Dimensions of American Working-Class History,* ed. Robert Asher and Charles Stephenson, 57–71 (Albany: SUNY Press, 1986); Michael Kazin, *Barons of Labor: The San Francisco Building Trades and Union Power in the Progressive Era* (Urbana: University of Illinois Press, 1987); and John Cumbler, "Migration, Class Formation, and Class Consciousness: The American Experience," in *Confrontation, Class Consciousness, and the Labor Process: Studies in Proletarian Class Formation,* ed. Michael Hanagan and Charles Stephenson, 39–64 (Westport, Conn.: Greenwood, 1986).

For the most part historians have written discrete histories of male and female workers. Some notable exceptions are Mary H. Blewett, *Men, Women, and Work: A Study of Class, Gender, and Protest in the Nineteenth-Century New England Shoe Industry* (Urbana: University of Illinois Press, 1988); Patricia Cooper, *Once a Cigar Maker: Men, Women, and Work Culture in American Cigar Factories, 1900–1919* (Urbana: University of Illinois Press, 1987); Edwin Gabler, *The American Telegrapher: A Social History, 1860–1900* (New Brunswick: Rutgers University Press, 1988); and Cindy Sondik Aron, *Ladies and Gentlemen of the Civil Service: Middle-Class Workers in Victorian America* (New York: Oxford University Press, 1987).

[12]The Renaissance and the American Revolution have been designated as periods that represented positive developments in Western history, yet at neither time did women's status or liberties improve. See Joan Kelly, "Did Women Have a Renaissance?" in *Becoming Visible: Women in European History,* ed. Renate Bridenthal and Claudia Koonz, 139–64 (Boston: Houghton Mifflin, 1977); and Linda Kerber, *Women of the Republic: Intellect and Ideology in Revolutionary America* (Chapel Hill: University of North Carolina Press, 1980).

[13]David Montgomery, "Thinking about American Workers in the 1920s," *International Labor and Working-Class History,* 32 (Fall 1987), 4–24; Susan Porter Benson, "Response," ibid., 31–38. Research on the significance of outwork during industrialization indicates that a gendered perspective can lead to different periodization of economic development. See Blewett, *Men, Women, and Work;* Christine Stansell, "The Origins of the Sweatshop: Women and Early Industrialization in New York City," in *Working-Class America: Essays on Labor, Community, and American Society,* ed. Michael M. Frisch and Daniel J. Walkowitz, 78–103, (Urbana: University of Illinois Press, 1983); Thomas Dublin, "Woman and Outwork in a Nineteenth-Century New Hampshire Town: Fitzwilliam, New Hampshire, 1830–1850," in *The Countryside in the Age of Capitalist Transformation: Essays in the Social History of Rural America,* ed. Jonathan Prude and Steven Hahn, 51–70 (Chapel Hill: University of North Carolina Press, 1985).

"Women's labor history" is the particular, the special, that which is different. Women's labor history thus remains segregated and ghettoized, with minimal impact on most studies of the working class.[14] Because working-class historians often subsume women's experience under men's, gender conflicts and power differences between men and women within the family and community tend to be invisible.[15] The family and community remain sexually undifferentiated. John Bodnar, for example, writes about the significance of family priorities and goals, but his vision of intrafamily conflict is limited to intergenerational friction; he gives little attention to possible gender antagonism.[16] In men's labor historiography the home remains a "haven" from the world of production; typically neither the oppression of women nor their unpaid labor receives attention or analysis.

Yet since men and women were differently situated in the family, the workplace, and the community, their experiences of these institutions may have diverged. Women's historians, Carroll Smith-Rosenberg explains, "insisted that women and men experienced, used, and conceived of the family, religion, work, and public and private space differently. The factory imposed distinctive burdens and offered divergent opportunities for women and for men."[17]

Indeed, feminist historians have shown that women's and men's experiences may not simply have diverged, they may even have been in conflict.[18] "Experience of class," Sally Alexander emphasized, "even if

[14]Feminists in various disciplines have begun to realize that feminist scholarship is not yielding the paradigmatic changes that many expected. See Judith Stacey and Barrie Thorne, "The Missing Feminist Revolution in Sociology," *Social Problems*, 32 (April 1985), 301–16; Nancy Hartsock, "The Feminist Standpoint: Developing the Ground for a Specifically Feminist Historical Materialism," in *Discovering Reality*, ed. Sandra Harding and Merrill B. Hintikka, 283–310, (London: Reidel, 1983); Helen Roberts, "Some of the Boys Won't Play Any More: The Impact of Feminism on Sociology," in *Men's Studies Modified: The Impact of Feminism on the Academic Disciplines*, ed. Dale Spender, 73–82 (New York: Pergamon, 1981). For a discussion of how feminist scholarship has both challenged and been shaped by traditional disciplines, see Ellen DuBois, Gail Paradise Kelly, Elizabeth Lapovsky Kennedy, Carolyn W. Korsmeyer, and Lillian S. Robinson, *Feminist Scholarship: Kindling in the Groves of Academe* (Urbana: University of Illinois Press, 1985).

[15]For a discussion of this point, see Blewett's Introduction to *Men, Women, and Work*, xiii–xxii. Herbert Gutman's well-documented and insightful research into immigrant and black work and family life, which justifiably earned him the designation of "father" of the new labor history, conflated working-class culture, community, and family with the experience of male workers. See Susan Levine, "Class and Gender: Herbert Gutman and the Women of 'Shoe City,' " *Labor History*, 29 (Summer 1988), 348.

[16]Bodnar, *Workers' World*.

[17]Carroll Smith-Rosenberg, "Hearing Women's Words: A Feminist Reconstruction of History," in her *Disorderly Conduct: Visions of Gender in Victorian America* (New York: Knopf, 1985), 18.

[18]Such was the case, for example, of men and women on the overland trail. See John Faragher and Christine Stansell, "Women and Their Families on the Overland Trail, 1842–1867," *Feminist Studies*, 2 (1975), 150–66.

shared and fully recognized, does not, as Thompson and others have suggested, produce a shared and even consciousness."[19] The meanings of working-class consciousness and culture incorporated in the new labor history have obscured the specificity of women's experiences, and therefore of men's. Thus while men's labor historians have explored the ethnic and racial diversity of working-class culture, they have tended to ignore differences consequent upon sex.

Not surprisingly, then, such topics as the sexual division of waged and unwaged labor have been left to women's historians. Susan Levine's review of historical research on shoe workers shows that most studies of the "shoe city" of Lynn have treated women as of only marginal significance. Only Mary Blewett explores women's role in depth. Blewett's research shows that market forces during early industrialization invaded the artisan family and that women became crucial to shoe work and labor protest throughout the nineteenth century. Furthermore, men and women shoe workers constantly debated the meanings of womanhood as an issue central to their labor politics and activism.[20]

Women's marginality in working-class history results from the conceptual categories employed and from assumptions about women workers as women and as workers. The conventional wisdom in labor history has been that women's primary roles were as wives, mothers, and daughters; male workers, by contrast, have been examined primarily as workers, not as husbands, fathers, and sons. Labor historians often assume that unlike men, women were transient members of the labor force, that women's family life, rather than their work experience, had the major impact on their behavior and consciousness, and that women's family role served as a conservative force on their behavior.[21]

A basic article of faith in working-class history has been that workers are historical agents. The new labor historiography has shown how male workers shaped their work, or at least actively resisted capitalists' power. Much of male workers' behavior at the workplace has been conceptualized as resistance and struggle to preserve control over their jobs and an autonomous craft culture. In developing these themes, men's labor histo-

[19]Sally Alexander, "Women, Class, and Sexual Difference," *History Workshop*, 17 (Autumn 1984), 131.

[20]Levine, "Class and Gender," 344–55; Blewett, *Men, Women, and Work.*

[21]Despite documentation of the inaccuracies of these assumptions, Eric Hobsbawm, for example, argued that women's consciousness resulted not from their work experiences, as men's did; but from their duties as wives and mothers. See his "Man and Woman in Socialist Iconography," *History Workshop*, 6 (1978), 121–38; but see the response by Sally Alexander, Anna Davin, and Eve Hostettler, "Labouring Women: A Reply to Eric Hobsbawm," *History Workshop*, 8 (Autumn 1979), 174–82. For an analysis of the overwhelmingly male language of work culture literature, see Alice Kessler-Harris, "Gender Ideology in Historical Reconstruction: A Case Study from the 1930s," *Gender and History*, 1 (Spring 1989), esp. 31–37.

rians often treat strikes and union activism as the quintessential form of worker resistance.[22] According to the resulting literature, union participation and femininity have been defined as antithetical; union participation has represented skill, economic independence, and commitment to work, while femininity has symbolized the lack of these characteristics.[23] Since trade unionism is often used as a measure of class consciousness, women's relatively low union participation has been considered evidence of their docility, apathy, and acquiescence in exploitation by employers. Such an approach not only underplayed women's labor activism, it also failed to explain why male workers sometimes participated in reproducing class relations that operated to subordinate them.[24]

The systematic nature of such biases and gaps in our understanding of the world of work signals the need to rethink existing concepts and frameworks before gender can be integrated into working-class history. Such an endeavor requires us to uncover the many ways in which gender has shaped the work process, the wage form, workplace conflicts, and class relations, as well as relations between men and women in the family, the community, the union, and the factory and office. It also requires us to explore what and when gender differences became significant for various racial and ethnic groups, and why identification of specific gender differences developed and changed.

Scholarship guided by this agenda is still in its infancy. Recent research in women's labor history has started to move beyond an "add women and stir" formula.[25] Studies of women and work have begun to discover the role gender plays in shaping work and people's experiences of it. But knowing that gender matters tells us little about how gender is developed and transformed and how gender operates in society. While more working-class historians now include some reference to women in their studies, most working-class histories continue to fall into the category of "sexless class."[26] As Marjorie Murphy put it, "gender analysis is seen as

[22]See, e.g., Montgomery, *Workers' Control in America* and *Fall of the House of Labor*; Stephen Meyer, "Technology and the Workplace: Skilled and Production Workers at Allis-Chalmers, 1900–1941," *Technology and Culture*, 29 (October 1988), 839–64; Dawley, *Class and Community*. For a critique of labor historians' preoccupation with evidence of class struggle and resistance, see Michael Kazin, "Struggling with the Class Struggle: Marxism and the Search for a Synthesis of U.S. Labor History," *Labor History*, 28 (Fall 1987), 497–514.

[23]Alexander, "Women, Class, and Sexual Difference," 145.

[24]On workers' cooperation in reproducing class relations at the workplace, see Michael Burawoy, *Manufacturing Consent: Changes in the Labor Process under Monopoly Capitalism* (Chicago: University of Chicago Press, 1979).

[25]See, e.g., Susan B. Reverby and Dorothy O. Helly, eds., *Beyond the Public and Private Dichotomy* (Ithaca: Cornell University Press, forthcoming).

[26]For a pertinent discussion of Canadian working-class history, see Bettina Bradbury, "Women's History and Working Class History," *Labour/Le Travail*, 19 (Spring 1987), 23–43.

an alternative to rather than an augmentation of class analysis."[27] What we need is not only augmentation but a recognition of the significance of gender for men's labor history. Women's labor history already has begun to develop answers and perspectives to meet this challenge.

Developments in Women's Labor History

Initial efforts in women's labor history, like women's history generally, began as what Gerda Lerner called "compensatory" or "contribution" history.[28] Motivated by the invisibility of women in existing studies, women's labor historians documented women's presence in paid production and their significant contributions to labor movements.

Some years ago Alice Kessler-Harris asked, "Where are the organized women workers?" and feminist researchers took up the question with energy.[29] They examined the conditions that facilitated or hindered women's labor force participation, such as cultural definitions of women's "proper place," family economic needs, and the availability of jobs for women within a community or time period. They discovered that women participated in unions and engaged in collective and at times militant labor activity, but that often women's efforts were stymied by the discriminatory tactics of a male-dominated labor movement.[30]

Women's labor historians provided important correctives to male-centered history by exploring topics related to women and women's concerns which had typically been ignored or demeaned. But women's labor historians' defense against the ways women had been treated by investigators of male workers too often allowed men's labor historians to shape the research agenda for the field as a whole. The focus, that is, was on showing that women were important in terms of the male model of his-

[27]Marjorie Murphy, "What Women Have Wrought: Review Essay," *American Historical Review*, 93 (June 1988), 654.

[28]Gerda Lerner, "Placing Women in History: Definitions and Challenges," *Feminist Studies*, 3 (Fall 1975), 5–14.

[29]Alice Kessler-Harris, "Where Are the Organized Women Workers?" *Feminist Studies*, 3 (Fall 1975), 92–110. On women's labor activism see Barbara Mayer Wertheimer, *We Were There: The Study of Working Women in America* (New York: Pantheon, 1977); Alice Kessler-Harris, *Out to Work: A History of Wage-Earning Women in the United States* (New York: Oxford University Press, 1982); Sharon Strom, "Challenging 'Woman's Place': Feminism, the Left, and Industrial Unionism in the 1930s," *Feminist Studies*, 9 (Summer 1983), 359–86; Ruth Milkman, ed., *Women, Work, and Protest: A Century of Women's Labor History* (Boston and London: Routledge & Kegan Paul, 1985).

[30]On the conditions affecting women's participation in the labor force, see, e.g., Tamara Hareven, "The Laborers of Manchester, New Hampshire, 1919–1922: The Role of Family and Ethnicity in Adjustment to Industrial Life," *Labor History*, 16 (Spring 1975), 249–65; Leslie Woodcock Tentler, *Wage-Earning Women: Industrial Work and Family Life in the United States, 1900–1930* (New York: Oxford University Press, 1979). On women's labor activism, see, e.g., essays in Milkman, *Women, Work, and Protest*.

tory. Most labor historians took for granted men's participation in the labor force. Beginning with the conception of men's and women's separate spheres of paid work and domesticity, men's labor historians assumed that men worked and women did not. Women's labor historians added women to labor history by demonstrating that women, like men, were present in the public sphere, worked for wages, and were active in labor struggles. The nature of women's work and the sexual division of labor were the starting points for analysis. While research on male workers emphasized men's role in creating or at least shaping the organization and definition of work, research on women focused on their adjustment to the existing job structure. Only recently have women's labor historians begun to examine the effects of changes in the labor process on women's work in paid production, how they exercised control over their work, and their relations with other workers and with employers. And only much more recently have men's labor historians begun to question whether men's labor force participation should be taken for granted.[31]

Women's labor historians, like feminist scholars more generally, have criticized existing scholarship for using the male norm as the universal standard. Women's labor historians have emphasized different questions and used different analytical frameworks and categories than those used to study men. One of the first fruits of this approach among women's historians generally was the documentation of a distinct "woman's culture" and "consciousness," indicating "a set of habits, values, practices, institutions, and way of seeing the world" which was based on cooperation and familialism rather than on competition and individualism.[32] Building on this discovery, women's labor historians explored the nature of working-class women's consciousness and the differences between women's and men's work culture and militancy. The specific character of women's work culture, family networks, and work relations helped to explain women's behavior, their militance and collective action, including their participation in strikes and food riots.[33]

[31]The various approaches to women's history overlap temporally.
[32]DuBois et al., *Feminist Scholarship,* 56. Temma Kaplan, e.g., sharply distinguishes between female and male consciousness in "Female Consciousness and Collective Action: The Case of Barcelona, 1910–1918," *Signs,* 7 (Spring 1982), 545–66. She found that women's consciousness in early-twentieth-century Spain was oriented toward preserving life and placing human need above property and profit. For a critique of the woman's culture approach, see Susan Levine, "Labors in the Field: Reviewing Women's Cultural History," *Radical History Review,* 35 (April 1986), 49–56.
[33]On women's work culture, see Barbara Melosh, *The Physician's Hand: Work Culture and Conflict in American Nursing* (Philadelphia: Temple University Press, 1982); Susan Porter Benson, *Counter Cultures: Saleswomen, Managers, and Customers in American Department Stores, 1890–1940* (Urbana: University of Illinois Press, 1986); Cooper, *Once a Cigar Maker;* Priscilla Long, "The Women of the Colorado Fuel and Iron Strike, 1913–

Whereas women's labor historians initially downplayed differences between men and women, later many began to consider sex differences as crucial. The study of women's culture both converged with and challenged analyses of workers' culture. Gutman and other working-class historians had demonstrated that forms of worker resistance other than participation in labor unions were possible and important to consider. This was a valuable insight, since trade unionism typically has involved a relatively small proportion of the American labor force. It also was important for revising conventional views of women's role in class struggles. Women workers, like men, adopted styles of organization and forms of resistance that fitted their needs, work schedules, and work cultures. Craft traditions and artisan pride were no longer considered the sole requisites for labor militance among male or female workers. Women's labor historians documented the ways in which female workers developed and used their own networks to get jobs, to learn skills, and to circumvent partriarchal supervisory rules. Women's informal socializing at work and in the community helped to forge solidarity and formed the basis for collective identity and labor militancy. In nineteenth-century Lowell, for example, single women textile workers developed nonartisan sources of militance at work and in the boardinghouses and protested low wages, long hours, and oppressive work rules.[34] More than a century later, in apparel plants in Rhode Island, activities such as birthday celebrations, wedding showers, and Christmas and retirement parties helped women workers to overcome age and ethnic divisions, contributed to building a communications network, and were key factors in women's resistance to management's manipulation of the piece-rate system.[35]

14," in Milkman, *Women, Work, and Protest,* 62–85; Susan Lebsock, *The Free Women of Petersburg: Status and Culture in a Southern Town, 1784–1860* (New York: Norton, 1984). On women's role in food riots, see Kaplan, "Female Consciousness and Collective Action"; and Dana Frank, "Housewives, Socialists, and the Politics of Food: The New York Cost-of-Living Protests," *Feminist Studies,* 11 (Summer 1985), 255–85; see also her essay in this volume.

[34] Thomas Dublin, *Women at Work: The Transformation of Work and Community in Lowell, Massachusetts, 1826–1860* (New York: Columbia University Press, 1979).

[35] Louise Lamphere, "Bringing the Family to Work: Women's Culture on the Shop Floor," *Feminist Studies,* 11 (Fall 1985), 519–540. Lamphere's research makes it clear, however, that women's culture may also be co-opted by management under other circumstances. On how family issues can shape women's resistance in the workplace, see Karen Sacks, "Computers, Ward Secretaries, and a Walkout in a Southern Hospital," in *My Troubles Are Going to Have Trouble with Me: Everyday Trials and Triumphs of Women Workers,* ed. Karen Brodkin Sacks and Dorothy Remy, 173–92, (New Brunswick, N.J.: Rutgers University Press, 1984). Louise Tilly's research suggests that women engaged in various forms of resistance, and that the types of household and production process were associated with levels and types of involvement in labor organizations. See her "Paths of Proletarianization: Organization of Production, Sexual Division of Labor, and Women's Collective Action," *Signs,* 7 (Winter 1981), 400–417.

Rather than view women workers as passive victims of capitalism, patriarchy, or woman's own nature, researchers on women's labor activism reconceptualized them as active agents in shaping their work lives. Once feminist historians discovered the existence of a distinct woman's culture, a separate world of homosocial bonds and autonomous women's networks, the version of woman as victim throughout history began to erode. Women did not passively and uncritically accept the "cult of domesticity" or capitalist labor relations. Feminist scholars showed how women, oppressed or not, used their networks and their culture to control their own lives and to shape the development of their societies.[36] Female slaves and industrial workers, previously studied in terms of their economic and social victimization, now were shown protesting and fighting to protect their rights and dignity.[37]

Many women's labor historians adopted a model of separate spheres which assumed that women's domestic values shaped their relation to work. Women's labor historians, like students of work generally, used different models to study male and female members of the working class. Those who researched male workers continued to employ a "job model," which focused on work as the primary factor explaining workers' behavior on and off the job. Those who studied women more typically used a "gender model," which focused on family circumstances to explain workers' relation to employment.[38]

Many studies of female work patterns concluded that a family's economic needs, along with ethnic definitions of woman's "proper place," determined whether a woman worked, the type of work she did, and how long she remained employed.[39] Joan Scott and Louise Tilly, for ex-

[36]E.g., Carroll Smith-Rosenberg, "The Female World of Love and Ritual: Relations between Women in Nineteenth-Century America," in her *Disorderly Conduct*, 53–75; Nancy Cott, *The Bonds of Womanhood: "Woman's Sphere" in New England, 1780–1835* (New Haven: Yale University Press, 1977); Mary P. Ryan, "The Power of Women's Networks: A Case Study of Female Moral Reform in America," *Feminist Studies*, 4 (Spring 1979), 66–86.

[37]For a discussion of the debate among women's historians regarding women's culture and the question of women's victimization vs. agency, see DuBois et al., *Feminist Scholarship*, 48–58.

[38]On the difference between gender and job models used by sociologists to study men, women, and work, see Roslyn Feldberg and Evelyn Glenn, "Male and Female: Job versus Gender Models in the Sociology of Work," *Social Problems*, 26 (June 1979), 524–38.

[39]Mary Beth Norton, "American History: Review Essay," *Signs*, 5 (Winter 1979), 328. On how family circumstances, ethnicity, and race influenced women's work patterns, see, e.g., Tamara Harevan, *Family Time and Industrial Time: The Relationship between the Family and Work in a New England Industrial Community* (New York: Cambridge University Press, 1981); Virginia Yans-McLaughlin, "Italian Women and Work: Experience and Perception," in *Class, Sex, and the Woman Worker*, ed. Milton Cantor and Bruce Laurie, 101–19 (Westport, Conn.: Greenwood, 1977); Beverly W. Jones, "Race, Sex, and Class: Black Female Tobacco Workers in Durham, North Carolina, 1920–1940, and the Development of Female Consciousness," *Feminist Studies*, 10 (Fall 1984), 441–51; Carole

ample, suggested that women moved back and forth between domestic and paid labor in response to family needs; Winifred Wandersee argued that women's short-term participation in paid employment and their low rate of unionization reflected women's commitment to family values rather than a search for self-realization.[40] Similarly, research on women's work culture and forms of labor militance has also emphasized women's domestic values.[41]

The studies of women's culture and consciousness dispelled many myths about women's passivity and uncovered the significance of women's forms of activism and militancy. Though this work left men's labor history largely untouched, it offered new questions and problems for future research, inching men's labor historians toward a more inclusive working-class history. Let us consider the implications of women's labor history for work being undertaken simultaneously by men's labor historians.

How, for example, can women's history modify the return to the study of labor organizations and leaders? Unless the new institutionalism is accompanied by a reconceptualization of labor activism, women workers will once again be hidden from history. Women's labor historians have provided much-needed information about women's participation in male-controlled unions, women's efforts to develop their own models of resistance, and the conflict between feminism and unionism.[42] A gendered labor history takes these issues further by exploring the ways in which gender bias is structured into the fabric of unionism. Rather than ask: Why have women been difficult to organize? it asks: What assumptions about gender have been structured into unions? How does union organization serve to recreate or challenge gender hierarchies? How has gender operated to define union issues in ways that make them irrelevant to women's concerns?

Shammas, "Black Women's Work and the Evolution of Plantation Society in Virginia," *Labor History*, 26 (Winter 1985), 5–28; Julia Kirk Blackwelder, "Women in the Workforce: Atlanta, New Orleans, and San Antonio, 1930 to 1940," *Journal of Urban History*, 4 (1977–78), 331–58; Barbara Klaczynska, "Why Women Work: A Comparison of Various Groups in Philadelphia, 1910 to 1940," *Labor History*, 17 (Winter 1976), 73–87; D. Harland Hagler, "The Ideal Woman in the Antebellum South: Lady or Farmwife," *Journal of Southern History*, 46 (August 1980), 405–18.

[40]Joan Scott and Louise Tilly, *Women, Work, and Family* (New York: Holt, Rinehart & Winston, 1978); Winifred D. Wandersee, *Women's Work and Family Values, 1920–1940* (Cambridge: Harvard University Press, 1981); also see Tentler, *Wage-Earning Women*.

[41]For a discussion and critique of this approach, see Kessler-Harris, "Gender Ideology in Historical Reconstruction."

[42]See, e.g., Nancy Schrom Dye, *As Equals and as Sisters: Feminism, Unionism, and the Women's Trade Union League of New York* (Columbia: University of Missouri Press, 1980); Meredith Tax, *The Rising of the Women: Feminist Solidarity and Class Conflict, 1880–1917* (New York: Monthly Review Press, 1980); Tilly, "Paths of Proletarianization"; Strom, "Challenging 'Woman's Place' "; Milkman, *Women, Work, and Protest*.

Women's labor history offers new insights into issues of skill as well. Men's working-class historians have equated skill with militance and have paid much more attention to skilled workers and their craft traditions than to unskilled workers who lacked an artisan heritage.[43] Since women were less likely to be found in artisan trades, women were less visible in working-class history. In turning their attention to those trades that lacked an artisan heritage—specifically trades, or aspects of trades, in which women worked—they have discovered that labor militance may be found among the unskilled and semiskilled as well as among the "labor aristocracy" and that organizing and militancy are not male preserves.[44]

Research on male workers often has ignored the role gender played in defining work as skilled.[45] But, as feminists have argued, the concept of skill itself is gender-bound. Abilities that women acquire informally in the home or in such "women's jobs" as sewing and typing often are defined as unskilled and go unrewarded by promotion or wages. Further, skill labels gave male workers leverage both as men and as workers. The craftworker's belief that skill was linked to manhood influenced the form and content of class conflicts and relations between male and female workers. Confrontations between capital and skilled male workers over the labor process took place on a gendered terrain, and strategies of male unionists and capitalists incorporated concepts of gender.[46]

[43]For a discussion of these points, see Jacques Rancière, "The Myth of the Artisan: Critical Reflections on a Category of Social History," *International Labor and Working-Class History*, 24 (Fall 1983), 1–27, and responses in ibid., 25 (Spring 1984), 37–46. For examples of research on artisans, see "The Skilled Worker and Working-Class Protest," special issue of *Social Science History*, 6 (Winter 1980). For a review of some of the major works on artisans, see Sean Wilentz, "Artisan Origins of the American Working Class," *International Labor and Working Class History*, 19 (Spring 1981), 1–22.

[44]On women in the needle trades, see Joan Jensen and Sue Davidson, eds., *A Needle, a Bobbin, a Strike: Women Needleworkers in America* (Philadelphia: Temple University Press, 1984); on women cigar workers see Cooper, *Once a Cigar Maker*; on women textile workers, Dublin, *Women at Work*; on assembly-line operatives in canneries, Vicki L. Ruiz, *Cannery Women, Cannery Lives: Mexican Women, Unionization, and the California Food Processing Industry, 1930–1950* (Albuquerque: University of New Mexico Press, 1987).

[45]Isaac Cohen, e.g., ignores the role of gender in his comparative analysis of British and American mule spinners' efforts to retain control over production despite introduction of new machinery. See his "Workers' Control in the Cotton Industry: A Comparative Study of British and American Mule Spinning," *Labor History*, 26 (Winter 1985), 53–85. Other examples are Walter Licht, *Working for the Railroad: The Organization of Work in the Nineteenth Century* (Princeton: Princeton University Press, 1983); Kazin, *Barons of Labor*; Bensman, *The Practice of Solidarity*.

[46]See Anne Phillips and Barbara Taylor, "Sex and Skill: Notes toward a Feminist Economics," *Feminist Review*, 6 (October 1980), 79–88; Ava Baron, "Contested Terrain Revisited: Technology and Gender Definitions of Work in the Printing Industry, 1850–1920," in *Women, Work, and Technology: Transformations*, ed. Barbara Wright et al., 58–83 (Ann Arbor: University of Michigan Press, 1987).

As a corollary, historians have tended to equate working-class men with the permanently employed and working-class women with transient laborers who worked only until they married or after they were divorced or widowed. Little attention has been given to the variability in male workers' participation in production and the large numbers of workers who periodically faced layoff and seasonal unemployment. Transience has been treated instead as a gender condition. Women's low level of union participation has been assumed to result from their impermanence in the labor force.[47]

At the same time, working-class activities related to reproduction and consumption have been given relatively little attention in studies of the working class. Even research on workers' participation in boycotts typically has treated it as an aspect of production rather than exploring the significance of women's role as consumer.[48] As Jeanne Boydston has noted, men's labor historians' overattention to the market economy and to paid labor is based on the assumption "that the working class bought its entire subsistence on the market, with cash."[49] But working-class families often depended on nonmarket resources, and on the labor of women and children within the household. Various forms of casual labor, including peddling, scavenging, and prostitution, were central to a working-class family's subsistence.

Because men's working-class historians have maintained a gender-blind theory of class relations, questions of sexual divisions and difference have been treated as subsidiary to the really important questions of class. Of major concern in men's labor history is working-class solidarity. From this vantage point, class divisions by race, ethnicity, and gender become problems to be analyzed and explained. In particular, women's "difference" is considered a limitation or deterrent to class action, interests, and unity. Thus David Montgomery treats women workers as yet another lever capitalists have used to divide the working class. He conceives of manliness as a particular type of class weapon, but does not

[47]For a discussion of this point, see Carole Turbin, "Reconceptualizing Family, Work, and Labor Organizing: Working Women in Troy, 1860–1890," *Review of Radical Political Economics,* 16 (Spring 1984), 1–16. For an exception, see Alexander Keyssar, *Out of Work: The First Century of Unemployment in Massachusetts* (New York: Cambridge University Press, 1986).

[48]E.g., Michael Gordon gives only passing mention to women's role in boycotts: "The Labor Boycott in New York City, 1880–1886," in *American Working Class: Explorations in American Labor and Social History,* ed. Milton Cantor, 287–332 (Westport, Conn.: Greenwood, 1979). Dana Frank, however, has demonstrated the power of housewives to force down food prices through their community-based boycotts: "Housewives, Socialists, and the Politics of Food"; see also her essay in this volume.

[49]Jeanne Boydston, "To Earn Her Daily Bread: Housework and Antebellum Working-Class Subsistence," *Radical History Review,* 35 (April 1986), 7–25.

treat gender as central to understanding working-class experience.[50] As Sally Alexander has explained, "Whether posited as objects of analysis, or included as part of the narrative, [women] can be present in marxist—and most labor—history, only as digressions from the real subject of history—class struggle; and their theoretical status is subservient to the study of modes of production."[51]

Conceptualizing Gender and Work

Clearly, the rich research in women's labor history provides valuable material and insights for constructing a gendered labor history. But a new direction in labor history appears to require more than a synthesis of existing research. Women's and men's labor historians have now exposed several critical conceptual problems and questions as well as numerous dead ends that force us to search for a new theoretical approach. Four problems stand out, however, as roadblocks to further progress.

First, women's labor history has remained ghettoized and segregated from men's labor history. To overcome this problem historians need to consider how the conceptual frameworks they use contribute to or alleviate the problem.[52] Second, despite numerous studies documenting the significance of gender at work, how and why sexual differences between men and women affect wages, job status, and class struggles remain unexplained. If gender is conceptualized simply as two categories of contradictory interests, it has little explanatory power. Third, while women's "resistance" has been documented, their "consent" to oppression, like that of men, remains undertheorized. This problem is part of the larger question of how to define the interplay between men's and women's gender and class interests and requires an examination of the construction of both feminine and masculine subjectivities alongside the development of class consciousness. Fourth, the emphasis on common gender interests of all women has left underdeveloped our understanding of differences and conflicts among women. Research on class, race, and ethnic diversity among women, for example, has uncovered the complexity of issues involved but it has provided no theory to explain the processes at work.

Poststructuralism has captured the attention of some women's labor historians because it speaks to the very issues that remain unresolved by existing approaches, offering ways to think about the challenges labor

[50]Montgomery, *Fall of the House of Labor.*
[51]Alexander, "Women, Class, and Sexual Difference," 127.
[52]On the dual problem of the overintegration of women's history into social history and its exclusion, see Joan Wallach Scott, "Women's History," in her *Gender and the Politics of History,* 16–27 (New York: Columbia University Press, 1988).

historians now confront: issues of subjectivity and identity, the categories of both "woman" and "women," the meanings and constructions of sexual difference, and ways to think about gender and its place in historical analysis.[53] This does not mean that poststructuralism offers the solution for transcending the problems that have long plagued feminists.[54] The key to developing a gendered labor history at this stage may be to maintain an open mind, to adopt those approaches we find useful, to adapt others when we can, and to put aside concepts and theories that block our understanding of the way gender operates.

The Ghettoization of Women's Labor History

While women's labor history has illuminated women's experiences and provided valuable correctiveness to male-centered history, it has not created a new narrative for labor history generally. Women's labor history has remained as "other" to men's labor history at least in part because it initially accepted the framework of class analysis as the basis for labor history. The new field thus elaborated upon rather than replaced a whole series of conceptual dualisms—capitalism/patriarchy, public/private, production/reproduction, men's work/women's work—which assume that class issues are integral to the first term of each pair and gender is important only to the second. Implicit in women's labor history has been some version of a dual systems approach to the study of class and gender, based on the theory that capitalism and patriarchy are distinct but mutually reinforcing systems of social relations.[55]

The particular dual systems theory mapped out by Heidi Hartmann has provided the general theoretical paradigm that has shaped much sub-

[53]Attention to these issues is not entirely new. Sociological theorists (e.g., symbolic interactionists) have addressed some of these concerns in the past. Some feminist anthropologists argue that poststructuralist insights into relations of domination and the connection between language and politics have been explored in feminist theory for more than forty years. See Frances E. Mascia-Less, Patricia Sharpe, and Colleen Ballerino Cohen, "The Postmodernist Turn in Anthropology: Cautions from a Feminist Perspective," *Signs*, 15 (Autumn 1989), 7–33.

Poststructuralism encompasses a wide range of theoretical trends, but is most often associated with Michel Foucault, Jacques Lacan, and Jacques Derrida, as well as with French feminist interpreters (Luce Irigaray, Julia Kristeva, Hélène Cixous). Despite significant differences among them, they share a theoretical core that allows discussion of them under the same general category.

[54]Ann Snitow believes that the tensions and contradictions in feminism cannot be transcended by theory alone; their resolution requires change in material conditions. See her "Pages from a Gender Diary: Basic Divisions in Feminism," *Dissent*, 36 (Spring 1989), 205–24. Thanks to Jacquelyn Hall for reminding me of this point.

[55]For examples of the dual systems approach, see Heidi Hartmann, "Capitalism, Patriarchy, and Job Segregation by Sex," *Signs*, 1 (Spring 1976, suppl.), 137–70; Zillah R. Eisenstein, ed., *Capitalist Patriarchy and the Case for Socialist Feminism* (New York: Monthly Review Press, 1979).

sequent empirical work on occupational sex segregation. Her call for a
focus on capitalism as well as on patriarchy in efforts to explain the sex
segregation of work was a major advance over previous formulations, for
she not only added considerations of relations between men and women
to an analysis of women's waged labor, she also argued that gender interests must be given as much weight as class interests. Numerous industrywide case studies of occupational sex segregation now document the
complex interplay between capitalism and patriarchy.[56]

Yet since the analysis of gender was thought to require a theory logically independent of class, the dual systems approach provided a theoretical rationale for men's working-class historians to continue to bracket
as unimportant to their research the mass of feminist research on working women and the sexual division of labor. Dual systems theorists accepted the principle that economic institutions and relations are gender-
neutral. As a result, their formulations forced few revisions in our
understandings of class and capitalism, and questions of sexual divisions
and sexual hierarchies continued to be of only peripheral concern in
male-centered labor history. For men's labor historians the sexual division of labor became an accepted fact rather than a historical problem to
be investigated.

Numerous feminist scholars have called for some kind of integrationist
approach to the class/gender dualism.[57] But how one forges such a synthesis, creates that integration, and dissolves the hyphen between capitalism and patriarchy is not self-evident. Efforts to integrate gender in
historical analysis have been limited largely because gender as a conceptual category has not been well theorized, and because feminist historians have only begun to unmask the gender biases inherent in such
traditional economic concepts and categories as work, class, wages, and

[56]Researchers disagree about the relative importance of workers and employers in creating and maintaining occupational sex segregation. See Ava Baron, "Women and the Making of the American Working Class: A Study of the Proletarianization of Printers," *Review
of Radical Political Economics*, 14 (Fall 1982), 23–42; Samuel Cohn, *The Process of Occupational Sex-Typing: The Feminization of Clerical Labor in Great Britain* (Philadelphia:
Temple University Press, 1985); Ruth Milkman, *Gender at Work: The Dynamics of Job
Segregation by Sex during World War II* (Urbana: University of Illinois Press, 1987). For a
review of British research see Sonya Rose, "Gender at Work: Sex, Class, and Industrial
Capitalism," *History Workshop*, 21 (Spring 1986), 113–21.

[57]For calls to rethink class analysis to incorporate gender, see Joan Acker, "Class, Gen-
der, and the Relations of Distribution," *Signs*, 13 (Spring 1988), 473–97; Joan Kelly, "The
Doubled Vision of Feminist Theory," in *Sex and Class in Women's History*, ed. Judith L.
Newton, Mary P. Ryan, and Judith R. Walkowitz (London and Boston: Routledge &
Kegan Paul, 1983); Iris Young, "Beyond the Unhappy Marriage: A Critique of the Dual
Systems Theory," in *Women and Revolution: A Discussion of the Unhappy Marriage of
Marxism and Feminism*, ed. Lydia Sargent, 43–69 (Boston: South End Press, 1981); Lise
Vogel, *Marxism and the Oppression of Women: Toward a Unitary Theory* (New Bruns-
wick, N.J.: Rutgers University Press, 1983).

skill.[58] As a result, scholarship integrating class and gender typically has fallen back on the language of interrelationship.

Earlier approaches to women's labor history demonstrated that questions about gender are crucial for any analysis of work and the economy. This research showed that an integrated labor history required one to transcend the separation of public and private spheres, to incorporate analyses of the family, consumption, and social reproduction in discussions of capitalist development and class relations.

Feminist scholars are reconsidering how women can be put back into the disciplines and whether producing separate bodies of research about women is sufficient. Research about women is still vital. At the same time, women's historians' concern with breaking down the divide between "history" and "herstory" has led to a new interest in gender relations.[59] Concerned scholars have sought to create a new synthesis of men's and women's history by exploring the ways men's and women's worlds, experiences, and cultures intersected. This is a valuable endeavor and important for the development of a gendered labor history. By itself, however, such an approach limits the integration of gender to the study of the relations between men and women, since in this formulation gender is considered important only if women are present. The rest of labor history could still proceed undaunted by calls for integration of gender. Studies on male workers, men's work, or predominantly male unions or activities could march on unfazed.

The field can be more decisively redirected only if gender is conceived as a fundamental category of all historical analysis.[60] Joan Scott's call for examination of the way meanings of sexual difference are constructed and used to signify power and hierarchy offers tremendous resources for a new understanding of the making of the working classes.[61] Attention to language—not just words but all forms of symbolic representation—

[58]The concept of the wage, e.g., not only is based on a male breadwinner model but also assumes that value is produced and that the wage is earned in the public sphere, at the site of production. On gender biases in the concept of the wage form, see Wally Seccombe, "Patriarchy Stabilized: The Construction of the Male Breadwinner Wage Norm in Nineteenth-Century Britain," *Social History,* 11 (January 1986), 53–76; on class see Harold Benenson, "Victorian Sexual Ideology and Marx's Theory of the Working Class," *International Labor and Working Class History,* 25 (Spring 1984), 1–23. On skill see Phillips and Taylor, "Sex and Skill"; on housework and productive labor see Bonnie Fox, ed., *Hidden in the Household: Women's Domestic Labour under Capitalism* (Toronto: Women's Educational Press, 1980).
[59]For excellent examples of this approach see Blewett, *Men, Women, and Work;* and Cooper, *Once a Cigar Maker.*
[60]See, e.g., Elizabeth Fox-Genovese, "Placing Women's History in History," *New Left Review,* 133 (May–June 1982), 5–29; Joan Wallach Scott, "Gender: A Useful Category of Historical Analysis," in her *Gender and the Politics of History,* 28–50.
[61]Joan Wallach Scott, "On Language, Gender, and Working-Class History," in her *Gender and the Politics of History,* 53–67.

reveals the significance of gender regardless of women's presence or absence and exposes the role of gender in historical events where previously we thought gender insignificant.[62] Scott's study of the Parisian garment trades in 1848, for example, integrates gender into working-class history by exploring the ways representations of the family and of sexual difference entered into the organization of labor and workers' critiques of capitalism. She focuses on how the various discourses constructed by and for tailors and seamstresses operated to shape workers' collective identities and political demands. Others have sought to incorporate analyses of symbolic representations into studies of workers' behavior. Jacquelyn Dowd Hall's study of the Elizabethton textile strike of 1929 exemplifies how an analysis of workers' language, dress, and gestures helps to uncover a strike's erotic undercurrent. It shows the links between women's labor militancy and gender conventions by exploring the ways women used their sexuality and gender-based symbolism as a protest style, and how the strikers' foes in turn sought to dismiss the protesters as being disorderly and unrespectable.[63]

This new research agenda is still evolving. An important goal is to revamp labor history in ways that will incorporate gender into labor history without either denying women's differences from men or segregating women into a separate sphere. Doing so requires conscious construction of a gendered labor history—a history that acknowledges rather than denies the gendered character of the historical concepts used to study both men and women, their institutions and social practices. A gendered labor history seeks to understand how gender operates, and the ways it has shaped and been shaped by economic institutions and relationships.

[62]On some of the pitfalls and promises of Scott's approach for history see Mariana Valverde, "Poststructuralist Gender Historians: Are We Those Names?" Labour/Le Travail, 25 (Spring 1990), 227–36. Criticisms of a poststructuralist historical approach can be found in Bryan D. Palmer, Descent into Discourse: The Reification of Language and the Writing of Social History (Philadelphia: Temple University Press, 1990); and Karen Offen, "The Use and Abuse of History," Women's Review of Books, 6 (April 1989), 15–16. For an interesting debate on this approach, see book reviews by Joan Scott and Linda Gordon of each other's works and their response in Signs, 15 (Summer 1990), 848–60.

[63]Joan Wallach Scott, "Work Identities for Men and Women: The Politics of Work and Family in the Parisian Garment Trades in 1848," in her Gender and the Politics of History, 93–112; Jacquelyn Dowd Hall, "Disorderly Women: Gender and Labor Militancy in the Appalachian South," Journal of American History, 73 (September 1986), 354–82. See also Ava Baron, "Questions of Gender: Deskilling and Demasculinization in the U.S. Printing Industry, 1830–1915," Gender and History, 1 (Summer 1989), 178–99; and Elizabeth Faue's analysis of gender and labor iconography, " 'The Dynamo of Change': Gender and Solidarity in the American Labour Movement of the 1930s," Gender and History, 1 (Summer 1989), 138–58.

Understanding Sexual Difference

An analysis of the gendering of work inquires when and why sexual differences become culturally and politically significant. How does gender come to have the capacity to affect wages and job status in ways that lead men to organize against women's entry into the labor market and capitalists to use gender as a divisive lever? In other words, the significance of sexual differences and the way they operate as a social force require explanation.

Most previous approaches have taken these differences for granted and emphasized the conflict and antagonisms between men and women.[64] "Categorical" theories, such as those that posit the existence of distinct sex/gender or patriarchal systems, treat sexual politics as relations between two internally undifferentiated groups of people with contradictory interests. Thus men's interests are opposed to women's interests, and men and women are related to each other in terms of power and conflict.[65] Women's historians, Elizabeth Fox-Genovese explains, "have tended to emphasize the distinctive attributes that differentiate the lives of all women from those of all men."[66] As a result, researchers have often treated gender as a coherent system of male domination rather than exploring layers of internal inconsistencies and the coexistence of multiple gender meanings within a society.

Categorical theories are not concerned with the process by which gender categories are constructed and do not consider why sexual difference is important in the first place. But the significance of sexual difference is precisely what needs to be explained. As Gayle Rubin aptly put it:

> Men and women are, of course, different. But they are not as different as day and night, earth and sky, yin and yang, life and death. In fact, from the standpoint of nature, men and women are closer to each other than either is to anything else—for instance, mountains, kangaroos, or coconut palms. Far from being an expression of natural differences, exclusive gender identity is the suppression of natural similarities.[67]

[64]Feminist theories as diverse as those of Shulamith Firestone, Michele Rosaldo, Nancy Chodorow, and Heidi Hartmann are all premised on essentialist assumptions about the sexes. On this point, see Nancy Fraser and Linda Nicholson, "Social Criticism without Philosophy: An Encounter between Feminism and Postmodernism," in *Universal Abandon? The Politics of Postmodernism*, ed. Andrew Ross, 83–104 (Minneapolis: University of Minnesota Press, 1988).

[65]For a critique of categorical theories of gender see Robert W. Connell, *Gender and Power: Society, the Person, and Sexual Politics*, 54–61 (Stanford: Stanford University Press, 1987).

[66]Fox-Genovese, "Placing Women's History in History," 12.

[67]Gayle Rubin, "The Traffic in Women," in *Toward an Anthropology of Women*, ed. Rayna Reiter (New York: Monthly Review Press, 1975), 179.

Debates among feminists about gender equality have taken on renewed vigor in recent years. Because so-called natural sexual differences have been used in the past to justify the exclusion of women from numerous occupations and activities, some feminists are understandably leery of such arguments. Research has revealed, however, that holding men and women to the same common standard has in effect reinforced women's social and economic inequality.[68]

Using the perspective of men's labor history as the starting point, women's labor historians have had to choose between demonstrating that women are "like men"—that, for example, they were just as militant as male workers—thereby ignoring difference; or that women and men differ in their relation to work, community, and family, thereby risking demeaning women's difference. Research that emphasizes the sameness of women and men potentially subsumes women workers' experiences under men's, but research that highlights women's differences runs the risk of essentialism. While it is important to explore the extent to which women had distinct experiences, arguments premised on gender differences and women's culture pose the danger of providing ahistorical explanations and reifying the very differences they seek to understand.[69] Analysis of working-class consciousness and culture must allow for the

[68]This outcome is revealed by recent research on divorce. See Leonore Weitzman, *The Divorce Revolution: The Unexpected Social and Economic Consequences for Women and Children in America* (New York: Free Press, 1985); Martha Fineman, "Implementing Equality: Ideology, Contradiction, and Social Change, a Study of Rhetoric and Results in the Regulation of the Consequences of Divorce," *Wisconsin Law Review*, 4 (1983), 779–884. On some of the problems involved in the debate on equality vs. difference, see Joan Wallach Scott, "The Sears Case," in her *Gender and the Politics of History*, 167–177; and Ava Baron, "Feminist Legal Strategies: The Powers of Difference," in *Analyzing Gender: Social Science Perspectives*, ed. Myra Marx Ferree and Beth Hess, 474–503 (Beverly Hills, Calif.: Sage, 1987). Alice Kessler-Harris, "The Debate over Equality for Women in the Work Place: Recognizing Differences," *Women and Work: An Annual Review*, 1 (1985), 141–61; Deborah L. Rhode, *Justice and Gender* (Cambridge: Harvard University Press, 1989) and her *Theoretical Perspectives on Sexual Difference* (New Haven: Yale University Press, 1990); Martha Minow, *Making All the Difference: Inclusion, Exclusion, and American Law* (Ithaca: Cornell University Press, 1990); and Nancy F. Cott, "Feminist Theory and Feminist Movements," in *What Is Feminism?* ed. Juliet Mitchell and Ann Oakley, 151–60 (New York: Pantheon, 1986). On the equality/difference debate pertaining to pregnancy and work see Wendy Williams, "Equality's Riddle: Pregnancy and the Equal Treatment/Special Treatment Debate," *New York University Review of Law and Social Change*, 13 (1984–85), 325–80; Herma Hill Kay, "Equality and Difference: The Case of Pregnancy," *Berkeley Women's Law Journal*, 1 (Fall 1985), 1–38; Ann C. Scales, "Towards a Feminist Jurisprudence," *Indiana Law Journal*, 56 (1980–81), 375–444; Lise Vogel, "Debating Difference: Feminism, Pregnancy, and the Workplace," *Feminist Studies*, 16 (Spring 1990), 9–32; and Lucinda Finley, "Transcending Equality Theory: A Way Out of the Maternity and the Workplace Debate," *Columbia Law Review*, 86 (October 1986), 1118–82.

[69]For discussion of the problems of this approach, see Linda Kerber, "Separate Spheres, Female Worlds, Woman's Place: The Rhetoric of Women's History," *Journal of American History*, 75 (June 1988), 9–39; and Ellen DuBois, "Politics and Culture in Women's History," *Feminist Studies*, 6 (Spring 1980), 28–36.

specificity of women's experiences and consciousness. But to the extent that woman is defined by what she is not—that is, not man—women remain marginal not only to working-class history but to workers' organizational strategies and policies.

Working women's limited choice between sameness and difference historically has meant either incorporation into men's unions or segregation and isolation. On the one hand, women's participation in male-dominated unions at best has been a mixed blessing. Numerous studies indicate that even when men have opened their doors to women, and even when women have been active union members, unions have given women's particular needs as workers low priority.[70] Men's work culture, reflected in unions, has muffled women's voices. In late nineteenth-century Pennsylvania, for example, male trade unionists gave little support to women sales and office workers' concerns about wages and hours because men and women understood and articulated these issues differently. Women discussed wages and hours in terms of equal pay for equal work and their desire for more personal time for leisure and family; men spoke of the requirements of a family wage and the need to reduce unemployment or to save motherhood.[71] Such limitations of unionism for women prevail as long as women are incorporated into unions on men's terms. On the other hand, efforts to develop independent all-female unions based on women's special organizational needs and work culture often have left women in a hostile environment isolated from men of their class and from women of other classes.[72]

We now need to go further in our understanding of men, women, and unions, to explore how constructions of sexual difference are built into union organization and structure. Some women's labor historians have begun to move beyond traditional dichotomies and to explore the connections and boundaries, the similarities and differences between women's and men's cultures.[73] In the work cultures of male and female cigar workers in the first decades of the twentieth century, for example, Patricia Cooper found similarities as well as differences. Both men and women workers sought autonomy at work, flexibility in the workday,

[70]On how male work culture was reflected in the cigarmakers' union, see Cooper, *Once a Cigar Maker;* on the printers' union see Baron, "Women and the Making of the American Working Class." Women organizers themselves sometimes found that to preserve unity they were forced to bracket women's concerns, as when the UE and UAW recruited women during World War II. See Milkman, *Gender at Work.*

[71]Gary Cross and Peter Shergold, " 'We Think We Are of the Oppressed': Gender, White-Collar Work, and Grievances of Late Nineteenth-Century Women," *Labor History,* 28 (Winter 1987), 23–53.

[72]Dye, *As Equals and as Sisters;* Robin Miller Jacoby, "The Women's Trade Union League and American Feminism," in Cantor and Laurie, *Class, Sex, and the Woman Worker,* 203–24; Kessler-Harris, *Out to Work.*

[73]Kerber, "Separate Spheres, Female Worlds, Woman's Place."

higher wages, and control over quality and quantity of production. As a result, men and women, despite differences in their skills and cultures, at times supported each other and organized together.[74]

Some women's historians have also begun to question the usefulness of emphasizing the separation between public and domestic spheres, pointing instead to areas where men's and women's behaviors, experiences, and circumstances are similar.[75] Whereas men's labor history often treated women workers as a homogeneous group of young, single daughters, this research emphasizes women's variable relation to production and to the family, documenting the role of women as contributors, as supporters of self and others, and even as household heads at various stages in the life cycle.[76] In an effort to correct the dichotomous, oppositional categories used to examine working-class men and women, some women's historians argue that we can better understand sexual difference by replacing concepts that are mutually exclusive to men and to women by a continuum that allows for a range of similarities and differences between and among women and men.

This research provides some important correctives to categorical theories and can help move us beyond dichotomies of public and private spheres. Yet it raises troubling questions for those concerned with issues of gender and class. If the differences between men and women are not sharply defined, then perhaps gender is not so salient a consideration. Indeed, Kessler-Harris raises the question whether gender identity was the lens through which women understood their work lives during the Depression.[77] While it is important to incorporate these insights into our exploration of gender, we must not obliterate the significance of gender as a category of analysis. In replacing mutually exclusive categories with those rooted in "non-dichotomous differences," we must go beyond conceptualizing gender as a linear continuum. We need to develop gender analysis in ways that allow for the historical specificity of gender identity while uncovering the ways gender assumptions are incorporated into social institutions and practices.

Feminists have searched for other ways to transcend this undesirable choice between sameness and difference. American "cultural feminists" believe that what is needed is a "woman-centered" understanding of dif-

---

[74]See Cooper, *Once a Cigar Maker.*

[75]See Kessler-Harris, "Gender Ideology in Historical Reconstruction." For a discussion of separate spheres in women's history, see Kerber, "Separate Spheres, Female Worlds, Woman's Place."

[76]See, e.g., Turbin, "Reconceptualizing Family, Work, and Labor Organizing."

[77]Kessler-Harris, "Gender Ideology in Historical Reconstruction." See also Jacquelyn Dowd Hall, James Leloudis, Robert Korstad, Mary Murphy, LuAnn Jones, and Christopher B. Daly, *Like a Family: The Making of a Southern Cotton Mill* (Chapel Hill: University of North Carolina Press, 1987).

ference in which women's differences become valued.[78] Similarly, some French feminists believe women's difference places women in a position to challenge and undermine male hegemony. Deconstruction attempts to subvert the hierarchical ordering in cultural constructions based on man/woman oppositions by emphasizing the importance of the second in a pair of hierarchical oppositions. From this perspective the failure to recognize difference denies women the potential power of their marginality. In this scenario, those on the margins are seen as the likeliest to disrupt the status quo.[79]

Yet to the extent that women's historians emphasize difference, albeit by defining it as positive, they accept the definition of woman as "other." And history provides abundant reminders that the existence of a woman's culture need not result in women's empowerment or in their inclusion within the general culture; rather, it may simply reinforce the cultural boundaries of sexual difference and women's proper place. The issue is not whether men and women are different but who has the power to define those differences and on what that power is based.[80] The question is not whether women are different from men but whether women are "different from *that which* men claim" women are.[81]

Joan Scott has opened up a new way to make gender visible and to explore how social institutions have incorporated gender into their structure by drawing our attention to the ways sexual difference has been used as a metaphor for expressing class relations and economic processes and thus as a key to investigating how gender came to characterize class relations while simultaneously reinforcing sexual hierarchy. In nineteenth century France, for example, debates about work and workers relied on notions of masculine and feminine for their meaning. As Scott explains:

> While middle class reformers in France depicted workers in terms coded as feminine (subordinated, weak, sexually exploited like prostitutes), labor and socialist leaders replied by insisting on the masculine position of the working class (producers, strong, protectors of their women and children). The terms of this discourse were not explicitly about gender, but they were strengthened by references to it. The gendered "coding" of certain terms

[78]Linda Alcoff, "Cultural Feminism versus Poststructuralism: The Identity Crisis in Feminist Theory," *Signs,* 13 (Spring 1988), 405–36.

[79]For discussion of the importance of power in defining difference, see Hester Eisenstein and Alice Jardine, eds., *The Future of Difference* (Boston: G. K. Hall, 1980). French feminists such as Hélène Cixous, Luce Irigaray, and Julia Kristeva reaffirm women's difference and point to women's marginality as a potentially powerful position from which to challenge the existing social order. See Elaine Marks and Isabelle de Courtivron, eds., *The New French Feminisms* (New York: Schocken, 1981).

[80]Hester Eisenstein, "Introduction," in Eisenstein and Jardine, *Future of Difference.*

[81]Collette Guillaumin, "The Questions of Difference," *Feminist Issues,* 2 (Spring 1982), 43.

established and "naturalized" their meanings. In the process, historically specific, normative definitions of gender (which were taken as givens) were reproduced and embedded in the culture of the French working class.[82]

Some of the critical questions we now need to address in examining gender and work pertain to the ways sexual difference is defined and manipulated. What are the historical conditions that heighten perceptions of sexual differences and when are these differences considered biological and natural rather than social? How are these differences articulated? How are they incorporated into the job structure, and into strategies of employers and workers and of various groups of men and of women?[83] Questioning sexual difference allows us to look at how gender is constructed, how it changes, and with what consequences. It is not only the discursive category "woman" that requires exploration, but the connection between such construction and the experiences of real women in historical situations. This is the challenge for the next stage in feminist research.[84]

The boundaries between the social and biological are neither clear nor fixed. Yet the ways in which the concept of gender has been used in feminist debates over the causes of working women's oppression have emphasized women's differences from men and separated our analysis of the social from the biological.[85] Indeed, the question how working men and women, capitalists and workers, constructed the relationship between gender and biological differences is precisely what needs to be explored to move the discussion of class and gender forward. Research has shown that neither the meaning of sexual differences nor that of gender equality was predefined at the outset. Not only the pursuit of gender equality but its meaning was at the root of the struggles between groups of men and women and between workers and their employers.[86]

[82]Joan Wallach Scott, "Gender: A Useful Category of Historical Analysis," in her *Gender and the Politics of History*, 48. See also " 'L'Ouvrière! Mot impie, sordide . . . ': Women Workers in the Discourse of French Political Economy, 1840–1860," in ibid., 139–63.

[83]Sally Alexander, "Women, Class, and Sexual Difference," *History Workshop*, 17 (Spring 1984), 127.

[84]For this reason we need to be careful how we adapt deconstruction for a gendered labor history. Mary Poovey believes that the logical conclusion of deconstruction "would be to argue that 'woman' is *only* a social construct that has no basis in nature": "Feminism and Deconstruction," *Feminist Studies*, 14 (Spring 1988), 52.

[85]Sandra Harding, "The Instability of the Analytical Categories of Feminist Theory," *Signs*, 11 (Summer 1986), 645–64. For attempts to locate the material basis for women's oppression by identifying the biological component of sexual difference, see the essays by Pat Armstrong and Hugh Armstrong and by Patricia Connelly in *The Politics of Diversity: Feminism, Marxism, and Nationalism*, ed. Roberta Hamilton and Michele Barrett (London: Verso, 1987).

[86]Kessler-Harris, e.g., examined the changes in male trade unionists' perceptions of women workers from the 1910s to 1920s, from a view that did not imply inequality to one that asserted female weakness and unreliability. See her "Problems of Coalition Building:

It is also at the root of contemporary feminist theorizing and political strategizing.[87]

Understanding "Consent" to Oppression

As we have seen, women's labor historians initially concentrated on establishing women workers as historical agents who actively resisted conditions that oppressed them. As women's labor history matured, the portrait of working-class women became more complex. Women's labor historians not only discovered a world of formal and informal modes of resistance, they also found that in some instances women appeared to accept and even to cooperate in reproducing the conditions that oppressed them. Women's historians conceded that in some cases, women opted to support the patriarchal family and its male members instead of aligning with other women. Mary Blewett, for example, shows that among shoe binders in New England both a family and a gender alliance were historic possibilities, but ultimately women formed a family alliance, supporting men's demands for a family wage rather than joining with female factory workers to obtain higher wages for women.[88] Further, a number of studies document women's desire to leave the labor force to take up domestic roles. The nineteenth-century immigrant women studied by Mari Jo Buhle supported socialism in the hope that they would be freed from wage earning to return to hearth and home, not because they wished to obtain independence through wage earning. In the same vein, working women in other places and at other times chose family rather than employment as their primary means of identification.[89]

Having established women as historical agents rather than merely as passive victims, how can we now account for women's lack of resistance

Women and Trade Unions in the 1920s," in Milkman, *Women, Work, and Protest,* 110–38. On changes in the rhetoric of sexual difference and gender inequality, see also Baron, "Questions of Gender," 178–99.

[87]Ava Baron, "Deconstructing Capitalist Patriarchy," paper presented at the Social Science History Association meeting, New Orleans, October 1987; Zillah Eisenstein, "Developing Feminist Theory: Sexually Particular, Equal, and Free," in her *Feminism and Sexual Equality* (New York: Monthly Review Press, 1984), 231–56.

[88]Mary Blewett, "Work, Gender, and the Artisan Tradition in New England Shoemaking, 1780–1860," *Journal of Social History,* 17 (December 1983), 221–48; also Jane Humphries, "The Working-Class Family, Women's Liberation, and Class Struggle," *Review of Radical Political Economics,* 9 (Autumn 1977), 25–41.

[89]Mari Jo Buhle, *Women and American Socialism, 1870–1920* (Urbana: University of Illinois Press, 1981); Tentler, *Wage-Earning Women;* Susan Estabrook Kennedy, *If All We Did Was to Weep at Home: A History of White Working-Class Women in America* (Bloomington: Indiana University Press, 1979). Scott and Tilly in *Women, Work, and Family* show that women in Europe sought work when it was consistent with the needs, values, and traditions of the family and rejected employment when it conflicted with family-centered goals.

to their oppression? A resistance/consent dichotomy cannot fully explain women's behavior.

One explanation is that women suffered from "false consciousness." This approach handles the problem of consent by relying on a theory of ideology. It sets up a dichotomy between authentic and false consciousness and between the real sources of oppression and their ideological construction. It assumes a separation between objective conditions of exploitation and subjective understandings of one's circumstances. This model rests on a notion of true consciousness as the legitimate basis of consent. Yet this explanation conflicts with the tenets of women's labor history by assuming women's ignorance and relegating women once again to passive instruments for the pursuit of others' interests.

Another approach is to interpret events by using women workers' culture or perspective. In this view, women make choices between their class and gender interests on the basis of their historically specific experiences.[90] Numerous studies document instances when women workers supported the sex segregation of work and men's higher pay. From the women workers' vantage point, such support provided positive advantages; for example, it increased female solidarity, or made men less competitive and more willing to cooperate with women's labor activity. Women selected the most beneficial choice on the basis of their assessment of the alternatives available.[91] This research provides some valuable insights into how working women viewed their world and the roles of class and gender in formulating these women's perspective and choices. But whereas theories of ideology throw out experience as a guide to "truth," this approach treats experience as relatively unproblematic and uses it as a key to historical explanation. Explanations for the form and content of women's culture and the link between structure and agency are still lacking.

Similar problems exist in explanations of male working-class behavior. The problem, however, is generally reversed: workingmen are assumed to have given priority to gender over class interests. Men's labor historians have tended to sidestep the issue by emphasizing male workers' resistance to capital and giving little attention to the conflict between men's class and gender concerns, or to how, as a result, they cooperated in or consented to their oppression by employers. According to the models of

[90]Disagreements about men's and women's support for the family wage system and their reasons for it illustrate the difficulty in examining the connection between class and gender interests and how people make choices between them. For discussion of the family wage see Humphries, "Working-Class Family," and Martha May, "The Historical Problem of the Family Wage," *Feminist Studies*, 8 (Summer 1982), 399–424.

[91]See, e.g., Kessler-Harris, "Gender Ideology in Historical Reconstruction." See also the essay by Dorothy Sue Cobble in this volume.

false consciousness and patriarchy, the family wage is either imposed upon male members of the working class as part of bourgeois hegemony or a strategy for protecting male interests.[92] False consciousness has generally been considered an inadequate explanation, for it contradicts working-class agency. Patriarchy assumes a material advantage for all men in oppressing women—an advantage that conflicts with their class interests.

Research on sex segregation and male unionists' efforts to exclude women from better jobs often assumes that men have distinct gender interests as men which somehow cut across class, race, and ethnic lines.[93] For example, Judith McGaw's insightful analysis of the consequences of technological change on men and women workers in the Berkshire paper industry nevertheless denies diversity in class experiences of masculinity, viewing manhood as an "interclass bonding experience."[94]

Existing theoretical models provide insufficient explanation for what men's interests are "as men." Rather than treat male power as a problem to be investigated, feminist theories often assume that men know what their gender interests are and that they have the power to obtain what they want.[95] Despite various efforts to uncover the motive force for patriarchy, an adequate theory is still lacking.[96] The exclusion of masculinity from studies of male workers not only universalizes the male experience as the norm; it also results in a distorted historical understanding of men's actions. For these reasons we need to historicize masculinity.

[92]Michele Barrett, e.g., has argued that the family wage was bad for the working class because it contributed to a sex-segregated labor force, created a reserve army of low-wage women, and acted to divide the working class. See her *Women's Oppression Today: Problems in Marxist Feminist Analysis* (London: Verso, 1980). For a critique of this approach, see Johanna Brenner and Maria Ramas, "Rethinking Women's Oppression," *New Left Review*, 149 (January–February 1985), 33–71. Jane Humphries, however, has argued that the family wage was good for the working class because it helped to strengthen the family and thus served as a source of sustenance for the working class as a whole. See her "Working-Class Family."

[93]In most cases only workingmen are considered to have gender interests; capitalists' role in gender segregation of work typically is considered to be based on their concerns as a class, not as a gender.

[94]See Judith McGaw, *Most Wonderful Machine: Mechanization and Social Change in Berkshire Paper Making, 1801–1885* (Princeton: Princeton University Press, 1987), and Mary Blewett's review, *Journal of Social History*, 22 (Winter 1989), 368–69.

[95]Workingmen, by contrast, are treated as less powerful in relation to capital than they are in relation to women.

[96]Some argue that men seek to control women's labor power in the home. See, e.g., Heidi I. Hartmann, "The Family as the Locus of Gender, Class, and Political Struggle: The Example of Housework," *Signs*, 6 (Spring 1981), 366–94. Others claim that men desire to control women's reproduction or sexuality. See e.g., Mary O'Brien, *The Politics of Reproduction* (Boston and London: Routledge & Kegan Paul, 1981); and Catherine A. Mackinnon, "Feminism, Marxism, Method, and the State: An Agenda for Theory," *Signs*, 7 (Spring 1982), 515–44.

But the history of working-class masculinity has yet to be written.[97] Most of what we know about masculinity in the nineteenth and early twentieth centuries is about the middle class. We have barely begun to uncover the ways workingmen's gender identity influenced the development of union policies and working-class politics.[98]

To understand men's or women's role in reproducing hierarchies of class and gender we must understand men's and women's efforts to construct and to defend a collective gender identity. Labor historians have limited examination of the subjective dimension to workers' cultural values and their role in shop-floor resistance and class struggles. To move beyond the resistance/consent dichotomy, research on the workplace now needs to explore questions related to subjectivity and identity.[99]

Poststructuralists' attention to subjectivity, to questions of how we give meaning to the material conditions and relations that structure our everyday lives, offers a fresh approach to questions concerning the conflict between class and gender interests. In dealing with an array of issues, women's historians have been stymied by theories of sexual difference which emphasize women's shared experiences and by inadequate alternatives for understanding interactions among gender, race, class, region, age, sexual preference, and a host of additional factors. But "experience" of class, gender, or any identifying characteristic and understanding of one's "interests" require one to signify oneself as a member of a particular group. Poststructuralism raises questions about the construction of a collective gender identity and about how such signification takes place, and illuminates the larger question of identity construction.

Feminist poststructuralists argue that language in the form of conflicting discourses constitutes women and men as conscious thinking sub-

[97]For exceptions see the chapters by Baron, Blewett, and Hewitt in this volume; also Baron, "Contested Terrain Revisited" and "Questions of Gender." A few books touch on working-class masculinity: Cooper, *Once a Cigar Maker;* Blewett, *Men, Women, and Work;* Nick Salvatore, *Eugene V. Debs: Citizen and Socialist* (Urbana: University of Illinois Press, 1982); David Halle, *America's Working Man: Work, Home, and Politics among Blue-Collar Property Owners* (Chicago: University of Chicago Press, 1984). For research on working-class masculinity in England see Paul Willis, *Learning to Labor: How Working-Class Kids Get Working-Class Jobs* (Westmead: Saxon House, 1977), and "Shop-Floor Culture, Masculinity, and the Wage Form," in *Working-Class Culture: Studies in History and Theory,* ed. John Clarke, Chas Critcher, and Richard Johnson, 185–98 (New York: St. Martin's Press, 1979); Cynthia Cockburn, *Brothers: Male Dominance and Technological Change* (London: Pluto, 1983); and the forum on masculinity in *Gender and History,* 1 (Summer 1989).

[98]Benenson, "Victorian Sexual Ideology"; and Alexander, "Women, Class, and Sexual Differences."

[99]Feminist scholars and labor historians have been reluctant to integrate psychological theories and political economy. On the need to make such integration, see Cora Kaplan, "Pandora's Box: Subjectivity, Class, and Sexuality in Socialist Feminist Criticism," in *Making a Difference: Feminist Literary Criticism,* ed. Gayle Greene and Coppélia Kahn, 146–76 (London: Methuen, 1985).

jects. The subject is not coterminous with the individual but is a position within a particular set of discourses. The unitary subject qua individual agent is deconstructed and replaced by a set of multiple positionings of subjectivities. Consent is not produced simply through repressive use of power; rather, subjects are constituted by discursive practices embedded in power relations.[100]

But it is important not to lose sight of human agency in the making of history. As Chris Weedon has argued, the subject is not the mere object of language but a person who exists "as a thinking, feeling subject and social agent, capable of resistance and innovations." Language is not hermetically sealed; meanings are constructed as part of a social world in which individuals may resist particular versions of meanings or produce new ones from the conflicts between existing discourses.[101]

Discourses may constitute individuals, but it is individuals trying to remake their world that constitute the stuff of history. Discourses, located in social institutions, mediate and shape our experiences. But discourses by themselves do not change the material conditions of life; they compete with each other for the allegiance of human agents. The agency of individuals is required before the social and political implications of a discourse can be realized.

Women's labor historians are beginning to take up questions concerning the construction of gender identity and its role in shaping workers' lives. Men's and women's efforts to defend their respectability as workers took place on a gendered terrain. These efforts shaped their work, the strategies they sought, and the ways they pursued them. Since both gender and class, as well as race and ethnicity, are integral to subjectivity, one cannot simply choose to privilege one identity or set of interests over another.[102] Poststructuralists' emphasis on the elusiveness of one's identity need not mean that efforts to secure a stable gender identity were unimportant in shaping workers' responses to changes in their work. In-

[100]For a discussion and critique on poststructuralism's theorizing on subjectivity, particularly poststructuralist psychoanalysis, see Julian Henriques, Wendy Hollway, Cathy Urwin, Couze Venn, and Valerie Walkerdine, *Changing the Subject: Psychology, Social Regulation, and Subjectivity* (London: Methuen, 1984), esp. 203–26. For an effort to apply Lacanian theory to the history of working-class politics and sexual difference, see Alexander, "Women, Class, and Sexual Difference."
[101]Chris Weedon, *Feminist Practice and Poststructuralist Theory* (Oxford: Basil Blackwell, 1987), 125. Some women's historians believe that a poststructuralist historical approach tends to ignore human agency. See, e.g., Louise Tilly, "Gender, Women's History, and Social History," *Social Science History*, 13 (Winter 1989), 438–62. However, the meaning of human agency is complex. Underlying current debates about the value of poststructuralism for historical analysis may be disagreements about how human agency is defined. I am grateful to Joan Scott for pointing this out.
[102]Elizabeth V. Spelman, *Inessential Woman: Problems of Exclusion in Feminist Thought* (Boston: Beacon, 1988).

deed, men's and women's efforts to obtain respectability as workers show the importance of the construction of gendered subjectivities for an understanding of class formation and strategies.[103]

Theories about work should draw attention to structures of power as well as to the significance of identity-securing strategies.[104] What is needed is a theory of gendered subjectivities—of what it means to be a man or a woman, of how people construct and understand such meanings, and of how these understandings are related to human agency and action. What are the terms, the discourses, the social practices, and the material power relations that influence working-class experiences? How are they formulated and changed? In sum, how are the meanings of being a woman and being a man formulated, and how have these formulations shaped men's and women's actions and the conditions under which they live and work?

Differences among Women

The category "woman" includes a wide range of women. Research that emphasizes woman's distinct morality or woman's separate culture or sphere sets up a false generalization, ignoring differences along such lines as class, race, ethnicity, religion, age, and region.[105] The "bonds of womanhood" did not mean universal sisterhood. The deep-seated distrust and divisions between white and black women and between middle-class and working-class women are now amply documented.[106] Clearly

[103]See, e.g., Baron, "Contested Terrain Revisited" and "Questions of Gender." Daniel J. Walkowitz examines female social workers' efforts to develop an identity that was both professional and feminine in "The Making of a Feminine Professional Identity: Social Workers in the 1920s," *American Historical Review*, 95 (October 1990), 1051–75.

[104]David Collinson and David Knights, " 'Men Only': Theories and Practices of Job Segregation in Insurance," in *Gender and the Labour Process*, ed. David Knights and Hugh Wilmott, 140–78 (Hampshire, Eng.: Gower, 1986).

[105]For a sampling of research on how women's lives have been shaped by relations of gender, race, ethnicity, and class, see Angela Davis, *Women, Race, and Class* (New York: Random House, 1981); Bettina Aptheker, *Women's Legacy: Essays on Race, Sex, and Class in American History* (Amherst: University of Massachusetts Press, 1982); Amy Swerdlow and Hanna Lessinger, eds., *Class, Race, and Sex: The Dynamics of Control* (Boston: G. K. Hall, 1983). For discussions of mutuality and conflict among women based on relations of gender, race, ethnicity, and class, see "Common Grounds and Crossroads: Race, Ethnicity, and Class in Women's Lives," special issue of *Signs*, 14 (Summer 1989). For a review of efforts to conceptualize the interrelations of class, race, and gender, see Karen Bodkin Sacks, "Toward a Unified Theory of Class, Race, and Gender," *American Ethnologist*, 16 (August 1989), 534–50.

[106]On racial divisions see, e.g., Jacquelyn Jones, *Labor of Love, Labor of Sorrow: Black Women, Work, and the Family from Slavery to the Present* (New York: Basic Books, 1985); Dolores Janiewski, *Sisterhood Denied: Race, Gender, and Class in a New South Community* (Philadelphia: Temple University Press, 1985). On class divisions see, e.g., Dye, *As Equals and as Sisters*; Stansell, *City of Women*, chap. 7; Kessler-Harris, *Out to Work*; Nancy A. Hewitt, *Women's Activism and Social Change: Rochester, New York, 1822–1872*

in some cases the class and race divide was wider and deeper than the gender gap. As Nancy Hewitt explained, "Women banded together to perform essential labor and then wielded their collective power in defense of same-class men and in defiance of other-class women."[107]

The plantation household brought black slave women and white mistresses together on the basis of sex and at the same time divided them on the basis of race and class.[108] Black slave women often found little help among white mistresses and forged their own sisterhood, which they used to defend themselves against whites and to strengthen the black community as a whole.[109] Race was no less salient for the relations among free black and white women.[110] Yet in some instances, black and white, male and female workers were able to overcome gender and race divisions. Tobacco and textile workers in the South during the 1930s, for instance, despite race and gender hierarchies, found sufficient common ground upon which to forge collective struggle against employers.[111]

Feminist theories have helped to explain the ways women were oppressed as "woman" but have provided fewer insights into how such categories as race, class, and gender intersected. As a result, women's historians studying the diversity of women's experiences were given little theoretical guidance. To explain the complexity of the relationship of sisterhood, racial and ethnic identity, and class solidarity, a trichotomy of class/race/gender developed. The problem with such an approach, as Alan Dawley put it, is that it "could not escape the coils of its own complexity, and in the end, depicted a set of infinite antagonisms which more or less canceled each other out."[112]

Difficulties in explaining the relation of class and race to gender raise a broader question: How can feminist thinkers incorporate differences among women and still formulate a theory about the oppression of woman as a social category? The conflict between "woman" and "women" is central to contemporary feminist debates about the direction of

---

(Ithaca: Cornell University Press, 1984), chap. 5. On the need to study regional differences see Jacquelyn Dowd Hall, "Partial Truths," *Signs,* 14 (Summer 1989), 902–11.

[107]Nancy A. Hewitt, "Beyond the Search for Sisterhood: American Women's History in the 1980's," *Social History,* 10 (October 1985), 307.

[108]On the relationship between black and white women in the slave South, see Elizabeth Fox-Genovese, *Within the Plantation Household: Black and White Women of the Old South* (Chapel Hill: University of North Carolina Press, 1988), and reviews by Christine Stansell, "Explosive Intimacy," *The Nation,* March 27, 1989, 417–22, and Jacquelyn Jones, "One Big Happy Family?" *Women's Review of Books,* 6 (February 1989), 4–6.

[109]Hewitt, "Beyond the Search for Sisterhood," 306–7. On varying notions of "community" among different groups of women, see "Communities of Women," special issue of *Signs,* 10 (Summer 1985).

[110]See, e.g., Lebsock, *Free Women of Petersburg.*

[111]Janiewski, *Sisterhood Denied.*

[112]Dawley, "Preface to Synthesis," 368–69.

feminist research and politics. Contemporary theory and practice require us to accept the significance of the concept of woman, the existence of a distinct "woman's point of view," and a shared set of interests, as well as to recognize diversity in sisterhood.[113] While some feminists emphasize differences, others are concerned that acknowledging such differences may eradicate the possibility of feminist theory and stand in the way of effective political action in mobilizing women qua women.[114]

Black feminists have begun to uncover the limitations of older explanations of women's triple oppression and to develop new ways to understand it.[115] Until recently feminists treated race, class, and gender in an "additive" way. This model assumed that various forms of oppressions could be explored separately; each could be added or subtracted, depending on which group was under investigation. Identity was conceived as divisible into distinct race, class, and gender parts.[116] Many feminists now believe it is impossible to isolate gender from race and class in order to uncover what women experience "as women in general." Rather they seek to incorporate difference into the very meaning of "being a woman." Moreover, previous explanations of differences among women used white middle-class women as the baseline for "adding on" other factors. Race, for example, was considered salient only for understanding black women. But despite its apparent invisibility, race is integral to an understanding of whites as well.

Replacing ahistorical and universal categories with historically and culturally specific ones is a key to this new conceptualization. Nancy Fraser and Linda Nicholson believe a feminist poststructuralism could provide the needed framework, since it "would tailor its methods and categories

[113]Denise Riley attempts to negotiate between the essentialism of "woman" and deconstruction of the category "women" in *"Am I That Name?" Feminism and the Category of "Women" in History* (Minneapolis: University of Minnesota Press, 1988). For a critique of this approach see Offen, "Use and Abuse of History."

[114]On the centrality of difference for feminist theory and politics, see Alcoff, "Cultural Feminism versus Poststructuralism"; Jana Sawicki, "Foucault and Feminism: Toward a Politics of Difference," *Hypatia,* 1 (1986), 23–36; Iris Young, "Difference and Policy: Some Reflections in the Context of New Social Movements," *Cincinnati Law Review,* 56 (1987), 535–50. On the value of incorporating women's diversity in women's studies, see Maxine Baca Zinn, Lynn Weber Cannon, Elizabeth Higginbotham, and Bonnie Thorton Dill, "The Costs of Exclusionary Practices in Women's Studies," *Signs,* 11 (Winter 1986), 290–303.

[115]Floya Anthias and Nina Yuval-Davis, "Contextualizing Feminism—Gender, Ethnic, and Class Divisions," *Feminist Review,* 15 (November 1983), 62–75. For a synthetic overview of black feminist thought, see Patricia Hill Collins, *Black Feminist Thought: Knowledge, Consciousness, and the Politics of Empowerment* (Boston: Unwin Hyman, 1990).

[116]On the problems with such "additive" theories see Spelman, *Inessential Woman;* and Deborah K. King, "Multiple Jeopardy, Multiple Consciousness: The Context of a Black Feminist Ideology," *Signs,* 14 (Autumn 1988), 42–72. On this and other problems with the way feminist theory has conceptualized race, see Hazel V. Carby, "White Women Listen! Black Feminism and the Boundaries of Sisterhood," in Centre for Contemporary Cultural Studies, *The Empire Strikes Back: Race and Racism in 70s Britain* (London: Hutchinson, 1982), 212–35, and her "Politics of Difference," *Ms.,* September–October 1990, 84–85.

to the specific task at hand, using multiple categories when appropriate and forswearing the metaphysical comfort of a single 'feminist method' or 'feminist epistemology.' "[117] Accordingly, some feminists have moved away from a concern with constructing a grand theory that would explain all forms of women's oppression and their causes. Only partial explanations are possible, since "woman" does not exist, only women in specific sets of social relations. Efforts to come up with feminist "truths," Jane Flax explains, require one to ignore internal differences in woman and relegate some women to the status of "other."[118] By assuming similarities of women's experiences of oppression across class and race, a concept of sisterhood may stand as a barrier to coalition building.[119] Recognition of differences among women may be a source of fragmentation and disunity, but it also might be used to multiply the sources of resistance to a particular form of domination.[120]

The project of integrating gender with axes of difference among women is twofold. First, we need to deconstruct the category "woman" by recognizing the experiential diversity among groups of women. Thus we must study the interconnectedness of, for example, race, class, and gender in defining subjectivity and experience. Second, we need to explore how workers and managers, and men and women of different races, ethnicities, ages, and religions, have constructed "woman" and "man" in ways that either ignore or highlight such diversity. We must examine how the languages of race, class, and gender were used to bolster each other or to deny their interrelatedness.[121]

Toward a Gendered Labor History

These problems point to the need for a new conceptual framework to incorporate gender into labor history. What, then, is gender, and how is it to be analyzed? It typically has been used to refer to culturally constructed differences between men and women, or simply as a synonym for women. But it has not been part of a well-developed theory of society or social change.[122] Gender has most often been envisioned as a single

[117]Fraser and Nicholson, "Social Criticism without Philosophy," 101–2.

[118]Jane Flax, "Postmodernism and Gender Relations in Feminist Theory," *Signs*, 12 (Summer 1987), 621–43.

[119]Bonnie Thornton Dill, "Race, Class, and Gender: Prospects for an All-inclusive Sisterhood," *Feminist Studies*, 9 (Spring 1983), 131–50.

[120]Sawicki, "Foucault and Feminism."

[121]On difference as experiential diversity among women, see Michele Barrett, "The Concept of 'Difference,' " *Feminist Review*, July 1987, esp. 30–33; on the value of examining the ways class and race ideologies are steeped in and spoken through gendered metaphors, see Kaplan, "Pandora's Box."

[122]For a useful discussion of the concept of gender, see Scott, "Gender: A Useful Category of Historical Analysis," 28–50.

dichotomy and treated as a static structure. As such, gender is reified; the ways gender is recreated and contested remain invisible. We are left with little understanding of how gender ideology is imported into production, or how it is developed, maintained, or changed as the labor process is transformed.[123] Instead gender must be recognized as multiplicities of co-existing genders and as a process embedded in social relationships, institutions, and processes.

The issue of where gender can be located is important, for if gender is thought to be constructed outside of production, then such supposedly gender-neutral categories as class, market, skill, and wages can remain intact; all that is required is to add gender to the analysis. In such approaches the gendered construction of job labels remains separate from an analysis of the meaning of work and the transformation of the occupational structure.[124] But skills are not simply ideological epiphenomena; they are part of a larger process by which the occupational structure itself is created. Changes in women's work accompanied changes in job processes and technologies. Shifts in the sex segregation of occupations are ideal situations in which to explore this interrelationship. If, rather than conceptualize gender as an external factor that impinges on social systems or relations at certain points or times, we think of how institutions and relations become gendered, our attention is directed to gender as an integral part of social existence.[125]

Gender, then, is constituted through people's lived experience within continually redefined and contested social activities and institutions. Gender is integral not only to relations between men and women, but also to a myriad of other relations of power and hierarchy, including those between employers and workers, men and boys, whites and blacks. As a social process, we need to think of *gender* not only as a noun but also as a verb. The study of gendering is concerned with how understandings of sexual difference shape institutions, practices, and relationships.

A gender analysis of work and economy means going beyond the study of women workers and women's work to study how gender affects and is affected by capitalist development and class formation. When we study

---

[123]Phillips and Taylor, "Sex and Skill," make an important contribution to our understanding of skill by exploring how men satisfied their gender interests by using their organizational strength to control the definitions of jobs. But instead of examining the ways gender and skill labels have developed historically, they argue that women receive lower pay and less prestige for the work they do simply because it is women who perform the work; that is, women bring their unequal status to the jobs they do. Their explanation for women's subordinate economic position hinges on the existence of a societal gender ideology that through some unspecified mechanism works its way into the sphere of production.

[124]Baron, "Questions of Gender."

[125]Acker, "Class, Gender, and the Relations of Distribution," 477.

the gendering of work, we look at how gender becomes a property of activities and institutions as well as of individuals.[126]

Gender is created not simply outside production but also within it. It is not a set of ideas developed separately from the economic structure but a part of it, built into the organization and social relations of work. In learning to work and in working, in struggles between workers and employers over the nature and meaning of work, both sides construct and contest definitions of masculinity and femininity. These contests over gender meanings provide clues as to how gendered subjectivities are constructed. Using the concept of gender in these ways may help us move forward in developing a gendered labor history. In this effort gender is transformed from a descriptive to an analytic category.

The essays in this volume bring us closer to constructing a gendered labor history, showing us ways to explore issues of work, economy, and class through the lens of gender, changing what we look for and what we see. No single method, approach, or theory of gender and work is advocated. To present a single approach would presuppose that we have transcended the theoretical problems before us and moved so far along in developing a gendered labor history that we have arrived at some new model that resolves those problems. No such consensus exists.

The essays in this book do not fall into conventional categories; they cut across them and add new ones. Efforts to categorize some as dealing exclusively with unions, the organization of work, or men's and women's activism in the workplace or community all fall short. For this reason the essays have been organized chronologically.

The essays examine how the cultural meanings attributed to sexual difference developed and changed and with what consequences for work and labor conflicts. Taken together, they show how gender decisively shaped the sexual division of waged labor and the structure of work and unions. This research demonstrates that conceptions of gender are not fixed, static entities; rather they continually change. It also documents gender as more than a simple dichotomy of masculine/feminine. At any point in time multiple gender meanings coexist within a society—meanings that are continually contested and transformed. Traditions of gender are both limiting and malleable; they become jumping-off points for change. With thematic differences, all of the essays too provide ways to

---

[126]Kessler-Harris, e.g., shows how conceptions of gender and equity are built into the "market." See her "Just Price, the Free Market, and the Value of Women," *Feminist Studies*, 14 (Summer 1988), 235–50; Baron, "Contested Terrain Revisited," shows how gender shapes struggles between employers and workers, choices of technology, and definitions of skill.

think about the question of how to integrate gender into labor history. But they do so in different ways.

Most of the essays (including those by Ava Baron, Nancy A. Hewitt, Eileen Boris, Angel Kwolek-Folland, Patricia Cooper, Dorothy Sue Cobble, Ileen DeVault, Mary H. Blewett, and Jacquelyn Dowd Hall) shed light on the links between work and the construction of collective gender identities. They show how workers drew their identity as men or women from their work and alternately infused their work with gendered meanings. Workers' concerns about their gender identity influenced their job choices, the ways they defined and did their work, and the strategies they chose to fight their employers. These essays provide new ways to understand how men and women workers attempted to construct and to defend a gendered identity in the context of the many discourses on gender and work simultaneously put forth by employers, unions, reformers, journalists, and others. In these studies we see workers as agents embattled, seeking to gain control over the discourse and the material conditions that defined their identities as men and women, as workers, and as family and community members.

A theme running through many of the chapters is that gender not only is apparent in relations between men and women workers but also is embedded in economic institutions and practices. Dolores Janiewski, Cobble, DeVault, Baron, and Blewett underscore the importance of exploring the significance of gender for economic phenomena by studying how gender shaped labor markets, work processes, and work relations. Rather than use different theoretical models to study men and women, as in the past, these authors show that gender is important for understanding men's as well as women's work and participation in the labor force.

Essays by Dana Frank, Elizabeth Faue, Blewett, Hall, and Hewitt tackle questions concerning labor militance and acquiescence from new angles. They expand upon research that now amply documents women's militancy within and outside of unions. These essays move beyond the conventional definition of labor activism by looking at how varying conceptions of masculinity and/or femininity shape men's and women's responses to work issues and labor conflicts.

Questions of how labor union policies were shaped by workers' conceptions of gender, and in turn how union policies and strategies affected relations among various groups of men and women workers, are taken up in several essays. Those by Nancy Gabin, Cobble, Hewitt, and Cooper confront how shifting definitions of gender equality shaped union policies and class and gender relations. The nature and definition of gender equality are part of the historical issues requiring the kind of exploration begun in this volume.

Many of the essays, especially those by Faue, Hewitt, Frank, Cooper, and Gabin, show how an understanding of gender can contribute to the "new institutionalism" in labor history. Their central questions pertain to the way gender has been incorporated into the labor movement and union structure. Looking at men's and women's different roles in the labor movement reveals only part of the picture. To study how the labor movement became gendered requires us to change the questions typically posed—from why women did not participate as fully as men in labor activism to how both men's and women's participation in the labor movement was shaped by assumptions about gender built into union organization, policies, and tactics.

Several essays reveal the intricate weave of race, ethnicity, and gender with class. Janiewski, Hewitt, Boris, Blewett, and Cobble look at how gender, race, and ethnicity shaped labor struggles and the ways these categories were alternately constructed by management and by workers to divide or unite workers along various lines. Further, they demonstrate that an additive analysis is insufficient to understand workers' experience and the forms of labor protest they developed. Workers' identities were not neatly compartmentalized into race, ethnic, class, and gender components.

Ava Baron's study of printers demonstrates that class and gender issues are not dual systems but facets of one reality. Her research underscores the value of examining gender for the study of male workers and men's work. She explores the significance of gender for understanding relations between men and boys and between adult male workers and their employers. Workingmen's understandings of gender structured their relations with others, grounded their views of market and skill, and shaped the ways they dealt with issues of wages and workers' control.

Men's relation to boys in the trade was particularly problematic for skilled male workers throughout the nineteenth and early twentieth centuries as apprenticeship unraveled during the transition from craft to industry. To printers, apprenticeship was more than a system of acquiring technical skills; it was an important link between their work and family roles, and an essential ingredient in acquiring manhood. Journeymen printers responded to changed economic and social circumstances after the introduction of the Linotype at the turn of the century by redefining masculinity and the criteria for determining competence. Struggles between employers and male workers over wages, training requirements, and definitions of skill were intimately connected to workers' efforts to construct a collective gender identity. But in their efforts to defend their craft and manly respectability, male workers became mired in contradictory definitions of manhood. Gender, then, is not a mere epiphenomenon that is imported from outside the workplace; it is created and recreated at work.

Dolores Janiewski places race and gender along with class consider-ations at the center of her study of labor-recruitment policies in the South. Inspired by Joan Scott's call for an analysis of how difference op-erates in the construction of meaning, Janiewski examines the ways suc-cessive southern elites defined class through the language of race and gender.

Two southern industries—textiles and tobacco—developed different strategies to resolve the conflict between the desire for the cheapest avail-able labor and the necessity of avoiding any apparent disruption of the racial and gender system. Successful labor recruitment was contingent on employers' ability to make work respectable for white men and women workers without threatening existing gender and race hierarchies. Em-ployers in both industries, in different ways, thwarted the emergence of a common class-based culture among southern women workers while rein-forcing the already established race and gender divisions. The new labor system incorporated notions of power that "naturally" subordinated all women and black men but that made class domination less visible. In-dustrialists encoded industrial paternalism with race and gender hierar-chies. A brotherhood of white men, which cut across classes to include planter, industrialist, millworker, and tenant farmer, disguised differ-ences in power and emphasized their common racial bond. At the same time, industrialists built on preexisting ideas that linked sexual dishonor with economic exploitation to block the potential bonds of black and white women and black and white men.

Mary Blewett's study of Fall River textile workers in the 1870s dem-onstrates the interconnected nature of class and gender politics and the ways market principles were imbued with gender meanings. She explores the relationship between changes in conceptions of masculinity and con-flicts between immigrant workers recruited from Lancashire, England, and their American textile employers. In order to produce cheap cloth and dominate the market, mill owners sought to transform Lancashire workers' norms of manly respectability into forms that enabled them to pay low wages while minimizing workers' resistance. Employers black-listed union organizers, forcing them to choose between two central as-pects of working-class manly respectability: their customary craft rights and their ability to earn a living while remaining in their community.

In these circumstances, immigrant spinners and weavers sought new ways to maintain their manly and craft respectability. During the strikes of the 1870s numerous versions of manliness were put forth by employ-ers and workers, native-born and immigrant workers, and men and women workers. Female activism, regarded by many working men as a dangerous challenge to manly respectability, became a crucial factor in the defeat of emerging union organization. By the early 1880s, the Lancashire tradition of popular radicalism was displaced by a definition of manhood based on the man as the primary family wage earner, acceptance of the market principle of supply and demand as the determinant of wages, and adoption of American-style working-class politics. Blewett not only documents the historically contingent nature of masculinity but also highlights the intraclass as well as interclass conflicts in gender meanings.

Eileen Boris examines assumptions about gender, ethnicity, and class expressed in controversies regarding New York tenement cigarmaking in the 1870s and 1880s. She looks both at the role of women as active agents in fighting to improve their working conditions and at how the concept of woman was deployed by various groups to highlight power hierarchies based on class and race.

The ensuing public debates about the location of work and of workers' rights during these decades drew heavily on the language of gender. Members of the Cigar Makers' International Union, which organized mostly white factory workers, held a version of masculinity which contained racial and gendered assumptions about workers' rights. Bohemian tenement workers held to traditional views of women's work appropriate in a family economy, while the CMIU took the position that a man should earn a family wage so that the woman could fulfill domestic duties and properly care for her children. Women, married and single, working in tenements and inside factories, drawing on different conceptions of femininity, defended their right to earn a wage. Manufacturers, too, large and small, invoked the language of gender to discuss class rights and obligations.

Workers and employers turned to the state to support their version of gender and class rights. Debates raged in legislative hearings and judicial briefs over the relation of public and private, the contradiction between republican notions of citizenship and manhood and racial ideas about tenement labor and about the rights of labor versus capital. Tenement cigarwork eventually came to an end with state regulation. Middle-class reformers, employing the ideology of domesticity, succeeded in shifting the terms of the debate.

Nancy Hewitt's study of the Latin cigarmakers of Tampa from the 1880s to the 1920s highlights the multiplicity of gender meanings and the ways divergent conceptions of manliness were intimately involved in shaping labor disputes. Hewitt compares the diverse conceptions of gender incorporated in the Cuban cigarworkers' union and community with that of factory owners, city fathers, and the CMIU, dominated by American men. Factory owners concurred that true manhood derived from individual economic success. Latinos forged solidarity across sex, skill, race, and ethnic boundaries. The CMIU chose Americanism and the family wage over class, gender, and ethnic solidarity. The common concern of Latin and Anglo male workers with virility led them to contest the proper place of women—rhetorically and pragmatically—in achieving virile unionism.

The story of Latin cigarworkers offers a picture of femininity in which women's difference from men supported rather than undermined women's militance; at the same time ethnic solidarity served to mute sexual conflict. Unlike their northern counterparts who fashioned a work culture different from men's, Tampa women shared many of the values and goals of the male cigarworkers with whom they worked. For the women as well as the men, virile unionism required the inclusion of women workers. But men's recognition of women's significance in labor militance did not imply equality. Like the Latin household, the union, conceived as a "family of labor," remained male-dominated even as the proportion of women in the cigar industry increased. Hewitt's portrait of virile unionism offers an alternative to the choice of either sexual difference or equality typically depicted in histories of women and unions. Tampa workers' version of virility highlights some of the limitations of a union strategy that allows for gender integration without gender equality.

Angel Kwolek-Folland examines the gendered metaphors used by workers and executives to describe the changing nature of work in the insurance industry between 1880 and 1930. By exploring the gendered terms in which the industry and its work were constructed, she looks beyond gender relations and the presence or absence of women workers to see gender as attached not simply to persons but also to institutions.

Gender spoke in multiple voices. By encoding work and work relations with sexual difference, both workers and executives attempted to make social phenomena appear natural and immutable. The industry used images of motherhood and family to promote its intangible product and to develop a maternalistic relationship with employees. "Corporate motherhood" suggested that the work was organized in a natural hierarchy rather than determined by economic needs or managerial considerations. Women and men, executives and workers described their dissatisfaction with their jobs as a function of gender relations rather than of work, corporate structure, bureaucratization, or position within the organization.

Women sales agents and managers both drew upon gender imagery to define themselves and their work. The "assertiveness" of which male sales agents boasted became "sauciness" and "impudence" in female agents. Women's adoption of leisure clothing for the office, however, at once contradicted their professed commitment to the job and reinforced gender hierarchies. Women managers and agents simultaneously flaunted their deviance, while also claiming their legitimate place, in gender terms.

Thus these women renegotiated the strain between their sense of the feminine self and the depiction of work as masculine.

Ileen A. DeVault's comparative analysis of labor-market choices made by relatively well-off working-class boys and girls in Pittsburgh in the 1890s takes a new tack on the construction of a sex-segregated labor market. She shows that questions about gender can be usefully applied to male as well as female workers. Women's scholars have argued that gender concerns decisively influenced women's job choices and labor activism. DeVault explores how gender considerations shaped both men's and women's participation in the labor force.

Young women who were concerned about "unfitting" themselves for their future roles as wives and mothers considered the feminine respectability of the job and tended to focus on immediate material advantages rather than on opportunities for promotion and long-term wage increases. Men, too, considered their future gender roles in making job choices. Since their goal was eventually to earn a family wage, long-term material benefits, job security, and possibilities for promotion influenced their job choices. In making these choices, young men also considered how jobs might enhance their manly respectability. While clerical work's nonmanual nature made its masculinity suspect, its relatively high wages and promise of steady employment contributed to a man's image as a breadwinner. Thus young men, particularly those native-born of working-class families, were confronted with contradictory definitions of masculinity in choosing clerical work.

Dorothy Sue Cobble documents the contested and contingent nature of sex segregation of work, cross-cut by racial divisions. She studies the gendering of an increasingly feminized and white food service from the turn of the century to the 1970s. In struggles with male unionists over the sex labeling of liquor service, waitresses drew on their notions of respectable work for women, their belief in gender equality, and their rights as unionists. Waitresses in each decade proclaimed the right to work and to be treated like their male co-workers. At the same time, they accepted a separate female sphere within this world of work and sought to expand its boundaries. Black and white waitresses in different ways defied the gender ideology and class arguments of waiters and pushed for new definitions of men's and women's work. The different economic realities that black and white waitresses confronted, along with craft traditions and shifting definitions of gender equality, help to account for the ways culinary workers drew the line between men's and women's work.

The story of how waiting work became gendered reflects the power of traditional gender ideology as well a its malleability. Waiters and waitresses constructed a discourse about nightwork for women which embraced conventional views of women's domestic and child-care responsibilities. But the two groups viewed such responsibilities differently. The legacy of each group's efforts to redefine the "family wage" and "craft interests" to its advantage had consequences for its ability to legitimate its claim to bartending work in the years ahead.

Jacquelyn Dowd Hall focuses on a strike at the Fulton Mills in Atlanta in 1914–15 to reveal the key role women's sexuality played in defining the social tensions that accompanied southern urban-industrial transformations. She examines the competing discourses of employers and their labor spies, workers, and reformers concerning the consequences of white women's working in the paid labor force in the New South.

The controversy surrounding Leo Frank and the murder of a young female pencil factory worker in 1913 helped to set the stage for debates about working women during the strike at the Fulton Mills. The union conceived of the strike as a battle for cultural legitimacy. Through language and pictures union organizers portrayed the brutality of mill work, depicted workers as respectable and hardworking, and developed themes of racial solidarity and worker unity. Spies sought to undermine strikers' self-representations. They depicted textile folks as living in a world of vice, immorality, and crime. Local strike leaders were portrayed as unmanly, and women were cast both as sexual predators and as victims. Middle-class reformers simultaneously pitied their white working sisters and feared the sexual dangers of women workers' newfound independence.

As the strike progressed, the labor and commercial press increasingly emphasized the number of women involved in the struggle and described strikers in female-coded terms. Images of workers shifted attention away from men to women and children. Attention focused on the victimization of women and children rather than on the issues of autonomy and control raised by the strikers. In effect, labor conflict was redefined and formulated as a gender issue.

Dana Frank investigates the gendered nature of labor strategies in three consumer organizing campaigns in Seattle of the 1920s. She shows how the labor movement's choice of tactics was colored and shaped by gendered assumptions that simultaneously reflected and reinforced men's and women's positions within the labor movement.

Her work corrects a central assumption of labor history that has equated worker resistance with activities related to production—unionism and the shop floor. From this vantage point women are seen as unorganized and nonmilitant. Women's labor historians have corrected this version to show women actively protesting to protect their rights as workers at the workplace and as housewives—supporting their husbands' strikes and participating in popular protests to protect and feed their families.

Frank deconstructs the production/consumption dichotomy by exploring both men's and women's labor protests in the sphere of consumption, focusing on boycotts, union labels, and cooperatives. Men's activism was not limited to the sphere of production, nor was women's to consumption. Workplace issues were fought out in both spheres. Her work helps to incorporate gender into the new institutionalism by redefining the "labor movement" to include a host of consumer organizing tactics as well as strikes.

Elizabeth Faue argues that to understand more fully both men's and women's participation in the labor movement one must explore the differential impact of the decline of community-based labor activism. As long as working-class union strategies were compatible with community organizing, women were active union participants. Indeed, the success of union strategies hinged on female networks rooted in community. As unions became more structured and bureaucratic, the community and women's participation became less salient.

Faue's study of the Minneapolis labor movement in the 1930s shows that the transformation of unions from community-based to bureaucratized institutions was neither inevitable nor gender-neutral. Bureaucratic rules built on gendered assumptions about the nature of union leadership and organizing. The application of such rules to men and women consequently pushed women to the margins of the labor movement. The ways labor movements defined labor solidarity, as inclusive or exclusive of women as workers and/or as wives of workers, was a critical aspect of the forms of labor militance such movements embraced.

Patricia Cooper's essay on Philco radio workers in the 1930s focuses on a sex-segregated occupational structure and male-dominated union. It deals with the thorny problem of the significance of sexual difference at work without either reviving categoricalism or eradicating the notion of difference altogether. Her essay challenges us to reconceptualize the supposedly homogeneous categories of workingman and working woman and to look more closely at variations in work relations between men and women workers. She demonstrates the fluidity of gender distinctions and how historical conditions allow for more or less questioning of the terms of sexual difference or for greater or lesser dichotomous extremes.

Like Faue, Cooper demonstrates how seemingly gender-neutral institutions and rules incorporated assumptions about gender. In this case, Cooper shows how a rationalized job structure incorporated into union contracts seemed to be gender-neutral but in fact was gender-biased and therefore perpetuated sex segregation and gender-based wage differentials.

Nancy Gabin's analysis of the United Auto Workers' policies on protective legislation and mandatory overtime in the 1960s helps to place in historical context contemporary dilemmas women confront in dealing with questions of gender equality at the workplace. Are women better off with "special treatment" or should they instead struggle to be treated "just like men"? Typically this question has been treated as "women's concern." Gabin makes the critical point that women's issues were also union issues, and then sets out to understand how the union dealt with gender equality by examining issues pertaining to hours of work: Would women, like men, be required to work overtime, or would men, like women, receive legal protection from such mandates?

Views of gender shaped the rights, duties, obligations, and protections that men and women believed they were due as workers. Contradictions between feminism and unionism deepened as UAW women fought to remove legislative limitations on their ability to work overtime and the UAW struggled to remove mandatory overtime requirements. The union supported the idea that gender equality meant that women should be treated like men; the obverse, that men could be treated like women so that both sexes might receive legal protection from excessive overtime, was never considered. As a result, women's victory was bittersweet; the union and the state left women adrift to deal with the contradiction between mandatory overtime and their ability to fulfill their obligations as wives and mothers.

Labor history currently is in a stage of transition. Whether a new synthesis will be reached and how it might further integrate women into the narrative of working-class history are issues still being debated. The research presented here contributes to these debates by demonstrating the significance of gender for understanding men, women, and work. This volume makes no claim to have discovered grand new solutions or to have transcended the theoretical problems now confronting the field. It does, however, offer ways to explore how gender shapes the world about which men's and women's labor historians write. By demonstrating some of the ways gender has been embedded in our institutions and practices and by showing the plasticity of gender as men and women, workers and employers have contested its meaning and its implications for class relations over two centuries of American history, the essays in this volume take us a step in the direction of constructing a gendered labor history.

CHAPTER TWO

An "Other" Side of Gender Antagonism at Work: Men, Boys, and the Remasculinization of Printers' Work, 1830–1920

Ava Baron

In 1834 General Duff Green, proprietor of the *Washington Telegraph* and United States government printer, announced his intention to establish the Washington Institute, a school to teach printing to boys. Five years earlier he had recruited approximately fifty boys to displace his journeymen. Members of the Columbia Typographical Society delighted in telling of Green's failure. Once the boys were initiated into the work, they claimed, they had begun "to feel the full throb of those principles of honor, magnanimity, and justice" characteristic of the craft printer. Still, the specter of their displacement by boys hung over the journeymen. They conceded the danger that boys could be used to degrade them and their work:

> There are no means of escape from the crisis which awaits us—it must be met, and met fearlessly, whether in the conflict we survive or fall! . . . Without a prompt and vigorous effort, united as one man throughout the Union, boys will usurp your places, and our honorable occupation will be numbered among the things that are gone! Can you, will you, submit to this humiliating condition?[1]

The conflict between Duff Green and the printers of the Columbia Typographical Society was one of many over what came to be called the

Material for this essay is drawn from my book manuscript "Men's Work and the Woman Question: The Transformation of Gender and Work in the Printing Industry, 1830–1920." Many thanks to Mary Blewett, Richard Butsch, Leonore Davidoff, Ileen DeVault, Nancy Hewitt, Susan Klepp, Priscilla Long, Keith McClelland, and Sonya Rose for comments, criticisms, and encouragement.

[1] Columbia Typographical Society, "Protest against the Washington Institute, Addressed to the Public Generally and Particularly to the Printers of the United States" (Washington, D.C.: Francis Blair, 1834), 11.

48   *Ava Baron*

"apprenticeship question." To both employers and journeymen the apprenticeship question was actually a composite of what typically are considered issues of class and workers' control—supply of labor, methods of training, the division of labor, work pace and work standards, and wages, hiring, and firing. Throughout the nineteenth century printers were among many craftworkers who complained bitterly about both the abuses and the decline of the apprenticeship system. In countless articles in their trade journals workers and employers labeled apprenticeship one of the most important problems they had to confront. Unions and employers' organizations established committees to study it; federal and state bureaus of labor produced reports on it; and state legislatures passed laws to regulate it.[2] The study of apprenticeship holds the potential to yield important new insights into craft unions and workers' control, the labor process and the social construction of skill. Yet the voluminous material on apprenticeship is relatively untapped. Most research on apprenticeship explores the early colonial craft system and focuses on the master-apprentice relation. The apprenticeship question that emerged after the first third of the nineteenth century in the United States, however, remains unexplored.[3]

Apprenticeship was also a question that deeply involved issues of gender.[4] At the heart of controversies between employers and workers over the selection and number of boys and the length and method of training were the criteria for determining both masculinity and competence. To adult workingmen apprenticed boys were what Simone de

[2]Builders, cigarmakers, plumbers, carpenters, musicians, wallpaper workers, leather workers, and iron molders similarly complained about the apprenticeship problem. For discussion of workers' response to apprenticeship and its decline in the United States, see Edward Bemis, "Relation of Labor Organizations to the American Boy and Trade Instruction," *Annals of the American Academy of Political and Social Science*, 5 (1894–95); James Motley, *Apprenticeship and American Trade Unions*, Johns Hopkins University Studies Series 25 (Baltimore: Johns Hopkins University Press, 1907), 11–12; New York State Bureau of Labor Statistics, *Annual Report*, 1886.

[3]William J. Rorabaugh, *The Craft Apprentice: From Franklin to the Machine Age in America* (New York: Oxford University Press, 1986); and William Mulligan, Jr., "From Artisan to Proletarian: The Family and the Vocational Education of Shoemakers in the Handicraft Era," in *Dimensions of American Working-Class History*, ed. Charles Stephenson and Robert Asher (Albany: SUNY Press, 1986), do address the apprenticeship system after industrialization, but their data are limited. Charles More, *Skill and the English Working Class, 1870–1914* (New York: St. Martin's Press, 1980), examines apprenticeship and the acquisition of skill in Britain. None of these works explores the gender implications of apprenticeship.

[4]The apprenticeship question was also inextricably linked to the woman question. Journeymen's concerns about unapprenticed boys and women were often articulated in similar terms, as threats to their relatively high wages and their positions as family providers. Yet there were also critical differences in the ways these men related these threats to boys and to women. I explore this theme in "Questions of Gender: Deskilling and Demasculinization in the U.S. Printing Trade, 1830–1915," *Gender and History*, 1 (Summer 1989), 178–99.

Beauvoir might have called an "other"—man was the reference, boy was the difference.[5] Workingmen contrasted themselves to these boys as a measure of their manliness; boys were what workingmen had once been, what they were not now, and what they feared resembling. Apprentices helped to bolster craftsmen's class and gender positions by highlighting the value of craft skills, the significance of training, and the achievement of manly respectability through work. Yet they also represented a threat to these workers' privileged positions as craftsmen and family providers.

During the initial period of proletarianization in the nineteenth century, American journeymen exhibited great antagonism toward boy apprentices and helpers. While research on gender at work has provided much information about women's work and on the relations between men and women workers, the gender implications of the apprenticeship question have been invisible.[6]

Gender is, as Gayle Rubin explains, "a socially imposed division of the sexes."[7] But it also is a process of constituting social relationships more broadly.[8] This process is based on understandings of sexual difference and involves more than relations between men and women. The adult white Teutonic males' constructions of the masculine and of sexual differences have relegated blacks and various ethnic groups as well as women and boys to the category of "other," as contingent beings. But boys posed a particular problem for men because they defined boys simultaneously as "not man" and as "in the process of becoming man." Examining man-boy relations enables us to see remarkable ways in which gender shaped workingmen's conceptions of what it meant to be a workingman, and how these understandings affected workplace issues.

---

[5]Simone de Beauvoir, *The Second Sex* (New York: Knopf, 1952).

[6]A large body of research documents various facets of gender antagonism at work and men's efforts to exclude women from skilled jobs, as well as gender cooperation. On the United States, see Ava Baron, "Women and the Making of the American Working Class: A Study of the Proletarianization of Printers," *Review of Radical Political Economics*, 14 (Fall 1982), 23–42; Mary H. Blewett, *Men, Women, and Work: A Study of Class, Gender, and Protest in the New England Shoe Industry, 1780–1910* (Urbana: University of Illinois Press, 1988); Patricia Cooper, *Once a Cigar Maker: Men, Women, and Work Culture in American Cigar Factories, 1900–1919* (Urbana: University of Illinois Press, 1987); Susan Levine, *Labor's True Woman: Carpet Weavers, Industrialization, and Labor Reform in the Gilded Age* (Philadelphia: Temple University Press, 1984).

[7]Gayle Rubin, "The Traffic in Women," in *Feminist Frameworks: Alternative Theoretical Accounts of the Relations between Women and Men*, ed. Alison M. Jaggar and Paula Rothenberg, 2d ed. (New York: McGraw-Hill, 1984), 165.

[8]Gender, in this respect, is an analytic category, not a description of the relation between the sexes. For a discussion of the concept of gender and its uses, see Joan Wallach Scott, "Gender: A Useful Category of Historical Analysis," in her *Gender and the Politics of History*, 28–50 (New York: Columbia University Press, 1988).

Acquiring Masculinity through Work:
The Apprenticeship Question before the 1880s

During the colonial period American printers, like other craftsmen,
continued the European custom of training boys in the "mysteries" of
their art through an extensive apprenticeship, typically lasting between
five and seven years. To printers, apprenticeship was more than a system
of acquiring technical skills; it was a boon to their craft respectability as
well. It was also an important link between their work and family roles
and an essential ingredient in acquiring manhood.

Entry into the ranks of journeymen required completion of the customary term of apprenticeship.[9] During his apprenticeship a boy developed
character and acquired proper values and behavior as well as technical
abilities.[10] The boy learned to be a man in class terms, and to be a worker in
gender terms.

To members of the typographical unions, completion of apprenticeship
symbolized passage simultaneously into manhood and into competent
worker status. "Competence" in the early decades of the nineteenth
century referred to a man's ability to earn a comfortable livelihood for
himself and his family.[11] One acquired an ability "to earn a competence"
by learning a craft. Through apprenticeship a boy became proficient
in a trade, obtained a means of earning a "family wage," and gained
a position of "honorable independence."[12] Journeymen's support for
the apprenticeship system was also a defense of the manliness of the
craft.

Printers considered their work a quintessential "manly art" because it
combined both intellectual and manual labor.[13] They understood the
work itself to contain the necessary ingredients for manliness. Journeymen generally couched their objections to women printers in terms of the
detrimental consequences to women themselves of doing "men's work."
Women, they said, could do the work, but they would be "unsexed" by
engaging in "masculine employment."[14] Boys, on the other hand, gradu-

[9]There is no evidence that an apprentice was required to demonstrate his ability by making or exhibiting a "masterpiece": Motley, Apprenticeship, 28.
[10]Bemis, "Relation of Labor Organizations," 85.
[11]Circular letter to the Master Printers of the City of New York, July 13, 1811, in
George A. Stevens, New York Typographical Union No. 6: Study of a Modern Trade Union
and Its Predecessors (Albany: J. B. Lyon, 1913), 68.
[12]Workingman's Advocate, June 16, 1866, 4.
[13]Printers' Circular, Feb. 1, 1867, 161, 162.
[14]Finchers' Trades Review, Oct. 1, 1864; for a fuller discussion of men's responses to
women printers, see Ava Baron, "Contested Terrain Revisited: Gender and the Social Construction of Skill in the Printing Industry, 1850–1920," in Women, Work, and Technology:
Transformations, ed. Barbara Wright et al., 58–83 (Ann Arbor: University of Michigan
Press, 1987).

ally acquired their masculinity during the apprenticeship term; engaging in manly work conferred masculinity on the apprentice.

But during the nineteenth century the conditions of apprenticeship changed, as capitalists replaced master printers as employers and journeyman became a permanent status. The struggle between employers and printers over the decline of appenticeship and its implications was prolonged and often intense.

Printers voiced various complaints about the apprenticeship system even in the first decades of the nineteenth century.[15] The proliferation of incomplete apprenticeships was one of the most vexing problems in the trade. Men bitterly complained about the ruinous system of "halfway" journeymen, or "two-thirders," whereby boys, usually apprentices who had run away before completing their apprenticeship, went to work for half or two-thirds of a regular journeyman's wages.[16]

Boys who ran away before completing their apprenticeship, by contrast to "regular boys," were characterized as "incapable of governing their passions and propensities," and therefore "plunge headlong into every species of dissipation, and are often debilitated by debauchery and disease before they arrive at the state of manhood."[17] Lack of manliness was equated with seduction, corruption, drunkenness, and general moral degradation. This moral dimension of manliness was rooted in discipline and self-control, which were associated with the practice of one's skill.

The New York Typographical Society surveyed the extent of the apprenticeship problem in 1810 and discovered numerous men working at printing who had not served a regular apprenticeship, as well as many boys hired to do printers' work at low wages.[18] The following years journeymen implored employers to stop hiring runaways. This practice, they said, encouraged boys "to elope from their masters," creating a "great grievance to journeymen, and also certain ruin to the boys themselves."[19]

Journeymen charged employers with using apprentices as cheap labor and flooding the trade with workers who knew only the simpler typeset-

[15]Sean Wilentz, *Chants Democratic: New York City and the Rise of the American Working Class, 1788–1850* (New York: Oxford University Press, 1984), 130–31; George A. Tracy, *History of the Typographical Union: Its Beginnings, Progress, and Development* (Indianapolis: International Typographical Union, 1913), 34–36.

[16]*Condition of Entrance to the Principal Trades*, Bureau of Labor Statistics Bulletin no. 13 (Washington, D.C.: U.S. Government Printing Office, 1906), 760.

[17]Circular letter to Master Printers, July 13, 1811, in Stevens, *New York Typographical Union No. 6*, 67–68.

[18]Ethelbert Stewart, *A Documentary History of the Early Organization of Printers*, U.S. Department of Labor Bulletin, 11, No. 61 (Washington, D.C.: U.S. Government Printing Office, 1905), 66–67.

[19]Circular letter to Master Printers, July 13, 1811, in Stevens, *New York Typographical Union No. 6*, 68.

ting work known as straight composition. These incompetents were unworthy and incapable of earning the union wage.[20] The halfways, printers argued, unfairly undercut the wages of the regularly apprenticed printers.[21] Employers' practice of taking on other "irregulars," such as adult male immigrants, as apprentices was considered equally "illiberal and unjust."[22]

Arguing in terms of justice and fairness to those who "deserved" a decent wage, journeymen began to adopt restrictions on the number of apprentices. Employers protested against these limitations and resented journeymen's unilateral infringement of long-standing craft customs and employers' traditional rights.[23]

A long and hard battle ensued during the 1830s. Journeymen boycotted, organized societies, and went out on strike. But efforts by local typographical societies to develop and enforce apprenticeship limitations throughout the 1830s and 1840s were ineffective. When the National Typographical Union was established in 1850, it declared the regulation of apprenticeship the most important issue printers faced.[24]

Journeymen adopted apprenticeship limits as a strategy to control the labor supply, defend their masculine rights, and sustain a family wage. Their dignity as workers and as men, journeymen claimed, required that they maintain the ability to determine their own worth and to set the price of their labor. They saw employers' efforts to override this right as an attempt to degrade and insult their manliness.[25] Therefore, at a mass organizing meeting of printers in 1850 the journeymen stood resolved and unanimous that they would not surrender their wages "to the unregulated, unlimited operation of the vaunted 'law of supply and demand.' "[26]

They believed that once a boy completed an apprenticeship and was certified as a competent worker, he should have the right to earn a "man's wages." Market fluctuations and lack of business were not legitimate grounds to reduce wages. During a strike in 1844, journeymen of the Franklin Typographical Society resisted their employers' efforts to reduce wages because business was dull, "as if the laborer was responsible

[20]Addison B. Burk, *Apprenticeship as It Was and Is* (Philadelphia: Philadelphia Social Science Assn., 1882), 7–8.
[21]New York State Bureau of Labor Statistics, *Annual Report*, 1886.
[22]Circular Letter to Master Printers, July 13, 1811, in Stevens, *New York Typographical Union No. 6*, 68.
[23]Stewart, *Documentary History*, 934; Paul H. Douglas, *American Apprenticeship and Industrial Education* (New York: Longmans, Green, 1921).
[24]The apprenticeship problem was largely responsible for the formation of the earlier National Typographical Association in 1836: Motley, *Apprenticeship*, 36.
[25]"Caution to Journeymen Printers," in *Printers' Scraps*, comp. Joel Munsell, vol. 9 (Albany, 1860), 56, in Typographic Collection, Manuscript Division, Columbia University Library.
[26]Address to National Convention of Journeymen Printers, 1850, in Stewart, *Documentary History*, app. A, No. 10, 981.

for the decrease in business." Men printers claimed they were justified in rejecting the principles of the market in order to earn the wages necessary to support their families.[27] Journeymen typically couched their demands for wage increases in terms of their ability to fulfill their role as family providers. The printers of Boston complained to the legislature in 1849 that their average earnings of $9.25 per week (some earned as little as $6) were insufficient to allow them to provide for their families. Similarly, the printers of New York and of Cleveland in 1864 justified their demands for wage increases by pointing to the increased cost of living. They cited retail prices of the necessary expenses for an average printer's family.[28]

The labor shortage after the Civil War intensified conflicts over apprenticeship as more employers took on apprentices or hired two-thirders. In September 1872 two hundred New York journeymen printers responded by going out on strike against five of the largest book and job offices to enforce apprenticeship limitations. The strike lasted sixteen weeks and cost the union over $15,000 in strike benefits and other expenses.[29]

Throughout the nineteenth century employers in country and small urban job shops sided with typographical unions in seeking stricter state controls over lengthy apprenticeships. This system allowed the employer to benefit from the skilled work of the apprentice during the last few years of the term without the payment of a full journeyman's wages. These employers took on as many boys as possible. But there were few opportunities for journeymen in small offices, and boys flocked to the cities in search of work.[30]

Employers in large urban printing firms welcomed apprenticed printers and two-thirders from small urban and country shops, rather than spend time and money to train apprentices. By the 1870s traditional indenture apprenticeships had become practically obsolete in large offices. These employers wanted to be able to discharge boys at their convenience, and boys preferred to have the right to leave for better job offers at will.[31]

[27]On the market as a social construct, see William Reddy, *The Rise of Market Culture: The Textile Trade in French Society, 1750–1900* (Cambridge: Cambridge University Press, 1984). On the family wage, see Martha May, "The Historical Problem of the Family Wage: The Ford Motor Company and the Five-Dollar Day," *Feminist Studies*, 8 (Summer 1982), 399–424; and Blewett, *Men, Women, and Work*, esp. chap. 5, for discussions of the significance of the family wage for workingmen.

[28]Massachusetts Legislature, "Remonstrance of Printers in Boston, Re: Remuneration Now Received for Their Labor," House Document no. 44 (February 1849), 2–3; *The Printer*, August 1864, 116.

[29]Stevens, *New York Typographical Union No. 6*, 460.

[30]Burk, *Apprenticeship*, 7–8.

[31]Stevens, *New York Typographical Union No. 6*, 456; Burk, *Apprenticeship*, 11–17.

But employers in small urban and country shops complained about investing time training an apprentice only to find that once his labor became profitable, he would leave.[32] One New York employer with a small shop explained that he did not take on apprentices because "the boys think they are men after a few months . . . and demand or look for men's positions. There is no way to hold boys till they become men."[33]

For the typographical unions the apprenticeship problem required battles on many fronts and precipitated strikes for various reasons. While some printing establishments, such as large newspaper offices, took on few apprentices, others, particularly small shops, employed more apprentices than the union allowed. In small shops printers struck to enforce the union stipulations on the ratio of apprentices to journeymen; in large establishments the union fought to prevent the hiring of nonunion printers, typically women, two-thirders, and others who had not completed a legitimate apprenticeship.[34]

By the 1880s apprenticeship laws were practically unenforced. An extensive study of apprenticeship in New York State in 1886 claimed that the apprenticeship law was a dead letter.[35] It was clear to journeymen and to employers that something had to be done, but they disagreed about the cause of the problem and its solution. Some blamed the subdivision of labor, others machinery. Unions blamed employers and foremen; employers pointed their fingers at the typographical unions.

Public sentiment increasingly opposed the old style of apprenticeship with its long term of indentured service and diffuse obligations by both boys and employers. Many considered apprenticeship un-American because it connoted a form of servitude and personal dependence.[36] Invoking negative images of race and dependency, Theodore DeVinne, president of the National Typothetae of America, an association of employing printers, labeled apprenticeship "a relic of feudalism and qualified slavery."[37] Employers in large urban shops wanted to rid themselves of legal and personal responsibility for boys. Apprentices were given wages in lieu of room and board. The old system of personalized mutual obligations had been displaced by market relations.[38]

Most employers, particularly those in large urban printing offices, were no longer printers themselves. They turned over the training of ap-

[32]*Inland Printer,* December 1890, 200.
[33]New York State Bureau of Labor Statistics, *Annual Report,* 1886, 123.
[34]U.S. Commissioner of Labor, *Annual Report,* 1901, 499–501; International Typographical Union Officers' Reports, 1920, 252; American Newspaper Publishers' Assn., *Annual Report,* 1924, 167–69.
[35]New York State Bureau of Labor Statistics, *Annual Report,* 1886, 100; Stevens, *New York Typographical Union No. 6,* 456.
[36]New York State Bureau of Labor Statistics, *Annual Report,* 1886, 99, 122.
[37]*Inland Printer,* November 1888, 107.
[38]New York State Bureau of Labor Statistics, *Annual Report,* 1886, 233–37.

prentices to their foremen or to other printers in the shop. Journeymen, who typically worked for piece wages, were reluctant to train apprentices because employers did not compensate them for lost work time.[39] This conflict of interests between men and boys at the point of production became more pronounced and more generalized in other types of printing establishments by the end of the nineteenth century.

By the 1880s even boys who had completed apprenticeships were not thoroughly trained in the entire craft. Many apprentices were taught only how to set straight matter and became what craft printers called mere "typestickers."[40] As a result, conflicts over apprenticeship focused more sharply on the division of labor, skills, and criteria for determining competence. As we will see, apprentices seriously jeopardized journeymen's class and gender interests in ways they had not done before.

Redefining Masculinity and Work: Class and Gender Implications of the Decline of Apprenticeship after 1890

The introduction of the Linotype into newspaper composing rooms after 1890 recast the class and gender issues involved in the apprenticeship question. Employers introduced methods of scientific management, subdividing the work and measuring workers' speed. Work on the composing machine, as one printer explained, made typesetting "as mechanical as it possibly can be under human agency." The machine operator had little time to think. "Iniquitous shop rules" had lowered the social esteem of craftsmen, one printer complained. At work the printer became "practically a prisoner . . . without the liberty to talk freely or see his friends, no matter how great the emergency."[41]

Before the introduction of the Linotype the work process was conducive to socialization as well as technical instruction of the apprentice. M. Nicholson, a journeyman printer, explained: "In the halcyon days preceding the linotype conversation in the composing room . . . was a great aid to the beginner, for he could hear arguments, disputes, sometimes a brief lecture, on almost every question." Journeymen developed a sense of proper grammar and acquired "an appreciable degree of culture in literary matters" which the boys in the office sought to emulate. The apprentice learned that a printer who made spelling or grammatical er-

[39]*Typographical Advertiser*, July 1867, 342.
[40]Tracy, *History of the Typographical Union*, 1098; Arthur R. Porter, Jr., *Job Property Rights: A Study of the Job Controls of the International Typographical Union* (New York: King's Crown Press, 1954).
[41]*Typographical Journal*, December 1913, 673, 674; March 1908, 253.

rors was ridiculed. The future printers "received their cue from this stimulating atmosphere." But composing machines limited opportunities for
this type of learning.[42]

The first Linotypes, combined with economic recession at the turn of
the century, increased unemployment and destroyed printers' job security.
By 1894, in New York City alone 266 machines had been installed, dis-
placing 480 printers. Conservative estimates indicated that one machine
displaced two printers.[43]

Unemployment was a threat to printers' independence, a central element of their masculinity throughout the nineteenth century. A man
without a job was not simply unemployed, he was "idle." The "strong"
man was juxtaposed against one who lived in enforced idleness. For a
man, lack of productive work induced a "sense of insecurity." The idle
man was weak, a "restless spirit." An unemployed man was a "deplor-
able spectacle."[44]

As well, unemployment jeopardized men's positions as family providers. Samuel Gompers, president of the American Federation of Labor,
explained to the Industrial Commission in 1899: "Man, by his physical
condition is the natural breadwinner of the family, and it is his duty to
work, and not only is it his duty, but he has the right to work, the right
to the opportunity to work." Therefore, he argued, when a two-thirder
was hired in preference to a journeyman, society did the worker and his
family a great injustice. The consequence, he continued, was "idle men
and busy children. . . . The boy is perhaps supporting the father."[45] The
threat of unemployment turned the so-called natural relation between a
man and his son upside down by making the boy productive and the man
idle. Such an unnatural situation could hardly be tolerated.

Faced with increased prospects of unemployment after the introduction of typesetting machines, union men sought to reduce the numbers of
apprentices and to limit further the types of work apprentices could
do.[46] By the 1890s journeymen argued that boys, lacking manhood,

[42]Ibid., November 1915, 609; December 1913, 673, 674.

[43]Stevens, *New York Typographical Union No. 6*, 466; George Barnett, "The Introduction of the Linotype," in his *Chapters on Machinery and Labor* (Cambridge: Harvard University Press, 1926), 6. In 1908 unemployment among printers in New York State was
21.6%. By the second decade of the twentieth century the increased size of newspapers had
somewhat reduced the extent of unemployment: in 1913 only 6.1% of printers in the state
were unemployed. See *New York Labor Bulletin*, 15, no. 3, whole no. 56 (September
1913).

[44]New York State Bureau of Labor Statistics, *Annual Report*, 1886, 23, 24.

[45]U.S. Industrial Commission, *Hearings: Report of the Industrial Commission on the Relations and Conditions of Capital and Labor*, vol. 7, *Manufacturers and General Business
and Testimony Taken November 1, 1899* (Washington, D.C.: U.S. Government Printing
Office, 1901), 620–21.

[46]Massachusetts Bureau of Statistics of Labor, *Annual Report*, 1907, 9–11; *Typographical Journal*, May 1916, 744.

could not operate the machines effectively: work on the new machines required manliness if it was to be done properly. The typographical union succeeded in keeping boys off machines until 1903, when they allowed them to practice during the last three months of their five-year apprenticeship.[47] The typographical unions' objections to publishers' use of boys to do "men's work" on typesetting machines frequently precipitated strikes.[48]

Restriction of apprentices to certain types of work differed distinctly from earlier practice. Embedded in this policy were changes in the ways printers understood masculinity and its relation to work. Previously union men had maintained that apprentices acquired their masculinity by engaging in the work. The custom, therefore, had been for journeymen to consider all work in a printing office appropriate for an apprentice.[49]

Rationales for limiting the number of apprentices also changed. Whereas earlier printers defended apprenticeship restrictions in terms of their right to set their wages, their role as family provider, and the manly respectability of the craft, now they justified the limits in terms of their rights to the job itself.

Journeymen also sought to curtail the labor supply by redefining the criteria for gauging workers' competence.[50] This strategy, too, entailed significant shifts in conceptions of masculinity. No longer were the completion of apprenticeship and the holding of a union card sufficient evidence of workers' abilities. The inadequacy of the apprenticeship system now also threatened the union as certifier of workers' skills.

Throughout most of the nineteenth century, union printers claimed that a completed apprenticeship demonstrated a worker's competence; it thus became the primary requisite for admission into a printers' association or a typographical union.[51] As one union member explained in his testimony to the Industrial Commission in 1899: "We hold, and believe we can safely maintain that a card of the International Typographical Union is prima facie evidence of a man's competency."[52]

[47]Elizabeth Faulkner Baker, *Displacement of Men by Machines: Effects of Technological Change in Commercial Printing* (New York: Columbia University Press, 1933), 117. In 1907 New York Typographical Local 6 adopted provisions that strictly regulated the work apprentices could do in newspaper offices during each year of apprenticeship, limiting work on machines to the last year of the term; Stevens, *New York Typographical Union No. 6*, 462–63.
[48]*American Newspaper Publishers' Association Bulletin*, Mar. 12, 1903; *The Unionist*, Aug. 7, 1899; New York State Bureau of Labor Statistics, *Annual Report*, 1890, case no. 2529.
[49]Barnett, "Introduction of the Linotype," 11.
[50]*Typographical Journal*, June 1909, 658.
[51]Stevens, *New York Typographical Union No. 6*, 454.
[52]U.S. Industrial Commission, *Hearings*, 583.

The power and prestige of the typographical union were based on the competence of its members. A union card, union men maintained, should be an assurance to the employer "that the bearer thereof is qualified to fill the position to which he is assigned."[53] Proper training made a man "worthy of his hire."[54] The advantage of the apprenticeship system and the union's control over it, printers explained, was that it prevented the labor market from being flooded with incompetent printers.[55] At least in part, union members constructed a defense of apprenticeship by appealing to employers' interests. They did not challenge the wage system or the idea that the employer was due a fair day's work for a fair day's pay. Balancing this equation, they maintained, required certain kinds of workers—manly ones, whom they identified as regularly apprenticed union members.

By the 1880s, however, a completed apprenticeship could no longer guarantee competence. Employers complained that possession of a union card was no assurance that the possessor was in fact a competent worker. Mark Crawford, president of the International Typographical Union (ITU), conceded in 1884 that there were incompetent men in the union and that their presence seriously challenged the adequacy of the union card as evidence of a printer's competence.[56] ITU president Martin Witter in 1886 expressed his fear that a large class of incompetents was being produced because of the lack of systematic apprenticeship training. These incompetents not only embarrassed the union but also were fatal to its prosperity and to the happiness of the new members themselves. "Dissatisfaction, jealousy, and in many cases recklessness were the result."[57]

By the 1880s competency requirements began to be specified in contracts between local typographical unions and employers.[58] Employers now sought to define competence in quantitative terms, measuring and evaluating workers' speed and performance in relation to the minimum output for machine composition. In this way, employers sought to have men prove their competence on a daily basis at work, not simply to obtain their jobs but to keep them.

Union men attempted to circumvent employers' standards by distinguishing competence from other criteria of workers' performance, such as carelessness, inefficiency, and inattention to the details of the work.[59]

[53] *Typographical Journal,* August 1912, 218.
[54] Report of the 28th Annual Meeting of the American Newspaper Publishers' Association (ANPA), New York City, Apr. 22–24, 1914, 32.
[55] U.S. Industrial Commission, *Hearings,* 583.
[56] Tracy, *History of the Typographical Union,* 1097.
[57] New York State Bureau of Labor Statistics, *Annual Report,* 1886, 203–4.
[58] Jacob Loft, *The Printing Trades* (New York: Farrar & Rinehart, 1944), 123.
[59] Chicago Typographical Union, minutes, vol. 4 (Mar. 27, 1892), 313–14, Chicago His-

They limited the meaning of competence to whether a printer had the ability to do the work, not whether or not his performance actually lived up to an established standard. Consequently, a foreman who discharged a man whose fitness for the work had already been determined had to "show deterioration as a workman or that general unfitness—physical, mental or moral—had come from them since employment."[60]

Manliness was coterminous with competence, which in turn was the foundation for their privileges as workingmen; it was also the basis on which they formulated challenges to employers' demands for speedup and changes in their work. To declare a man incompetent, then, was to challenge his manliness. Workingmen claimed that masculine character-istics were required for mechanical typesetting work. In contrast to their earlier claims, they maintained that these were abilities a man brought to the work. Workers discharged for incompetence lost not only their jobs but their manliness. A foreman's right to judge competence also gave him the power to determine who was a man. If a man's competence was successfully challenged, he lost all his "job property rights." A print-er's job, what he called his "situation," became his property, and it ac-crued the same rights and protections given to owners of other types of property.[61] The union protected the job rights of every man "provided he does good work and can set 3,700 ems per hour, leaded slugs, or 3,200 ems per hour, solid slugs."[62] For these reasons, a foreman's arbitrariness had to be controlled. As James O'Leary put it to the members of the Chicago Typographical Union when he appealed charges of incompe-tence, "For myself I do not plead, but beg for the cause of manhood that you halt the insidious soul destroying practices too long indulged in by the cravenhearted."[63]

Competence was deemed so central to journeymen's ability to fulfill their manly responsibilities and to their masculine identity that those la-beled incompetent, union men believed, became despondent, broken in spirit and even suicidal. Men should be spared "the temptations and dan-gers which come from incompetency," concluded the ITU president.[64]

Workingmen had redefined and narrowed the meaning of competence in light of new work standards. But in doing so, they put their masculin-ity on a shaky foundation. By the 1890s even a man who had once been

torical Society; Porter, *Job Property Rights*, 36–44; Stevens, *New York Typographical Union No. 6*, 529.

[60]Chicago Typographical Union, Executive Committee minutes, vol. 12 (Nov. 22, 1914), 130, Chicago Historical Society.

[61]For an extended discussion of printers' application of property rights to jobs in com-posing rooms, see Porter, *Job Property Rights*.

[62]"Report of the Machine Committee," in Chicago Typographical Union, minutes, vol. 5 (Sept. 29, 1895), 307.

[63]Chicago Typographical Union, minutes, vol. 8 (July 29, 1906), 305.

[64]*Typographical Journal*, November 1911, 525; suppl., October 1911, 32.

declared competent could lose his ability to perform his job. Masculinity and competence were no longer enduring characteristics.

When the Linotype was introduced, many older journeymen who could not learn to operate the machine or who could not work up to the production standard were forced to retire or to find other means of employment. Journeymen could no longer claim to be masters of their craft. Some were simply displaced by the new technology while others were forced to revert to the status of learner. Many took courses at typesetting schools established by employers, machine manufacturers, and typographical locals.

The new standards for judging competence on the Linotype emphasized workers' endurance and intensified the conflict between journeymen and apprentices by favoring younger over older workers. The line between the apprentice as boy and the journeyman as man became less distinct. Given these circumstances, journeymen justifiably perceived apprentices as their rivals.

Changes in work conditions, the speeding up of production on machine work, the adoption of time wages, and new standards of competence made it increasingly difficult for journeymen to assume responsibility for an apprentice's on-the-job training. Journeymen abandoned systematic attempts to teach boys at work, since their manhood as well as their job property rights now depended on their ability continually to work up to specified production norms.[65]

Although journeymen contributed to the demise of apprenticeship by forfeiting their role in training, they also feared the implications of a weakened apprenticeship system. The increased specialization of apprentices on one aspect of work jeopardized their future claims to competence and hence to manhood. Accompanying specialization was what printers saw as "a loss of independence, and, to some extent, a sense of helplessness."[66] A union printer pointed to the serious consequences to boys who had been deprived of a proper apprenticeship. Only those instructed in every branch, he said, were "practically equipped for the battle" when they reached manhood.[67]

As in the past, printers voiced their objections to employers' misuse of boys in paternalistic terms. But around the turn of the century, they combined paternalism with a critique of capitalist values of profitmaking. Now they identified a conflict between masculininty and a system of wage earning. Journeymen blamed employers' greed for "the neglect of our boys."[68] The president of the ITU decried employers' practice of

[65]Tracy, *History of the Typographical Union*, 1099.
[66]*Inland Printer*, September, 1895, 594.
[67]*Typographical Journal*, Apr. 1, 1898, 271.
[68]*Inland Printer*, December 1897, 303.

keeping an apprentice on a particular task once he became proficient at it, "solely because his highly specialized service reduces the cost of production a fraction of a cent a column."[69] Often the apprentice was given no instruction at all, but simply picked up whatever knowledge he could.[70] A union printer lamented: "Now the boy is not engaged for the purpose of making a man of him, but rather to make money out of his labor."[71]

Encoded in union men's version of competence was a critique of capitalism articulated in gendered terms. They juxtaposed their fatherly responsibilities for the boys' welfare with the boys' development of manly character and conflated protecting this next generation of men with safeguarding the future of manly work itself. Inadequate training in the entire craft and a specialized division of labor, said the ITU president, spelled "not only economic loss but the possible ruination of men." A man's competence gave him a sense of manly independence which an incompetent worker lacked. Further, an apprentice specialized in one aspect of the craft was deprived of his manly honor, for he was forced to "steal the trade" by working below union wages in order to support his family. An incompetent obtained employment by "some form of misrepresentation as to his abilities," only to be turned out as soon as the quality of his work became apparent. The man came to be known as an incompetent, and as a result, "the poor unfortunate has no place to go and is welcomed nowhere, except it be in a saloon of the lowest class. . . . If the incompetent is a father, then these conditions are almost sure to breed criminal tendencies among his children."[72]

For such reasons, the union should examine the effects of an inadequate apprenticeship training "on the boy and the man," not just on the cost of production, said the president in 1911. A "mock apprenticeship" was the parent of misfortunes. When a young man secures his first job upon becoming a journeyman and finds he is not much of an artisan, that he is below par, and that "probably he has no real right to call himself a printer," the knowledge comes as a shock. The boy's discovery of his defects leads him to periods of depressions, which "break down his spirit and leave the youth enveloped in the dark gloom of utter hopelessness." Employers dismiss such arguments as mawkish, but "those who are students of the development of character and manhood will not dismiss these features as negligible."[73]

[69]*Typographical Journal*, suppl., October 1911, 32.
[70]New York State Bureau of Labor Statistics, *Annual Report*, 1886, 216–17, 297; *Inland Printer*, December 1897, 303.
[71]*Typographical Journal*, March 1908, 251.
[72]Ibid., suppl., October 1911, 32; December 1913, 678.
[73]Ibid., suppl., October 1911, 32.

To union men competence had become contingent upon biological traits, not just acquired skills. Using the language of eugenics then in vogue, these men articulated their defense of work as manly in terms of the special masculine aptitudes and innate abilities they brought to the work, which made them better printers than others. "If we are to have skilled journeymen we must have the right kind of material to work with," union officers maintained.[74] These views of the relationship between masculinity and work shaped the ways union men dealt with the apprenticeship question. They claimed that not all boys had the ability to become competent printers. Therefore a boy's aptitude for printing should be established before he became an apprentice or gained admission as a journeyman.

Middle-class reformers often advocated training in skilled trades for lower-class boys. Overseers of the Poor placed homeless boys in apprenticeships and later established industrial training schools.[75] Of the twenty-seven trades listed in an 1886 report of the Overseers of the Poor, printing was one of three in which the majority of lower-class boys were placed.[76] The union strongly opposed these efforts, arguing that such boys were not fit to be printers—"teaching a trade to a miscellaneous lot of boys who merely played with type when the spirit moved them was an expensive way of making useless motions." The boys who should be trained as printers were the ones who already had selected printing as their life's occupation.[77]

Union men traced the decline in printers' general level of competence to the admission of the wrong kind of boys as apprentices. The Linotype made the attraction of "desirables" as apprentices a problem for the union. The ITU Committee on Supplemental Education identified the devaluation of manual labor and decline of craft respectability as the reasons why more qualified young men did not seek to become printers. Drawing on images of freedom, patriotism, and nativism, the union articulated a version of masculinity in which white, working-class, native-born sons were the heirs to true manhood; these were the qualities necessary to be a competent craftsman. "Americanism" was incompat-

[74]Ibid., suppl., August 1921, 216–17.

[75]Employers made ethnicity an important factor in selecting boys for admission to their training schools. They claimed that boys of certain nationalities, especially German, were interested in attaining high levels of proficiency and demonstrated special aptitude: Carl De Witt Davis, *A Study of the School of Apprentices of the Lakeside Press* (Chicago: R. R. Donnelley, 1922), 39–40. In 1886 35% of the parents of apprentices were native-born Americans; 24% came from Ireland, Scotland, and Wales; and 6% came from England: New York State Bureau of Labor Statistics, *Annual Report*, 1886, 106.

[76]First was farming; second was the machine trade: New York State Bureau of Labor Statistics, *Annual Report*, 1886, 91.

[77]*Typographical Journal*, January 1915, 23.

ible with the indignities and penalties being imposed on "free men." Boys "with spirit and red blood in their veins will not submit to such tyrannies." Boys seek more "manly pursuits," printers claimed. To attract the best American youths, union printers warned employers, "you will have to treat them less like prisoners of necessity and more like men."[78] Their voices linked manliness with craftwork in terms that conflated workers' rights with the requisites of masculinity.

Union men's rhetoric in the late nineteenth and early twentieth centuries sometimes combined the contradictory language of the physical fitness revival, which focused on the possibility of improving one's physical abilities through exercise, with that of eugenics and Darwinism, which emphasized heredity and innate biological capacities. The lack of an apprenticeship system in printing offices allowed boys to be indiscriminately employed without regard to their fitness for the trade, lamented one printer.[79] Since the bosses were willing to take on any kind of boy, the union should require testing and qualifications. The best way to rid the trade of incompetents was to head them off in the beginning by requiring apprentice applicants to take an examination to ascertain their aptitude for the trade. The boy should also be examined by a physician to ensure that he had the "bodily capacity" for the work.[80]

Union men's new appeals to inherent aptitudes were consistent with changes in their views concerning the relationship between work and masculinity. Men's self-respect now became linked to the idea that they alone could do certain kinds of work. Union men no longer argued that the work itself was masculine; now they claimed that they brought their masculinity to the work they did. Men made better compositors than women, they said, because men had inherent masculine characteristics, such as physical endurance, which allowed them to work longer on the typesetting machines. Women typesetters' physical limitations and natural temperaments made them less competent than men as typesetters.[81]

Being male was not sufficient to qualify one as a printer, however; not all males were equally suited to the work. Some boys, like all women, were considered too "delicate" to withstand the "long hours and constant mental and bodily strain" required by the printer's work. Therefore, "extreme care must be used in selecting boys who possess the necessary educational qualifications and are mentally and physically fit-

---

[78]Ibid., March 1908, 253.

[79]*Inland Printer*, February 1898, 629. On Americans' concern to maintain the viability of the nation through eugenics and physical fitness in the early twentieth century, see Harvey Green, *Fit for America* (New York: Pantheon, 1986), chap. 9.

[80]*Typographical Journal*, December 1896, 425–26; June 15, 1897, 465–66.

[81]Baron, "Contested Terrain."

ted." If unfit boys were kept out of the printing business, one printer claimed, "consumption and other tubercular complaints would not be so remarkable for their ravages in the trade."[82]

Union printers and employers sought to define the criteria for competence by controlling aptitude tests and certification exams. Union printers sometimes charged that employers were unfair because they included questions that were "foreign" to the business. Journeymen claimed that employers brought boys into the trade indiscriminately, without regard for the lad's tastes and abilities.[83]

Employers countered that the union's criteria obstructed boys' opportunities to "rise in the world."[84] Employers claimed that their aptitude tests selected those who would be most efficient at the work. They evaluated an apprenticeship applicant's morals, physical appearance, mental alertness, physique, and physical health, as well as the industriousness and thrift of his parents.[85]

Employers suggested and developed a number of solutions to the apprenticeship problem. They called for the old apprenticeship requirements of proficiency in all aspects of printing to be replaced by a system of certification of competence in specialized branches or types of work.[86] But the major strategy employers pursued by the end of the nineteenth century was to establish a system of school training.[87] The Linotype was designed to do straight composition and therefore reduced employers' demands for apprentices to do this type of work. Further, by 1909, when time wages had supplanted the piece wage system, employers wanted to remove training from the shop floor because teaching apprentices distracted journeymen and lowered output. Printing, employers claimed, was a science, not an art, and therefore could and should be taught in schools as a set of general principles.[88]

[82]*Typographical Journal,* December 1896, 425–26; June 15, 1897, 465–66; suppl. August 1920, 245; December 1896, 425–26; June 1897, 465–66.
[83]Ibid., September 1900, 228.
[84]Ibid., August 1904, 132.
[85]See generally issues of *ANPA Bulletin* in the early twentieth century.
[86]*Inland Printer,* April 1888, 516.
[87]Employers made numerous efforts to replace apprenticeship with various types of training programs and trade schools throughout the nineteenth century. In the 1830s some employers established their own training schools. In the 1850s and 1860s employers attempted to circumvent the union's apprenticeship restrictions by hiring untrained women and providing them with six weeks of on-the-job training. Such efforts were largely unsuccessful. See Baron, "Women and the Making of the American Working Class."
[88]On the Linotype and need for apprentices, see Baker, *Displacement of Men by Machines,* 117. The movement to replace piece wages with time wages followed in the wake of the Linotype. By 1909 piece rates were virtually obsolete: Loft, *Printing Trades,* 45; Barnett, "Introduction of the Linotype," 10. On printing taught as a science, see Douglas, *American Apprenticeship,* 179.

By the end of the nineteenth century the development of scientific management, the passage of state compulsory education laws, and new work processes bolstered employers' efforts to train printers outside the apprenticeship system. The number of manual training schools grew rapidly in the 1890s, from fifteen schools with 3,300 students in 1894 to forty schools with 13,900 pupils in 1897.[89]

Employers supported schools, as newspaper publishers put it, to "war with the Union."[90] Most of the technical and trade schools for printing established by employers, such as the New York Trade School, the Winona Technical Institute in Indianapolis, the Wentworth Institute in Boston, and the Dunwoodie Institute in Minneapolis, were avowedly antiunion.[91] As one union executive explained in 1886: "If a boy become [sic] a full-fledged mechanic in a technical school, he would not know anything about unions, nor would he have any sympathy with their rules and regulations."[92] The goals of these schools were not simply to teach technical aspects of the work but to socialize pupils into a nonunion work culture. As one school director explained in 1911, boys learned "ideals, discipline, and loyalty [to the company], right along with technical training."[93]

Union printers saw employers' schools as training grounds for incompetents. School graduates had no knowledge whatever of the art of printing, according to the union. Such schools produced not printers but "freaks" or "botches" who were incapable of the work. Freaks did not operate the machinery; they "assaulted" it. One union man cited a school graduate who had broken thirteen spacebands within the first two hours of employment. Such instances of incompetence union men claimed were common. But of greatest concern to them was that despite incompetence, some graduates managed to gain admission to the union. "They get cards," one union man explained. "Nobody knows how—but they get 'em."[94]

[89]Douglas, *American Apprenticeship,* 179.

[90]*ANPA Bulletin,* May 10, 1923.

[91]*The Unionist,* Sept. 11, 1906, 2. On trade schools used to train boys as strikebreakers, see Douglas, *American Apprenticeship,* 315–16; John Clyde Oswald, *Printing in the Americas* (New York: Gregg, 1937), chap. 28; Loft, *Printing Trades,* 214. The United Typothetae contributed an endowment of $225,000 to the Carnegie Institute of Technology in Pittsburgh: Oswald, *Printing in the Americas,* 361. Several state associations of employing printers maintained schools in various states. The New York Typothetae, in conjunction with the American Machine Typesetting Company, established a technical school to train typesetters during the struggle with the union over the eight-hour day in 1906: *The Unionist,* Sept.11, 1906, 2. Some printing plants, such as the Lakeside Press of Chicago and Foote & Davies of Atlanta, even established their own training schools.

[92]New York State Bureau of Labor Statistics, *Annual Report,* 1886, quoted in Bemis, "Relation of Labor Organizations," 85.

[93]Quoted in Loft, *Printing Trades,* 223–24.

[94]*Typographical Journal,* August 1912, 217–18.

Union printers disagreed about what measures to take to deal with incompetents. Some union members supported instituting examinations to qualify for union membership. Others favored including incompetents as members to prevent them from being hired as cheap, nonunion labor. Still another group maintained that those who could set only straight matter should not be called journeymen and should not be admitted into the union.[95]

Union men were caught in a double bind. On the one hand, the apprenticeship system as it existed by the late nineteenth century was unenforced and impractical. In its current form it jeopardized their class and gender positions. Yet the replacement of apprenticeship with technical training schools created other class and gender crises for men printers. It is not surprising, therefore, that typographical union locals advocated a variety of solutions to the apprenticeship problem and that the national union developed no consistent position on training schools until the early twentieth century.[96]

Union members argued the merits and demerits of trade school education for decades.[97] Whereas in the nineteenth century, the ITU dismissed trade schools as "jokes," by the first decade of the twentieth century the ITU was forced to accept trade schools in the hope of influencing their direction. "The trade school is here," the ITU president declared in 1907.[98] In 1915 the ITU established a Commission on Vocational Training to determine the aims, purposes, and net results of such schools. The union explained to the members: "We are face to face with a condition that will prove a menace to the trade or an advantage to it dependent largely on how we handle the question now."[99]

By the early twentieth century the typographical union found it increasingly difficult to legitimate training solely on the basis of intuition and rule-of-thumb methods of work. The ITU eventually acceded to the new terms of craft legitimation. They made numerous efforts to establish training programs and schools under their own control.[100] The ITU Course in Printing, developed in 1908, aimed to supersede the rule-of-thumb approach by teaching students the principles involved in printing.

[95]New York State Bureau of Labor Statistics, *Annual Report*, 1886, 203; *Typographical Journal*, August 1912, 218, and October 1904, 393.
[96]See Tracy, *History of the Typographical Union*, 1098–1100; New York State Bureau of Labor Statistics, *Annual Report*, 1886, 159–63; *Typographical Journal*, suppl. August 1915, 256–59.
[97]Some typographical locals were more vehemently opposed to trade schools than others. *New York State Department of Labor Bulletin*, no. 30 (1906), 367.
[98]Quoted in Tracy, *History of the Typographical Union*, 909.
[99]ITU communication, Jan. 11, 1915, in Chicago Typographical Union, minutes, vol. 12 (Feb. 28, 1915), 200–201.
[100]The AFL considered establishing its own training schools in the early 1900s. The New York Typographical local established a school in 1909.

Instruction at the workplace would be reduced, the union explained, since graduates of the course, "having mastered the principles . . . will be able to reason out what should or should not be done."[101]

From 1908 to 1913 more than 4,300 students took the course. Recognizing that having a good theoretical knowledge of the work was necessary if the printer was "to maintain his reputation of being the happy medium between artist and mechanic," printers established technical clubs that offered programs and lectures designed to increase the printers' understanding of the craft. Ultimately, however, these various union efforts failed for want of sufficient financial resources.[102]

Ultimately both the union and employers sought state intervention to resolve the apprenticeship question. The compromise solution was a system of publicly funded vocational education. Employers had succeeded in their efforts to create a new form of industrial training in schools.[103] The union accepted the idea of technical schools but rejected those financed and controlled by employers. Employers accepted the union position that schools should supplement rather than displace apprenticeship. Apprenticeship came to mean a combination of classroom instruction and job experience.[104]

Despite these compromises, employers and printers continued to battle over the nature and organization of these schools.[105] The establishment of formal schooling supplemented by entrance and exit exams led union printers to fear that they would lose control over admission to the trade and over the definition of competence.

For printers throughout the nineteenth century skill was a form of property. But by the end of the century journeymen began to consider their positions as skilled workers a property right that they could pass along to their sons as part of their role as family provider. In earlier decades printers' sons entered a variety of trades, but by the 1890s generational inheritance became markedly high among printers; sometimes a printer's son had a right to a job at the same firm as his father.[106] The

[101]Report from *Typographical Journal* in ANPA, *Labor Bulletin,* Apr. 11, 1908.

[102]*Inland Printer,* July 1897, 410; Douglas, *American Apprenticeship,* 317.

[103]By 1912 employers and organized labor together supported a federal bill to provide public funds for industrial education. This was part of a general movement supported by the National Association of Manufacturers and the AFL: Douglas, *American Apprenticeship,* 326.

[104]*Typographical Journal,* suppl., August 1917, 206.

[105]Employers continued to dispute the union's limitations on the numbers of apprentices. Even after the development of publicly funded vocational schools in 1925, publishers complained of insufficient numbers of trained operators. While union shops had only 1 apprentice to 16 journeymen, nonunion shops had a ratio of 1 to 5.6. The solution of this problem, publishers argued, was creation of more trade schools to supplant the apprenticeship system altogether. See *ANPA Bulletin,* May 6, 1925.

[106]Philadelphia Social History Project data (based on U.S. census returns from 1850–1880), Chicago local newsletter reports of new members, and biographical sketches of

replacement of the apprenticeship system with training schools threatened to disinherit printers' sons and to undermine men's roles as family providers.[107] Union men believed that the schools would refuse to admit their sons.[108] The development of "objective" criteria of "fitness" and "adaptability" meant limitations on the ability of union members to pave the way for family and friends to enter the trade.[109]

In some areas, particularly in large cities, where the number of apprenticeship opportunities fell short of the demand, union men debated the consequences of giving printers' sons preference over those of nonprinters. A member of the New York Typographical local complained that printers' sons had little opportunity to become apprentices in union shops. As he saw it, union printers' sons should be given preference over sons of nonprinters in learning the trade: "It is their undoubted right to be given an opportunity to follow in the footsteps of their fathers." Others expressed fear of retaliation and foresaw large pools of nonunion printers if sons of nonprinters were discriminated against. In many smaller cities, however, the inheritance of positions was not considered a problem because there were sufficient apprenticeship opportunities.[110]

Union limitations on the numbers of apprentices as a solution to the unemployment problem lessened the possibility of their own sons' entry into the craft. One printer lamented: "Year after year the unions draw the apprenticeship limit a little tighter, until today, in some branches of the trade, at least, an enterprising and hopeful father who desires his son to become a disciple of the art preservative is met with a complete rebuff."[111] Thus employers were not entirely to blame for this crisis in men's ability to fulfill their fatherly responsibilities to their sons. In the

---

Providence, Rhode Island, Typographical Union members from 1762 to 1907 reveal few identifiable father-son printer pairs. Although these data do not enable one systematically to identify all father-son pairs, the rarity with which they appear (11 sons in a sample of 180 printer-headed Philadelphia households from 1850–1880) suggests they were exceptional. For more discussion of job inheritance among Canadian and British printers, see Wayne Roberts, "The Last Artisans: Toronto Printers, 1896–1914," in *Essays in Canadian History*, ed. Gregory S. Kealey and Peter Warrian (Toronto: McClelland & Stewart, 1976), 128; and Cynthia Cockburn, *Brothers: Male Dominance and Technological Change* (London: Pluto, 1983), 114.

[107]Douglas, *American Apprenticeship*, 181; *The Unionist*, September 1902, 2. For discussion of inheritance of skilled positions in other trades, see Geoffrey Crossick, *An Artisan Elite in Victorian Society: Kentish London, 1840–1880* (Totowa, N.J.: Croom Helm, 1978), esp. chap. 6; Takao Matsumora, *The Victorian Glass Makers: The Labour Aristocracy Revisited* (Manchester: Manchester University Press, 1983), 72–75; and Stephen Hill, *The Dockers: Class and Tradition in London* (London: Heinemann, 1976).

[108]Bemis, "Relation of Labor Organizations," 80–84.

[109]*Typographical Journal*, November 1915, 610.

[110]*Typographical Journal*, June 1914, 760; August 1914, 199–200, 202, 262; September 1914, 429.

[111]*Inland Printer*, February 1898, 629.

transition to new conceptions of masculinity the union had adopted class and gender strategies that were internally contradictory.

Throughout the period the issues raised by journeymen printers concerning wages, working conditions, and hiring and firing were influenced by their relation to boy apprentices. These issues touched the very core of these men's gender and work concerns. But the nature of these concerns and the ways they were articulated shifted dramatically and had important ramifications for their relations with boys as well as with their employers.

During most of the nineteenth century printers couched their gender arguments in terms that left the wage relation intact. They accepted the premise of a fair day's work for a fair day's pay, and combined it with arguments for a family wage. Efforts to define a fair day's work became a battle over identifying manly workers. By the end of the century workingmen were articulating a version of masculinity that led them to voice new concerns about the nature of capitalism. But the terms they adopted set limits on their ability to maintain manly dignity through work. They became mired in contradictory strategies. The men developed new and different reasons for excluding boys from "men's work." The new terms for defining sexual differences formulated masculinity not as an all-or-nothing characteristic but as a matter of degree. Being a male was a necessary but not sufficient criterion of the capacity for manly work. Manliness was now measured at work by performance. Men had to prove their competence and reaffirm their manliness every day. Manly competence, once attained, was not guaranteed for life. Struggle with employers over work pace and standards were more than class issues; they were forumulated and fought in gendered terms.

CHAPTER THREE

Southern Honor, Southern Dishonor: Managerial Ideology and the Construction of Gender, Race, and Class Relations in Southern Industry

Dolores Janiewski

Southern employers behaved and spoke in ways designed to enhance awareness of racial and gender differences as they muted the recognition of any possible conflict between their own interests and those of white members of the laboring class. Tobacco planters in the seventeenth-century Chesapeake initiated the process that created racial distinctions and reorganized preexisting sexual divisions of labor. From these dominant practices antebellum and postbellum industrialists molded an industrial labor force. Each successive group of employers contributed to a managerial ideology that deflected attention from class to gender and racial issues. These conceptions of race and gender became a part of the social conventions by which southern whites located men and women, blacks and whites, within their social order long after slavery had ended. If we can understand the development of those notions of essential racial and gender differences and inequalities, we are on our way to understanding how and why sexual and racial divisions have become so deeply entrenched in the labor force.

Research on the segementation of the labor market has yielded important insights into the construction of differences between groups of workers, but its practitioners have often written as though managers operated freely in a cultural vacuum, guided only by their own economic interests. Identifying employers' motivations almost exclusively in class terms, they have ignored or downplayed gender and racial considerations.[1] Intent on explaining divisions among workers, they have concen-

[1]For a pioneering effort in this literature, see Richard C. Edwards, Michael Reich, and David M. Gordon, eds., *Labor-Market Segmentation* (Lexington, Mass.: D.C. Heath, 1975), and their later effort: David M. Gordon, Richard Edwards, and Michael Reich, *Segmented Work, Divided Workers: The Historical Transformation of Labor in the United*

trated on the workplace and the labor market—that is, on the sphere of production. While recognizing that workers bear other identities—racial and gender identities being among the most important—they have insisted, implicitly or explicitly, on the primacy of class. They have failed to give sufficient recognition to the dominant class interest in *reproducing* the members of their society as gendered and racially conscious beings. They have generally written "labor" history rather than integrating their work into the comparative study of gender, race, and class and analyzing the terms by which each of those relationships is represented by and to the members of each social group.[2]

Even Ruth Milkman's prize-winning, *Gender at Work* would be enhanced by more attention to issues that a study of the construction of southern labor markets and the sexual and racial divisions within them cannot avoid. Milkman's argument that ideology plays "a central role in reproducing the sexual division of labor once it has crystallized in a particular labor market" needs to be extended to include the role of ideology in the initial creation of sexual and racial divisions of labor and their persistence despite such major shifts as emancipation and the wartime recruitment of women into "men's jobs."[3] Preexisting assumptions about gendered labor, beyond the scope of Milkman's and similar workplace studies, shaped the managerial strategies she emphasizes and constrained the ability of unions and women workers to overcome them. An examination of one crucial aspect of the creation of a sexually and racially divided labor force in the South can help to trace the origins of conceptions of gendered labor which continue to influence twentieth-century labor relations outside as well as within the South.

Taking inspirations from Joan Scott's appeal for labor historians to examine "how people construct meaning" and "how difference (and therefore sexual difference) operates in the construction of meaning," let us examine a language created by a dominant class that stressed "identity" and "difference."[4] Emphasizing racial differences and gender differences among members of the "dominant" race, the language fashioned by southern employers submerged the reality of class domination. Daniel A. Tompkins, one of the most prominent ideologues of the New South,

States (Cambridge: Cambridge University Press, 1982).

[2]See Joan Scott, "On Language, Gender, and Working-Class History," *International Labor and Working-Class History*, 31 (Spring 1987), 1–13, and the replies by Bryan D. Palmer and Christine Stansell in the same issue for a spirited discussion of the need for labor historians to engage in an encounter with poststructuralists and cultural anthropologists.

[3]Ruth Milkman, *Gender at Work: The Dynamics of Job Segregation by Sex during World War II* (Urbana: University of Illinois Press, 1987), 157.

[4]Scott, "On Language, Gender, and Working-Class History," 1.

wrote plainly in 1901: "The white man loves to control, and loves the person willing to be controlled by him. The negro readily submits to the master hand, admires and even loves it."[5] Having accentuated the masculinity of the "master"race, Tompkins conflated a labor system with a sexual and racial system when he asserted that "love" for the inferior was achieved at the cost of submission. A common inheritance "naturally" endowed southern white men of every class with the right to dominate the "naturally" subordinated members of southern society, who included all women and black men.[6] His language, like that of his fellow manufacturers, rendered invisible the control his class of white men exerted over the other white men, women, and children who worked in their factories.

Origins

Tompkins deliberately used language that harkened back to the origins of labor relations in the South. Already acculturated into a society where a sexual division of labor allocated the major share of agricultural labor to men and domestic labor to women, the men who sought to establish a cash-crop economy in the southern colonies designated men as their primary labor supply. The original labor market involved a master's purchase of the laborer's person on a temporary or permanent basis. Slavery replaced indentured labor when the potential supply of European labor decreased and the price of African slaves declined. Slave owners embraced the idea of race as a way to represent the essential distinction between persons who could be enslaved and those who could not. Denying to Native Americans and Africans the rights of "freeborn Englishmen," slave owners simultaneously raised the status of members of their own race above that of even a temporary "unfree" person. They also lessened the danger arising from the expansion of a class of poor, recently freed indentured servants who were becoming a potentially rebellious class by the 1670s. Poorer whites, no longer required to perform the most servile labor, gained a stake in a system that replaced class with

[5]Daniel A. Tompkins, *Cotton and Cotton Oil* (Charlotte, N.C.: Published by the author, 1901), 47.
[6]This emphasis on language should not be taken as total acceptance of Scott's position that language constructs either gender or class. Like her critics Bryan Palmer and Christine Stansell, I do not wish to privilege gender or language (or race) over the actual activities in which southerners, male and female, constructed their social existence. See Bryan D. Palmer, "Response to Joan Scott," *International Labor and Working-Class History*, 31 (Spring 1987), 14–23, and Christine Stansell, "A Response to Joan Scott," ibid., 24–29.

race as the primary form of identity and difference in the planter-generated labor and linguistic system.[7]

White male property owners, architects of southern law, created a social order in which they could exercise legitimate authority over the other, subordinated members of their society in racial and gender-specific forms. To ensure the creation and reproduction of two races, the laws necessarily regulated sexual, social, and productive relations. As gender relations among the dominant racial group developed into a form of domestic patriarchalism, white women concentrated on domestic labor, the reproductive work of bearing "legitimate" heirs, and became the exclusive reproductive and sexual property of their fathers and husbands.[8] Simultaneously laws forbade white women to tend tobacco and refused to recognize them as productive laborers for purposes of taxation. Slaves, both women and men, became legally defined as productive and reproductive property whose labor and children belonged to their masters.[9] On one side of the racial divide, the law intervened directly to maintain the chastity of one group of women. On the other side, it offered no support for a slave woman's refusal of sexual access. Southern planters claimed exclusive control over sexual, productive, and reproductive property in racially and sexually distinct forms.[10]

Male members of the property-owning classes forged an ideological defense for the sexual and racial order they had constructed. They assumed the power to define and defend "virtue and decency" as well as "the barrier, which nature, as well as law, has erected between the white and black races."[11] Especially among the lower classes, when familial discipline and social ostracism failed to prevent such transgressions, their judicial arm punished violators of the moral code.[12] Applying the rules that had evolved in other patriarchal caste systems, they insisted that

[7]Edmund Morgan, in *American Slavery, American Freedom: The Ordeal of Colonial Virginia* (New York: Norton, 1975), makes these arguments about the shift from indentured white labor to enslaved black labor in Virginia.

[8]See Alan Kulikoff, *Tobacco and Slaves: The Development of Southern Cultures in the Chesapeake, 1680–1800,* Institute of Early American History and Culture (Chapel Hill: University of North Carolina Press, 1985), 166, 382.

[9]Winthrop Jordan, *White over Black: American Attitudes toward the Negro, 1550–1812* (New York: Norton, 1977), 167–78.

[10]As discussed by Gerda Lerner in *The Creation of Patriarchy* (New York: Oxford University Press, 1986), 100.

[11]John Campbell, "Negro Mania—The Negro and Other Races of Man," in *The Industrial Resources, Statistics, etc. of the U.S., and more particularly of the Southern and Western States,* 3 vols., comp. James D. B. De Bow, 2:197 (1852–53; rpt. New York: A. M. Kelley, 1966); James H. Hammond, "Progress of Southern Industry," in ibid., 3:34–35.

[12]See Victoria Elizabeth Bynum, "Unruly Women: The Relationship between Status and Behavior among Free Women of the North Carolina Piedmont, 1840–1865" (Ph.D. diss., University of California, San Diego, 1987), 174–203.

white women's sexual restraint offered the only safeguard for the purity of the superior race in a system where children bore the racial identities of their mothers.[13] Defining black women as a "class of females who set little value on chastity and afford easy gratification to the hot passions of men," they denied black women the honor they extolled in white women who possessed a reputation for chastity.[14] In effect proslavery ideologues portrayed slaves as a different order of being from themselves. Slaves were "innately and immutably immoral," licentious, and perpetually childlike; their only legitimate "family" was the one headed by the white planter.[15] As in other slave systems, for these slave women "economic exploitation and sexual exploitation were . . . linked" through the self-justifying language and actions of a male slave-owning group.[16] The logic of a patriarchal slaveholding society divided women into the respectable and the disreputable; the moral natures of these different sorts of women marked the classes and the races as made up of entirely different orders of beings.

In a world ideally organized according to this model, labor would be performed only by the degraded caste—the slaves—and the superior group would act only as master. Indeed, labor itself would function as a mark of degradation. All whites would own slaves; all blacks would be enslaved. In the words of Linton Stephens, brother of the Confederate vice president, "menial services and manual labor" would be confined to a "class of men defined by blood" rather than "a class marked by poverty."[17] All white women would be kept securely within the family economy and be supported by propertyholding male protectors. Most southern whites, however, could not ascend into the ranks of slaveholders and planters. Many white males had to engage in "the degradation of physical toil." Sometimes they might be required to work for their economic superiors. Relatively prosperous nonslaveholders might still conform to an attenuated version of the slaveholder's ideal by keeping their womenfolk out of the fields and exercising authority over the family labor force. But there were poor white women who had lost their male providers. Some white men could not even relieve their wives and daughters of "those domestic drudgeries" that impaired "delicate purity."[18]

[13]William Harper, "Memoir on Negro Slavery," in De Bow, *Industrial Resources*, 3:220, 228; Mary Douglas, *Purity and Danger: An Analysis of the Concepts of Pollution and Taboo* (London: Routledge & Kegan Paul, 1966), 125–27.

[14]Harper, "Memoir on Negro Slavery," 220; Campbell, "Negro Mania," 203.

[15]Margaret A. Burnham, "An Impossible Marriage: Slave Law and Family Law," *Law and Inequality: A Journal of Theory and Practice*, 5 (July 1987), 189.

[16]Lerner, *Creation of Patriarchy*, 100.

[17]Quoted in Lawrence Shore, *Southern Capitalists: The Ideological Leadership of an Elite, 1832–1885* (Chapel Hill: University of North Carolina Press, 1986), 44.

[18]James D. B. De Bow and William Daniell, *American Cotton Planter*, March 1854, quoted in Shore, *Southern Capitalists*, 35, 19.

Such class realities blurred the "unerring lines" that were supposed to mark the "distinction between the species" in a region whose leaders insisted "that capital and labor . . . should be represented by the master and the slave."[19] Somehow the frustrations of men unable to fulfill the social ideals had to be dealt with so that the labor and language system could remain compelling and mutually reinforcing.

The "thousands of poor, degraded whites among us" posed a problem once they began "to understand that they [had] rights."[20] As a potential employer reported, a "poor white man would feel affronted to be asked to engage in servile labor." For white women the association of labor with degradation was intensified by slavery's linkage of sexual dishonor with economic exploitation. Any occupation that placed a white woman near a black laborer, male or female, inflicted "a degree of degradation to which she could not condescend" and which her menfolk could not countenance. Wealthier whites, who sought to use the labor of white men and especially white women, faced a potential conflict between access to necessary labor and the maintenance of a racial and sexual hierarchy carefully constructed by the planters. Unless they could make work "respectable for white persons," either racial chaos, class conflict, sexual disorder, or economic disaster might occur.[21] If southern employers were to use white labor without endangering "our institutions," labor's "symbolic load" must be overcome while poorer whites must be reassured that they were indeed raised to the "general level" of other whites, as such planters as Jefferson Davis had promised them.[22]

Creating an Industrial Work Force in a Slave Economy

So long as tobacco, sugar, and cotton earned prices high enough to subsidize the purchase of slaves, planters could avoid the ideological contradictions their labor and linguistic system had created. But men who sought to develop manufacturing in the South could not easily escape the dilemma. Depending on the "size and character of the local labor pool, the regional price for slaves, the migratory patterns of whites, and the willingness of blacks and whites to enter the mills at prevailing wage

[19]Campbell, "Negro Mania," 203; South Carolina Institute, *Second Annual Report*, November 1850, quoted in Shore, *Southern Capitalists*, 37.
[20]William Gregg, *Essays on Domestic Industry* (1844), and J. H. Taylor, "Manufactures in South Carolina," *De Bow's Review*, January 1850, both quoted in Shore, *Southern Capitalists*, 30, 34.
[21]Charles T. James, "Cotton and Cotton Manufactures at the South," in De Bow, *Industrial Resources*, 1:241.
[22]Taylor, "Manufactures in South Carolina," quoted in Shore, *Southern Capitalists*, 34; Douglas, *Purity and Danger*, 124, 227; Jefferson Davis, March 1859, quoted in Shore, *Southern Capitalists*, 65.

rates, or even to work for wages," manufacturers decided on their own particular strategy.[23] Textile mills, needing water power and usually too undercapitalized to buy slaves, clustered in the Piedmont areas at the fall lines, where the available labor pool typically included white women and children unwanted in the agricultural economy. Tobacco factories gradually hired whites but the majority of their workers were slaves, purchased or hired. The numbers of white women and children in the industry increased in the 1850s, when the price of prime male slaves rose beyond the reach of manufacturers. But their employers maintained separate work sites for the newly hired whites and the remaining slaves.[24] Thus the sexual and racial divisions of labor developed by southern planters now shaped the choices of manufacturers.

Even as manufacturers conformed their recruitment policies to the "size and character of the local labor pool," they sought to justify the social and political consequences of their decisions. Those who hired white workers claimed that the practice encouraged their recruits to become "firm and uncompromising supporters of our institutions" by raising "this class from want," "beggary," and "moral degradation to a state of . . . moral and social respectability.[25] William Gregg, a pioneering textile manufacturer in South Carolina, solicited votes in the 1840s on "the ground that he had built a factory which gave work to poor white people."[26] Yet such a rationale could be completely convincing only if employers demonstrated their commitment to "the barrier which nature, as well as law, has erected between the white and black races." They had to exclude slaves from their workplaces so that whites would not be forced into "degrading positions where they would compete with blacks."[27] Providing additional reassurance, the supporters of the decision to hire white labor pointed to the dangers posed by the alternative choice. James Hammond, the last senator from South Carolina before the Civil War, argued that a slave mechanic was "more than half freed" and warned that such a slave would become "the most corrupt and turbulent of his class."[28] The mill that relied heavily on the labor of white women and children would be a refuge for the "afflicted" and would "improve not only the physical but the moral and intellectual conditions of our

[23]Randall M. Miller, "The Fabric of Control: Slavery in Antebellum Southern Textile Mills," *Business History Review,* 55 (Winter 1981), 471–90.

[24]Joseph Clarke Robert, *The Tobacco Kingdom: Plantation, Market, and Factory in Virginia and North Carolina, 1800–1860* (Gloucester, Mass.: Peter Smith, 1965), 197, 215–16.

[25]James, "Cotton and Cotton Manufactures," 241.

[26]Daniel A. Tompkins, *Cotton Mill, Commercial Features* (Charlotte, N.C.: Published by the author, 1899), 205.

[27]Quoted in Peter Rachleff, "Black, White, and Gray: Working-Class Activism in Richmond, Virginia, 1865–1890" (Ph.D. diss., University of Pittsburgh, 1981).

[28]Hammond, "Progress of Southern Industry," 34–35.

citizens." Children would be given "light and honorable employment." Any male hand "who shall utter any slanderous word reflecting upon the good name of any female engaged in the establishment" was threatened with discharge from the mill of one particularly upright textile operator.[29] In short, employers could choose to make their jobs "respectable for white persons" through ostentatious attention to their morality and the elimination of black workers from their factories. Adherents of this view insisted that slave labor should be confined to agriculture and white labor to manufacturing while predicting that a mixed-race labor force "would be in hostile array to our institutions."[30]

Employers who owned or hired slaves had to defend themselves against charges that industrial employment undermined slavery. Their defense of their policies harked back to Jefferson's warnings against the creation of a propertyless mob of white workers. Their spokesmen agreed with William Harper that such laborers, "kept in strict subordination, will be less dangerous than . . . a class of what are called free laborers."[31] They could point to the difficulties of persuading a sufficient number of whites to overcome their "notable reluctance . . . to accept employment in the cotton mill."[32] Yet the rising prices of slaves in the 1850s made their choice an expensive proposition.[33] Hampered by limited capital, the shortage of labor, and perplexing ideological dilemmas, southern manufacturers found it difficult to develop a successful labor recruitment strategy in the antebellum South.

After Emancipation

Emancipation removed the possibility of using slave labor and the ideological imperative of making a labor recruitment strategy appear compatible with slavery. Yet employers still needed great ideological dexterity. The war had shattered the social order into "demoralized and trembling fragments of society and law";[34] defeat had brought impoverishment and the collapse of the labor system. They had to devise a

[29]Quoted in Gary Freeze, "Poor Girls Who Might Otherwise Be Wretched: Society, Gender, and the Origins of Paternalism in North Carolina's Early Cotton Mills, 1836–1880," in Jeffrey A. Leiter et al., "Hanging by a Thread: Social Change in Southern Textiles," in process.

[30]South Carolina Institute, *Second Annual Report,* and Taylor, "Manufactures in the South," quoted in Shore, *Southern Capitalists,* 37, 34.

[31]Harper, "Memoir on Negro Slavery," 234.

[32]Quoted in Gavin Wright, *Old South, New South: Revolution in the Southern Economy since the Civil War* (New York: Basic Books, 1986), 128.

[33]James, "Cotton and Cotton Manufactures," 241.

[34]Zebulon Vance to Joseph Brown, January 1865, quoted in Shore, *Southern Capitalists,* 89.

recruitment strategy that would appear responsive to the political, economic, and social exigencies of the post–Civil War South. An agricultural system in disarray promised to give them easier access to labor. At the same time it raised the question whether freed people had "deteriorated as laborers." Some employers insisted that "young negroes are not equal to those of the older generation who were raised by whites."[35] The decision to hire white widows and their children could make employers who recruited those victims of the war appear patriotic and charitable. But the strategy of using white labor also risked worsening class divisions already widened by the war. Denying that the nature of black labor had been radically altered by emancipation, some employers claimed to prefer a black worker because "it is in his nature to submit to authority . . . and he does not want money or property enough to rise in rebellion against capital."[36]

Southern manufacturers faced ideological pressure from an unaccustomed direction. As the *Vicksburg Republican* proclaimed in April 1868, "The Republican Party is pledged to elevate labor, to educate the masses." Thomas Settle, a leading Republican in North Carolina, campaigned for the support of poorer whites, whom he promised to rescue from "moral servitude" to the power of planters and the degradation of labor the antebellum system had caused.[37] At the same time, southern manufacturers found it difficult to ignore the desires of planters, who still controlled most of the South's surviving resources. The planter spokesmen insisted that abolition should "be limited, controlled," so as to "make the change as slight as possible both to the white man and to the negro, the planter and the workman, the capitalist and the laborer." Edmund Rhett insisted that freedmen be "kept as near to the condition of slavery as possible and as far from the condition of the white man as is practicable."[38] Though manufacturers loudly proclaimed the New South, they ignored the heirs to the Old South at their peril.[39] Emancipation had not freed manufacturers from dealing with the ideological conflicts between antebellum conceptions of appropriate gender, race, and labor relations and the "free labor" ideology espoused by radical Republicans.

Manufacturers found it impossible to avoid involvement in the politi-

[35]R. Barnwell Rhett, Birmingham, Nov. 13, 1883, and Robert M. Patton, Birmingham, Nov. 12, 1883, in U.S. Senate Committee on Education and Labor, *Capital and Labor Investigation*, vol. 4, *Testimony* (Washington, D.C.: U.S. Government Printing Office, 1885), 153, 48.
[36]John W. Lapsley, planter and ironmaker, Birmingham, in ibid., 166.
[37]Quoted in Shore, *Southern Capitalists*, 135, 141.
[38]Quoted in ibid., 103.
[39]See Jonathan M. Weiner, *Social Origins of the New South: Alabama, 1860–1885* (Baton Rouge: Louisiana State University Press, 1978) for the way planters thwarted industrial development in one southern state.

cal arena. Republicanism appeared to offer the proper political vehicle for an aspiring industrial class. But southern Republicans were torn between a commitment to maintain a class of independent producers and a push toward an industrial economy of powerful employers and propertyless wage earners. They might best have pursued the first goal by promoting an interracial alliance between lower- and middle-class blacks and whites. But "moderate" Republicans warned against the dangers of economic radicalism and black equality as they sought to promote a favorable business climate to lure capital southward. The Democratic party counterattacked by proposing a cross-class alliance based on a common commitment to white supremacy which managed to "redeem" the South from a party divided by the interests of enterpreneurs, yeomen, and freedmen. The Ku Klux Klan and similar paramilitary groups aided the success of the ideological appeal.

Manufacturers were not simply bystanders during this political and cultural counterrevolution. Some prominent manufacturers joined Democrats in preaching a new gospel that was more in tune with the interests of entrepreneurs. Henry W. Grady, the champion of this New South, boasted of a "perfect democracy, the oligarchs leading in the popular movement" toward "diversified industry." In such a South blacks would be barred "from no avenue in which their feet are fitted to tread" but would never be permitted to regain the "negro supremacy" imposed during Reconstruction.[40] In the words of the *Manufacturers' Record*, " business principles" would triumph over "politics" in shaping the regional and national agenda.[41] By the 1890s Daniel Tompkins, another New South spokesman, declared that because "the people of the North realize that an excess of zeal in the cause of freedom does injury, we are now all free in the South, free to enter upon manufacturing enterprises and to help develop American resources and promote American civilization."[42] Combining ideological appeals to the dignity of labor, white supremacy, and economic development with attacks on "agrarianism" and racial equality, prominent industrialists and Democrats sought to blend Old and New South ideologies into a political message that could cement an alliance between agrarian and industrial elites nationally while splitting members of the lower classes along racial lines.

Drawing on antebellum precedents, the agrarian elites and their commercial and industrial allies fashioned a language that would stir the emotions and inspire the loyalties of the embittered, impoverished white males whose families and whose labor they wished to use in their mills

[40]Henry W. Grady, "The New South" (1886) and "At the Boston Banquet" (1889), in Grady, *The South: Some Addresses* (Charlotte, N.C.: Observer Printing House, 1910).
[41]"A Southern Triumph," *Manufacturers' Record*, 18 (Aug. 23, 1890).
[42]D. A. Tompkins, "Manufactures" (1899), in Grady, *The South*.

and factories and, increasingly, on tenant farms. The antebellum concern for racial purity served as a focal point for fears of a drastically altered sexual and political economy while it deflected attention from the actions of elites who were aiding and benefiting from the transformation. The loss of control over white women and fears about their exploitation as they entered the public workplace were translated into charges of assault by black rapists. Proclaiming themselves to be white women's protectors against the black menace, white men reasserted their control over white women and over blacks. Lynching and political campaigns for white supremacy reaffirmed white male solidarity through physical and rhetorical violence.[43]

Manufacturers joined in campaigns led by landed elites in the Black Belt to disfranchise black voters. E. C. Venable, of the Venable Tobacco Company, assured the Workingmen's Club of Petersburg, Virginia, that "God had given the country to the white race and blacks were not going to rule any longer in Petersburg."[44] The president of Erwin Cotton Mills granted permission for a parade in support of a disfranchisement amendment to the North Carolina constitution in 1900. The parade was led by a man holding a "White Supremacy" banner and included a white float carrying sixteen young women dressed in white and bearing streamers with the slogan "Protect us with your vote."[45] Such explicit defenses of white virgins against the "black beast" expressed the anger of men whose masculinity was threatened by the dissolution of the patriarchal and racial foundations on which their identities rested. Symbolically ministering to the "injuries of class," the elite rhetoric masked the actual shift of power from poorer to wealthier whites by the passage of many disfranchising statutes enacted in the name of white solidarity. Many of the laws drove the lower classes, white as well as black, from the southern electorate at the very time that the Populist movement was seeking, like the Republicans thirty years earlier, to create a class-based alliance.[46]

Yet, as Richard Edmonds of the *Manufacturers' Record* understood, manufacturers could never so enthusiastically embrace the cause of white supremacy as to exclude blacks altogether from the pool of potential

[43]See Jacquelyn Dowd Hall, "The Mind That Burns in Each Body: Women, Rape, and Racial Violence," in *Powers of Desire: The Politics of Sexuality,* ed. Ann Snitow, Christine Stansell, and Sharon Thompson, 328–49 (New York: Monthly Review Press, 1983), and Cal M. Logue and Howard Dorgan, eds., *The Oratory of Southern Demagogues* (Baton Rouge: Louisiana State University Press, 1981).

[44]Quoted in William D. Henderson, *Gilded Age City: Politics, Life, and Labor in Petersburg, Virginia, 1874–1889* (Lanham, Md.: University Press of America, 1980), 243.

[45]Dolores E. Janiewski, *Sisterhood Denied: Race, Gender, and Class in a New South Community* (Philadelphia: Temple University Press, 1985), 91.

[46]According to J. Morgan Kousser, *The Shaping of Southern Politics: Suffrage Restriction and the Establishment of the One-Party South* (New Haven: Yale University Press, 1974), the goal was to disfranchise poor whites and poor blacks.

workers. The danger of class conflict among whites could never be entirely eliminated. As one writer to the *Record* warned, "White laboring
men looking in the mirror and seeing in their lineaments a kinship of
race and right with the ruling classes, clamor for a revolution." The same
writer welcomed black workers as allies against such dangers. "The negro cannot do without us, and we cannot spare him. . . . He is an indispensable factor of our industrial system. . . . The negro, seeing in the
color of his face the emblem of his inferiority, willingly submits to the
menial pursuits of life." Edmonds reluctantly printed opposing views demanding the expulsion of blacks from the South and encouraging "white
labor" to "[force] them all out of the State," but his New South could
never become entirely a white man's country.[47] Farsighted businesssmen
avoided total endorsement of racial annihilation or removal because it
obviously would limit their own options. Somehow labor recruiters in
the New South must acknowledge the tenets of white supremacy while
limiting its full implementation in its most virulent form.

Textile and Tobacco Recruitment Strategies

In parallel with their political resolution of the postwar crisis, New
South manufacturers resolved their ideological dilemmas by adapting
prewar recruitment strategies to postwar conditions. The textile industry
continued to rely on the "family labor system" and its ideological coun-
terepart, industrial paternalism.[48] Such a strategy enabled mill owners to
expand a white labor force by attracting women, girls, and young children, who had previously labored only within the family economy. At
the same time the supervisors found a welcome model for their efforts to
discipline the workers in the patriarchal head of the farm family.[49] A
continued commitment to a white labor force fitted the ideological and
material interests of textile manufacturers. Interconnected labor processes made a homogeneous and unified labor force a major asset. Furthermore, this strategy enabled textile manufacturers and their allies to
redefine the "family" so as to exclude blacks. The "colored people" were

[47]C. J. Haden, "Why Georgia Is the Empire State of the South," *Manufacturers' Record*,
24 (Oct. 13, 1893); W. Silbert Wilson, "Free Discussion of Southern Matters" and "Correspondence: The Negro and Immigration" (Nov. 24, 1893).
[48]Philip Scranton, "Varieties of Paternalism: Industrial Structures and the Social Relations of Production in American Textiles," *American Quarterly*, 36 (Summer 1984), 235–
57.
[49]William Lazonick argues that the family labor system offered the primary model for
textile labor relations in England before the textile industry emerged in the United States:
"The Subjection of Labour to Capital: The Rise of the Capitalist System," *Review of Radical Political Economics*, 10 (Spring 1978), 6–9.

"with us still but they are not part of our families as they were then."[50]
Shifting from an interracial to an interclass "family," textile officials reinforced the struggle for the same goal they were pursuing in the political
arena.

Although a few efforts were made to use black labor in postwar mills,
textile executives in the 1880s and 1890s were insisting that "the question of the employment of colored labor in the finer processes of manufacturing" would be discussed only "by those who know nothing about
it." The head of the Georgia school system testified before a Senate committee that because blacks lacked "purity of life" and did not recognize
the "marriage relation," it was essential that they "be under the control
of the white race." He considered black membership in a mill village
family simply untenable. A Georgia mill executive provided another reason for excluding blacks: "The whites won't work with the colored." He
also objected to using black workers in the mills because "they think
they are as good as you."[51] In 1893, when the *Manufacturers' Record*
polled its readers on the issue of "colored mill help," the majority concluded that "white labor will not work with the negro at the machine.
You cannot mix them in a cotton mill. . . . You will not live to see a
cotton mill run successfully by negro operatives."[52] Statistical evidence
revealed the results of these managerial beliefs. Whereas in 1890 14.2
percent of southern textile operatives were black males and 2.95 percent
were black females, by 1910 only 1.33 percent were black males and
0.76 percent were black females.[53] As manufacturers anxiously sought to
attract the "better class" and increasingly avoided experiments with
black labor or an integrated labor force, textile labor became defined
ever more rigidly as white.[54]

This industrial strategy also eased the dangers that might arise from
the presence of large numbers of white women who lacked the protection
of an independent patriarchal family economy. Manufacturers averted a
potential crisis in gender relations caused by conditions that forced white
women into the public realm by giving them and their children employment that was "well adapted to their strength" and by subjecting them
"to elevating social influences" in sheltered workplaces where they visi-

[50]Gusatvus J. Orr, Atlanta, Nov. 21, 1883, in U.S. Senate, Committee on Education and
Labor, *Capital and Labor Investigation*, 4:676.

[51]Testimony in ibid., 589, 671, 539.

[52]"Colored Help for Textile Mills," *Manufacturers' Record*, 24 (Sept. 22, 1893); "Negroes Not Suited for Mill Work," ibid. (Oct. 6, 1893); "More Views about Colored Mill
Help," ibid. (Oct. 13, 1893).

[53]Wright, *Old South, New South*, 178.

[54]David Carlton, *Mill and Town in South Carolina, 1880–1920* (Baton Rouge: Louisiana
State University Press, 1982), 115.

bly remained under white male protection and care.[55] Yeomen who could not control their own family economies on the land might thankfully come to a mill village, where they could personally ensure the respectability of their wives and daughters who labored in the mill. The sons they reared in the mill village might aspire to a new patriarchal status as overseers and supervisors.[56] Certainly the racial and gender ideologies of the period would not permit "the working of negroes, particularly negro men beside white women within walls. . . . No association which might permit the possible lessening of the negro's deference toward white women would be allowed.[57] Now more than ever, textile manufacturers had to recognize that the "right" labor was white.

Such a recruitment strategy made the textile industry less likely to be seen as bringing social degradation on its female workers even as it was being attacked for taking women away from the home.[58] When criticisms were voiced, textile manufacturers were quick to refute them. When Hugh Wilson of the *Abbeville* (S.C.) *Press and Banner* dared to suggest that a mill worker learned nothing of the "duties and work of a womanly life—the life which nature and the laws of our civilization intended," manufacturers deplored his slander of the "virtuous women who prefer to earn their bread by honest toil."[59] Denunciations came just as rapidly in response to Clare de Graffenried's "Georgia Cracker in the Cotton Mills," which appeared in *Century* in 1891. This report described mill families as huddled together "irrespective of sex or relationship" in a society where "moral distinctions" were unknown. While women and children labored for long hours in the mills, de Graffenried reported, husbands sat "sunning their big lazy frames."[60] Richard Edmonds of the *Manufacturers' Record,* one of the leading proponents of the New South ideology, attacked de Graffenried's article for "misrepresentation."[61] Rebecca Felton, a leading Georgia suffragist

[55]See, e.g., Anne Firor Scott, *The Southern Lady: From Pedestal to Politics, 1830–1930* (Chicago: University of Chicago Press, 1970), chaps. 4–6; *The Cotton Mills of South Carolina: Their Names, Locations, Capacity, and History* (Charleston, S.C.: News and Courier Book Presses, 1880), 22.

[56]Wright, *Old South, New South,* 142.

[57]Holland Thompson, *From the Cotton Field to the Cotton Mill: A Study of the Industrial Transition in North Carolina* (New York: Macmillan, 1906).

[58]William P. Few, "The Constructive Philanthropy of a Southern Cotton Mill," *South Atlantic Quarterly,* January 1909.

[59]*Abbeville Press and Banner,* Aug. 22, 1883; *Charleston News and Courier,* Sept. 6, 1883.

[60]Clare de Graffenried, "The Georgia Cracker in the Cotton Mills," *Century,* February 1891, 483–98. This article and the controversy it generated are fully explored by LeeAnn Whites in "The de Graffenried Controversy: Class, Race, and Gender in the New South," *Journal of Southern History,* 54 (August 1988), 449–78.

[61]*Manufacturers' Record,* Feb. 7, 1891.

and political activist, defended the "industrious, honest, virtuous, well-behaved, law-abiding and God-fearing women" who had been unfairly accused of being "indifferent to the moral law." Felton denounced the charge of immorality as an "outrage upon womanly virtue and modesty" which threatened to undermine white supremacy.[62] In the opinon of defenders of the textile industry, any suggestion that the mill village patriarch had failed his fatherly duty to defend the "purity" of his "daughters" or that white women could be guilty of sexual misconduct threatened to subvert the industry's claim to be an agent of white supremacy. White supremacists, such as Felton, vigorously denounced black depravity and allowed no one to place white mill workers at the same moral level as blacks.

Solid adherents of the sexual and racial assumptions of New South ideology, white workers vigorously objected whenever individual mill owners sought to hire black workers. They were outraged by any suggestion that their conduct or moral worth could be equated with that of blacks.[63] Managers frequently claimed that their white workers would never tolerate black labor in the mills.[64] In 1897 white workers at Fulton Bag and Cotton Factory attacked the "nasty, black, stinkin' nigger wimmin" brought to work in the factory.[65] Charleston textile workers denounced the efforts of the "negro-loving" president of the Vesta Cotton Mill to hire black workers as leading to "either social degradation or starvation wages." The head of the local textile union shared the white-supremacy podium with the president of Erwin Mills in the 1900 campaign to disfranchise blacks in North Carolina. When a newspaper inadvertently referred to both mill workers and blacks in a sentence dealing with common health problems, the workers objected to the implication that they were "some lower order of human beings." Such resentment led the South Carolinia legislature in 1915 to pass a law prohibiting the employment of blacks in the state's textile mills.[66] As Daniel Tompkins expressed it in an extended discussion of the feasibility of hiring black labor in the mills, "The Anglo-Saxon laborer is . . . in possession of this industry, and it is yet to be proven whether the colored race can compete in it."[67] Ironically, manufacturers' success in appealing

[62]*Augusta Chronicle*, May 10, 1891, as developed in Whites, "De Graffenried Controversy."

[63]Melton A. McLaurin, *Paternalism and Protest: Southern Cotton Mill Workers and Organized Labor, 1875–1905* (Westport, Conn.: Greenwood, 1971), 60–61, 107.

[64]"Colored Help for Textile Mills," *Manufacturers' Record*, 24 (Sept. 22, 1893).

[65]Wright, *Old South, New South*, 189.

[66]Carlton, *Mill and Town in South Carolina*, 158–60, 245.

[67]Daniel A. Tompkins, "The Cultivation, Picking, Baling, and Manufacturing of Cotton from a Southern Standpoint," paper delivered to the New England Cotton Manufacturers' Association, Atlanta, Oct. 25, 1895.

to racial solidarity among their white workers limited their ability to play one group of workers off against another.

Because the textile industry came to represent the promises of the New South to impoverished white southerners, the need to maintain white solidarity constrained the recruitment strategies of mill owners to a greater extent than it did those of other manufacturers. Employers in other industries were better able to use black labor. Testimony at Senate hearings in 1883 made it clear that Alabama iron mills and Alabama mining companies could "employ colored laborers . . . for ordinary laboring work, preferring them to whites." A wealthy woman from Birmingham felt equally free to denounce poor whites as the "most hopeless, helpless, trifling set of people in the entire South"; nothing could be done with those women except "to employ them in factories." Even blacks, she reported, considered themselves higher than "poor white trash."[68] Apparently industrial patterns in Alabama, and particularly in the iron and steel industry, allowed employment policies and even public attitudes among the elites to differ significantly from those of the textile industry.

Given their considerably smaller labor requirements (one-half those of textile manufacturers in 1890, one-fifth in 1910), tobacco processors found it easier to recruit both black and white workers without running the risks that limited textile employers (see Tables 3.1 and 3.2). Practice of industrial slavery in the antebellum years gave them access to a pool of already trained black workers.[69] In addition, the processing of tobacco easily lent itself to two tiers of labor, those who prepared the leaf (the primary task before the war) and those who made the final products, whereas the work of the textile industry was more interconnected and horizontal. Tobacco manufacturers continued their antebellum tradition of using black labor in the nonmechanized parts of the process while increasing the number of white workers in newer parts of the industry, especially those being mechanized, which were not already identified with blacks.

As far as the virtue of their white female employees was concerned, tobacco manufacturers evidently felt the same compulsions as their counterparts in textiles. Allen & Ginter, the first company to produce cigarettes in the South, hired young white women in Richmond to roll

[68]Henry J. Evans, mayor of Chattanooga and iron manufacturer, and Mrs. Ward, Birmingham, in U.S. Senate Committee on Education and Labor, *Capital and Labor Investigation*, 4:169, 345.

[69]See Robert S. Starobin, *Industrial Slavery in the Old South* (New York: Oxford University Press, 1970), 49, 211–12. Ironically for those historians who celebrate paternalism on the slave plantation, the industry that actually employed a higher percentage of slaves displayed fewer paternalistic tendencies than the one that relied on white labor. See, e.g., Dwight Billings, Jr., *Planters and the Making of the "New South": Class Politics and Development in North Carolina, 1865–1900* (Chapel Hill: University of North Carolina Press, 1979), 60–61, 101–4, 116–18.

Table 3.1. Percentages of textile employees who were black or female, 1890–1960

	1890	1910	1930	1940	1960
Total	482,110	898,992	1,183,400	1,170,014	963,040
Black	1.2%	1.3%	2.2%	2.1%	4.5%
Female	49.9%	45.6%	41.8%	40.8%	44.0%

Source: Richard L. Rowan, *The Negro in the Textile Industry, Report No. 20: The Racial Policies of American Industry* (Philadelphia: University of Pennsylvania Press, 1970), 54.

cigarettes while pledging to provide "clean" employment by avoiding the "mingling of the sexes." Their spokesmen reported that they hired only the daughters of "respectable artisans" after carefully investigating their "character and habits."[70] The *Manufacturers' Record* rejoiced at the "almost paternal care . . . exercised over . . . a hundred young girls" in the employ of W. Duke & Sons, and reported that "immorality among them is absolutely unknown."[71] The Dukes insisted that they guarded the "moral purity" of their white female employees and required them to be "self-respecting" and "religious" in order to keep their jobs.[72] Into the 1930s the same factory continued to discharge white women whose sexual activities became the subject of gossip.[73] In that same decade a cigarette advertisement depicted white women standing in their white uniforms, like so many spotless vestal virgins, beside their machines. Manufactuers offered black female tobacco workers neither protection from sexual harassment nor the opportunity to represent the industry. Some foremen sought sexual favors from black women as the price of keeping their jobs. Other tobacco employers publicly boasted of treating black women roughly and rating them "by their muscles" in language that clearly separated them from the virtuous white virgins who worked in other parts of the industry.[74] Perhaps impelled by the actual presence of black women in the industry, tobacco employers, like their contemporaries in textiles, symbolically placed white women in a higher moral class than black women.

Tobacco manufacturers reinforced the racial hierarchy within the tobacco factory. Segregation, while never legally enacted for the tobacco industry, divided the labor force spatially and ideologically.[75] In the New

[70]*Richmond Industrial South*, June 17, 1882; *Frank Leslie's Illustrated Newspaper*, Feb. 10, 1883.
[71]*Manufacturers' Record*, 19 (May 2, 1891).
[72]Washington Duke, quoted in *Raleigh News and Observer*, Apr. 5, 1896.
[73]Janiewski, *Sisterhood Denied*, 97.
[74]Emma L. Shields, "A Half-Century of the Tobacco Industry," *Southern Workman*, September 1922, 420–21.
[75]John Cell, *The Highest Stage of White Supremacy: The Origins of Segregation in South Africa and the American South* (Cambridge: Cambridge University Press, 1982).

Table 3.2. Race and sex of tobacco workers in Kentucky, North and South Carolina, and Virginia, 1890–1940 (percent)

	1890	1940
Total	16,977	43,516
White Male	19.7%	30.7%
Female	8.2%	23.7%
Black Male	47.4%	22.4%
Female	24.7%	23.1%

Source: U.S. Department of Commerce, Bureau of the Census, Sixteenth Census, *The Labor Force* (Washington, D.C.: U.S. Government Printing Office, 1942).

South black workers could be included in the tobacco industry only on a segregated basis.[76] Factory managers continued the antebellum practice of calling blacks by their first names while insisting that they be "Mr. [Surname]" to black subordinates. Thus the factories were organized to honor "the wise and beneficent purpose of keeping separate races which are, by nature, widely different in color, social qualities, and moral tendencies."[77] Like other people marginalized by class, general, or racial hierarchies, black tobacco workers, particularly women, cleaned the dirt from the products of nature, becoming discolored themselves in the process. White women, on the other side of the color line, tended the machines of civilization, turning out cloth or cigarettes, while they wore white uniforms as testimony to their immunity to pollution. Like other dominant groups, southern manufacturers retained "their stock of women within their control" while implicitly justifying "social hierarchies and supremacy in terms of natural attributes," such as blackness, virginity, and dirt.[78]

The recruitment strategies of the tobacco and textile industries, which often coexisted in the same communities, complemented each other. Both industries carefully avoided excessive competition with agricultural em-

[76]Howard Rabinowitz, *Race Relations in the Urban South, 1865–1890* (New York: Oxford University Press, 1978), argued that segregated labor was the only kind available to blacks from the time of emancipation. See also Janiewski, *Sisterhood Denied,* 95–126.

[77]Quoted from *Baptist Missionary Herald,* January 1874, in Rachleff, "Black, White, and Gray."

[78]Leonore Davidoff, "The Rationalization of Housework," in *Dependence and Exploitation in Work and Marriage,* ed. Diana Leonard Barker and Sheila Allen (London: Longmans, 1976), draws on Mary Douglas's work on "purity and danger" to analyze domestic service as a ritual of pollution and purity mediating between nature and culture. Members of the subordinate sex and class are required to do the cleaning; they themselves are "unclean" and must be segregated lest they pollute members of the "washed" classes. See also Kate Young, Carol Wolkowitz, and Roslyn McCullagh, *Of Marriage and the Market: Women's Subordination Internationally and Its Lessons* (London: Routledge & Kegan Paul, 1981), xix; Joel Williamson, *The Crucible of Race: Black-White Relations in the American South since Emancipation* (New York: Oxford University Press, 1984), 115–24, 249–58, 306–10, 418–22.

ployers. Each gained access to a plentiful and relatively cheap supply of labor through their access to the work of white children and young women. The tobacco industry had the additional advantage of hiring the still cheaper labor of black men, women, and children. For the most part both effectively kept their wage levels down while restricting better-paying occupations to experienced white males. Both strategies success-fully accommodated industrial requirements to the demands of a racially and sexually stratified society.

Honor and Dishonor in Textile and Tobacco Factories

Weaving together the threads of honor and dishonor, southern manu-facturers clothed their actual deviations from tradition in the garb of per-fect fidelity to its racial and sexual practices. Like all employers, they could not operate purely from an economic calculus. Preexisting divi-sions within the potential group of workers were recognized and rein-forced because they suited the economic, political, and ideological interests of southern manufacturers and other elites. Treating all workers as interchangeable parts could have provoked widespread resistance to their power and perhaps subverted their authority. Like their slave-owning predecessors and their planter and merchant contemporaries, they feared the creation of a class-based alliance among the poorer mem-bers of their society. To avert that danger, they sought to instill a racial and gender consciousness while portraying themselves as defenders of white workers' interests.

The entrenchment of male authority appealed to patriarchal values al-ready a familiar part of life. When workers referred to their employers as being "like a daddy," they recognized the process by which they were being reared into a new way of working, for it echoed experiences of the past. Paternalism, a system of "mutual obligations—duties, responsibili-ties, and ultimately even rights"—would bind white workers and em-ployers together by transforming "power relationships" into "moral" obligations.[79] Employers offered their white male workers "white skin" privilege in compensation for their loss of real control over human and economic resources. A brotherhood of white men bound together planter, industrialist, landlord, millworker, and tenant farmer in defense of an ideal that denied their conflicts of interest and disguised the real differ-ences in power. Even as the private patriarchy of the yeoman's indepen-dent household dissolved, white men could take part in the symbolic

---

[79]See Eugene D. Genovese, *Roll, Jordan, Roll: The World the Slaves Made* (New York: Random House, 1976), 5, for the first part of the definition; Howard Newby, Colin Bell, David Rose, and Peter Saunders, *Property, Paternalism, and Power: Class and Control in Rural England* (Madison: University of Wisconsin Press, 1978), 28, for the second part.

construction of a public patriarchy that demonstrated their superiority over the subordinated members of southern society. Politicians, industrialists, and planters wielded power in the name of the white brotherhood while selected members of the lower classes exercised more limited authority in their behalf. Although an early advocate of this New South strategy had declared in 1881, "In the fabric of thought and of habit which we have woven for a century we are no longer to dwell," textile and tobacco manufacturers clearly wove together old and new threads for the "era of progressive enterprise" to which they were leading other southerners.[80]

That era began to unravel in the 1920s as the costs of the policy began to mount for the textile industry and as the tobacco industry grew more confident that it no longer needed to fear the consequences of a disgruntled labor force. Costly paternalism and family labor gave way to a more impersonal, bureaucratic managerial style that sought to raise productivity in the crisis-ridden textile industry. Emboldened by the Depression, the tobacco industry sought to speed up its workers, white and black alike, at a time when they apparently had little choice but to submit. Ironically, the forms of social cohesion reinforced or imposed by managerial strategy offered the workers a way to resist. Mill villages, once mobilized, could become class-conscious supporters of workers' actions. The violation of their sense of racial entitlement could radicalize white tobacco workers unwilling to accept conditions they likened to slavery. Perceiving the need for allies, black tobacco workers could seek aid from other members of their community and might even reach across racial lines to their newly enlightened white counterparts. Unions might gain adherents among white workers who felt betrayed when "daddy" was revealed to be only a businessman.[81] Power relationships in the factory had begun to shed their moral, familial, fraternal, and racial disguise.

Managers were able to regain control through a series of concessions, innovations, and continuities. Mill owners sold village housing, scattering the cohesive working-class communities that had begun to challenge them. With the encouragement of employers and their unions, white tobacco workers continued to define certain jobs and departments as white and to maintain a racial and sexual differential in pay, promotion, and benefits. Black workers lost jobs to mechanization and to the segregation that denied their entrance to other occupations in the tobacco industry.

[80]*Charleston News and Courier*, Dec. 27, 1881.

[81]Janiewski, *Sisterhood Denied*, 77, 153–78; George Sinclair Mitchell, *Textile Unionism in the South* (Chapel Hill: University of North Carolina Press, 1931); Herbert J. Lahne, *The Cotton Mill Worker* (New York: Farrar & Rinehart, 1944); Nannie Mae Tilley, *The R. J. Reynolds Tobacco Company* (Chapel Hill: University of North Carolina Press, 1985), 374–414; and Augusta V. Jackson, "A New Deal for Tobacco Workers," *Crisis*, October 1938, 322–24.

When their unions too militantly addressed the issues of racism and corporate power, the government withdrew its protection and the more conservative labor movement turned its back. A feminist movement that
could engage the loyalties of women across the racial and class boundaries did not emerge to mobilize women's energies or to redefine the
"virtuous woman." Occupied by domestic concerns, a persistent legacy
of the gender system, women could function as workers only by dividing
their energy between two workplaces. Male power remained firmly entrenched in union, factory, and the surrounding community, providing a
useful foundation for modern hierarchies of power.

Workers nevertheless made some advances. Some black workers gained
access to formerly all-white textile mills as the breakup of the village
family removed one major barrier to blacks after World War II. Once
installed, they became the major support for new union drives.[82] A combination of black agitation, the civil rights movement, and federal policy
eventually forced the integration of the tobacco labor force and its union
in the 1960s, after black workers had shrunk to a small minority of the
work force. Affirmative action altered some of the gender inequalities.
Gradually the seniority lists and the occupational structure yielded to a
more integrated labor force, albeit primarily at the entry level. Racial
and gender divisions narrowed but did not close.[83]

The fabric of control woven by planters and industrialists was raveled
and reworked in the transitions from the Old to the New South and now
to the Sunbelt. Employers never recruited or managed workers as though
they were colorless and sexless. They drew upon tradition to allocate
work, power, honor, and resources while modifying the preexisting patterns to their purposes. In the process they restricted their employees'
ability to challenge their power but set limits on their own freedom of
action. Obviously southern manufacturers displayed concern about the
reproduction of a system of sexual, class, and racial domination that was
not confined merely to their factories. Accentuating the issue of race in
explosive connection with sex, they hindered the emergence of class-
based alliances among the working and laboring groups in their society.

[82]Harriet L. Herring, *Passing of the Mill Village: Revolution in a Southern Institution*
(Chapel Hill: University of North Carolina Press, 1949); Richard L. Rowan, *The Negro in
the Textile Industry, Report No. 20; The Racial Policies of American Industry* (Philadelphia: University of Pennsylvania Press, 1970), 69; Janiewski, *Sisterhood Denied*, 172–76;
and Dolores Janiewski, "Seeking a 'New Day and a New Way': Black Women and Unions
in the Southern Tobacco Industry," in *"To Toil the Livelong Day": America's Women at
Work, 1790–1980*, ed. Carol Groneman and Mary Beth Norton, 161–78 (Ithaca: Cornell
University Press, 1987).

[83]Mary Frederickson, "Four Decades of Change: Black Workers in Southern Textiles,
1941–1981," *Radical America*, 16 (November–December 1982), 27–44; Mimi Conway,
Rise Gonna Rise: A Portrait of Southern Textile Workers (Garden City, N.Y.: Doubleday,
1979).

Simultaneously they enhanced their own power as the dominant partners in three overlapping sets of relationships. Skillfully they mastered the craft of domination but they could never create an impenetrable fabric. While ultimately relying on power, they also had to resort to persuasion to secure allies for themselves. They always remained vulnerable to economic crisis, political challenge, and the possibility that the subordinate members of their society might somehow disentangle themselves.

CHAPTER FOUR

Manhood and the Market: The Politics of Gender and Class among the Textile Workers of Fall River, Massachusetts, 1870–1880

Mary H. Blewett

Fall River textile workers with different cultural and work traditions battled over the political meaning of masculinity and over strategies of class action during a decade of rapid change, economic depression, and popular struggle in the 1870s. Manhood acquired new meanings within a nexus of complex economic forces, most important of which was the power of mill agents to determine market strategy. This power gave employers the authority to set new work conditions that influenced workers' conceptions of gender and union strategy.

By "gender" I mean appropriate masculine and feminine behaviors that are worked out in political controversy and become socially established as expressions of the fundamental "natures" of men and women. Central to this conflict over the meaning of working-class masculinity were struggles between powerful and less powerful men and conflicts between working-class men and women over the lessons of history and the opportunities for labor politics in New England. The specifics of these political conflicts in Fall River can help us reconstruct the contingencies of mid-nineteenth-century ideas about working-class masculinity and the family wage.

Patriarchal masculinity and the family wage are closely tied historically but in ways that (in many accounts) seem reactive to sweeping social and economic changes rather than a result of intense political contests between classes and sexes. Though the origins of the family breadwinner wage norm among Lancashire textile workers in the mid–nineteenth century remain unclear, we know that its adoption in the 1870s by the trade union movement reduced the standard of living and of English working-class women and increased their domestic struggles.[1]

[1] For an overview of gender and class analysis of nineteenth-century British workers, see

A study of the role of immigrant textile workers from Lancashire in the popular struggles of Fall River can clarify the ways in which masculinity and the family wage became defined for American trade unionists. These struggles involved the rhetoric and customs of skilled workers; the uses of violence and respectability as public demeanors; contests over leadership in labor protest and union strategy; household arrangements about domestic work; measures of bodily strength; women workers' expectations in regard to manhood; attitudes of native-born American workers toward geographical mobility and individual rights; and the responsibilities of sons to fathers and of workingmen to the radical politics of the Lancashire past.

The key struggle in Fall River took place between the mill agents and the immigrant mule spinners and weavers from Lancashire, part of a massive emigration sponsored by British trade unions after the American Civil War. Lancashire workers dominated the local work force culturally and politically by 1875 and tried to reconstruct in New England their heritage of popular radicalism and labor politics from old England. At the same time, Fall River capitalists attempted to dominate the domestic market for cotton print cloth and purge their English workers of "their chronic insubordination."[2] During the course of these conflicts, the

Sonya O. Rose, "Gender at Work: Sex, Class, and Industrial Capitalism," *History Workshop Journal*, 27 (1986), 113–31. On the family wage in nineteenth-century America, see Martha May, "Bread before Roses: American Workingmen, Labor Unions, and the Family Wage," in *Women, Work, and Protest: A Century of Women's Labor History*, ed. Ruth Milkman, 1–21 (Boston: Routledge & Kegan Paul, 1985). On the family wage in nineteenth-century England, see Wally Seccombe, "Patriarchy Stabilized: The Construction of the Male Breadwinner Wage Norm in Nineteenth-Century Britain," *Social History*, 11 (1986), 53–76, and Jane Lewis, "The Working-Class Wife and Mother and State Intervention, 1870–1918," in *Labour and Love: Women's Experience of Home and Family, 1850–1940*, ed. Jane Lewis (Oxford: Basil Blackwell, 1986). On the experience of working-class women, see Laura Oren, "The Welfare of Women in Labouring Families: England, 1860–1950," *Feminist Studies*, 1 (Winter–Spring 1973), 107–25; Nancy Tomes, "A 'Torrent of Abuse': Crimes of Violence between Working-Class Men and Women in London, 1840–1875," *Journal of Social History*, 11 (Spring 1978), 329–45; Ellen Ross, " 'Fierce Questions and Taunts': Married Life in Working-Class London, 1870–1914," *Feminist Studies*, 8, (Fall 1982), 575–602.

[2] On the emigrations, see Charlotte Erickson, "The Encouragement of Emigration by British Trade Unions, 1850–1900," *Population Studies*, 3 (1949), 248–273. On managers' views of insubordination, see *Fall River News*, Mar. 6, 1875. For conservative assessments of this radical challenge, see *Commercial Bulletin*, Aug. 28 and Oct. 2, 1875; *Providence Journal*, Sept. 29, 1875; and the views of William Jennings of the Merchants Mills in *Fall River News*, Oct. 22, 1875. For the nature of popular radicalism in Lancashire, see Edward P. Thompson, "Class Consciousness," in *The Making of the English Working Class* (New York: Random House, 1963), 669–729. On Lancashire radicalism among textile workers in the early nineteenth century, see Cynthia Shelton, *The Mills of Manayunk: Industrialization and Social Conflict in the Philadelphia Region, 1787–1837* (Baltimore: Johns Hopkins University Press, 1986). The mule spinners in New England and Lancashire have been studied comparatively by William Lazonick, "Industrial Relations and Technical

meanings of masculinity within the ideology of Fall River labor protest were challenged and transformed.

In the aftermath of that struggle, during the winter of 1881–82, Robert Howard, secretary of the National Mulespinners' Association, brought the social reformer Lillian Chace Wyman to Fall River to interview blacklisted textile workers. Howard and Wyman visited the home of one "elderly" English mule spinner, "Mr. W." His little house was the essence of Victorian domesticity, clean and neat with pictures on the wall, lace-edged towels, and a stack of firewood that promised "good cheer." During the visit his "old wife," the mother of seventeen children, rose from her easy chair to treat a troop of neighborhood children to candy and offered tea to her guests after the interview, in which she took no part.[3] Mr. W. appeared to have been the sole support of his large family until the children were of an age to work in the mills.

To Mr. W., the secret blacklist was an assault on his manhood. The blacklist barred him from his trade in Fall River by common agreement among the mill owners. His choice was to stay in the city and take less skilled work, losing his place among his brother spinners, or to look for a spinning job in a distant town far from his friends and union. "It was a heavy heart I had that night—for I'm gettin' to be an old man, and my old woman . . . , she broke down a-cryin'." Like many other spinners, Mr. W. had been told only that he was being fired for poor work. Over the next few weeks he found other jobs, only to be discharged again and again until by chance he discovered his name on the blacklist in some mill office. He was relieved to find that the blacklisting was in retaliation for labor reform politics or union activity and not a judgment on his ability to spin. As Mr. W. put it: "You may think it a weakness in me but that pleased me, and it pleased the old woman, and made her proud to think they couldn't find fault with me." This husband and wife shared the view that (despite his age) skill and strength were the measure of his worth as a man.

From the moment that Lancashire spinners landed in Fall River, however, the measure of skill and strength was always at issue in New England textile factories. The mill agents used the cheapest raw cotton and the best machinery, paid the lowest wages in the region, and demanded

Change: The Case of the Self-acting Mule," *Cambridge Journal of Economics*, 3 (1979), 231–62, and by Isaac Cohen, "Workers' Control in the Cotton Industry: A Comparative Study of British and American Mule Spinning," *Labor History*, 26 (Winter 1985), 53–85.

[3] Lillian Chace Wyman, "Studies of Factory Life: Black-listing at Fall River," *Atlantic Monthly*, November 1888, 605–12. All quotes are from this source except for Fall River as a "mean" place: *Boston Herald*, Feb. 24, 1875. On the blacklist, see Massachusetts Bureau of Labor Statistics (hereafter MBLS), *First Annual Report* (1870), 326, and *Second Annual Report* (1871), 80–82.

ever more intense physical exertions from their operatives to produce massive quantities of inferior cloth, the defects in which the printing process would conceal. They controlled the domestic market for print cloth by having the capacity to glut it with the cheapest possible goods.[4] Fall River became known among operatives as "the hardest place for work and the meanest place for wages" in New England. Before he was blacklisted, Mr. W. got into trouble with his mill superintendent by complaining about violations of the ten-hour law of 1874 and the speeding up of the mules, objecting that the additional strenuous physical effort would be "the death of me yet." His superintendent timed the motions of the spinning frames with his watch to keep them going at full speed until the old English spinner "cursed him in his heart for the fatigue and pain that he was suffering as he toiled."

Mr. W. had been proud of his activities as a union leader in Lancashire and spoke with great bitterness about the strikebreaking spinners or "knobsticks" of New England who had defeated the recent strike of 1879. After months on the blacklist, poverty forced him to sign away his union membership and return to work, promising to remain silent about grievances and never again to participate in a strike. This act signaled a shameful abandonment of the Lancashire traditions of union activity that had formed the basis of his resistance. Remembering the sting of this defeat, he sprang to his feet and cried out, "I'm humiliated,—I'm less of a man than I was!" His view of respectable masculinity was based on the value of his work, his physical ability to perform it satisfactorily on his own terms, and his right to work as a spinner in Fall River, rights that the mule spinners' trade union sought to protect.

Both his manhood and his customary rights as a spinner were threatened by the geographical mobility of other New England textile workers, who often served as strikebreakers, and by the blacklist, which forced spinners to choose between their craft and their community. Spinners regarded their own emigration from Lancashire to New England (and their

---

[4]Between 1870 and 1872, eighteen corporations in Fall River built five additional cotton mills, while fifteen new corporations constructed seventeen more mills, enormously increasing the city's productive capacity (which had already surpassed that of Lowell in 1870) and the indebtedness of its corporations: *Fall River News*, Jan. 16, 1875. This expansion of production required 6,000 more workers by 1872; the work force more than quadrupled between 1865 (2,654) and 1875 (11,514). By 1880, Fall River produced 32% of all the cotton print cloth in the country. These mills, in combination with adjacent mills in Rhode Island, Connecticut, and southeastern Massachusetts, dominated the national market with 57% of production: Thomas Russell Smith, *The Cotton Textile Industry of Fall River, Massachusetts* (New York: King's Crown, 1944), 50–65, and Frederick M. Peck and Henry H. Earl, *Fall River and Its Industries* (Fall River, 1877), 68. Also see the report of the Labor Council of Boston on the 1875 strike in *Fall River News*, Mar. 6, 1875. On the contrasting competition, small firm size, and specialization of the textile industry in England, see William Lazonick, "Competition, Specialization, and Industrial Decline," *Journal of Economic History*, 41 (March 1981), 31–38.

occasional well-publicized return in small groups) as a collective political
act, unlike the random movements of individuals in search of work. Mr.
W.'s sense of humiliation and loss of manhood also reflected the defeat
of Lancastrian popular radicalism in that bitter decade of class struggle
in Fall River. By 1881, union men such as Mr. W. had grudgingly accepted a definition of manhood in the workplace based on the goal of a
wage that permitted the husband to be the sole support of his family, the
exclusive control of the spinners' union by men, their acceptance of market forces and geographical mobility as determinants of wage levels, and
their participation in American-style politics rather than popular radicalism. This craft-union definition of masculinity, however, left spinners vulnerable to the power of the mill agents to determine their wages and the
conditions of the workplace where they expended their skill, strength,
and manhood.

Mr. W. had once embodied the cultural and political heritage of England's most militant industrial region. In the early nineteenth century,
the Lancashire spinners resisted the introduction of the self-acting mule
and with it new workers called minders, while the hand-loom weavers
fought the use of the power loom. Both also opposed the employment of
women and children in the factories, viewing them as not only cheap labor but easily coerced. Men regarded control of their trade as crucial in
struggles with their employers. By mid-century the resistance of male
weavers to women as workers had faded as both sexes commonly tended
the steam-driven looms in Lancashire factories, while spinners accepted
self-acting mules. As a result of the general reformation of the terms of
industrial work, male workers had shed their public image as "Lancashire brutes" and became known as sober, conscientious, self-educated, and
serious men who operated consumer cooperatives like small businesses
and enjoyed the employers' acceptance of their unions. Even after the defeat of their efforts to control the nature of their work and the general
decline of popular radicalism, especially after the failure of Chartism in
the 1840s and the passage of the ten-hour law, spinners and weavers developed different organizations and strategies to defend their interests.[5]
Issues of gender strategy remained central to their approaches.

The spinners' organizational strategy drew the self-acting mule minders into their union, renamed them spinners, and successfully limited admission into the trade to young men and boys, although the fight to keep
women out of mule spinning continued in nineteenth-century Lancashire
and proved a notable failure in Scotland. The chief argument used
against the introduction of women to mule spinning was not the strenu-

[5]On the development of the spinners' and weavers' unions in Lancashire, see H. A.
Turner, *Trade Union, Growth Structure and Policy* (Toronto: University of Toronto Press,
1962), 108–68.

ous physical requirements of the work but the need for men to supervise other men and the boys hired as piecers and helpers.[6] Spinners from Lancashire brought with them to Fall River their belief that the effective organization of small numbers of skilled male workers in one community would enable them to counter the mill agents' argument that market forces determined wages.

The weavers' organizations, by contrast, permitted free entry to their occupation by both men and women, often cooperated with nonmembers (even nonweavers) during strikes, and involved a membership that moved freely about Lancashire in search of better work and wages. Unlike the spinners, they were concerned primarily to establish a standard list of wages in Lancashire, not to gain control over who performed the work in what locale. For the men and women weavers, the issue was regional organization, not the sex of the union members.

The Lancashire workers who arrived in Fall River in increasing numbers in the late 1860s and early 1870s also brought with them an experience of industrial relations that had developed along with the employers' acceptance of their unions in the mid-century compromise between capital and labor in English textiles. Worker and "master" acknowledged mutual responsibilities. Workers treated their employers with deference, and employers agreed to negotiate with union men. In Lancashire this deferential relationship had involved complex behaviors that protected and secured the respectability and sober-minded demeanor of working-class men.[7] Immigrant workers quickly learned, however,

[6]Ibid., 128–29. On men as spinners, see Lazonick, "Industrial Relations and Technical Change." For a different view of male control of mule spinning, see Mary Freifeld, "Technological Change and the 'Self-acting' Mule: A Study of Skill and the Sexual Division of Labor," *Social History,* 11 (1986), 319–44. Mule spinners in Fall River had made regional organization their goal since 1858 (see David Montgomery, *The Fall of the House of Labor* [Cambridge: Cambridge University Press, 1987], 156–59), but they lost most of their local strikes, and the regional drive remained visionary until the more promising attempts by the weavers in 1875.

[7]Patrick Joyce, *Work, Society, and Politics: The Culture of the Factory in Later Victorian England* (Brighton: Harvester, 1980), analyzes mid-century Lancashire as a culture of internalized deference, class harmony, and cooperation based on key structural elements in the experience of factory work: the convergence of home and work in the family wage economy of factory workers and the maturation of mechanization. Other factors that characterized this system were the decline of popular protest, the acceptance of union organization by employers, the passage of the Factory Acts and limited suffrage, and the general prosperity of the textile industry at mid-century, although Joyce acknowledges (50–82) that popular radicalism remained alive in the weaving centers of Burnley and Blackburn and in Yorkshire towns with "primitive" forms of mechanization. My research, especially as regards the instrumentality of deference, supports the critical review of Joyce by Neville Kirk in *Bulletin of the Society for the Study of Labour History,* 42 (Spring 1981), 41–43. Lancashire workers came to Fall River in several waves of immigration and therefore represented somewhat different experiences. Many of those who arrived in the 1840s and 1850s fought for the Union cause in the Civil War, while later arrivals from England had endured the Preston strike of 1853–54 and the "cotton famine" in the early 1860s. On Lancashire

that the capitalists in Fall River regarded the doffed caps and politeness of Lancashire workers as marks of servility and unmanliness and rejected their expectations of mutuality with hostility and open contempt. In the absence of deferential politics in Fall River, spinners and weavers searched for new ways to confront the power of their employers while maintaining their respectable manhood.

The complex meanings of masculinity for the immigrant mule spinners and weavers of Fall River began to emerge during a strike in 1870. When the employers announced a wage cut for all workers on June 30, the spinner's union tried to draw them into Lancashire-style negotiations. Representatives of the 500 spinners, speaking for the thousands of other textile operatives who were thrown out of work by the stoppage of spinning operations, offered to compromise.[8]

The Fall River agents, unwilling to deal with the union, refused even to acknowledge the mule spinners' formal statements. The strike leader William Isherwood, who had been blacklisted in Lowell in 1867 for activity in support of the ten-hour day, called their response "silent contempt." The mill agents then recruited mule spinners from other textile cities and towns in New England as strikebreakers. Deferential politics had failed.

The Fall River spinners now sought other means to preserve the respectability and sober demeanor of workingmen. Determined to avoid overt violence against the out-of-town spinners who began to arrive at the central railroad depot, they depended on persuasion and appeals to the dignity and manliness of the mule-spinning craft. These appeals were backed by verbal threats "to look out for squalls if they went to work" and union funds to pay train fares back home. The spinners' union denied using any compulsion against strikebreakers and represented their position as "repeatedly and respectfully" entreating the mill owners to negotiate.[9] In this way the strike leaders could avoid any negative con-

---

during the American Civil War, see William O. Henderson, *The Lancashire Cotton Famine, 1861–1865* (Manchester: Manchester University Press, 1934); Edwin Waugh, *Home-Life of the Lancashire Factory Folk during the Cotton Famine* (Manchester, 1867); R. Arthur Arnold, *The History of the Cotton Famine* (London, 1864); and John Watts, *The Facts of the Cotton Famine* (London, 1866). For an overview of British immigrants, see Rowland T. Berthoff, *British Immigrants in Industrial America, 1790–1950* (Cambridge: Harvard University Press, 1953). John T. Cumbler's study of Fall River explores the social institutions that textile workers brought with them from Lancashire to Fall River—lodges, pubs, workingmen's clubs—but not the ideology and politics: *Working-Class Community in Industrial America: Work, Leisure, and Struggle in Two Industrial Cities, 1880–1930* (Westport, Conn.: Greenwood, 1979), 148–53. On the role of New England textile workers in late-nineteenth-century labor politics, see Montgomery, *Fall of the House of Labor,* 154–70.

[8] On the 1870 strike, see MBLS, *Second Annual Report* (1871), 47–93; *Fall River News,* July 21–Sept. 16, 1870; *Boston Herald,* Aug. 26–30, 1870.

[9] *Boston Herald,* Aug. 30, 1870; MBLS (1871), 47–93.

nection with public violence which might tarnish their respectability as
men fit to negotiate with their employers.

The mill agents sought to provoke a violent reaction by the spinners in
order to discredit them and convince the community that the union leaders were reckless and irresponsible. Mill agents heightened tensions during the strike by calling in false alarms and prompting fire companies to
drench the crowds protesting in front of the mills. They also persuaded
the mayor to hire special police and summon the state militia, while they
encouraged undercover agents to spy on striking spinners and circulate
reports of drunkenness and potential bloodshed.[10]

The only incident of violence toward a strikebreaking spinner in 1870
demonstrates the care with which striking spinners and their allies
among the weavers divided the responsibilities for intimidating strikebreakers in an effort to protect the manly respectability of the spinners'
union. The victim was Isaiah Sanderson, a Scottish immigrant farmer
who had worked as a spinner for only three years and who had been
enticed back to spinning at the Durfee Mill with promises of a house for
his family. Sanderson, new to the trade, had refused to join the spinners'
union but expected trouble and afterward kept his mouth shut. To make
an example of him to others, a noisy crowd waiting outside the mill
kicked, stoned, and gave him "a tremendous pounding" as he quit for the
night after two days at work.

The street crowds who surrounded Sanderson were composed mostly
of women and children, and his attackers were probably weavers. They
supplied the howls and jeers, the fists and blows, to humble a disloyal
male and to protect the reputation of the spinners as law-abiding citizens
and respectable men. These crowds were backed up by the tenants of
corporation housing nearby, armed with stones and dirt clods ready to
shower the strikebreakers at a signal. State police called in by the city
authorities discovered the majority of them were women sitting at their
windows with stones concealed in their aprons.[11] The spinners, entirely
absent from the tumult, remained law-abiding and respectable men. The
dissociation of masculinity from overt violence served class politics in
1870 and demonstrated an active, even violent public role for women
and children during strikes as long as male authority remained unchal-
lenged in labor protest.

The striking mule spinners in 1870 also resisted the mill agents' attempts to justify the use of strikebreakers on the grounds of supply-and-
demand ideology. Mill agents claimed that market forces determined the
supply of labor, which in turn set the local wage level. If spinners' wages
were too low, they were told, they should go to other mill towns where

[10] MBLS (1871), 76–82, esp. 78.
[11] Ibid., 57–62 (for Sanderson), 68–74, 84 (on the women's role).

there was a demand for their skill. For the agents, any attempt to oppose market forces, such as intimidating strikebreakers by collective action, represented coercion and interference with individual rights and natural economic laws.[12] Strike leaders feared that the dispersal of union men would cripple attempts to resist wage cuts and sought instead to fix the responsibility for the wage cut on decisions made by the Fall River mill agents, not by the market—decisions that the spinners believed could be changed by negotiations between the union and the mills.

Mill agents also tried to denigrate spinning as a manly trade by insisting that "girls run mules easily and successfully" in other Massachusetts mills. In response, the spinners argued that they worked harder and faster at their Fall River machines than spinners anywhere else in New England, walking twenty-five miles and more each eleven-hour day, with only one young boy to help piece up broken yarns: "a pretty good day's work for any man." Spinners described the job as "so hard" that many could not work the entire month at the mill, but had to "stay away from it and rest." The striking spinners continued to oppose any use of women in spinning, insisting that men were "better" and "cheaper" and that the exhausting work was "not a fitting employment for females."[13]

As long as the spinners led organized protest in the city, their customary opposition to women in their trade shaped their sense of proper gender arrangements in the spinning rooms even as their wives and daughters yelled and threw stones in the streets. Their highly visible role as strike leaders, however, meant the blacklist and either removal from the trade or departure from Fall River. Those spinners who stayed on in the city after 1870 to work at less skilled jobs automatically lost their status as craftsmen and their positions in the union. This association of masculinity with the craft and union proved vulnerable to the combined determination of Fall River capitalists to tame their Lancashire workers by isolating their leaders.

After two months without work or a strike fund, other textile workers slowly returned to the mills. Leaders of the spinners' union such as William Isherwood were blacklisted and forced from their corporation tenements, while other strikers reluctantly signed contracts pledging not to join a union and went back to work.[14] However, all parties to the 1870 strike took the long view: the spinners organized in secret, the weavers waited for reinforcements, and the mill agents tried to identify and blacklist all leaders.

[12]See the debate between the Spinners' Committee and "Mill Operative" and "Main Street," who supplied the manufacturers' view of the strike, in *Fall River News*, July 23, 26, 30; Aug. 8, 13, 15, 16, 18, 20, 1870.
[13]*Fall River News*, Aug. 8, 1870.
[14]*Fall River News*, Sept. 9, 1870; MBLS (1871), 90.

Some immigrant mule spinners in Fall River apparently had wives who were weavers. The involvement of wives in factory work as well as in active labor protest could undermine the traditional sexual division of labor within the household. In 1871 an English-born mule spinner described a pattern that he claimed was familiar to the families of employed spinners in Fall River whose wives worked in the mills as weavers or in other operations. He helped prepare their daily food, rising at 5 A.M. to start the breakfast while his children and wife slept, help- ing to make and put the "dinner" into the pails, and after work "help- [ing] along supper until she gets home."[15] Explaining his involvement in housework to his astonished interviewer, the spinner reported that he and his wife cooked and cleaned the house together on Sundays and took a "nap" after dinner, the only chance for intimacy in a work- week of nearly seventy hours. Shared housework made it possible for his wife, with the help of her twelve-year-old daughter, to tend ten looms rather than six to eight looms usual for women weavers, and earn more on piecework.

Brought up in England as a factory girl, his wife had worked since their marriage except for periodic intervals of six months to bear and care for a new child. Luckier families who had immigrated with kin de- pended on an older female relative to take care of the children during working hours and ease the burden on both husband and wife.[16] As the mills continued to expand production and supply plenty of factory work, even household responsibilities seemed negotiable among family mem- bers, and routine housework alongside a working wife did not seem to undermine a spinner's sense of manliness.

Failing to locate sufficient native-born labor for the twenty-two new cotton mills built in a frenzy of activity between 1870 and 1872, Fall River managers sent recruiters to Lancashire to hire more English opera- tives. According to a story told by a female weaver, one Fall River man- ufacturer confided to an overseer his eagerness to employ "green horns" from Lancashire. "Yes," the overseer replied, "but you'll find that they have brought their horns with them."[17] However, Fall River agents were convinced that they could dominate these historically unruly people as easily as they controlled the national market for print cloth. A tide of immigration in the early 1870s swelled the numbers of Lancashire work- ers already resident in the city. As the depression of 1873 produced wage cuts and deteriorating work conditions, Lancashire workers controlled local labor activity. The different strategies and modes of organization of

[15]MBLS (1871), 476–79.
[16]Ibid., 478–79, 481.
[17]The quote is from a meeting of rebellious female weavers who called on their male co-workers to use their "horns": *Fall River News*, Jan. 18, 1875.

Lancashire spinners and weavers during two crucial strikes in 1875 reveal intraclass conflict over the meaning of masculinity and desirability of autonomous female activism and labor protest.

Hard times after the onset of the 1873 depression threatened male workers' craft standards and gender identities by intensifying their workloads. Working-class men perceived these pressures on their bodily strength and stamina as an assault on their right to spin according to the requirements of the craft and on their ability to support their families. The Lancashire immigrants who arrived after 1870 confronted unfamiliar working conditions that drove the pace of work beyond endurance. Their first reaction was to channel their political energies into the final push in 1874 for the ten-hour day in Massachusetts.[18] But Fall River managers responded to statutory limitations on daily labor by significantly speeding up work processes and pushing daily operations beyond the legal limit. Protecting their capacity to produce the cheapest print cloth in New England remained Fall River's key to dominating the domestic market.

New England mill agents also refused to supply their spinners with the help of minders and piecers (customary in Lancashire), the supervisory aspects of which helped define spinning as man's work. Instead, a spinner had the assistance of only one young "back boy" to help piece up (repair) the multiple strands of yarn spun from cheap cotton during the back-and-forth motions of the huge frames. By depriving them of the ability to supervise younger male workers, employers in Fall River undercut the male authority of mule spinners. These pressures produced a "Fall River walk," brisk and quick. Few spinners, even the young and vital ones, had the stamina to work out the full month of six-day weeks, eleven hours a day, without laying off as "sick" for several days to regain their strength. "Sick spinners" routinely filled the jobs of exhausted men for several days each month. The employers' practice of defining a spinner's work as just beyond a man's physical powers, an abuse the operatives called the "grind" or "lashing the help," undermined his pride in his strength and skill.[19]

Wage cuts during the depression of 1873 meant less income to spend on food to sustain overtaxed strength and vitality. English spinners and weavers had legendary appetites for beer and beef. After a sweating spinner had walked his daily twenty-five miles and more back and forth at

---

[18]On ten-hour protest, see *Fall River News, Boston Herald,* and *Boston Advertiser,* Apr. 3, 1874; *Lawrence American,* Apr. 4, 1874; *Lawrence Journal,* Apr. 11, 1874. On post–Civil War labor politics, see David Montgomery, *Beyond Equality: Labor and the Radical Republicans, 1862–1872* (Urbana: University of Illinois Press, 1981).

[19]On the necessity of "sick" spinning, see MBLS (1871), 482; Wyman, "Studies of Factory Life," 611; *Fall River News,* Aug. 8, 1870. On the "grind," see MBLS, *Thirteenth Annual Report* (1882), 348–54.

the mules in a brutally hot spinning room, beer supplied carbohydrates for the thirsty body and anesthetic for overstrained muscles and nerves. Temperance organizations in Fall River categorized all alcohol consumption as drunkenness and all beer halls as "rum-shops." These middle-class attitudes enabled mill agents to castigate beer-drinking English workers as drunkards and to argue that "more sickness is caused by beer than by overwork." During hard times, workers hid dinner pails filled with cheese and bread rather than the customary cold meat, and spinners objected to the substitution of salmon for beef, the perennial New England solution to feeding apprentices cheaply.[20] A man's physical well-being, especially under the exhausting conditions of Fall River factories, required red meat and plenty of beer.

Overseers also denied spinners their customary time to oil and clean their machines by setting the piece rate for spinning yarn so low as to require almost total concentration on machine operations. Although managers bought new spindles that were supposed to be self-lubricating, the accumulation of cotton waste on and near mules whose unoiled gears scraped metal against metal caused a disastrous fire in the Granite Mill during the fall of 1874. The official inquest criticized as cowardly the behavior of mule spinners who saved themselves, while the women and children trapped on the upper floors were burned alive or jumped to their deaths. The spinner whose unoiled machine had produced the sparks that ignited cotton waste and filled the upper floors with flame and smoke was a half-trained young fellow, "only a boy not yet as thoughtful as a man," who had neglected his duties to his mules under the pressures of keeping up with the movements of the older, experienced men in the spinning room. Fall River overseers, unlike their English counterparts, posted the daily work record of each spinner to create competition among operatives. As one Lancashire immigrant put it: "If a man is not able to get as much off his mules as the others, he is, of course ashamed, and becomes a butt of ridicule to his fellow-workmen. A boy of seventeen likes to feel like a man . . . and will be tempted to neglect his machinery."[21] By encouraging such competition the mill agents not only redefined the pace of work but encouraged the measure of manhood to assume a new and deadly potential.

[20]MBLS (1871), 49, 469–70, 476–86. For budgets and diets of Fall River mule spinners and weavers in 1874, see MBLS, *Sixth Annual Report* (1875), 284–90; in 1875, *Fall River News*, Mar. 6, 1875. On beer drinking, see MBLS (1882), 209, 219, 254–60.
[21]Henry Sevey, editor of the radical Fall River *Labor Journal* and an 1874 immigrant from Lancashire, defended the Granite Mill spinners by fixing responsibility for the deaths on the managers, who provided fire buckets but no water and no means of escape from the upper floor: *Labor Journal*, Sept. 26 and Oct. 3, 1874 (Fall River Historical Society). For the state's investigation of the fire, see MBLS (1875), 142–77.

After a year of wage cuts and intensifying workloads, the mill agents of Fall River decided in late 1874 to stimulate prices in the depressed market for print cloth by limiting production. But when other New England textile mills shifted to producing print cloth, Fall River returned to full capacity in January 1875. By cutting wages by 10 percent, they flooded the market with the cheapest cloth and defeated their upstart competitors.[22] Fall River spinners and weavers had already accepted a 10 percent cut in early 1874, and at a meeting of male weavers on January 6, 1875, which excluded women, they seemed ready to accept the additional cut. But the women weavers, inspired by their Lancashire heritage of popular radicalism, organized to oppose any further acquiescence. They shamed and pushed their reluctant male co-workers into the only successful weavers' strike in the city in the nineteenth century.[23] During the strike and its aftermath, the gender politics of Lancashire workers focused on the emerging differences between men and women workers over labor protest, the challenge of activist women to male leadership, and the differing priorities accorded regional organization by weavers and spinners.

Female operatives first organized themselves across ethnic and skill lines. They were led by women weavers from Lancashire but included cardroom workers and native-born Americans and French-Canadian immigrants. They demanded that the men, both weavers and spinners, act quickly and decisively to prevent a pattern of recurrent wage cuts. English women pointed to the effectiveness of resistance on the long-term (if not the short-term) relations of capital and labor in Lancashire. Activist women formulated the strike's successful strategy: suspend work at the three mills whose agents had instigated the wage cut while allowing the other mills to make cloth, meet their contracts, and pay their workers, who then contributed a share of their wages to the strike fund.[24]

In their public call for a meeting, the women weavers indicated that the source of their anger was their exclusion from decision making, their own view of the lessons of history and politics in Lancashire, and their disapproval of the behavior of the male workers.

[22]*New York Times,* Jan. 23, and Mar. 15, 1875.
[23]On the exclusion of women weavers from the key meeting at which male weavers decided not to strike in early January 1875, see letter to the editor, *Boston Globe,* Feb. 23, 1875.
[24]*Fall River News,* Jan. 18, Feb. 22, Mar. 8 and 17, 1875. The terms of the contracts with the cloth printers for Fall River goods in the spring of 1875 made it impossible for the manufacturers to respond with a lockout. When they negotiated subsequent contracts, the Fall River agents insisted on reserving the right to close all the mills if workers struck any one mill: *Commercial Bulletin,* Aug. 28, 1875. The official celebratory history of the strike prepared by the Weavers' Union acknowledged the role of the women weavers in the origins of the strike but ignored their activities and named none of them: A Workingman, *History of the Fall River Strike* (Fall River, 1875).

Dissatisfied with the dilatory, shilly-shally and cowardly action of many of the chief conductors of our late meetings, we, the female operatives have decided to meet together and speak and act for ourselves, as we and our children are as much interested in, and are as great sufferers by, this late movement of the manufacturers. . . . Every reduction they succeed in establishing, renders us less liable to resist the next.[25]

The January 16 meeting at which the women weavers dared the men to act reverberated with direct, public challenges to working-class manhood. Addressing their complaints to the only man present, Lancashire-born Henry Sevey, editor of the Fall River *Labor Journal,* they shouted insults: "Come on, you cowards! You were [be]got in fear, though you were born in England." They were reminding the male weavers that they were the sons of the hand-loom weavers of Lancashire who had fought tenaciously for their rights. It was time for the sons to show their "horns" as their fathers had done, with bold action and imaginative strategy.

The next day a group of male weavers approached Robert Borden, treasurer of the Crescent Mill, and presented their demands to him before a *Boston Globe* reporter.

A delegation of 6 tall, blonde, blue-eyed Englishmen, they held their hats in their hands and their tongues in their mouths until the Treasurer spoke to their leader when he stepped respectfully to the counter and said in a marked North Country accent: "Wael, I suppose ye're awaere we are come to see ye, sir, about our little grievances, and thaet's about the figger thaet we think will bring us back t'our looms."

When Borden protested that the manufacturers suffered more than the weavers from hard times, their barely concealed anger flared briefly.

"More of a hardship, sir?" interrupted a giant bearded Yorkshire man, with flushed pale face and tears standing in his eyes, "more of a hardship, sir? Ah if ye knew—"
"We haeve to live upon our daily wages," another said in a low suppressed voice, "and back of thaet we've no money, sir; while you've plenty to back-set you, I hope."

As the men went away disappointed, the reporter remarked to Borden: "That's a gentlemanly set of strikers." "Yes," Borden replied, "I make them gentlemanly."[26] The next day, the male weavers and the spinners joined the women's strike.

[25]*Fall River News,* Jan. 18, and Feb. 22, 1875.
[26]*Boston Globe,* Jan. 18, 1875.

In addition to intimidating strikebreakers as they had done in 1870, the women weavers took a more public role in labor protest, appearing regularly on platforms with male strike leaders, agitating at strike meetings, and traveling throughout southeastern Massachusetts and Rhode Island, canvassing for support. They expanded the goals of strike activity by advocating equal pay for equal work, the removal of all children under the age of fourteen from millwork, and the recruitment into the mule spinners' union of those young women who were just beginning to spin warp yarn on primitive ring-spinning frames. Memories of the activities of their own mothers and grandmothers in support of radical politics and the Chartist movement may have inspired some of these Lancashire women. Their new forms of activity and influence on strike policy in Fall River reflected the lessons they had learned in labor protest both in England and in America and their concerns as women workers.[27]

During the 1875 strike women workers challenged the hegemony of the mule spinners over labor protest in Fall River since the 1850s. Discouraged by past failures and hard times, many male workers had opposed the decision to strike in January. Among them was the Lancashire-born labor reformer Thomas Stephenson, whose *Lawrence Journal* competed with Henry Sevey's *Labor Journal* for the support and direction of the textile operatives of New England. Stephenson had pilloried Sevey's unmanly conversion to support of the women's strike at their January 16 meeting by calling him another "Adam in the garden of old" who was manipulated "as the weaker vessel" by "babbling Amazons." When he charged that Sevey lacked "ordinary manly courage and determination," he may have been echoing the views of many male workers until the strike was won.[28] When it was over and the wage cut had been rescinded, the Fall River weavers and their activist women controlled local labor politics.

[27]*Fall River News*, Feb. 15, 22; Mar. 1, 8, 13, 15, 17; Apr. 5, 1875. Cassie O'Neil, a representative of the women weavers of Fall River, advocated the organization of women weavers and ring spinners in Lowell as well as equal pay for equal work during a mule spinners' strike shortly after the successful weavers' strike in Fall River: *Boston Herald*, Apr. 25, 1875; *Lowell Courier*, Apr. 26, 1875. For O'Neill on child labor, see *Fall River News*, Mar. 1, 1875. Women strikers formed their own organization for a few weeks and adamantly refused to accept any compromise with the manufacturers: *Boston Journal*, Jan. 18, 1875; *Boston Herald*, Feb. 1, 1875. The *New York Times*, Sept. 29, 1875, described the public activities of protesting women during the events of 1875 as more violent and "disgusting" than those of the men. For intriguing but undeveloped evidence on women's involvement in Lancashire radical politics, see James Epstein, "Understanding the Cap of Liberty: Symbolic Practice and Social Conflict in Early Nineteenth-Century England," *Past and Present*, 122 (February 1989), 75–118. On the activities of English women in support of Chartism, see Dorothy Thompson, "Women and Nineteenth-Century Radical Politics: A Lost Dimension," in *The Rights and Wrongs of Women*, ed. Juliet Mitchell and Ann Oakley, 112–38 (New York: Penguin, 1976).

[28]*Fall River News*, Feb. 22, 1875.

As a result of the success of the strike in March, the weavers began to organize a regional association of textile operatives to establish a standard list of wages and agitate for factory legislation that would make New England the Lancashire of America.[29] This prospect alarmed mill agents throughout the region. For mule spinners, the appeal of a standard wage list and a regional organization lay in making both the blacklist and strikebreaking spinners obsolete in New England. During and after the 1870 strike, the mule spinners had tried unsuccessfully to develop contacts with mule spinners in the principal textile centers of New England to prevent strikebreaking. However, for many New England born textile workers, male and female, geographical mobility, initially from farm to factory, meant their right to seek to better themselves. As one Fall River operative critical of English ways said: "Individual ideas, rather than the collective, rule in this country."[30]

Many American workers and manufacturers alike rejected as spiritless and unmanly the claims of immigrant spinners and weavers to a right to work in their trade in their chosen community. Charles Nordhoff, labor reporter for the *New York Herald,* wrote on the Fall River situation: "No man is a slave who had the right to migrate and the spirit to do it, the courage and endurance necessary for the struggle with life." Nordhoff contrasted the attitudes of English and American workers. "[Lancashire weavers] know only weaving, and nothing else, and regard it as their only work . . . and they will starve rather than do anything else." English trade unions teach a man that he has

> a vested right in their trade and a right to live by it. . . . He remains in Fall River; he does not attempt any other work; he is simply a Fall River weaver, and stands and suffers on that ground. . . . I cannot help but think the American would show the greater pride and independence in his course. . . . He would accept the conditions, quietly do his work well, but with a determination to get out of the business as soon as he could move himself away.[31]

[29]*Fall River News,* Apr. 5, 1875. That year the *Sixth Annual Report* of the MBLS (186–87) advocated a major reform of Massachusetts factory legislation along the lines of English law: *Fall River News,* Apr. 30, 1875. The leadership of the new textile workers' organization seemed to consist of the leaders of the Weavers' Association (many of whom were pre–Civil War immigrants from Lancashire), who initially had opposed the January strike. No women appeared as speakers at the regional convention: *Fall River News,* May 22, 1875; *Boston Herald,* May 21 and 22, 1875. After the successful weavers' strike in Fall River, the nearby New Bedford textile workers demanded an increase in wages and got it almost immediately. Weavers in the mill villages of Rhode Island also demanded increased wages and organized in support of a ten-hour law; see the weekly *Province Sun,* January to December 1875. For an assessment of the success of the weavers' strike by the conservative press, see *Commercial Bulletin* (Boston), Aug. 26, 1875.

[30]*Fall River News,* Feb. 19, 1875; MBLS (1882), 300.

[31]*New York Herald,* Oct. 19, 1875.

Furthermore, many American workers, male and female, were young, single boarders in New England textile cities rather than members of resident families, for whom relocation posed difficult problems. As one Lancashire weaver put it in 1875: "Ay, but we are too poor to move away; we owe money, mayhap; and where shall we go?" English workers came to associate Yankee willingness to move about the region looking for better work as playing into the hands of hostile employers. Lancashire operatives deplored the by-word in Fall River, "If you don't like it, get out," and spoke of the American as "proverbial for his submission."[32] Other English spinners and weavers who had immigrated before 1870 had developed connections with native-born workers in New England textile cities. While participating in the ten-hour movement, they learned to use the rhetoric and ideology of Yankee rights and republicanism to defend their resistance to their employers. As a result, the older immigrants served as mediators between American labor reformers and the newly arrived English people. But the dominance of labor protest in Fall River in 1875 by weavers inspired by Lancashire-style popular radicalism endangered this coalition.

In the summer of 1875, as the weavers organized throughout eastern Massachusetts and Rhode Island, the mill agents decided to try again to destroy their small competitors by cutting wages back to prestrike levels and glutting the market with cheap goods. The Fall River weavers' response was extraordinary: they rallied the American and French-Canadian workers and collectively withheld their labor in a deliberate effort to influence the price of print cloth for their own purposes. On July 31 they voted overwhelmingly not for a strike but for what they pointedly called a one-month "vacation." Workers wildly applauded a resolution that if the Fall River mills could not pay decent wages for weaving, they had no moral right to the print goods market. Next they resolved that if other manufacturers could pay more for the work, then "they have the best right to it," and the Fall River mills "must stand their chance of being burst up."[33] This defiant act, which drew on their heritage of popular radicalism, openly denied the validity of a morally neu-

---

[32]Ibid., Oct. 13, 1875. On English attitudes toward American textile workers, see MBLS (1882), 338, 224. On the pre–Civil War period, see Norman Ware, *The Industrial Workers, 1840–1860* (1924; Chicago: Quadrangle, 1964), 76–78, 116–18; Phillip T. Silvia, Jr., "The Spindle City: Labor, Politics, and Religion in Fall River, 1870–1905" (Ph.D. diss., Fordham University, 1973), 12–58; Sylvia Chace Lintner, "A Social History of Fall River, 1859–1879" (Ph.D. diss., Radcliffe College, 1945), 123–30.

[33]The Fall River manufacturers regarded all competitors who during the depression had shifted from wide goods to print cloth as "outside" of their "legitimate" business and were determined to rid the market of the oversupply (as they saw it) of 10,000 looms that interfered with their dominance of the print cloth market: *Fall River News*, July 19, 22, 24, 30, 1875. For the vacation decision by the weavers' organization, see ibid., Aug. 2, 1875. The *Fall River News* of July 30, 1875, indicates that the male weavers were less sympathetic to the vacation than the women weavers. On the radical challenge of the vacation movement, see *Commercial Bulletin*, Aug. 28, 1875. During their vacation, the weavers formally joined

tral market run by natural laws and laid bare the struggle in New England between labor and capital over wages and workers' rights. The mill agents were determined to crush this unprecedented threat to their power, whatever the cost. The ferocity of this struggle exposed the spinners to the historic charge of brutality and recklessness.

After a month of vacation with production booming in other mill towns and no price increase in the market, the operatives abandoned the strike. However, the mill agents, eager to demolish both the spinners' and the new weavers' organizations, decided to lock out their employees and starve them into submission. Within several weeks the workers were "clemming," as the Lancashire folk said: they were literally wasting away with hunger. That hunger and the refusal of the mill agents to employ workers who would not sign away their union memberships tapped a politically primitive response from the angry Lancashire workers on September 27, the day the mills finally reopened.

Inspired by one elderly male labor activist with memories of the customs of late-eighteenth-century food riots in Manchester, England, hundreds of men and women strikers marched to city hall yelling, "Bread!" "Tyranny!" They carried signs that read "15,000 white slaves for auction" and bore poles on which were impaled loaves of bread. As their forebears had done occasionally since the 1790s, they demanded their right to be fed, and threatened to take food wherever they could find it if they were refused. To underscore their anger at being told to return to work or go to the state poor farm, one woman striker hit the mayor on the head with a loaf of bread. English men and women joined together in desperation to demand from American authorities their customary right to feed their families even while they resisted their employers. The historic and cultural significance of the food riot was clear to Lancashire people but baffling to everyone else (even to the mayor, who literally did not know what hit him) except the conservative press in Boston and Providence, whose editors well understood the revolutionary import of Manchester-style bread riots in New England.[34]

---

the national union of textile operatives and agitated for a ten-hour law in Rhode Island: *Fall River News*, Aug. 10 and 17, 1875.

[34]During the second month out of work, growing dissension among the spinners, carders, and weavers and their leaders over the correct course of action and the desertion of their cause by supporters in the community prompted the manufacturers' decision to try to force them to sign yellow-dog contracts before they returned to work: *Fall River News*, Aug. 14; Sept. 4, 11, 13, 16, 1875. Some of the strike rhetoric was cast in terms of the rights of American citizens in a free country, but the actions on Sept. 27 were inspired by the Lancashire past; see Edward P. Thompson, "The Moral Economy of the English Crowd in the Eighteenth Century," *Past and Present*, 50 (February 1971), 76–136. One of the chief sources of this inspiration was the seventy-five-year-old strike leader Jonathan Biltcliffe: *New York Herald*, Sept. 25–28, 1875; *Boston Herald*, Sept. 28, 1875. According to the labor reformer Jennie Collins, the person who hit the mayor on the head was a woman: letter to the editor of *Boston Globe*, reprinted in *Fall River News*, Oct. 6, 1875. Sheila

The spectacle of the bread riot split the textile operatives of different ethnic groups into confused and hostile camps. French-Canadian and American workers were appalled and alienated by demands for bread, threats of looting, and rumors of arson and violence. The local French-language newspaper denounced the food riot as led by a "ridiculous mob." These cultural divisions and the defeat of the vacation strategy convinced the Lancashire mule spinners that the weavers' union, with its contingent of female agitators and its emotional displays of desperation and rage, had led the strikers into disaster. Mill owners used the disorderly conduct of bread rioters in the streets of Fall River to recast the spinners and weavers as Lancashire brutes and later to characterize all union men as "English and Irish scum."³⁵

For many spinners, a violent demand for bread as the only alternative to the horrors of the state poor farm was no manly way to behave in public or to deal with their employers. Worst of all, returning operatives signed away their union memberships. The weavers' union disappeared and the spinners' union went underground. After 1875, the spinners recaptured the leadership of labor politics in Fall River, which turned toward moderation and caution. The men followed their leader, Robert Howard, who first made his own men "as obedient and docile and harmonious as the parts of a mule frame."³⁶ The dream of a weavers' Lan-

Rowbotham argued that women played a central role (if often inspired by female duty to family) in bread riots in nineteenth-century western Europe: *Women, Resistance, and Revolution* (New York: Vintage, 1974), 99–107. Also see Malcolm I. Thomis and Jennifer Grimmett, *Women in Protest, 1800–1850* (New York: St. Martin's Press, 1982), chap. 2. On the events of Sept. 27, see *Fall River News,* Sept. 27, and the testimony at the trials of those accused of participating in a riot, Sept. 29 and Oct. 2, 1875; and reports from special correspondents in the *New York Times,* Sept. 28 and 29, 1875; *New York Herald,* Sept. 25–28, 1875. For statements by William H. Jennings of the Merchants Mill on the "peculiar" and intolerable activities of the Lancashire weavers, see *Fall River News,* Oct. 22, 1875; for the conservative press, *Providence Journal,* Sept. 29, 1875, and *Commercial Bulletin,* Oct. 2, 1875.

³⁵On Oct. 2, 1875, *L'Echo du Canada,* the French-Canadian newspaper in Fall River, described the events of the bread riot on Sept. 27 as dangerously violent and peculiarly alien: Lintner, "Social History of Fall River," 158–59. One of the defense lawyers for the six men arrested for rioting, a Yankee labor reformer, strongly denied any "premeditation or collusion or purpose" on the part of the crowd that besieged city hall for bread and defended his clients on the basis of their right to peaceable assembly: *Fall River News,* Oct. 2, 1875. After a lost strike in Lowell in the late spring of 1875, mule spinners seemed skeptical about the possibilities of regional organization. On the return of the vacationers to the mills, see *Fall River News* and *New York Herald,* Oct. 13, 16, 19, 1875. On unionists as "scum," see MBLS (1882), 341. On anger and masculinity, see Peter N. Stearns, "Men, Boys, and Anger in American Society, 1860–1940," in *Manliness and Morality: Middle-Class Masculinity in Britain and America, 1800–1940,* ed. J. A. Mangan and James Walvin (Manchester: Manchester University Press, 1986).

³⁶*Boston Globe,* Aug. 18, 1879. Robert Howard's account of the labor unrest in Fall River in the 1870s obliterated all mention of divisions over the 1875 strike, the role of women weavers, and the bread riot: "Progress in the Textile Trades," in George E. McNeill, *The Labor Movement: The Problem of To-day* (Boston, 1887).

cashire in New England, a place where men and women would participate equally in work and union activity, faded along with their organization.

A spinners' strike in 1879 demonstrated the vulnerability of textile workers who abandoned popular radicalism and regional organization. Conducting themselves with courtesy and patience for three long years while accepting the economic laws of the marketplace, the mule spinners waited until print cloth prices had finally risen, then reminded the mill owners of their past promises to rescind wage cuts when good times returned. Still clinging to their power over the postwar print cloth market, the mill agents refused to negotiate, recruited strikebreakers from other New England textile centers, and, most important, increased the numbers of ring spinning frames run by women and young boys in their mills. Any amount of yarn spun on ring frames represented fewer jobs for mule spinners. The reality of unskilled female ring spinners producing quantities of warp yarn in the Pocasset Mill during the 1879 strike prepared the mule spinners to listen to arguments in favor of "thinning" the labor market by the withdrawal of all women, or at least all married women, from factory work. "The comfort and dignity of man begins," one speaker told them, "when he has a home and domestic circle engaged in promoting his happiness." Unable to restrain the increasingly desperate spinners from using violence to intimidate strikebreakers, the leaders of the lost strike in 1879 were blacklisted to a man.[37] For many of them, the working woman at her ring spinning frame had become the new enemy.

The meanings of masculinity for spinners and weavers became central to the conflicts between the cultural and political traditions of Lancashire and the conditions of work and life in Fall River during the turbulent decade of the 1870s. Initially mule spinners and weavers attempted to transplant the deferential politics of the mid-century system of industrial relations from England to New England. In doing so, they protected their respectable masculinity in ways that they believed served class politics in general and indicated some flexibility in gender relationships during labor protest and within their households as long as their leadership of the community of workers remained uncontested. The use of popular

[37]On the 1879 strike, see *Providence Journal*, May 9, 13, 1879; *Boston Herald*, June 16–Oct. 7, 1879; *Boston Globe*, June 13–Aug. 25, 1879; MBLS, *Eleventh Annual Report* (1880), 53–68. Cumbler suggested that although some union militancy continued in the city after 1879, French-Canadian workers, who as a community were often divided over the wisdom of militancy, became an increasingly significant and conservative portion of the work force of spinners and weavers. On the increasing conservatism of the mule spinners in Fall River, see Cumbler, *Working-Class Community*, 173–94. Ring spinning began to replace mule spinning in American textile production in the 1890s; the mule spinners never attempted to organize the female ring spinners until then.

radicalism by rebellious women during the 1875 weavers' strike revealed
serious conflicts among men and women workers over the leadership
and direction of class activities in Fall River.[38] Yet the success of the
weavers in early 1875 had indicated ways to resolve the dangers of a
geographically mobile labor force in New England and even challenged
the ideology of supply and demand as well as the power of their employers to manipulate the market. But this activism also threatened male control of the spinning trade, the authority of mule spinners in labor
politics, and the respectable masculinity of mule spinners by association
with public riot and disorder.

After the failure of the weavers' attempt to influence the print cloth
market, the spinners returned to a strategy of moderation that restored
their sense of proper masculine leadership but offered no means to confront either the power of their employers at work and in the market or
their ability to transform the nature of spinning itself by employing
women on new technology. Despite a keen sense of loss among male activists such as Mr. W., who remembered the radical politics of Lancashire, the mule spinners were advocating a family wage. Skilled and
respectable union men bowed to the forces of supply and demand and
voted for political candidates who supported craft unions. After the
events of the 1870s, Robert Howard, the secretary of the mule spinners'
union, built a political career that eventually led to the state senate and a
prominent role in the Massachusetts Knights of Labor. As union men
embraced electoral politics as the key to labor reform, women's involvement in union activity continued to diminish.

Conflicts over the meanings of masculinity in Fall River factories and
in labor protest were not simply stumbling blocks to the establishment of
a Lancashire in New England; more important, they provide evidence of
intraclass conflict and cultural discontinuity in meanings assigned to
working-class gender.[39] They also represent one powerful but largely un-
recognized element in the complex interconnections among people
caught up in immigration, industrialization, and cross-cultural adjustment in late-nineteenth-century America. Finally, the variety of forms

[38]The events of the 1870s in Fall River provide indirect evidence on gender politics
among Lancashire workers and on the militancy and agency of English women textile
workers. This evidence complements Thomis and Grimmett, *Women in Protest;* Rose,
"Gender at Work"; and Carol Morgan, "Working-Class Women and Labor and Social
Movements of Nineteenth-Century England" (Ph.D. diss., University of Iowa, 1979).

[39]For treatments of working-class masculinity that suggest cultural and cross-class continuities, see Peter Stearns, *Be a Man! Males in Modern Society* (New York: Holmes &
Meier, 1979), chap. 4; and Judith A. McGaw, *Most Wonderful Machine: Mechanization
and Social Change in Berkshire Paper Making, 1801–1885* (Princeton: Princeton University
Press, 1987), chap. 9.

that working-class masculinity took in Fall River culture and politics in the 1870s demonstrate the contingencies rather than the eventualities in the meaning of masculinity and the content of the family wage in nineteenth-century America.

CHAPTER FIVE

"A Man's Dwelling House Is His Castle": Tenement House Cigarmaking and the Judicial Imperative

Eileen Boris

In January 1885 New York's highest court struck down a statute that prohibited cigarmaking in New York City and Brooklyn tenement houses where cooking, sleeping, and the daily activities of life took place. Their decision in the case *In re Jacobs* displayed the gendered subtext of the law through its interpretation of privacy and contract. Unconvinced that the measure was passed to promote the public health, the Court of Appeals relied upon the emerging judicial understanding of "free labor" to argue that a man's property and personal liberty could not be taken away without due process of law. "This law was not intended to protect the health of those engaged in cigarmaking, as they are allowed to manufacture cigars everywhere except in the forbidden tenement-houses," declared the New York court. At a time when medical authorities already were exposing the deadly effects of nicotine, it asked, "What possible relations can cigarmaking in any building have to the health of the general public?" Guided by the rights of "free labor," the right to contract and the rights of property, the court never considered the actual conditions in tenement houses or their impact on the larger society. By claiming that "if the legislature has the power under the Constitution to prohibit the prosecution of one lawful trade in a tenement-house, then it may prevent the prosecution of all trades therein," *Jacobs* became a

Research for this paper was facilitated by a Howard University Research Grant in the Humanities, Social Science, and Education. I thank Stuart Kaufman and Peter Albert of the Samuel Gompers Papers for access to their files, especially the materials compiled by Leslie S. Rowland on tenement house cigarmakers in New York City from the 1870s to 1900. This paper relies heavily on Rowland's pioneering research, which was conducted in 1970–71 for a seminar directed by the late Herbert Gutman at the University of Rochester. I take full responsibility, however, for the interpretation.

hurdle that stymied regulation of industrial homework for the next half century.[1]

The judges who sought to save the cigarmaker from the paternalism of the state affirmed his paternalism within the family: "It cannot be perceived how the cigarmaker is to be improved in his health or his morals by forcing him from his home and its hallowed associations and beneficent influences, to ply his trade elsewhere." Individual (male) freedom to engage in work "by which he earns a livelihood for himself and family," individual (male) choice "to do his work where he can have the supervision of his family and their help" could not succumb to what the judges labeled an arbitrary law. The justices failed to notice that wives and children were not merely "help" for the male cigarmaker, but central to the production of cigars by the largely Bohemian immigrant group that worked in the tenements. Nor did they consider that the cigarmaker no longer was an independent artisan but an employee working in a divided labor process and thus hardly the independent citizen of Republican ideology.

In its tone and reasoning, *Jacobs* expressed a set of assumptions that illuminate the interplay of gender, ethnicity, and class in law and public policy. This decision framed the discourses of disease, dirt, and exploitation under which the battle over industrial homework was waged during the last decades of the nineteenth century. But its significance goes beyond the particular subject of tenement homework. As an early example of legal undermining of labor legislation, *Jacobs* reveals the assumptions about gender which stood at the center of both the contest between capital and labor and the conflicts within a working class divided by sex, ethnicity, and skill in Gilded Age America.

Rather than focus on the state in relation to either class struggle or women workers,[2] let us explore the more complex interaction between

[1]*In re Jacobs*, 98 N.Y. 98 (1885), 113–14, 105–6; 83 U.S. (16 Wall.) 36 (1873), 83–130 (dissenting opinions). The most comprehensive analysis of *Jacobs* is in William E. Forbath, "The Ambiguities of Free Labor: Labor and the Law in the Gilded Age," *Wisconsin Law Review*, no. 4 (1985), 795–96. For the best discussion of contract, see Amy Dru Stanley, "Contract Rights in the Age of Emancipation: Wage Labor and Marriage after the Civil War" (Ph.D diss. Yale University, 1990). For medical testimony on the impact of tobacco, see Elizabeth Stow Brown, "The Working-Women of New York: Their Health and Occupations," *Journal of Social Science*, 25 (December 1888), 78–92; see also "The Cigar Makers' Perils: The Mass Meeting's Committee before Doctor Day," *New York Sun*, Oct. 1, 1874; Demos, "Correspondence from New York," *Workingman's Advocate*, Nov. 14 and 21, 1874, 2.

[2]On the state and class conflict, see, e.g., Leon Fink, "Labor, Liberty, and the Law: Trade Unionism and the Problem of the American Constitutional Order," *Journal of American History*, 74 (December 1987), 904–25; Christopher Tomlins, *The State and the Unions: Labor Relations, Law, and the Organized Labor Movement in America, 1880–1960* (New York: Cambridge University Press, 1985); and William Forbath, "The Shaping of the American Labor Movement," *Harvard Law Review*, 102 (April 1989), 1109–1256, none of

the power of courts and legislatures, working-class militancy, and hierarchies within the working class. Concepts of manhood and womanhood, understanding of gendered behavior provide the lens through which workers adopted strategies and learned lessons from their struggles; indeed, gender shaped this history. As the historian Joan Scott has noted, "nineteenth-century worker protest movements offered analyses of social organization that interpreted 'experience' even as they appealed to its objective impact on people's lives. In the process they provided individuals with forms of social consciousness based on common terms of identification and so provided the means for collective action."[3]

Women as cigarmakers and as the wives and daughters of cigarmakers actively fought to better the conditions of their craft in the 1870s and 1880s. Yet "woman" was not an actual agent but the most powerful of symbols under the social conditions that generated *Jacobs*. She was the object/beneficiary of working-class masculinity and the degraded opposite of the craftworker. White, "Teutonic" male workers drew more narrowly the bonds of mutuality, excluding large numbers of women workers, as they associated tenement production with the alien and fought for their right to a family wage. Homework, they argued, undermined American values and the home life behind those values, to which the family role of women was central.

Homework also represented a new form of slavery. "The manufacturers say that they have inaugurated the tenement system for our benefit and at our request," Samuel Gompers told a crowd of strikers in 1877. "Yes, as the slave kneels and holds up his hands for the shackles."[4] Associating slavery with weakness and dependency and dependency with loss of masculinity, Gompers and his supporters combined nativism with racism and male supremacy in defense of their restricted vision of the working class. Tenement house manufacturing joined competition from

---

which considers gender as integral to the story. A whole literature has developed on protective labor legislation for women workers. See, e.g., Judith Baer, *The Chains of Protection: The Judicial Response to Women's Labor Legislation* (Westport, Conn.: Greenwood, 1978); Ann Corinne Hill, "Protection of Women Workers and the Courts: A Legal Case History," *Feminist Studies*, 5 (Summer 1979), 247–73.

[3] Joan Scott, *Gender and the Politics of History* (New York: Columbia University Press, 1988), 94. For the significance of analyzing the language of gender to understand working-class movements, see ibid., 53–67 and 93–112.

[4] "A Translation of an Article in the *Social-Demokrat*," Oct. 24, 1875, in *The Samuel Gompers Papers*, vol. 1, *The Making of a Union Leader, 1850–86*, ed. Stuart B. Kaufman et al. (Urbana: University of Illinois Press, 1986), 66–67; see also "Report on the Trade Union Activities of the United Cigarmakers of N[orth] A[merica] in 1874," trans. from *Social-Demokrat*, Jan. 24, 1875, in ibid., 58. For the slavery image, see Demos, letter to *Workingman's Advocate*, Nov. 11, 1874; Jacob Riis, *How the Other Half Lives* (New York, 1891), 136; "The Tenement Horrors," *New York Herald*, Oct. 5, 1874; "Cigar Makers Speaking," *New York Sun*, Oct. 31, 1877.

"coolie" or Chinese labor and women working on molds as an assault on white manhood, on their Republican freeborn rights. This working-class version of Republicanism championed the rights of man and linked the notion of a virtuous citizenry with economic equality. It had emerged out of the cauldron of Reconstruction politics as the dominant political philosophy among organizing workers, but had its roots in the emergence of artisan self-activity earlier in the century. Laboring women had attempted to assert themselves into the Republican equation of natural rights with the superiority of the producing classes. But their quest after "self-rule" ran aground upon the competing conception of a specifically female virtue that substituted domesticity for citizenship. Free labor doctrines, which became embodied in the Fourteenth Amendment, embedded a gendered dichotomy: free labor contrasted with slave labor; but to be a slave was to be unmanly, a dependent and thus like a woman. Such a set of interpretations shaped the terrain upon which workers resisted home labor.[5]

Ultimately the battle against tenement house cigarmaking, both on the shop floor and in the courts, was crucial in shaping the racialist, masculinist voluntarism of the American Federation of Labor (AFL). The lessons learned by Gompers and the Cigar-Makers' International Union (CMIU), however, developed out of their understandings of gender, race, and class. Fought for the most part by groups of men against each other, this contest attempted to resolve the relation between home and workplace and what activities properly belonged to whom in which arena. In the process, the voices and needs of the mainly female and immigrant homeworkers became mute.

The Tenement House System and Early Efforts to Abolish It

Tenement house cigarmaking developed as an employer response to the economic depression of the 1870s. But it also grew out of changes in tax laws, which increased the cost of imports while taxing tobacco and tobacco products made in this country. Deskilling of the craft, through the introduction from Germany of the mold that separated bunchmaking from rolling, also fueled this reorganization of production. So did an abundant labor supply in the form of the immigrants who began arriving

[5]For a stimulating analysis along these lines, see Gwendolyn Mink, "The Lady and the Tramp: Gender, Race, and the Origins of the American Welfare State," in *Women, the State and Welfare*, ed. Linda Gordon (Madison: University of Wisconsin Press, 1990), 92–122. See also Forbath, "Ambiguities of Free Labor"; Sean Wilentz, *Chants Democratic: New York City and the Rise of the American Working Class, 1788–1850* (New York: Oxford University Press, 1984), 61–103; Christine Stansell, *City of Women: Sex and Class in New York, 1789–1860* (New York: Knopf, 1986), 146–53.

in 1869 from worn-torn Bohemia. A few manufacturers were using the system in 1872; at least 50 were doing so, often in multiple houses, as late as 1888.[6]

The size of the tenement cigarmaking population also varied. They accounted for about four-fifths of the entire New York product in 1877, the year of the great strike of the cigarmakers, when at least 1,000 families (5,000 people) worked in the tenements, and between a seventh and an eighth of the entire trade by 1885. After the licensing of homework in tenements as a regulatory measure, still 775 families (4,075 people) are known to have been making cigars in 1901; others were doubtless doing so without licenses. While such figures represented approximations at best, most observers agreed that the introduction of the suction table and other new technologies (such as bunching machinery in the mid-1880s), along with the union label (introduced in 1880 for higher-priced cigars), essentially had diminished, if not destroyed, the system by the first decade of the new century.[7]

To make up for the federal tax on American-made tobacco and tobacco products, a manufacturer would buy or lease a tenement house

[6]My understanding of the transformation of the cigarmaking industry relies on Patricia A. Cooper, *Once a Cigar Maker: Men, Women, and Work Culture in American Cigar Factories, 1900–1919* (Urbana: University of Illinois Press, 1987), 10–40; and Dorothee Schneider, "The New York Cigarmakers' Strike of 1877," *Labor History,* 26 (Summer 1985), 325–52, supplemented by original materials in the Rowland files. See also Edith Abbott, *Women in Industry* (New York: Appleton, 1910), 190–201; Bureau of the Census, *Twelfth Census, 1900,* vol. 9, *Manufacturers,* pt. 3, "Special Report on Selected Industries" (Washington, D.C.: U.S. Government Printing Office, 1902), 669–71; J. R. Dodge, "Statistics of Manufactures of Tobacco," in *Tenth Census, 1880: Report on the Production of Agriculture* (Washington, D.C.: U.S. Government Printing Office, 1883), 13–30; Samuel Gompers, *Seventy Years of Life and Labor: An Autobiography* (New York: Dutton, 1925), 1:106–8; "Effect of Foreign Born on Cigar Making Trade," in U.S. Congress, House, *Reports of the Industrial Commission,* vol. 15, pt. 3, 57th Cong., 1st sess. (Washington, D.C.: U.S. Government Printing Office, 1901), 385–88. "The Cigar Makers' Strike," *New York Herald,* Oct. 17, 1877, reported Sutro & Newmark to be the first company to introduce the system.

[7]Abbott, *Women in Industry,* 195–202; [Adolph Strasser], "Appendix: Cigar-Makers' International Union," in *The Labor Movement: The Problem of Today,* ed. George E. McNeill (Boston, 1887), 603; testimony of Strasser, U.S. Senate, Committee on Education and Labor, *Report of the Committee of the Senate upon the Relations between Labor and Capital,* 5 vols. (Washington, D.C.: U.S. Government Printing Office, 1885), 1:451; testimony of Samuel Gompers, reprinted in Kaufman et al., *Gompers Papers,* 1:291–92; for 1883, see "President's Biennial Report," *Cigar Makers' Official Journal* (hereafter, *CMOJ*), September 1883, and "The Tenement-House Cigar Law," *New-York Tribune,* Sept. 30, 1883 (which reports 25 firms as operating tenements with about 5,000 workers); State of New York, *Thirteenth Annual Report of the Bureau of Labor Statistics for the Year 1895* (Albany, 1896), 552. Robert W. De Forest and Lawrence Veiller, for example, concluded in their report on New York tenements in 1900 that "through the invention of a machine called the suction table, the manufacture of cigars is being gradually removed into factories; and it is the opinion of those best acquainted with the trade, that it will soon disappear from the tenement-houses": *The Tenement House Problem: Including the Report of the New York State Tenement House Commission of 1900,* 2 vols. (New York, 1903), 1:53.

capable of holding up to twenty families and bond it as a single factory. Often he would maintain a block of tenements, referred to as a "nicotine hive," linking their outside gates. He would keep one apartment for storage, office, and packing purposes and rent the ground floor to a grocer or saloonkeeper. He then would compel employees to rent apartments of two or three small rooms for more than the going rate as a condition of employment, withholding the rent from their wages. If a worker had earned less than the month's rent the first week, often the employer would provide credit in the tenement store, further emeshing the cigarmaker in relations of dependency, much as the owner of a company town tied workers to their jobs through debt and the threat of eviction. As one correspondent of *The Workingman's Advocate* complained, "the independent spirit necessary to a good citizen, is endangered by the experiment of stringent rules, allowing the boss and his tools to enter the rooms at any time to watch and control the working, thus making a penitentiary of a place where the tender, sacred family ties should rule supreme."[8]

Not only did the tenement house employer save factory rent and utilities by forcing his workers to use their homes as his place of production, but he profited from rearranging the labor process so that stripping and casing became incorporated in the cigarmaker's job. In the factory, he would have to hire workers for both of these processes; in the home, the cigarmaker's children prepared the tobacco, as it were, for nothing. His greatest advantage came from the low piece rates. One reporter calculated that "a man who could earn in a factory a little over $2 a day, would net only about $5 a week" in a tenement.[9] Tenement house workers, however, neither worked the same hours as factory cigarmakers nor labored alone. Given the meagerness of the piece rate, which continuously fell during the 1870s, fourteen-hour days were common; some cigarmakers even worked on Sunday.[10] They worked as

[8]Letter from P. to *Workingman's Advocate*, Aug. 22 and 29, 1874. For the dependency and workings of the system, see the testimony of Vincenza Vesprer, in U.S. Congress, House, *Testimony Taken by the Select Committee of the House of Representatives to Inquire into the Alleged Violation of the Laws Prohibiting the Importation of Contract Laborers, Paupers, Convicts, and Other Classes*, 50th Cong., 1st sess. (Washington, D.C.: U.S. Government Printing Office, 1889), 373–77. Vesprer was at the time working in the factory but was still required to live in her boss's tenement, a situation that suggests deterioration by the late 1880s. See also testimony of Samuel Gompers in ibid., 394–96; "Pestilence in the Cigar," *New York Sun*, Sept. 26, 1874; "Perils of Tenement Workshops," *New-York Tribune*, Sept. 28, 1874. For the phrase "nicotine hive" and a description of such tenements, see "The Wonderful Strike," *New York Sun*, Nov. 27, 1877; "The Cigars of Death," *CMOJ*, February 1880.

[9]"Pestilence in the Cigar," *New York Sun*, Sept. 26, 1874. This article provides the most astute analysis of the profits to be gained: about $2,500 on rents, $650 savings on stripping, and close to $500 for casing, for each house.

[10]"The Cigar Trade," *New York Times*, Sept. 28, 1874. This article estimated 6,000 tenement homeworkers.

part of a family group: mother, father, children, and older relative, or a boarder.[11]

Among these workers, Bohemians predominated, and women were the more proficient. More than half of the nearly 13,000 Bohemians in New York City were cigarmakers.[12] Most were from rural regions where the women rolled cigars in manufactories while their men continued to farm or practice other crafts. Unable to find work upon immigration, Bohemian men either learned bunchmaking or rolling from their women, some of whom had found work in cigar workshops soon after their arrival, so that together they could form a cigarmaking team. One Czech worker defended the tenement system: "Women could make better cigars than men, and it was therefore necessary that the wives should help their husbands in making cigars."[13]

Despite women's skill, manufacturers considered their husbands to be the heads of the cigarmaking teams. Sharing a belief in male dominance, the women themselves attempted to maintain the patriarchal family structure of the Old World. The journalist Jacob Riis reported one woman as saying, as she continued her household duties, " 'Aye . . . it would be nice for sure to have father work at his trade.' Then what a home she could make for them, and how happy they would be." The newspapers could suggest that the Bohemian women offered a model for women's-rights advocates, but these immigrants accepted their inherited gender system and thus accepted elevation of the father as the leader within their unit of family labor.[14]

Unionized cigarmakers had no trouble with such a gender division of power. From the beginning, the organized cigarmakers' campaign against

[11]For one graphic description, see "A Scrap of Truth," *Progress,* June 23, 1885. See also "A Tenement Trade," *New-York Daily Tribune,* Sept. 23, 1874; "The Wonderful Strike," *New York Sun,* Nov. 27, 1877, also describes the tenements. See also "Tenement Cigar Factories Endanger the Public Health," *CMOJ,* January 1880. These various reports note that the families of the Bohemians were not large, suggesting that work with tobacco led to sickly children and lowered fertility.

[12]The precise numbers of Bohemians in the city are difficult to determine because they were first counted in "Austria-Hungary (including Bohemia)." In 1880 this figure was 16,937; it rose to 47,514 in 1890, when a separate table lists the number of Bohemians as 12,322. See Kate Holladay Claghorn, "The Foreign Immigrant in New York City," chap. 9 of *Reports of the Industrial Commission on Immigration,* vol. 15 (Washington, D.C.: U.S. Government Printing Office, 1901), 467 (table 8), 469 (table 14). One 1874 report listed Bohemian cigarmakers as including 4,000 women and between 2,000 and 3,000 men. It was generally assumed that over half of the Bohemians were cigarmakers. See "Pestilence in the Cigar," *New York Sun,* Sept. 26, 1874.

[13]Abbott, *Women in Industry,* 196–201; "Foreign Life in New York," *New-York Tribune,* Nov. 7, 1877; "Samuel Gompers and the Early Cigarmakers' Unions," in Kaufman et al., *Gompers Papers,* 1:45–46; for the Czech man's appraisal, "The Tenement Horrors," *New York Herald,* Oct. 5, 1874. For another claim of female superiority, see "A Tenement Trade," *New-York Daily Tribune,* Sept. 23, 1874.

[14]Riis, *How the Other Half Lives,* 142; Jane E. Robbins, "The Bohemian Women in New York," *Charities,* Dec. 3, 1904, 194–96.

the tenement house system combined a discourse of horror and disease with a ideology of gender that resembled Victorian notions of womanhood, manhood, and home life but was rooted in artisanal culture. Skilled workers believed in respectability, hard work, masculinity, and protection of the weak. Women's wage labor was not incompatible with domesticity, although wage labor under exploitive conditions sullied womanhood and destroyed child life.[15] Masculinity was central to the work culture of cigarmakers, who associated the deskilling of their craft with its feminization. White maleness certainly defined the CMIU, which in the late 1870s reacted to defeats by the tenement house manufacturers by turning to an exclusiveness that would characterized the AFL well into the next century.[16] But they connected this cultural assault against tenement cigarmaking with an attack on the economic exploitation inherent in the system. This outrage at the bosses and capitalists would be lost in later campaigns waged by middle-class social workers against industrial homework.

At a time when ethnic benevolent societies had more members than the cigarmakers' union, the CMIU clung to its strict policy of accepting as members only those who made hand-rolled cigars until 1875, when a new constitution theoretically opened the union to all, regardless of skill, ethnicity, or gender. This change came in the midst of an economic recession, after the numbers in the two New York locals had dropped below 50, and following successful organization by the United Cigar Makers, a small group of German-speaking unionists who initially organized about half of the registered cigarmakers in 1874. Led by Gompers and Adolph Strasser, who was soon to become president of the CMIU, the United Cigar Makers ignored craft distinctions, as well as gender and ethnic differences, and created separate language sections (English, Bohemian, German). It offered a benefit program, an idea that, incorporated in the CMIU became the basis for an increase in dues which effectively excluded the poorer paid, the less skilled, women and the immigrants. At that time, the reemerged CMIU became an "American" union, again without ethnic sections. But in a period of high unemployment and recession, the union embraced only a fraction of cigarmakers, either in or outside of the tenements.[17]

[15]Stansell, *City of Women;* David Montgomery, "Workers' Control of Machine Production in the 19th Century," *Labor History,* 17 (1976), 485–509; Sherri Broder, "Informing the 'Cruelty': The Monitoring of Respectability in Philadelphia's Working-Class Neighborhoods in the Late Nineteenth Century," *Radical America,* 21 (July–August 1987), 34–47.
[16]Cooper, *Once a Cigar Maker;* for the impact of the tenement homework struggles, see Gompers, *Seventy Years,* 1:183–91.
[17]For a summary of these developments, see Schneider, "New York Cigarmakers' Strike," 331–34; Cooper, *Once a Cigar Maker,* 19–21; Bernard Mandel, *Samuel Gompers: A Biography* (Yellow Springs, O.: Antioch Press, 1963), 21–23. In 1873 the CMIU consisted of 84

The first significant attack against tenement manufacturing set a pattern that would continue throughout the century. Charging that contagious diseases lurking within the tenements threatened "the neighborhood and the city" as well as the consumer of cigars, trade unionists appealed to the health of the public to rid themselves of the tenement menace to their economic well-being. They demanded in September 1874 that the New York City Board of Health strictly enforce laws relating to the tenements. John Swinton, the labor journalist elected chair of a multiethnic meeting, contrasted the harms of the system with the humanity of the crowd, who became noble (male) citizens of the republic, fighting for the welfare of the entire community, rich and poor alike, trying "to guard your families, to protect your health, to elevate your lives and your manhood."[18]

Fifty "turn-in jobbers," as tenement house workmen still were called, most of them employees of one man, protested this meeting at one of their own a few days later and attempted to hold a mass meeting the following Sunday. Chaired by their foreman, David Reiss, these meetings suggested the splits within the ranks of cigarmakers by place of employment, as well as the power of the manufacturers—who sent letters of support to one meeting—over their tenement workers. Reiss argued, in terms that the Court of Appeals would return to a decade later, "If any kind of cigar making is injurious, every kind is." Taking the line that would be sustained by the City Board of Health, he claimed that working in a factory was more injurious because there were more workmen. The *New York Sun* reported him as exhorting "his fellow workmen simply to stand up manfully for their right to pursue their self-supporting occupation in the way that best suited them."[19]

When it came to gendered understandings of masculinity, Reiss and the tenement house men shared with John Swinton and the journeyman cigarmakers, as the factory workers were being called, a discourse that associated manhood with freedom. But while both groups saw women and children as under the power of their men, they had different conceptions of what was best for these subordinates. The tenement workers

locals with 3,771 members; in 1884, membership had dropped to 54 locals with 2,167 members, suggesting the impact of the depression, the degradation of the craft, and the inability and unwillingness of the CMIU to enroll the new immigrant and female cigarmakers. See [Strasser], "Appendix: Cigar-Makers' International Union," 602. Later in the same report, however, Strasser notes growth from 126 locals in 1881 to 185 in 1883, compared to the nadir of 17 locals in 1877.

[18]"Death in the Tenements," *New York Sun*, Sept. 28, 1874; see also "Perils of Tenement Workshops," *New-York Tribune*, Sept. 28, 1874.

[19]"The Cigar Men's Quarrel," *New York Sun*, Sept. 29, 1874; "The Tenement Horrors," *New York Herald*, Oct. 5, 1874; "Home News," *New-York Tribune*, Oct. 5, 1875; "Tenement Cigar Making," *New York Sun*, Oct. 5, 1874.

held a more traditional idea of family economy, to which their foreman appealed, even though he accepted the Victorian ideology of separate spheres. "It was better for men to work in their own homes, because they could work when they pleased and by the help of their wives and children, who could not work in outside factories, they could make much more money," Reiss argued. Then he charged, as the manufacturers' association would do during the 1877 strike, that the CMIU "opposed the tenement system . . . because they wished to prevent women from working and earning money." Rather than a plea for women's freedom, this claim must be understood as women's right to work at home, to earn money within the confines of both domestic ideology and the actual restraints that family labor imposed.[20]

Bohemian tenement workers themselves looked at the matter from a practical rather than an ideological viewpoint. They explained the necessity of having their more proficient wives working alongside them and highlighted the economic need that lay beneath the discourse of health, family, and freedom: "Working at home a family can make $25 a week if they work fourteen or fifteen hours a day, but that cannot be done in the shops." Against such a position, shop workmen argued "that a union of all the cigar makers would fix uniform good wages for all the men, and would release the women to attend to household duties and the children to go to school." Thus while some men in both groups embraced the more modern concept of the family wage, its tenets were central to the definition of masculinity set forth by union workers. In addition, trade unionists defended working-class women's right to motherhood, as they attacked the conditions that led "mothers [who] while nursing their babes made cigars, so that the infants inhaled the deadly nicotinous odor."[21]

In a series of powerful articles for the German-language *New York Volkszeitung,* written a few years later in the midst of the campaign to legislate tenement cigarmaking out of existence, Samuel Gompers most forcefully articulated this understanding of womanhood and home life, which would come to dominate organized labor under the AFL. He indicted the poison of the tenements not only for sapping the health of workers but for destroying the moral fiber of the home. Dust, scraps, stems, and filth impeded the housekeeper's efforts "to keep her apartment somewhat clean" in these places without water, and the pressures of piecework robbed families of home life. The housewife served smoked sausage for dinner instead of cooking, and the parents sat on the only

[20]"Tenement Cigar Making," *New York Sun,* Oct. 5, 1874; "Tenement Horrors," *New York Herald,* Oct. 5, 1874.
[21]"Tenement Horrors," "Tenement Cigar Making," "Home News," *New York Tribune,* Oct. 5, 1874.

chairs to eat it while their children crouched like animals. Not only was the work of such small children criminal (they should have been in school), but Gompers implied that homework destroyed the very basis of life, the mother-child bond. "In one room we saw a mother who had just begun to nurse her child but had not interrupted her work of making wrappers." Other mothers, he reported, rolled cigars while their dying babies seemed to cry, " 'How can I stay alive in such a place?!' " Intent upon exposing the evils of tenement house work, he was unable to see the heroic struggles of whole families or the resourcefulness of such mothers. Respectability and sentimentality clothed his vision of the family and women's place within it.[22]

The Board of Health—whose investigation was conducted, like most official visits, with due notice to employers, who then set about cleaning up—rejected such an interpretation. Its assumptions matched those of the tenement manufacturers. It concluded that "the compensation of the factory worker is generally greater per capita than in the tenements, but, by employing every member of the family old enough to work, many earn money who would otherwise be idle, and the aggregate income is greatly increased, enabling the purchase of many comforts not within reach of the factory worker. Children too young to be trusted from home, and the disabled, rheumatic old people, instead of depleting, add to the family income." A citizen's committee rebutted all the report's points and focused on the $3 a week earned for sixteen-hour days by the entire family, reminding the public that "the factories are but working places for adults for a stay of nine hours a day, whereas the tenements is [sic] the home of the whole family, and their exclusive residence." Its own investigation showed that the factories were superior on all counts. The cigarmakers called for the removal of the board, but in their weak state lacked the political and moral clout to affect the tenement system. Later inspections under the tenement house laws called the Board of Health study into further question.[23]

The year 1874 would not be the last time that the CMIU turned to the state to eradicate its tenement competitors. The union called upon Congress in late 1878 to amend the revenue law to prohibit cigar manufacturing in rooms used for dwelling or domestic purposes. Wives would be

[22]"A Translation of a Series of Articles by Samuel Gompers on Tenement-House Cigar Manufacture in New York City," in Kaufman et al., *Gompers Papers*, 1:172–73, 180–87.

[23]The most complete report on the investigation, the citizens' committee response, and union protest meetings is found in "Cigar Making," *Workingman's Advocate*, Feb. 15, 1875; see also "The Cigar-Makers' Protest," *New York Times*, Dec. 28, 1874; "Cigar-Making in Tenement-Houses: Report of the Sanitary Inspectors to the Board of Health," *Tobacco Leaf*, Nov. 11, 1874; "Tenement-House Cigar-Making," *New-York Tribune*, Aug. 5, 1879; "Tenement House Cigar Factories Endanger the Public Health," *CMOJ*, January 1880; "Homes of Poor People," *New-York Tribune*, Jan. 8, 1882.

unable to rock cradles while they worked because the cradle was a domestic piece of furniture; this and other features would make tenement house manufacturing too expensive to carry on and thus end the system. While the original proposal clearly applied the prohibition to wage or salaried workers, the one passed in committee by the Senate appeared to cover small manufacturers, a charge that led to its defeat. Strasser retorted, in terms that tied the CMIU's defense of an unsullied domestic sphere to increasingly nativist rhetoric: "There can be no doubt that the law, if rigidly enforced, would effect small manufacturers to a certain degree, especially those who are living and working with their families in *Chinese Bunks.*"[24] Frustration at the federal level would send the economically weak CMIU to the New York State Legislature.[25]

The Meaning of the Great Strike of 1877

This turn to legislature lobbying—with its virulent, near-hysterical onslaughts against the tenement house "pest holes"—was a reaction to the failure of the trade's general strike in 1877. As one employer later reflected, "at the time of the great strike, the factory hands were idle and the workers in the tenement houses were busy. The tenement-house system thus broke the strike and the labor unions have worked ever since to break up the tenement-house system."[26] His memory, however, was more self-serving than accurate, for the relation of tenement to shop proved less problematic in 1877 than it would become afterward.

"The Factories Now Following the Lead of the Tenements. Cigar Making Generally Suspended Throughout the City," announced the *New York Sun.* Inspired by the railway rebellion of that summer, nearly 15,000 New York cigarmakers, about three-quarters of the trade, walked out in mid-October demanding higher wages. Many in the shops earned $4 per 1,000, but were asking for $5, while those in the tenements were paid $2 or $3 per 1,000.[27] Generally tenement workers asked for a $1 raise, sometimes with a $1 reduction in rent. Some insisted that their

[24]"Legislation against Tenement House Factories," *CMOJ,* March 1879; "Read and Judge," *CMOJ,* May 1879. See also "Tenement House Cigar Making," *New York Herald,* Feb. 22, 1879; "The Tax on Tobacco," *New-York Tribune,* Feb. 13, 1879.

[25]Strasser argued in his "Biennial Report," *CMOJ,* September 1879: "In the state of New York it should be agitated as a sanitary measure, and as a revenue measure in Congress, at Washington. Public opinion on the subject should be assiduously kept alive."

[26]Louis Hass, of Kerbs and Spiess, quoted in "Cigar-Making in Tenement-Houses," *New-York Tribune,* Mar. 14, 1883.

[27]"The Cigar Makers' Strike," *New York Sun,* Oct. 16, 1877; "Dissatisfied Cigarmakers," *New-York Daily Tribune,* Aug. 6, 1877; "Strike of Cigar-Makers," *New York Times,* Aug. 29, 1877; "The Cigarmakers' Strike," *New York Herald,* Sept. 8, 1877; see also Schneider, "New York Cigarmakers' Strike of 1877."

employer/landlords provide gas and light "on the floors" as well as higher wages. By mid-November they also demanded that their homes "be cleaned and whitewashed" and "that only union men should be employed."[28] Shopworkers asked for varied rates for strippers, bunchers, and rollers. Some employers reduced the wage rates of the factory labor force and ended these men's customary right to smoke at work; others saw an opportunity to slash the wages of all.[29]

CMIU Local 144, led by Gompers, organized the strikers into the Cigar Makers Central Organization, with Strasser as president and Marie Hausler, a Bohemian factory worker, as vice president. Each shop, factory, and tenement sent delegates to this central committee, which collected and allocated strike funds (including the entire treasury of Local 144), ran commissaries, and coordinated strategy. In December the strikers operated a cooperative factory to generate funds for the cause. In its organization and mutual aid practices, including assessments to aid strikers, the central body resembled the CMIU.[30]

From the start, women and tenement house workers had equal representation. Thus, when the Central Organization polled workers on striking a given employer, those in the tenements counted just as much as those in the shops and often forced the inside workers out. Women were fully enfranchised. These somewhat overlapping groups were extremely militant. For example, Bohemian women strikers were accused of "having molested other girls" at work in one major factory. Rollers at Mendel Brothers struck for $1 more, but the tenement house workers asked for $2. When a number of the shop men reported to work a few days later, the tenement workers, "partly by persuasion, partly by intimidation, prevented the shop-workers from going in, and induced them to join the strike." When Benjamin Lichtenstein of Lichtenstein Brothers, one of the largest employers of tenement labor, early on "induced" the actual owner of one tenement to evict several families in his employ, tenants "hustled him out of the house together with foreman Mr. Schmidt and threw many packages of tobacco belonging to Lichtenstein on the sidewalk." Though previously unorganized, the tenement workers joined

[28]*New York Times*, Oct. 18, 1877. See also "The Striking Cigar-Makers," *New York Sun*, Nov. 11, 1877.

[29]E.g., "Strike of the Cigar-Makers," *New-York Daily Tribune*, Sept. 6, 1877; "The Cigar Makers' Strike," *New York Sun*, Oct. 16, 1877; "Discontent with Wages," *New-York Tribune*, Oct. 16, 1877; "The Great Cigar Strike," *New York Sun*, Oct. 17, 1877; for a final tabulation, "The Cigar-Maker's Fair," *New York World*, Dec. 28, 1877, reports 15,000 went out, but only 300 to 400 went back even at their old wages.

[30]"The Wonderful Strike," *New York Sun*, Nov. 27, 1877; "Changed Aspect of the Strike," *New York Times*, Dec. 9, 1877; Gompers, *Seventy Years*, 1:140–55; Schneider, "New York Cigarmakers' Strike of 1877."

the union, sometimes en masse as with 500 employees of Straiton &
Storm, perhaps the largest manufacturer in the nation.[31]
Yet the CMIU-dominated leadership ignored the behavior of women
and tenement workers. They separated the first from the realm of worker
and condemned the second as the source of their woes. Putting an end to
the tenement system by raising prices so it would no longer be profitable,
allowing all to work in factories, became their chief goal. Blame at the
time centered on the system and not on the individuals caught in its web.
But when the strike was lost, the CMIU attacked those whom they had
portrayed as victims. Gompers recalled, "They [tenement house workers]
all went out on strike without organization or discipline. We union men
saw our hard-earned achievements likely to vanish because of this reckless precipitate action without consultation with our union."[32]
The more desperate plight of the tenement workers, who had no resources to fall back on, certainly drained the strike fund. By late October
many of these Bohemian families had pawned or sold their household
furniture.[33] The series of evictions that began in November, for they had
not paid rent to their employers during the strike, created another battleground that took up limited resources and energy. Each eviction required
a search for a new apartment to rehouse the family. While some individuals provided free housing and lawyers volunteered services, such reset-
tlement still proved costly. Employers went to extremes to force people
out into the streets: one small manufacturer "removed the doors and
windows from the rooms of a family of strikers"; a larger firm "started a
sweatroom on the first floor . . . for the purpose of driving families out."
In less than two months employers secured 1,980 warrants for ejection;
only 680 actually were dismissed. They claimed to have filled up the tenements with new workers after throwing out the old.[34]
Yet the evictions also provided some of the strike's finest moments as
workers organized to support each other and publicize the manufacturers'

[31]"The Cigarmakers' Struggle," New York Sun, Nov. 16, 1877; "Ordering Men to
Strike," ibid., Oct. 23, 1877; "Striking Cigar Makers Winning," ibid., Oct. 11, 1877; "Demands on Employers," New-York Daily Tribune, Oct. 17, 1877; "The Striking Cigar-
Makers," New York World, Oct. 18, 1877; "Great Uprising of Cigar-Makers in New
York," CMOJ, October 1877. See also "The Offer to Cigarmakers," New York Sun, Nov.
17, 1877.
[32]"Increasing the Great Strike," New York Sun, Oct. 18, 1877; [Strasser], "To the Cigarmakers of the U.S. and Canada," CMOJ, December 1877; Gompers, Seventy Years, 1:147.
[33]See the report in New York World, Oct. 24, 1877.
[34]"Strikers Getting Excited," New York World, Nov. 8, 1877; "The Cigarmakers'
Strike," New York Sun, Nov. 3, 1877; "A Lull in the Cigar-Makers' Strike," New-York
Tribune, Nov. 3, 1877; "Ejecting Striking Cigar-Makers," New-York Tribune, Nov. 8,
1877; "The Long Strike Waning," New York Times, Nov. 8, 1877; "Seventy-three Families
Ejected," New-York Tribune, Dec. 5, 1877; "Dispossessing Cigar-Makers," New-York Tribune, Nov. 21, 1877.

heartless tactics. With music playing and flags waving, the cigarmakers ushered families with their household goods onto wagons and toward a new life. The display of American and German, but not Bohemian, flags reflected the leadership's combination of patriotism with insensitivity to Bohemian nationalism at a time when the fight for an independent Czechoslovakia still engaged Bohemians abroad. An even more colorful procession opened the cooperative factory; shops held their own flags and banners, declaring, "No more tenement houses for cigarmakers," "A fair day's pay for a fair day's work," and "Heaven frowns upon those who grind the faces of the poor." Tenements along the parade route also displayed mottoes.³⁵ Such parades were devices to build community support, which was evident in neighbors', shopkeepers', and even landlords' offers of housing and rent money. The city's nineteen Bohemian benefit societies pledged all their funds to the strikers, and unionists of other trades collected funds.³⁶

Gender provided the most powerful of all symbols, however, in this struggle between labor and capital. The Faborsky incident demonstrated how assumptions about domesticity, motherhood, and gender traits could create sympathy for the strikers. Faborsky was a leader of the strike against Levy & Uhlman, which was evicting him as a warning to the nearly hundred other residents of its tenement. His wife "lay writhing [in labor] and groaning on a rude pallet" as city marshals removed their furniture to the street. While the employers claimed the woman was "shamming," the papers emphasized her condition, reporting that the bed, when placed back in her tenement, caved in and further injured her. In contrast to the cruel employers stood the kindhearted saloonkeeper who offered to pay the rent and the protesting strikers who cried "shame." "They treated her most shamefully and unmanly," the *Cigar Makers Official Journal* reported. Outrage erupted again when a pregnant woman on a picket line was "seized with premature labor" after being pushed down by policemen. To unionists, the police, like the courts, seemed to have been bought off by the employers.³⁷

³⁵"Brooklyn Joining the Strike," *New York Sun*, Nov. 9, 1877; for other incidents of brass bands and flags assembled to meet evicted tenement workers, see "Dark Outlook for the Cigar-Makers," *New-York Tribune*, Nov. 17, 1877; "Strikers Move Out to Martial Music," *New-York Tribune*, Nov. 28, 1877; "Jubilant Strikers," *New York World*, Dec. 7, 1877.

³⁶"The Cigar-Makers' Strike," *New York Times*, Nov. 4, 1877; "Cigar Strike Notes," *New York Herald*, Nov. 9, 1877; "The Cigar-Makers' Strike," *New York World*, Nov. 14, 1877; "Persistency of the Cigar-Makers," *New-York Tribune*, Nov. 24, 1877 (on landlords who refused to cooperate with employers); "The Striking Cigar-Makers," *New York World*, Nov. 22, 1877 (on an old woman who offered her house rent-free); "The Strike of the Cigar-Makers," *New-York Tribune*, Nov. 14, 1877 (on landlord noncooperation); "The Cigarmakers' Struggle," *New York Sun*, Nov. 16, 1877 (on contributions from the street railway union).

³⁷"Stripping a Home," *New York Sun*, Nov. 8, 1877; "Ejecting Striking Cigar-Makers," *New-York Tribune*, Nov. 8, 1877; "Strikers Getting Excited," *New York World*, Nov. 8,

Women workers also gained symbolic value by virtue of being "women." The papers also reported that male strikers were "abusing" working women as they left the cigar factories.[38] The employers promoted the hiring of "American girls" to take the place of the foreign strikers, resolving in a defense of *their* manhood (against the strikers who would dictate the way they ran their businesses) "that females more readily learn the trade than males." Indeed, the Cigar Manufacturers' Association defended their use of the tenements by claiming that the opposition was "nothing more than a movement on the part of the Cigar-Makers' Union to throw out of business many women who could not or would not work in shops." Yet, as they readily admitted when it came to employment of women in the shops, here were "workers whose services may be depended upon at low wages." And women did not demand "smokes." By late November they had hired about four thousand women, although it was claimed that except for the packing and sorting of cigars, their employment was "anything but a success." Indeed, Levy & Uhlman had dismissed "young girl apprentices" and taken back their sixty to eighty tenement families. When the strike collapsed in early January, however, *The World* intensified the ideological battle over women's place in the trade by proclaiming, "American Girls Bringing Victory to the Manufacturers."[39]

The concept of rights became engendered, though in the public debate during the course of the strike, gender became attached to class. The district courts may have defended the "rights" of women strikebreakers to work; they certainly supported such tenement women as Emma Giess, who, when charging another woman with assault, justified her home cigarmaking as allowing her to earn "enough money to live on . . . and I would rather do that than live on charity."[40] But these "rights" interfered with the right claimed by the CMIU men to defend their families. Gompers most powerfully linked manhood with protection of women and the family wage. He rallied the strikers at a mass meeting

---

1877; "Cigarmakers' Strike," *New York Herald,* Nov. 8, 1877; "Brooklyn Joining the Strike," *New York Sun,* Nov. 9, 1877; untitled news notes in *CMOJ,* November 1877; "The Cigar-Makers' Strike," *New York World,* Nov. 10, 1877.

[38]E.g., "The Cigarmakers," *New York Sun,* Nov. 15, 1877.

[39]"The Cigar-Makers' Strike," *New York Times,* Nov. 12, 1877; "The Cigar-Makers' Strike Extending," *New-York Daily Tribune,* Oct. 24, 1877; "Girls Making Good Cigars," *New York Sun,* Nov. 26, 1877. For the problems with and faced by the female apprentices, see "Cigar-Makers Still Determined," *New York Times,* Nov. 18, 1877, which reports that some of the Levy & Uhlman women were fired for "ruin[ing] more tobacco than could be replaced with a month's wages." For an attack on the work of these women, see "The Wonderful Strike," *New York Sun,* Nov. 27, 1877. For the manufacturers' victory through using them, "The Cigar-Makers' Strike," *New York World,* Jan. 5, 1878; "Is the Cigar Strike Ended?" *New York World,* Jan. 1, 1878.

[40]"The Cigar-Makers Strike," *New York World,* Nov. 16, 1877.

in Brooklyn: "The time has come when speaking is of little avail. We are now called upon as men and fathers of families to make one grand effort to better our miserable condition, which has been thrust upon us for the past five years, and, if required, we must force a different condition of affairs." "Their manhood and rights as fellow-men were at stake," he explained, warning the manufacturers that if they "imported" any Chinese, "they would be responsible for any violent action that might be taken to protect their wives and children, and provide them with bread. (Applause)."[41]

The concept of rights was too powerful to be confined to Gompers's working-class cult of masculinity. Working-class men also held a high opinion of their women, who were comrades in the struggle for workers' rights. After all, female members of the CMIU made up nearly half the audience at many rallies. As one unionist from Cincinnati declared, "I would to Heaven, we had women in Cincinnati, such as you have in New York, all glory to them! They are genuine women, and as mothers, sisters, shopmates, we can work hand and heart with them, in killing oppression and elevating our trade."[42]

Moreover, rights could be seen apart from the breadwinner's protective role. While Bohemian men resented employers' strategies to curtail the ability of their families to earn a living wage, single women working inside factories stood up for natural rights. The strike activist Marie Hausler, who charged that the tenement system degraded women, expressed "the disappointment her countrymen had felt on discovering that the tyranny of the old country had been imitated in the new." But Gompers and his supporters linked rights with gender identity as they urged the Bohemians to "strike for your rights like men and [the bosses] can no longer play the despot."[43]

Employers, though not a monolithic group, shared with Gompers this language of gender. Larger manufacturers, many of whom also had tenements, dominated the National Cigar Manufacturers' Association (NCMA), which had forty members in November 1877. This group had locked out employees after the strike was on its way and evicted tenants. It defended the tenement house system as "adopted with the object of benefiting the operatives and at their request, as the cigarmaker claimed *he* could do the full amount of work and attend to household duties at the same time." But soon the NCMA abandoned this stance as the de-

---

[41]"The Cigar-Makers' Strike," *New-York Daily Tribune*, Oct. 31, 1877; "Great Mass Meeting in Cooper's Institute," *CMOJ*, January 1878; "The Cigar-Makers' Strike," *New York World*, Nov. 9, 1877.

[42]"As Determined as Ever," *New York Sun*, Nov. 1, 1877; "The Cigar-Makers' Strike," *New York World*, Oct. 31, 1877; "Correspondence," *CMOJ*, November 1877.

[43]"Cigar Makers Locked Out," *New York Sun*, Oct. 21, 1877; "General Strike of Cigar Makers," *New-York Daily Tribune*, Oct. 15, 1877.

fender of mothers who had to stay at home and merely asserted the right of employers to structure the production process as they saw fit.[44]

Meanwhile, small manufacturers condemned the NCMA, and some even sympathized with the strikers, with whom they held a common notion of male respectability. D. Hirsch, the employer of Samuel Gompers, blamed the tenement house system for the strike and for the plight of cigarmakers."The cigar-makers, as a class, are very respectable and intelligent people, who would be contented with reasonable treatment from their employers," he told the *New York Times*, "but that they have been compelled to submit to repeated reductions until they have finally been reduced to a point almost of starvation."[45] Yet even among this group, class solidarity prevailed. Though many "opposed" the tenement system "because it ruins our trade," they could "not go against those manufacturers who have them." For in the struggle of capital against labor, as one declared, "I can not go against bosses."[46]

By mid-December the strikers faced a lockout, with the NCMA announcing they had all the hands they required and would not employ any connected to the union. Some employers had enough stock to wait out the strike; others began to manufacture cigars in Pennsylvania, Long Island, and New Jersey. The union countered in a war of propaganda, claiming that fewer than five hundred cigarmakers went back as scabs. Increased picketing of factories and a greater number of confrontations with police signaled the strike's growing ineffectiveness by the first of the year. Though the cigarmakers led by Gompers's local attempted to reorganize the industry into a single organization with delegates from each shop, unity—between immigrants and native-born, women and men, skilled and less skilled, shop and tenement—dissipated with the end of the strike.[47]

[44]"Statement," *Tobacco Leaf*, Oct. 24, 1877; "The Cigar-Makers' Strike Extending," *New-York Daily Tribune*, Oct. 24, 1877; "The Strikers Still Firm," *New York Times*, Oct. 24, 1877; "The Cigar-Makers' Strike," *New York World*, Oct. 24, 1877; "The Cigar-Makers' Strike," *New York Times*, Nov. 12, 1877.

[45]"The Cigar-Makers' Strike," *New York Times*, Sept. 2, 1877. See also, in *New York Sun*, "Cigarmakers' Strike," Oct. 19, 1877; "The Cigarmakers' Strike," Nov. 2, 1877; "Cigar Makers Locked Out," Oct. 21, 1877; "Secrets of Cigar Making," Dec. 3, 1877.

[46]"What the Tenement House Monopolists Say" and "Opinions of Manufacturers Opposed to Tenement House Factories," both in *CMOJ*, March 1879; "Tenement-House Cigars," *New York World*, Jan. 13, 1878.

[47]For leaving the city, "The Strike of the Cigar-Makers," *New-York Tribune*, Nov. 14, 1877; "The Cigar-Makers' Strike," ibid., Dec. 12, 1877; for the number of shops that gave in, "Cigar-Makers Still Determined," *New York Times*, Nov. 18, 1877; for the end of the strike, "The Cigar Manufacturers," *New York Times*, Dec. 16, 1877; "Events of the Grand Strike," *CMOJ*, December 1877; "A Clique of Conspirators," *CMOJ*, January 1878; "Turbulent Cigarmakers," *New York Sun*, Jan. 6, 1878; "Ending the Cigar Strike," *New York Sun*, Feb. 4, 1878. For the attempt to unify the industry, see "Cigar-Makers' Plans," *New-York Tribune*, Jan. 18, 1878.

By then the tenement house workers had joined the mold, female workers, and "coolies" as the tools by which manufacturers drove down the wages of the true cigarmakers, skilled northern European/Anglo-Saxon male workers.[48] The cause certainly suffered because so many lacked homes apart from their workplaces. The CMIU could have built on the desire of tenement workers to improve conditions instead of turning on them and refusing them membership in the union as long as they worked in the tenements. They could have squarely blamed the manufacturers, who after all had responded to the tenement workers' militancy with their trump card: eviction. Instead, the Great Strike taught the CMIU to be weary of the unorganized and unskilled immigrants, often female, because they could drag the more skilled, organized sector down with them. That this response was not unrealistic, given the power of capital and the weakness of labor, did not make it inevitable. For employers themselves were divided, and some members of the CMIU, who would secede to form the Cigarmakers' Progression Union (CPU), would offer an alternative by attempting to organize tenement and shop workers alike.[49]

To Albany: The Pitfalls of Legislation

After the Great Strike, the cigarmakers tried to win by legislation what they could not through contract. The state legislature in Albany became their new battleground; the union actively entered electoral politics and rallied its members to campaign against incumbents who voted against labor's interest.[50] A tenement house bill finally passed in 1883, with help from an unexpected supporter, the young representative from New York

[48]For a typical complaint/attack on the forces undermining cigarmakers, see "The Dangers That Surround Us," *CMOJ*, August 1879.

[49]At the end of the strike some members of the central committee declared that "the endeavor [by the Internal Revenue Service] to abolish the tenement-shop was a trick of the manufacturers, and another delegate excitedly warned the strikers that if they consented to the abolition they would be digging their own graves." Since President Strasser had pressed for the tax change in the first place, the report may be an exaggeration, but it suggests some differences of opinion among strike activists. See "Cigar-Making in Tenement-Houses," *New-York Tribune*, Jan. 10, 1878, and "Home News," ibid., Jan. 11, 1878. It was possible for homeworkers to organize as the tenement workers of Sutro & Newmark did in 1880; see "New York Notes," *CMOJ*, May 1880. By contrast, when 450 factory employees at Kerbs & Spiess struck, the tenement house workers, about 120 families, remained working; see "The Striking Cigarmakers," *New-York Tribune*, Dec. 31, 1880.

[50]For the text of the initial bill, see *CMOJ*, February 1880; of the bill first passed, see "On the Warpath," ibid., April 1882; for brief discussions, Mandel, *Samuel Gompers*, 30–33; Gompers, *Seventy Years*, 1:186–97; Ruth Shallcross, *Industrial Homework: An Analysis of Homework Regulation Here and Abroad* (New York: International Affairs, 1939). For the history of this battle, see "The Tenement House Bill," *CMOJ*, April 1880; "Dull Day in the Capitol," *New York Times*, Jan. 15, 1881; "At the State Capital," *New York Times*, May 1, 1884; "Measures Affecting Laboring Men," *New-York Tribune*, May 1,

City's silk stocking district, Theodore Roosevelt. In the test case, *In Re Paul*, however, the Court of Appeals declared it unconstitutional on a technicality. Soon afterward the legislature passed a more precisely drafted bill and the stage was set for judicial review on whether the police power of the state or right to property would prevail.[51]

The bill made it a crime to manufacture cigars in tenements used for living purposes in all cities of 50,000 population or over (New York and Brooklyn).[52] To safeguard small manufacturers, however, it exempted shops on the first floor of tenements where cigars were also sold. While enforcement belonged to the city's sanitary inspectors, the bill permitted the trade unions or any citizen to report violations, a measure no doubt reflecting the CMIU's distrust of the Board of Health, which supported the manufacturers.[53]

While the employers countered through the courts,[54] smaller manufacturers and some of the larger ones complied until the justices pronounced a decision. The CMIU gloated over the impact of the acts, announcing that men in factories went on full time after the 1884 law.[55] Large

---

1884. For the stealing of the bill in 1882, see "Closing Hours at Albany," *New York Times*, June 3, 1882; for the union's political action, see "Report of Delegate to the Labor Congress of Pittsburgh," *CMOJ*, December 1881; "Legislative Notes," *CMOJ*, January 1883; "Vote on the Tenement-House Cigar Bill," *CMOJ*, October 1883.

[51]The initial bill referred only to tenement houses in its title but its provisions also included dwelling houses. Because it was mislabeled, the court ruled against it. For Roosevelt's role, see n. 62 below. For the *Paul* decision, see "Court of Appeals: In the Matter of the Application of David A. Paul," *CMOJ*, February 1884; for the regrouping to pass an amended bill, "The Decision of the Court of Appeals," ibid.

[52]See "The Tenement Cigar Law," *New-York Tribune*, Oct. 9, 1884; decision reprinted in *CMOJ*, October 1884.

[53]"On the Warpath," *CMOJ*, April 1882; "Laws of 1884, Chapter 272," *Second Annual Report of the Bureau of Statistics of Labor of the State of New York for the Year 1884* (Albany, 1885), 387–88; for union enforcement, see "Defend the Tenement House Law," *Progress*, Sept. 28, 1883; "The Cigar Act in Force," *New York Times*, Oct. 2, 1883. On the actions of the New York Board of Health, which the union charged was in the pay of the manufacturers, see *CMOJ*, February 1883. On the policing of the cigar manufacturers, see report in *CMOJ*, June 1884.

[54]"The Cigar Tenement-House Act," *New York Times*, Oct. 13, 1883. For the conditions under which Paul worked, see "The Tenement House Cigar Bill," *CMOJ*, December 1883. See also *In the Matter of the Application of Peter Jacobs for Writs of Habeas Corpus and Certiorari, etc., Case on Appeal* (New York, 1884), 9–15. Jacobs, an English immigrant, lived in a seven-room apartment in a tenement house of only four apartments. Paul's own apartment stretched the entire side of a floor, from back to front. The manufacturers got an opinion on the first act even before it went into effect, so as to plan their legal strategy. A lower-court judge declared the law valid because the legislature had the right to enact improvements for the public health. See "An Attempt to Obtain a Decision," *CMOJ*, August 1883. For a discussion of this strategy, see "Before the Courts," ibid., October 1883. See also "A Test Case," *New York Times*, May 16, 1884.

[55]"The Tenement-House Cigar Law," *New-York Tribune*, Oct. 2, 1883; "Complaints of Tenement House Manufacturers," *CMOJ*, October 1883; for a negative report on the impact, see "The Cigarmakers," *John Swinton's Paper*, Feb. 3, 1884.

manufacturers who had abandoned the system also heralded the bill; others who had retained the system foresaw hundreds of families unemployed or making less money in factories than they supposedly did at home, while many employers would move out of the city to Pennsylvania or New Jersey, "where the farmers and their families can sit at home and make cigars," claimed Louis Hass of Kerbs & Spiess. Many believed the law to be unconstitutional because "it will vitiate many contracts." Both the *New York Times* and the *New-York Tribune* echoed manufacturers and their legislative supporters in editorials against the bill, claiming that its true purpose was to increase union control over the trade, prevent "women from making a living," and raise employers' expenses.[56]

Such opinions reflected debates in Albany which not only foreshadowed the arguments made before the courts but also exposed the class issues underlying the tenement house controversy, and revealed that these issues often were expressed in gendered terms and mixed with questions of ethnicity. One senator argued before the governor in 1883 that "a factory was not a fit home; that the American people had a different view of the subject of home; that it meant privacy, decency and morality." Cigarmaking in homes was a "nuisance" to the public health, contended Edward Grosse, the first sponsor of the bill in 1880. "Highly injurious to the workman, and especially to the health of his wife and children," it demoralized family life because children, who could not be properly educated, failed to learn the difference between a workshop and a dwelling.[57]

Opponents of the bill, however, rejected Grosse's evidence in favor of the authority of the Board of Health, contending that the legislature could delegate the power to investigate to this local body, but not declare a nuisance itself. Although one representative pointed out that government had removed a whole class of manufacturing—the slaughterhouses—from the tenements, and that it had the power to protect citizens, others claimed that such acts violated a man's "right to carry his business with him and with his family wherever he or that family resides," as Thomas Alvord of Onondaga County explained, echoing the *Slaughter-House* dissents. Alvord provided the classic defense of the rights of men, rights that inhered in the realm of patriarchal power,

---

[56]"Cigar-Making in Tenement-Houses," *New-York Tribune*, Mar. 14, 1883; "The Tenement-House Cigar Law," ibid., Sept. 30, 1883; editorials in ibid., Oct. 15, 1883, and Jan. 30, 1884; *New York Times*, Oct. 2, and Dec. 7, 1883.

[57]"Argument before Governor Cleveland," CMOJ, March 1882; "The Tenement House Bill in the Assembly," ibid., May 1880. The CMIU thought the issue so important that it reprinted the first debate in 1880 over the course of six months; later debates merely present variations on themes raised in the first one. See "On the Hygiene of Occupation," in *A Treatise on Hygiene and Public Health*, ed. Albert Henry Buck, 2 vols. (New York, 1879), 1:42, cited in Kaufman et al., *Gompers Papers*, 1:203–4.

which bill supporters doubted applied to those whose only choice was unemployment or living and working in the same space: "A man's dwelling house is his castle; he has a right to use that dwelling house, whether he uses it as a tenant or uses it as an owner, as long as it is not detrimental to public health and as long as it does not affect his neighbors in his immediate vicinity wrongfully, as he pleases." As a proponent of nineteenth-century liberalism, Alvord conceived of man as separate, as the individualist making his own way. Government would merely ensure that he did not hurt his fellows. Since Alvord rejected the idea that the bill was to protect the public health, it thus interfered with a man's freedom. Man alone, however, could not make cigars under this system; as one legislator reminded his colleagues, it took the whole family.[58] Yet both sides of this debate accepted the separation of public from private, one to reject state interference in the home, the other to distinguish proper from improper activities there. All discussed the impact of such homework mainly on the male household head.

Such analysis drew upon the Republican notion of citizen in a struggle over what generated slavery:[59] tenement-house manufacturing, which in forcing a man to work in his home as a condition of employment interfered "with the liberty of the working men," as Grosse claimed, or "communistic" unions that attempted to draw men into factories to fight the battle of labor against capital, a division that an upstate Republican such as Alvord refused to recognize.[60] The CMIU men had accepted their status as wage earners; while often owning their own tools and possessing skill, cigarmakers were even less accurately described as independent proprietors than the butchers who had been so designated by Justice Stephen J. Field in his famous *Slaughter-House* dissent.[61] The question became what conditions made men free rather than whether women who worked at home did so freely, for most such women assumed that the

[58]"The Tenement House Bill in the Assembly," *CMOJ*, July, August, and October 1880; "The Tenement-House Cigar Factories," ibid., October 1881.

[59]An employer named Straiton used a metaphor that was central to Northern Republicans: "The condition of absolute subjection in which these unions hold the men is worse than the condition of the negro slaves"; quoted in "A Thousand Cigar-Makers Strike," *New-York Tribune*, Feb. 19, 1884.

[60]"The Tenement House Bill in the Assembly," *CMOJ*, August 1880; "Tenement House Cigar Factories," ibid., October 1881; see also comments by Mr. Mitchell on "soulless communism" in ibid., September 1880. For the support of taxpayers and homeowners, see Grosse's comments in ibid., May 1880, and Representative Cohen's, June 1880. For another image of tenement house slavery, see the comments of Representative Wren in ibid., July 1880.

[61]On this point, see "Cigarmakers' Strike," *New York Herald*, Nov. 15, 1877: "The striking workmen . . . did not wish to interfere in any manner with the private management of the factories; all they demanded was a fair and living rate of wages." The CMIU's conflict with the Knights of Labor perhaps stemmed in part from their different conception of themselves. On slaughterhouses and the cases about them, see Forbath, "Ambiguities of Free Labor."

system existed for their benefit, and viewed their presence in the home as a proper recognition of their responsibilities as mothers, wives, and housekeepers.

Theodore Roosevelt believed in freedom as a precondition for citizenship, but such an association led him to link protection of tenement workers with preservation of the American way, a culture associated with proper relations among men, women, and children within the family. Before the Assembly in 1884 he explained how the dirt, disease, and child labor in the tenements led him to suspend his belief in laissez-faire. In terms that emphasized the menace of unassimilated children who failed "to learn our language, to acquire our notions of what the rights of citizenship demand," Roosevelt argued for ending tenement house cigarmaking not merely as a hygienic measure, not merely to facilitate enforcement of the child labor laws, but to maintain a notion of Republican citizenship that was gendered and racialist.[62]

Briefs submitted in the two cases brought to test the law sharpened the arguments heard in the legislature. When the case brought by David Paul went before the Court of Appeals in 1883, the lawyer for the defense portrayed the manufacturers as heroes for allowing "these poor people to substantially pursue their old industry at home." Wives and children became the proper helpmeets for free men. The law was unconstitutional because it interfered with private property and personal freedom, disfranchised citizens or deprived them of rights without due process, and negated the newly minted right to contract under the U.S. Constitution. The lawyer for the union, by contrast, emphasized that regulating unwholesome trades fell under the proper use of the police power of the state; he relied on the majority decision in the *Slaughter-House* case rather than on the dissent.[63]

This line of reasoning predominated in the brief prepared for *In Re Jacobs* the next year. Defense lawyers responded by denying the force of the police power in this instance: "the State cannot under the pretense of prescribing a police regulation, encroach upon the just rights of the citizen, secured to him by the Constitution." That cigarmaking was allowed on the first floor negated the public health argument and revealed the act for what it really was, an attempt at coercion. Indeed, they contended that the cigarmakers were actually healthier than average.[64] Thus the leg-

[62]"Bill: In Assembly, April 8, 1884," *CMOJ*, May 1884; Theodore Roosevelt, "A Judicial Experience," *Outlook*, 91 (Mar. 13, 1909), 563–64, and *An Autobiography* (New York, 1913), 79–81; Howard Lawrence Hurwitz, *Theodore Roosevelt and Labor in New York State, 1880–1900* (New York: Columbia University Press, 1943), 77–87.

[63]"The Tenement House Cigar Bill," *CMOJ*, December 1883.

[64]Morris S. Wise would point out that the death rate in the cigar tenements was only 9 per thousand, compared to 31 for the city as a whole. Such numbers are meaningless unless they are controlled for the age structure of the population; they also fail to take into ac-

islature, these lawyers argued, could not interfere with "the natural right of every man to labor for the support of himself and his family, at such times and in such manner as his own will of convenience dictates." Conceiving of skill as property, the defense turned wage laborers into propertyholders, contending that the law "breaks up their property." Moreover, the tenement house law would substitute the "promiscuous association" of the factory for family industry, not only driving laborers into the factory and ending economic competition but violating the family, regulating its domesticity, and exposing young girls to the physical and moral "mischiefs" of the shop floor.[65]

The *Jacobs* decision accepted all these arguments. The tenement manufacturer Louis Haas rejoiced: "I never anticipated any other result from the start. The law was clearly in violation of the spirit of American institutions." The *Cigar Makers' Official Journal* announced, "Slavery Declared to Be Liberty," and President Strasser demanded that the court be impeached if possible; if the legislature failed to remedy the wrongs of workers, the only option was "brute force."[66] The concept of a man's right to liberty of contract won out over the cigarmakers' belief in a man's responsibility to support his family with dignity and through his skills. This new understanding of masculinity reflected even as it shaped the class positions of men in the emerging age of corporate capital. Yet it was predicated on the separation of home from marketplace, an idea central to the Victorian concept of women's place. The irony was that this doctrine developed out of a case that, by sanctioning wage earning within the home, exposed as false such dichotomies as home and work, private and public.

The Aftermath of *Jacobs*

Judicial defeat pushed Gompers and ultimately the AFL away from a direct reliance on the state as an instrument for gaining trade union

---

count sickness and disability. See "Men's Right to Work at Home," *New York Times*, Feb. 9, 1884. By contrast, *CMOJ* reported that tenement house deaths constituted 56% of total mortality, as reported by the Board of Health. See "Monstrous Facts," February 1884.

[65] "The Legal Argument," *CMOJ*, January 1884; "Respondent's Points," "Supplemental Point," and "Appellant's Points," in *In the Matter of the Application of Peter Jacobs*, 8–9, 14–17, 1–3. For earlier presentation of the arguments of the defense team, see "Before the Courts," *CMOJ*, October 1883.

[66] *In re Jacobs*, 98 N.Y. 98 (1885); "Cigar-Making in Tenement-Houses," *New-York Tribune*, Jan. 22, 1885; "Slavery Declared to Be Liberty," *CMOJ*, February 1885; "Cigars and Politics—Another Death-Dealing Decision," *John Swinton's Paper*, Oct. 19, 1884; see also "The Unclean Bench," *John Swinton's Paper*, Oct. 12, 1884; "Proceedings of the Sixteenth Session of the CMIU," *CMOJ*, October 1885; "Retrospect and Prospect," *Progress*, Jan. 24, 1885.

goals,[67] confirming the position of socialist dissidents among the cigarmakers but with different conclusions. Rather than build a workingmen's party, the CMIU choose to "accomplish through economic power what we had failed to achieve through legislation."[68] The campaign for tenement house legislation had another related consequence: it strained existing divisions among New York cigarmakers. German socialists (many of whom were recent immigrants) not only objected to high dues but condemned the electoral politics of the CMIU. They withdrew from the union in mid-1882 to form their own organization, the Cigarmakers' Progressive Union (CPU), which over the next eighteen months grew to include nearly 67 percent of the city's cigarmakers (as opposed to 5 percent in the CMIU), particularly those in the tenement houses.[69]

This split further weakened workers in their contests against manufacturers. The Knights of Labor took advantage of the internecine warfare to negotiate contracts with employers which gave their district assembly a closed shop. But by September 1886, when the Knights failed to deliver on their promises to employers, a reunited CMIU stepped into the resulting vacuum, and for the next year and a half most large employers abandoned the tenement house system out of fear that it would destroy factory competition.[70]

Gompers and Strasser emerged strengthened from these faction fights—as did the more elitist, closed union structure that they had forged. But the split that formed the CPU suggests that we must not regard Gompers and his allies as the heroes in this initial fight against exploitive homework: the choice in the early 1880s was not to keep the current tenement house system or to prohibit it. Organization promised a

[67]As Gwendolyn Mink argues, however, the AFL did forge an alliance with the Democratic party by the Progressive Era to maintain its own autonomy. See her *Old Labor and New Immigrants in American Political Development* (Ithaca: Cornell University Press, 1987), esp. 236–60.

[68]"Defend the Tenement House Law," *Progress*, Sept. 28, 1883, 5, reprinting comment from the *New York Volkszeitung* against legislation; "A Failure Once More," ibid., Oct. 24, 1884, 1; for Gompers's account of the legislative campaign, see his *Seventy Years*, 1:183–97; see also Mandel, *Samuel Gompers*, 29–37.

[69]"The Great Trade Unions," *John Swinton's Paper*, Oct. 21, 1883; "Hear Both Sides," ibid., Dec. 23, 1883; "A Local Conflict," *CMOJ*, April 1882; "Deliberate Misrepresentation," *CMOJ*, May 1882; "Progressive Scabs," *CMOJ*, August 1882; "The Lock-Out," *CMOJ*, August 1883; "Proceedings of the 15th Session of the CMIU," *CMOJ*, September 1883 (suppl.). For Gompers's interpretation, see his *Seventy Years*, 1:199–204.

[70]"A Lockout Impending," *New York Tribune*, July 16, 1883; "Deliberate Deception," *CMOJ*, April 1884. The best account of the struggle in New York with the Knights is in *Fourth Annual Report of the Bureau of Statistics of Labor* (Albany, 1887), 523–39; see also "The Culmination of the Rivalry between the CMIU and the Cigarmakers' Progressive Union of America," in Kaufman et al., *Gompers Papers*, 1:365–409; "The Battling Cigarmakers," *John Swinton's Paper*, Feb. 14, 1886; "Bolt of CPU from K of L into CMIU," *John Swinton's Paper*, Aug. 1, 1886. For the employers giving up the tenement system, see "Tenement House Cigars," *New York Times*, Dec. 20, 1887.

third way, and there was some basis for believing that the workers themselves would reject the conditions in the tenements. Although the 1884 legal contest occurred in the context of declining production and an oversupply of labor,[71] cigarmakers, including those in the tenements, continued to press their demands on the shop floor as well as in the legislative halls. Bohemian tenement house and shop workers continued to meet together; during a 1886 lockout, the mothers who worked in the tenements joined the young single women who labored in the factories in rooms rented by CPU locals to discuss proposals set forth at more public meetings attended only by men. The immediate interests of the two groups of women could conflict, but the single women's expectations that they would soon marry and would become tenement house workers upon motherhood provided a basis on which to formulate a unified set of demands. Such actions suggest that these workers were capable of trade unionism if they were educated instead of written off as the New York equivalent of "coolie" labor. Like Marie Hausler, they demanded their rights as workers. But disunity within the class—based on politics, gender, skill, and race/ethnicity—hampered such efforts.[72]

The tenement house system persisted into the late 1880s and 1890s.[73] On one hand, the system was fought on the terrain of trade unionism: organization of factories, contract negotiations, strikes, and the union label. Locals with any tenement house workers, the residue from the CPU, were forbidden to maintain such workers in good standing as long as they labored at home. Such a stand committed the CMIU against organizing the less skilled.[74]

[71]While the numbers of cigarmakers rose during the first half of that year, from January until June the number of cigars manufactured decreased by a quarter of a million. At a time when about 8,000 people worked in the tenement houses, there were at least 3,000 surplus cigarmakers in the city. See "The Cigar Trade," *CMOJ,* June 1884; state of the trade reports in *John Swinton's Paper,* Oct. 26 and Nov. 16, 1884; "Cigar-Making in Tenement-Houses," *New-York Tribune,* Jan. 21, 1885, quoting one unionist on numbers out of work; for number of tenement workers, "Respondent's Points," in *In the Matter of the Application of Peter Jacobs,* 14.

[72]These strikes were reported most often in *John Swinton's Paper;* see "Strikes in This City," Dec. 9, 1883; "The Cigarmakers," Sept. 20, 1885; see also "Doings of the Workingmen," *New-York Tribune,* Feb. 18, 1884. For work resuming in the tenements, "Doings of the Workingmen," *New-York Tribune,* Feb. 11, 1884. For the trade unionism of tenement women compared with that of factory women, see "Settled by the Girls: The Congress of the Female Cigarmakers," *New York Times,* Jan. 24, 1886.

[73]"Tenement House Cigars," *New York Times,* Dec. 20, 1887; "Going Back to Their Old Plan," ibid., Dec. 21, 1887; see report in *John Swinton's Paper,* Jan. 9, 1888. Such manufacturing continued even during the period when the Manufacturers' Association sought to restrain it. See listings by the Label Committee of New York City, "Filthy Tenement-House Factories," *CMOJ,* April 1887, which reports 26 houses with 546 families.

[74]For the upholding of the label, see "Their Labels Protected," *New York Times,* Mar. 9, 1888, on a court decision against one tenement-house manufacturer who used labels that looked like the union's. In June 1893 *CMOJ* began consistently to print lists of tenement

On the other hand, the trade unions appealed to "an enlightened and humane public opinion," as the Working Women's Society of New York City resolved, which would abolish the tenement menace. A combination of middle-class reformers and young working women, this society focused on the "suffering women and children" in the tenements, with their health and morality in danger. Such a portrait of victimization was hardly new; middle-class reformers had painted a similar one of garret seamstresses before the Civil War. By the late nineteenth century, their appeals generated public investigation, entrenching this image of the homeworker in the popular imagination.[75]

A more generalized sweatshop peril had replaced the cigar tenement houses by the time the New York Bureau of Labor Statistics reported on the conditions of cigarmakers in 1895, ten years after *Jacobs* and three years after the state's first regulation of homework as a sanitary measure.[76] All the themes of earlier exposés found ample confirmation. Home cigarmakers were exploited, they lived in cramped squalor, and, with all members of the household pressed into service, they had a degraded family life. Men failed as breadwinners and their women failed as housewives and mothers. Children could not claim their right to schooling and play. In the end, the Bureau of Labor rejected these factories in the tenements not because of their working conditions or even the threat of disease they supposedly carried to the consumer; it rejected them because they were improper homes.

Commenting on *Jacobs*, the Progressive Era feminist Rheta Childe Dorr later argued, "The tradition [of the innate sacredness of The Home] is strongest in strong men. . . . It sways legislatures and the courts, which, being composed entirely of men . . . have no more than a theoretical knowledge of Home. *In this day the presence of manufacturing in a home turns that home into a factory.*"[77] Like Samuel Gompers thirty years before, Childe Dorr maintained the separation of public from private, work from home, the very discourse that butressed many an argument against the women's suffrage she also supported. Like the New York Bureau of Labor in 1895, she would bring the state into the home

house factories. It also published warnings against specific cigar brands whose tenement origins employers were attempting to disguise. See "Tenement House Cigars," May 1895. For the barriers against tenement workers in the union, see the exchange between union locals 90 and 141 against the Strasser decision in *CMOJ*, June and July 1891. The 1891 Report of the Committee on the Constitution affirmed such action by denying membership to Chinese laborers and tenement house workers; see "Proceedings of the Nineteenth Session of the Cigar Makers' International Union," *CMOJ*, October 1891 (suppl.).

[75]"Against Tenement House Cigar Factories," *CMOJ*, February 1888; see Stansell, *City of Women*, 147–54.

[76]New York State Bureau of Labor Statistics, *Annual Report*, 1896, 545–61; for the 1892 bill, "A Blow at Sweating Shops," *New York World*, Apr. 21, 1892.

[77]Rheta Childe Dorr, "The Child Who Toils at Home," *Hampton*, April 1912, 183.

to save the private from itself, asserting the right to interfere in a man's freedom, not only as a health measure by way of the police power of the state, but also in the best interests of women and children, a rationale for state action championed by an important sector of women reformers.[78] *Jacobs* had narrowed the meaning of the police power of the state by proclaiming *men's* right to community protection; men's freedom to contract justified women's necessity to labor at home. Blocked by such an interpretation of the Fourteenth Amendment, labor standards legislation increasingly became restricted. Working men would negotiate contracts; women and children would be protected by the state. Despite its claim to voluntarism, the AFL would lobby the state in the interest of skilled male workers, which called for laws that reduced the labor supply, such as legislation to protect women and children and to restrict immigration. The union had become a man's castle. Men, no matter their class, agreed: women's place was at home, whether or not that home served as a waged workplace. In promoting this sexual division of social space, working-class men stymied their own efforts to protect the factory from tenement labor by refusing to organize home-based workers.

[78]On the reevaluation of "social feminists," as historians once called this group of women reformers, see Eileen Boris, "Women, Politics, and Feminism," *American Quarterly,* 41 (March 1989), 196–203; Alice Kessler-Harris, "The Debate over Equality for Women in the Workplace: Recognizing Difference," in *Women and Work: An Annual Review,* vol. 1 (Beverly Hills, Calif.: Sage, 1985), 141–61; and Nancy F. Cott, "What's in a Name? The Limits of 'Social Feminism'; or, Expanding the Vocabulary of Women's History," *Journal of American History,* 76 (December 1989), 809–29.

CHAPTER SIX

"The Voice of Virile Labor": Labor Militancy, Community Solidarity, and Gender Identity among Tampa's Latin Workers, 1880–1921

Nancy A. Hewitt

Members of the Cigar Makers' International Union (CMIU) were proud of their craft and of their manhood. They forged brotherly bonds in the workplace, at saloons that served as union headquarters, and on the well-worn paths trod by tramping artisans. Cigarmakers frequently and forcefully challenged employers' prerogatives and asserted their own. Poor stock, unfair dismissals, overbearing foremen, violation of apprentice laws and "victimization of members" were as likely as wage disputes to inspire walkouts. In most areas of the country, the manliness of craft locals was a direct extension of an exclusively male membership. As Patricia Cooper concluded after a close study of work culture among CMIU members, "Women could hardly be manly."[1]

Tampa's Latin cigarworkers were as quick as their northern counterparts to take offense at highhanded employers. Yet they were organized along industrial (not craft) lines and their labor actions were not entirely male affairs. In the seven years after the industry's founding in 1886, local factories suffered at least fourteen strikes. In half of them, women and men walked out together; female workers made up 12 to 22 percent of the disaffected.[2] The Tampa workers style of unionism, Latin heritage,

I thank Steven Lawson, Louis Pérez, Susan Porter Benson, David Roediger, Ava Baron, and two anonymous readers for their thoughtful critiques of earlier versions of this essay. Research for this article was funded in part by the National Endowment for the Humanities and aided by the generosity of fellow Tampa historians, Robert Ingalls and George Pozzetta.

[1]Patricia Cooper, *Once a Cigar Maker: Men, Women, and Work Culture in American Cigar Factories, 1900–1919* (Urbana: University of Illinois Press, 1987), 220 and chaps. 1 and 3 generally.

[2]Commissioner of Labor, *Tenth Annual Report: Strikes and Lockouts*, 2 vols. (Washington, D.C.: U.S. Government Printing Office, 1894), 1:138–47. In Tampa the word

and embrace of female members led the CMIU to attack them as un-American and unmanly.[3] The vehement response of the local labor press indicated that Latins held different views of both patriotism and manhood. Characterizing the CMIU as "a barn of white livered dung hill cocks," they proclaimed themselves "the voice of virile labor."[4]

In Tampa, the potency of the union depended on class leaders' ability to forge a common shop-floor identity out of the distinct life experiences of Afro-Cuban, white Cuban, Spanish, and Italian women and men. An examination of the city's labor relations is particularly valuable for assessing the role of gender in workplace organizing. The sexual division of labor in the local cigar industry distinguished but did not isolate male from female workers, while the Latin legacy of machismo was counterbalanced by the joint efforts of women and men on behalf of Cuban independence. The intertwining of family, community, and shop-floor issues in pursuit of both Cuban independence and workers' control ensured that non-wage-earning Latins would play critical roles in labor battles as well.

From the cigar industry's founding through the massive 1920–21 strike, women's increased participation in the labor force and rising militancy along with the introduction of machines and the attendant deskilling of cigar work transformed their place in the labor movement and responses to it by employers, city fathers, union officials, and male co-workers. The tale of Tampa's early cigar industry is one of labor militancy dominated by men. On the day the first factory opened, Cuban workers successfully struck against the hiring of a Spanish foreman. Yet this shop-floor action taken by men could not be separated from community-wide concerns shared by women, rooted in Cubans' century-long struggle against Spanish imperialism in their homeland. Indeed, it was as much war as work that shaped Cubans' gender assumptions, political strategies, and labor activism at the turn of the century. The Ten Years' War (1868–1878) against Spain, the repression that followed defeat, and the labor militancy of cigarworkers which accompanied political rebellion encouraged both owners and employees to flee the island for south Florida. Once there, women, including many who joined anti-colonial insurgencies, responded to labor demands and family necessity

---

Latin was used to describe an immigrant community composed of Cubans, Spaniards, and Italians.

[3] See *Cigar Makers' Official Journal* (hereafter *CMOJ*), September and November 1900 and November 1901, for the best examples of CMIU's linkage of patriotism and manhood in its attacks on Latin labor.

[4] *La Federación*, Dec. 14, 1900 (original in English). This paper was the voice of La Resistencia, the Latin union discussed below. *La Federación* published English-language editorials though most articles were printed in Spanish.

by entering the work-force in record numbers. When the battle for *Cuba Libre* erupted again, they served as role models for *patriotas* in both community and factory-based organizations.[5]

The war for Cuban independence begun in 1895 followed insurgent patterns of the past—a loosely organized command directed decentralized fighting units that were dependent on community networks (including women) for munitions, matériel, and medical care. Its ideological focus was new, however, shaped by the ideas of the émigré José Martí, who began to articulate a more radical nationalist vision in the 1880s. A founder of the Cuban Revolutionary Party, he argued that independence required the collective support of all the island's and émigrés' progressive forces. Martí insisted that the movement integrate Afro-Cubans and women, sympathetic Italians, Puerto Ricans, even Spaniards, and cigar manufacturers as well as workers into its efforts.[6]

In Tampa, men and women formed more than forty revolutionary clubs, both single-sex and mixed, and joined in factory-based activities that crossed ethnic and racial lines. Expeditionary forces sent to Cuba were racially integrated and were often funded by the efforts of female kin and club members, and women sometimes served alongside men on the battlefield. Like the earliest strikes, war focused attention on manly virtues but could be sustained only by the joint efforts of both sexes.[7]

When U.S. troops entered the war in 1898, they found the island's forces wanting, though the insurgents were then on the verge of victory. Offended by a seeming lack of discipline, a loose command structure, racial mingling, and the ragged clothing and decrepit appearance of their allies, U.S. officers and publicists attacked Cubans' national pride and collective manhood. The correspondent George Kennan reported, "In courage, in honesty, in capacity, and in all that goes to make true manhood, . . . American soldiers were immeasurably superior to Cubans." The Cuban " 'is a treacherous, lying, cowardly, thieving, worthless, half-breed mongrel,' one U.S. officer from the Fifth Army Corps concluded;

[5]See Joan Marie Steffy, "The Cuban Immigrants of Tampa, Florida, 1886–1898" (M.A. thesis, University of South Florida, 1975), and Nancy A. Hewitt, "Cuban Women and Work: Tampa, Florida, 1895–1901," paper presented at the American Historical Association conference, Washington, D.C., December 1987. Among the most famous of the émigré heroines was the tobacco stripper and Tampa resident Carolina Rodríguez.

[6]Martí visited Tampa several times in the 1890s, making his message of solidarity clear in his choice to stay with the Afro-Cubans Ruperto and Paulina Pedroso during his trips to the city. The supporters of *Cuba Libre* also included a few resident Italians, such as Orestes Ferrera, who fought with the insurgent forces in Cuba and then returned to Ybor City to marry one of the youngest Cuban émigré orators, María Luisa Sánchez. See Louis A. Pérez, Jr., *Cuba between Empires, 1878–1902* (Pittsburgh: University of Pittsburgh Press, 1983), chaps. 5 and 7.

[7]See Steffy, "Cuban Immigrants," and Hewitt, "Cuban Women and Work."

'born of a mongrel spawn of Europe, crossed upon the fetiches of darkest Africa and aboriginal America.' "[8]

Championing their own centralized and hierarchical command and conventional military operations, U.S. army officers dismissed the rebels's accomplishments, claiming that the insurgent army had "borne no testimony to its desire for a free Cuba."[9] Translating supposed military incompetence into certain political incapacity, North American leaders justified the imposition of "protectorate" status on the newly "liberated" island. In Tampa, rabid military rhetoric was muted by citizens' ongoing contact with Cuban émigrés and by the local economy's dependence on Cuban labor. Still the merging of jingoism and racism, attacks on Cubans' manhood and their national pride, and suspicions regarding their military and political aptitude shaped responses to labor agitation in the century to come.

The role of gender in defining the intertwined worlds of war and work, factory and community, labor militancy and political radicalism was complex. The cigar cities of Ybor City and West Tampa were neither southern versions of the great garment centers (where women formed the backbone of the industry) nor eastern variants of western mining camps (where wives and daughters supported men's organizing efforts). Tampa does not even fit the model of other cigar cities, where men and women labored in distinct systems of production in separate workplaces. There younger, unmarried women of new immigrant groups, producing cigars by the team method, constructed a work culture distinct from and largely incompatible with that formed earlier by older, married men of nineteenth-century immigrant stock who crafted whole cigars by hand.[10]

In Tampa women and men of the same ethnic background labored in the same factories, sometimes side by side, performing both individual handwork and less skilled teamwork, sharing economic, political, and familial goals. In general, women and men received equal pay for equal

[8]Quoted in Pérez, *Cuba between Empires*, 204, 206.

[9]Ibid., from report on Fifth Army Corps in *New York Times*, Aug. 7, 1898, 201. Such complaints are especially interesting in view of the fact that U.S. forces were neither well organized nor well disciplined themselves during the Cuban expedition.

[10]See Cooper, *Once a Cigar Maker*, chaps. 5 and 8, on cigar work culture elsewhere in the United States. On women's work culture generally, see Susan Porter Benson, *Counter Cultures: Saleswomen, Managers, and Customers in American Department Stores, 1890–1940* (Urbana: University of Illinois Press, 1986); Barbara Melosh, *"The Physician's Hand": Work Culture and Conflict in American Nursing* (Philadelphia: Temple University Press, 1982); and Sarah Eisenstein, *Give Us Bread but Give Us Roses: Working Women's Consciousness in the United States, 1890 to the First World War* (London: Routledge & Kegan Paul, 1983). For a situation more similar to that of Tampa cigarmakers in the sharing of work space, family space, and some skills, see Mary H. Blewett, *Men, Women, and Work: Class, Gender, and Protest in the New England Shoe Industry, 1780–1910* (Urbana: University of Illinois Press, 1988).

work, though women held fewer highly skilled positions. Women pre-dominated among "strippers" (who separated the tobacco leaf from the stem) and banders and made up a growing component of bunchers and rollers. Only the jobs of *resagadores, lectores, selectores,* and *escogedores*— those who selected tobacco leaf by color and texture, read to cigarmakers as they worked, and picked and packed cigars—were closed to women.[11] Non-wage-earning wives and daughters were also critical to the success of hundreds of *chinchales*—home-based shops established by skilled men seeking greater economic autonomy. Thus in Tampa the roles of female and male cigarworkers, though distinct, were sufficiently inter-twined to give the edge to cooperation over conflict in both workplace and union.

The cigar work force, predominantly Cuban into the 1910s, labored and lived in the ethnic enclaves of Ybor City and West Tampa. Ybor City was incorporated into the city proper in 1887; West Tampa was offi-cially annexed in 1924. Despite their different administrative relations with Tampa, the two ethnic areas, which were also the city's only indus-trial centers, had more in common with each other than with the central city that divided them. There Anglo-Americans and native-born blacks predominated in the population. In Ybor City large numbers of white Cubans, Afro-Cubans, Spaniards, and Italians resided in mixed neighbor-hoods, while in West Tampa one found more Afro-Cubans and native-born blacks, though white Cubans still formed the bulk of the residents. By 1900, immigrants employed the term *Latin,* and later *Tampeño,* to describe the mix of Cubans, Spaniards, and Italians who inhabited the two communities.[12]

For Cuban women and men, who formed the city's first industrial la-bor force and shared work spaces and wartime memories, virile union-ism was not exclusively masculine. A cooperative wartime ethos was reinforced by socialist, anarchist, and communist speakers who regularly appeared in Tampa's cigar centers through the 1930s. Some were "out-side agitators," such as Eugene Debs, Enrico Malatesta, and Elizabeth Gurley Flynn; others were resident radicals, such as the *escogedor* Carlos Baliño, the editor Pedro Estévez, and the stripper Altagracia Martínez. Each emphasized community solidarity over individual machismo as the

[11]And even here there were exceptions. One or two women appear as *lectores* in early records among Tampa Cubans and Puerto Rican workers. Women entered the ranks of *escogedores* in the 1930s primarily, under the pressure of employers.

[12]Gary Mormino and George Pozzetta, *The Immigrant World of Ybor City: Italians and Their Latin Neighbors, 1885–1900* (Urbana: University of Illinois Press, 1987), chaps. 2 and 3. Intermarriage, which increased over the course of the early twentieth century, re-quired such a general term, since fewer and fewer residents of Ybor City and West Tampa could claim a single ethnic heritage. Even among early arrivals, many were children of mixed-race Cuban and Spanish parents.

source of labor's strength. In its purest form, modeled on the teachings of Martí, this solidarity embraced not only women and men but also blacks and whites and Italians and Cubans.

This vision of labor solidarity set Tampa's Latin workers at odds with employers, the CMIU, and city fathers. Despite differences of ethnicity and class, these three groups accepted a definition of virility that was exclusively male. Tampa's large factory owners, including Spaniards, Germans, Anglos, and even some Cubans before 1900, viewed upward mobility and individual economic success as the reflection of true manhood. CMIU leaders broadened the definition to include communities of skilled labor, which still excluded women, blacks, and certain new immigrants.

City fathers viewed patriarchy as a necessary accompaniment to virility, turning a protective if patronizing eye to women, children, and honest workmen. But they were intolerant of challenges to the status quo and hurled charges of un-Americanism at "uppity blacks," "outside agitators," and "ludicrous women." For city elites and the CMIU's old immigrant leaders, manhood and patriotism were joined, the sole property of a select circle.

Such visions of proper social and sexual order were often tested by Latin laborers. On Labor Day in 1899, for example, local unions staged a massive parade, composed "principally [of] cigar makers and their families." Its central feature was "a float, on which sat enthroned, the 'Queen of Labor,' a very dark brunette, while around her stood young Cuban girls." The accompanying legend read: "Labor Knows No Color, Creed, or Class." A local reporter claimed that the tableau "would have met with more approval from the discerning public, had the attendants been colored and the queen white. The dusky belle was somewhat of a startling innovation."[13]

Employers and civic leaders, holding still-fresh memories of the "American" defeat of Spain and the financial rewards of a cigar boom, temporarily forgot their earlier claims that "the torch, the knife and the bomb" were about to lay "Ybor City in ruins and [fill] her streets with blood."[14] The CMIU and leading trade journals refreshed their memories. In 1898 the *Cigar Makers' Official Journal* chided Cubans for being the only ethnic group to remain "aloof" from the CMIU, assuring them that the " 'junta' will no longer be needed here" to ensure workers' rights.[15] According to *Tobacco Leaf*, a manufacturers' journal, "the outrageous tyranny of anarchistic unionism as practiced in Tampa" seri-

[13]*Tampa Morning Tribune* (hereafter *TMT*), Sept. 5, 1899.
[14]Ibid., Mar. 12, 1887, quoted in Robert P. Ingalls, *Urban Vigilantes in the New South, 1882–1936* (Knoxville: University of Tennessee Press, 1988), 40 and chap. 2 generally.
[15]*CMOJ*, August 1898.

ously threatened the trade. The training of "strictly American help (women for preference)" would be the "only salvation" of Tampa's Clear Havana industry.[16] Both unionists and employers feared ethnic difference. Yet CMIU leaders still hoped to assimilate patriotic Cuban workers into their brotherhood, while industry officials sought to replace explosive immigrant men with disciplined Anglo daughters.

Cuban labor leaders meanwhile applauded the efforts of Latin daughters. In the aftermath of the 1899 strike, La Sociedad de Torcedores de Tampa, popularly known as La Resistencia, embraced a number of new *gremios,* or branches. The union's newspaper, *La Federación,* viewed the formation of a Gremio de Despalilladoras, composed entirely of women, as a reflection of the "great enthusiasm among the strippers for building and maintaining a strong organization." Female banders soon formed a *gremio* as well, proclaiming that "no good reasons exist to hinder women from joining" La Resistencia. *La Federación* took the occasion to proclaim: "Workers of the International! By your turning to the bosom of the family, the vigor of the Society of Cigar Workers of Havana from Mexico to Canada has achieved complete unity."[17]

For Latin leaders, vigor and unity required the inclusion of women in the labor movement. Perhaps men's acceptance of women was eased by the concept of the union as a "family of labor" and by the fact that the sisterhood of cigar laborers was composed mostly of less skilled and less well-paid workers, many with male relatives in the trade. Still, the gradual increase of women from 10 percent to nearly 40 percent of the local cigar industry labor force between 1885 and 1920 would strain Latin men's acceptance of female comrades even as women became ever more central to the industry's and the union's success.

More surprisingly, the CMIU asserted its interest in organizing Tampa women, choosing strippers as the first line of attack in breaking the Latin grip on local labor. The union's most recent experience with women was hardly encouraging. Having taken control of a spontaneous women's strike in New York City in the spring of 1900, the International sank over $200,000 into the effort, which fizzled into failure by autumn. Despite women's valiant efforts in the struggle, many CMIU men "drew the conclusion that the women strikers were simply not worth helping" and that only strikes composed of "strictly union men" should be assisted.[18] Yet as the New York strike drew to a close, CMIU leaders were again turning to women to expand their power.

Patriotism and proper sex roles were the banners raised by the CMIU. La Resistencia's vaunted solidarity was merely the result, it claimed, of a

[16]*Tobacco Leaf,* Oct. 17, 1900.
[17]*La Federación,* Dec. 8, 1899, and Nov. 2, 1900. Original in Spanish.
[18]Cooper, *Once a Cigar Maker,* 256.

few macho tyrants' imposing their will on the worthy but passive majority. Despite American contributions to Cuban independence, the CMOJ complained, La Resistencia's leaders "threaten us with extinction if we do not sacrifice our manhood and womanhood and our fealty to American institutions." We "will never submit to become slaves of a transplanted despotism ruled absolutely by a horde of irresponsible leaders," the local organizer assured his brothers. The report concluded with the last stanza of "My Country, Tis of Thee."[19]

La Resistencia, meanwhile, challenged its opponents' virility. In a proclamation to "The People of Tampa," its leaders argued that current troubles were due to "the absorbent spirit, absolute and unjust," of the CMIU, which boasted "a strength it did not have, and of course found itself failed when the test came." Accusing their organizers of trying "to take refuge in the folds of the banner of patriotism," La Resistencia avowed its own internationalism, noting that it was "composed of several nationalities, including many Americans."[20] It then charged the CMIU with defying "all principles of trade unionism" by "using as tools the new union of strippers," an unmanly act for those wedded to the family wage and male exclusivity in the union.[21]

Criticisms turned to indictments when "an armed mob" of CMIU recruits attacked the Seidenburg factory. Within minutes the mob had moved on to a second factory, where men let loose a "fusillade of bullets" into windows where sat "men and women, unaware of the imminence of danger."[22] CMIU's manliness had taken a violent turn; La Resistencia made it clear that its version of virility rested on broad-based support, not brute force.

City fathers on the Board of Trade, whose main concern was to forestall disruptions of the industry, now chose sides; CMIU violence ensured their sympathy for the female strippers. It was women, then, who finally determined the fate of the dueling unions. The Gremio de Despalilladoras, whose 1,248 members made up nearly one-quarter of La Resistencia's total membership, met in the "Greatest Women's Meeting Ever Seen in Tampa" and "Voted against recognizing [the] Strippers' Union of the International."[23] With that vote they ensured their union's victory. The CMIU, having chosen women as its weapon, was now held hostage by them.

[19]*CMOJ*, November 1900.

[20]Printed in *TMT*, Nov. 10, 1900. La Resistencia's membership among cigarmakers was said to include 334 Americans and 1,558 Cubans (as well as lesser numbers of Italians and Spaniards) out of a total of 2,880.

[21]Ibid., Nov. 16, 1900. It is unclear whether the members of La Resistencia or the *Tribune* editors translated these passages into English.

[22]Ibid.

[23]*Tampa Weekly Tribune*, Nov. 22, 1900.

In the strike's aftermath, *La Federación* attacked the CMIU as "a traitor to the Working Class," employing violence against its own constituency and promising accommodation to its natural foes. The use of force was disparaged as traitorous, but collusion with capitalists was considered the greater sin. Pointing to a circular in which the CMIU described itself as a "conservative organization" of "American working men" and La Resistencia as a body of "malcontents," the editors admitted they were "malcontents with the existing social conditions." Any "workingman that applies the word 'malcontent' to his fellow wage slave is a poltroon," they went on. "It is not the voice of virile Labor that ever is heard expressing 'contentment' with existing conditions." Nor is it "the voice of honorable Labor that ever breathes race or national distinctions," which serve only as "levers for the capitalist."[24]

In July 1901 *La Federación*'s vision of virile unionism was severely tested when local factory owners announced plans to open branches outside of Tampa. La Resistencia struck one of them, and the owners hired CMIU replacements. A general strike of the industry followed. This time La Resistencia found not only the CMIU and trade journals arrayed against it but civic leaders as well.

In negotiating with the Board of Trade just before the strike, La Resistencia's "committee of sixty," which included six strippers and was headed by a "mullato," directly confronted Tampa business leaders with their commitment to crossing boundaries of skill, race, and sex.[25] Two days later the *Tampa Tribune* called La Resistencia "the most powerful influence in the city today, and, considered numerically, . . . the strongest organization in the State of Florida." No longer limiting itself to cigarworkers, the union organized *gremios* among "clerks, cooks, waiters, bakers, bartenders, porters, draymen, laundry workers, etc.—in fact, all classes of help that are employed in places of business that derive their support from Resistencia."[26]

With manufacturers threatening to abandon Tampa and unionists flaunting their power, the *Tribune* noted that "public sympathy has naturally changed." Though supportive of "the honest workman, who, by the sweat of his brow, toils to make an honorable living for those dependent upon him," they would no longer tolerate "designing labor agitators." Declaring that "the strike must be stopped," the editor advocated "deporting those who are responsible for the trouble as it exists."[27]

It was the confounding of categories that appeared most troublesome. Honest men who worked to support a family and needy women who

[24]*La Federación*, Dec. 14, 1900. Original in English.
[25]*TMT*, July 25, 1901, and *United States Tobacco Journal* (hereafter *USTJ*), Aug. 17, 1901. The strike committee was headed by union secretary J. G. Padilla.
[26]*TMT*, July 27, 1901.
[27]Ibid., Aug. 7, 1901.

were well trained and disciplined were acceptable. But laborers who joined trade associations—particularly those that embraced all classes, sexes, and races; threatened to mute occupational, economic, and familial hierarchies; and were led by foreigners and rabble-rousers—were not to be tolerated.

With widows, wives, and daughters of cigarmakers prominent among its burgeoning strippers' *gremio*, La Resistencia continued to rely on community-wide support, nonviolent militancy, decentralized leadership, and an ethos of mutuality. City fathers, with wives and daughters safely ensconced in social clubs and charitable societies, turned to verbal and physical assaults organized through a secret citizens' committee. They justified their vigilante actions in the name of patriotism, private property, the patriarchal family, and free enterprise.

To local union leaders the absence of pickets and lack of violence throughout the five-month strike demonstrated their version of virility. Community solidarity was so complete that picket lines were unnecessary. Members concentrated instead on providing over 5,000 workers and their dependents with the means of survival. Opening soup houses, fund raising in Havana and Key West, and sharing scarce resources among neighbors were the primary vehicles for sustaining the needy.[28]

Meanwhile, on the night of August 5 the citizens' committee unveiled its version of manly action by kidnapping thirteen male Resistencia leaders and abandoning them on the coast of Honduras.[29] Though the committee supposedly applauded "honest workmen" who supported families, at least half of the men deported left behind dependent wives and children. The following week, landlords began to evict strikers and their families. In September mounted police raided soup kitchens and spilled the soup into the street.

Virile labor relied increasingly on female leadership as men were "deported" or left town to find work. Women who came to the fore were also threatened with violence. On August 23 the *Tribune* reported that the "officers of the strippers union of La Resistencia"—including Luisa Herrera and Altagracia Martínez—"have been notified to leave the city at once." Latin women responded with both appeals to individual vulnerability and proclamations of collective strength. The wives of kidnapped leaders wrote the governor, requesting an investigation into the disappearances. Though petitioning as "distressed wives and mothers," they argued that the union's demands were "just and equitable" and the kidnappings "contrary to the laws of any civilized country." At the same

---

[28]See Durward Long, "La Resistencia: Tampa's Immigrant Labor Union," *Labor History,* 6 (1965), 192–213; Hewitt, "Cuban Women and Work"; *TMT,* Aug. 20, 1901. On this and other strikes in the cigar centers, see also Ingalls, *Urban Vigilantes,* and Mormino and Pozzetta, *Immigrant World of Ybor City,* chaps. 4 and 5.

[29]Long, "La Resistencia"; *TMT,* Aug. 7 and 8, 1901.

time, striking strippers appealed to "the American Women of Tampa to use their influence to stop the abductions." Luisa Herrera took a more aggressive approach, advising cigarworkers that they would all "leave Tampa and allow it to rot as a grinning skeleton."[30]

As the strike dragged on, male ranks were further diminished by arrests for vagrancy. In the breach, Cuban and Italian women organized a march on the mayor's office. When demonstrators were confronted by the sheriff and a "party of armed citizens," Altagracia Martínez spoke out, challenging attacks on honest workers, while next to her a comrade unfurled an American flag. Such activity, reminiscent of the efforts of *patriotas* in the battle for *Cuba Libre*, led male workers to memorialize their female comrades in the strike's aftermath. It also led, after a second demonstration, to the decline of vagrancy arrests.[31]

Neither individual courage nor collective nonviolence led to victory, however. City fathers, certain that their economic well-being, American pride, even their manhood were threatened by La Resistencia, employed all the resources at their disposal to break the association. The trade press supported them. *Tobacco Leaf* recognized but demeaned the solidarity of the workers—"They will starve and let their families starve sooner than be called scab or strikebreaker." On October 9 the editor attacked La Resistencia as "foreign in its origins, foreign in race, foreign in tongue, and antagonistic to our laws, customs, and government."[32] A week later, the assassination of President William McKinley by a self-proclaimed anarchist further fueled Anglo fears of aliens and radicals.

More important, the CMIU, though it opposed the "anarchistic methods" employed by civic leaders, refused to support the strikers. Still hoping to gain favor in the area, the organizer George French criticized the "many good men in La Resistencia" for following leaders who "simply make trouble for themselves." Worse still, the local trades assembly of the American Federation of Labor endorsed the citizens' committee's actions, claiming they were "done in the best interest of organized labor and would be beneficial to the entire labor situation."[33] The CMIU brotherhood had room for like-minded followers; the local AFL apparently doubted there were any among Latins.

[30]*TMT*, Aug. 23 and 29, 1901; Letters to Governor William Sherman Jennings, 1901, in Jennings Papers, Box 6, Florida State Archives, Tallahassee (Robert Ingalls provided me with this citation); Herrera quoted in *Tobacco*, Aug. 23, 1901. See also *USTJ*, Aug. 31, 1901.

[31]Emilio Del Río, *Yo fuí uno de los fundadores de Ybor City* (Tampa: By the author, 1972), 64–65; *TMT*, Oct. 5, 1901. Río's book was one of those that memorialized the labor *patriotas*.

[32]*Tobacco Leaf*, Oct. 9, 1901.

[33]*CMOJ*, September 1901 (see also August 1901); *Tampa Union and Chronicle*, Aug. 8, 1901.

Frightened by La Resistencia's racial, ethnic, and sexual solidarity, city fathers, manufacturers, the CMIU, and local AFL affiliates all chose Americanism and manhood over class conflict and cross-sex organizing. By Thanksgiving 1901 the strike was over and the voice of virile labor momentarily silenced. Over the next decade, the CMIU organized those Latin laborers they viewed as so misguided in their first choice of leaders, and discovered that they could be persuaded to take on a new union label more easily than they could be compelled to change their version of virility.

Between 1902 and 1910 the CMIU labored diligently to convince Tampa workers of the benefits of "American-style" unionism, including the ability of a union man to support a family on his wage alone. In 1908 the organizer A. Sineriz called it "a disgrace to any community or craft" for women to be "in the factories working" while men spent their wives' and daughters' earnings in barrooms and worse places. Sineriz claimed that even if a "man take [sic] care of the children, his care is not the care of the mother, and the children grow up seeing their father the tyrant of the family, and they cannot have respect for him but fear, and are prepared to accept any other kind of tyranny."[34] For Sineriz, the only alternative to the family wage was social chaos.

His analysis revealed two key concerns of CMIU organizers in Tampa: the unconventional role of women in the industry and the apparent power of tyrannical, radical male leaders. Sineriz was especially agitated when in 1908 a visit by Big Bill Haywood reinvigorated " 'the old "died in the wool," "never say die" remnant' of La Resistencia." The focus on a few despotic leaders, however, did not mean that the CMIU had faith in the bulk of workers. Visiting Tampa in 1909, national president George Perkins deplored "the misguided and impatient demands of the masses," noting how rare was "the man who has the courage to stand for what he thinks."[35]

When a second lengthy strike erupted in 1910, the image of radical Latin leaders misdirecting sheeplike masses vied with that of impatient Latin masses forcing the hands of rational CMIU leaders. These images converged with equally contradictory ones of women as both dependent and aggressive, resulting in a fluid mosaic of arguments regarding the cause and effect of labor agitation. Though CMIU leaders now served as

[34]A. Sineriz, "Report from Tampa," in *CMOJ*, October 1908.
[35]George Perkins, CMIU president, quoted in George E. Pozzetta, "Italians and the Tampa General Strike of 1910," in his *Pane e Lavoro: The Italian American Working Class* (Toronto: Multicultural History Society of Ontario, 1980), 35; *CMOJ*, December 1909. See also George Perkins to Samuel Gompers, June 27, 1910, in American Federation of Labor (AFL) Papers, microfilm, reel 36. Of course, Perkins's remark assumes that the only man who truly stands for what he thinks is one who supports the CMIU's programs without exception. Robert Ingalls provided me with this citation.

the voice of virile labor, they often agreed with characterizations of Latin workers put forth by civic leaders, if not with their methods of handling them. Local union spokesmen walked a hazardous line between gaining community-wide support and sustaining American-style unionism.

As much a lockout by employers as a walkout by workers, the 1910 strike involved 10,000 men and 2,000 women. Erupting in an atmosphere charged with tension, the struggle quickly flared into violence and gained the attention of the national press.[36] In 1910 virility was tested by brute force. Vigilantism against strikers was applauded by the *Tribune*, but worker-induced violence of any kind was decried and denied by *El Internacional*, the local Latin voice of the CMIU.

Initially Anglo editors seemed to agree with *El Internacional's* disclaimers, noting that in "all previous cigarmakers strikes . . . there has been nothing of this sort." Indeed, the *Tribune* concluded that "the Latin-Americans are inspired to their defiance of the law . . . by the belief that they are backed . . . by the other unions of this city, largely composed of Americans."[37] In an odd twist of logic, city fathers were suggesting that it was working-class Anglos who were to blame for Latin labor's turn to violence.

Mayor D. B. McKay pointed to other distinctions among the workers, differentiating "good citizens" from the "lawless element." The "good citizens" apparently included many dependent women. Under the headline "The Slaughter of the Innocent," *Tribune* editor Goode M. Guerry detailed the destitution of helpless women and children. A week later he ran a "Human Document of the Strike," the tale of a middle-aged mother of six, a stripper married to a cigarmaker with "hopelessness in her voice and the tragedy of want upon her face," who described the intimidation and starvation imposed upon her family by the "well-paid leaders of the cigarmakers."[38]

Disputing Guerry's patronizing portrait, the local socialist leader S. Elliott denounced manufacturers who locked laborers out and city fathers who refused to aid needy families. Though equally appalled by the depredations heaped upon "helpless women and children," he expressed outrage at Guerry's "remedy": "Seize their Fathers by Stealth! Kidnap their brothers and husbands!, shrieks the Editor. . . . Deprive them of their natural protections and turn [them] over, naked and alone, to the tender mercies of . . . the Manufacturers Association and the American Tobacco

[36]See Pozzetta, "Italians and the Tampa General Strike," and Ingalls, *Urban Vigilantes*, chap. 4, for accounts of the shootings, lynchings, arson, and beatings that accompanied the 1910 strike.
[37]*TMT,* Sept. 16, 1910.
[38]*USTJ,* Sept. 24, 1910; *TMT,* Oct. 11, 1910.

Trust."[39] Blasting civic leaders for their hypocrisy, Elliott joined them in viewing women as helpless victims of the class struggle.

The *Tribune* agreed in part, charging civic leaders with "submissiveness," "evasions" of responsibility, and even "downright cowardice." Guerry described Tampa's citizens as "hopelessly and pitiably impotent" and challenged the "guiding and controlling elements" of the city to assert the "manhood" that could save Tampa from ruin. On September 20 two Italian immigrants, suspected of attempting to assassinate a cigar factory bookkeeper, were lynched, but no one took credit for the deed. In response to escalating violence and charges of cowardice and in the "interest of the weak—the wives and children of fanatics—," "three hundred loyal citizens finally went forth to afford protection to those in danger."[40]

This new citizens' committee broke up gatherings of workers, attacked the offices of *El Internacional* and the Labor Temple, assisted in the arrests of union leaders and pickets, and closed down soup kitchens. The committee soon swelled to "nearly a thousand members," the "backbone of the business community." Still claiming that "a few agitators" had aroused "the passions" of Latin laborers, the committee believed that their removal would end the troubles. "The backbone of the strike has been broken," the *Tribune* declared on October 20th, two months after the strike began—and three months before it actually ended.[41]

As in 1901, landlords and police used evictions and arrests to force cigarworkers back to work, and again such tactics heightened militancy among women. Men formed the bulk of the strikers and took the brunt of the violence, but working-class women proved that their duties as "preservers of the fireside and the home" extended into the streets as well.[42]

Throwing off the dependency with which the press enshrouded them, a group of Italian women gathered near the Arguelles factory in November to keep strikebreakers out. Six were arrested by prowling citizen patrols and fined $50 each for disturbing the peace. Though satisfied that "you dependents were enticed to do what you did by someone behind you" who hoped to "appeal to the sympathies of the court," Judge Drumright chose to punish the women as he would "any other violator of the law." The *Tribune* derided the women's actions as "ludicrous." Claiming that the "deluded members of these unheralded minstrels" had tried to

[39]S. Elliott to Editor, *El Internacional*, Oct. 7, 1910. Original in English.

[40]*TMT*, Oct. 1 and 18, 1910.

[41]Accounts of the citizens' committee activities are from *USTJ*, Oct. 15, 1910, and *TMT*, Oct. 18 and 20, 1910. See also Joint Advisory Board (of CMIU) to Gompers, Oct. 17, 1910, in Gompers Letter Book, AFL Papers, reel 149. On the lynching of Angelo Albano and Categne Ficarrotta, see Ingalls, *Urban Vigilantes*, 95–99.

[42]Quote from *CMOJ*, January 1910.

"scratch and bite" the "citizen police," a reporter was certain they would "give a performance quite diferent [sic]," and more decorous, when they appeared before the judge. The *United States Tobacco Journal* found less humor in the incident, labeling the "mob of Italian women . . . armed with clubs" as "viragos."[43]

El Internacional championed the "six ladies." One letter writer chided "Judge Drumwrong" and the deputies for showing the "lack of natural respect" that women deserved.[44] The paper used the women's arrest to attack "the arbitrariety of that Trinity"—"manufacturers, citizens, and officers of the law"—which understood "only the terms of brute force." Combining support for female militancy with claims for women's special treatment, the Latin labor press thus merged late-nineteenth-century images of bold *patriotas* with newer models of fragile womanhood.

Working-class women had few platforms from which to voice their own views. One of the few extant female strike documents appeared, however, in the same week as the women's arrest. Twenty-eight female strikers, half Cuban and half Italian, published a manifesto "to the Workers of Tampa in general and in particular to our Comrades, the Women." The authors insisted on "our obligation" to "assist and maintain our dignity which has been stepped on a thousand times by our constant enemy," the manufacturers. Calling on the legacies of Joan of Arc, Louise Michel, Teresa Claramunt, and others, they proclaimed, "It is our duty to protest" against those "who degrade our sons" for degradation of them "is degradation of us."[45] Here women themselves merged models of revolutionary heroism with paeans to motherhood.

Despite this evidence of Latin women's "strength of soul," as one supporter called it, weakness of body won out.[46] Arrests and evictions depleted union ranks, financial resources dwindled, citizen patrols squelched protest, and strikers drifted back to work. In January the CMIU declared the strike over, without gaining recognition.

The 1910 strike tested the CMIU's virility and enshrined vigilantism as the response of civic leaders. More overtly and continuously violent than the previous decade's struggle, the battle also revealed more complex interweavings of class, ethnicity, and gender. National trade journals collapsed all three categories, declaiming against foreign tyrants and working-class viragos alike. Local opponents, more reluctant to denigrate

[43]*TMT*, Nov. 16, 1910; Nov. 15, 1901; *USTJ*, Nov. 19, 1910. *Virago* is an archaic word for a noisy, domineering woman or an Amazon.

[44]Mrs. A. Kossovsky to Editor, *El Internacional*, Nov. 18, 1910. Mrs. Kossovsky was an outspoken socialist organizer who frequently published letters in *El Internacional*. The rest of this paragraph quotes from the editorial of that issue. Original in English.

[45]"A los Trabajadores de Tampa" (1910), Labor Union Manifestos, microfilm of *El Internacional* and related papers, reel 1, University of South Florida Library, Tampa.

[46]Octavio J. Monteresy to Editor, *El Internacional*, Nov. 18, 1910. Original in Spanish.

the Latin labor on whom their economic success depended, placed primary blame on outside agitators and misguided militants. They portrayed the mass of workers and of women as dependent and weak, if temperamental and at times laughable. The national CMIU leadership harbored similar views of the Latin masses, and blamed the strike's defeat on the failure of foreigners to adjust to American-style unionism. As for women, they ignored their manifestos and militancy, claiming that their only role was to encourage their male kin to divide their "love . . . between [their] firesides and the union."[47] Latin men also employed images of "helpless women and children," suggesting limits to their faith in a female version of virility. Militant women sought to reassure their male comrades by presenting themselves as wives and mothers as well as workers and by calling on historical images of heroic women, including martyrs, to justify their efforts.

In the decade before the next general strike, increases in the proportion of women cigarworkers and of women without male kin in the trade coincided with a gradual escalation in tensions between the sexes, testing the limits of Latin solidarity. At the same time, cigarettes and automation threatened hand rollers with extinction as memories of joint struggle in pursuit of *Cuba Libre* faded. During this same period the CMIU, though it remained the voice of organized Latin labor, was unable to suppress the radical remnant or institute the family wage. Instead, its representatives sought to emphasize the dangers of impulsive strikes and to incorporate Latin women as well as men into American-style unionism.[48]

On November 10, 1916, the increasing contradictions regarding women's place in the local labor movement surfaced in *El Internacional* with particular clarity. An editorial asked, "Why is it that our female comrades never take interest in the matters we discuss? Despite abundant evidence to the contrary, the editorial read as if women were new to cigar work. "Woman is no longer an object of luxury for a rich man's parlor, or a cook for a poor man. She is permitted to go to the shop and earn her wages just like a man does . . . but she must take the responsibility that goes with it." Taking a progressive position from the perspective of the CMIU, the editor argued that women "should not be forgotten" when a committee is appointed "for any purpose." Such appointments, however, were intended not "to force men to be more liberal, but to train women in complying with their duties." The editor proceeded to distin-

[47]*El Internacional*, Feb. 2, 1911, and *CMOJ*, January 1910.
[48]Women were being enrolled in a separate and secondary section of the CMIU across the country. See Cooper, *Once a Cigar Maker*, chap. 7 and 8. What was different in Tampa was workers' insistence that the CMIU allow industrial-style organization, which included women in the same union locals as men.

guish between male and female activists: "woman is a perfect comple-
ment to man" because "while he can act more readily and decidedly, she
can think more quickly." Women were also touted as "more moral" and
"more reliable."

These patriarchal assumptions about sexual hierarchy and gender identity intruded into Latin labor circles along with the CMIU's influence.
They confronted an increasingly independent coterie of women workers
who did not make reliability their key concern. On the very day *El Internacional's* editorial appeared, women strippers walked out at the Lozano
& Sidelo factory. Obtaining wage increases there without a fight, the
instigators moved on to Perfecto, Garcia & Bros., from which "joint
[male and female] committees spread the idea" of calling for an increase
of $3 per thousand cigars on all jobs. At a mass meeting later that day,
workers called for a general walkout in hand-rolling factories, potentially putting 10,000 people out of work. Some 1,500 workers had already left their benches when a committee was appointed to seek CMIU
"recognition and aid."[49]

The spontaneity and militancy of the movement was recognized as the
work of women. Celestino Vega, a factory owner, sought "protection"
for his male rollers when a "disorderly mob of strikers rushed into the
factory deriding and hooting the workers.... [W]omen, leading the
mob, called the men at work 'females' and offered their skirts to those
who refused to quit."[50]

Male workers soon took control of the strike, however, calling for an
increase for hand rollers, most of whom were men. Meanwhile strippers
and banders in the same branch of the industry—the ones who apparently harassed Vega's workers—proceeded with their own efforts. Within
two weeks the hand rollers agreed to settle the strike for an increase of
$1 per thousand for themselves, apparently abandoning the demands of
their sister strikers in other departments. Meanwhile the *despalilladoras
de capa*, the more skilled women who stripped wrapper leaves and who
had received some concessions from individual factory owners, wanted
to stay out until their less skilled sisters, the *despalillidoras de tripa*, who
stripped filler leaves, obtained concessions as well. The close vote on returning to work (1,384 to 1,266) and the fact that West Tampa workers
formed the bulk of those who voted against the settlement suggest deep
cleavages—of geography and gender—in strikers' ranks.[51]

El Internacional opposed the strike, arguing that its continuation
would have ended with "lamentations from the wives and children of

[49]*TMT*, Nov. 11, 1916. For a similar women-led walkout a few months earlier, see ibid.;
July 15, 1916. Original in English.
[50]Ibid.
[51]Ibid., Nov. 17 and 25, 1916.

workers, . . . due to hunger and misery." Taking the position of national CMIU leaders, the editor attacked "the radicalism in vogue" and singled out women for their "blind enthusiasm." The writer queried his comrades, "May a man now say what he thinks without exposing himself to the dangers of being insulted by his female comrades who offer him their skirts?"[52]

El Internacional was caught in the middle of changing gender identities and expectations, yet the editor's adoption after the 1916 incident of CMIU perspectives regarding female workers indicated how completely out of touch he was with the rising militancy of local women. Male workers were less out of touch than ambivalent. Some refused to follow a woman-led walkout. Others first joined women on strike committees, then formed their own, and ultimately accepted a settlement most beneficial to men. Women themselves sent mixed messages. Was offering their skirts to men a derogation of femaleness? Or was it an attempt to shock reluctant comrades by flaunting the role reversal strippers inaugurated by leading the walkout? Was it a singular act of defiance or part of a larger challenge to gender prescriptions in pre–World War I Tampa?

The 1916 episode revealed the hold that new and more conservative versions of virile labor had taken on Latin men as women gained greater prominence in local factories. World War I intensified women's pursuit of autonomy and heightened tensions over women's roles and rights in society at large. The war also exacerbated tensions between male and female cigarworkers across the country.[53] Yet in Tampa, ethnic solidarity, resulting from the increased employment of "American girls," once again helped mute sexual conflict. Moreover, as advocates of nationalism and internationalism vied once more for the hearts and minds of the working class, resurgent radicalism reinvigorated the unity of Latin workers.

In Tampa, American women made their greatest gains during the war as pickers and packers, positions that had long been male preserves. Here as elsewhere, peace in Europe meant war in the cigar industry.[54] Nationally, the strike of 1919 conflated issues of patriotism, class conflict, and gender. Locally, it forced Latin men's reconsideration of women's expanding roles and Latin women's acknowledgment of ethnic loyalties.

In an effort to exacerbate conflicts among workers and stem the tide of walkouts, Tampa employers offered a wage increase to the mostly

[52]*El Internacional*, Dec. 1, 1916. Original printed in Spanish and English.
[53]For an analysis of gender conflict in the cigar industry nationally, see Cooper, *Once a Cigar Maker*, chap. 10.
[54]Cooper notes (ibid., 295) that Tampa workers had won a modest 8% increase in 1918 after a brief strike by workers, only half of whom were CMIU members. On supposed links between the Bolshevik revolution and Tampa strikes of 1919, see *TMT*, April 27, 1919, and *USTJ*, Nov. 19, 1919.

male hand rollers. Refusing to repeat the errors of 1916, however, the workers rejected any offer that would "leave the clerks, strippers, banders, etc. to 'paddle their own canoe.'" *El Internacional*'s editor now applauded such action: "They realize that labor will ever be subservient ... so long as they stand divided."[55]

This change of heart seems to have been due in large part to manufacturers' employment of Anglo women. Blaming the "unstable labor situation" in Tampa on "a large foreign element of an excitable and undependable race," factory owners hoped native-born women would stabilize labor relations. Instead, the move increased tensions along lines of ethnicity and skill and solidified bonds between Latin women and men. The resulting strike was described by the trade press as a "foreign-language agitation against employment of American women." Tampa's cigar workers, they claimed, were demanding the "complete discharge of all American women who are packers" because of the lower wages paid them. Those wages were justified by the fact that women handled "scrap cigars not requiring the same skill as the packing of the high class lines."[56]

Local labor leaders argued that they were demanding not dismissal of but equal pay for their female comrades. "Do the manufacturers desire to benefit the women," asked *El Internacional*'s editor, "by offering them employment that they may be self-supporting, but at a lower rate than that paid men ... ? Why if a woman does a man's work, should she be paid less than a man?"[57] In the cigar centers, where the notion that women worked for pin money had not yet fully taken hold and where piece rates had always varied by job rather than sex, arguments for equal pay did not challenge tradition. Still, local labor leaders may have hoped to discourage further female employment by such a demand.[58]

No satisfactory settlement was reached in 1919, and the issues resurfaced in 1920 in a struggle that both workers and manufacturers viewed in Manichean terms. *Tobacco Leaf* claimed, "The issues at stake in this controversy are by no means local.... The cigar manufacturers in Tampa are fighting the battle of the entire cigar industry." Richard B. Lovett, president of the Florida State Federation of Labor and leader of a Tampa local of railway carmen, responded in a letter to Gompers: "You no doubt realize that this ... struggle is the pivot upon which the entire Union or non-Union movement in the cigar industry, especially in the

[55]*El Internacional*, December 1919. Original in English.
[56]*USTJ*, Nov. 19 and 22, 1919.
[57]*El Internacional*, Aug. 22, 1919. Original in English.
[58]This supposition seems plausible because in other job categories Tampa workers jealously guarded wage distinctions based on fine gradations of skill, most of which worked to the detriment of women.

south, rests."[59] Between April 1920 and December 1921, cigar factory employees in Ybor City and West Tampa were on strike or locked out for a total of eleven months, fighting over the closed shop, limits on apprentices, women's wages, and the introduction of automation. Solidarity within the Latin community was severely tested during the prolonged strike, as was the capacity of virile labor to adapt to a changing sexual and ethnic division of labor.[60]

City fathers and employers continued to interweave xenophobia with antilabor diatribes and to conflate patriotism, patriarchy, and virility. They insisted that the people who fomented the trouble were "not even men of family, and . . . have no love for any country." The *United States Tobacco Journal* claimed that these agitators "are not taxpayers; they are not home-builders; they are not men that will marry and settle down; they are . . . destroyers, not only of manufacturing, but cities and even homes." Mayor McKay voiced these same concerns before the local Business and Professional Women's Club, and the *Tribune* concurred: "The closed shop is not American, it is of soviet Russia, of purse-proud Prussianism, of revolution and of hell." The "real workman," insisted the *Tobacco Journal*, feels that "getting strike benefits each week is a reflection on [his] manhood."[61]

Latin women challenged this portrait, noting the convergence of familial and working-class obligations. One housewife, whose cigarmaking husband and daughter left Tampa to find work, asserted, "I would feel the humiliation too keenly to confess to my relation to them were they to prove so disloyal and treacherous as to return to work in Tampa under the present conditions, and we would all prefer to starve than submit to such a disgrace." Her feelings were shared by large numbers of workers. "Our only hope of salvation," intoned *El Internacional*, "lies in class consciousness and solidarity," Black cigarmakers, both Cuban and native-born, directed the same message to their comrades: "We must stand by the white workers . . . if we betray them we will betray ourselves, our children, our family and our race."[62]

[59]*Tobacco Leaf,* July 1, 1920; Richard B. Lovett to Gompers, Sept. 13, 1920, in AFL Papers, reel 36. Robert Ingalls provided me with the latter citation.
[60]See Durward Long, "The Open–Closed Shop Battle in Tampa's Cigar Industry, 1919–21," *Florida Historical Quarterly,* 47 (October 1968), 101–21. Long discusses the attempts of the Cigar Manufacturers' Association to drive small shops out of business during this period, since many of them were more sympathetic to workers. He also documents the tremendous support provided Tampa strikers by the CMIU. In terms of deskilling, the shift to packing cigars on end in round cans rather than flat in boxes was as important to skill maintenance as was the introduction of machines.
[61]*Tobacco Leaf,* June 10 and July 1, 1920 (see also *USTJ,* Dec. 4, 1920; *USTJ,* May 8, 1920; *Tampa Citizen,* Aug. 13, 1920; and *TMT,* Sept. 8, 1920.
[62]*Tampa Citizen,* Sept. 3, 1920; *El Internacional,* May 7, 1920 (original in English).

Particularly in the years surrounding World War I, Latins reinforced workplace solidarity through the organization of community-based consumer cooperatives. As early as 1908, Latins began establishing food cooperatives in Ybor City. Between 1918 and 1921, some two dozen cooperatives were founded in the Latin enclaves. In addition, Cuban and Italian families sustained a range of consumer boycotts, including a bread strike in 1915, a potato, meat, and onion boycott in 1917, and a rent strike in 1919. Local Latins also organized on a community-wide basis to support a range of political causes, raising funds to support the Russian Revolution, the Mexican Revolution, the Tom Mooney defense fund, the Ettor and Giovannitti defense fund, and later the Sacco and Vanzetti defense.[63] Thus *tampeños* brought a well-developed sense of community solidarity and cooperation to strike actions in the postwar period.

The CMIU marveled at the strength of Tampa's striking Latins. The organizer R. S. Sexton described the scene as "one of the most remarkable . . . that was ever heard of." He noted that there had been "no disturbance of any kind" among the nearly 8,700 strikers, "no picketts [sic] around the factories, the committee says they don't need any as they have no fear that the strikers will desert the ranks."[64]

Attempts by city fathers to aid striking families were rejected in favor of working-class solidarity. Workers refused charity from Anglo organizations, most run by wives of manufacturers or members of the citizens' committee; one, the Children's Home, was housed in a refurbished cigar factory. Lovett initially voiced consternation over workers' reactions, but later expressed admiration for "the foresight of those starving Latin families" who refused to leave their "children to the tender mercy of men [or women] who will try to squeeze the lifeblood out of [them] while living."[65]

The insistence of civic leaders that they sought only to assist needy families and the rejection of this rationale by workers reflected the larger issues of the strike: paternalism and elite control on the one side versus labor militancy and workers' control on the other. City fathers looked to their wives for assistance in 1920, while manufacturers looked to Anglo women workers. The packers' union, employers argued, was depriving native-born women of work to which they were "peculiarly suited," and, by slowing down production, were throwing "strippers, selectors and cigar makers" out of work as well.[66]

[63]See Mormino and Pozzetta, *Immigrant World of Ybor City*, 151, 152, 157–59; *El Internacional*, Sept. 5 and 12 and Nov. 7 and 14, 1919.
[64]Sexton to Gompers, July 31, 1920, in AFL Papers, reel 36. Robert Ingalls provided me with this citation.
[65]Letter printed in *Tampa Citizen*, July 30, 1920.
[66]*TMT*, July 7 and Aug. 8, 1920.

Working-class Latins repudiated both elite aid and factory owners' arguments. Packers' Local 474 claimed that employers' hiring practices were merely a strategy to reduce wages, noting owners' resistance to hiring Anglo women as apprentices. Women's inability to do "the strong work, as the men are forced to do while learning the trade," underscored their unsuitability for the work. Yet, the packers noted, "the fact is that every female member of the union is American-born, not a single one of them Latin."[67] This last point demonstrated that the packers did not discriminate on the basis of sex or ethnicity, but their claims of female frailty, which buttressed specifically male definitions of virility, also reflected divisions in the local.

On November 6 cigarworkers throughout the nation observed Tampa Day, donating a day's wage to strikers' families. Tampa's locals issued a long statement on the occasion, announcing among other items support for working women yet fear that "the abundance of labor will give the manufacturer the opportunity to eliminate from his shop all dignified and civic [i.e., unionized and Latin] women." These dignified and civic women, children in tow, had led the "Biggest Labor Parade Ever Seen in Tampa" two months earlier. In addition, women workers and wives began traveling, many for the first time during a strike, to find jobs or join husbands, demonstrating, according to *El Internacional*, "the solid determination of the workers to be treated as human beings." In October close to 3,000 strikers, about half of them women, voted to continue the strike.[68] Community solidarity was strong, though it failed to embrace Anglo women, who were geographically as well as culturally isolated from *tampeños*.

Throughout the fall, employers insisted that Tampa's cigar benches were filling up with "girl packers" from across the country, who "found working conditions superior to their expectations." These Anglo girls, "earning twice as much as they have been accustomed" to, were the wave of the future, according to *Tobacco Leaf*. Yet "a careful survey" by *Tampa Citizen* reporters suggested that it was predominantly black women who were entering the factories. The *Citizen* concluded that manufacturers' hopes of "employing unskilled American girls" are "swiftly fleeting with the knowledge that American girls cannot be secured as long as they are forced to work at the same benches with negro girls."[69]

To replace ethnic solidarity with racial conflict was hardly a victory, yet manufacturers and civic leaders insisted that the strike was being con-

[67]Local 474 to *El Internacional*, Aug. 13, 1920. See also issue of Aug. 20, 1920. Original in English.
[68]*Tampa Citizen*, Nov. 12, 1920; *TMT*, Sept. 7, 1920; *El Internacional*, Sept. 10, 1920 (original in Spanish); *TMT*, Oct. 15, 1920; *CMOJ*, September 1920.
[69]*Tobacco Leaf*, Aug. 26, 1920; *Tampa Citizen*, Aug. 13, 1920.

tinued only "by every possible manipulation of the excitable and easily influenced minds of the Latin cigarmakers."[70] When they finally were forced to give up the struggle, the "excitable" Latins sought to circumvent new policies that would divide workers. *Selectores,* for instance, "decided to pool [their] salaries," ensuring that "each will receive equal pay and there will be no throat-cutting," rather than accept differentials instituted by employers.[71] Virility still meant solidarity, not individual achievement. Yet with more women, and more non-Latin women, entering the industry and with the most highly skilled jobs now subject to female intrusions, the sexual tensions glimpsed in 1916 grew, abetted by major transformations of the Tampa industry.[72]

The 1920–21 strike was expensive for everyone involved. Loss of markets and inventory depletions encouraged employers to replace more skilled Latin men and women with less skilled Anglo women, to hasten automation of the stripping and rolling processes, and to move entire factories farther north. The costs to the CMIU, in dollars and prestige, heightened national leaders' ambivalence about organizing Latin labor and diminished their commitment of resources in future strikes. Finally, transformations in the industry increased women's presence yet lowered their wages, leading Latin women and men to follow somewhat different paths in seeking job security. These gender-specific choices appeared within the year.

Only nine months after the cigarworkers returned to their jobs, they were once again on strike. It was apparently West Tampa strippers, confronted with short pay, who first "walked out in protest"; this walkout led within a "few hours" to "a general strike." Strippers and cigarmakers then both asked for better wages. *El Internacional* supported the spontaneous walkout, claiming that employers had unjustifiably slashed cigarworkers', and especially strippers', wages. Claiming that most strippers were "poor mothers and widows . . . compelled to work to support their tiny ones," *El Internacional* shamed owners for not even having "the gentleness to notify these poor women before hand of their greedy scheme."[73]

[70]*TMT,* Jan. 2, 1921.

[71]Reported in *El Internacional,* Feb. 5, 1921, a day after workers returned to the factories. Original in English.

[72]In 1920 Tampa produced 227,800,000 cigars and the industry employed some 40% of the city's workers. (The percentage had been 56.2 in 1910.) In 1929, 504.8 million cigars were produced in Tampa, though the proportion of the city's workers engaged in cigar production fell to about 25%. Automation thus allowed cigar manufacturers to increase production while reducing the work force. Moreover, a higher percentage of the work force was female in 1930 (c. 43%) than in any previous decade. See Ingalls, *Urban Vigilantes,* 149, 150, 185; A. Stuart Campbell, *The Cigar Industry of Florida* (Gainesville: University of Florida Press, 1939), 8, 55–56.

[73]*Tampa Citizen,* Nov. 25, 1921; *El Internacional,* Nov. 25, 1921 (original in English).

Frustrated by the failure of the manufacturers' earlier victory to lift the threat of labor tumult, the *Tampa Times* reminded its readers, "The manhood of this city has controlled equally aggravating situations in the past, and it is not to be feared that they will fail or hesitate in their plain duty now." Assuming that the strike was the work of "outside agitators," the *Tribune* demanded of workers, "If there is no man among you . . . big enough to stand up and denounce such leaders . . . , then hand the job over to some woman, and watch her kill off these drones, even as the queen bee will not let the drones live to eat the honey her busy, honest workers have made!" To aid workers in coming to their senses, a citizens' committee quickly congregated and ran local CMIU leaders out of town.[74]

Anglos' Janus-faced view of women—as simultaneously queen bees tolerating only busy workers and passive drones easily led astray by male agitators—conflicted with *El Internacional*'s portrait of desperate but determined mothers. The response of George Perkins, national CMIU leader, to reports of "disturbances and violence" in Tampa presented still another perspective. He assured Gompers that such activities occurred "in only one factory, and that was started by the women strippers." Admitting that some strikers were arrested and fined and that a few agitators were "deported," he insisted that the "Tampa papers are full of the wild stuff as usual" and that communications from workers were "on the hysterical side. . . . It remains," he concluded, "that cigarmakers of Tampa rushed headlong into a wild strike."[75] Thus, two decades after first seeking to organize Latin workers via the strippers, CMIU union leaders bridled at their unruly behavior, their penchant for radicalism, and the role of "hysterical" women as coconspirators.

Still arguing for unity, male cigarworkers nonetheless felt increasingly threatened by the influx of Anglo women and perhaps as well by the initiative of their Latin sisters, especially when, as in 1916, militant strippers refused to subordinate their interests to those of men. The union men who portrayed them as "poor women" who "have the misfortune of having to earn a living" were confronted in real life by strong-minded, strong-willed comrades with their own sense of priorities.

Before the meeting called to decide whether the strike should continue, strippers proclaimed that they "would stay out on strike regardless of the outcome of the vote." Recognizing that they "could hold up a return to normalcy," strippers acted "independently throughout the strike, keeping aloof from the decisions of the leaders."[76] The vote for the strike was

[74]*TMT*, Nov. 23 and 26, 1921; *Tampa Times*, Nov. 28, 1921.
[75]Perkins to Gompers, Nov. 29, 1921, in AFL Papers, reel 36. Robert Ingalls provided me with this citation.
[76]*Tampa Times*, Nov. 26, 1921, and *TMT*, Nov. 27, 1921. Although the only descriptions

close, with most of the winning majority coming from the West Tampa districts, where female strippers initiated the walkout.

Within a few days of the referendum, the all-male worker-members of an industry-wide arbitration committee ended the strike. With local union leaders still missing, national CMIU leaders apathetic, and workers divided, the men claimed that continuation of the strike was futile. No further mention appears of the strippers' threat to boycott a return. The tensions inherent in the women's manifesto were buried with the strike.

In the following decades women came to dominate cigar manufacturing. A few skilled women sustained hand-rolling traditions for select customers; most made the transition to machines, where they were joined by native-born women. By the mid-1930s, male union leaders represented a shrinking and increasingly feminized work force. Women came to prominence in the industry and union, then, only in the decade of their demise. Thus no full-blown female version of "virile" unionism ever emerged in Tampa.

The legacy of labor activism in Tampa was not that the city became a hotbed of working women's militancy, as Lawrence and New York's Lower East Side did. Instead, Tampa's Latin workers sought to empower their class through a melding of male leadership and female comradeship, of labor confrontation and community solidarity, of locally controlled struggle and internationalist ideals. The early experience of Spanish persecution provided Cuban laborers in particular with a broad political vision that muted cultural traditions of male dominance.

The voice of virile labor emerged from male-headed households, male-dominated unions, and a sexual division of labor that benefited men. Yet it could not be the voice of men only; it required women's integration into and support of the Latin family, economy, community, and labor movement. Out of struggles for political liberation and workers' control Latin laborers forged a form of virile unionism that, though not gender-neutral, was gender-integrated. Often resting on rhetoric of victimized women and maternal martyrdom, it still provided openings for female militancy, which was applauded by male co-workers when it was in harmony with their agenda.

Women's prominent if subordinate role in virile unionism in Tampa suggests the ways in which women's family and wage-earning roles could converge to support a radical vision of class and community. Here domesticity did not inhibit women's involvement in political and economic concerns, but rather served as a resource—for financing independence,

---

of women's independence come from Anglo papers, the strippers' proclamation suggests that they are not exaggerating substantially here.

supporting home-based production, and sustaining strikers. Though the inability of women to sustain an autonomous female voice indicated the limits of this nexus for fully egalitarian sexual relations within the working class, it yet provides a blueprint for an organizational strategy that integrates women and men. It also demonstrates the importance of the larger political as well as economic context in shaping a work culture sufficiently shared by women and men to sustain labor militancy and community solidarity over three decades.

CHAPTER SEVEN

Gender, Self, and Work in the Life Insurance Industry, 1880–1930

Angel Kwolek-Folland

In 1924 Glover Hastings, superintendent of agencies for the New England Mutual Life Insurance Company, described life insurance to an agents' training class as "the standing together . . . of hosts of manly men to defend each other's homes from the enemy that shoots on the sly and in the dark."[1] Such metaphors of manhood and womanhood were common in the life insurance field, as workers at all levels in the industry addressed the changing nature of their work at the turn of the century.[2]

The uses of gendered language to describe work and work relations stemmed from at least two interrelated sources. First, executives and workers in life insurance drew on gender metaphors as a primary way to

A fellowship from the American Association of University Women supported a portion of the research for this essay. The three companies that so generously provided access to their corporate records made my work possible, and I am only one of the beneficiaries of their commitment to the importance of history. In addition, the generous and careful assistance of several archivists made my work much easier. James Mann of the Metropolitan Life Insurance Company Archives, Arline Schneider of the Equitable Life Assurance Society of the United States Archives, and Phyllis Steele of The New England Archives all located sources, answered questions, carefully read several versions of this research, and—perhaps most important—took an enthusiastic interest in the work. Finally, my debt to several friends and colleagues is enormous. In conversations both specific and general, Ava Baron, Gail Bossenga, Nupur Chaudhuri, Sara Evans, Brendan Fletcher, Joseph Hawes, Linda Nieman, Ann Schofield, Peg Wherry, and Sue Zschoche helped me to refine and redefine my interpretations of gender and work.

[1] Elizur Wright, quoted in Glover S. Hastings, typewritten notes, Home Office Training School File, Historical Collection, Corporate Library, The New England, Boston (hereafter TNE). See also E. Marie Little, "Life Insurance" (Nov. 9, 1915), 6, in Bureau of Vocational Information Papers, Schlesinger Library, Cambridge, Mass. (hereafter BVI).

[2] I am using Rosabeth Moss Kanter's inclusive definition of corporate "workers" as both "managers, professionals, and technical personnel" and "paper-handlers, record-keepers, and date-manipulators": *Men and Women of the Corporation* (New York: Basic Books, 1977), 4. Kanter argues that assumptions about gender become part of the structure of work relations. This essay is, in part, an effort to look more closely at the historical development of the relationship between corporate structure and gender which she outlined.

delineate difference. Enlisting the late-nineteenth-century vocabulary of separate spheres, which used dualistic gender terms and relationships drawn from biology to describe nonbiological phenomena, workers and executives expressed their culture's specific obsession with categories of maleness and femaleness as signifiers of difference.[3] Second, the changing demography of the office work force challenged the male-defined and -populated nineteenth-century workplace. Between about 1880 and 1930, young, white, middle- and working-class women entered the formerly all-male world of business in the United States as clerks, typists, bookkeepers, secretaries, and stenographers. In 1870 women made up only 2.5 percent of the clerical labor force; by 1930, 52.5 percent of all clerical workers were women. By the 1880s, life insurance employed more women workers than any other area of the private service sector.[4]

Workers in the insurance industry expressed gender in multiple voices. Executives and managers used images of manhood and womanhood to explain and legitimate their product and production process to the public and to workers. In the process they articulated a theory of work relations in gendered terms. Workers explicated their own alternative conceptions of the meaning of work through gender.[5] Both explanations

[3]Gender "systems" in the West historically have viewed femaleness and maleness as opposites, and used them as an analogue for difference. This emphasis on the separation of manhood and womanhood, while an ancient Western image, was emblematic of the nineteenth century. See Michel Foucault, *The History of Sexuality,* vol. 1, *An Introduction* (New York: Vintage, 1980). For examples of gendered expression in political and social realms, see Paula Baker, "The Domestication of Politics: Women and the American Political Society, 1780–1920," *American Historical Review,* 89 (June 1984), 620–47; and Mary P. Ryan, "The American Parade: Representations of the Nineteenth-Century Social Order," in *The New Cultural History,* ed. Lynn Hunt, 131–53 (Berkeley: University of California Press, 1989).

[4]Elyce Rotella, *From Home to Office: U.S. Women at Work, 1870–1930* (Ann Arbor, Mich.: U.M.I. Research Press, 1981), 2–105. Carole Srole notes, for example, that insurance companies in Massachusetts reflected the national trend toward female dominance in clerical positions in the industry by the 1880s: "'A Position That God Has Not Particularly Assigned to Men': The Feminization of Clerical Work, Boston, 1860–1915" (Ph.D. diss., University of California, Los Angeles, 1984), 29. For the relation between manhood and business, see Peter Filene, *Him/Her/Self: Sex Roles in Modern America,* 2d ed. (Baltimore: Johns Hopkins University Press, 1986); Joe L. Dubbert, *A Man's Place: Masculinity in Transition* (Englewood Cliffs, N.J.: Prentice-Hall, 1979); and Irvin Wyllie, *The Self-made Man in America: The Myth of Rags to Riches* (New Brunswick, N.J.: Rutgers University Press, 1954).

[5]Gender "systems" generally define normative values, deviance, and social and personal expectations for biological males as well as females. For an analysis of the socially defined basis of gender attribution, see the Introduction to Suzanne Kesseler and Wendy McKenna, *Gender: An Ethnomethodological Approach* (New York: Wiley, 1978), 1–20; and Sherry B. Ortner and Harriet Whitehead, *Sexual Meanings: The Cultural Construction of Gender and Sexuality* (New York: Cambridge University Press, 1981). For an excellent theoretical discussion of the application of categories of gender difference to the historical process, see Joan W. Scott, "On Language, Gender, and Working Class History," in her *Gender and the Politics of History* (New York: Columbia University Press, 1988), 53–67.

infused discussions about the meaning of work in life insurance with powerful cultural and intensely personal meanings. Conceptions of manhood and womanhood defined the meaning of work, the experience of workers, and the limits and possibilities of institutional organization.[6] Men and women in the life insurance industry used gendered metaphors and images to express their understanding of the relationship between personal and institutional definitions of the work experience.[7]

Life insurance is a service industry in its product, its reliance on corporate structure, and its often genuine (and fiscally sound) concern with the health and welfare of its clients and employees. From its commercial origins in the 1840s to the early twentieth century, life insurance changed from a maligned and publicly suspect operation to a well-regulated and respectable business. During that process, the industry in some cases anticipated much that was to take place within the American business community generally.[8] The evolution of status, wage, and gender distinctions between workers, of the corporate bureaucracy and division of labor which were typical of business growth in the late nineteenth century, became noticeable in the life insurance industry by the 1880s.

Life insurance executives looking for ways to make their business appealing found gender imagery both a "natural" and a useful tool.[9] Although any business relies to some extent on reputation, good customer relations are critical in life insurance. The industry "manufactures" and sells financial security, basing its operations on complex and precise

[6]As Joan W. Scott has put it, "gender is a primary way of signifying relationships of power . . . a primary field within which or by means of which power is articulated": "Gender: A Useful Category of Historical Analysis," *American Historical Review*, 91 (December 1986), 1069–70.

[7]Recent work in cultural and cognitive anthropology suggests that an analysis of language—particularly metaphor and metonymy—can uncover the links between individual self-conception and cultural actions and roles. See, e.g., Naomi Quinn and Dorothy Holland, eds., *Cultural Models in Language and Thought* (New York: Cambridge University Press, 1987); and George E. Marcus and Michael M. Fischer, *Anthropology as Cultural Critique: An Experimental Moment in the Human Sciences* (Chicago: University of Chicago Press, 1986). Quinn and Holland argue that metaphor and metonymy are modes of cognition. Metaphor "maps structures from one domain to another," and metonymy "structures a domain in terms of its elements." Metaphor links physical and abstract understanding; metonymy provides "salient examples," ideals, or stereotypes, which are then enacted and socialized through ritual.

[8]The literature on the "managerial revolution" is voluminous. The best general work is still Alfred D. Chandler, *The Visible Hand: The Managerial Revolution in American Business* (Cambridge: Harvard University Press, 1977). For an analysis of this change within the life insurance industry, see Angel Kwolek-Folland, *The Business of Gender: Men and Women in the Office, 1870–1930* (Baltimore: Johns Hopkins University Press, forthcoming).

[9]In a similar way, the early aviation industry used women pilots to demonstrate the simplicity and safety of mechanical flight: Joseph J. Corn, "Making Flying 'Thinkable': Women Pilots and the Selling of Aviation, 1927–1940," *American Quarterly*, 31 (1979), 556–71. I am grateful to Patrick B. Nolan for calling my attention to this article.

computations, accurate and thorough record keeping, and financial investing. The intangible nature of its product and the all but invisible process of production make the public's goodwill of paramount importance.[10] By 1900, life insurance executives had articulated a philosophy of service which justified their product. In their public pronouncements regarding the social purpose of life insurance and in the symbols they attached to their companies, executives incorporated gender in a philosophy I have called "corporate motherhood." Because of their emphasis on security and family protection and their concern with creating a positive public image, life insurance executives perhaps tended more than most to think of their mandate in social terms. Nevertheless, social legitimacy was particularly important in life insurance, which fought an uphill battle for public acceptance until the early twentieth century.

Executives had two interconnected purposes in mind when they used images of motherhood and family: first, to calm the fears of the public and stimulate sales; and second, to encourage a paternalistic relationship with employees. Both Metropolitan Life and New England Life executives repeatedly referred to their companies as "families." This emphasis initially came from the roots of the business in the family partnerships of the 1840s and 1850s. It became increasingly metaphorical, however, as companies grew and altered their organizational and recruiting structures. By the 1920s, Metropolitan Life's "family of 40,000" described an ideal of harmonious public and employee relations, not reality.[11]

Symbols of womanhood emphasized the security of the industry, enhancing its persona by inferring that a company's relationship with the public was that of a mother with her children. Company logos, advertising, and descriptions stressed the nurturing and protective aspects of life insurance with images of domestic womanhood. Metropolitan Life and the Equitable both used the symbol of a mother to suggest the protection and care they offered. In 1859 Equitable adopted as its logo a vignette of an allegorical female figure with shield and spear protecting a mother holding a child in her arms.[12] This vignette varied slightly over time,

---

[10]This is not to suggest that life insurance companies sold an unnecessary product. In fact, given the economic transformations of the nineteenth century, life insurance filled a critical need left by the breakdown of older forms of financial security, such as family partnerships, land, and workers' associations.

[11]Metropolitan Life Insurance Co., *A Family of 40,000: How Health and Happiness Are Provided for Its Members* (ca. 1926), in Metropolitan Life Insurance Company Archives, New York (hereafter MLICA). See also "Family Affairs," *New England Pilot,* 1 (May 1916), 165; and "One Big Family," *New England Pilot,* 13 (August 1927), 1, both in TNE.

[12]John Quincy Adams Ward executed a statue for the Equitable in 1871, based on an emblem designed for use on the company's policies in 1860. See Lewis I. Sharp, *John Quincy Adams Ward: Dean of American Sculpture* (Newark: University of Delaware Press, 1985), 184; and R. Carlyle Buley, *The Equitable Life Assurance Society of the United States, 1859–1964* (New York: Appleton-Century-Crofts, 1967), 1:106–7.

modifying but not abandoning the symbolic connection between the company and motherhood. In an advertising theme of 1900, a portrait of mother and child, titled "The Equitable Mother," referred to the security of families insured by the company. The New England used a picture of Priscilla Alden at her spinning wheel to illustrate the company in 1886. Between 1908 and 1954, this image appeared on life insurance policies and some promotional items. This was both a localized symbol of colonial antecedents and a larger invocation of Victorian associations of home, hearth, and domesticity.[13] The ideology of corporate motherhood and its attendant symbols marked a major departure from the notion that business was a public, male arena driven by men and masculine values.

The symbols of corporate motherhood also tied a company's product to its production process, articulating an ideal of employee relations. The industry's vision of companies as mothers to the public harmonized with descriptions of the maternal relationship between companies and their employees. In an address of 1920 titled "Mother Metropolitan," company president Haley Fiske told a gathering of sales agents that the Metropolitan was a mother to both its clients and its employees. Referring to his audience as "my dear boys," Fiske said, "If Mother is this great Company, and if these millions of people [clients] are her children, then you are the elder brothers," whose job it was to become part of the client's "family circle," to become their "confidante and advisor."[14] Fiske patterned his vision of corporate motherhood and service on that of the ideal middle-class Victorian woman: a nurturing and concerned figure, intrinsically benevolent and forgiving. Within the corporate family, male sales agents were eldest sons, carrying the ideal of service to the consumer/child.[15]

In addition to these symbolic references to motherhood and family, Metropolitan Life, Equitable, Aetna Life, and New England Life all provided benefits to their employees to convince them that the companies were concerned about their welfare.[16] By the 1890s, these companies

[13]Photographs in Equitable Life Assurance Society Archives, New York (hereafter ELASA), MLICA, and TNE; Phyllis E. Steele, special collections coordinator, "Uses of Company Symbols," July 28, 1988, in TNE.

[14]Haley Fiske, "Mother Metropolitan," in *Life Insurance Addresses and Papers*, vol. 3 (Privately bound, n.d.), 25–26 (MLICA).

[15]*The Intelligencer: In Memoriam—Haley Fiske, 1852–1929*, 20 (Mar. 6, 1929), 17 (MLICA).

[16]As early as 1896, Metropolitan Life provided lunchrooms with free tea or coffee and athletic facilities. In 1913 Metropolitan Life opened a sanatorium at Mount McGregor, New York, for the care of tubercular employees. In 1921 the Equitable inaugurated a rest camp for "Equitable girls who are convalescent or whose state of health demands a period of rest and quiet." Employees also could use the camp for vacations. The stated purpose of the rest camp was to keep "our people well and efficient": "Metropolitan Life Insurance Company Highlights, 1868–1983," 2, in MLICA; A. R. Horr, vice president, "Memorandum for Heads of Departments," Feb. 18, 1921, in ELASA. See also Priscilla Murolo, "White-

sponsored employee lunchrooms, rest and recreation facilities, and sports events. This package was formalized in the years just before World War I. In the mid-teens, for example, Metropolitan Life created a Welfare Department, headed by Mrs. Gean Cunningham Snyder, to oversee the health and job satisfaction of the company's female employees. Metropolitan hoped through this device to "increase the efficiency and happiness of its employes."[17] The Welfare Department's mandate clearly grew out of the need to undermine worker discontent. Initially, however, it was based on the gender-specific belief that female employees required special maternal protection and guidance when they were far from home and family and so prey to a variety of temptations. Metropolitan developed the concept of corporate motherhood further around 1921, with the creation of the position of "house mother," whose duties were "indicated by her title":

> She is glad to consult with women Clerks as to their relations with their associates and superiors in the office, their domestic affairs, and their personal worries. She will willingly advise them in regard to any difficulties in or out of the office, or their residences and surroundings. Women Clerks who do not live with near relatives may feel free to ask her advice about boarding-places or living accommodations.

The house mother extended corporate motherhood to men as well. The company stressed that while the house mother "is expected, primarily to be of assistance to the women Clerks, . . . yet she is only too glad to advise with any men Clerks to whom she can be of help."[18] In fact, the welfare idiom often took on clearly gendered tones. Athletic facilities at

---

Collar Women: The Feminization of the Aetna Life Insurance Company, 1910–1930," paper delivered to the American Historical Association Conference, December 1985. For early-twentieth-century "welfare capitalism" in industry, see Richard Edwards, *Contested Terrain: The Transformation of the Workplace in the Twentieth Century* (New York: Basic Books, 1979), 90–97, and Stewart D. Brandes, *American Welfare Capitalism, 1880–1940* (Chicago: University of Chicago Press, 1976). An excellent discussion of the development of management styles in the twentieth century, and particularly the growth of the "human relations" school in the 1930s, is M. Christine Anderson's "Gender, Class, and Culture: Women Secretarial and Clerical Workers in Twentieth-Century America" (Ph.D. diss., Ohio State University, 1986), 75–108.
[17]Marie Louise Wright, "City Cruel Only to Girls Who Are Not Efficient, Says Guardian of 2,000," *Evening Mail*, May 8, 1913, n.p. (MLICA).
[18]Metropolitan Life Insurance Co., *Rules Governing Home Office Clerical Employees* (1921), 20, MLICA. Such programs were not unique to life insurance. The National Cash Register Company initiated the earliest industrial employee welfare program in the United States in the mid-1890s. The NCR program included many of the same features found among employee benefits in the life insurance industry. The NCR plan, however, like those of manufacturing concerns generally, was not part of the general business philosophy; nor was it tied to public image and product acceptance, as the plans of the life insurance companies were. Rather than merely an attempt at "worker control," in other words, life insurance welfare programs were part of the public justification of the industry.

Metropolitan Life, for example, were open to both men and women, as were courses in "self-improvement." For women only, however, Metropolitan Life provided sewing rooms and instructors so that women workers could make their own clothing. Higher wages would have enabled them to buy clothing, but wages would not have expressed so directly the company's message of benevolent motherhood.

The rhetorical uses of such symbols as motherhood and family also found expression in the physical spaces of life insurance offices, reinforcing the gendered environment of work relations. Designers and executives recreated the images and ambience of home within the office. They suggested domestic environments by the sizes of rooms (individual offices were smaller than areas where the "family" gathered together), residential fixtures and furniture, and decorative elements. Metropolitan Life's executive library and dining room in the 1890s repeated design elements common to Victorian domestic appointments: mantel clocks, candelabra, framed wall mirrors, a bearskin rug. The executive offices of New England Life's Milk Street building from the 1920s to 1941 were arranged like well-appointed parlors or libraries, with table lamps, leather couches, fireplaces, paintings, books, carpets, and display cabinets. Thus an essentially domestic environment was replicated within the public confines of the office. These "private" spaces within a "public" place reinforced the personalized overtones of the terms *home office* and *family*.[19] The emphasis on domesticity in these decorative details focused on and used cultural assumptions about gender which physically explicated gender differences as status differences, and vice versa.

Office spaces and decoration reinforced not only public corporate status but notions about private, individual gender. Highly articulated private offices set those who possessed them apart from other workers, and in very visible ways emphasized the individualism and masculinity of their occupants. The fact that all of their occupants were men generated crucial repercussions for the significance of gender in business. First, it pulled the male role as husband and father—as domestic family member—directly into the workplace by recreating a private space within a public arena. Thus the private side of a man could be expressed in his public workplace. As one author put it: "He brings his whole life to his office now, where before he left part of it at home, for there was no place for it in his commercial existence. His office is now *his* office, where before he seemed merely to be occupying a space apportioned to

[19] For a discussion of the implications of spatial division and segregation for gender relations, see Kwolek-Folland, *Business of Gender*; and Angel Kwolek-Folland, "The Gendered Environment of the Corporate Workplace, 1880–1930," in *The Material Culture of Gender/The Gender of Material Culture*, ed. Kenneth L. Ames and Katharine Martinez, Winterthur Conference Proceedings (New York: Norton, forthcoming).

him.""[20] Second, the private office designed to express a man's domestic side, his essential self as opposed to his commercial self, represented a form of property ownership and thus a traditional proof of manhood. This was especially critical in the corporate setting of a service industry such as life insurance. Corporate organization generally muted individual choice and autonomy, a phenomenon heightened by the feminized persona of a life insurance corporation. The implication was that men without private offices were not only lower in status within the company, they were also less manly as individuals. The private office, arrayed in its domestic symbolism and watched over by female secretaries or "office wives," thus was a mark of manhood as well as status.

Gendered imagery had a decided instrumental influence on how companies presented their product to the public and explained their relation to their employees. Life insurance rhetoric combined a feminized vision of the production process as a benevolent and nurturing spiritual force with imagery that stressed the familial nature of corporate relations and the company as a mother both to employees and to clients. Gendered images painted the inherently unstable and threatening picture of unregulated masculine business with a stable and nonthreatening gloss of motherhood and fatherhood, of women and men within the family serving their public children. This use of gender metaphors drew its emotive power from the specific tensions of the nineteenth-century gender dichotomy. Much as woman's task within the middle-class family was to tame the competitive and chaotic urges of men, so the mother company guided and stabilized the public. The public face of life insurance, in other words, conflated the separate worlds of Victorian manhood and womanhood, pulling privatized images of home and family into the public world and using that imagery to legitimize both a product and a production process.[21]

Gender metaphors had the advantage of being both expandable and mutable, highly specific and personal. The use of gendered terms and metaphors in the insurance industry in the United States at the turn of the twentieth century converted Victorian social ideals of manhood and womanhood into models for a corporate work ethic. The industry's image of business as a family relationship integrated public and private social gender roles. In the process, the industry used beliefs about manhood and womanhood to legitimate both its product and its production process. From the managerial perspective, the use of gender to describe work relations suggested that corporate work was based on a natural

[20]Randolph Sexton, *American Commercial Buildings of Today*, pt. 1 (New York: Architectural Books Publishing Co., ca. 1928), 11–12.

[21]This mingling of public and private is an intriguing adoption of the tenets of the "social motherhood" movement of the period from the 1890s to 1920.

hierarchy of the sexes rather than on an economic structure or the needs of managerial capitalism. Corporate motherhood defused and confused the reality of structural paternalism: womanhood had a symbolic existence that masked the hierarchical realities of corporate organization. Corporate work was thus experienced in an ideological context that blurred personal and public definitions of gender in the interests of organizational efficiency.

Both men and women workers accepted and used the same natural and corporate definitions of manhood and womanhood to explicate status, to express a commitment or lack of it to labor, and to assert a sense of self in relation to others in the workplace. Gendered language provided a way for workers to describe their experiences and understand the meaning of labor within their lives as a whole. It also functioned to conflate the distinctions between an individual's experiences as a worker and as a private person, and to this extent reinforced the corporate uses of gendered images.

Although economic and demographic factors were the basis for the changing nature of labor in life insurance from 1870 to 1930, some managers and workers in the industry held women in particular and womanhood in general responsible for men's subordination to the new bureaucratic structures. Women were, after all, one of the most visible signs of the changed business environment.[22] In 1933 an Equitable clerk, Charles H. Vanse, contrasted the environment at Equitable to what it had been in the 1890s: "Now-a-days one is surrounded by an ocean of permanent waves and one's requests (not orders) are received with a smile while one's vocabulary has been refined to such an extent that 'Oh Well' is about as near as one can come except that the 'Old Timers' occasionally relapse into the old version." Vanse remembered the predominantly male office as a place of action. He attributed the politeness, refinement, and enforced cheerfulness he described to the presence of women; women had altered the vigorous, independent masculine office relations beyond recognition. Further, such changes in vocabulary and attitude affected not only the experience of work but the behavior of male managers and executives outside the workplace. In Vanse's account and others, the feminized character of office labor seemed to be a direct result of the feminization of the workplace. The newly "civilized" worker had lost his manhood in the gendered office.[23] The presence of

---

[22]Carole Srole discusses male clerks' perception that women workers lowered men's wages in the 1870s. She points out that in reality reductions were caused by general economic depression: " 'A Position That God Has Not Particularly Assigned to Men,' " 100–110.

[23]Charles H. Vanse, "How Well Do I Remember," *Equitable Spirit*, 1 (April 23, 1934), n.p. (ELASA). "The Romance of Park Place," in V.F., H.O., 1876–1893, MLICA, relates the story of a fistfight between two male clerks at Metropolitan Life in 1889. Cindy Aron

women altered both the social behaviors of the workplace and the association of work with manliness. The experience of office manhood thus took on new and disturbing implications.

Management theorists echoed Vanse's fears. For some, women's presence in offices raised the issue of dependency, and the dangers of that dependency for males. In 1932 one management educator, George Frederick, argued that American executives and managers had become "paralyzed" and "petulant" because they had turned so much of their work over to women. Such dependency was an offense not against corporate order but against nature. "After all, there is something a bit silly in seeing a husky man in an office chair so helpless that there isn't a paper . . . or a utensil he knows how to lay hold upon, without asking a frail little woman on the other side of the room to go get it for him." He likened this businessman to a "spoiled child" whose mother had to pick up after him.[24] The dependency Frederick observed stemmed from the stratification of office work and the job specialization of the corporate structure. Workers under managerial capitalism did not control or participate in the entire process of production, only in parts of it. Frederick, however, like Vanse, described such fragmentation as a relationship between men and women, as the result of a gender system rather than economic or organizational imperatives.

The expression of the fragmentation, dichotomy, and subordination of office work in gendered metaphors seems to have been typical office rhetoric by at least the 1920s. Observations made by women workers about men in offices echoed the infantile image of the business manager or executive. Many secretaries who responded to a survey conducted by the Bureau of Vocational Information (BVI) in 1925 complained about the irrationality of male demands in the workplace. They referred to men as "temperamental," "difficult to work for," moody, and "disagreeable."[25] By the 1920s, the image of childlike men had become a part of the popular image of male office workers. In 1928 a former secretary, Grace Robinson, lamented that "the man one works for has, more than likely, a healthy, well nourished temper that all its life has been permitted to cavort about naked, untrammeled, and undisciplined."[26] Women as well as men, workers as well as theorists, described their dissatisfaction

---

notes changes in the behavior of male clerks in federal offices as they adjusted to the introduction of women clerks in *Ladies and Gentlemen of the Civil Service: Middle-Class Workers in Victorian America* (New York: Oxford University Press, 1987), 164–65.

[24]George Frederick, "The Secretary-less Business Man," *Office Economist*, 14 (July–August 1932), 4.

[25]See, e.g., no. 1607, folder 384b; no. 1092, folder 371b; no. 1778, folder 384; and no. 1629, folder 383a, in BVI.

[26]Grace Robinson, "The Rocky Road to Secretarial Success," *Liberty*, Apr. 21, 1928, 22.

with fragmentation and lack of control as a function of gender relationships rather than job, position, or corporate structure.

Life insurance executives encouraged the view that all workers, male and female, were dependents in a system of benevolent familial alliances. Both the specialized ideology of corporate motherhood and the structural paternalism it legitimized stressed the childlike nature of workers, voicing the notion that male as well as female corporate employees were undisciplined dependents. Corporate motherhood addressed the issue of dependency by lumping men and women together, asserting the commingling of prescribed male and female behavior, and describing an employee who was loyal and obedient regardless of sex. Yet deep-rooted cultural assumptions of male dominance and female subordination could not be overridden so easily. In fact, the implicit challenge to the gender hierarchy posed by the image of corporate motherhood gave the issue of subordination a highly personal cast.

Descriptions of the childlike and subservient qualities of male office workers linked men to stereotyped images of women, suggesting that the childlike male was emasculated. This idea placed men at the same subordinate level as women and threatened to upset the finely balanced power structures of both the gender dichotomy and corporate status. Male workers tried to shape office gender relations in ways that would emphasize male dominance.[27] Several former secretaries in the BVI survey observed that employers preferred to hire women who did not have college educations because such workers would be less independent and self-assured. One respondent noted that "there is not a little prejudice . . . against the college girl; she's less easily blind folded and men don't like to be 'seen through.' " Another claimed that "some of the men in the concern like to have high school graduates; enjoy the feeling of superiority over their secretaries."[28]

This apparent preference for employees who were female and who were younger and less well educated than their bosses seems to have been borne out in reality. The youth of female office workers was both a subject of comment and a demographic fact throughout the period. Photographs of the Metropolitan Life office staff taken in the 1890s suggest a predominantly young female work force. So prevalent were young women office workers in insurance, in fact, that the term *girl* was shorthand for *clerical worker.*[29] In 1915 Metropolitan Life reported that the

[27]A Young Agent, "The Psychology of the Bull Pen," *Manager's Magazine*, 3 (July 1928), 18.
[28]No. 911, folder 371b, and no. 1093, box 31, folder 373, BVI.
[29]Photographic files, MLICA. See, e.g., "A Wonderful Village" (Nov. 6, 1911), 2, in V.F. Employees 1867–1960 (I), MLICA.

average age of its male clerks was 31, that of female clerks 27.[30] A respondent to the BVI survey noted that

> One [employment] agency has said that they find it hard to place a young woman in secretarial work when she attains the age of thirty or thirty-five. . . . The advertisements in the papers seem to bear that statement out. . . . Whereas when I started out I was turned away for lack of experience, today I notice the advertisement calls especially for the inexperienced.[31]

The youthfulness of female insurance workers stemmed in part from the ideological and economic attractions of office work to young, never-married women. The best-paid and most prestigious of positions open to young women, office jobs also were surrounded by a mythology that emphasized the highly personal, even intimate nature of male-female relations in the office. The "office wife," popular literature claimed, could marry the boss and become his real wife.[32] Age played an important role in this mythology, and pointed to its deeper social and sexual meanings.

[30]*Welfare Work for Employees* (company brochure, 1915), 7 (MLICA). Though extreme youth was less usual among clerical workers than in other female employment sectors, the Women's Educational and Industrial Union's 1914 report on education indicated that nearly 44% of women in office service began working in offices before they were 16: *The Public Schools and Women in Office Service* (Boston, 1914), 51. Younger women continued to predominate in clerical work into the Depression. See Harriet A. Byrne, for the U.S. Department of Labor, *The Age Factor as It Relates to Women in Business and the Professions*, Women's Bureau Bulletin no. 117 (Washington, D.C.: U.S. Government Printing Office, 1934).

[31]Annie R. Walford to Emma Hirth, director of BVI, May 29, 1925, box 31, folder 373, BVI. A survey made by the Women's Bureau of the Department of Labor in 1931 showed that 63.5% of the female clerical labor force were under the age of 20. Elyce Rotella's computations on the clerical labor force based on census returns indicate that female clerical workers were younger overall than the general female work force: about half were between the ages of 16 and 24: *From Home to Office*, 113. The Minnesota Department of Labor in 1919 showed six female "children" (between ages 10 and 16) employed as stenographers or typists. In 1920 the department reported fourteen female "children." In neither year were any male "children" reported in those categories. See *Seventeenth Biennial Report of the Department of Labor and Industries of the State of Minnesota, 1919–1920* (Minneapolis, 1921), 118. Women office workers also tended to be younger than their male counterparts. Federal census reports of 1920 indicate that 51% of all female clerks were between the ages of 17 and 24, in contrast to 35% of all male clerks. For stenographers and typists, the federal census showed a smaller range, but a tendency toward younger women. Fifty-five percent of all male stenographers and typists were between 17 and 24. For women, that figure was 62%. See Byrne, *Age Factor*, 17. The census figures were computed from Bureau of the Census, *The Fourteenth Census of the United States Taken in the Year 1920*, vol. 4, *Population, 1920, Occupations* (Washington, D.C.: U.S. Government Printing Office, 1922), Table 6. The category included all clerks except those in stores, and in shipping and weighing.

[32]This theme is discussed in greater detail in Kwolek-Folland, *Business of Gender*. See also Donald R. Makosky, "The Portrayal of Women in Wide Circulation Magazine Short Stories" (Ph.D. diss., University of Pennsylvania, 1966).

Commonly held notions of appropriate age and gender relations paired an older man with a younger woman. The idea of a young male boss employing an older female secretary upset both the traditional age hierarchy and notions of male dominance. The proper role for an older women—mother—precluded sexuality or sexual attraction in the boss-secretary relationship. This idea divested such a relationship of its power via marriage imagery (the "wedding" and thus transcendence of two status levels or power levels, the office wife and the corporate family man) and of its potent sexual tensions as well.[33]

The evolution of corporate bureaucracy in life insurance associated gender traits with particular jobs; and gender divisions described the hierarchy of positions within a corporation, replicating differences of status. Thus the people in the lower positions within a business were associated with a wide array of feminine qualities, those in the upper reaches with masculine qualities. A woman manager was expected to adopt masculine business behaviors and beliefs; a male secretary, attributes increasingly defined as feminine. For a woman to display features or attitudes of dominance—age, position, or behavior—undermined both the status hierarchy and the gender system. As we have seen, however, men often attributed their own perceived subordination to the presence of women. Crucial components of male self-definition, in other words, hinged on the meanings womanhood assumed in the corporate context. This uncanny reversal of the hierarchy ascribed to women levels of control and dominance which their definition as subordinates denied.

This inversion of power suggests that patriarchal attitudes and structures in the life insurance industry applied as much to men as to women workers. On the one hand, the attitudes of top managers and executives included the sense that all employees were boys and girls under the care of watchful and protective parents: the executive father and the mother company.[34] Insurance work involved some degree of subordination and inequality for both men and women. Yet experience bore out the organizational presumption of female inferiority. By 1930, notions of appropriate work for men and women, the promotional hierarchy of life insurance corporations, even company buildings created a job segregation by gender and separate promotional tracks, status levels, and pay scales for male and female workers. Thus in life insurance, as in other industries, women did not enjoy the opportunities for advancement open

[33]Some male employers stated a preference for "older" women, emphasizing that they were more "motherly" and therefore removed the issue of sexuality from the workplace. Rosabeth Kanter has observed that "stereotyped informal roles," such as mother, "pet," "seductress," and "iron maiden," entrap women's sexuality, defusing and containing its potential for disruption: *Men and Women*, 233–34.
[34]See President Haley Fiske to Third Vice President Francis M. Smith, May 8, 1928, in V.F., Haley Fiske, Personal, MLICA.

to men.[35] As the role reversal evident in men's sense of dependency illustrates, however, male workers also experienced powerlessness within the corporation. What seems to have been operative in corporate work experience was the increasing degree to which descriptions of gender acted as descriptions of labor relationships, and the concurrent importance of gender roles to ideas about the self.

Women insurance sales agents and managers created definitions of their work which simultaneously drew on and undermined masculine and corporate imperatives. The problems and possibilities of their arguments reveal the complex relations between the genders of work and the self in life insurance offices. Women agents and managers participated in the male world of sales and management even as they asserted a female role in business. They usurped the language of management and sales to describe their work, and consciously departed from male values.[36] In particular, female agents and managers claimed their superiority to men as *workers*, arguing for the recognition of natural female skills in the life insurance workplace.

The life insurance product, as opposed to the producing company itself, was couched in masculine terms. Companies emphasized life insurance sales as a masculine calling, much like the clergy or the law. At the instrumental level, sales pitches aimed life insurance primarily at male breadwinners and played on the desire for what one historian has called "economic immortality."[37] Life insurance removed death from the feminized regions of sentimentality and placed it in the masculinized realm of rationalism. The industry demonstrated that death could be tabulated, categorized, predicted, and given a cash value through actuarial tables and statistics. As a product, then, life insurance aimed predominantly, although not exclusively, at men.

The meaning of saleswork in life insurance, however, was open to interpretation, and sales literature stressed a complicated mixture of behaviors for agents and managers. Sales demanded competitiveness but also cooperation; agents needed to be enthusiastic but rational; they had to be both self-effacing and aggressive servants of society and their company. The life insurance product and customer also were problematic. Clients

[35]The major exposition of patriarchy as the causal factor in women office workers' subordination is Margery Davies, *Woman's Place Is at the Typewriter: Office Work and Office Workers, 1870–1930* (Philadelphia: Temple University Press, 1982).

[36]Companies began at least as early as the 1890s to hire women sales agents and to create "women's agencies" in order to capture the increasing market of working and career women. Reflecting Victorian assumptions on the division of gender, companies assumed that women agents would appeal to women customers. For a complete discussion of this issue, see Kwolek-Folland, *Business of Gender.*

[37]Viviana Zelizer, *Morals and Markets: The Development of Life Insurance in the United States* (New Brunswick, N.J.: Transaction, 1983), 58. Zelizer perceptively discusses the cultural and ideological context of the life insurance product.

were both recalcitrant enemies and grateful beneficiaries; life insurance was both a monetary exchange and social stewardship. Above all, life insurance sales was a "manly calling." It is in the context of these contested and masculinized meanings that women sales agents defined their work.[38]

Women agents, aware of the gendered basis of their employment, requisitioned gender relations and images to legitimate their work. Newsletters printed by women's agencies, for example, used gender to position the agencies within the larger corporate structure. In 1903 Florence Shaal's Equitable agency began to publish a newsletter for agents titled *The Little Sister to the Equitable News,* calling attention to its derivative and gendered relation to the company's newsletter.[39] Marie Little's agency published the *Little Upstart* from 1916 to 1918, using the manager's name as a pun for the position of her agency within the company (and perhaps to take the menace out of *upstart*). As the titles of these journals imply, they borrowed their rationale for existence from the house journals for agents published by Equitable and other companies. Their main purpose, like that of the company journals, was to encourage sales, create solidarity within the agency, and instruct agents on sales technique and attitude.[40] At the same time, however, the women's newsletters acknowledged their diminutive stature and derivative nature. Drawing on the analogy of the company as a family, their titles stressed their childlike, subordinate, and nonthreatening stature.

The *Little Upstart* consciously tried to set the women's agency apart from male agencies. One early issue asserted ascribed female qualities against the masculine tradition of the house papers: "We rather glory in our sauciness and impudence and pride ourselves upon the jewel of our inconsistency, and we snap our fingers at precedent and tradition. We want to have a sweetish number [of the newsletter] bubbling over with sentiment and have deliberately planned it."[41] The use of such terms as *sauciness, impudence,* and *inconsistency* and the implication that sentiment was an appropriate management tool cut two ways. On the one hand, they recognized common beliefs about women's nature and behavior: women were childish and inconsistent. Thus the writer laid claim to an accepted, if arguable, image of womanhood.[42] On the other,

[38]For a discussion of life insurance and the masculinized definition of saleswork, see Kwolek-Folland, *Business of Gender.*

[39]Unfortunately, no copies of this newsletter survive. However, it was quoted in *Equitable News,* 50 (February 1904), 10 (ELASA).

[40]Editorial in *Little Upstart,* 1 (July 1916), 1 (ELASA).

[41]*Little Upstart,* 5 (November 1916), 1 (ELASA).

[42]Pamela N. Warford, "The Social Origins of Female Iconography: Selected Images of Women in American Popular Culture, 1890–1945" (Ph.D. diss., St. Louis University, 1979), 3–5.

she inverted the implications of that image by suggesting that these were business strengths rather than womanly weaknesses. *Sauciness* and *impudence* could be translated in the male language of management as *fighting spirit* and *aggressiveness*. The behavior was generic to sales, but it was expressed in a very different way. Sauciness and impudence were *not* behaviors prescribed for such female corporate workers as typists, or for managers of either gender.

This validation of female assertiveness usurped male-centered definitions of aggressive sales behavior. The use of *sauciness* and *impudence* in this context recognized women's minority position in management and sales; but it also accommodated aggression into the canon of female business behavior. It turned impudence into an element of a female success ethic, legitimizing it as a female version of male aggression. The writer set female agents apart from male and other female workers without stepping beyond the bounds of acceptable female behavior. At the same time, however, she challenged masculinized definitions of management's role and turned female weaknesses into work skills commensurate with those of men.

We can see a similar assertion of female values at the expense of male and corporate codes of behavior in the issue of office clothing for agents. Office clothing illustrates women workers' use of alternative primary structures of self-definition which undermined official power structures and replaced them with alternative possibilities.[43] Women's office dress emphasized sexuality, suggesting that women workers were not wholly committed to their labor in ways management wanted. Popular women's magazines and company journals and newsletters contributed to this impression by suggesting in words and pictures that the female office worker was dressing to attract a husband.[44] Clothing styles were an aspect of female office behavior that management consistently found particularly offensive. The business educator and theorist Edward Kilduff expressed it best:

> The secretary should realize that a business employer silently criticizes the secretary who wears clothing more suited for social affairs than for office

[43]Judith Smith, "The 'New Woman' Knows How to Type: Some Connections between Sexual Ideology and Clerical Work, 1900–1930," paper presented at the Berkshire Conference on Women's History, 1974. Smith emphasizes the freeing of sexuality denoted by a change in women's office dress. Valerie Steele has argued that the shift in women's clothing styles between 1869 and 1930 was from one sort of erotic expression to another, rather than from repression to sexuality. See her *Fashion and Eroticism: Ideals of Feminine Beauty from the Victorian Era to the Jazz Age* (New York: Oxford University Press, 1985).

[44]Lauretta Fancher, "His Secretary Speaking," *Collier's*, 83 (Apr. 13, 1929), 28, 40; Merle Thorpe, "The Lady's Engaged," ibid. (May 25, 1929), 43, 70. The issue of women's dress and their emphasis on marriage is a constant theme in the journals of life insurance companies. See, e.g., *Pacific Coast News*, 1 (Apr. 22, 1921) (MLICA).

work . . . Some women secretaries do not seem to realize that it is a business
mistake to wear their "party" clothes to the office, that it is not in keeping
with the general scheme of a business office to be "dressed up."[45]

This sort of admonition had been common from the time women began
to work in offices. In one of the earliest advice books to prospective
women office workers in 1898, Ruth Ashmore counseled women to purchase sensible, dark clothing. She claimed that wearing fancy dress at
work suggested to employers that a woman was more interested in parties and the social whirl than in earning a living.[46]

Male business clothing had developed by the 1890s into a kind of uniform that was also worn outside the office by middle-class men. The
middle-class male's subdued dark suit asserted his commitment to his
job, and carried the implication that office work was an essential component of his self-image in and out of the workplace.[47] Early office
clothing for women essentially was a simplified version of middle-class,
daytime domestic attire—a dark skirt and a white or dark long-sleeved
blouse. Such clothing was not a uniform associated with office work in
the same way as a male's dark suit. Significantly, however, it was closer
symbolically to male office attire than female dress after about 1915.

Gradually female workers did develop a "uniform" for office wear,
and it was precisely this uniform that managers found so disconcerting.
By the 1920s, women's office wear was the same as their leisure wear
and implied—certainly to management—that women office workers
were not wholly committed to their job. Elaborate hair styles, jewelry,
perfume, light sandals, and dresses of soft, colorful fabrics told management that women office workers had not sold their entire consciousness
to the demands of the typewriter or Dictaphone. In addition, such clothing stressed differences between male and female, accenting femininity
and sexuality and reinforcing the gender dichotomy. On one hand, of
course, leisure clothing underscored female subordination and the perception that women's primary interest lay in marriage rather than in office work. On the other, it placed women outside the structure of
business: it acted as an assertion of self and womanhood which challenged business values, the divisions of status and dominance, and even
manhood. Management certainly viewed women's office attire from both
these perspectives, seeing such clothing as a statement of female distance

[45]Edward Kilduff, *The Private Secretary: The Duties and Opportunities of the Position*,
rev. ed. (New York: Century, 1924), 59.
[46]Ruth Ashmore, *The Business Girl in Every Phase of Her Life* (Philadelphia: Curtis,
1898), 8–9. This work first appeared in 1895.
[47]Valerie Steele, in her analysis of Victorian clothing, observes that "the clerk's shiny
black suit functioned both as a badge of respectability and as an involuntary sign of his
relatively humble position in the social order": *Fashion and Eroticism*, 83.

from the commitments of corporate labor and as a badge of the feminized office—a reminder of the explosive potential of sexuality and of management's ultimate inability to control the social construction of a worker's gendered self.

In the *Upstart*'s attention to women's fashion, its admonitions to dress "appropriately" and "sensibly," the newsletter echoed prescriptions leveled by management at clerical workers, secretaries, and other managers. Like male-oriented management journals, the *Upstart* proffered constant advice about dressing for saleswork. One article cautioned that "Little Agents should always wear smartly tailored suits," because tailored suits placed their wearers on a businesslike plane and were closer to male office attire. They made women sales agents conform with male managerial definitions of proper business clothing. Further, such requests urged women agents to identify themselves with their careers by projecting an image of commitment and serious intent.[48]

However, the newsletter's comments on dress also alluded to interests at variance with corporate business aims. In keeping with its contrary agenda, clothing columns in the *Upstart* came under such headings as "Flivel and Drivel." Unlike advice to male agents, *Upstart* articles focused on fashion as often as on practicality and business image. And they indicate that some women agents avoided the tailored suit. Under the title "Who's Who in Bankruptcy," the editor mentioned that "Marie Smith is sporting a charming new blue crepe de chine frock, all bespangled with beads, most handsome and expensive."[49] Such comments recognized that women sales agents had a distinct interest in clothing and fashion at odds with the practical matters of life insurance sales, and suggested that female agents shared something of the perspective of other women office workers.

The political quality of women's language and behavior grew out of a problem of self-definition: How could one remain a woman in a man's world? This question underlay much of women's work experience in offices, and female sales agents and managers addressed it in a variety of ways. Aware of their outsider status, women agents used humor to assert difference and to mask or deflect dissatisfaction and criticism. The language and tone of the *Upstart*, for example, sometimes poked fun at the rituals of life insurance sales, rituals that largely excluded women. One article commented that many items in the *Upstart* might seem "hackneyed to the seasoned agent. . . . [But] we hope our blasé readers will kindly remember that few of our agents have had the educational advantages of the conventions, and of listening to the wiseacres air their knowl-

[48]*Little Upstart,* 1 (July 1916), 5 (ELASA).
[49]Ibid., 11 (May 1917), 2 (ELASA).

edge at these assemblies."[50] Here the newsletter suggested the pomposity and exclusivity of the male management style. This type of attack on the agent conventions was unprecedented in the house journals. While it may have been the unspoken opinion of some agents, it never appeared in print.

The issue of deviance was particularly important to women agents because it touched on the intimate relation between individual and social gender. The mingling of notions about gender and the labor experience among office workers becomes clearer in the context of women workers' distinctions between their role and that of men. Women sometimes denied their subordinate position at work by asserting their superiority to male workers, using gender awareness to conflate the organizational hierarchy, stand it on its head, and deny its relevance to their sense of women's role. To avoid the perception that they were out of place, women managers and agents could infuse their work with culturally prescribed feminine values, using assumptions about women's nature to assert female superiority and difference. On the one hand, they spoke and acted as outsiders, not bound by company prescriptions, flaunting their deviance from the corporate structure. On the other hand, they claimed that women's approach to sales and management was superior to that of salesmen and male managers, that they were more appropriate insiders than men in this industry. Marie Little, speaking before a class on "Business Today" held at the New York University School of Commerce in 1915, asserted this perceived difference between male and female life insurance agents. Little explained that a woman agent was more appropriate to the business. Life insurance was inherently not "'a man's world,' . . . for most insurance is for women. Woman is the homemaker, the true instinct of her is home. Who then should be better able to sell insurance [than] women who know the needs of the home? . . . Woman in the insurance field finds her true vocation." Little claimed that women were more committed than men to the higher ideals of life insurance and the client's welfare because of intrinsic female qualities. She asserted that male agents were more interested in making a sale than in telling the truth; women were "more conscientious than men and, therefore, that very fact will make their statements more conscientious."[51]

For all their assertions of difference, women agents still faced the fact that saleswork required certain generic, male-defined behaviors. One of the primary attributes of the male sales agent was competitiveness. Both the *Upstart* and the *Little Sister* urged competition among women agents, but the language varied from that of the male-oriented journals, which often used agricultural metaphors to explain the role of male sales agents. Customers were viewed as fertile fields for the right man—the

[50]Ibid., 3 (September 1916), 1 (ELASA).
[51]Little, "Life Insurance," 9, 11.

ambitious, energetic, enthusiastic man who worked hard. As an article in the house journal for Equitable, *Items for Agents,* put it in 1909, life insurance "lies as an immense farm before you; every possible implement for working it is furnished by the Society. It is up to you to sow the seed and gather the crop."[52]

A short piece in the *Upstart* titled "Her Garden" implied a smaller and more intimate field of endeavor. In a larger sense, however, the garden was the "Laboratory of Life." This metaphor echoes the industry philosophy that life insurance sales was a noble calling of benefit to all humanity, but stresses its particular suitability as a career for women. The article used the symbolic meanings of various flowers and herbs to describe the qualities needed by agents. These characteristics were identical to those of salesmen generally—ambition, enthusiasm, loyalty—but included others foreign to the vocabulary of male management: "Violets for Modesty; and Mignonette to make you sweet. . . . We will need lots of Red Clover for Industry, and Oh, I pray that my Hollyhocks will grow for in garden language they mean Ambition. Over here, I shall plant White Crysanthemums [sic] for Truth and Shamrocks for Loyalty."[53] Striving for modesty and sweetness were not part of the male canon of management; in fact, while male managers stressed teamwork and sympathy, male cooperation and sensitivity had as their ultimate goal a conquered rather than a coaxed customer. Modesty and sweetness, though were important components of cultural womanhood, projected as specifically female elements of business success.

One issue of the *Upstart* devoted entirely to the career of the agency manager Florence Shaal made clear the differences between male and female approaches to management and sales success. One author claimed that Shaal was "the good comrade of her women, ready to give of her very best to help and encourage them; rejoicing in their successes and sympathizing in their failures and discouragements as though they were her own."[54] Other encomiums to Mrs. Shaal in this issue stressed this same sense of female solidarity and an almost inherent lack of competitiveness. While male managers admonished that all leadership included this personalized empathy with subordinates, the female agents whose articles appeared in the *Upstart* added the distinct notion that such personalism was a feminine trait and the mark of a female management style that set women apart from men.[55]

[52]*Items for Agents,* 2 (Jan. 14, 1909), 7 (ELASA).
[53]A.A.R., in *Little Upstart,* 3 (September 1916), 3 (ELASA). See also "Policies and Posies," Ibid., 9 (March 1917), 5 (ELASA).
[54]Imogen Burnham, "An Appreciation," ibid., 5 (November 1916), 2 (ELASA).
[55]For the persistence of this belief, see Ann Hughey and Eric Gelman, "Managing the Woman's Way," *Newsweek,* Mar. 17, 1986, 46–47. This article argues for a distinct female management style, based on such "natural," "instinctive" female qualities as "sympathy," "sensitivity," and "a lack of the killer instinct."

The distinctions female agents made between manly and womanly job attributes is clearly revealed in the different behaviors ascribed to "business girls" and "business women." Women office workers, after the advent of female professionalism around 1900 to at least 1930, stressed the feminine qualities of the business or office girl and the masculine qualities of the business woman. The heroine of a *Saturday Evening Post* story of 1915 had ambitions to be a business woman, the owner of her own advertising agency. In contrast to the office girls she saw around her, she aspired to a "career." Office girls were clock watchers, uncommitted labor, destined forever to be low-paid subordinates.[56] Their relations to their work described by respondents to the BVI survey also reveal this distinction between "girls" and "women" in business. One woman, a former secretary, commented that "I really feel that the business world rubs the bloom from a woman." Another emphasized that secretarial work "tends to make a business woman of her, thereby tending to detract sweet feminine qualities."[57] Thus business women were more like men in their attachment to their work and their allegiance to business values.

In their assertion of the distinctions between male and female managers, *Upstart* writers addressed this issue of gender deviance directly. They emphasized that Mrs. Shaal, though a manager, had retained her womanhood: "A business woman has been defined by other men besides Shakespeare as 'a woman impudent and mannish grown,' but such a description does not apply to Mrs. Shaal. Dainty, refined, with a magnetic charm of manner, . . . she has had such a brilliantly successful career, and yet has lost nothing of her womanly grace and charm."[58] In affirming Shaal's essential femininity, the author denied that management positions necessarily turned women into men. Marie Little addressed the issue of deviance this way: "I think it only fair to remind you that tradition says all life insurance agents are bores. In that case, however, I never found yet a woman agent that was a bore. It seems that that quality is enjoyed by the men alone, and we will let them have it."[59] Little's comment reassured her listeners that to become an agent or manager did not mean that a woman had to become like a man. Further, she suggested that female agents were not bound up in the self-definitions business promoted for women, but approached sales on their own terms. The goal of female life insurance managers and agents, in other words, was to retain social definitions of womanhood and use those attributes as a means of

[56]Maude Radford Warren, "Green Timber," *Saturday Evening Post*, pt. 1, Nov. 20, 1915, 3–5, 38–39, 41–42; pt. 2, Nov. 27, 1915, 19–20, 52.
[57]No. 862, folder 372a, and no. 1641, folder 384b, BVI.
[58]Burnham, "Appreciation," 2.
[59]Little, "Life Insurance," 3.

engaging the work commitment of other women. One way to accomplish this feat—to be a manager without being manly—was to choose a profession not at odds with cultural definitions of woman's place. Advocates saw life insurance sales, like other evolving "women's professions" such as teaching, nursing, and social work, as uniquely suited to women because it called forth and used so-called natural aspects of womanhood.[60] Thus, in the life insurance industry, women could become managers and sales agents without having to adopt male business values. Rather, they could emphasize feminine traits, such as modesty and sweetness. Further, they could draw parallels between such masculine characteristics as aggression and such feminine ones as impudence. In that way work could be an expression of the female self rather than a negation of womanhood. By simultaneously presenting themselves as antagonists to corporate norms—as outsiders—and asserting their close match to the industry's rhetoric of social service—as insiders—they could carve out a female space within a male world.

In the life insurance industry, work could be defined and expressed by an individual's commitment to gender. A woman who wished to escape the deadening aspects of office work, to step outside the time and space of wage labor and into management or sales, had to adopt male business values and behaviors defined as male—to become *like* a man. A woman who became a manager surrendered her female self; a man who did so fulfilled his masculine self. The issue for women agents and managers was not simply political or economic equality of opportunity and experience; it was whether an individual chose a position of strength or one of weakness within an economic and social system shaped by powerful cultural assumptions regarding the gendered self.

Social and individual gender in the office were composed of images and expectations that reinforced and delineated each other. This process was based, ultimately, on the explanations of experience, on the symbols, images, and metaphors available to connect the abstract qualities of hierarchy, status, and power relationships to the specific experiences of managing people, selling insurance, and typing reports. The discussions about manhood and womanhood, the concern with gender deviance, the gendered uses of space and bodily expression fused the economic and social concerns of the life insurance corporation to the individual concerns of workers. The social constructions of gender expressed in the life insurance industry fitted within and informed both the experience of work and the underlying economic and organizational structures of the corporate work system.

[60]For the development of female professions, see Sheila Rothman, *Woman's Proper Place: A History of Changing Ideals and Practices, 1870 to the Present* (New York: Basic Books, 1978), 42–60.

To the extent that definitions of gender behavior were caught up in the experience of work in life insurance, they both legitimized and challenged the power relationships of the corporate labor system. Both men and women in the industry accepted and used a dichotomy of gender to explicate status, to express a commitment or lack of it to labor, and to assert a sense of self in relation to others. The gender analogies of life insurance allowed workers to express a crucial aspect of their personal lives—who they were as men or women—in their work. Glover Hastings and Marie Little, among others, meshed both personal and corporate understandings of gender to explicate their sense of what their work meant. By using gender, workers could draw on a common language and reshape it, describing and defining their work in ways that reinforced rather than undermined their sense of womanhood and manhood.

That workers made their accommodation in gendered terms was in part a response to the structural inequities of the corporation—to the fact that wages, hiring, and status were segregated by sex. In addition, life insurance workers shared the images articulated by executives for other purposes. Executives, after all, used gender symbols precisely because they provided a vocabulary common both to the public and to workers, an Esperanto that bridged differences of class or motivation. Personal concepts of gender, however, imposed constraints and created possibilities that also shaped the institutional system. Managers seldom were able to impose their own dress codes or make actual the corporate family. The social gender system of the life insurance workplace was a product of the way such institutional and personal visions and imperatives were resolved.

CHAPTER EIGHT

"Give the Boys a Trade":
Gender and Job Choice in the 1890s

Ileen A. DeVault

When Pittsburgh's working-class press asked, "What Shall be Done with Daughters?" its answer, in part, was "Teach them all the mysteries of the kitchen, the dining-room and the parlor."[1] No mention was made of wage earning. For sons, the answer was quite different. "Give the Boys a Trade. . . . You will be insuring the happiness and comfort of your sons, the welfare of those who come after them, and discharging a solemn duty you owe to society and the country."[2] What was the significance of this difference?

Because women in the United States historically have not been encouraged to work outside the home, a considerable literature within women's history has dealt with the factors contributing to or militating against their wage-earning activities. We find this emphasis in studies on the feminization of certain occupations, on women's union activities and militance, and on the history of women wage workers in general. This juxtaposition of issues has supplied many of the most exciting connections made in working-class women's history, forcing us to consider the experiential intersections between family and community issues and workplace concerns.[3]

I thank the following people for their comments on this essay: Ava Baron, Marjorie DeVault, Tony Fels, Dana Frank, Lori Ginzberg, and David Montgomery. Patricia Cooper and Walter Licht also commented on a version of this essay presented at the Social Science History Association, November 1988. Though none of these people will be completely satisfied with my responses, they all helped me clarify my thoughts in important ways.

[1]*National Labor Tribune*, Oct. 11, 1879 (hereafter *NLT*).

[2]Ibid., Apr. 16, 1892.

[3]The following very partial list represents a much larger body of scholarship. General works include Alice Kessler-Harris, *Out to Work: A History of Wage-Earning Women in the United States* (New York: Oxford University Press, 1982), and Leslie Woodcock Tentler, *Wage-Earning Women* (New York: Oxford University Press, 1979). One of the best-known works on the feminization of an occupation is Margery W. Davies, *Woman's*

Historians of male wage workers have not similarly had to begin by asking why men entered the labor force. For men, wage earning has been taken for granted. "Men's history" therefore provides no framework sufficient to delineate how young men have viewed their occupational opportunities and choices. But this is exactly the question before us now. Comparing women's job choices with men's does more than simply add a new twist to our understanding of men's lives, however. Such a comparison initially highlights the similarities in the processes of decision making by men and by women. Ironically, these similarities in and of themselves ultimately force us to confront the ways in which expectations about gender roles influence the job choice process. This attention to gender has the potential to provide the most fruitful links between men's family, community, and workplace concerns, just as it has done in regard to women.

We can move toward such a gendered understanding of job decisions by exploring the options faced by teenaged women and men seeking training and employment for office work in Pittsburgh, Pennsylvania, in the 1890s. Clerical work turns out to be an ideal occupation to examine. Working-class families did not necessarily sit down and make "career decisions" as we think of them today with and for their children. Many, perhaps most, did not enjoy the material conditions necessary for such a procedure; others took for granted progressions within occupations or from one occupation to another. At the same time, when a young person from a working-class family decided to seek office employment, it *was* a decision, since clerical work required specific off-the-job training. Thus, while it might be very difficult to discuss, for example, individual or family "choices" to have young working-class men become common laborers, the movement of similarly placed young men into office work allows us to discuss, albeit gingerly, a range of conscious choices and decisions. This process, in turn, provides us with insight into broader issues of job choice, giving us a new realm of exploration for understanding the history of men's as well as women's labor force experiences.

By the 1890s, hundreds of Pittsburgh's young people gained clerical skills in the city's public school system each year. The high school's commercial department, established in 1868, had always focused on transmitting specific business skills. Enrollment records for the school

---

Place Is at the Typewriter: Office Work and Office Workers, 1870–1930 (Philadelphia: Temple University Press, 1982). Examples of the use of such arguments in discussions of women's union activities include the articles in Ruth Milkman, ed., *Women, Work, and Protest* (Boston: Routledge & Kegan Paul, 1985), as well as Carole Turbin, "Beyond Conventional Wisdom: Women's Wage Work, Household Economic Contribution, and Labor Activism in a Mid-Nineteenth-Century Working-Class Community," in *"To Toil the Livelong Day": America's Women at Work, 1780–1980,* ed. Carol Groneman and Mary Beth Norton (Ithaca: Cornell University Press, 1987).

through the 1890s provide a picture of the young people who sought office employment.[4] During that decade the department's student body grew rapidly, simultaneously with changes in its composition. Concurrent with the feminization of the clerical work force, the proportion of young women in the program grew dramatically, especially after the introduction of typewriting into the curriculum in 1894. From the mid-1890s through the first decade of the twentieth century, then, the program's students were about half men and half women.[5]

Who were these aspiring clerical workers? Between 45 and 55 percent of the Commercial Department's students came from working-class families,[6] a percentage lower than working-class representation in the city's population as a whole. But if the Commercial Department underrepresented the working class as a whole, it had an extremely high level of skilled workers in its clientele. While only about 19 percent of Pittsburgh's male workers held skilled manual jobs at the turn of the century, 35 percent of Commercial Department fathers did.[7]

The Commercial Department, then, did not exactly mirror Pittsburgh's residents. The least advantaged members of the population, unskilled workers, were unlikely to have children attending the program. In fact, the high representation of skilled workers' children suggests that the Commercial Department served an elite group within the working class itself. Homeownership figures for the students' families confirm this impression. While only a little over a quarter of the city's population owned homes in 1900, almost half of the Commercial Department students' parents owned their residences in that year.[8] The nativity of Commercial Department students in 1900 also reinforces the idea that the program served a middle group of the city's population. In comparison with the

[4]The extant Commercial Department enrollment records list approximately 3,100 students enrolled from 1890 through 1903. The following collective portrait is based on a sample of 1,844 of these individuals, and a subsample of about 600 of them found in the 1900 census as well.

[5]Pittsburgh, Board of Education, 26th Annual Report (1894), 2; Ileen A. DeVault, "Sons and Daughters of Labor: Class and Clerical Work in Pittsburgh, 1870s–1910s" (Ph.D. diss., Yale University, 1985), 183–86.

[6]Children whose families were headed by manual workers made up 46% of the program's student body. When we examine only fathers' occupations, this predominance of working-class students becomes even clearer: 19% of the fathers were in the unskilled category and 35% in the skilled category, for a total of 54%. See DeVault, "Sons and Daughters of Labor," 203–6.

[7]John Bodnar, Roger Simon, and Michael P. Weber have estimated that manual workers made up 72% of Pittsburgh's male wage earners in 1900: Lives of Their Own: Blacks, Italians, and Poles in Pittsburgh, 1900–1960 (Urbana: University of Illinois Press, 1982), 64, table 4. See also Andrew Dawson, "The Paradox of Dynamic Technological Change and the Labor Aristocracy in the United States, 1880–1914," Labor History, 20 (1979), 325–51.

[8]U.S. Department of Commerce, Census Office, Twelfth Census of the United States, Taken in the Year 1900: Population, Part II, vol. 2 (Washington, D.C.: U.S. Government Printing Office, 1902), 709, table 107. Twenty-six percent of Pittsburgh's population owned their own homes in 1900, while 49% of the Commercial Department parents did.

population of the city as a whole, foreign-born residents were greatly underrepresented in the department, while U.S.-born Pittsburghers were overrepresented.[9]

Why did these relatively well-off working-class adolescents decide to educate themselves for office work? Examining the comparative qualities of clerical work and other job possibilities for both women and men both demonstrates the general factors involved in job choice at the turn of the century and begins to explicate the operation and implications of gender differences.

Our thinking about women's job choices in the late nineteenth century has been informed, as were the choices of women at the time, by the relatively few occupations open to them. Both female socialization and employers' prejudices limited the jobs considered by women at the turn of the century.[10] Most of these wage-earning women were young, single, and living with their parents. Clerical workers provide the extreme example of this tendency: as a group, they were younger than other women workers and even more likely than others to be single and living at home.[11] What considerations did such young women bring to their perusal of the available jobs?

Most studies of wage-earning women begin by examining economic considerations, including both wage levels and the steadiness of employment. Even the relatively well-off working-class women contemplating clerical jobs would have considered the immediate material benefits of their options for wage earning. A young woman who was not self-supporting would contribute to her family's income, either directly, by handing her wages over to her parents, or indirectly, by using her earnings to buy her own clothing or to supply other needs.[12] At the same

[9]Almost half (49%) of the program's students were the native-born children of native-born parents. Most of the rest were children of foreign-born parents (42%). Foreign-born students made up only 6% of the student body, and 3% of the students were black. See DeVault, "Sons and Daughters of Labor," 208, table 4.2. The comparable figures for Pittsburghers aged 15 to 19 in 1900 are 34%, 43%, 18%, and 5%. See U.S. Department of Commerce, Twelfth Census, 1900: Population, 338, table 32.

[10]Elyce J. Rotella, From Home to Office: U.S. Women at Work, 1870–1930 (Ann Arbor, Mich.: UMI Research Press, 1981), 30–37; Valerie Kincade Oppenheimer, The Female Labor Force in the United States: Demographic and Economic Factors Governing Its Growth and Changing Composition, Population Monograph Series, no. 5 (Berkeley: Institute of International Studies, 1970), 68–70.

[11]Rotella, From Home to Office, 115; Davies, Woman's Place Is at the Typewriter, 74–76.

[12]U.S. Department of Labor, Fourth Annual Report of the Commissioner of Labor, 1888: Working Women in Large Cities (Washington, D.C.: U.S. Government Printing Office, 1889), 64–65. This study found firm evidence for the participation of women workers in family economies. Of the women studied, 86% lived at home; more than half contributed their entire earnings to their family. The study also reported that "the 5.25 persons to each family [of a working woman] were supported by 2.78 persons at work." Also see Rotella, From Home to Office, 41–43, 50–51; Mary P. Ryan, Womanhood in America: From Co-

time, since these young, single women did not plan to support themselves permanently, their concerns would have focused on initial and relatively short-term wages, not on opportunities for promotion and wage increases over the course of years.[13]

This short-term view of wage earning both grew out of and influenced more subjective opinions of their choices as well. Looking forward to their futures as wives and mothers, young women entering the labor market sought "appropriate" employment that would either prepare them for or at the least not "ruin" them for their future roles.[14] Questions of propriety in wage earning quickly shaded over into murkier issues of the relative status of different occupations. Individual women combined different aspects of all these considerations in their employment decisions.

In Pittsburgh as elsewhere in the country, women faced a labor market in which only a few jobs were open to them—jobs highly segregated by sex. Although domestic service and the needle trades remained the top two female occupations in 1900, over half of Pittsburgh's women wage earners worked in other "typical" female jobs in the city's cigar, electrical manufacturing, food, and other industries.[15] The women students of the Commercial Department left no journals or memoirs describing how they thought about employment and the various occupations open to them. However, locating these individuals and their families in the 1900 federal census provides some clues. In order to recreate the options as perceived by young women preparing for clerical work and thereby illustrate women's job choices, in what follows I compare office jobs with the other three most common occupations of the sisters of the aspiring female clerical workers: sales, the needle trades, and teaching.[16]

---

lonial Times to the Present: (New York: New Viewpoints, 1979), 124; Tentler, *Wage-Earning Women*, 85.

[13]Gary Cross and Peter Shergold, " 'We Think We Are of the Oppressed': Gender, White-Collar Work, and Grievances of Late Nineteenth-Century Women," *Labor History*, 28 (1987), 38–42, 48–49.

[14]Kessler-Harris, *Out of Work*, 128.

[15]U.S. Department of Commerce and Labor, Bureau of the Census, *Occupations at the Twelfth Census, 1900* (Washington, D.C.: U.S. Government Printing Office, 1904), 682–83, table 43. Elizabeth Beardsley Butler described many of these jobs in her study for the Pittsburgh Survey, *Women and the Trades* (1909; rpt. Pittsburgh: University of Pittsburgh Press, 1984). In her article "Technology and Women's Work: The Lives of Working-Class Women in Pittsburgh, 1870–1900," *Labor History*, 17 (1976), 58–72, Susan J. Kleinberg overstated the impact on women workers of Pittsburgh's heavy industrial base. In fact, Pittsburgh's female labor force participation rates were comparable to those of other late-nineteenth-century expanding midwestern industrial cities such as Buffalo, Cleveland, and Detroit.

[16]I located 424 of the female Commercial Department students in the 1900 manuscript census. The families of these women included 261 female siblings listed as gainfully employed, 106 of them as clerical workers. Of 155 sisters who did not seek clerical jobs, 21% worked as teachers, 24% as saleswomen, and almost 24% in the needle trades. See

Table 8.1. Working conditions and benefits for four female occupational groups, 1890s

Occupational groups	Weekly wages[a]	Weekly hours[a]	Unemployment (percent)[b]		Benefits/conditions[c]
			1890	1900	
Clerical workers	$8.00–9.00	54–57	5%	9%	Might be paid for
Clerks	6.92		4	7	vacations, illness
Stenographers					Safe, clean working
and typists	9.55		8	13	conditions
Bookkeepers	9.08		5	9	
Teachers	12.00 (50 weeks) 16.67 (36 weeks)	32½ (school hours)	38	58	Summers off Crowded market Supervision of personal life
Saleswomen	6.00–7.00	58	8	13	Seasonal overtime and unemployment Poor working conditions
Needle trades	6.00	58	11	21	Seasonal
Milliners	7.24		–	26	Wide range of working conditions
Dressmakers	6.50		–	18	
Seamstresses	5.50		–	19	
Factory operatives	4.84		–	–	

[a]*Annual Report of the Secretary of Internal Affairs of the Commonwealth of Pennsylvania*, pt. 3, *Industrial Statistics* (Harrisburg, 1894), sec. A; U.S. Bureau of Labor, *Work and Wages of Men, Women, and Children*, 11th Annual Report of the Commissioner of Labor, 1895–96 (Washington, D.C.: U.S. Government Printing Office, 1897); and U.S. Bureau of Labor, *A Compilation of Wages in Commercial Countries from Official Sources*, 15th Annual Report of the Commissioner of Labor, 1900 (Washington, D.C.: U.S. Government Printing Office, 1900). For saleswomen and the needle trades, also see Elizabeth Beardsley Butler, *Women and the Trades* (1909; rpt. Pittsburgh: University of Pittsburgh Press, 1984), 408–9. For teachers' wages, see Lila Ver Planck North, "Pittsburgh Schools," in *The Pittsburgh District: Civic Frontage*, ed. Paul Underwood Kellogg (New York: Survey Associates, 1914), 269; Pittsburgh Board of Education, *37th–38th Annual Report* (1905–6), 11–12.

[b]U.S.Department of the Interior, Census Office, *Report on Population of the United States at the Eleventh Census: 1890*, pt. 2 (Washington, D.C.: U.S. Government Printing Office, 1897), 712–13, table 118; U.S. Department of Commerce and Labor, Bureau of the Census, *Occupations at the Twelfth Census, 1900* (Washington, D.C.: U.S. Government Printing Office, 1904), 682–83, table 43.

[c]See Ileen A. DeVault, "Sons and Daughters of Labor: Class and Clerical Work in Pittsburgh, 1870s–1910s" (Ph.D. diss., Yale University, 1985), 87–105.

Table 8.1 presents the material conditions of women in these four occupational categories—clerical work, teaching, sales, and the needle

DeVault, "Sons and Daughters of Labor," 96–97. These three occupations also showed up most commonly in late-nineteenth-century discussions of the female jobs "replaced" by office work.

trades. Teaching provided the highest wages, though teachers also experienced the highest levels of unemployment. Clerical wages and working conditions compared favorably with both saleswork and the needle trades. Both clerical work and teaching required some sort of formal training before one entered the job market. In return for this investment in time, energy, and money, women in these jobs gained material benefits in terms of both wages and working conditions. Although average wages were not as high for clerical workers as for teachers, there were many more office positions available. Investment in clerical training provided a more sure "return."

Young women's choices took into account much more than simply material conditions, however. Even as opportunities for women's wage earning increased, ethnic divisions contributed to and reinforced the hierarchy of desirability within the female job market. Table 8.2 illustrates these divisions. Immigrant women dominated the ranks of domestic servants and of workers in specific manufacturing occupations, such as tenement cigar makers. Other manufacturing jobs drew most heavily upon native-born women with immigrant parents. Saleswork also attracted women of foreign parentage, though native-born women with native-born parents were represented in this occupation beyond their proportion in the female work force as a whole. Teachers included almost equal proportions of native-born women with native-born and with foreign-born parents. Virtually all of the city's clerical workers were born in the United States; 50 percent of them had American-born parents, while the parents of another 42 percent were immigrants, mostly of German and Irish stock.[17] These divisions developed from the convoluted interaction of English-language requirements for some jobs, employers' prejudices and desires for a malleable work force, and the preferences and prejudices of the women workers and their families.[18]

These ethnic variations highlight the less tangible qualities of clerical work for Pittsburgh's female wage earners. The female labor market exhibited the tensions inherent in the widening economic and social gap between native-born or old immigrant group workers and the city's new immigrants from southern and eastern Europe. Maintaining the ethnic identifications of certain occupations encouraged native-born women and those from the old immigrant groups from northwestern Europe to enter the labor force. Both clerical occupations and teaching provided waged work virtually "untainted" by any peer contact with the new

[17]U.S. Department of Commerce and Labor, Bureau of the Census, *Statistics of Women at Work* (Washington, D.C.: U.S. Government Printing Office, 1907), 286–89, table 28.
[18]See Ryan, *Womanhood in America*, 120–21; Kessler-Harris, *Out to Work*, 137–38; Maurine Weiner Greenwald, Introduction to Butler, *Women and the Trades* (1984), xvii.

Table 8.2. Nativity of Pittsburgh's female labor force, 1890, 1900, 1910, by job category (percent)

	Native-born			
	(native-born parents)	(foreign-born parents)	Foreign-born	Nonwhite
1890				
Total female work force	25.1%	36.5%	37.3%	4.1%
Clerical workers	40.3	51.1	8.3	0.4
Teachers	47.6	44.9	6.8	0.7
Saleswomen	35.2	54.7	10.0	0.2
Needle trades	30.4	49.1	18.4	2.1
Servants	18.6	27.1	48.6	5.7
Female population	31.3	38.5	27.5	2.7
1900				
Total female work force	28.4	37.6	26.7	7.3
Clerical workers	50.1	42.5	6.9	0.5
Teachers	46.5	45.5	7.5	0.5
Saleswomen	35.3	51.5	13.0	0.2
Needle trades	31.4	47.8	17.7	3.1
All manufacturing occupations	27.9	49.2	20.6	2.3
Servants	17.8	28.4	41.0	12.8
Female population	33.2	39.1	23.5	4.2
1910				
Total female work force	30.6	36.6	24.6	8.3
Clerical workers	50.7	43.5	5.5	0.4
Teachers	49.0	41.1	9.4	0.5
Saleswomen	37.8	50.4	11.2	0.6
Needle trades	35.1	41.2	19.1	4.7
Servants	15.6	21.1	46.2	17.1
Female population	34.0	37.7	23.6	4.7

Sources: U.S. Department of the Interior, Census Office, *Report on Population of the United States at the Eleventh Census: 1890*, pt. 2 (Washington, D.C.: U.S. Government Printing Office, 1897), 712–13, table 118; U.S. Department of Commerce and Labor, Bureau of the Census, *Occupations at the Twelfth Census, 1900* (Washington, D.C.: U.S. Government Printing Office, 1904), 682–83, table 43; U.S. Department of Commerce, Bureau of the Census, *Population: 1910* (Washington, D.C.: U.S. Government Printing Office, 1914), 4: 591–92, table VIII.

immigrants.[19] Given teaching's limited employment opportunities and crowded applicant pool, the rapid growth of clerical work made it an ideal aim for young native-born women.

[19]Native-born teachers came into contact with immigrants, but as their superiors, not as their peers.

Several other qualities of clerical work also contributed to its high status in the female working-class job market. A stenographer or typist in a working-class family reflected the family's material well-being. If not exactly the conspicuous consumption of the middle classes, it was a kind of "conspicuous employment," representing a family's investment in time, education, and accouterments.[20] Clerical work required first of all a specific and relatively high level of education. At a time when only a small portion of teenagers attended school beyond the eighth grade, sending a child to school beyond the compulsory age of fourteen suggested to friends and neighbors a secure and comfortable standard of living.[21] Having a daughter attending the high school also implied that the family could afford to forgo her household work and take advantage of the ready-made clothes and store-bought foodstuffs becoming increasingly available at the turn of the century. But the Commercial Department was not just "high school": the program trained these young women for the top of the working-class female occupational hierarchy.[22]

Office employment also required a high standard of clothing; just entering the clerical job market called for a substantial investment in appropriate attire.[23] Even if a working-class clerical worker kept her entire salary for herself and therefore did not need to dip into the family coffer to maintain her wardrobe, she had to own at least parts of the wardrobe simply in order to apply for jobs. Over the years, women office workers and their advocates often discussed what came to be known as "the clothes problem." Possible solutions to the "clothes problem" all required substantial material resources and therefore contributed to the conspicuous employment qualities of clerical work.[24]

Furthermore, while most female clerical workers evinced little interest in advancing into middle management positions, clerical work did hold out the promise of a different sort of "promotional opportunity." Encouraged by rumor, fiction, and suggestive jokes, young women working in offices could always hope to marry the boss—or his dashing young

[20]This is a variation on what Hanna Papanek identified as wives' work of "family status production." See Papanek, "Family Status Production: The 'Work' and 'Non-Work' of Women," *Signs: Journal of Women in Culture and Society,* 4 (1979), 775–81.

[21]Of the children eligible for high school in Pittsburgh in 1908, 5.1% were enrolled: U.S. Immigration Commission, *The Children of Immigrants in Schools* (Washington, D.C.: U.S. Government Printing Office, 1911), 9.

[22]Susan B. Carter and Mark Prus, "The Labor Market and the American High School Girl, 1890–1928," *Journal of Economic History,* 42 (March 1982), 166.

[23]Remington Typewriter Company, *How to Become a Successful Stenographer* (n.p., 1916), 62, 65–66; Peter R. Shergold, *Working-Class Life: The "American Standard" in Comparative Perspective, 1899–1913* (Pittsburgh: University of Pittsburgh Press, 1982), 169, table 44, and 199, table 56. A woman's tailored wool suit cost $10 in Pittsburgh in 1901, one-eighth of the average Pennsylvania family's clothing expenditure in that year.

[24]Remington Typewriter Company, *How to Become a Successful Stenographer,* 62–63; *Phonographic World,* June 1900, 593 (hereafter *PW*).

son. Though these highest of hopes were rarely fulfilled in reality, office work did provide women with employment that did not isolate them entirely from male companionship, even if actual tasks were segregated by sex. Fellow clerical workers, company sales personnel, and visiting businessmen all became part of an expanded pool of marital possibilities.[25]

Clerical work thus occupied a special position within Pittsburgh's female job market, one that allows us to examine women's occupational choices and the complex interaction between material and subjective considerations and short- and long-term goals. In respect to material considerations such as wages, hours, seasonality, and working conditions, office work enjoyed considerable advantages over female occupations other than teaching. In the case of teaching, a tight job market often outweighed that occupation's other benefits. The rapid expansion of clerical work at the turn of the century provided constant openings for qualified young women. At the same time, clerical work also offered less tangible status benefits. The conspicuous nature of the training and apparel necessary for entry into a clerical job reinforced ethnic and intra-class divisions, within both the female job market itself and the city's working-class neighborhoods. Work in Pittsburgh's offices also held a special appeal to young working-class women as popular fiction contributed to fantasies of socializing with bankers and industrial magnates in downtown streets.

This brief outline of the factors considered by young women entering the clerical work force illuminates the basic considerations that went into women's job choices. The immediate material conditions of a job, such as wages and working conditions, were important whether the individual woman was self-supporting or planned to contribute to her family's wage pool, directly or indirectly. Beyond this consideration, less objective factors also entered into women's decisions. Especially for the young women who made up the majority of women wage earners at the turn of the century, more subtle distinctions involving status gradations played a large role in decisions once material goals were achieved. Such considerations operated both for the individual young woman and for her family. Maintaining a young working woman's personal honor was believed to affect her marriage changes in the future and also reflected her family's social standing in the community.

Young men's objectives upon entering the job market were both similar to and different from women's. Men, like most women, might first hold an immediate objective: to gain employment and contribute to the

[25]See DeVault, "Sons and Daughters of Labor," 326–36; short stories in NLT, Apr. 20 and Aug. 3, 1899, and in PW, 1905; Cross and Shergold, " 'We Think We Are of the Oppressed,' " 47–48.

economy of their family of origin.[26] Men also held an explicitly gendered long-range objective. In line with their assumptions that they would eventually become the primary wage earners of their own families, they took into account a range of factors that influenced their future earning capabilities. Necessity forced many young men (even among those who aspired to clerical employment) to focus on the first objective; immediate earning power, at almost any level, outweighed considerations of long-term benefits. Others enjoyed material conditions that allowed them to concentrate on the second objective, participating in extended training in order to gain future benefits. For these young men, short-term economic gain became incidental, or, in some cases, temporarily irrelevant.

In moving toward both short- and long-term objectives, four categories of considerations came into play. The first category includes the material benefits of different jobs—wages foremost, but also hours and other working conditions. These material benefits had both short- and long-term aspects; beginning wages often varied widely from the possible peak earning rate for an occupation, and peak earnings were reached at different ages. In addition, hours of work and safety provisions on the job played an important role in determining the overall length of a man's working life.[27] Beyond these material conditions, young men also had to consider the training required for different jobs: was there any? how was it acquired? how did it affect the course of earnings over time? Often closely related to training was the opportunity for promotion. Were low beginning wages or a long and possibly expensive training period eventually rewarded by compensatory remuneration of one sort or another? Finally, perceptions of the status of various occupations also played a role in young men's job decisions. These status perceptions involved competing cultural values arising from class and ethnicity as well as from the rapidly changing ideals of the dominant culture. Occupational status was worked out from the interplay of these values. Young men's job decisions took into account all of these factors.

The task of comparing clerical work with other job opportunities is trickier for men than it is for women, if for no other reason than that men have a wider range of options before them, even when limitations imposed by class and ethnicity are taken into consideration. An examina-

[26]Shergold assumes that children stop contributing to family income at 21 years of age: *Working-Class Life*, 80. Other research has found variously that most people married in their early twenties and that half remained single into their late 20s: John Modell, Frank F. Furstenberg, Jr., and Theodore Hershberg, "Social Change and Transitions to Adulthood in Historical Perspective," in *Philadelphia: Work, Space, Family, and Group Experience in the Nineteenth Century: Essays Toward an Interdisciplinary History of the City*, ed. Theodore Hershberg (New York: Oxford University Press, 1981), 324.

[27]See Roger L. Ransom and Richard Sutch, "The Labor of Older Americans: Retirement of Men On and Off the Job, 1870–1937," *Journal of Economic History*, 46 (1986), 23–26.

tion of the occupations of the brothers of the male Commercial Department students illustrates the problem.[28] Among a group of 118 brothers who were not themselves in clerical jobs, occupations ranged from laborers through sausage makers, wire winders, glassworkers, carpenters, draftsmen, machinists, tobacco dealers, dentists, brokers, and many others. However, when grouped together by characteristics of skill, industry, and status, the most common of the brothers' occupations fall into three groups. The first group consists of sales jobs—low-level white-collar positions enjoying social status roughly equivalent to that of clerical work. Over 18 percent of the clerical workers' brothers held sales positions, well over the representation of salesworkers in the work force as a whole.[29] The second group consists of skilled trades for which the time required to be spent in training was basically equal to that devoted to formal education for clerical positions. Over 28 percent of the brothers entered skilled trades. The third group represents less choice than necessity. It consists of those jobs whose very short training periods matched their low returns in both social status and wages. Laborers and unskilled or semiskilled factory workers make up this group. Over a quarter of the aspiring clerical workers' brothers found employment in such jobs, 17 percent as laborers and almost 9 percent in miscellaneous factory jobs.

We can begin to explore the comparative advantages and disadvantages of these three groups of jobs, and thereby to explicate men's job choices, by examining wage rates. Though wages alone cannot tell the entire story, they do highlight a number of the objectives young men pursued when they sought jobs.

Pittsburgh's male clerical workers, like male office workers elsewhere, earned about $15 a week at the turn of the century. Within and among different clerical occupations, men's wages varied widely. These variations seem to reflect long-term opportunities for male clerical workers. Thus male clerks' earnings averaged about $11 a week but ranged from a low of $3 to a high of almost $29. Bookkeepers earned on average over $19 a week, though here the range of wages was astounding, from a minimum of $5 per week to a maximum of $40 per week. Such wide variations in earnings within occupational categories suggest changes over the course of years. Beginning their careers at fairly low wages, male

---

[28]Of the male students, 214 were found in the 1900 manuscript census. The families of these men included 201 male siblings listed as gainfully employed, 83 of them as clerical workers.

[29]Salesmen made up about 3.5% of the male work force in 1890, 1900, and 1910: U.S. Department of the Interior, Census Office, *Report on Population of the United States at the Eleventh Census: 1890*, pt. 2 (Washington, D.C.: U.S. Government Printing Office, 1897), 712–13, table 118; Bureau of the Census, *Occupations at the Twelfth Census, 1900*, 682–83, table 43; U.S. Department of Commerce, Bureau of the Census, *Population: 1910* (Washington, D.C.: U.S. Government Printing Office, 1914), 4: 591–92, table VIII.

clerical workers could hope eventually to earn $30 to $40 a week. This career view of clerical jobs becomes even clearer when the wages for these jobs are compared with the wages of male stenographers, the most rapidly feminized occupation. The range of stenographic pay for men was relatively small, from $10 to $15. The predominance of women stenographers affected these male wages, as did assumptions that while a man might *begin* his career as a stenographer, he would soon move on to a different and more highly paid position. As one observer noted, "What gentleman engaged in the position of stenographer, does not look forward to the day when he will be the dictator, and someone else will be occupying the position he now occupies?"[30]

Like the wages of male clerical workers, the wages of Pittsburgh's salesmen varied greatly, from a minimum of $8 a week to $40 or more. Most of this variation arose from the different situations in which salesmen found themselves, and particularly from the distinction between retail and wholesale positions.[31] Retail salesmen earned between $8 and $25 a week. Early-twentieth-century observers attributed these variations to years on the job.[32] At the same time, salesmen for manufacturing firms earned considerably higher wages than their retail counterparts. Researchers for a 1900 federal study examined the wage records of fourteen of the country's major corporations and found that these companies' traveling salesmen earned an average of about $2,000 a year, or $40 a week. The minimum reported was $1,079 ($21.58 a week) and the maximum was $5,000 a year ($100 a week).[33]

To some extent, retail and wholesale jobs represent the difference between entry-level sales positions for men and their possible long-term financial benefits. For salesmen, then, both the range of wages within the two types of sales jobs and the difference in the overall wages between them provide evidence of the long-range material benefits of sales jobs for young men. These differences are also apparent in the age and marital status of men in the two types of sales jobs. Census figures reveal that salesmen in stores tended to be young (about 40 percent were under twenty-four years of age in the 1890s) and a majority of them were sin-

[30]*PW*, March 1889, 144; DeVault, "Sons and Daughters of Labor," 121–23.

[31]U.S. Bureau of Labor, *A Compilation of Wages in Commercial Countries from Official Sources: 15th Annual Report of the Commissioner of Labor, 1900* (Washington, D.C.: U.S. Government Printing Office, 1900), and *Work and Wages of Men, Women, and Children: 11th Annual Report of the Commissioner of Labor, 1895–96* (Washington, D.C.: U.S. Government Printing Office, 1897); Meyer Bloomfield, ed., *Readings in Vocational Guidance* (Boston: Ginn, 1915), 527.

[32]John R. Commons and William M. Leiserson, "Wage-Earners of Pittsburgh," in *Wage-Earning Pittsburgh*, ed. Paul Underwood Kellogg (New York: Survey Associates, 1914), 132.

[33]Jeremiah W. Jenks, for U.S. Department of Labor, "Trusts and Industrial Combinations," Bulletin no. 29 (Washington, D.C.: U.S. Government Printing Office, 1900), 684.

gle. In 1900, over half of the salesmen in stores were unmarried, while only a third of commercial travelers were.[34] To some extent, then, the different sales occupations represented different life stages. However, the retail sales ranks did include some older, married men as well. Sheer numbers worked against movement from retail to wholesale positions, since retail workers made up at least 80 percent of all Pittsburgh salesmen. While some of these men's colleagues eventually moved from retail into wholesale positions, others remained in an occupation dominated by men less encumbered by family responsibilities, a situation that worked to lower wages. Salesmen's wages have thus suggested to us not only the movement up from beginners' wages but also the operation and limitations of one set of promotional opportunities.

The wages of skilled manual workers illustrate a different type of career ladder and the training it required. Of the 28 percent of the clerical workers' brothers who entered skilled trades, 11.5 percent became machinists, while almost 8 percent entered the building trades and just over 6 percent became skilled workers in the iron and steel industry. The young men who entered these occupations began with low wages and few skills, but counted on reaching the ultimate security provided by skilled trades. Table 8.3 illustrates the average earnings possible for three of these skilled occupations: machinists, carpenters, and plumbers. The table does not include skilled occupations in the iron and steel industry because comparable data are not available. The most highly skilled workers in iron and steel, such as rollers and heaters, earned as much as $35 to $45 a week at the turn of the century.[35] Theoretical fifty-two-week earnings for these men reached $2,000 and over, but in fact many worked only half to three-quarters of the year, so that they actually earned only $1,000 to $1,500 annually.[36]

All of these skilled trades required some sort of training period, though not always a formal apprenticeship. In the iron and steel mills, both working-class tradition and employer policies encouraged a process

[34]U.S. Census Office, *Report on Population . . . 1890*, pt. 2, 712–13, table 188; U.S. Bureau of the Census, *Occupations at the Twelfth Census, 1900*, 682–83, table 43.

[35]Jones & Laughlin Steel Corporation, Pittsburgh Works, Payroll and Tabulating Department, "Earning Records, 1862–1901," in Archives of Industrial Society, Hillman Library, University of Pittsburgh, records a maximum for heaters of $42.00, for rollers of $45.50; John A. Fitch, *The Steel Workers* (New York: Charities Publication Committee, 1910), 301–5, gives $37.32 as a maximum for heaters, $44.58 for rollers.

[36]David Brody, *Steelworkers in America: The Nonunion Era* (New York: Harper & Row, 1969), 39–40. See also Alexander Keyssar, *Out of Work: The First Century of Unemployment in Massachusetts* (Cambridge: Cambridge University Press, 1986), 58 and 308–19, tables A.1, A.2, A.4. Charles A. Gulick, Jr., claimed that even in the "prosperous year" of 1910 it was probably impossible to work more than forty-five weeks: *Labor Policy of the United States Steel Corporation* (New York: Columbia University Press, 1924), 63. The NLT constantly noted which mills were open or shut, and the general market conditions for iron and steel.

Table 8.3. Annual earnings possible in three skilled occupations, Pittsburgh, 1890–1908

	Average weekly wages	Earnings for 52-week year	Workers unemployed 1–3 months (percent)	Earnings for 39-week year
Machinists				
1890s[a]	$12.25	$ 637.00	8.7%[b]	$ 477.75
Before 1904[c]			9.0[d]	
Union scale:				
Minimum	16.20	842.40		631.80
Maximum	21.60	1,123.20		842.40
1906[e]	18.49	961.48		721.11
Carpenters				
1890s[a]	16.74	870.48	14.8[b]	652.86
1890s[f]	18.79	977.08		732.81
1903 (union)[g]	21.00	1,092.00	18.3[d]	819.00
1906[e]	21.02	1,093.04		819.78
1907–1908[c]				
Union scale	24.00	1,248.00		936.00
Nonunion	21.00	1,092.00		819.00
Plumbers				
1890s[a]	18.53	963.56	8.9[b]	722.67
1894 (union)[c]	21.00	1,092.00		819.00
1901 (union)[c]	24.00	1,248.00	9.0[d]	936.00
1907 (union)[c]	27.00	1,404.00		1,053.00

[a]U.S. Department of Labor, *Wages in the United States and Europe, 1870 to 1898*, Bulletin no. 18 (September 1898), 678, 673, 681.

[b]U.S. Department of the Interior, Census Office, *Report on Population of the United States at the Eleventh Census: 1890*, pt. 2 (Washington, D.C.: U.S. Government Printing Office, 1897), 712–13, table 118.

[c]John R. Commons and William M. Leiserson, "Wage Earners of Pittsburgh," in *Wage-Earning Pittsburgh*, ed. Paul Underwood Kellogg (New York: Survey Associates, 1914), 140, 154, 162.

[d]U.S. Department of Commerce and Labor, Bureau of the Census, *Occupations at the Twelfth Census, 1900* (Washington, D.C.: U.S. Government Printing Office, 1904), 680–81, table 43.

[e]Peter R. Shergold, *Working-Class Life: The "American Standard" in Comparative Perspective, 1899–1913* (Pittsburgh: University of Pittsburgh Press, 1982), 46, 62.

[f]*Annual Report of the Secretary of Internal Affairs of the Commonwealth of Pennsylvania*, pt. 3, *Industrial Statistics* (Harrisburg, 1894), B.3.

[g]*Annual Report of the Secretary of Internal Affairs of the Commonwealth of Pennsylvania*, pt. 3, *Industrial Statistics* (Harrisburg, 1903), 469 (returns from United Brotherhood of Carpenters and Joiners).

whereby men worked their way up from unskilled to skilled positions. This process could take years, though gaining a position through relatives who worked at the same mill might speed it up some.[37] The other occupations under consideration had more formal apprenticeships,

[37]Commons and Leiserson, "Wage-Earners of Pittsburgh," 141–42; Fitch, *Steel Workers*, 13, 141–42.

though their actual operation depended on union strength in the particular trade. Plumbers and steamfitters maintained the strictest apprenticeships, ranging from three to five years in length. The 1907 union scale, for example, specified four classes of workers: the steamfitters themselves, earning $24.00 a week; junior steamfitters, or "second men," young men in the last years of their apprenticeships, earning $16.50 a week; "experienced helpers," apprentices after their first three months at the trade, earning $13.50; and "inexperienced helpers," who earned only $9.00 a week.[38]

Other trades encountered situations that made it impossible for them to regulate apprenticeships fully. Carpentry apprenticeships supposedly took three years in the mid-1890s, but even then, many carpenters never served any at all. On the one hand, many young men picked up carpentry skills without formal training. On the other hand, by the turn of the century mechanization began to minimize skills further, as carpenters increasingly only put together pieces produced in planing mills.[39] Machinists experienced the most dire consequences of the increased division of labor. Despite their increasing numbers, by 1907 only about a third of Pittsburgh's machinists were "all-round" men, able to operate a wide range of machines. The rest were "specialists," operating a single machine that performed a single function. The all-round men, generally members of the machinists' union in Pittsburgh, still maintained formal apprenticeships and received the highest wages.[40]

In all these occupations, then, young men could expect to earn moderate wages during several years of training before achieving the high wages of the skilled positions. Unlike the formal education required for clerical positions, training for skilled trades combined immediate earnings with future possibilities.

Of course, many young men did not have the luxury of plotting out this type of long-term strategy. Over a quarter of the aspiring clerical workers' brothers found employment as laborers or factory operatives. These jobs usually required no experience; starting wages equaled peak wages. Almost 17 percent of the brothers were listed as laborers in 1900. Some of these men may in fact have been working in entry-level positions in the skilled trades, but others were concerned more with immediate employment than with future opportunities. Laborers earned between $7 and $12 a week, depending on the employing industry. Easy entrance created a highly competitive situation. Many were hired by the day or by

[38] *Annual Report of the Secretary of Internal Affairs of the Commonwealth of Pennsylvania*, pt. 3, *Industrial Statistics* (Harrisburg, 1894), sec. B.

[39] Ibid., B.4; Walter E. Weyl and A. M. Sakolski, for U.S. Department of Commerce and Labor, *Conditions of Entrance to the Principal Trades*, Bulletin no. 67 (1906), 690, 694.

[40] Commons and Leiserson, "Wage-Earners of Pittsburgh," 140–41; Weyl and Sakolski, "Conditions of Entrance," 686–89.

the hour as casual laborers; even the high unemployment figures given in the 1890 and 1900 census probably underestimated the tenuous nature of this type of employment.[41]

The almost 9 percent of the brothers employed in miscellaneous factory jobs worked in positions virtually unknown to their fathers, in the new world of semiskilled factory work. Businesses such as the Westinghouse electrical supply plants in East Pittsburgh hired these young men at weekly wages between $9 and $12. Though these wages barely differed from those for laboring jobs, factory employment provided more job security. These positions also represented the city's expanding industries. While skilled industrial trades declined in the city's traditional industries such as iron and steel and glass, the new factory jobs expanded.[42] They provided steady work to an increasing portion of the city's work force.

This discussion of wage rates faced by male clerical workers and their brothers has thus touched on at least three out of our four initial job choice objectives: immediate and long-term financial gains, promotional opportunities, and training requirements. How did the perceived status of various jobs—the fourth objective—enter into the picture? As we will see, status distinctions involved all of the factors already discussed and more.

A short story in Pittsburgh's working-class press in 1898 began with the following mock job advertisement: "Wanted—A bright boy to begin at the bottom of the ladder in my office and gradually work up by his own conscientious efforts until I can take him into partnership and marry him to my only daughter."[43] This male version of the typical success-through-marriage story of women's fiction offered both romance and promotion. Not only fiction promulgated such dreams of success. Journals directed toward clerical workers assured their male readers that advancement was not only possible but forthcoming. The encouragement offered actually held out two possibilities for promotion. The most widely talked about was also the least likely: the young man's meteoric

[41]Shergold, *Working-Class Life*, 240–41, table 2; Commons and Leiserson, "Wage-Earners of Pittsburgh," 119–21. In 1890, 27.47% of laborers were unemployed for one to twelve months; in 1900, 37.58%: U.S. Census Office, *Report on Population ... 1890*, pt.2, 712–13, table 188; U.S. Bureau of the Census, *Occupations at the Twelfth Census, 1900*, 682–83, table 43.

[42]U.S. Department of Commerce, Bureau of the Census, *Thirteenth Census of the United States, 1910: Manufactures, 1909, Reports by States, with Statistics for Principal Cities* (Washington, D.C.: U.S. Government Printing Office, 1912); Commons and Leiserson, "Wage-Earners of Pittsburgh," 135; Glenn E. McLaughlin, *Growth of American Manufacturing Areas: A Comparative Analysis with Special Emphasis on Trends in the Pittsburgh District* (Pittsburgh: University of Pittsburgh, Bureau of Business Research, 1938), 195.

[43]"An 1897 Boy's Story," *NLT*, Apr. 7, 1898.

rise to partnership and wealth. Arguing against the effortlessness of fiction, other authors emphasized individuals' skills and initiative, stating repeatedly that promotion within business bureaucracies came from individual effort.[44]

But less sensational promotional goals also existed. In the course of a *Phonographic World* debate over the merits of business versus railroad office work, one of the railroad proponents pointed out that, in addition to promotional opportunities, railroad work assured the clerical worker of employment unaffected by business failures.[45] Especially for working-class youths, well aware of the vagaries of the economy, this kind of bureaucratic stability might have been as attractive as the more sensational success stories.

The actual availability of promotional opportunities is quite difficult to ascertain. For example, the majority of railway officials in the late nineteenth century began their railroad employment in clerical and sales positions, although, as Stuart Morris has pointed out, "the number of higher executive positions relative to the total number of employees was never very high."[46] Some railroad clerks realized this. The *Locomotive Firemen's Magazine*, commenting in 1902 on the formation of the Brotherhood of Railway Clerks two years earlier, pointed out that some clerks had finally "realized that all clerks could not hope to be 'general managers' and most of them would spend their days trying to 'figure out' how a $40-salary can be made to pay the expenses of an American family."[47] The same situation prevailed in banks, especially as they expanded and the number of low-level clerical workers mushroomed, and in virtually all offices; as businesses elaborated office hierarchies, they created many more clerical than managerial positions.[48] Nonetheless, for young men making initial job choices, rumors of possible futures might easily outweigh less alluring realities.

The male students of Pittsburgh's Commercial Department began their working careers as clerks, bookkeepers, and stenographers. For example, Charles Fuhr, John Flood, Joseph Crowley, and Jacob Baschkopf all worked as bookkeepers when they were twenty-five years old. Ten years

[44]*PW*, March 1889, 145; May 1889, 183; April 1905, 261–67; January 1905, 67; *Accountics*, April 1897, 10–13.

[45]*PW*, June 1889, 215. See the debate in *PW* over chances for promotions in railroad versus business offices: May, June, July, and August 1889, 183, 215, 237, 277 and November 1890, 70. *PW* also ran many notices of railroad employees' promotions. An ad for the Success Shorthand School in *PW*, January 1905, 89–90, tells the stories of young men stuck in clerical ruts until they learned shorthand and advanced to other clerical jobs.

[46]Stuart Morris, "Stalled Professionalism: The Recruitment of Railway Officials in the United States, 1885–1940," *Business History Review*, 47 (1973), 324.

[47]Quoted in Harry Henig, *The Brotherhood of Railway Clerks* (New York: Columbia University Press, 1937), 11.

[48]See DeVault, "Sons and Daughters of Labor," 18–79.

later, none of them listed his occupation as "bookkeeper," though none was a captain of industry, either. Jacob Baschkopf worked as an insurance inspector. Joseph Crowley, after working for over fifteen years as a bookkeeper, had become an undertaker. John Flood worked as an office manager in the central business district, while Charles Fuhr had become an auditor in the bank in which he had started his employment. These examples reflect the range of promotional possibilities open to the Commercial Department students. Much of their upward progression came through bureaucratic promotions. Banks provide the clearest examples of this progression. By the turn of the century, few young men expected to enter banking employment as a clerk, teller, or bookkeeper and end up owning a bank. But banks were known for their job security; once employed by a bank, a man could expect to progress by logical steps through its departments. The other side of the bank employment coin, however, was that job security and bureaucratic promotions were often guaranteed only within a single bank.[49] If Charles Fuhr, working as an auditor in 1915, had chosen in that year to seek a job at another bank, he might have had to start again at the bottom as a simple bookkeeper.

Overall, an examination of the former Commercial Department students fails to reveal any significant job mobility for these male clerical workers. Beginning their employment careers as low-level clerical workers, they generally stayed within the confines of that occupational rank.[50] Looking at our range of male occupations, then, we see that, although popular perceptions suggested great promotional possibilities for clerical workers, the reality of clerical work was more connected to the stability of bureaucratic employment. Long-term prospects could be best in clerical work, although wholesale positions, often sharing the same promotional ladder and pool, were quite comparable. Skilled workers might hope to be self-employed someday, but even that was a more modest aim than the clerical worker's dream of commercial or financial greatness. And, as mentioned earlier, even without such astounding success, the bureaucratic stability of employment in banks, railroads, and other large corporations outweighed the vagaries of industrial employment—accident, age, and technological obsolescence chief among them.

Looking at the more immediate future, however, young men who desired clerical employment faced a crucial obstacle. Unlike other occupations, office jobs could be obtained only after a course of formal and nonremunerative education. For Pittsburgh's young men, therefore, cler-

---

[49]Amos Kidder Fiske noted in 1904 that a bank's chief clerk, the second in command under the cashier (one of the bank's officers), had usually risen through the ranks, and that some banks hired only at the very bottom rungs, with the expectation of promoting their employees: *The Modern Bank* (New York: Appleton, 1904), 198–99.

[50]DeVault, "Sons and Daughters of Labor," 307–38, discusses the career trajectories of Commercial Department students.

ical work entailed many of the same social considerations it did for women. The characteristics of "conspicuous employment" operated in similar ways. Education for clerical work not only provided necessary skills but also imparted a level of social status in and of itself. Similarly, young men, too, had to invest in a new set of clothes in order to enter office employment. At the same time, however, these status considerations functioned differently in men's decisions than in women's. Clerical work's status features played an important role in some young women's decisions to enter the labor market at all. Since young men did not face the decision whether to work for wages or not, conspicuous employment characteristics were more equivalent to material considerations in their decisions to seek clerical work.

At the same time, ambiguous (and often contradictory) distinctions between manual and nonmanual labor contributed to young men's perceptions of the social status of office employment. The United States has always fostered a schizophrenic view of manual labor.[51] One set of traditions has glorified the individual who worked with his hands and scorned those who didn't—lawyers, politicians, financiers. Certainly Pittsburgh's workers upheld a working-class version of this tradition in the late nineteenth century, basing trade union and political power on their belief that it was their labor that created the city's—and the nation's—wealth.[52] The alternate tradition argued that "Americans very naturally are disinclined to manual labor."[53] Although middle-class observers tended to decry this tendency among workers' sons, many workers seem to have understood and supported their children's decisions. Even the city's "aristocracy" of skilled labor often tried to escape from the very work they glorified, becoming full-time unionists or politicians or, in the case of clerical training, seeking something "better" for their sons. Less skilled industrial workers found less to glorify in their work and more to gain from having their sons escape it. One commentator quoted in the National Labor Tribune pointed out that "many of the men who are metaphorically weeping over the desperate position of the

[51]See, e.g., Daniel T. Rodgers's discussion in The Work Ethic in Industrial America, 1850–1920 (Chicago: University of Chicago Press, 1978), esp. 180.

[52]See DeVault, "Sons and Daughters of Labor," chaps. 4 and 5, as well as NLT for 1870s–1890s; Francis G. Couvares, The Remaking of Pittsburgh: Class and Culture in an Industrializing City, 1877–1919 (Albany: SUNY Press, 1984); Leon Fink, Workingmen's Democracy: The Knights of Labor and American Politics (Urbana: University of Illinois Press, 1983); Gregory S. Kealey, "Labour and Working-Class History in Canada: Prospects in the 1980s," Labour/Le Travailleur, 7 (Spring 1981), 67–94; David Montgomery, "Labor and the Republic in Industrial America: 1860–1920," Le Mouvement Social, 111 (April–June 1980), 201–15; Richard J. Oestreicher, "Industrialization, Class, and Competing Cultural Systems: Detroit Workers, 1875–1900," in German Workers in Industrial Chicago, 1850–1910: A Comparative Perspective, ed. Hartmut Keil and John B. Jentz (De Kalb: Northern Illinois University Press, 1983).

[53]NLT, Sept. 7, 1893.

young American who is barred out from the opportunity to learn a trade would not have their own sons serve an apprenticeship."[54] "No matter what you do," another author argued, "whether it be bookkeeping, measuring milk, handling a pick or running an engine, it is the man, not the work . . . that makes him and his labor, respectively, respected or despised."[55]

For young men choosing to enter office occupations, two central signifiers of masculinity appear to be operating in contradiction. On the one hand, there is the glorification of (hard) manual labor as intrinsic to masculine identity. On the other hand, there is what could be called a "social" definition of masculinity, based on the ability of the "real man" to support his family. The latter is embodied in calls for the "family wage," the former in defenses of male predominance in jobs in which the entrance of other groups, especially women, threatened to displace men.[56] In fact, clerical work did not fall into this last category. Since the clerical sector was the most rapidly expanding sector of the labor market at the turn of the century, women could enter office jobs without posing this type of threat. In addition, the sex segregation of individual jobs within the clerical sector ensured that women would be seen as even less competition in this way.[57] In this setting, then, the social definition of masculinity was more crucial; a man's image of himself as a family's breadwinner could very well outweigh any sense that manual labor alone embodied masculinity. Clerical work, which implied steady wages for many years, could therefore seem to be superior to most turn-of-century industrial jobs, which carried with them the threat of premature disability or death.[58]

[54]*NLT*, May 16, 1895. See the quote from John Fitch, below, for an example of middle-class concerns.

[55]*NLT*, Sept. 7, 1893.

[56]Cf. Martha May, "Bread before Roses: American Workingmen, Labor Unions, and the Family Wage," in Milkman, *Women, Work, and Protest*, 1–21, and Ava Baron, "Contested Terrain Revisited: Technology and Gender Definitions of Work in the Printing Industry, 1850–1920," in *Women, Work, and Technology: Transformations*, ed. Barbara Wright et al., 58–83 (Ann Arbor: University of Michigan Press, 1987).

[57]Between 1870 and 1920 the U.S. work force as a whole increased by 328%. In comparison, the clerical occupations increased by 3,818%. Alba M. Edwards, for U.S. Department of Commerce, Bureau of the Census, *Comparative Occupation Statistics for the United States, 1870–1940* (Washington, D.C.: U.S. Government Printing Office, 1943), 104–12. As late as 1900, women made up only 29.2% of clerical workers in the United States: U.S. Department of Labor, Women's Bureau, *Women's Occupations through Seven Decades*, Bulletin no. 218 (1947), 75, 78. Only the job category of stenographers and typists was fully feminized at this time, with women making up 76.6%. The next closest category consisted of "bookkeepers, cashiers, and accountants," which was only 29.1% female in 1900: Davies, *Woman's Place Is at the Typewriter*, 178–79, table 1.

[58]On the psychological reverberations of the male role of family provider, see Jessie Bernard, "The Good-Provider Role: Its Rise and Fall," *American Psychologist*, 36 (January 1981), 1–12.

By the turn of the century, new ethnic divisions appeared within the male labor force as well, exacerbating other social distinctions among occupations. The new immigrants from southern and eastern Europe filled the unskilled and semiskilled jobs created by technological innovations and the further subdivision of labor in the skilled trades. John Fitch found the results of this development in Pittsburgh steel mills in 1908: "Many American boys fancy that they degrade themselves by entering into competition with a Slav for a job. Accordingly, lacking experience and hence skill, they shut themselves out of the avenues of approach to the better mill positions."[59] Already by 1900, foreign-born workers made up 39 percent of Pittsburgh's male work force, while clerical, sales, and many skilled manual jobs were dominated by native-born men. Table 8.4 illustrates these divisions. Thus, just as the female labor market was stratified by nativity and ethnicity, so was the male labor market.

Like clerical work for women, clerical work for men occupied a unique niche in the job market. While other available jobs provided either comparable material benefits or similar social status, clerical work seemed to provide it all. For young men who could afford to defer immediate earnings in order to gain the necessary training, clerical work's long-term material benefits proved well worth the effort and the wait. In addition, just as it did for women, clerical work's social status also appealed to native-born working-class men. For these young men, clerical work fitted into their expectations of being future family-wage earners.

This description of young men's decisions to become clerical workers illustrates working-class men's job choice considerations. While their economic circumstances forced many young men to consider the immediate material conditions of a job first and foremost, their long-term job horizon ensured that they would always be cognizant of a job's extended benefits. Young women, assuming that their futures held marriage, were concerned with the relative propriety of the various jobs open to them. In the constricted female job market, clerical work was the only occupation that not only held out the potential for meeting appropriate partners but also might actually increase a woman's social status. For this reason, the status of clerical work might actually encourage a woman to enter the paid labor force even if she had no pressing financial reason for doing so. Young men, of course, would not be persuaded to enter the labor force because of a job's status; they expected to be employed most of their lives. They were, however, as concerned as women with how marriageable different jobs made them. For young men, marriageability depended less on status or propriety than on the stability and level of future earn-

[59]Fitch, *Steel Workers*, 145.

Table 8.4. Nativity of Pittsburgh's male labor force, 1890, 1900, 1910, by job category (percent)

	Native-born			
	Native-born parents	Foreign-born parents	Foreign-born	Non-white
1890				
Total male work force	24.6%	27.4%	43.5%	4.5%
Clerical workers	48.5	37.4	13.4	0.8
Salesmen (stores)	43.2	36.8	19.9	0.1
Carpenters	41.7	23.7	33.9	0.7
Machinists	32.9	30.3	36.6	0.2
Laborers	11.8	19.0	62.3	6.9
Male population	30.7	35.7	30.2	3.4
1900				
Total male work force	26.4	27.9	38.9	6.8
Bookkeepers and accountants	53.6	34.6	11.6	0.2
Salesmen	43.1	36.1	20.0	0.7
Carpenters	46.3	24.4	28.3	1.0
Machinists	35.5	35.6	28.6	0.3
Laborers	11.2	20.0	57.3	11.5
All manufacturing occupations	23.4	30.3	42.7	3.7
Male population	32.1	35.8	27.3	4.9
1910				
Total male work force	28.0	27.3	39.1	5.6
Bookkeepers and accountants	55.4	33.9	10.4	0.3
Salesmen (stores)	44.8	33.1	21.6	0.5
Carpenters	38.6	23.5	36.1	1.7
Machinists	30.2	32.9	36.5	0.5
Laborers (blast furnaces, rolling mills)	6.6	14.6	76.2	2.6
Male Population	35.0	34.1	28.9	5.0

Sources: U.S. Department of the Interior, Census Office, *Report on Population of the United States at the Eleventh Census: 1890*, pt. 2 (Washington, D.C.: U.S. Government Printing Office, 1897), 712–13, table 118; U.S. Department of Commerce and Labor, Bureau of the Census, *Occupations at the Twelfth Census, 1900* (Washington, D.C.: U.S. Government Printing Office, 1904), 682–83, table 43; U.S. Department of Commerce, Bureau of the Census, *Population: 1910* (Washington, D.C.: U.S. Government Printing Office, 1914), 4: 591–92, table VIII.

ings. Men's perceptions of their future familial role as primary bread winner thus led them to focus more on long-term economic considerations when they chose an occupation. In fact, for relatively well-off working-class men, considerations of such things as future earnings and employment stability might well have overshadowed immediate benefits.

As we noted earlier, studies of women's wage-earning choices have looked at the ramifications of those choices for women's union activities and militance and for the feminization of certain occupations. The same sort of work can be profitably done for men, as well. If young women's individual and collective activities in the labor market were affected by their assumptions that they would one day marry and no longer have to work for wages, how were young men's activities influenced by their knowledge that they would have not only to go on supporting themselves and/or contributing to the family coffers, but also to support first a wife and then a growing family? The task now facing scholars of "men's labor history" is to apply the insights on men's job choices suggested here to different male workers' situations.

In my own research on clerical workers, understanding the context of young men's job choices helps decipher the ambiguous class position of office jobs. On the one hand, clerical work was only marginally at the top of the job market for men, although it was more clearly so for women. On the other hand, for both men and women, clerical work reinforced other tendencies toward separation of a native-born working-class elite from the largely immigrant unskilled workers of the turn of the century. In addition, contradictory notions of masculinity in manual and nonmanual occupations operated in the context of an expanding office work force made up of both men and women. The combination of all these intersecting factors does not explain away clerical work's ambiguities, but it does make them more comprehensible.

Thinking about men's job choices suggests profitable research that could be carried out on a number of other topics as well. For example, looking at the very different motivations between the job choices of young men entering the skilled trades and unskilled jobs, what can we say about the role played by family concerns? The often desperate "decisions" made by young men in taking unskilled jobs suggests a possible link between the economic powerlessness such unskilled workers experienced on the job and their family responsibilities. What effect did this linkage have on unskilled workers' collective actions? How did the existence of other wage earners in a family influence these male workers' behavior? At what point did they become willing to risk their own wages?

For organized skilled workers at the turn of the century, the linkage between workplace and family concerns is just as crucial, though in different ways. These men chose (and often worked to gain over the course of years) trades that would provide not only themselves but their entire families with what they assumed would be a comfortable standard of living. The unionist's ideal "family wage" would cover not only food, clothing, and shelter, but also comforts such as the pianos so many middle-class observers expressed surprise to see in turn-of-the-century skilled workers' homes.[60] Again, understanding the job choices made in an effort to attain this standard of living may help us to comprehend the force with which skilled workers responded to attacks on their "manhood."

It seems redundant (but is unfortunately not unnecessary) to say that this response emphasizes the gendered nature of the famed "manliness" of turn-of-the-century skilled workers. Davis Montgomery has described how "the workers' code celebrated individual self-assertion, but for the collective good, rather than for self-advancement."[61] The process by which these skilled workers chose their jobs suggests an intermediate step: between the "collective good" of the union and the "self-advancement' of the individual stood the smaller collective unit of the male-headed household. The sense of what it meant to "be a man" thus not only holds the potential of explicating workers' relationships with their employers and supervisors but also redounds back to their original choices of occupations, and in so doing prefigures family roles and relationships. These examples only begin to touch on the ways in which exploring male workers' job decisions may open up new areas for research. Just as it has done for women's labor history, raising these issues holds the potential of uncovering new insights into the connections between men's workplace concerns and their family and community experiences. A labor history that fully takes gender into account in this way will be that much richer and, perhaps, that much more true to the realities of working-class life in the past.

[60]One example of middle-class observers' attitudes is seen in Margaret F. Byington, *Homestead: The Households of a Mill Town* (1910; rpt. Pittsburgh: Center for International Studies, University of Pittsburgh, 1974), 85.

[61]David Montgomery, *The Fall of the House of Labor: The Workplace, the State, and American Labor Activism, 1865–1925* (Cambridge: Cambridge University Press, 1987), 204.

CHAPTER NINE

"Drawing the Line":
The Construction of a Gendered Work Force
in the Food Service Industry

Dorothy Sue Cobble

Whether one consumes a five-course dinner at the top of New York's World Trade Center or hurriedly sips coffee in the lowliest neighborhood café, one enters a world constructed by gender. The labor segmentation of the food service work force defies geographical, ethnic, and class boundaries. It has endured in the face of unionization, the changed consciousness of women, and the passage of laws prohibiting discrimination based on sex.

Scholars have analyzed the phenomenon of job segregation by sex from a variety of perspectives. Some view it as a divide-and-conquer strategy adopted by employers wary of a unified working class. Others argue that the creation of female job ghettos characterized by low pay and status is a necessary cornerstone in a patriarchal-capitalist system desirous of and dependent on women's subordinate role in the family. A third approach assumes that the sexual division of labor is the rational result of women's failure to augment their "human capital."[1]

Thanks go to *Labor History* for allowing me to use material from my essay " 'Practical Women': Waitress Unionists and the Controversies over Gender Roles in the Food Service Industry," which appeared in vol. 29 (Winter 1988), 5–31. Special thanks also to Ava Baron, Maurine Greenwald, Alice Kessler-Harris, and Michael Merrill for their helpful comments on earlier drafts of this essay.

[1]For an introduction to the labor segmentation argument and the Marxist-feminist literature, consult Natalie Sokoloff, *Between Love and Money: The Dialectics of Women's Home and Market Work* (New York: Praeger, 1980), chaps. 3–6. The patriarchal dimension to sex segregation has been persuasively argued by Heidi Hartmann, "Capitalism, Patriarchy, and Job Segregation by Sex," in *Women and the Workplace: The Implications of Occupational Segregation,* ed. Martha Blaxall and Barbara Reagan (Chicago: University of Chicago Press, 1976), 137–69. The human capital theory is discussed in Donald J. Treiman and Heidi I. Hartmann, eds., *Women, Work, and Wages: Equal Jobs for Equal Value* (Washington, D.C.: National Academy Press, 1981), 17–24, 53–54, and by Mary Huff Stevenson, "Wage Differences between Men and Women: Economic Theories," in *Women*

Most recently researchers have turned their attention to the process by which sex segregation developed in specific industries and occupations. These case studies have revealed the sexual division of labor to be more complicated and historically contingent than current theories acknowledge. Sex-segregated work patterns appear to be a product of economic, political, and social forces whose relative power varies over time and place. Susan Hirsch has argued that management actions "were the primary force behind the sex-typing of jobs" at the twentieth-century Pullman Company, for example. Similarly, Ruth Milkman has shown how employers in the auto and electrical industry maintained a gender-stratified labor force despite workers' protests and the disruptions of World War II. Yet in the printing industry, Ava Baron found that while structural factors linked to capitalism and patriarchy foreclosed certain possibilities, the workers themselves, especially the male printers, exerted considerable influence over the gendered work arrangements that existed in that trade.[2]

The food service industry is a particularly promising arena for extending our understanding of the maintenance and reordering of the sexual division of labor. Bitter controversies over the gender definition of certain jobs have racked the industry throughout the twentieth century, and the record of these disputes has been preserved in the work rules, contracts, convention proceedings, newsletters, and correspondence of local food service unions.[3] These documents offer a remarkable unfiltered lens through which to view the actions of working-class men and women, both white and black. From the turn of the century into the 1970s, wait-

---

Working: Theories and Facts in Perspective, ed. Ann Stromberg and Shirley Harkess, 89–107 (Palo Alto: Mayfield, 1977).

[2]Susan Hirsch, "Rethinking the Sexual Division of Labor: Pullman Repair Shops, 1900–1969," *Radical History Review*, 35 (April 1986), 31; Ruth Milkman, *Gender at Work: The Dynamics of Job Segregation by Sex during World War II* (Urbana: University of Illinois Press, 1987), esp. chap. 7; Ava Baron, "Women and the Making of the American Working Class: A Study of the Proletarianization of Printers," *Review of Radical Political Economics*, 14 (Fall 1982), 23–42.

Scholars whose work is rooted in literary paradigms have also questioned the inherited theoretical perspectives on sex segregation which assume an explanatory scientific mode. For these poststructuralists, the focus of inquiry shifts from the search for causes to the construction of meaning, from the assertion of universality to the illumination of historical and situational contingency. As the historian Joan Scott has argued, it is only when we understand what the gendered categories of "woman worker" and "male worker" signified that we can begin to tell "the story of the creation of a gendered workforce." Two of Scott's influential essays are "Gender: A Useful Category of Historical Analysis" and "The Sears Case," both in *Gender and the Politics of History*, 28–50 and 167–77 (New York: Columbia University Press, 1988).

[3]A complete list of the primary sources used in my research on food service workers may be found in "Sisters in the Craft: Waitresses and Their Unions in the Twentieth Century" (Ph.D. diss., Stanford University, 1986), 538–80.

ers, waitresses, and bartenders formed locals organized along sexual and racial lines in such major cities as Chicago, San Francisco, Los Angeles, Cincinnati, and St. Louis.[4] Operating in a local market, these individual culinary organizations had considerable autonomy in developing their own internal union regulations, contract proposals, and political agendas. With few exceptions, they chose staff and officers from among their own ranks. Moreover, since food service locals, like many other craft-oriented nonfactory unions, often took primary responsibility for the hiring and job assignment of workers, the gender categorization of jobs was debated in open meetings of the membership as well as in negotiation sessions with employers. Thus the records of these race- and sex-segregated locals offer the historian access to the gender formulations of working-class men and women in a rare form: one undistorted by middle-class interpretation or dominated by white male labor officialdom.

The words and deeds of food service workers, both white and black, belie the conventional notion that sex-segregated work resulted solely from either the actions of employers or the exclusionary policies of male trade unionists. In certain industries, men *and* women unionists exerted considerable influence over the nature of the gendered labor force of which they were a part. Their definitions of "gender equality" and their goals as male and female workers were critical in determining where the sexual boundaries would be drawn.

Beginning in the late nineteenth century, culinary unionists established a permanent toehold in the industry with the chartering of the Hotel Employees and Restaurant Employees Union (HERE). These AFL-affiliated locals survived the employer onslaughts of the pre–New Deal period and experienced unprecedented growth in the 1930s and 1940s. By the early 1950s, more than a quarter of all workers in eating and drinking establishments were organized under the HERE banner, and in labor strongholds such as San Francisco, New York, and Detroit unionization approached 80 percent.[5]

---

[4]Although cooks, dishwashers, and miscellaneous kitchen workers also formed labor organizations, my research focuses primarily on waiters and waitresses. Bartending is also analyzed as a related trade.

[5]Consult Cobble, "Sisters in the Craft" chaps. 3 and 4, for a history of union organizing in the industry. For statistics on food service unionization, see Leo Wolman, *Ebb and Flow in Trade Unionism* (New York: National Bureau of Economic Research, 1924), 118–121; Philip Taft, "Brief Review of Other Industries," in *How Collective Bargaining Works*, ed. Harry A. Millis (New York: Twentieth Century Fund, 1942), 924–25; *Catering Industry Employee*, May 1949, 8, and January 1954, 2; *Officers' Report*, Hotel Employees and Restaurant Employees [HERE] International Union, 1953, 48, in HERE International files, Washington, D.C.; U.S. Department of Labor, Bureau of Labor Statistics, *Industry Wage Survey: Eating and Drinking Places, June 1961*, Bulletin no. 1329 (June 1962), 9.

Food service workers became unionized as the hotel and restaurant industry expanded and feminized. In 1900 barely 100,000 workers were employed in commercial table service and the majority were male; by 1970, food service was the number one retail industry in America and 92 percent of all waiting work was done by women.[6] Bartending remained a male preserve much longer than waiting: less than 3 percent of the craft's practitioners were female by 1940; twenty years later women still made up under 11 percent of all bartenders. But in the last two decades, bartending was feminized faster than almost any other occupation: by 1986 women represented 44 percent of the trade.[7]

Shifts occurred in the racial composition of the work force as well. Over the course of the twentieth century, the proportion of black food service personnel declined, particularly among waiters. Blacks dropped from a third of all waiters at the turn of the century to 12 percent by the 1940s. The ranks of black waitresses also thinned, although not so dramatically, as black women were underrepresented in the waitress craft: after peaking at 12 percent in 1920, they dipped to 5 percent by 1970. Although the number of black men and women bartenders were small, averaging less than 5 percent over the course of the twentieth century, their representation dwindled even further once bartending began its rapid feminization. The proportion of black women bartenders, for example, fell from 8.2 percent in 1950 to 3.4 percent in 1970.[8]

[6]A. M. Edwards, for U.S. Department of Commerce, Bureau of the Census, *Sixteenth Census of the United States: 1940: Comparative Occupational Statistics, 1890–1940* (Washington, D.C.: U.S. Government Printing Office, 1943), 72; Joseph A. Hill, for U.S. Department of Commerce, Bureau of the Census, *Women in Gainful Occupations, 1870–1920*, Census Monographs 9 (Washington, D.C.: U.S. Government Printing Office, 1929), 83; U.S. Department of Commerce, Bureau of the Census, *Nineteenth Census of Populations, 1970: Subject Reports, Occupational Characteristics* (Washington, D.C.: U.S. Government Printing Office, 1973), 27. For a fuller discussion of the expansion and feminization of waiting work, consult Cobble, "Sisters in the Craft," chap. 1.

[7]Edwards, *Sixteenth Census, 1940: Comparative Occupational Statistics* 56, 165, (table 14), 172 (table 15); U.S. Department of Commerce, Bureau of the Census, *Seventeenth Census of Population, 1950*, vol. 4, *Special Reports*, pt. 1 (Washington, D.C.: U.S. Government Printing Office, IB-21, and *Eighteenth Census of Population, 1960: Subject Reports, Occupational Characteristics* (Washington, D.C.: U.S. Government Printing Office, 1963); 8, 18; *Catering Industry Employee*, May 1988.

[8]The complicated reasons for these shifts will not be addressed here. I explore this issue in *Dishing It Out: Waitresses and Their Unions in the Twentieth Century* (Urbana: University of Illinois Press, 1991). See U.S. Department of Commerce, Bureau of the Census, *Thirteenth Census of the United States, 1910: Population*, vol. 4, *Occupational Statistics* (Washington, D.C.: U.S. Government Printing Office, 1913), 432–33; Edwards, *Sixteenth Census, 1940: Comparative Occupational Statistics, 1870–1940*, 165 (table 14), 172 (table 15); U.S. Department of Commerce, Bureau of the Census, *Sixteenth Census of the United States, 1940: Population*, (Washington, D.C.: U.S. Government Printing Office, 1943); *Seventeenth Census, 1950*, vol. 4 pt. 1, *Special Reports*, IB-35; *Eighteenth Census, 1960: Occupational Characteristics*, 28; *Nineteenth Census of Population, 1970: Subject Reports, Occupational Characteristics* (Washington, D.C.: U.S. Government Printing Office, 1973), 26–27 (table 2).

The white women who moved into waiting work were an unusually homogeneous group. Primarily native-born, they shared blue-collar and farming backgrounds and were drawn from the "old" Northern European immigrant groups (German, Irish, Scandinavian, English, and Welsh). More than women in clerical and factory work, they tended to live in nontraditional family settings (a high proportion were divorced, separated, or, if single, living apart from their family of origin) and to be primary wage earners. Especially before the 1930s, waitresses often lived alone, with dependents, or with other waitresses in small apartments and furnished rooms. Restaurant work attracted these "women adrift" because it provided them with free meals, companionship, and the possibility of a living wage. Until the 1960s, the vast majority of waitresses worked full-time, spent a substantial number of years in their trade, and tended to perceive their work status as permanent.[9]

Waiters and bartenders, on the other hand, were more likely to be foreign-born. Only 36 percent of waiters were native-born whites in 1930 in contrast to 78 percent of waitresses. Male culinary workers were also a more diverse group ethnically: Irish, German, and American predominated, but Italian, Greek, Spanish, French, Russian, and Eastern European were not uncommon. And unlike their sisters in waiting work, in family status male food and drink dispensers resembled the male work force at large.[10]

Both, however, shared an allegiance to certain working-class institutions and ideologies. As active unionists, they partook of a class culture that included elements of the craft traditions of the AFL. Collective advancement of their craft and the preservation of their union organizations were of utmost importance. Food service workers fought to establish and maintain work rules that clearly defined the craft boundaries of their work. They also respected the inherited jurisdictional claims of the various culinary trades.[11] These craft practices were seen as

---

[9]U.S. Department of Commerce, Bureau of the Census, *Sixteenth Census of the United States, 1940: Occupational Characteristics* (Washington, D.C.: U.S. Government Printing Office, 1943), 144–45; *Seventeenth Census, 1950: Special Reports*, vol. 4, pt. 1, 1B-151, 157; *Eighteenth Census, 1960: Occupational Characteristics*, 192, 202; *Nineteenth Census, 1970: Occupational Characteristics*, 774, 760. Cobble, "Sisters in the Craft," chaps. 1 and 2, provides full documentation on the ethnic, racial, and family backgrounds of waitresses.

[10]U.S. Department of Commerce, Bureau of the Census, *Fifteenth Census of the United States, 1930: Population*, vol. v, *Occupations* (Washington, D.C.: U.S. Government Printing Office, 1933), 76, 85; San Francisco Board of Education, Attendance and Guidance Bureau, *The Restaurant Industry in San Francisco: Occupational Study No. 8* (San Francisco, August 1932), 12; Edward Paul Eaves, "A History of the Cooks' and Waiters' Unions of San Francisco" (master's thesis, University of California, Berkeley, 1930), iii–iv; *Mixer and Server*, April 1922, 51; Meredith Story, "To Serve the Public: Waiters in New York, 1875–1910," Social Science Collection, University of California, Berkeley, c. 1980.

[11]When international unions were chartered by the AFL, they were given exclusive control or "ownership" of certain kinds of work. No other labor organization could legiti-

essential to preserving not only organizational interests but the dignity and working conditions of the occupation. These class loyalties shaped the positions of men and women on gender issues just as did their economic and family status.[12]

Despite the dramatic changes that transformed the nature of public food consumption in the twentieth century and the heterogeneity of the industry, stratification by sex persisted. Waitresses worked in a myriad of environments, from bustling, high-pressured lunch counters to genteel tearooms to red-carpeted cocktail lounges, but invariably they were segregated into the lower-paying jobs and faced the prospect of downward mobility as their youth and attractiveness faded. Male waiters held the more prestigious, higher-paying jobs and could realistically aspire to promotion to captain or maitre d'. Similarly, bartenders and cooks—members of the most thoroughly masculinized culinary crafts—occupied the highest rung in the food service hierarchy in terms of status, pay, and benefits.

Nevertheless, beneath this seemingly still surface of unchanging sexual hierarchy, the gender labeling of particular jobs was being contested. The line separating men's work from women's work was continually redrawn. Culinary workers challenged employers' sexual preferences in hiring and engaged in acrimonious debates within their own organizations as to the proper gender definition and division of work. Three disputes stand out as particularly revealing: the quarrel over whether women should serve liquor, the retention of nightwork ordinances against women, and the preservation of bartending for men only.[13] The concerns

---

mately represent workers doing those tasks unless the jurisdictions were redefined. Local union charters carried similar "rights." The National Labor Relations Act policy of elections for representation undermined chartered jurisdictional rights; the culinary industry, however, did not come under the provisions of the act until 1955.

[12]When we examine the structural bases for the consciousness of working-class men and women, it is critical to look at both the impact of the workplace (or the point of production) and the home. Labor historians have concentrated on the workplace while historians of women typically root their analyses of women's culture in the home. It is also important to note that not all "family-based cultures" and "work cultures" are the same. Unlike the immigrant women described by John Bodnar, waitresses experienced a family culture and responsibilities that reinforced their activism in the public sphere rather than undermined it. See Bodner, "Immigration, Kinship, and the Rise of Working-class Realism in Industrial America," *Journal of Social History*, 14 (Fall 1980), 45–65. Carole Turbin makes a similar point about Troy laundresses in "Beyond Conventional Wisdom: Women's Wage Work, Household Economic Contribution, and Labor Activism in a Mid-Nineteenth-Century Working-Class Community," in *"To Toil the Livelong Day": America's Women at Work, 1780–1980,* ed. Carol Groneman and Mary Beth Norton, 47–67 (Ithaca: Cornell University Press, 1987). For an introduction to the literature on women's work cultures, see Micaela di Leonardo, "Women's Work, Work Culture, and Consciousness," *Feminist Studies,* 11 (Fall 1985), 491–518.

[13]Other debates included whether women should be organized, what they should be paid, and how the ratio of men to women in individual establishments should be determined. See Cobble, "Sisters in the Craft," chaps. 3, 4, 7, and Cobble, " 'Practical Women':

of waitresses are articulated in all three debates; the attitudes of waiters and bartenders emerge most clearly in the latter struggles.

Shall Waitresses Serve Liquor?

Waiters' locals in the early twentieth century often barred women from membership and required that employers replace unorganized female workers with male union members. As women organized their own locals, however, and showed no sign of disappearing from the industry, male culinary workers adjusted their strategies: most dropped their exclusive claim to union waiting work and repealed their constitutional bans on female membership.[14] Nevertheless, in the early 1930s, when the repeal of Prohibition revived liquor service, waiters saw an opportunity to retain at least one high-paying stratum of the occupation. Using both the legislative and internal union arenas, they submitted resolutions to exclude women from liquor service to culinary local joint executive boards (LJEBs), HERE International conventions, and state and municipal politicians.

Waitresses objected vehemently to these proposals. They blocked convention resolutions that included blanket restrictions on liquor service by women, and their active lobbying halted similar bills in state legislatures. The Boston waitresses' local, for instance, reported that the bill before the Massachusetts legislature banning women from liquor service in taverns "would have passed but for the efforts put forth by Sister [Eva] Rankin and a committee chosen by the organization. Our girls stormed the legislature, obtained a lot of publicity, and won."[15]

Waitresses drew on their belief in women's right to employment and on certain notions of gender equity to counter arguments against their serving liquor. Expanding the "family wage" concept to include women, Kitty Donnelly, who served Waitresses' Local 107 of Cleveland for close to thirty years as business agent and who had been widowed at an early age with three sons to support, wondered whether the "brothers" supporting such restrictive proposals "realize [that] there are a lot of self-supporting women who head families?"[16] Veteran officer Kitty Amsler of Missouri underscored the economic hardship these proposals would have on waitresses. Such legislation "would throw 5,000 waitresses out

Waitress Unionists and the Controversies over Gender Roles in the Food Service Industry," *Labor History,* 29 (Winter 1987–88), 5–31.

[14]Cobble, "Sisters in the Craft," chap. 3.

[15]*Catering Industry Employee,* March 1934, 37; August 1935, 17.

[16]A biographical portrait of Kitty Donnelly can be found in *Mixer and Server,* September 1921, 150, and *Catering Industry Employee,* January 1930. The quote is from *Catering Industry Employee,* May 1933, 27.

of work," she pointed out; "women are equal to men, [and] such distinctions shouldn't be made between the sexes." Equally strong outrage was directed at the seeming paternalism of these resolutions. "How come . . . the Bartenders and Waiters are looking after the morals of the Waitresses? Who says I will be disgraced . . . if I serve a glass of beer?" Southern California organizer Bee Tumber queried.[17]

Waitresses also stressed their rights as unionists and their jurisdictional claim to any work that fell within the purview of the waiting craft. Drawing attention to the impact of such legislation on their union, the members of Chicago Local 484 proclaimed that "such legislation would eliminate the waitresses as a majority of eating places have retail licenses to sell liquor." San Francisco waitresses held that any resolution that banned women from liquor service or that "used the words served or serving" was "discriminating against bona fide waitresses."[18]

By 1936 waitress unionists had persuaded their union brothers to drop such blanket prohibitions, but they opened the way for the success of prohibition on female bartenders by conceding the legitimacy of male claims to "ownership" of certain kinds of work. The allegiance of white waitresses to their craft heritage and to deeply held notions of gender separatism prompted Kitty Donnelly, like many other waitress unionists, to narrow her protest to the restrictions on women *serving* liquor, not *mixing* liquor.

Moreover, a long-standing concern over preserving the respectability of waitressing and a reluctance to invade male-defined terrain led many waitresses to specify the kinds of establishments in which it would be acceptable for women to serve liquor. Generally, those establishments that served *only* liquor were seen as the domain of men. There, male culture reigned supreme and women were not only interlopers but without protection and power. Donnelly, for example, hoped that "the girls will get work in serving it [liquor] on a 50–50 basis with the boys," but she added that she drew "a line to beer being served by girls in beer halls unless there is food served with it." She even allowed that cocktail waitresses should be banned unless they were also serving food.[19]

Local 48 waitresses drew the line at exactly the same spot as Donnelly. They voted in 1942 to "take no application from any girl who works in a tavern" or in any establishment that did not serve food, and to instruct the secretary "to write to Lt. Governor De Witt protesting the employment of women in bars." The waitresses' local also supported the LJEB

[17]*Catering Industry Employee*, April 1935, 30; August 1935, 17; May 1933, 17; April 1935, 30; May 1935, 32; June 1935, 27, 48.
[18]Ibid., April 1935, 30; *Proceedings*, HERE, 1941, Resolution 38, introduced by San Francisco Local 48.
[19]*Catering Industry Employee*, May 1933, 27.

policy discouraging "employment of women in cocktail lounges and bars." Other waitresses' locals reached similar conclusions. Facing a flurry of protest letters from waitress officials in Chicago, Buffalo, Seattle, and Santa Barbara, Chicago Bartenders' Local 376 amended its 1936 resolution "prohibiting the employment of women in premises licensed for retail sales of liquor" to except establishments "where the serving of food is the principal part of business." The complaining letters ceased.[20]

Black waitresses in Chicago, however, fought not only to preserve liquor service but to have their work as cocktail waitresses in taverns accepted as legitimate. In 1934 Local 444, Chicago's all-male "colored" waiters' local, applied to the International for reinstatement. Concerned with rebuilding their organization and aware of the extensive number of taverns on Chicago's South Side, the waiters' local seized upon the recent introduction of alcohol as the propitious moment to assert an exclusive male claim to cocktail work. Rather than appeal to the black women workers in the taverns to join the union, Local 444, under the leadership of Livert "St. Louis" Kelly, picketed the bars and threatened the owners with violence if women were not replaced with men from Local 444. As a result, some two to three hundred black cocktail waitresses lost their jobs.[21]

In reaction, black cocktail waitresses organized and requested that the international charter a separate local for black women. Having a union, they hoped, would help them "recover their jobs" and prevent interference "on the part of pickets and union leaders . . . with their efforts to earn a livelihood as waitresses." When both George McLane, a pivotal Chicago culinary official,[22] and the international refused their request for a separate charter—in part because of protests from Local 444—the women hired a Chicago attorney, Mrs. Georgia Jones Ellis, and sought the backing of the Women's Bureau. Obtaining a letter of introduction

[20]Executive Board (EB) minutes, San Francisco Waitresses' Local 48, Oct. 27, 1942, and Local Joint Executive Board (LJEB) minutes, Mar. 17, 1942; May 19, 1942; Aug. 18, 1942, in HERE Local 2 Files, San Francisco; *Catering Industry Employee*, March 1936, 25.

[21]Chartered in 1926, Local 444 had allowed dues payments to lapse. See General Secretary-Treasurer to McNeal, President 444, Aug. 2, 1944, and General Secretary-Treasurer to Virginia Blanton, Secretary 444, May 7, 1934, in reel 10, Defunct Union Locals, HERE International files.

[22]George McLane, president of the Chicago Bartenders' local, has been described by Matthew Josephson and others as part of the "Al Capone syndicate," which moved from illicit rumrunning to pushing various racketeer-supplied liquor at bars where they controlled the teamster and culinary locals. Most likely, "St. Louis" Kelly was tied in with McLane and thus desired to have his men working there instead of women because of the greater ease in conducting his illegal scams. He needed experienced union waiters in the taverns, for instance, to push certain brands of beer. For a fuller discussion of the racketeering elements in Chicago, consult Jay Rubin and M. J. Obermeier, *The Growth of a Union: The Life and Times of Edward Flore* (New York: Historical Union Association, 1943), 48–73, passim, and Matthew Josephson, *Union House, Union Bar: A History of the Hotel and Restaurant Employees and Bartenders International Union, AFL-CIO* (New York: Random House, 1956), 211–15, 234–61.

from black congressman Oscar De Priest, Ellis traveled to Washington and met with the head of the Women's Bureau, Mary Anderson, to plead her case. Anderson dispatched Ethel Erickson, a Women's Bureau field agent, to Chicago with instructions to "get the facts" regarding the "displacement of the colored waitresses," and she wrote to John Fitzpatrick, president of the Chicago Federation of Labor, asking his cooperation.[23]

Erickson's report from Chicago revealed a dismal situation. On the basis of interviews with tavern owners, waitresses, union officials, newspaper reporters, attorneys, and the Chicago Urban League, Erickson accused the black waiters' local of requiring kickbacks from the men it dispatched and of planning to put the newly unemployed waitresses "on the street to hustle," thus setting up in one stroke two illegal sources of revenue. The justifications put forward by the male union officials regarding the need to protect the morals of the women were obviously disingenuous, she contended. Removing the black women from their cocktail jobs made them more vulnerable, it appeared, especially since these taverns were not (yet) operating as brothels. Equally important, none of the women complained of "any special problem of morality"; and since most were older, married women with dependents, in Erickson's view they were quite capable of protecting their own morals.[24]

The situation was finally "resolved" when the international, under pressure from the Women's Bureau, decided "that these colored waitresses [will] be invited to join our present colored local in Chicago, Local 444." After Fitzpatrick advised them that "the door of the union had been closed against them and now it was opened and they should go in and secure membership and the future would take care of itself," the black waitresses accepted. "I regard this as a very happy ending to a nasty situation," Fitzgerald wrote Erickson. "If they put 50 or 60 women into that union, I imagine they will have the balance of power, that is, if I know women." Attempting to close on a jocular note, Fitzpatrick inadvertently touched the core of a potentially serious problem for the black waitresses: the power imbalance within the local union.[25]

Once inside the local, the women continued to push for the expansion of their job rights and their power vis-à-vis their male union brothers. Although it is difficult to imagine a local so recently hostile to female employment and plagued by such an unsavory reputation as capable of

[23]Ethel Erickson to John Fitzpatrick, Aug. 6, 1934; Oscar De Priest to Mary Anderson, Apr. 26, 1934; and Anderson to Fitzpatrick, Apr. 26, 1934, all in file "HERE," box 865, Record Group 86, Women's Bureau Records, National Archives, Washington, D.C. (hereafter RG 86).

[24]Memo, Erickson to Anderson, Aug. 6, 1934, and Erickson to Fitzpatrick, Aug. 6, 1934, in ibid.

[25]Edward Flore to Anderson, Aug. 20, 1934, and Fitzpatrick to Erickson, Aug. 25, 1934, in ibid.

support for female rights, it appears that black women held their own under extremely inhospitable circumstances. By 1935 Local 444 had at least one female business agent, Kathleen Slate, who, with the backing of women within the local, successfully organized cocktail waitresses.[26]

By the late 1930s, the dispute over whether women should serve liquor receded into the background. Waiters now turned to new tactics to thwart the influx of women. In the 1940s and 1950s frequent and bitter disputes over jobs were played out in negotiations with employers and in conflicts between waiters' and waitresses' unions within their LJEBs and the international. Waiters also aggressively defended legislation prohibiting women from working at night. Although waitresses met these challenges head on, waiters' locals succeeded in slowing—but not halting—the feminization of the industry, and in many instances men maintained their monopoly of the higher-status, better-paying waiting jobs.

The Campaign for Restrictions on Nightwork

In the decades after World War II, the battle over the gender segregation of waiting work was fought out in the legislative arena. Waiters' locals pushed for the passage of new protective laws banning nightwork for women hotel and restaurant employees and they fought tenaciously against the repeal of existing laws.[27]

Before the war, the majority of waitresses had sided with their brothers.[28] In the 1920s and again in the 1930s, waitresses from New

[26]*Catering Industry Employees*, June 1935, 30.

[27]Nightwork restrictions typically forbade work between the hours of midnight and 6 A.M., but a few statutes banned work between 10 P.M. and 7 A.M. By 1920, six states outlawed nightwork for all working women, and an additional twelve states prohibited nightwork in some occupations. For an overview of the nightwork issue, consult Sheila Rothman, *Woman's Proper Place: A History of Changing Ideals and Practices* (New York: Basic Books, 1978), 156–65; Elizabeth Baker, *Protective Labor Legislation with Special Reference to Women in the State of New York* (New York: Columbia University Press, 1925), 233–51; Judith Baer, *The Chains of Protection: The Judicial Response to Women's Labor Legislation* (Westport, Conn.: Greenwood, 1978), 86–88; U.S. Department of Labor, Women's Bureau, *Night Work Laws in the United States*, Bulletin no. 7 (1920); Florence P. Smith, for Women's Bureau, *Labor Laws for Women in the States and Territories*, Bulletin no. 98 (1932); Clara M. Beyer, for Women's Bureau, *History of Labor Legislation for Women in Three States*, Bulletin no. 66 (1929); and Ronnie Steinberg, *Wages and Hours: Labor and Reform in Twentieth-Century America* (New Brunswick, N.J.: Rutgers University Press, 1982).

[28]The early legislative drives also relied on the energies of the National Consumers' League, the Women's Trade Union League (WTUL), and other female reform groups. For examples of the arguments used, refer to Consumers' League of New York, *Behind the Scenes in a Restaurant: A Study of 1017 Women Restaurant Employees* (New York, 1916), 17, 28–29, 32, and *The Forty-eight-Hour Law: Do Working Women Want It?* (New York, 1927). See also *Monthly Bulletin*, New York WTUL, March 1932, reel 22, collection IV (Records of the New York WTUL), and *1926–29 Convention Report*, 14, reel 8, collection

York City, Buffalo, Syracuse, and even Kansas City joined with their brother trade unionists in testifying on behalf of New York State's nightwork prohibitions. These waitresses spoke against repeal of the restrictions, one explained, "to help our Brother Locals, for we do know that if the bill had been passed a great many of the men would be out of work now."[29] They correctly assumed that many employers preferred to hire women and would do so if nightwork restrictions were lifted. Although they were being denied opportunities for advancement and the bigger tips that nightclub work and dinner service brought, loyalty to their male co-workers and fellow union members took precedence.

The waitresses who did oppose restrictions on nightwork before the 1940s emphasized their need for the more lucrative evening service and their rights as primary breadwinners. The director of inspection for the New York State Department of Labor confessed to Elizabeth Baker in the early 1920s that enforcement of nightwork prohibitions was difficult because the "women themselves are not in sympathy with being deprived of work at night when tips are higher." The *New York Times* reported that some waitresses testified on behalf of repeal because "they could make more money in night work and wanted to be able to take advantage of this opportunity." Unorganized and rank-and-file waitresses tended to be more opposed to nightwork restrictions than their leaders, who, it can be surmised, had stronger union and working-class loyalties. The union leaders who did condemn nightwork laws cited the family responsibilities of their members. "A great many of our women are working to support themselves and their children, the same as the men, and are certainly entitled to do so," Jennie Philcox declared. A second waitress official insisted that many women wanted to work at night because they had "a family to support where there is no husband to depend on. I do think they should be consulted as to their wishes in the matter."[30]

IX, in WTUL Papers, microfilm ed., Stanford University, Green Library. The Communist Party's 1926 "Platform of the Class Struggle" listed prohibition of nightwork among its demands for working women. Consult Robert Shaffer, "Women and the Communist Party, USA, 1930–1940," *Socialist Review*, 46 (May–June 1979), 80. The international union remained uncommitted during this period. See Flore to Anderson, Feb. 6, 1930, in file "HERE," Box 865, RG 86.

[29]*Mixer and Server*, February 1929, 35, and March 1929, 43; *Catering Industry Employee*, March 1930, 19, and June 1930, 36–37; *New York Times*, Mar. 4, 1931; Vee Terry Perlman, *The Minimum Wage Muddle* (1934), in file "Min wage/1934," box 906, RG 86. Cobble, "Sisters in the Craft," chap. 1, documents the increasing preference of employers for women as eating out became a pastime for the middle-class as well as the elite, as restaurant service moved away from its adherence to formal European service, and as the relaxing of Victorian attitudes toward women who mixed publicly with men made waitress work more acceptable to the public and to native-born white women seeking wage work.

[30]Baker, *Protective Labor Legislation*, 336; *New York Times*, Feb. 27, 1930; *Catering Industry Employee*, June 1930, 36–37, and October 1930, 36–37; *Mixer and Server*, June 1929, 43, and May 1928, 69; Perlman, *Minimum Wage Muddle*.

228   *Dorothy Sue Cobble*

These spokeswomen, like many other prominent waitress leaders, adapted the family wage argument to support women's claims to better jobs. A few even defended a woman's right to independence as well as a living wage. "We do not wish to be dictated where we should work or what hours of the day we should work," one activist proclaimed. Another defiantly questioned the authority of the men who were so eager to protect women. "Who says I can't work after 9 at night?" she asked. Their notions of gender equity included individual autonomy and personal freedom for women wage earners equal to those of men.[31]

By the postwar period, the majority of waitresses unequivocally opposed restrictions on nightwork. A variety of factors prompted this shift. As a result of the need for female labor in the expanding food service industry and the widespread use of female workers during the crisis of World War II, a large number of waitresses now actually worked at night.[32] Thus the economic issues involved were now more pressing: the retention of union jobs for women was at stake as well as the distribution of future work. Moreover, the prominence of male culinary workers in the postwar campaigns clarified the basic adversarial relation between the sexes on this issue and undercut the loyalty of waitresses to their brother unionists.[33]

As each side fought for what it perceived as its own self-interest,[34] their rhetoric revealed the clear economic and gendered nature of their concerns. Male culinary officials frequently relied on the family wage concept, narrowing it to apply to men only. "Night work for women would take away jobs from men, particularly during the period of highest earnings which rightfully should be reserved for men who support families," one wrote. Underneath the plea for higher wages lay a concern for maintaining traditional gender relations. "A man begins to lose faith in himself" when he becomes "dependent upon his wife as a wage-earner,"

[31]*Catering Industry Employee,* May 1935, 32; June 1935, 48.
[32]During World War II, protective legislation was perceived as hampering the war effort; as a result, all but five states exempted women from the laws restricting nightwork. Consult Philip S. Foner, *Women and the American Labor Movement: From World War I to the Present* (New York: Free Press, 1980), 353–54.
[33]In the postwar era male culinary unionists replaced the National Consumers' League and other women's groups as the principal proponents of the legislation. Working-class women appeared as a major element in the coalition favoring repeal. My "Sisters in the Craft," 427–45, provides a detailed account.
[34]In the long run, male workers misperceived their own economic interest; ultimately they were undermining their own working standards and unions by competing with their female co-workers. In fact, by reinforcing an artificial division of labor among food servers, nightwork legislation crowded women workers into daytime jobs, where women worked for less money, thus undermining conditions within the industry and encouraging the replacement of men. Moreover, since many local and state HERE organizations protected the short-term interests of their male members at the expense of the immediate needs of their female members (and the long-term interests of both), women within HERE and unorganized female workers found it increasingly difficult to see the union as their ally.

reasoned one Cleveland unionist. "When this happens the woman will become domineering and independent." A third made clear the commitment to gendered divisions in the workplace as well as at home. "We must impose, by law if necessary, priority of jobs for male workers," he wrote in 1945. Even if "the industrial activities of women" were restricted, they might still "find employment in housekeeping, secretarial work, nursing, and education."[35]

Waiters emphasized that nightwork would protect the "weaker sex" and preserve the ever-vulnerable female moral character. Extensive nightwork was detrimental to the health and well-being of future mothers and it subjected women to dangerous nighttime travel. They warned of moral decay when "glamour replace[s] craftsmanship as illustrated in one leading Manhattan hotel where their waitresses are garbed in transparent skirts and in another Manhattan hotel where the [low-cut] Faye Emerson neckline is the fad."[36] In briefs submitted to the state legislature in 1950, the New York State Culinary Alliance, a state federation of culinary locals, claimed that "the moral reasons" to prohibit nightwork were "as valid today as they were 25 years ago." Drawing on the 1908 Brandeis brief, submitted in defense of an Oregon statute limiting the daily hours of female laundry workers to ten a day, the alliance wrapped up its case as if forty-two years had changed nothing. "Medically, physically, socially, and morally there is a difference between men and women, and the difference is one that the State has the right and indeed the duty to recognize and protect."[37]

The position of the State Culinary alliance clashed with the postwar views of most waitresses.[38] Some of the waitresses had raised the question previously; at the 1945 Culinary Alliance meeting "there was practically an open fight on the floor," according to Gertrude Lane, secretary of New York City's Local 6. The waitresses "became very voluble,"

[35]Vera Freeman and Harry Newman, for New York Department of Labor, Division of Research and Statistics, *Some Aspects of the Nightwork Problem with Special Reference to Restaurant Industry*, Publication B-23 (Albany, 1940), 33; *Mixer and Server*, May 1928, 69; *Catering Industry Employee*, May 1945, 29.

[36]Freeman and Newman, *Some Aspects of the Nightwork Problem*, 33; Miguel Garriga to Ed Miller, May 13, 1948, in File "HERE," box 865, RG 86; "Women and Night Work in Restaurants," anonymous typescript (c. 1948), 3, 11–12, in folder "Night Work," HERE Local 6 files, New York; *Hotel and Club Voice*, Aug. 16, 1941, 2.

[37]Brief submitted by New York State Culinary Alliance, Dec. 7, 1950, 6–7, 11–12, 14–17, in folder "Night Work", HERE Local 6 files. See Muller v. Oregon, 208 U.S. 412 (1908), for the text of the Brandeis brief. Other reasons cited included "the correlation between juvenile delinquency and broken homes—where the mother is out of the home because of nightwork" and "the opportunities and inclination for crime, including sexual crimes, [being] greater after midnight than in broad daylight."

[38]Freeman and Newman found, for example, that of 139 restaurant workers interviewed, only 16 favored nightwork restrictions for women: *Some Aspects of the Nightwork Problem*, 13–14, 32–33.

pointing out that nightwork restrictions would keep them from working the supper jobs, typically the best-paid waiting work. New York City waitresses agitated "to work Broadway 'hot spots' at night because there [were] . . . greater tips there and greater opportunities." Upstate New York waitresses protested the limitation on their working night banquets in restaurants—"a purely economic question," according to Helen Blanchard. She added that "the girls in upstate New York want particularly to work . . . where the tips are higher," and to have their share of the work in twenty-four-hour counter and table service restaurants.[39] By emphasizing the economic dimension of the debate, Blanchard hoped perhaps to sidestep the stickier issues concerning women's physical and moral nature.[40]

Waitresses' locals in Buffalo and Rochester—two separate-sex locals that broke with the State Culinary Alliance on the issue and lobbied for repeal—voiced economic concerns first, but they also attempted to refute the gender-based objections raised by their opponents. They agreed in 1949 on a variety of propositions: (1) nightwork restrictions kept women out of the most lucrative work (dinner shifts and cocktail service); (2) nightwork had no ill effect on women's health or morals; (3) nightwork prohibitions did not keep women from being molested; and (4) women should be able to choose the hours of work that were best suited to their particular needs.[41] Thus they rejected the notion of women's fragile health and moral character and questioned the logic protecting women from male aggression by keeping them home at night. Lastly, they asserted the right of women themselves to determine when they worked and how best to meet the demands of work and family, repudiating the concept of a paternalistic state that adjusted the workplace to ensure that women would not shirk their family duties.

---

[39]Transcript, 1945 Women's Bureau Conference for Trade Union Women, 252–58, in box 898, RG 86; minutes of Women Bureau's Labor Advisory Committee meeting, June 4, 1946, 2, in box 1529, RG 86; memo, Constance Williams to Frieda Miller, Apr. 29, 1947, in file "Bulletin no. 233," box 991, RG 86; Gertrude Lane to Hugo Ernst, Nov. 12, 1946, in reel 145, Local Union Records (hereafter LUR), HERE International files, Washington, D.C.; *Hotel and Club Voice*, Mar. 26, 1949, 1; *Voice of Local 1*, August 1949, 7, and July 1950, 1, in folder "Night Work," HERE Local 6 files, New York.

[40]A sympathetic culinary business agent, Charles Darling, interviewed by the Women's Bureau that same year, revealed that the attitudes of waitresses in Connecticut differed little from those of waitresses in New York. In Connecticut "it was the women members who urged that the union support the relaxation of restrictions to allow women to work until 1 A.M. in restaurants." The women took this position, according to Darling, because they "don't make anything" on day shifts. "At night they can make more money because they get more in tips at dinner, banquets or from persons drinking, and consequently they 'don't mind' nightwork": interview by Martha Ziegler, Women's Bureau agent, June 25, 1947, in box 676, RG 86.

[41]Freeman and Newman, *Some Aspects of the Nightwork Problem*, 2, 33–4, 100.

Wage-earning women on both sides of the debate claimed that their position was consistent with fulfillment of women's responsibilities at home. One waitress who opposed repeal feared that "late working hours would deprive the home of the necessary care and love that children and family need." She did not "think women working at night and making a few dollars more . . . would create the desired equality for women."[42] Most waitresses, however, disputed the idea that restricting women's nighttime hours would make them better mothers. Interviews with night-workers in a variety of industries revealed that they favored nightwork precisely because it allowed them *more* time with their family. They could sleep during the day while their children were in school, spend time with them in the late afternoon and early evening, and work at night after putting them to bed. This scenario depended, of course, on the presence of another adult at night. Because so many waitresses were divorced and separated, they argued less frequently that nightwork would allow them time with their children than did many other wage-earning women. They emphasized instead that nightwork opportunities enabled them to provide financially for their children.[43]

Waitresses and waiters appear to have perceived the economic conse-quences of nightwork legislation correctly. Waitresses' locals such as Rochester's Local 22 reported declining membership in the late 1940s as a direct result of nightwork legislation. Women's Bureau investigators also ran across concerned HERE officials who explained that "the men, particularly the waiters, don't like what has happened now that the wo-men's night work law has been abolished" and "men are losing their jobs." An official New York State study surmised that since "one-half of all restaurants stay open past 12, it is estimated that 7,500 to 8,000 women might be employed in restaurants if the law were repealed." These economic considerations, in addition to the fact that working-class women themselves preferred to make their own decision in the matter, lend validity to the opinion of contemporary scholars that the disadvan-tages of nightwork prohibitions (more than almost any other protective statute) outweighed their advantages.[44]

Unfortunately, waitresses who advocated repeal never acquired full support from their historic allies, the WTUL and the Women's Bureau. Both organizations reviewed their stance toward nightwork in the years

[42]*Voice of Local 1*, October 1948, 2.

[43]See the synopsis of nightwork studies in transcript, 1946 Conference for Women Unionists, 237, in box 897, RG 86; "Summary of Material on Effect of Night Work," mimeo, in file "Trade Union Women's Conference, October 1946," box 1696, RG 86.

[44]*Catering Industry Employee*, June 1949, 32; Ziegler-Darling interview; U.S. Depart-ment of Labor, Women's Bureau, *Night Work for Women in Hotels and Restaurants*, Bul-letin no. 233 (1949), 12; Freeman and Newman, *Some Aspects of the Nightwork Problem*, 2; Baer, *Chains of Protection*, 86–87.

after World War II, but by 1948 they reaffirmed their allegiance to protective legislation, including nightwork prohibitions.[45] Without the backing of these key organizations, the movement for repeal was only partially successful. No new states adopted nightwork legislation after the war, and by 1949 eight states had either relaxed their regulations, continued their wartime suspension of the laws, or, as in the case of Pennsylvania, repealed nightwork altogether. But in a handful of states, legislation specifically regulating nightwork for adult women in restaurants remained on the books until the 1960s.[46]

Thus, as in the dispute over women serving liquor and as will be seen in the response of waitresses to the bartender campaigns, in some circumstances waitresses defied both the dominant gender ideology and the class arguments put forward by their union brothers; they pushed for new definitions of "women's jobs" and "men's jobs" which would serve the interests of their sex. In other circumstances, however, they acceded to the status quo. In the case of nightwork, economic necessity prompted their challenge. Indeed, protest against nightwork prohibitions swelled over the course of the twentieth century as increasing numbers of waitresses—swept into such nontraditional areas as dinner and banquet work, evening cocktail service, and late-night café jobs by the unrelenting demands for female service labor—realized that their own nighttime jobs were at risk.[47] It is important to note that the promise of future jobs or the concept of economic opportunity was not enough to overcome their allegiance to their union brothers; only the more basic defense of one's economic livelihood could justify that break.

The economic motivations of waitresses were buttressed by cultural resources peculiar to their situation as wage-earning women. In challenging the boundaries of their work sphere, waitresses drew on such working-class concepts as the family wage and craft interest, but they reinterpreted these ideas to their advantage. Thus they contended that single and divorced women deserved a family wage, just like male heads of household. And since most night jobs could be encompassed within the generally accepted parameters of the waitress craft, they cited the jurisdictional traditions of their various locals in conjunction with their craft heritage as waitresses in legitimizing their claims. Yet, as the con-

---

[45]Cobble, "Sisters in the Craft," 427–45, traces the controversy over nightwork in the WTUL and the Women's Bureau. According to my evidence, their judgment that nightwork restrictions resulted in slight economic damage did not conform to the picture that emerged from the testimony of restaurant workers in studies done by state agencies, and even in discarded and unpublished studies found in the bureau's own files.

[46]Freeman and Newman, *Some Aspects of the Nightwork Problem,* 19–20, 26; Steinberg, *Wages and Hours.*

[47]In particular, attitudes changed during the war. See memo, Constance Williams to Frieda Miller, Apr. 29, 1947, in box 991, RG 85.

troversy over female bartenders will reveal, the craft mentality left waitresses an ambiguous legacy: it encouraged them to claim certain jobs as
their own—those that fell within the boundaries of waiting work—but
undercut their ability and desire to resist the postwar union campaigns
that argued for the preservation of bartending for men.

The Bartender Campaigns

Buoyed by the 1948 U.S. Supreme Court decision upholding the Michigan law that forbade women to work as bartenders, bartender locals
launched a full-scale legislative crusade aimed at excluding women from
their trade.[48] They were backed by HERE International, which issued a
pamphlet featuring successful local campaigns to date—some 17 states
prohibited "barmaids" by 1948[49]—and encouraged similar drives in other
states. By 1953 the international's officers proudly reported new state laws
and local ordinances in places "such as Ohio (1949), Oregon (1952),
Washington (1952), Michigan (1950) and Illinois (1951) to cite a few."[50]
The motivations of bartenders were clearly economic, but deep-seated
beliefs about gender lent force to them. Noting the reluctance of employers to discharge the women bartenders hired during the war, Bartenders'
Local 503 announced that "the dispensing of Alcoholic Beverages
[should] be restricted to men only, to enable our members to get back to
work." Others worried that barmaids lowered the standards of the craft
by working for less. Some even feared that having women behind the bar
threatened the very survival of bartending as an occupation. Barmaids, it
was pointed out, would give critical ammunition to the prohibitionists'
efforts to create dry districts.[51]

[48]See the U.S. Supreme Court decision dated Dec. 20, 1948, in Goesaert v. Cleary, no.
49, October Term, 1948, and the discussion of this case in Susan Hartmann, *The Home
Front and Beyond: American Women in the 1940s* (Boston: Twayne, 1982), 131; *New
York Times*, Dec. 21, 1948, 27; Baer, *Chains of Protection*, 111–21.
[49]*Barmaid*, like *waitress*, may be seen as a pejorative feminization of the standard term,
bartender, which, like *waiter*, commonly referred only to a man who practiced the craft.
Nevertheless, at times *barmaid* is used here instead of *female bartender* because it reflects
the language of the period and is a less cumbersome way of distinguishing the male and
female groups within the occupation.
[50]*Anti-Barmaid Laws*, December 1948, 3, in reel 30, General Office Records (hereafter
GOR), and *Proceedings*, HERE Convention, 1953, both in HERE International files. By
the 1960s twenty-six states prohibited women from working in mining, bartending, and
other occupations. See Barbara A. Babcock et al., *Sex Discrimination and the Law: Causes
and Remedies* (Boston: Little, Brown, 1975), 261.
[51]*Catering Industry Employee*, December 1936, 42; February 1937, 51; March 1937,
38; October 1940, 33; *Hotel and Club Voice*, Jan. 15, 1947, 4; *Voice of Local 1*, October
1950, 3; *Officers' Reports*, 1949, 26, in HERE International files; *New York Times*, Sept.
1, 1936.

234 Dorothy Sue Cobble

Bartenders displayed a variety of assumptions about femininity and masculinity in making their case. Linking skill with masculinity, they contended that women were incapable of being "proficient mixologists." Male bartenders lacked sex appeal, but by virtue of being male they possessed a superior competence in the technical aspects of mixing drinks. Women were not "emotionally or temperamentally suited for the job," either. One union official went so far as to argue that "a bartender must be a good conversationalist or know when or when not to talk, and you show me the woman who knows that." In addition, women's "moral and physical well-being" was menaced by exposure to alcohol and endangered by unruly, unrestrained male patrons.[52]

The push for restrictive legislation drew on a deeply embedded commitment to preserving what one Michigan official described as "the sacred professional realms of the male." Bartending "should remain a cloister for men," the International General Executive Board intoned. "Women should be encouraged to apply themselves to table service."[53] Bartenders for generations had prided themselves on being the priestly overseers of the exclusively male drinking "societies" that were entrenched in particular taverns and bars. The tavern "functioned as the poor man's counterpart to a private social club." These establishments, "bastions of male fellowship and independence," had been and were to remain a public space reserved solely for the expression of male culture—a space where men didn't "have to work at being gentlemen." At times a woman might enter if she was escorted by a man or if she was in a subordinate, thoroughly feminized role, such as that of the bar girl who solicited drinks with the implicit assumption of sexual favors to follow, or that of the stripper. A woman behind the bar, however, undercut

---

[52]*Catering Industry Employee*, April 1939, 45; October 1942, 18; January 1943, 29; February 1943, 31; April 1943, 30; *Hotel and Club Voice*, Jan. 15, 1947, 4; Aug. 16, 1941, 2; *Voice of Local 1*, October 1950, 3; *Officers' Reports*, 1949, 26, in HERE International files; Edith Carroll, "Barmaids Come Back," *New York Times Magazine*, Mar. 18, 1945, 27; *New York Times*, Aug. 19, 1946. The historian Susan Hartmann (*Home Front and Beyond*, 132) has argued that the gallantry behind these laws is suspect. Female bartenders may actually be subject to fewer moral and physical dangers than cocktail waitresses, who lack the protection of a bar between them and the patrons. It is also possible that the higher status of bartending would help insulate women from customer abuse. Nevertheless, many women who have moved into nontraditional jobs have been subjected to hostility and abuse, especially if they work among many men. Moreover, union male bartenders considered it their responsibility to protect unescorted women and cocktail waitresses from physical abuse (see *Catering Industry Employee*, March 1945, 18). Who would back up the lone female bartender?

[53]*Michigan Hotel Bar-Restaurant Review*, July 1942, 1–2; *Catering Industry Employee*, February 1935, 21, 36; *Proceedings*, HERE Convention, 1938, in HERE International files.

not only the strict segregation between the sexes but challenged the traditional hierarchical gender relations that reigned in the tavern society.[54]

The aversion of male bartenders to opening their ranks to women was shared by the American public. "The tavern hostess or barmaid . . . is a disgrace," one Chicago columnist wrote, "one step away from the lowest form of livelihood. It's a very sordid situation." The American public had long condemned women who handled liquor and publicly mingled with men, and now they also deemed women eminently corruptible by liquor and incapable of exerting the authority over customers required of the bartender.[55]

Although waitresses had balked at waiters' earlier attempts to legislate their banishment from establishments that served liquor, they now raised few objections to legislation banning them from bartending, despite the numbers of women who had filled such jobs during the wartime shortage.[56] When HERE president Ed Flore announced that "we are secure in the conviction that service at public or private bars is exclusively the employment of male employees" and that "this thought has been generously concurred in by the female members of our International Union," he apparently spoke the truth. The Portland waitresses' union refused to dispatch women as bartenders because "this is not proper employment for women," and its members joined with bartenders in picketing a place where two women dispensed beer. Many waitresses' locals included clauses in their work rules and agreements forbidding women to tend bar. The members of the Los Angeles local, according to their business manager, Mae Stoneman, had "strict instructions not to pour, open, [or] mix [liquor], or even pick up a piece of garnish on penalty of a stiff fine, suspension, or even expulsion."[57]

Reports from Ohio, where waitresses lobbied on behalf of a law "forbidding the employment of women, except owners and/or owners' wives,

[54]The quotes are from Jon M. Kingsdale, "The 'Poor Man's Club': Social Functions of the Urban Working-Class Saloon," *American Quarterly*, 25 (October 1973), 472–89, and Carroll, "Barmaids Come Back," 27. James Spradley and Brenda Mann, *The Cocktail Waitress: Women's Work in a Man's World* (New York: Wiley, 1975), contains an extended anthropological analysis of male and female tensions in bars and the American male bartender's tenacious protection of his "sacred male space" behind the bar; see esp. 1–14, 144–48. For a historical discussion of the centrality of taverns to working-class male culture, see Roy Rosenzweig, *Eight Hours for What We Will: Workers and Leisure in an Industrial City, 1870–1920* (Cambridge: Cambridge University Press, 1983), 35–65, 93–126.

[55]*Catering Industry Employee*, December 1934, 25.

[56]Consult *Catering Industry Employee*, 1940 through 1953, and the HERE International correspondence files.

[57]*Catering Industry Employee*, June 1941, 3; February 1941, 32; Mae Stoneman to Bob Wasson, Apr. 25, 1944, in reel 628, LUR, and contract between the Restaurant and Hotel Employers Council of Southern California and Los Angeles LJEB HERE, 1962–1967, both in HERE International files.

as bartenders," reveal some of the explanations voiced by those wait-resses who publicly supported the legislation. According to the *Catering Industry Employee*, the waitresses testified that "tending bar is a man's job, and that handling kegs, beer cases, packing coolers and similar work ... [was] unsuited to women." The union brief claimed that wait-resses favored restrictive legislation because a woman serving liquor "can turn away from an unruly or uncivil customer and refuse to approach his table while the girl tending bar must remain near at hand" and because many "felt more secure working where a male bartender was on duty" and preferred having "a man to back up" their decisions. The brief also noted that waitresses supported the crusade because plenty of jobs ex-isted for them as waitresses.[58]

Although the Ohio waitresses conceded differences between men and women in physical strength and recognized the lack of authority an iso-lated female interloper would have in a situation reserved for the expres-sion of male culture and camaraderie, they and other waitresses rejected many of the other arguments put forward by their brothers. Kitty Am-sler, a St. Louis waitress officer since 1917, voiced her "complete accord with the opinion that women have no place behind the bar," but in a letter to the international questioned the logic of the bartenders: "If women bartenders are grist for the Dry Mill why aren't the wives and daughters of the licensee who appear to be excepted by most of the state laws you exhibit?" Other waitresses sniffed at women's so-called inca-pacity to mix drinks and saw no need to have their morals defended.[59]

The decision of waitresses to claim the serving of liquor as their own while allowing the mixing to be done by men is best understood within the context of competing economic and ideological (gender and class) considerations. As the Ohio waitresses noted, the retention of jobs was not so pressing an issue in the postwar years as it had been in the 1930s. Indeed, white waitresses were enjoying a surplus of jobs in the 1940s and 1950s. Those few who had moved into bartending during the war found it easy to transfer back into waitressing. Moreover, the restrictive policies advocated by bartender locals were legitimized by strongly held societal proscriptions against women's invading the sacred male space of the bar—proscriptions that many waitresses accepted.[60] When pressed in an

[58]*Catering Industry Employee*, June 1949, 15; "Brief in Support of Legislation to Pro-hibit Employment of Women Bartenders in Ohio" (c. 1949), 3, in reel 30, GOR, HERE International files.
[59]Kitty Amsler to Hugo Ernst, Jan. 5, 1949, in reel 229, LUR, HERE International files; Hotel and Restaurant Employees International Alliance and Bartenders International League of America, *Fifty Years of Progress: A Brief History of Our Union, 1891–1941* (Cincinnati, 1941), 68.
[60]Sociological studies of the social relations of food service employees in the workplace as well as my own research suggest that another factor relevant to the hesitancy of wait-

interview to explain why barmaids for so long were not accepted in the union, Gertrude Sweet finally pointed to certain gender concerns: "Men . . . women as well . . . simply felt that it was not the place for a woman to work in a bar."[61]

Finally, for many waitresses, to be a bartender was not only unladylike but unwaitress-like. In disputes with the waiters, the proud craft traditions of waitresses fueled their protests. Waiters were attempting to claim aspects of waiting work that to a skilled waitress properly fell within the boundaries of her craft. With the bartenders, the opposite was true: the craft heritage shared by food service workers lent credence to the bartenders' claim that the work "belonged" to them. As San Francisco's veteran waitress leader Jackie Walsh explained some years later in regard to the admission of bar girls: "There wasn't anything really wrong with having them in except that they weren't bona fide waitresses nor did they do waitress work. . . . In other words they were not qualified craftsmen."[62]

Significantly, the single organized protest came from black women bartenders in Chicago. In 1951, when the Chicago city council adopted an ordinance forbidding women "to dispense alcoholic beverages," 300 barmaids belonging to the all-black Waitresses', Bartenders', and Cooks' Local 444 refused "to pay dues until the matter [was] cleared up." The officers of Local 444 contemplated replacing the female bartenders with men but in the end decided they were "not in a position to force the issue." Women continued to be dispatched from the hiring hall and the local even included women in their bartender training program, hiring Lilli Belle Curry, a former local 444 officer, and two other black women as instructors.[63]

In 1961, however, the old city ordinance was finally enforced and some 400 black female bartenders lost their jobs. With few equally lucrative options open to them and outraged at this discrimination, they

---

resses may have been the real power exercised by the bartender. A waitress literally cannot perform her work if the bartender does not cooperate. Waitresses, it appears, perceived waiters more as equals; bartenders were seen as having greater authority and status. See Cobble, "Sisters in the Craft," 98–108, 509–13, and earlier accounts of food service workers such as William Whyte's classic *Human Relations in the Restaurant Industry* (New York: McGraw-Hill, 1948).

[61] Interview with Gertrude Sweet by Shirley Tanzer, Aug. 2, 1976, for the University of Michigan/Wayne State Oral History Project, "Twentieth-Century Trade Union Woman: Vehicle for Social Change" (New York Times Microfilm, 1979), 21.

[62] Interview with Jackie Walsh by Lucy Kendall, March–November 1980, for the Women in California Collection, 122, California Historical Society Library, San Francisco.

[63] "1955 Report," typed sheet attached to letter, Local 356 to GP, Oct. 14, 1958; Local 444 to GP, May 13, 1952; Murray Washington to GP, July 3, 1954; Willis Thomas, secretary-treasurer, Local 356, "On the Job: Bartenders Training Program" (c. 1958), (Local 356 had absorbed the 900-member Local 444); all in reel 10, Defunct Union Records, HERE International files.

protested. Since their local refused to help—despite having collected dues from them for years—the barmaids organized community support. They picketed city hall, demanding repeal of the ordinance, and advertised their economic plight through placards emphasizing their right to a wage capable of supporting their families: "City Fathers Unfair to Working Mothers," "Help Us Keep Our Children Educated," "The Right to Work Is the Right to Live." Black community newspapers carried their story, stressing the lack of concern shown by the city council and the union as to whether "these Negro women, many of them mothers," were employed or were to be "thrown on ADC's Relief Rolls. Unlike white girls," the paper continued, "these women . . . have little or no recourse except to apply for relief. Those who have been able to find jobs are largely working as baby sitters, housemaids, 'day workers,' part-time waitresses . . . and mail order house employees," the reporter noted.[64]

In desperation the women wrote the international for assistance, stating that their local officers "told us there is nothing they can do" and pointing out that "many of us have families to raise and are not experienced in any other field." Ed Miller's curt reply offered little consolation and in fact was rather disingenuous in view of the active support of the international for state and local barmaid ordinances. "Please be advised that the International Union had nothing to do with the law in Chicago, Illinois, and the matter is entirely up to the local union in Chicago."[65] Without the backing of either the international or their local union, many black barmaids permanently lost their "career union jobs"—as the black newspaper *New Crusader* dubbed them—even though eventually the ordinance was overturned.

These protests by black women erupted precisely because of their more extreme economic situation and their distinct cultural inheritance as black women and black trade unionists. Because of the discrimination against black women in the food service industry, their economic alternatives were more limited than those of white women. In addition, because their daily experience largely conflicted with the reigning ideology of "separate spheres," both black men and women were less encumbered with the desire to conform to these gender prescriptions, especially when "moral protection" conflicted with economic need. Lastly, because of the history of discrimination against them from their international and at times even from their co-workers, black waitresses did not fully embrace the white craft traditions so firmly revered by their white union brothers and sisters. They had never been thoroughly accepted as either ladies or sisters in the craft. Thus, unlike white waitresses, black women boldly

[64]*New Crusader* (Chicago), Feb. 11 and 18, 1961.
[65]Mrs. Leila Adkins et al. to Ed Miller, Feb. 23, 1961, and Miller to Adkins, Mar. 2, 1961, in reel 30, GOR, HERE International files.

proclaimed their right to serve liquor in taverns even where no food was available as well as their right to mix drinks.

The bartender campaign was ultimately a losing one, but the policies advocated by male unionists and tolerated by their union sisters slowed the feminization of bartending after World War II considerably. Municipal and state ordinances prohibiting female bartenders were sustained throughout the 1960s; women did not move into bartending in any numbers until the 1970s, when lawsuits charging sex discrimination under Title VII of the Civil Rights Act of 1964 finally emerged victorious.[66] After close to a century of resistance, the union opened its doors to women.

The policies pursued by male and female culinary workers frequently not only determined the gender boundaries within the industry but critically affected the rate of feminization of certain categories of work. The protective legislation put forward by male culinary unionists retarded the movement of women into food service jobs and restricted them to the least lucrative categories of the trade. Nevertheless, although waiters and bartenders devised similar defensive strategies, waiters were never as successful in implementing these restrictive measures. The reasons are manifold. First, women entered waitressing earlier—that is, before unionization—and in greater numbers. By 1920 women outnumbered men in the waiting craft and by the 1950s the occupation had become thoroughly feminized. Bartenders, on the other hand, were undisturbed by female competitors until after World War II.[67] Second, although the entry of women into waiting work was retarded by moral judgments by the public at large, the public never felt strongly enough against waitresses' *serving* liquor to countenance widespread restrictive legislation. Societal proscriptions against female bartenders, in contrast, were deeply felt, and the campaign to block women's entry into the craft was waged at the height of the "feminine mystique."

Third, as members of a classic male preserve, bartenders supported exclusionary policies unanimously. Male waiters, on the other hand, were divided in their response to female co-workers. Instead of excluding women from the union entirely, from the earliest days a sizable number had argued for their organization, had admitted them into their locals, and in fact had even recognized them as sister craftswomen. Thus waiters who advocated restrictive policies never had the complete and enthusias-

[66]Baer, *Chains of Protection*, 111–21; Hartmann, *Home Front and Beyond*, 131–33. See Babcock et al., *Sex Discrimination and the Law*, 269–71, for accounts of litigation related to the mixing of liquor by women.

[67]The shifting attitude of male unionists can be closely correlated with the number of women in their trade. Where the numbers are small, an exclusionary policy is feasible. At a certain point, however, when a critical mass of women is reached, new policies—usually equal pay and organizing—are advocated.

tic backing of their fellow craftsmen which the bartenders enjoyed. Moreover, waiter officials of mixed-sex locals faced opposition from women members within their own union. The vast majority of bartender officials were free of such political and organizational hindrances.

Of course, where and when *female* food service workers drew the line also played a critical role in shaping the gendered labor force. The elite position of men within the industry was sustained in part by the reluctance of unionized waitresses to challenge men's claim to own both the waiting work in the fancier, more formal all-male houses[68] and the coveted work of mixing and pouring drinks. Yet when external forces such as Prohibition, World War II, and the unremitting demand for female service work over the course of the twentieth century opened up new categories of waiting work, women ensured the institutionalization of these changes. Organized into craft-based, sex-segregated locals, they effectively *defended* against attempts to deprive them of liquor service and nightwork. In fighting to secure the occupational advances that were thrust upon them, they permanently extended the boundaries of the territory labeled "female" and facilitated the feminization of their trade.

The process by which men and women food servers formulated their stance on the disputes over "men's work" and "women's work" was not simple or straightforward: they delicately balanced economic, gender, and class considerations. Waitresses, for example, considered not only their economic interests as primary wage earners but their working-class traditions as practicing craft unionists and adherents of a communitarian "moral economy" perspective.[69] Their shifting definitions of gender

[68]These policies were not challenged until the 1970s. The protests arose from the filing of lawsuits (often naming the union as a defendant) by waitresses individually and in small groups rather than from protests by waitress locals or officers. Louise Kapp Howe details the background of a pivotal New York City suit initiated by the American Civil Liberties Union on behalf of two waitresses who sought to work in such classic all-male bastions as the 21 Club and the Four Seasons. Local 1, named in the suit, claimed that the union had no control over hiring. See Howe, *Pink-Collar Workers: Inside the World of Women's Work* (New York: Avon, 1977), 103–42, and *New York Times*, Nov. 11, 1976. See Babcock et al., *Sex Discrimination and the Law*, 271, for a discussion of another case, Evans v. Sheraton Park Hotel, 503 F.2d 177 (1974), in which a "dissident" group of union waitresses charged that Local 507's separate-sex structure resulted in waiters' being assigned the more lucrative types of banquet work.

[69]The concern evidenced by waitresses over protecting the jobs of their union brothers can be seen as deriving in part from this working-class tradition. The concept of "moral economy" was first developed by E. P. Thompson in "The Moral Economy of the English Crowd in the Eighteenth Century," *Past and Present*, 50 (February 1971), 70. Maurine Greenwald argues that Seattle working-class women subscribed to this concept in determining who had a legitimate claim to wage work: "Working-Class Feminism and the Family Wage Ideal: The Seattle Debate on Married Women's Right to Work, 1914–1920," *Journal of American History*, 76 (June 1989), 118–149.

equality and economic need also affected their ultimate position. At times these considerations reinforced each other, as with the issue of liquor service and ultimately with nightwork. Their defense of their jurisdictional claims, as practitioners of a craft, their desire for economic advancement, and their repudiation of the particular conceptions of gender advocated by their male counterparts all combined to lead them into sharp conflict with their union brothers. At other points, as during the bartender campaigns, their concerns competed, forcing them to pursue one allegiance at the expense of another. Their desire for economic opportunity and gender equality was circumscribed by their loyalty to craft traditions and their notions of gender separatism.

The policies pursued by unionized waitresses reveal the complicated nature of working-class feminism, a world view that incorporated many identified strands of middle-class feminism while remaining distinctly working class. Like many equal-rights feminists, they proclaimed their desire to be treated the same as their male co-workers. They also believed in the right of women to work outside the home and to be visible actors in the public sphere.[70] Simultaneously, however, they accepted and defended a separate female sphere within this work world. Instead of challenging the classification of work as either men's or women's and demanding an end to the separate-sphere ideology, waitresses focused on upgrading the jobs labeled female and extending the boundaries of their female sphere.[71] They sought equality through separation—an approach not too far removed from that adopted by domestic feminists of the late nineteenth century. Indeed, many waitresses as late as the 1970s defended their separate-sex locals with their separate dispatch procedures for men and women against lawsuits alleging sex bias and discrimination.[72] Union leaders such as Detroit's Myra Wolfgang also vehemently opposed the Equal Rights Amendment and pushed for the retention of protective

[70]Although the scope of this essay does not allow for a discussion of the impact of ethnicity on the cultural resources available to union waitresses in their ideological debates, I have argued elsewhere that the equal-rights individualist tradition was more available to them than to many other working-class occupational groups because of their native-born status and Old World ethnic backgrounds. For a more extended analysis, see Cobble, "Sisters in the Craft," 45–50.

[71]As Temma Kaplan has noted: in defending what many working-class women perceive as the rights accorded them by the sexual division of labor, such women have taken actions that have had "revolutionary consequences": "Female Consciousness and Collective Action: The Case of Barcelona, 1910–1918," *Signs: Journal of Women in Culture and Society,* 7 (Spring 1982), 545–66.

[72]A federal court ruled in Evans v. Sheraton Park Hotel, 503 F.2d 177 (1974), that the maintenance of two sex-segregated locals constituted an "unlawful employment practice" within the equal employment provisions of the Civil Rights Act of 1964. The waitresses in this local divided over the issue.

legislation.[73] In these moments, waitresses often argued from difference, pointing to the special needs of women.

The strategies of waitresses over the course of the twentieth century do not fall into neat compartments, however. As Joan Scott has argued in regard to feminists in general, waitresses did not "oscillate between demands for equality and affirmations of difference": rather, they attempted "to reconcile theories of equal rights with cultural concepts of sexual difference."[74] Rejecting absolutist solutions, waitresses formulated approaches on the basis of the particular situation confronting them. Rejecting the conservative parameters of the debate, they sought an equality based not on sameness but on difference.

[73]An unidentified newspaper clipping (c. 1957) in file 24, box 3, Bertha Metro Collection, California Historical Society, San Francisco, tells of waitresses who testified on behalf of maximum hours laws for women and other protective legislation; see also typed sheets headed "News Release on Myra Wolfgang," Nov. 12, 1976, 2, in Photo Records, HERE International files. For opposition to the ERA see *Hotel and Club Voice,* Apr. 19, 1947, 7; Mar. 29, 1947, June 18, 1949, 4; *Proceedings,* HERE Convention, 1953, 178–79; Bernard Rosenberg and Saul Weinman, "Young Women Who Work: Interview with Myra Wolfgang," *Dissent* (Winter 1972), 32–33; House General Subcommittee on Labor and Committee on Education and Labor, *Hearings to Amend the Fair Labor Standards Act of 1938,* 88th Cong. 1st sess. December 1963, 116; Myra K. Wolfgang, "From Testimony Presented before the Subcommittee on Constitutional Amendments of the Senate Committee on the Judiciary on May 6, 1970, in the course of Hearings on Proposed 'Equal Rights' Amendments to the Constitution," *Congressional Digest,* 50 (January 1971), 19–23.

[74]Scott, "Sears Case," 176. See Nancy Cott, *The Grounding of Modern Feminism* (New Haven: Yale University Press, 1987), for a discussion of the many strands of middle-class feminism. The classic accounts of domestic feminism include Daniel Scott Smith, "Family Limitation, Sexual Control, and Domestic Feminism in Victorian America," in *Clio's Consciousness Raised,* ed. Mary S. Hartman and Lois W. Banner (New York: Harper & Row, 1974), and Kathryn Kish Sklar, *Catharine Beecher: A Study in American Domesticity* (New Haven: Yale University Press, 1973). Alice Kessler-Harris also has questioned the use of the poles of difference and equality in the writing of the history of feminism. Consult Kessler-Harris, "The Debate over Equality for Women in the Work Place: Recognizing Differences," in *Women and Work: An Annual Review,* vol. 1, ed. Laurie Larwood, Ann Stromberg, and Barbara Gutek (Beverly Hills, Calif.: Sage, 1985), 145–53.

CHAPTER TEN

Private Eyes, Public Women: Images of Class and Sex in the Urban South, Atlanta, Georgia, 1913–1915

Jacquelyn Dowd Hall

> Can women who have been looked at for too long ever master the art of looking back?
>
> Martha Banta, *Imaging American Women*

In the fall of 1985, historians and archivists in Atlanta, Georgia, made a startling discovery. They found hundreds of labor spy reports, stored and forgotten in the basement of the Fulton Bag and Cotton Mills, once the city's largest textile factory.[1] Hired in 1914, shortly before a protracted strike, the detectives who filed these reports masqueraded as workers, lived in the mill village, and infiltrated the union. They remained after the conflict ended, acting as management's eyes and ears in the mill, serving the more generalized needs of local manufacturers, and tracking the sentiment surrounding the trial, conviction, and subsequent lynching of Leo Frank, a Jewish factory superintendent accused of murdering a thirteen-year-old girl.

Earlier versions of this essay were presented at the annual meeting of the Organization of American Historians, St. Louis, Mo., Apr. 6, 1989, and at the Seminar on Race, Class, and Gender in Southern History, University of California Graduate Program in Southern History, University of California, San Diego, June 23, 1989. It owes a great deal to the research assistance of Lawrence Boyette. Thanks to Ava Baron, Pamela Dean, Sarah Deutsch, John D'Emilio, Peter Filene, Leon Fink, Julia Greene, Nancy Hewitt, John Kasson, Robert Korstad, James Leloudis, Susan Levine, Kathleen Much, Mary Murphy, Christine Stansell, and Joel Williamson for their incisive comments. My greatest debt is to Glenda Gilmore, who worked with me on this project from start to finish. I am also grateful for a research grant from the Institute for Research in Social Science of the University of North Carolina at Chapel Hill and for the financial support of the National Endowment for the Humanities and the Andrew W. Mellon Foundation, which enabled me to complete this essay at the Center for Advanced Study in the Behavioral Sciences.

[1] Robert C. McMath, Jr., "History by a Graveyard: The Fulton Bag and Cotton Mills Records," *Labor's Heritage*, 1 (April 1989), 4–9; Fulton Mills Collection, Price Gilbert Memorial Library, Georgia Institute of Technology, Atlanta. I owe a special debt to Bob McMath for inviting me to use these papers soon after they became available.

The South's textile barons left few paper trails, so these accounts are bound to attract the attention of historians eager for intimate details of management policy and labor strife.[2] Obviously, such evidence calls for special caution. The spies were agents of domination, and they fashioned their stories for particular readers—the powerful men they hoped both to manipulate and to serve. Their writings inscribed visually based modes of surveillance and portrayal, what feminist film critics call the "male gaze." The spies saw without being seen, revealed secrets without themselves being revealed. Their portrayals, by definition, were not reciprocal.[3] They were also deeply gendered, for they sexualized women and denigrated the manliness of mill village men.

Yet the spy reports' self-interestedness is part of their value, for these documents tell us as much about their writers and the conventions that directed their pens as about the workers they profess to portray. This reflexivity has a further advantage. It alerts us to the assumptions and strategies of the spies' adversaries, the trade unionists and reformers who sought to intervene on the workers' behalf. The workers who appeared in the trade unionists' photographs and the reformers' broadsides, like those who animated the spy reports, bore little resemblance to the flesh-and-blood individuals who worked in the mill. Read together, however, and with an eye to relations of dialogue and dominance, these warring images may indeed reveal secrets—about how visions of workers are constructed and deployed; about the shifting meanings of labor conflict when class and gender issues are transposed; about the modernization of sex and the discursive face of power.[4] By showing us a society in ferment, they also challenge the notion that the New South remained an isolated, cohesive, and backward region.

[2]For historians' relatively uncritical reliance on informers' reports, see Paul Thompson, *The Voice of the Past: Oral History* (New York: Oxford University Press, 1988), 40, 101. The literature on labor espionage itself, however, is quite thin. See U.S. Congress, Senate, *Violations of Free Speech and Assembly and Interference with Rights of Labor: Hearings before the Subcommittee of the Committee on Education and Labor on S. Res. 266*, 74th Cong., 2d sess. (Washington, D.C.: U.S. Government Printing Office, 1936); Darryl Holter, "Labor Spies and Union-Busting in Wisconsin, 1890–1940," *Wisconsin Magazine of History*, 68 (Summer 1985), 243–65; Charles K. Hyde, "Undercover and Underground: Labor Spies and Mine Management in the Early Twentieth Century," *Business History Review*, 60 (Spring 1986), 1–27; Gene Caesar, *The Incredible Detective: The Biography of William J. Burns* (Englewood Cliffs, N.J.: Prentice-Hall, 1968); Frank Morn, *"The Eye That Never Sleeps": A History of the Pinkerton National Detective Agency* (Bloomington: Indiana University Press, 1982); Dirk Hoerder, ed., *Plutocrats and Socialists: Reports by German Diplomats and Agents on the American Labor Movement, 1878–1917* (Munich: K. G. Saur, 1981); and William M. Reddy, "The Batteurs and the Informer's Eye: A Labour Dispute under the French Second Empire," *History Workshop*, 7 (Spring 1979), 30–44.

[3]Laura Mulvey, "Visual Pleasure and Narrative Cinema," *Screen*, 16 (Autumn 1975), 6–18; Judith Mayne, "Feminist Film Theory and Criticism," *Signs: Journal of Women in Culture and Society*, 2 (Autumn 1985), 81–100.

[4]James Clifford, "On Ethnographic Authority," in James Clifford, *The Predicament of Culture* (Cambridge: Harvard University Press, 1988), 14, 23.

C. Vann Woodward, the South's foremost historian, made his mark in the 1940s and 1950s by attacking the notion of consensus and continuity, long before the consensus school of American history came under assault from other quarters. Yet even Woodward, by deflating the pretensions of the New South's pro-industry and pro-northern-capital boosters, encouraged the impression that the defeat of Populism and the triumph of Jim Crow in the 1890s ushered in an era of suffocating stagnation, relieved only by the jolt of World War II. This assumption has been reinforced in recent years by a recrudescence of consensus theories among southern scholars of every political stripe.[5]

Neither Woodward nor his critics saw women as historical actors, nor did gender conflict figure in their debates. That neglect is not surprising; more puzzling are the regional lacunae in the burgeoning field of women's history. Historians of women have produced a copious literature on the impact of industrialization, urbanization, consumerism, and commercialized leisure on working-class women in the Northeast and Midwest. But these modern workers, pioneers of a new heterosocial subculture, disappear below the Mason-Dixon line. Here feminist historians find no Sister Carries, no "women adrift," no "charity girls," only the familiar figures of a reactionary sexual mythology: the promiscuous black woman and the passionless white lady.[6]

[5]C. Vann Woodward, *Thinking Back: The Perils of Writing History* (Baton Rouge: Louisiana State University Press, 1986), 59–79; Morgan Kousser and James M. McPherson, eds., *Region, Race, and Reconstruction* (New York: Oxford University Press, 1982), xvii. Among those Woodward calls the "New Continuarians" are Dwight B. Billings, Jr., *Planters and the Making of a "New South": Class, Politics, and Development in North Carolina, 1865–1900* (Chapel Hill: University of North Carolina Press, 1979); David Goldfield, *Cotton Fields and Skyscrapers: Southern City and Region, 1607–1980* (Baton Rouge: Louisiana State University Press, 1982); Jonathan M. Wiener, *Social Origins of the New South: Alabama, 1860–1885* (Baton Rouge: Louisiana State University Press, 1978); George B. Tindall, *The Persistent Tradition in New South Politics* (Baton Rouge: Louisiana State University Press, 1975). A number of recent studies, however, reinforce Woodward's emphasis on discontinuity. Edward L. Ayers, *The Promise of the New South: Life after Reconstruction* (New York: Oxford University Press, 1992), for instance, argues that the New South was even newer than Woodward imagined. See also David L. Carlton, "The Revolution from Above: The National Market and the Beginnings of Industrialization in North Carolina," *Journal of American History*, 77 (September 1990), 445–75; Don H. Doyle, *New Men, New Cities: Atlanta, Nashville, Charleston, Mobile, 1860–1910* (Chapel Hill: University of North Carolina Press, 1990); Glenda Gilmore, "Gender and Jim Crow: Women and the Politics of White Supremacy in North Carolina, 1896–1922" (Ph.D. diss., University of North Carolina at Chapel Hill, 1992); Steven Hahn, "Class and State in Postemancipation Societies: Southern Planters in Comparative Perspective," *American Historical Review*, 95 (February 1990), 75–98; Anne Goodwyn Jones, *Faulkner's Daughters* (manuscript in progress); and James L. Leloudis, "'A More Certain Means of Grace': Pedagogy, Self, and Society in North Carolina, 1880–1920" (Ph.D. diss., University of North Carolina at Chapel Hill, 1989).

[6]Theodore Dreiser, *Sister Carrie* (New York: Doubleday, 1900); Kathy Peiss, "'Charity Girls' and City Pleasures: Historical Notes on Working-Class Sexuality, 1880–1920," in *Powers of Desire: The Politics of Sexuality*, ed. Ann Snitow, Christine Stansell, and Sharon Thompson, 74–87 (New York: Monthly Review Press, 1983); Joanne J. Meyerowitz,

The interweaving stories of the Fulton Mills strike and the Leo Frank case, as revealed in the competing versions of pro- and antilabor sources, confound such flat and timeless generalizations. They indicate the depth of the anxiety generated by the growth of a permanent working class with its own forms of heterosociability and social crime. They allow us to glimpse a major source of this anxiety: women in action, creating a new sexual system and challenging an older, rural-based patriarchal order. Attention to these women suggests the inadequacy of interpretations that stress the white South's monolithic sexual conservatism, pointing instead to the region's entanglement in national developments, to women's sexual agency, and to the competing discourses that constituted the public's response.[7]

I

Jacob Elsas, a German Jewish immigrant, founded the Fulton Bag and Cotton Mills in 1889, building houses for his employees in an area known first as the Factory Lot and then as Cabbagetown. Atlanta tripled in size over the next thirty years, and Fulton Mills grew with the city. By 1914, when Jacob's son Oscar took over the presidency, Fulton Mills was producing sheeting, twine, and cotton and burlap bags at branch plants throughout the country. Approximately 1,300 people worked in its Atlanta headquarters alone. Thirty-five percent of these employees were women, and 12 percent were boys and girls under sixteen.[8]

Women Adrift: Independent Wage Earners in Chicago, 1880–1930 (Chicago: University of Chicago Press, 1988), and "Sexual Geography and Gender Economy: The Furnished Room Districts of Chicago, 1890–1930," *Gender and History*, 2 (Autumn 1990), 274–96; and Estelle Freedman and John D'Emilio, *Intimate Matters: A History of Sexuality in America* (New York: Harper & Row, 1988), 171–235. There is an extensive literature on the South's split image of female sexuality, a subject that was the focus of my own earlier work: Jacquelyn Dowd Hall, *Revolt against Chivalry: Jessie Daniel Ames and the Women's Campaign against Lynching* (New York: Columbia University Press, 1979); and " 'The Mind That Burns in Each Body': Women, Rape, and Racial Violence," in Snitow et al., *Powers of Desire*, 328–49.

[7] For other glimpses of the emergence of new patterns of sociability and sexual behavior in the South, see Barbara Shaw Anderson, "Struggling with the Burdens of Feminine Virtue: The Case of Ida Ball Warren in North Carolina, 1914–1916" (master's thesis, University of North Carolina at Chapel Hill, 1988); Jacquelyn Dowd Hall, "Disorderly Women: Gender and Labor Militancy in the Appalachian South," *Journal of American History*, 73 (September 1986), 354–82; Jacquelyn Dowd Hall, James Leloudis, Robert Korstad, Mary Murphy, Lu Ann Jones, and Christopher B. Daly, *Like a Family: The Making of a Southern Cotton Mill World* (Chapel Hill: University of North Carolina Press, 1987), 225–36, 252–88; and Rebecca Lallier, "A Place of Beginning Again: The North Carolina Industrial Farm Colony, 1929–1947" (master's thesis, University of North Carolina at Chapel Hill, 1990).

[8] U.S. Department of Commerce, Bureau of the Census, *Eleventh Census of the United States* (Washington, D.C.: U.S. Government Printing Office, 1895), 1:454, and *Donald B.*

Fulton Mills had a reputation as a "hobo mill." Its high turnover rate was seen as a telltale sign of poor working conditions and a shabbily maintained company town. In truth, the Factory Lot resembled other working-class communities in the urban South, and the owners had much in common with their peers. Mill village conditions varied widely, but the outdoor privies, unpaved roads, poverty, and disease that marked the Factory Lot were not at all unusual.[9]

Three things, however, set Elsas's firm apart. One was a labor contract that codified—and thus revealed—the unilateral nature of labor relations in the mills. Unlike most mill owners, who simply hired and fired at will, Elsas required each worker to sign a contract specifying that the company assumed no responsibility for work-related injuries and that it could discharge and evict employees without warning at any time. Workers, on the other hand, were obligated to pay for damage to equipment, fined for minor infractions, and compelled to forfeit a week's wages if they quit without giving notice. Fulton Mills' other distinctions were vagaries of fate: Elsas had the bad luck, first, to come under the intense scrutiny of federal investigators during the strike, and second, to leave behind, in the form of the labor spy reports, an extensive record of the

Dodd and Wynell S. Dodd, *Historical Statistics of the South, 1790–1970* (University: University of Alabama Press, 1973), 74; *Davison's Textile Blue Book, 1910–1911* (New York: Davison, 1910), 69; "100th Anniversary Fulton Cotton Mills," *Textile Industries*, December 1968, 63–64; Memorandum for Secretary Wilson, by Robert M. McWade and John S. Colpoys, Aug. 18, 1915, in Fulton Bag Company, Case File 33/41, Record Group 280, Federal Mediation and Conciliation Service Records, Suitland Branch, National Archives (hereafter McWade and Colpoys Memorandum); Inis Weed, "Preliminary Report," July 28, 1914, in Records of the U.S. Commission on Industrial Relations, U.S. Department of Labor, box 10, Record Group 174, National Archives, Washington, D.C. (hereafter RG 174). The Records of the U.S. Commission on Industrial Relations are also available on microfilm: Melvyn Dubofsky, ed., *U.S. Commission on Industrial Relations, 1912–1915, Unpublished Records of the Division of Research and Investigation: Reports, Staff Studies, and Background Materials* (Frederick, Md.: University Publications of America, 1985).

[9]In 1911 the U.S. Bureau of Labor found little difference in the living standards of workers in three typical mill settings: Atlanta; Greensboro, N.C.; and Burlington, N.C. Families in all three communities suffered from serious illnesses, dietary deficiencies, and decrepit surroundings. See U.S. Congress, Senate, *Report on Condition of Woman and Child Wage-Earners in the United States*, vol. 16, *Family Budgets of Typical Cotton-Mill Workers*, prepared by Wood F. Worcester and Daisy Worthington Worcester, 61st Cong., 2d sess. (Washington, D.C.: U.S. Government Printing Office, 1911), 19–171. For mill owners' treatment of their employees during this period, see Edward H. Beardsley, *A History of Neglect: Health Care for Blacks and Mill Workers in the Twentieth-Century South* (Knoxville: University of Tennessee Press, 1987). For mill village life, see Hall et al., *Like a Family*; I. A. Newby, *Plain Folk in the New South* (Baton Rouge: Louisiana State University Press, 1989); and Allen Tullos, *Habits of Industry: White Culture and the Transformation of the Carolina Piedmont* (Chapel Hill: University of North Carolina Press, 1989).

offstage attitudes and behavior other self-proclaimed paternalists successfully concealed.[10]

The earliest sign of the labor trouble that would engulf the mill came
in October 1913, when several hundred weavers and loom fixers staged a
work stoppage in protest over the firing of a loom fixer and the company's decision to increase the amount of time required for giving notice,
a ploy designed to curb workers' mobility and thus to squelch the most
common form of everyday resistance in the southern mills. This walkout,
conducted mainly by men, was self-initiated and short-lived, but in its
wake the workers organized Local 886 of the United Textile Workers
Union of America (UTW).[11]

Elsas responded by contracting with the Philadelphia-based Railway
Audit and Inspection Company, as well as with several smaller southern
firms, to plant undercover "operatives" in his mill.[12] He also began firing union members, and in May 1914, workers walked out again. Their
initial demand for the reinstatement of the discharged employees gradually expanded to include appeals for higher wages, shorter hours, an end
to child labor, and the abandonment of the "present vicious contract system." This time the unionists mobilized men, women, and children alike,
precipitating what one UTW organizer called "the first big strike of organized workers in the cotton mills of the South."[13]

The Fulton Mills walkout was not in fact southern mill hands' "first
big strike." But 1914 did mark the first time that the UTW and the
American Federation of Labor (AFL) poured significant resources into

---

[10]*Journal of Labor*, May 29, 1914, 4; Operative 16, Mar. 11, 1915, box 3, file 37,
Operative Reports, Fulton Mills Collection, (hereafter Operative Reports); Alexander M.
Daly to Dr. Charles McCarthy, July 31, 1914, RG 174. For the useful metaphor of "on-
stage" and "offstage" behavior, see James Scott, *Weapons of the Weak: Everyday Forms of
Peasant Resistance* (New Haven: Yale University Press, 1985), 25.

[11]For the best account of the tensions leading up to this first strike, see "In the Matter of
Fulton Bag & Cotton Mills, Atlanta, Georgia, before the United States Commission on
Industrial Relations; Testimony Taken in Atlanta, Georgia," vol. 1, "Testimony for the
Complainants," 3–13, Strike Records, Fulton Mills Collection (hereafter Strike Records).
These hearings are summarized in Alexander M. Daly, "Sworn Testimony Taken before
William C. Massey, Notary Public, in and for the City of Atlanta, and State of Georgia, of
about Forty Witnesses," n.d., RG 174 (hereafter Daly, "Sworn Testimony").

[12]According to Gary M. Fink, "Labor Espionage: The Fulton Bag and Cotton Mills
Strike of 1914–1915," *Labor's Heritage*, 1 (April 1989), 13, 17, the Railway Audit and
Inspection Agency, a large interstate business, had been involved in the coalfield wars in
Colorado and had provided strikebreakers in textile disputes from Maine to Georgia. The
mill also dealt with such firms as the Graham Agency of Knoxville, Tennessee; Day's De-
tective Agency of Augusta, Georgia; and Sherman Services of New York.

[13]Inis Weed, "Final Report on Strike in Fulton Bag and Cotton Mills in Atlanta, Georgia,
and Conditions in Nearby Mill Towns," Sept. 19, 1914, 2, RG 174 (hereafter Weed, "Final
Report"); *Journal of Labor* (June 19, 1914), 4; *Report of Proceedings of the Thirty-fourth
Annual Convention of the American Federation of Labor* (Philadelphia, Nov. 9–21, 1914),
341.

the South. Reeling from the southward shift of the textile industry and pressed from the left by the Industrial Workers of the World (IWW), the UTW had recently announced a southern organizing drive. Meanwhile, the AFL, alarmed by the surge of women into the industrial work force, authorized a special assessment on the membership of its affiliated unions to organize women workers. The Fulton Mills strike provided a perfect opportunity to launch both ventures. Once the walkout began, both the UTW and the AFL focused their attention on Atlanta, sending a total of seven organizers to the city and maintaining a tent colony for evicted workers during the year-long conflict.[14]

The strike drew reinforcement from other quarters as well. Atlanta's craft unions enjoyed considerable political influence, and the Atlanta Federation of Trades tried to arbitrate and publicize the conflict.[15] The local affiliate of the Men and Religion Forward Movement, a militant evangelical organization, also came to the workers' defense. Both the Federal Conciliation Service and the United States Commission on Industrial Relations investigated the strike, and both issued reports sympathetic to the union.[16]

[14]The Knights of Labor in the 1880s and the National Union of Textile Workers in the 1890s had led extensive organizing campaigns in Georgia. The AFL's one-cent assessment was levied by the Executive Council on Feb. 28, 1914, in accordance with a resolution adopted at the AFL's 1913 convention. It yielded funds that amounted to perhaps one-ninth of the AFL's regular organizing budget (e.g., $2,088.58 as compared to $18,588.43 during the month of July 1914). The funds were used to pay portions of the salaries of eighteen organizers (four of whom were women). Of these people, three women and three men, in addition to UTW president Golden, were active in Atlanta. See *Report of Proceedings of the Thirty-fourth Annual Convention*, 20, 58, 331; *American Federationist*, September 1914, 743. This campaign reflected a realization that women were in the work force to stay, but it did not signal a serious, long-term commitment to bring them into the AFL on an equal basis with men. For the AFL's historical hostility toward women workers, see Alice Kessler-Harris, *Out to Work: A History of Wage-Earning Women in the United States* (New York: Oxford University Press, 1982), 152–66. For the organization's limited shift in attitude, see Ann Schofield, "Rebel Girls and Union Maids: The Woman Question in the Journals of the AFL and the IWW, 1905–1920," *Feminist Studies*, 9 (Summer 1983), 335–58.

[15]The literature on labor politics in Atlanta and in the South generally is quite thin. For the salience of class issues and the participation of skilled workers in city politics, see Eugene J. Watts, *The Social Bases of City Politics: Atlanta, 1865–1903* (Westport, Conn.: Greenwood, 1978), esp. 73–74; Mercer Griffin Evans, "The History of the Organized Labor Movement in Georgia" (Ph.D. diss., University of Chicago, 1929), 258–59; Thomas Mashburn Deaton, "Atlanta during the Progressive Era" (Ph.D. diss., University of Georgia, 1969), 143–44; and Thomas M. Deaton, "James G. Woodward: The Working Man's Mayor," *Atlanta History: A Journal of Georgia and the South*, 31 (Fall 1987), 11–23.

[16]Harry G. Lefever, "The Involvement of the Men and Religion Forward Movement in the Cause of Labor Justice, Atlanta, Georgia, 1912–1916," *Labor History*, 14 (Fall 1973), 521–35; McWade and Colpoys Memorandum; Herman Robinson and W. W. Husband to Secretary of Labor William B. Wilson, July 24, 1914, Federal Mediation and Conciliation Service Records; Daly to McCarthy, July 31, 1914; Daly, "Sworn Testimony"; Weed, "Preliminary Report" and "Final Report."

The UTW's chief representatives on the scene were Charles A. Miles, who had led the AFL's battles against the IWW in New York, and Sara Conboy, a Boston Women's Trade Union League activist who would soon become the UTW's highest-ranking female official. Miles in turn persuaded the union to hire a local woman, O. (Ola) Delight Smith, a telegrapher who had been blacklisted after a 1907 strike. Dubbed the "Mother Jones of Atlanta," Smith was a talented labor journalist and president of the national Ladies Auxiliary of the Order of Railroad Telegraphers.[17]

Smith had no experience in organizing textile workers, but she moved quickly to capitalize on her skills as a publicist, combining the pen with the camera in a campaign designed both to encourage collective self-confidence among the workers and to garner public support. Working closely with Miles, she recruited a moving picture company to film the picket line, then invited the workers to free screenings in a local theater. Sporting a hand-held camera and adapting the formulas pioneered by Jacob Riis and Lewis Hine, she darted about the mill village, snapping pictures of child laborers, evicted families, defiant workers, and company spies. She also hired local commercial photographers to help document the strike. She then captioned those images, mounted them on cardboard, and displayed them in store windows, in order to expose the sneering arrogance of the company's agents and underscore the strikers' poverty and respectability.[18]

[17]On Miles and Conboy, see Robert E. Snyder, "Women, Wobblies, and Workers' Rights: The 1912 Textile Strike in Little Falls, New York," *New York History*, 60 (January 1979), 51–52; Meredith Tax, *The Rising of the Women: Feminist Solidarity and Class Conflict, 1880–1917* (New York: Monthly Review Press, 1980), 266–67; Alice Henry, *Women and the Labor Movement* (New York: Macmillan, 1927), 95; *A Look at the Record* (n.p., n.d. [UTW, 1976]), 9–12, 14, pamphlet celebrating the 75th anniversary of the United Textile Workers of America, in the Robert F. Wagner Labor Archives, Tamiment Institute Library, New York University; Textile Workers of America, *Proceedings of the Nineteenth Annual Convention*, Baltimore, Oct. 20–25, 1919. On Smith, see *Journal of Labor*, June 12, 1914, 7 (quote), and Oct. 17, 1913, 5; and Jacquelyn Dowd Hall, "O. Delight Smith's Progressive Era: Labor, Feminism, and Reform in the Urban South," in *Visible Women: An Anthology*, ed. Nancy Hewitt and Suzanne Lebsock (Urbana: University of Illinois Press, forthcoming). Of the six people who were, at one time or another, paid by the AFL campaign to organize women workers, only O. Delight Smith was assigned exclusively to Atlanta. She earned considerably less than the other organizers, and her entire salary of approximately $20 a week came from the AFL's special fund. See correspondence in Frank Morrison Letterbooks, Perkins Library, Duke University: Morrison to Charles A. Miles, June 13 and June 16, 1914, vol. 387; Morrison to Mrs. E. B. Smith, Dec. 1, 1914, vol. 401; Morrison to Miles, June 16, 1914, vol. 387.

[18]Operative H. J. D., June 3, 1914, box 2, file 15; Operatives J. W. W. and A. E. W., June 6, 1914, box 1, file 2, Operative Reports. Smith compiled and annotated three albums of photographs, which she titled "Conditions," "Evictions," and "Tent City." Along with 16 additional prints, these photographs form a unique collection of 136 images. They can be found at the George Meany Memorial Archives in Washington, D.C. Copies of the photographs are available at the Southern Labor Archives, Special Collections, Georgia State University, Atlanta. Some copies are also located in "Exhibits," Fulton Bag Company, Federal Mediation and Conciliation Service Records. For this photographic record, see Clifford M.

Smith's use of photography placed her squarely within the Progressive tradition, for the camera furnished progressivism's preeminant mode of proof. Lewis Hine had traveled through Georgia for the National Child Labor Committee in 1913, and Smith was surely familiar with his work. Like him, she created ensembles of images and words.[19] Smith, however, did more than appropriate established forms. Hine and the child labor reformers used the camera to persuade an indifferent public to endorse legislative reforms. Smith's photographs had a similar purpose, insofar as they aimed at marshaling public backing for the union. But by showing the strikers to themselves, in action and as a collectivity, she sought to foster insurgency, not to heal class divisions.

The camera was not the unionists' only weapon. They made use of words and rituals as well. They organized parades that contradicted the mill owner's charge that the strikers' ranks were limited to a few malcontents. Smith wrote a column called "From the Strikers' Camp," in which she emphasized the workers' gallant domesticity. The *Journal of Labor* editorialized that these workers were not " 'floaters.' . . . [T]hey were men who had worked for years in the mills . . . of the class which creates all the wealth of the state." Their strike was conducted along "dignified, conservative lines."[20]

Organizers also appealed to white racial solidarity in their attempt to overcome the image of textile workers as a pariah class. Union literature designed for a national as well as a local audience played on the theme of "white slavery" in the southern mills. Unionists circulated pictures of the black men hired by the company to evict workers from their homes, with captions such as "Put out by a Nigger." "Just imagine," wrote UTW president John Golden, "white southern Americans, . . . little white children . . . thrown into the streets by negroes . . . all because their parents dared to join a labor union."[21]

The spies' job was to counter this multifaceted campaign. Their reports, which the mill owners fed to reformers, government investigators, and

Kuhn, "Images of Dissent: The Pictorial Record of the 1914–15 Strike at Atlanta's Fulton Bag and Cotton Mills," paper presented at the annual meeting of the Organization of American Historians, St. Louis, Mo., Apr. 6, 1989. It was Kuhn who first brought this material to my attention. For the documentary tradition on which Smith drew, see Peter B. Hales, *Silver Cities: The Photography of American Urbanization, 1839–1915* (Philadelphia: Temple University Press, 1984); and Alan Trachtenberg, *Reading American Photographs: Images as History, Mathew Brady to Walker Evans* (New York: Hill & Wang, 1989).
[19]Hales, *Silver Cities,* 168. The National Child Labor Committee apparently supplied copies of Hine's Georgia photographs to the *Atlanta Georgian,* which published them without attribution during the 1914 child labor campaign. See photographs in *Child Labor Bulletin,* 2 (August 1913), 24, and 3 (February 1915), 35. They are reprinted in *Atlanta Georgian,* June 29, 1914, 1.
[20]*Journal of Labor,* June 5, 1914, 5; Sept. 26, 1914, 3; Sept. 19, 1914, 2; Oct. 3, 1914, 3; and Oct. 31, 1913, 4 (quotes).
[21]Ibid., July 24, 1914, 2.

national union officials, sought to contest photography's claim to unmediated truth. Where the unionists pictured a struggle waged by virtuous white men and women, the spies conjured an urban underworld composed of hobos, whores, and street urchins. Their aim was to discredit the local leaders and contradict the union's self-representations, thus dividing the rank-and-file and undermining the strike's public support.[22]

The spies ran with the young men of the village, whiled away their time on street corners and in Decatur Street dives, and infiltrated what they portrayed as an interracial crime ring that traded in bootleg whiskey, cocaine, and prostitution. They acted as provocateurs, fostering and exaggerating the underworld they described.[23] They shaped their narratives for particular readers, and their pens, like the photographer's eye, were guided by social conventions.

In fact, the spy reports belonged to a century-old literary tradition that had been given new life by muckraking reformers: a secrets-of-the-city genre of urban reportage. Tours of urban lowlife, written by novelists, journalists, and reformers for middle-class audiences, depicted the city as a dark continent peopled by the degraded and vicious poor. Similarly, textile folk, as construed by the spy reports, inhabited a hidden city dominated by vice, immorality, and crime.[24]

The spies drew distinctions between the rough and the respectable, the dangerous and the dependable, employing a trope that had long been a staple of writings on working-class life.[25] In their rendition, floaters dominated the more innocent members of the union. Stable workers were illiterate, vulnerable, and easily deluded; they resented the "Rough Necks" but could not escape their influence.[26]

This split image of workers dated back to the beginnings of the Industrial Revolution, but the spy reports added a modern permutation: these rough workers did not steal to survive; they were perverse consumers,

[22]Hales, *Silver Cities*, 163; [Oscar Elsas] to B. Z. Phillips, Jan. 22, 1915, box 1, file 1, Operative Reports (hereafter Report to B. Z. Phillips).
[23]Report to B. Z. Phillips.
[24]Kasson, *Rudeness and Civility*, 72–111; Morn, *Eye That Never Sleeps*, 87; Report to B. Z. Phillips; Operative 16, Dec. 23, 1914, box 3, file 31; Operative 16, Mar. 22, 1915, box 3, file 37; Operative 16, Oct. 8, 1915, box 3, file 44, Operative Reports.
[25]For the political uses of various representations of the working class, see Joan Wallach Scott, "A Statistical Representation of Work: La Statistique de l'industrie à Paris, 1847–48," in Joan Wallach Scott, *Gender and the Politics of History* (New York: Columbia University Press, 1988), 113–38; Christine Stansell, *City of Women: Sex and Class in New York, 1789–1860* (New York: Knopf, 1986); and Meyerowitz, *Women Adrift*.
[26]Operative 470, Aug. 1, 1914, box 2, file 20; Operative 16, Mar. 22, 1915, box 3, file 37 (quote); Operative 16, Dec. 27, 1914, box 3, file 31; R. H. Wright to Harry G. Preston, Sept. 23, 1914, box 1, file 6; Wright to Preston, Oct. 14, 1914, box 1, file 10; Operative 16, n.d., box 3, file 33, Operative Reports.

exploiting the greed and pleasures of the marketplace. The Magnolia Pharmacy allegedly sold cocaine as well as Coca-Cola; restaurants offered gathering places where customers could get a quick meal while laying plans to "holdup, burglarize, [and] blow safes." Strikers-turned-streetwalkers were said to pillage Decatur Street stores, using "umbrellas, muffs and cloaks to hide the loot."[27]

Constructions of gender shaped the spies' message. As depicted in their reports, mill village ringleaders lacked the manliness required by trade unionism. Possessing neither self-control nor self-respect, they combined weakness and gullibility with criminal aggression. The spies ridiculed these men's claims to the role of "father of this movement." Rather, outside organizers were responsible. Male strikers appeared mainly as yeggs, highway robbers, and bootleggers, too busy dodging the cops to maintain a tent city or run a union.[28] Mill women were usually cast either as sexual predators or as prey. The spies charged that lewd women from the union gathered in a popular saloon on payday to "tempt those now at work in the Mill to drink with them and quit work."[29] They saw women in the tent city as a source of contagion, as the dangerous carriers of venereal disease.

Because they viewed the factory as sexualized space, the spies routinely used seduction as a means of infiltration. Operative 429, who passed himself off as an aspiring dance instructor, spent days trying to get a date with Lillie Priest, a mill worker with an inviting smile and a reputation as a "very gay girl." Finally she let him take her dancing and to a movie. "I have made a good impression with her," he reported, "and I am sure I will know everything on her mind shortly." The dance instructor also charmed (or said he charmed) Mary Kelleher, a UTW organizer. He wined and dined her and forwarded her letters to his boss in Philadelphia.[30]

[27]Report to B. Z. Phillips.

[28]Operative 16, n.d., box 3, file 37 (quote), and Report to B. Z. Phillips. A "yegg" was an itinerant burglar, especially a safecracker. The self-described yegg Jack Black defined the type as "highly secretive, wary; forever traveling, always a night 'worker.' He shuns the bright lights, seldom straying far from his kind, never coming to the surface. Circulating through space with his always-ready automatic, the yegg rules the underworld of criminals": Black, *You Can't Win* (New York: Macmillan, 1926), 5. There is a good deal of evidence that rank-and-file leaders such as H. Newborn Mullinax were in fact the founders and the mainstays of the union. These men were skilled weavers and loom fixers and long-time employees, not the hobos the spies made them out to be. See Mullinax, "Personals from Textile Workers," *Journal of Labor,* Jan. 9, 1914, 5; and "In the Matter of Fulton Bag & Cotton Mills."

[29]Report to B. Z. Phillips.

[30]Operative 429, Sept. 7, 1916, box 4, file 48 (quote), and Sept. 17 (quote), Sept. 21, Oct. 6, and Oct. 7, 1916, box 4, file 49; "Operative 16 Reports on Mrs. Kellar Organizer," Nov. 6, 1915, box 3, file 44, Operative Reports.

Even O. Delight Smith was not exempt from the spies' translation of
female activism into illicit sexuality. Indeed, they devoted particular effort to decoding her sexual character and using it to undermine her leadership position. Their tactics ranged from rumormongering to blackmail
and entrapment. They staked out her house and peeped through the windows until the lights went off. They observed her drinking beer at the
German Cafe until long past midnight. A man claimed that he saw her
registering at a hotel with UTW organizer Charles Miles but promised to
keep the secret if she would have "intercourse" with him. He said that
Smith refused but procured another woman—from whom he promptly
caught gonorrhea.[31]

This was not O. Delight Smith's first experience with attempts to use
her private life to undermine her public role. She had worked as an organizer for the Order of Railroad Telegraphers, riding in cabooses and
handcars, staying in hotels, and dodging efforts to " 'catch me' with a
man in my room."[32] What set the Atlanta case apart was the apparent
collusion of her husband, Edgar B. Smith, with those who sought to do
her in.

In the midst of the strike, Edgar initiated divorce proceedings, represented by Fulton Mills's law firm. He alleged that he had found his wife,
drunk and "about half dressed," at home with a drifter named Pat Calahan. But his main charge was that Delight had "mapped out a line of
conduct for herself entirely at variance with the duties of a good wife"
and that she wouldn't stay "at home where all good women ought to
be." Delight, in turn, accused her husband of circulating rumors detrimental to her "reputation of chastity" and advising and abetting the men
who were trying to force her out of her job.[33] In the end, the jury refused
her request for a divorce with alimony and granted her husband a divorce instead. It went further, giving him but denying her the right to
remarry.[34]

[31]Operative 12, July 25 and 26, 1914, box 2, file 16; Operative 39, July 25 and July 26,
1914, box 2, file 17; Operative 15, Aug. 1, 1914, box 2, file 18; Operative 16, Dec. 27,
1914, box 3, file 31 (quote), and June 7, 1915, box 3, file 41, Operative Reports.

[32]*Journal of Labor,* Apr. 7, 1950, 1–2.

[33]Calahan appears in various sources as "Pat Calahan," "Pat Callahan," and "J. Callahan." See Mrs. O. L. Smith v. Edgar B. Smith, Libel for Divorce, Depositions of Defendant,
Aug. 17, 1915; Petition of Mrs. O. L. Smith, Aug. 3, 1915; and Mrs. O. L. Smith v. Edgar
B. Smith, Divorce Suit, Aug. 27, 1915, all in Superior Court of Fulton County, Fulton
County Courthouse, Atlanta. By the time the case went to court, Edgar was no longer
being represented by Rosser, Brandon, Salton, and Phillips. It is clear, however, that the
company sought to exploit the Smiths' marital difficulties and that Edgar Smith's inquiries
about his wife to UTW officials helped to undermine her position in the union. See E. B.
Smith to American Federation of Labor, Nov. 29, 1914, vol. 401, Morrison Letterbooks;
and undated, unsigned, handwritten note in box 3, folder 4, Strike Records.

[34]*Atlanta Georgian,* Jan. 19, 1917, 8; Foreman's report, Mrs. Ola L. Smith v. Edgar B.
Smith, Jan. 18, 1917; Mrs. O. L. Smith v. E. B. Smith, Petition for Divorce, and Cross-bill

Smith's nemesis was a wily and ambitious Railway Audit and Inspection Company detective named Harry Preston, and the interaction between them is particularly revealing. Preston had disliked Smith from the start, with an intensity that did not extend to the other UTW organizers.[35] The reasons for his animus are not altogether clear, but they were certainly aggravated by frustration. Try as he might, Preston could not worm his way into Smith's confidence. Nor could he establish a stable link between her outward behavior and her inner substance; he could not read her character or fathom her meaning.

Preston's depictions of Smith's words and actions were wildly contradictory. On the one hand, she was a foul-mouthed rabble-rouser whose "usual tirade" consisted of calling the company and its minions " 'Liars, Pimps, Thugs, etc.' " On the other hand, it was her job to counsel moderation. He watched her every move and expression, hoping for signs that his campaign was taking effect, predicting—prematurely, as it usually turned out—that she could not stand the strain. Early on, he reported that Smith had told him "that she was worn out . . . and was almost sick, and she could not keep it up much longer." Long before Smith actually fell from grace, Preston was reporting that "the 'cockey' walk . . . she used to have [is] all gone, and she goes around like a smacked 'a—' now, (excuse [the] expression, it fits so perfectly)."[36]

It was, above all, Smith's partnership with Charles Miles that played havoc with Preston's powers of deduction. When she failed to take a back seat to the national UTW organizer, Preston decided that the two were locked in a power struggle and that Smith was trying to seize control of the union. When they continued to work together harmoniously, he jumped to the conclusion that they were entirely "too friendly." Unable to turn up any evidence of adultery, he hypothesized that Miles was a weakling who hoped the strikers would return to work so that he could "retire gracefully" with the excuse that the strikers had deserted him. Preston changed course again when Miles did eventually retreat, leaving Smith in charge of the strike. Then he maintained that the two

---

by deft. and second verdict for defendant upon his Cross-bill in Fulton Superior Court, June 7, 1917, Superior Court of Fulton County. According to state law, three terms of court were necessary in divorce actions. The court impaneled a special jury for each term of court. Absolute divorce was granted only on the verdict of two concurring juries; the second jury determined the rights of the parties and could impose "disability of remarriage on the guilty party." Disabilities could be removed in subsequent proceedings. See Franklyn Hudgings, Ll.B., *What Everybody Should Know about the Law of Marriage and Divorce* (New York: New Century, 1935), 23.

[35]Operative 115, Oct. 14, 1914, box 1, file 10; R. H. Wright to Harry G. Preston, Oct. 14, 1914, Operative Reports.

[36]Operative 115, July 3, 1914, box 1, file 6 (quote); Operative 115, July 6 (quote), July 11, July 13 (quote), and July 25, 1914, box 1, file 7; Operative 115, Sept. 14, 1914, box 1, file 9 (quote), Operative Reports.

organizers had been planning to run away together until Pat Calahan "broke in to Miles's arrangements."[37]

Preston's peregrinations illustrate a phenomenon with a long historical pedigree: the tawdry mudslinging directed at female trespassers who disrupt the hierarchies of the public sphere. But the spy's confusion was also emblematic of social relations in an increasingly pluralistic, mobile society. How, after all, could one read appearances in a metropolis of strangers, a world where social identity was no longer taken for granted and the self could become "a series of dramatic effects"?[38]

Northern Victorians cherished character and feared the impostor who undermined social confidence by passing for something he was not. In the antebellum South, white men were less concerned with probity than with appearances; for them a man's honor depended on public acceptance of the self he projected. In either case, an accusation of lying, of projecting a false self, was a grave insult. But by World War I, urban-dwelling southerners—along with other Americans—were coming to "accept the idea of a social system filled with liminal men in pursuit of the main chance." A new success ethic made the confidence man less an object of fear than a model for ambitious young men to emulate. Personality and corporate gamesmanship replaced character as the keys to mobility in a fluid social world.[39]

Preston, for instance, was no run-of-the-mill nineteenth-century strike-breaker. He was a more protean modern figure: the confidence man in a gray flannel suit. He had appeared on the stage under the name Henry Greenhough. He could sing, and he worked his way into the union and the Men and Religion Forward Movement by arranging the music for their meetings. He had nothing but scorn for ordinary workers and concentrated his attention mainly on the UTW organizers, whose company he much preferred. He was seated as a delegate and honored guest at the

[37]Operative 115, Aug. 28 and Sept. 1, 1914, box 1, file 8; Operative 457, Dec. 11, 1914, box 2, file 27, Operative Reports; Fink, "Labor Espionage," 21; Frank Morrison to Mrs. E. B. Smith, Oct. 20, 1914, vol. 397, and Morrison to Charles A. Miles, Oct. 24, 1914, vol. 398, Morrison Letterbooks.

[38]Mary Ryan, *Women in Public: Between Banners and Ballots, 1823–1880* (Baltimore: Johns Hopkins University Press, 1990); Kasson, *Rudeness and Civility*, 94 (quote).

[39]Bertram Wyatt-Brown, *Honor and Violence in the Old South* (New York: Oxford University Press, 1986); Edward L. Ayers, *Vengeance and Justice: Crime and Punishment in the 19th-Century South* (New York: Oxford University Press, 1984); Kenneth S. Greenberg, "The Nose, the Lie, and the Duel in the Antebellum South," *American Historical Review*, 95 (February 1990), 57–74; Warren I. Susman, " 'Personality' and the Making of Twentieth-Century Culture," in *New Directions in American Intellectual History*, ed. John Higham and Paul K. Conkin (Baltimore: Johns Hopkins University Press, 1979), 212–26; Karen Halttunen, *Confidence Men and Painted Women: A Study of Middle-Class Culture in America, 1830–1870* (New Haven: Yale University Press, 1982), xiii–xviii, 198–210 (quote, 198); Peter Filene, *Him/Her/Self: Sex Roles in Modern America* (Baltimore: Johns Hopkins University Press, 1986), 69–93.

annual convention of the Massachusetts Federation of Labor, had a private meeting with the executive board of the UTW, dined with President Golden, and attended the UTW annual convention in Scranton. After the strike, he moved quickly up the corporate ladder. By 1920 he was back in Atlanta as the Railway Audit and Inspection Company's southern district manager.[40]

If Preston was a modern "liminal man," Smith was a boundary-crossing New Woman whose reflection in the spy reports was understandably fragmented and opaque. Luckily, Smith's writings and photographs permit us to supplement the spy's version with a highly literate woman's self-representations. That wider lens discloses a complex social identity. It also suggests that in O. Delight Smith, Preston met an impressive adversary, a woman fighting on uneven ground, yet still managing quite often to give as good as she got.[41]

For one thing, as the private eyes were spying on Mrs. Smith, Mrs. Smith was spying on them. She had her own "inside man" in the mill, who kept her informed about the company's machinations. She prided herself on her physical courage: "These pictures were taken by myself," she boasted, "while thugs and spotters were ever around me." Several cameras were "knocked from my hand and smashed before I succeeded in collecting these."[42] Her candid shots of company spies reversed the usual power relations between the seer and the seen, alerting us to the problems with the metaphor of a "male gaze"—which positions women as the Other, the more or less helpless targets of objectification.

Moreover, Smith's columns in the *Journal of Labor* provide a rare glimpse of a little-noticed phenomenon: working-class feminism in the urban South. For years before the textile strike, she offered a running commentary on everything from the need for labor unity to "the penalty of being a woman." Like Charlotte Perkins Gilman, she warned of the dire effects of dependency on women's characters. She gave short shrift to the institution of marriage, "which very seldom helped to compensate matters but on the other hand made matters worse." She argued that the chief threat to a woman's autonomy lay in her vulnerability to character

[40]Fink, "Labor Espionage," 13, 17, 24–28, 31; Operative 115, July 19 and July 26, 1914, box 1, file 7; Operative 115, Sept. 24, 1914, box 1, file 9; Harry Preston Reports, Jan. 18, 1920, box 7, file 120, Operative Reports.

[41]Smith's costs, of course, should not be minimized. She lost her job and left Atlanta. But she also persuaded the divorce court to remove the restrictions on her right to remarry, married for love, and resurfaced in Oregon, where she eventually earned the sobriquet "first lady of the Oregon labor movement." See Hall, "O. Delight Smith's Progressive Era"; and *Oregon Labor Press*, Dec. 12, 1958.

[42]Operative 115 to Oscar Elsas, July 7, 1914; Operative 115, July 9, 1914 (quote), box 1, file 7, Operative Reports; O. Delight Smith, inscription on second page of album titled "Conditions," Meany Archives (quote).

assassination, a vulnerability that bred a nagging fear of "what others say." When the "tongues of loafing men go wagging," she argued, women must rely on a sense of inner worth, not on male protection.[43]

Yet there were chinks in Smith's armor, inconsistencies, if not in her thought, at least in her rhetorical strategies. She spent pages in defense of female ambition, then bowed to custom by arguing that if only men were unionized, a woman could stay at home where "she rightfully belongs." Independence, she assured her readers, "has not taken from the True Woman one iota of that sweet feminine quality." She attacked the double standard, but she offered no brief for women's desire.[44]

These, of course, were precisely the conventions that Smith's enemies eventually invoked. Harry Preston's vendetta had a personal edge: he went after Smith partly because she seemed to lack feminine sweetness, not just because she was on the wrong side of a labor-management dispute. The divorce court punished her for both her work and her sexuality.

The difficulty of Smith's position can be read not only in her columns but also in her gestures, as caught and framed by the camera's eye. Posing in front of the union commissary with Charles Miles and another union man, Smith looks resolute yet curiously askew (fig. 10.1). The body language of the men conveys energy and determination. Their shoulders are set; they gaze directly into the camera, their heads and bodies joined in straight axial lines. Miles raises his chin belligerently. Smith stands to the side, avoiding the symbolic position in the center of the group which often reflects tokenism rather than collegiality. She appears as tall as the men; like Miles, she raises her chin. Yet she turns away, tilting her head back and to the side in a customary feminine gesture. The axis of her pose is broken, suggesting inconsistency, especially in contrast to the determined set of her mouth. The women photographed in the strikers' camp take a different stance. They occupy the background, but they face the camera more directly (fig. 10.2). Pictured in the camp kitchen, they perform private tasks in a public setting. They are not creating a new public role but asserting their right to an established one, whose normal venue they have been denied. Smith's presence in front of the commissary announces her bid to occupy new public space. But her stance hints at the precariousness born of the distance between possibility and aspiration.[45]

[43]*Journal of Labor*, Feb. 26. 1909, 5; Aug. 20, 1909, 5.

[44]Ibid., Feb. 26, 1909, 5; Feb. 19, 1909, 2; Aug. 20, 1909, 5.

[45]See Martha Banta, *Imaging American Women: Idea and Ideals in Cultural History* (New York: Columbia University Press, 1989), for a perceptive analysis of how pictorial images create "social types" and of women's uses of those images in their self-representations. I am grateful to Pamela Dean and to Helen Langa, "Narratives of Women's Propriety and Protection in Some Documents Concerning the Fulton Bag and Cotton Mill

Figure 10.1. The man on the left is H. N. Mullinax, the secretary (not the president) of Local 886. To his left are UTW organizers Charles Miles and O. Delight Smith. The photograph was taken by a local professional photographer, Duane A. Russell. George Meany Memorial Archives, Washington, D.C.

Whether they were written by small-time criminals, proto-efficiency experts, or aspiring bourgeois, the spy reports exposed the complexities of social life in a world that drew a thin line between con men and social climbers and allowed elites to rely on criminals to maintain their power.[46] More important for our purposes, the reports unmasked the class and gender conflicts that accompanied urban-industrial transformations. How pervasive were those conflicts? What do they reveal about the New South's sexual culture? To address those questions, we must bring other

Strike in Atlanta, 1914–1915," seminar paper, University of North Carolina at Chapel Hill, 1988, for help in reading this visual evidence. More generally, I am indebted to Langa and to the other students in my fall 1988 women's history course for their insights and camaraderie. They helped clarify my thinking at many points.

[46]For the efforts of detectives to adopt the trappings of modern advertising and represent themselves as "industrial harmonizers and conciliators," see Sidney Howard, *The Labor Spy* (New York: Republic, 1924), 17–19, 21. For the argument that Fulton Mills did in fact use spies as proto–efficiency experts, see Gary M. Fink, "Efficiency and Control: Labor Espionage in Southern Textiles," paper presented at the annual meeting of the Organization of American Historians, St. Louis, Mo., Apr. 6, 1989; and Deborah Kim Dawson, "The Origins of Scientific Management in the Textile Industry" (master's thesis, Georgia Institute of Technology, 1990).

Figure 10.2. The kitchen tent at the strikers' camp. Established by UTW organizers in August 1914, the camp housed from two to three hundred families throughout the winter of 1914–1915. George Meany Memorial Archives, Washington, D.C.

perspectives and other layers of meaning into play. Let us turn, then, to the new social circumstances of working-class women and to the tensions those circumstances aroused, as they manifested themselves in the fatal drama of the Leo Frank case and reverberated in the Fulton Mills strike as well as in more quotidian debates.

II

The years preceding the Fulton Mills strike were marked by profound changes in urban life. Atlanta's population mushroomed, and its female labor force increased at an even dizzier rate. By 1920, 42 percent of all Atlanta women aged sixteen and older had joined the work force. Only the Massachusetts textile cities of Fall River, Lowell, and New Bedford and the white-collar city of Washington, D.C., had higher rates of female employment.[47] Traditionally, a large black population accounted for the

[47]Julia Blackwelder, "Mop and Typewriter: Women's Work in Early Twentieth-Century Atlanta," *Atlanta Historical Journal,* 27 (Fall 1983), 24; Joseph A. Hill, *Women in Gainful Occupations, 1870 to 1920,* Census Monographs, 9 (Washington, D.C.: U.S. Government Printing Office, 1929), 11, 146.

high levels of gainfully employed women in southern cities, and black women continued to work in much greater proportions than whites. But from 1900 to 1920, as the city's population expanded by 123 percent (from 89,872 to 200,616), the number of black women wage earners in Atlanta advanced by only 60 percent. Meanwhile, employment among white women jumped by 276 percent. This disparity was due in part to a leveling off of the laundry and household service jobs to which black women were confined and in part to the exclusion of blacks from the textile and clerical jobs that drew white women into paid labor. The result was a marked change in the racial composition of the city's female work force. In 1900 white women constituted only 28 percent of wage-earning women. By 1920 they accounted for 48 percent.[48]

Such developments might have caused consternation in any case. But the living situations of these new wage-earning women made their presence in the city more disturbing still. In 1900, Atlanta, like most southern locales, ranked far below cities such as Chicago in the percentage of wage-earning women living apart from their families. By 1920, however, approximately one-fifth of working women in both Atlanta and Chicago were living "adrift." Single white women, migrating to the city to work in department stores and offices, accounted for most of this change.[49]

Middle-class observers in Georgia, like their counterparts throughout the country, responded to the surge of white women into wage labor with pity, puzzlement, and disapproval. They assumed that black women should work and would probably be sexually active. The tendency of the mill village to breed immorality was also axiomatic. The behavior of the young women in the expanding service sector was harder to read. Free from parental supervision and prey to the temptations of the city, they were a new phenomenon, and their visibility on the urban landscape aroused more general concerns about the female working class. Working mothers, it seemed, were threatening family life; wage-earning daughters were prone to promiscuity or vulnerable to abuse; children were being

[48]Hill, *Women in Gainful Occupations*, 145–46; U.S. Department of Commerce, Bureau of the Census, *Fourteenth Census of the United States, 1920* (Washington, D.C.: U.S. Government Printing Office, 1922), 3:222. It should be emphasized that the rate of labor force participation among black women increased more slowly than that of whites because so many black women were *already* working. Moreover, the black population rose less quickly than the white (76% versus 154%). The changes in the structure of the female work force remain striking nevertheless, and they seem to have been due mainly to the forces that pushed white women off the farms, on the one hand, and the exclusion of black women from urban job opportunities, on the other.

[49]The comparison with Chicago is based on Meyerowitz, *Women Adrift*, 4–5; and U.S. Department of Commerce and Labor, Bureau of the Census, *Statistics of Women at Work* (Washington, D.C.: U.S. Government Printing Office, 1907), 29. Information on the 1920 Bureau of the Census study and other figures are from Hill, *Women in Gainful Occupations*, 139, 143–45, 333–36. The eleven cities included in Hill's study were Fall River, Mass.; Providence, R.I.; Rochester, N.Y.; Paterson, N.J.; Cincinnati, O.; Indianapolis, Ind.; St. Paul, Minn.; Kansas City, Mo.; Louisville, Mo.; New Orleans, La.; and Atlanta.

warped by factory labor. These worries helped nourish an antiprostitution campaign and a debate over child labor.[50] At their most sensational, they also fed the vendetta against Leo Frank.

In July 1913, Frank, a pencil factory superintendent, was arrested and charged with assaulting and murdering a thirteen-year-old employee named Mary Phagan. A jury found Frank guilty and the judge sentenced him to death. The case became a cause célèbre in the spring of 1914, a few months before the Fulton Mills strike, when national Jewish organizations rallied to Frank's defense. Appeal followed appeal, until, in April 1915, the United States Supreme Court denied a plea by Frank's attorneys to reverse the death sentence on the grounds that a mob atmosphere had prevailed during the trial. On June 21, 1915, two months after the Fulton Mills strike ended, Governor John Slaton commuted Frank's sentence to life imprisonment. Three weeks later, a band of prominent citizens from Phagan's hometown, the nearby suburb of Marietta, took Frank from his prison cell and lynched him.[51]

The furor against Leo Frank turned on the vulnerability of factory girls, and the case provided a forum for the expression of intense racial, class, and religious antagonisms. Frank's attorneys, as well as the country's major newspapers, invoked virulent racist stereotypes in their effort to shift the blame for Phagan's murder to Jim Conley, a black janitor who was the prosecution's chief witness.[52] Frank's opponents, on the other hand, cast the superintendent as the embodiment of rapacious capitalism. The former Populist leader Tom Watson and the William Randolph Hearst–owned *Atlanta Georgian* helped whip that perception into murderous rage. Although the spies tried hard to furnish evidence to the contrary, there is no indication that the Fulton Mills walkout was sparked by anti-Semitism. But once the strike began, prejudice undoubtedly fueled popular antagonism toward the Jewish mill owner, and resentment against Elsas spilled over into the outcry against Leo Frank.[53]

[50]For an excellent survey of urban middle-class concerns during this period, see Paul Boyer, *Urban Masses and Moral Order in America, 1820–1920* (Cambridge: Harvard University Press, 1978), 191–219.

[51]The standard study of these events is Leonard Dinnerstein, *The Leo Frank Case* (New York: Columbia University Press, 1968).

[52]*Journal of Labor*, May 2, 1913, 14; Steven Hertzberg, "Southern Jews and Their Encounter with Blacks: Atlanta, 1850–1915," *Atlanta Historical Journal*, 23 (Fall 1979), 21; Eugene Levy, " 'Is the Jew a White Man?': Press Reaction to the Leo Frank Case, 1913–1915," *Phylon*, 35 (June 1974), 212–22. The evidence indicates that Conley was probably guilty of the crime.

[53]The Elsases contributed to Frank's defense. Oscar's son-in-law, Benjamin Z. Phillips, who sat on the company's board of directors and served as the firm's general counsel, helped oversee the spy network. Phillips was also a law partner of Governor Slaton's, and their firm defended Leo Frank. For the spies' accounts of anti-Semitism among the workers and UTW organizers, see Special Work, June 3, 1914, box 3, file 14, and July 3, 1914, box 1,

As they probed the nature of Frank's alleged crime, southerners also confronted the emergence of a modern sexual system that acknowledged a wide range of human desires even as it hedged them about with new psychological constraints. Public outrage rested in part on the tenacious belief that Mary Phagan had been sexually molested, despite strong evidence that no rape had occurred. Yet at Frank's commutation hearings, his attorney conceded that Phagan may indeed have been raped, an act that he defined as "the carnal knowledge of a female, normally accomplished, forcibly and against her will." Rape, he maintained, was "one of the natural conditions of life . . . it takes all the law and the religion to keep it within reasonable bounds, and then [they] don't quite succeed." A natural expression of male sexuality, rape was particularly irresistible to black men, who were seen not as deviants but as criminals, though less bound than white men by civilization's restraints. If Phagan was raped, it stood to reason that she was raped by the janitor, Jim Conley; anyone who knows the Negro, Frank's lawyer explained, "knows that the prize above life itself to him is the privilege of debasing a white woman."

The prosecution agreed that the girl had been molested. But partly because the evidence of rape was so flimsy and partly to deflect attention from Conley, they charged Frank with perversion, implying that he had engaged in cunnilingus or some other form of nonprocreative sex. These rumors of "perversion" probably did more than anything else to damn Frank in the court of public opinion.[54] And the rumors portrayed him less as a rapist than as an unmanly practitioner of sodomy or pedophilia, forms of male sexual expression that became objects of intense concern as the Victorian fixation on the "hypersexual girl" gave way to fears of the "psychopathic man" (who was seen not as a rapist but as a homosexual or child molester).[55]

There has been a good deal of speculation about why so many white Georgians chose to blame Leo Frank rather than Jim Conley for Mary Phagan's murder. The reasons were tangled and contingent, rooted as

---

file 6; and the following reports of Operative 16: Apr. 16, 1915, box 3, file 38; May 3, 1915, box 3, file 39; May 27, 1915, box 3, file 41; June 20, June 21, June 25, and June 28, 1915, box 3, file 42, all in Operative Reports.

[54]"Transcript of hearing before Governor John M. Slaton on request for commutation of death sentence of Leo Frank" [1915], 144, 148–49, Leo Frank Collection, box 1, folders 1–8, Special Collections, Robert W. Woodruff Library, Emory University; Dinnerstein, *Leo Frank Case*, 19; Clark Jack Freshman, "Beyond Pontius Pilate and Judge Lynch: The Pardoning Power in Theory and Practice as Illustrated in the Leo Frank Case" (honors thesis, Harvard College, 1986), 52–53.

[55]For this transition, see Elizabeth Lunbeck, " 'A New Generation of Women': Progressive Psychiatrists and the Hypersexual Female," *Feminist Studies*, 13 (Fall 1987), 513–43; and Estelle Freedman, " 'Uncontrolled Desires': The Response to the Sexual Psychopath, 1920–1960," *Journal of American History*, 74 (June 1987), 83–106, esp. 97–98, 100–101.

much in the particular circumstances of the case as in underlying forces. Among them were the anxieties inspired by urbanization, industrialization, and the rise of a modern sexual order. At the turn of the century, the image of the black rapist, cut loose from the bonds of slavery and purportedly retrogressing into criminality, had signified for whites the most frightful possibilities of social change. Those fears had crested in the Atlanta riot of 1906, Georgia's worst conflagration in an era of extreme racial violence. Apologists for lynching continued to rely on the notion of white women as the passionless victims of sexual assault. But as the twentieth century wore on, it became increasingly difficult to ignore the possibility that women had sexual urges of their own. Disfranchisement and segregation eliminated blacks from electoral politics and pushed them out of sight, if not out of mind, while capitalist development brought new social tensions to the fore.[56] As a result, white women and children—in the guise of wage earners, prostitutes, and street children—joined recalcitrant blacks as emblems of a society out of whack. In that context, the charge that a factory supervisor had molested a white woman in his employ acquired explosive cultural meaning.

But the fate of "Little Mary Phagan" meant different things to different people, for there was no agreement about how the figure of the white working girl should be construed. Were women's identities—and thus their social needs—rooted in race, class, or gender? Was their sexuality a site of exploitation or of experimentation? Were they victims or agents of a sexual revolution?

The *Atlanta Georgian,* which used the Frank case to transform itself into one of the most widely read daily newspapers in the South, offered Mary Phagan as a symbol of the respectable working-class woman besieged, willing to die in defense of her chastity. Yet the *Georgian's* typical daily reporting featured stories of female desire, not testimonials to female virtue. A poem to working girls published in 1914 turned on the temptations of the city:

---

[56]For the argument that racial extremism subsided as whites convinced themselves that the "Negro problem" had been solved, see Joel Williamson, *A Rage for Order: Black-White Relations in the American South since Emancipation* (New York: Oxford University Press, 1986), 42–43, 83–86, 117–51, 240–44. John Dittmer, *Black Georgia in the Progressive Era, 1900–1920* (Urbana: University of Illinois Press, 1977), on the other hand, underscores the continued salience of racial issues during the Progressive Era. For an intriguing analysis of the gender dynamics of the Frank case, see Nancy McLean, "The Leo Frank Case Reconsidered: Gender and Sexual Politics in the Making of Reactionary Populism," *Journal of American History,* 78 (December 1991), 917–48. McLean argues that the denunciation of Leo Frank illustrates the South's sexual conservatism. My emphasis is on the conflicts aroused by the modernization of sex.

Lonely girl, little lonely girl!
Below you gleam the city lights—
Could your throbbing feet whirl on in dance
Dare you toss your head and take your chance
With the beasts that prowl o 'nights?
An eddy of life, perhaps, might whirl
A comrade or joy your weary way.
The street you dream might yield delight—
You long for color and friends at night
Who work so hard by day.[57]

Young women who did take their chances became the central characters in the crime and scandal stories that were the *Georgian*'s stock in trade. And the heroines of these tales, who ran the gamut from society girls who decamped with bigamists to reformatory inmates who went over the wall, were pacesetters in a nationwide revolution in morals and manners, not figures in a regional morality play.[58]

This is not to say that the *Georgian* celebrated women's rebelliousness. Adhering to Progressive Era convention, the paper often suggested that its protagonists had been drugged or forced into "white slavery" and stressed the "weird and unnatural tragedy" that was their actions' inevitable result.[59] Yet such ritualistic punishments were glosses on the main theme: a fascination with women's sexual agency that the *Georgian* both reflected and helped to create.

The *Journal of Labor*, mouthpiece for the Atlanta Federation of Labor and for the city's labor elite, took a different approach. It refused to sexualize Mary Phagan's death, casting her more as a victim of capitalism in general than as a symbol of women's physical vulnerability. The *Journal* argued that Phagan differed little from "the girl who has her life sapped away slowly by occupational disease or is maimed or killed by machinery at her work." It editorialized against a plan to erect a statue of the "martyred child" on the grounds of the state capitol, suggesting the endowment of a hospital ward for working girls instead.[60]

The agitation triggered by the Leo Frank case fed into a broader questioning of the implications of new patterns of women's work, a questioning that, in turn, helped shape the response to the Fulton Mills strike. In

[57]*Atlanta Georgian*, June 5, 1914, editorial page.
[58]See ibid., July 6, 1914, 1; July 23, 1914, 1; June 25, 1914, 1.
[59]Ibid., July 4, 1914, 1.
[60]*Journal of Labor*, May 2, 1913, 4; Sept. 5, 1913, 4. This is not to say that the *Journal* ignored the sexual dimensions of the case altogether. Its coverage was generally restrained, but at one point it called on its male readers to accept responsibility for finding the "fiendish brute" who committed the murder: ibid., May 30, 1913, 4.

1908, for instance, the *Journal of Labor* featured a spirited discussion at the Universalist Church on the merits of wage work for white women. One man said that "girls these days wanted to dress better than their daddy could afford. They expect to work until they get married, they like to be independent of their father, and this same independence continues after marriage, and makes life miserable for both parties." His remarks "got the ladies all on their feet about the same time." The group decided to conduct a survey of how many women worked out of "stern necessity" and how their wages compared with men's. At the next meeting, the investigators reported that few Atlanta women worked for "pin money"; indeed, 90 percent of the city's department store clerks and 100 percent of its textile operatives had to work, and they did so at wages considerably lower than men's.[61]

Five years later the *Journal* warned that women's economic disadvantages had led to a feminization of poverty in the city. The city warden, who was in charge of doling out "the pittance allowed by the municipality for the poor," reported that he had had 5,000 calls for help in 1913, 1,000 more than in 1912 and four times more than in 1903, when his office had been established. These pleas were equally divided between blacks and whites, and most came from women who were the sole supporters of their families. Some could not find work, but many were employed at jobs that paid far less than a living wage. Charity, the *Journal* insisted, served as an economic makeshift that subsidized "face-grinding employers." The solution it proposed was the organization of women workers and equal pay for equal work.[62] The warden's report also provided ammunition for the *Journal*'s campaign on behalf of the striking textile workers, for many of the women who relied on charity for survival apparently worked at Fulton Mills.

Unfortunately, this focus on women, however well meaning, could go only so far in illuminating the issues raised by the Fulton Mills strike. Labor historians have often subsumed women and children under the category of "worker," writing about the working class as if it consisted only of adult men. Contemporary observers made the opposite mistake. Preoccupied with gender boundaries and confronted by an industry that relied on a family labor system that seemed to threaten the authority of male household heads, crusading journalists, reformers, and craft unionists alike increasingly made their appeals for public sympathy in terms that shifted attention away from the bid for workers' control reflected in the strikers' protest against the contract system and the firing of union members. Ignoring male workers, they highlighted the anomalous posi-

[61]Ibid., Nov. 13, 1908, 6; Nov. 20, 1908, 7.
[62]Ibid., Nov. 7, 1913, 4; Jan. 9, 1914, 4.

tion of wage-earning women and children instead. In the process, strikers' interests as workers disappeared, as did their collective agency.

At first, as we have seen, the *Journal of Labor* and the UTW had construed the strikers as "intelligent, industrious men." But as the conflict unfolded, they increasingly stressed the number of women involved and described the strikers in general in female-coded terms.[63] The UTW's most widely circulated photograph featured a skinny, barefooted boy seated alone on a curb. The caption identified the child as Milton Nunnally, "Age 10 Years," a Fulton Mills worker who had "received for 2 weeks wages only 64 cents" (fig. 10.3). This picture was distributed as a postcard throughout the country and reprinted by numerous newspapers and journals. Child labor, suggested the unionists and the reformers, caught mill workers in a cycle of ignorance and poverty. Women started work too young, then gave birth to stunted children who in turn became "slaves of the mill." The remedy was state intervention in the form of child labor legislation and compulsory education laws. Such laws targeted lazy mill fathers and greedy manufacturers alike, both of whom bore responsibility for what the *Georgian* termed "The Coming De-Generation."[64]

This tendency of gender issues to override class issues reached its apogee in the Men and Religion Forward Movement, whose quarter-page bulletins in Atlanta's major papers brought the strike to citywide attention. Initially an evangelical movement aimed at masculinizing the churches by recruiting male members and adopting modern business methods and aggressive advertising, the group quickly became an effec-

[63]Ibid., Oct. 31, 1913, 4. For the prevalence of "control strikes" and an upsurge in rank-and-file militancy during this period, see David Montgomery, *Workers' Control in America: Studies in the History of Work, Technology, and Labor Struggles* (Cambridge: Cambridge University Press, 1979), 91–112. For the feminized representation of textile workers, see Lawrence J. Boyette, "Gender, Working-Class Culture, and Unionization: A Test Case" (diss. prospectus, University of North Carolina at Chapel Hill, 1988).

[64]Kuhn, "Images of Dissent," 4–5; *Atlanta Georgian*, June 24, 1914, editorial page (quote); June 21, 1914; June 28, 1914. For an earlier controversy in which reformers substituted a concern for the domestic situation of women and children for a confrontation with class exploitation, see LeeAnn Whites, "The De Graffenried Controversy: Class, Race, and Gender in the New South," *Journal of Southern History*, 54 (August 1988), 449–78. It is important to note, however, that this was a characteristic of the American reform tradition, not a peculiarity of the South. By 1915, most reformers had turned from direct organization to protective legislation as the best means of solving the problems of women workers. Kathryn Kish Sklar argues that Progressive reformers pursued such gender-specific solutions in part because of the American tradition of limited government and the weakness of class as a vehicle for political action: Sklar, *"Doing the Nation's Work": Florence Kelley and Women's Political Culture, 1860–1930* (New Haven: Yale University Press, forthcoming). For a provocative discussion of the tendency of male trade unionists to assume that women's gender, not their membership in a class, defined their primary identity, see Patricia J. Hilden, "Women and the Labour Movement in France, 1869–1914," *Historical Journal*, 29 (1986), 809–32. Sklar's and Hilden's work underscores the need to place southern history in a broad comparative perspective.

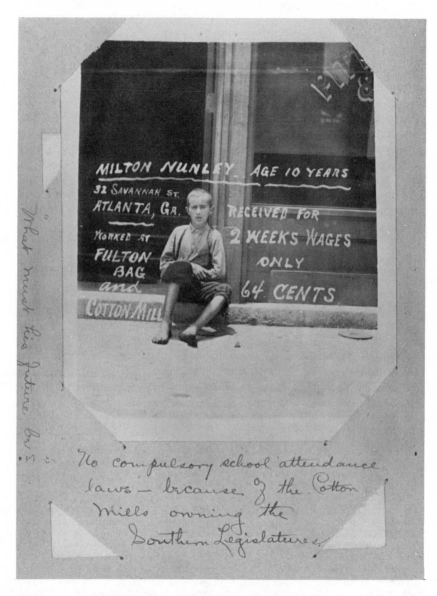

Figure 10.3. Made into a postcard, this photograph of Milton Nunnally, a ten-year-old boy who worked briefly at Fulton Mills, became the most widely circulated image of the strike. Elsas countered by arguing that Nunnally was hired at the insistence of his mother, who swore that the boy's father had deserted him and that he had to work. The mill owner also asserted that Nunnally had been discharged for idleness and that his mother ran a house of assignation. George Meany Memorial Archives, Washington, D.C.

tive proponent of the social gospel. The Atlanta chapter was among the nation's most outspoken and long-lived.[65]

Like the spies—and unlike the craft unionists—these evangelical reformers saw the working-class district as sexualized space. They believed that 75 percent of Atlanta's prostitutes came from the "cotton mill strata, often right from the Fulton district." The prostitute, to their mind, was a passive victim, drawn "by forces she does not understand, lured by lies or driven by want." The solution they proposed was a "living wage" that would enable men to keep their wives and daughters at home—out of the mills and, by extension, out of the brothels. In 1912 these ministers and businessmen led a campaign to shut down the city's red-light district. When the strike broke out, they continued to focus on the exploitation of women and children or to represent mill workers in general in feminine terms: "weak mentally, spiritually, and bodily," neither the men nor the women could do much to help themselves.[66]

In the case of O. Delight Smith, we were able to counter such images of victimization with a writer/photographer's self-representations. Mill workers left behind less evidence of how they saw themselves. Yet even the hostile reports of the labor spies are shot through with evidence that belies the reformers' assumptions about women's passivity. Indeed, for glimpses of women's agency—of women acting up and looking back—we must turn from prolabor sources to the problematic documents with which we began.

What set the spies apart from other visitors to the Satanic mills was the ease with which they blended into the urban underworld. To be sure, they spotlighted the rough and neglected the respectable; their accounts reveal their prejudices (or their eagerness to confirm the prejudices of their employers). But at least they show us a community in motion. Their descriptions of street life are often more matter-of-fact, and in some ways more valuable, than those of the reformers and government investigators on whom historians traditionally rely.

The Men and Religion Forward Movement, for instance, purveyed an image of the mill village as a "graveyard . . . of the living" where lost souls huddled together in "row after row of houses . . . dreary, drab, mo-

[65]Lefever, "Involvement of the Men and Religion Forward Movement"; Gail Bederman, " 'The Women Have Had Charge of the Church Work Long Enough': The Men and Religion Forward Movement of 1911–1912 and the Masculinization of Middle-Class Protestantism," *American Quarterly*, 41 (September 1989), 432–65.

[66]"Digest of Two Interviews with the Rev. G. R. Buford," RG 174; Harry G. Lefever, "Prostitution, Politics, and Religion: The Crusade against Vice in Atlanta in 1912," *Atlanta Historical Journal*, 24 (Spring 1980), 13; *Atlanta Constitution*, June 13, 1914, 5. See also "Atlanta Vice Commission Reports" and "Atlanta's Segregated District Gone," *Vigilance*, November 1912, 28–30.

notonously the same."[67] In fact, the Factory Lot stood beside the Georgia
Railroad only a mile from the city's center, it was traversed by two street-
car lines, and its outskirts accommodated many families that did not
work in the mill, along with shopkeepers who maintained a thriving
commercial district.[68] The graveyard came to life in the spy reports, and
women popped up everywhere in this lively public space.

In the world of the spy reports, women's roles were active, if often
unsavory. Mill girls pursued men they liked and fended off those they
didn't. They negotiated a city that provided many new sites and situations for sexual contact, and they engaged, however unequally, in a system of sexual bartering and exchange. In one report, a spooler broke a
board over the head of a married man who pinched her; in another, a
woman tried to blackmail her boyfriend into marrying her by promising
to "play shut mouth" about his crimes.[69] Lillie Priest, the "very gay girl"
courted by Operative 429, proved more than a match for the charming
dance instructor. He suspected her of being a double agent, employed as
an informer by the company but also working for the union. He was
certain that she was "stuck on" him. But every time he managed to make
a date, she thwarted him by bringing a girlfriend along. "I was compelled through circumstances," he complained, "to entertain them both."
He confronted Priest with his suspicions, but she put him off with "a
plausible story (all lies)." In the end, the detective was ordered back to
Philadelphia, probably at the behest of Elsas, who had decided that 429's
reports were full of "hot air."[70] Lillie Priest disappeared from the record,
apparently still working both sides of the street.

Three female figures illustrate the difference between the reformers'
and the spies' representations. A typical Men and Religion Forward
Movement bulletin invoked an image of a "little girl not over twelve, her

[67]*Atlanta Constitution*, June 6, 1914, 7. This image was echoed and elaborated by W. J.
Cash, Frank Tannenbaum, and others. See Cash, *The Mind of the South* (New York:
Knopf, 1941), 204, and Tannenbaum, "The South Buries Its Anglo-Saxons," *Century*, 106
(June 1923), 205, 210–11.
[68]Only in the 1930s did Cabbagetown become a mill-dominated community rather than
a working-class neighborhood. For these changing residential patterns, see Stephen W. Gra-
ble, "The Other Side of the Tracks: Cabbagetown—a Working-Class Neighborhood in
Transition during the Early Twentieth Century," *Atlanta Historical Journal*, 26 (Summer/
Fall 1982), 51–66; and Gretchen E. Maclachlan, "The Factory Lot in 1900: Urban or Rural," seminar paper, Emory University, 1986. Maclachlan found that households in which
all employed members worked at the mill constituted fewer than half of the 155 households
in the Factory Lot.
[69]Operative 331, Aug. 15, 1922, box 6, file 106; Report to B. Z. Phillips, Operative
Reports. See Kathy Peiss, *Cheap Amusements: Working Women and Leisure in Turn-of-
the-Century New York* (Philadelphia: Temple University Press, 1986); Stansell, *City of
Women;* and Meyerowitz, *Women Adrift,* for studies of similar milieus.
[70]Operative 429, Sept. 21, Sept. 26, and Oct. 7, 1916, box 4, file 49, Operative Reports.

pink dress fluttering against the grime, [running] through a forbidding door to work." The girls in the spy reports occupied a more ambiguous milieu. These accounts showed Big Annie Parr and her sidekick May Parkman donning overalls and caps instead of fluttering pink dresses. Cross-dressing, the two women dodged the cops and "hobo[ed] out of town." Parr and Parkman were adopting a strategy familiar to rebellious working-class girls of the time, who sometimes wore men's clothing in order to earn men's wages and enjoy men's mobility. Before the emergence of a homosexual subculture in the cities, cross-dressing also enabled women to live in same-sex relationships.[71]

In short, the women who frequented the assignation houses on Decatur Street may have been meeting their lovers, exchanging sex for treats, or using their bodies for political advantage rather than sinking helplessly into prostitution, as the reformers believed. For them, sex could mean pleasure or danger; it suffused the politics of everyday life. The spies tell us little about the economic disadvantages that led women to barter sex for support; nor do they acknowledge women's vulnerability to sexual violence. But their images of working-class women do subvert the old mythology that cast women's virtue in the racial polarities of black and white. In the process, they add a new figure to the New South stage: the white working-class woman who saw no contradiction between fighting the mill boss and charting new sexual terrain.

III

Despite the combined efforts of the textile workers, the reformers, and the craft unions, Fulton Mills prevailed, in part because of its sheer implacability. Asked by a federal investigator what he considered the best way to break a strike, Oscar Elsas responded, "I'd just as soon get guns and mow 'em down as not." He refused to submit to any form of mediation or even to meet with labor leaders. Taking refuge in the tent city, two to three hundred families held out through the winter, only to see themselves replaced by an endless pool of labor recruited from the city and the surrounding countryside. As this war of attrition continued, local and national support faded away. Finally, in May 1915, the UTW closed the camp and admitted defeat. By then most of the strikers had

[71] *Atlanta Constitution,* June 6, 1914, 6, 7; Report to B. Z. Phillips. For this phenomenon, see D'Emilio and Freedman, *Intimate Matters,* 124–25; Jonathan Katz, *Gay American History: Lesbians and Gay Men in the U.S.A.* (New York: Crowell, 1976), 209–79; and Box-Car Bertha, *Sister of the Road: The Autobiography of Box-Car Bertha,* as told to Dr. Ben L. Reitman (New York: Macauley, 1937).

moved on to other mills, though some remained in Atlanta trying "secretly to continue the fight."[72]

At issue in the strike were the aspirations of men, women, and children who were among the nation's most exploited workers. Different observers interpreted those aspirations differently, and their interpretations depended on varying constructions of workers' identities. But in each version, assumptions about gender figured centrally. Neither the craft unionists' emphasis on wages nor the reformers' stress on domesticity nor the spies' preoccupation with sexuality tells us how textile workers imagined and invented themselves.[73] Yet words are actions; outsiders' labels help create the fund of interpretive possibilities from which identity can be drawn.[74] Observers' reports can be fruitfully interrogated for clues to the lives of both the seers and the seen. And the downfall of O. Delight Smith, like the murder of Leo Frank, reminds us that images help construct relationships of power.

[72]Weed, "Final Report" (quote); *Journal of Labor,* Sept. 4, 1914, 6; McWade and Colpoys Memorandum, 7; Operative 16, May 12, 1915, box 3, file 40, Operative Reports (quote).

[73]This study, of course, is concerned with observers' representations, not workers' identities. For the latter, we would have to draw on sources that are less hierarchical and more dialogic, sources that allow those who have usually been the objects of surveillance and reform a voice in the representational process that produces our understanding of the past. For this issue, see Clifford, "On Ethnographic Authority," 21–54. For a study of southern textile workers that relies heavily on oral history—a source that is, by its nature, created in dialogue—see Hall et al., *Like a Family;* and Jacquelyn D. Hall and Della Pollock, "History, Story, and Performance: The Making and Remaking of a Southern Cotton Mill World," in *Reconstructing American Literary and Historical Studies,* ed. Günter H. Lenz, Hartmut Keil, and Sabine Bröck-Sallah (Frankfurt am Main: Campus and New York: St. Martin's Press, 1990), 324–44. For studies that take the complexity of women workers' identities as a central concern, see Susan Porter Benson, *Counter Cultures: Saleswomen, Managers, and Customers in American Department Stores, 1890–1940* (Urbana: University of Illinois Press, 1988), 229 and passim; Alice Kessler-Harris, "Gender Ideology in Historical Reconstruction: A Case Study from the 1930s," *Gender and History,* 1 (Spring 1989), 31–49; Ardis Cameron, *Neighborhoods in Revolt: The Laboring Women of Lawrence, 1860–1912* (Urbana: University of Illinois Press, forthcoming); and Carole Turbin, "Beyond Dichotomies: Interdependence in Mid-Nineteenth-Century Working-Class Families in the United States," *Gender and History,* 1 (Autumn 1989), 293–308.

[74]Nancy Fraser, "The Uses and Abuses of French Discourse Theories for Feminist Politics," paper presented to the Program in Social Theory and Cross-Cultural Studies, University of North Carolina at Chapel Hill, Apr. 14, 1989.

CHAPTER ELEVEN

Gender, Consumer Organizing, and the Seattle Labor Movement, 1919–1929

Dana Frank

"The labor man fights at the point of production, where he is robbed; the labor woman fights at the point of consumption, where she is robbed." With this phrase trade unionists in Seattle, Washington, in the 1920s summed up gender relations in their movement. It was a tidy conceptualization, assigning to men the sphere of trade union activity, to women the sphere of politicized consumption, as together they battled their respective exploitations in a common movement.[1]

The reality of their movement and of the respective spheres of men and women was, however, far less neat. Male trade unionists embraced consumer organizing tactics in an effort to match employers' power at the workplace; women trade unionists turned away from the politics of consumption to fight for legislation to protect them at the point of production; while the female family members of trade unionists engaged in a host of campaigns involving both production and consumption.

Nonetheless, the motto points to a central aspect of Seattle trade unionists' world: the ways in which the labor movement's tactics were deeply gendered. Every choice of tactic grew out of trade unionists' assumptions about the proper place of women and men at the workplace and in the workers' movement; every choice reflected, as well, the different material relations of men and women to production and consumption. Each choice, in turn, continually recast women's and men's position in the movement. At the same time, it shaped the ability of the working class as a whole to counter the power of the city's employers.

Between 1919 and 1929 AFL labor unionists in Seattle took up three consumer tactics: cooperatives, boycotts, and union label promotion.

Great thanks to Ileen DeVault, Nancy Cott, Alan Dawley, David Montgomery, and Karin Stallard for their generous advice, and especially to Ava Baron.
[1] *Co-operator*, June 1920, 3; July 1920, 3.

Each yields clues not only to the relationship between consumer organizing and gender dynamics in the U.S. labor movement, but also to the declining power of American labor in the 1920s and to the relationship between the American working class—male and female—and the rise of consumerism in the twentieth century.[2]

To understand fully the gendered nature of the labor movement we need to begin by expanding our definition of the labor movement to encompass the broad range of activities that can be grouped under the category of consumer organizing. Promotion of union labels, cooperatives, boycotts, and other tactics involving organized consumption have been integral to the U.S. trade union movement since the nineteenth century. They were crucial to the success of the Knights of Labor, for example, as networks encouraging class-conscious shopping spread among Knights throughout the country in the 1880s.[3] But labor historians, with a few exceptions, acknowledge these activities only in a very perfunctory fashion.[4] We still tend to think of the strike as the solitary tactic of the U.S. labor movement. The old labor history was in fact better on this front; most studies of the boycott, for example, date from the second

[2]On the U.S. labor movement in the 1920s, see Irving Bernstein, *The Lean Years: A History of the American Worker, 1920–1933* (Boston: Houghton Mifflin, 1960); J. B. S. Hardman, *American Labor Dynamics in the Light of Post-War Developments* (New York: Harcourt, Brace, 1928); David Montgomery, *The Fall of the House of Labor: The Workplace, the State, and Labor Activism, 1865–1925* (New York: Cambridge University Press, 1987); Frank Stricker, "Affluence for Whom?—Another Look at Prosperity and the Working Classes in the 1920s," *Labor History*, 24 (Winter 1983), 5–33; David Brody, "The Rise and Decline of Welfare Capitalism," in his *Workers in Industrial America: Essays on the Twentieth-Century Struggle* (New York: Oxford University Press, 1980), 48–81; Robert H. Zieger, *The Republicans and Labor, 1919–1929* (Lexington: University of Kentucky Press, 1969). On consumer culture, Richard Wightman Fox and T. J. Jackson Lears, *The Culture of Consumption: Critical Essays in American History, 1880–1980* (New York: Pantheon, 1983); Stuart Ewen, *Captains of Consciousness: Advertising and the Social Roots of the Consumer Culture* (New York: McGraw-Hill, 1976); and the classic by Robert and Helen Merrell Lynd, *Middletown: A Study in Modern American Culture* (New York: Harcourt, Brace & World, 1929).

[3]Gerald Grob, *Workers and Utopia: A Study of Ideological Conflict in the American Labor Movement, 1865–1900* (Evanston, Ill.: Northwestern University Press, 1961), 44–57; Claire Anna Dahlberg Horner, "Producers' Cooperatives in the United States, 1865–1890" (Ph.D. diss., University of Pittsburgh, 1978); Richard Jules Oestreicher, *Solidarity and Fragmentation: Working People and Class Consciousness in Detroit, 1875–1900* (Urbana: University of Illinois Press, 1986), 109, 116–17, 129, 224, 227–28; Leo Wolman, *The Boycott in American Trade Unions* (Baltimore: Johns Hopkins University Press, 1916); Harry Wellington Laidler, *Boycotts and the Labor Struggle* (New York: John Lane, 1914).

[4]The recent exceptions are Gregory R. Zieren, "The Labor Boycott and Class Consciousness in Toledo, Ohio," in *Life and Labor: Dimensions of American Working-Class History*, ed. Charles Stephenson and Robert Asher (Albany: SUNY Press, 1986), 131–46, and "The Propertied Worker: Working-Class Formation in Toledo, Ohio, 1870–1900" (Ph.D. diss., University of Delaware, 1981), chap. 10; Michael Gordon, "The Labor Boycott in New York City, 1880–1886," *Labor History*, 16 (Spring 1975), 184–229; David Scobey, "Boycotting the Politics Factory: Labor Radicalism and the New York City Mayoral Election of 1884," *Radical History Review*, nos. 28–30 (September 1984), 280–325.

decade of this century.[5] New labor historians have lacked interest in the twentieth-century American Federation of Labor—less militant, less democratic, and thus less politically appealing than the IWW or CIO.[6] Yet the AFL has been American labor's main province of consumer organizing.[7]

Once we step back and define the labor movement from this broader perspective, a new sphere of women's relations to trade unionism then opens up. For consumer organizing activities historically have involved women quite prominently—though not, it is important to note, exclusively. Yet historians of women's labor history have thus far given little attention to consumer organizing activities. The first generation of women's labor history has appropriately focused, rather, on two issues: first, on the barriers and encouragements to women's membership and activism as trade unionists themselves—including their position in the wage labor force, their situation and responsibilities outside it, and the attitudes of male unionists[8]—and second, on women's roles in strike support work, whether it be their own strikes or those of their menfolk. This literature stresses women's networks of support growing out of household and neighborhood as well as the paid workplace.[9] Both concerns,

---

[5]Laidler, *Boycotts and the Labor Struggle;* Wolman, *Boycott in American Trade Unions;* see also Delia Randall, *The Labor Boycott: A Bibliography,* 2d ed. (New York: Works Progress Administration, 1938).

[6]For the generational distinctions in labor history, see David Brody, "The Old Labor History and the New: A Review Essay," *Journal of Social History,* 4 (Spring 1971), 277–85; David Montgomery, "To Study the People: The American Working Class," *Labor History,* 21 (Fall 1980), 485–512.

[7]Laidler, *Boycotts and the Labor Struggle;* Wolman, *Boycott in American Trade Unions;* Zieren, "Labor Boycott and Class Consciousness"; Ernest Spedden, *The Trade Union Label* (Baltimore: Johns Hopkins University Press, 1910).

[8]See, e.g., Carole Turbin, "Beyond Conventional Wisdom: Women's Wage Work, Household Economic Contribution, and Labor Activism in a Mid-Nineteenth-Century Working-Class Community," in *"To Toil the Livelong Day": America's Women at Work, 1780–1980,* ed. Carol Groneman and Mary Beth Norton, 47–67 (Ithaca: Cornell University Press, 1987), and "And We Are Nothing but Women: Irish Working Women in Troy," in *Women of America: A History,* ed. Carol Ruth Berkin and Mary Beth Norton, 202–22 (Boston: Houghton Mifflin, 1979); Mary H. Blewett, "The Sexual Division of Labor and the Artisan Tradition in Early Industrial Capitalism: The Case of New England Shoemaking, 1780–1860," in Groneman and Norton, *"To Toil the Livelong Day,"* 35–46, and "Work, Gender, and the Artisan Tradition in New England Shoe Making, 1780–1860," *Journal of Social History,* 17 (December 1983), 221–48; Alice Kessler-Harris, *Out to Work: A History of Wage-Earning Women in the United States* (New York: Oxford University Press, 1982), and "Where Are the Organized Women Workers?" in *A Heritage of Her Own: Toward A New Social History of American Women,* ed. Nancy F. Cott and Elizabeth Pleck, 343–66 (New York: Simon & Schuster, 1979); Sharon Hartmann Strom, "Challenging 'Woman's Place': Feminism, the Left, and Industrial Unionism in the 1930s," *Feminist Studies,* 9 (Summer 1983), 359–86; Maurine Weiner Greenwald, *Women, War, and Work: The Impact of World War I on Women Workers in the United States* (Westport, Conn.: Greenwood, 1980).

[9]Ruth Milkman, *Women, Work, and Protest: A Century of U.S. Women's Labor History* (Boston: Routledge & Kegan Paul, 1985); Meredith Tax, *The Rising of the Women: Fem-*

however, tend to bring us back to the strike. Paralleling historians of male workers, women's historians have looked for militance, workplace identities, and feminism. Consumer organizing activities often evince none of these characteristics, yet they nonetheless shaped class conflict.

Expanding the study of the labor movement to include consumer organizing opens up a host of new issues involving gender and labor activism. It reveals a broader array of the kinds of women in the labor movement. It moves our focus from single women to married; from young women to those in their thirties, forties, and fifties; from women who worked in the narrow range of employment to which females have historically been restricted to women from families whose members worked in a wide range of trades. Simultaneously it shifts our attention from an exclusive emphasis on women wage earners to a much broader range of women—some of them wage earners, but just as many not. Both attempted to integrate a political understanding of their responsibilities as unpaid workers in the home with an understanding of male family members' labor struggles. Finally, the inclusion of consumer organizing forces us to explore how gender dynamics shaped trade unionists' choices of tactics and broadens our study of male workers' labor activism.

Ultimately, we need to use a different conceptual vocabulary to understand the question of women and the labor movement. We have tended to accept the "labor movement" as a given, based on strikes, organizing drives, and tactics at the point of production and at times in relation to the state, and then ask how women fit into that history. I think we need instead to stress more fully the particular incarnation of trade unionism at each point in time, and then ask how that formation was gendered. Susan Levine has argued that the Knights of Labor allowed for much greater participation by women than did their successor, the AFL, because the movement theoretically and structurally allowed for the integration of both women's waged labor and their domestic roles into a larger class-based movement.[10] We need to extend this insight into the twentieth century.

To examine consumer organizing also requires close attention to women's unwaged work in the home. Each time trade unionists imposed a boycott, called for observance of the union label, or celebrated consumer

---

inist Solidarity and Class Conflict, 1880–1917 (New York: Monthly Review Press, 1980); Susan A. Glenn, "Partners in the Struggle: Gender and Class Consciousness among Jewish Women Garment Workers," paper delivered at the Organization of American Historians Conference, Apr. 5, 1987; Susan Levine, Labor's True Woman: Carpet Weavers, Industrialization, and Labor Reform in the Gilded Age (Philadelphia: Temple University Press, 1984). For a theoretical perspective, see Temma Kaplan, "Female Consciousness and Collective Action: The Case of Barcelona," Signs, 7 (Spring 1982), 545–66.
[10] Levine, Labor's True Woman.

cooperatives, they asked women (and men) to reshape their shopping and spending habits in service to class interests. Consumer tactics extended the labor movement, in other words, beyond employer-employee relations at the waged workplace, involving only the wage-earning union member (male or female), to a politicization of the daily choices through which women expended their families' earnings to convert wages into their families' sustenance. Thus when we examine consumer organizing we must look closely at the ways in which trade unionism embraced both a politics of production and a politics of consumption.[11]

Seattle unionists undertook three successive consumer organizing campaigns between 1919 and 1929: first, cooperatives; second, a citywide boycott; and finally, union label promotion. A wide range of organizational strategies were available to Seattle's working class, some based on production, some on consumption, some incorporating both. Each cast gender in a distinctive mold. The choice of strategy to employ, and, on a citywide basis, the mix of strategies, determined in part the relations between women and men in the labor movement; conversely, the relations between women and men in the movement influenced the choice of strategy and the degree to which it succeeded.

Cooperatives

The Seattle labor movement is best known for its general strike of February 1919. The strike was led by AFL locals, which had moved leftward during World War I as a flood of Wobblies migrated into the city to take jobs in the shipyards and related war-boom industries. By 1919 Seattle's unions counted 52,000 members (out of a total city population of 250,000), 4,000 of them female.[12] Workers in the service, transportation, and building trades, as well as shipyard and other metal-trades workers, all enjoyed the closed shop. These organized workers were almost exclusively white, either native born, immigrants, or the children of immigrants from Scandinavia, Britain, or Canada. By war's end they had constructed a class-based cultural and institutional world that is difficult fully to grasp from a contemporary perspective. Seattle's labor movement in 1919 could boast, for example, its own daily newspaper with a circulation of 100,000, its own filmmaking company and theater, a string of trade-sponsored recreational halls, and a trades union savings and loan.

[11]For a theoretical formulation of these questions, see Batya Weinbaum and Amy Bridges, "The Other Side of the Paycheck: Monopoly Capital and the Structure of Consumption," *Monthly Review,* 28 (July–August 1976), 88–103; see also Ellen Willis, " 'Consumerism' and Women," in *Woman in Sexist Society,* ed. Vivian Gornick, 658–65 (New York: Basic Books, 1972).
[12]Washington [State] Bureau of Labor, *Twelfth Biennial Report, 1919–1920* (Olympia, 1920), 33–34.

At the center of the movement lay the Central Labor Council, which co-ordinated not only cross-trade workplace solidarity but the ideological fertility and vision at the center of the Seattle movement.[13]

Seattle's wartime and immediate postwar militance paralleled that of working-class communities throughout the United States in those years; indeed, its general strike is the most frequently cited national exemplar of such radicalism. Similarly, in its rapid movement rightward after 1922, the Seattle labor movement exemplifies the national shift in the decade from militance to apathy. Seattle thus serves as a slightly exaggerated but highly representative example of national trends in the 1920s.

From Seattle's war-fueled upsurge sprang a flourishing cooperative movement. From 1918 to 1920 Seattle's organized workers built two cross-city chains of consumer and producer cooperatives. The first, the Seattle Consumers' Co-operative Association, identified itself with strict Rochdale principles of one member, one vote, and patronage dividends to members. It expanded horizontally across the city, neighborhood by neighborhood, until by 1920 it numbered 1,070 member families, with nine consumer branches plus a cooperative jewelry store, a tailor shop, and a fuel yard.[14] The second chain, the Co-operative Food Products Association, was more directly integrated into the trade union movement. It began when the butchers' union organized a cooperative meat market after a 1917 strike, then expanded swiftly in late 1918 and 1919 to sausage production, a slaughterhouse, a milk condensary in the country, and five neighborhood distributive branches off a cluster of market stalls downtown; its membership similarly peaked at around 1,000 families.[15]

[13]For background on the Seattle labor movement in 1919 and the 1920s, see Robert Friedheim, *The Seattle General Strike* (Seattle: University of Washington Press, 1964); Harvey O'Connor, *The Revolution in Seattle* (New York: Monthly Review Press, 1964); Anna Louise Strong, *I Change Worlds* (New York: Henry Holt, 1935); Jonathan Dembo, "A History of the Washington State Labor Movement, 1885–1935" (Ph.D. diss., University of Washington, 1978); and Dana Frank, "At the Point of Consumption: Seattle Labor and the Politics of Consumption, 1919–1927" (Ph.D. diss., Yale University, 1988).

[14]On the growth and philosophies of the Seattle Consumers' Co-operative Association, see *Seattle Union Record*, daily ed. (hereafter *SUR*), Jan. 28; Feb. 3 and 12; Mar. 7, 11, 12, 14, 20, 29; Apr. 2, 12, 23; and June 7, 1919; Jan. 7, 1920; *Seattle Union Record*, weekly ed. (hereafter *SURW*), Feb. 12; Mar. 1, 15, 29; Apr. 3, 8, 9, 12; and June 7, 1919; Carl Lunn, "How We Cooperate Out West," *Life and Labor*, September 1920, 205; *Co-operation*, July 1919, 108, and September 1919, 135; *Co-operative Consumer*, January 1918, 13, and April 1918, 6; *Northwestern Co-operative News*, Sept. 1, 1919, 5; Earl Shimmons, "The *Seattle Union Record*," 31, in Harry Ault Papers, University of Washington Manuscripts Collection, pt. 1, box 7, folder 9; *Forge*, July 5, 1919; Co-operative League of America, *Report of the Proceedings of the First American Co-operative Convention, Springfield, Illinois, September 25–27, 1918* (Springfield: Co-operative Association of America, 1919), 122.

[15]On the Co-operative Food Products Association, see its monthly newsletter, *The Co-operator;* U. G. Moore, "The Rise and Fall of the Seattle Food Products Association," *Co-operation*, January 1923, 9; Co-operative League, *Proceedings*, 109–23, 257–60; Frank, "At the Point of Consumption," chap. 2.

The co-ops' heyday, however, was brief. The cost of living began to drop in June 1920, removing one of the main impulses behind the movement. The 1921–22 recession then cut into members' ability to invest capital in the two chains. A series of disastrous defeats for labor ate away at the vision of fundamental social change on which the movement had always depended. By 1922 all the co-ops had failed, tumbling down one after the other in a bitter chain of financial failure and personal recrimination.[16]

At the heart of this briefly flourishing "cooperative moment" lay a vision of the integration of relations of production and consumption. Cooperation, as preached by its enthusiasts, promised to buttress traditional trade unionism by guaranteeing a source of food during strikes; at the same time it would lower prices, thus offering the workers, in a time of inflation, protection against erosion of their wages. At the same time cooperation presented itself as a path to fundamental social change: the workers' autonomous sector would gradually integrate consumer and producer cooperatives in an ever-expanding network (inspired by the British example) that would ultimately supplant capitalism, allowing the workers, in effect, to secede from the union of labor and capital.[17]

Men were numerically dominant in the movement, despite consumer cooperation's theoretically "female" place in the sphere of consumption. Male members of almost every union in the city, of every political persuasion, and from both the leadership and the rank and file, turned with enthusiasm to the cooperative movement after the war. Unlike other consumer organizing campaigns undertaken by Seattle trade unionists in the 1920s, however, the cooperative movement sought to politicize consumption not only in order to restructure and gain leverage on relations at the paid workplace but also to restructure relations of consumption itself. On the one hand, producer cooperatives could usher in workers' self-management, while sustaining struggles at remaining capitalist workplaces; on the other hand, consumer cooperatives would end exploitation by evil "middlemen" in the sphere of consumption.

Detailed examination of the Cooperative Food Products Association (CFPA) shows that women's activities were contained largely in a series of neighborhood-based women's co-op clubs. Two prominent women activists originally conceived these clubs as seeds for neighborhood buying clubs that would eventually evolve into new branch stores and in the process draw more trade union families into the movement. But as

[16]See Frank, "At the Point of Consumption," chap. 2, for an extended analysis of the causes of the co-ops' failure, as well as the sources cited in nn. 14 and 15 for both chains.

[17]The best sources on the theories underlying cooperation are *Co-operator;* the Cooperative League's national journal, *Co-operation;* and the repeated articles extolling cooperation in *SUR* in 1919, esp. in late spring.

women joined and expanded these clubs, they instead undertook largely social and educational activities. They spent their meetings hearing guest lecturers from the labor or cooperative movement or discussing key texts on cooperation. The women appear to have taken great pleasure and pride in the social and aesthetic aspects of their clubs. Reports of club meetings thanked the hostess for her generous hospitality or praised her social graces. One meeting report read, "Beautiful flowers and foliage were donated by the members, making the room and tea table very lovely with autumn colors." The women's clubs also organized social events for the whole co-op movement, to unite it citywide or to tie it in, on a neighborhood basis, with particular trade unions. Describing a 1920 Christmas ball, one prominent woman activist captured perfectly the women's faith in the social component of cooperation: "The general opinion in Seattle is that in the Labor Movement we do not play enough. And I think that if the co-operators can in the social way bind our people together, we will be accomplishing a great thing." She had expressed the same viewpoint the previous May: "Co-operation will be the solution not only for consumer and producer, but will make life more sociable and neighborly in our communities."[18]

The co-op women were at the same time quite self-conscious about women's unique economic relation to the cooperative movement. From their point of view, women, first of all, spent the workers' money. Jean Stovel, trying to persuade fellow unionists to enlist their wives and mothers in the cooperative movement, argued, "WOMEN do 90 per cent of the shopping. . . . They spend the money you earn. Their purchasing power is one of the most effective weapons in the hands of labor today." "You spend the money your husband earns," the CFPA newsletter's women editors reminded readers. In some ways we can sum up their attitude as "shopping as social change." Listen to the way one educational director concluded an article on women in the movement: " . . . anything that is for the good, for the humane, the noble, and unselfish, ideas and principles, we, the women of the co-operative clubs, are interested in helping and patronizing."[19]

All this women's co-op activism took place, however, within a very male-controlled movement. All but one of the chain's original directors and committee members were male. The only two women in the leadership were in charge of the educational department. When rank-and-file women attempted to influence co-op policy, the men appear to have simply ignored them. Women members of the West Seattle club, who be-

[18]Quotes: *Co-operator,* October 1920, 6–7; *Co-operation,* February 1921, 32; *Co-operator,* May 1920, 7. For the women's clubs, see monthly reports in *Co-operator.*

[19]Quotes: *Co-operator,* August 1920, 6; June 1920, 3; March 1921, 4. See also July 1920, 3; March 1921, 4.

lieved they had amassed enough members to warrant a branch store in their neighborhood, repeatedly visited trustees' meetings in 1920 to ask for a store. The trustees repeatedly thanked them for their interest in the co-op's affairs but equally politely ignored their request.[20]

But in the winter of 1920–21 the Cooperative Food Products Association suddenly voted four women onto its board of trustees. Only a year earlier, the chain had ignored a statewide resolution calling for equal representation by gender on co-op boards. In the fall of 1920, however, the chain had entered a steep decline in membership and patronage. The women's clubs, however, were booming.[21] The male leaders apparently realized that women's patronage and interest in the movement held the key to the future survival of the movement; if they had to share power to save the movement, then they would share it.

The women's priorities within the movement as a whole were often quite different from the men's. In 1920 the women united their clubs in a citywide co-op women's federation, took over the women's lounge at the central store, and, after the men refused to add dry goods to the co-op's stock, set up their own dry goods sales operation financially independent of the main chain. With the funds generated by that operation they established a "Women's Exchange," which took in and distributed clothes and other articles and then sold them at minimal markup or, increasingly, donated them to charity. The women also used this fund to buy themselves a silver tea service to use at meetings.[22]

The cooperative's women, unlike the CFPA in general, thus intermixed with little apparent anxiety money-making activities, charity work, business expansion, and women's home production. Blocked from using regular CFPA resources for their projects, the women nonetheless pursued what they themselves perceived to be cooperative activities. Their projects, along with the club meetings in members' homes, created literally a women's space within the movement—they took over the women's rest room at the main store for their educational department and women's clothing exchange. Similarly their independently purchased tea service made possible proper attention to a quintessentially female cultural ritual.[23]

[20]Ibid., August 1920, 1–2; September 1920, 7; October 1920, 7; December 1920, 5.

[21]Ibid., May 1920, 6; August 1920, 2; December 1920, 5; September 1920, 2; December 1920, 5; January 1921, 2; February 1921, 7; March 1921, 3; June 1921, 5; *Co-operation,* January 1920, 12; February 1921, 32; Moore, "Rise and Fall," 9–10.

[22]*Co-operator,* April 1920, 7; June 1920, 7; July 1920, 6; September, 1920, 1, 6; October 1920, 5; November 1920, 5; December 1920, 7; January, 1921, 4; February, 1921, 1–2; March 1921, 5; June 1921, 5.

[23]Some observers would argue that the silver tea service symbolized the embourgeoisement of these working-class women, their aspiration to middle-class culture. I do not agree that this is necessarily the case. See, for an alternative perspective, Lizabeth Cohen, *Making a New Deal: Industrial Workers in Chicago, 1919–1929* (New York: Cambridge University

Women's activities in the second chain, the Seattle Consumer's Cooperative Association (SCCA), paralleled those in the Food Products Association. The SCCA may in fact have had more women on its board of directors; Carl Lunn, its leader, referred at one point to five women sitting with him on the board, but the total number of directors is unclear. Like their counterparts in the CFPA's women clubs, SCCA women organized social and educational activities. Lola Lunn, Carl's wife, planned numerous branches of an SCCA "Women's Co-operative Study Club" that would "give information concerning the Rochdale co-operative system, . . . study every phase of the movement, . . . carry into the homes the need and benefit of co-operation, . . . give social entertainments, . . . start classes among children and . . . assist with the general educational activities." Women of the Hillman City SCCA branch did organize a Women's Co-operative Guild in November 1919, and laid plans for "vigorous social and educational features." They presented a Christmas entertainment for children including songs, recitations, and vaudeville stunts.[24]

The women and the men of Seattle's postwar cooperatives, in sum, had divergent definitions of what their movement was really all about: the men concerned themselves largely with financial matters, the women with social ones. The men made decisions about dividends, upper-level investments, and the broad future of the business, and the women turned to charity, self-education, and parties. While the division of labor within the movement reflected the sexual division of labor within the larger society, it also shaped a unique female working-class political vision and sense of the ideal direction of the class movement. Briefly, the co-ops were flexible enough to accommodate both—though, again, within a framework in which the men retained the ultimate power to shape the movement.

The Boycott

A second campaign in postwar Seattle involved consumer organizing not as class secession, but as class war. In March 1920 the Central Labor Council declared a boycott of Seattle's largest department store, the Bon

Press, 1990), chap. 3. For a more extended discussion of the class culture and class politics of workers and consumption in 1920s Seattle, see Frank, "At the Point of Consumption."

[24] Quotes: Lunn, "How We Cooperate," 209–10; *SURW*, Nov. 15, 1919. On the Women's Co-op Study Guild, see also Co-operative League, *Proceedings*, 256–60; *SUR*, Apr. 22, July 1, July 8, and Aug. 9, 1919, and Feb. 2, 1920. A Washington State Women's Co-operative Guild was formed in January 1920, its "chief purpose" "to develop the educational and recreational phases of the Co-operative movement": *Co-operation*, February 1920, 28.

Marche, then in the process of being constructed by nonunion labor.[25] Three large postwar developments converged to spark this boycott. First, in the aftermath of the general strike Seattle's employers had launched a fierce drive for the open shop, decimating unions across the city in 1919 and 1920.[26] The labor movement's leadership, after losses in seventeen strikes and lockouts, increasingly felt that the strike no longer tactically served them.[27] Electoral actions similarly failed, further contributing to interest in the boycott.[28] The city's department stores, moreover, were the leaders of the employers' association, and symbolized the class enemy.[29] Second, in 1919 that same body of employers and bankers had imposed a boycott on advertising in the *Union Record,* labor's newspaper, and then attempted to shut down the paper altogether with charges of espionage. The *Record* wanted not only to retaliate but to force the department stores—traditionally a major source of revenue for all newspapers—to renew advertisements in its pages.[30] Finally, the decision to

[25]Minutes, Seattle Central Labor Council (hereafter CLC), February and March 1920, in Records of the King County Central Labor Council, box 8, University of Washington Manuscripts Collection.

[26]Samuel Zimand, *The Open Shop Drive* (New York: Bureau of Industrial Research, 1921), 13; Margaret Jane Thompson, "Development and Comparison of Industrial Relations in Seattle" (M.B.A. thesis, University of Washington, 1929), 65–66; Francis R. Singleton, *Seattle and the American Plan,* pamphlet reprinted from *Business* in Ault Papers, pt. 1, box 5, folder 17; Washington Bureau of Labor, *Twelfth Biennial Report,* 18–19; "How Seattle Fights Unfair Labor Unions," *Iron Age,* October 21, 1920, 1055–56; Minute Books, Seattle Chamber of Commerce, Oct. 19, 1920, in Seattle Public Library; Mark Litchman to Miss Baritz, Feb. 3, 1920, in Mark Litchman Papers, University of Washington Manuscripts Collection, pt. 1, box 1, folder 27; Christy Thomas, "Seattle's New Labor Policy," *Review of Reviews,* 62 (November 1920), 516–20; see also *SUR* throughout 1919 and early 1920.

[27]Reports of Agent 106, Oct. 18, 23, and 28, 1919, Broussais C. Beck Papers, University of Washington Manuscripts Collection, box 1, folder 16; Dec. 1, 1919, folder 18; Dec. 15, 19, 1919, folder 19.

[28]Dembo, "Washington State Labor Movement," 275–79; Mary Joan O'Connell (Sister Mary Veronica), "The Seattle *Union Record,* 1918–1928: A Pioneer Labor Daily" (M.A. thesis, University of Washington, 1948), 116, 151–58; *SUR,* November 1919, January and February 1920; Minutes, CLC, Jan. 20 1920; Agent 106, November 1919, Beck Papers, box 1, folders 17 and 18; Jan. 21, 1920, folder 20; Feb. 20, 1920, folder 21; Mark Litchman to Joseph Gilbert, Sept. 21, 1920, Litchman Papers, pt. 1, box 1, folder 29; Litchman to Moses Baritz, Feb. 3, 1920, folder 17.

[29]On the decision to boycott the Bon Marche, see Minutes, CLC Jan. 28, 1920, and Minutes of the Executive Board, CLC, Feb. 2, Mar. 10 and 15, 1920, King County Central Labor Council Records, Box 15; Thompson, "Development and Comparison," 66–67; *SUR,* Jan. 29 and Feb. 5, 1920; in Beck Papers: Agent 106, Feb. 28 and Mar. 3, 1920, box 1, folders 20 and 22, and Agent 17, Feb. 6, 1920, box 2, folder 3.

[30]On the advertising boycott, see *SUR,* Feb. 18 and Apr. 24, 1920; O'Connell, "Seattle *Union Record,*" 84, 201; Earl W. Shimmons, "The Labor Dailies," *American Mercury,* 15 (September 1928), 85–93; *Business Chronicle,* January 1919, clipping in Harvey O'Connor's notes for *Revolution in Seattle,* O'Connor Papers, Archives of Labor and Urban Affairs, Walter Reuther Library, Wayne State University, pt. 2, box 3; in Ault Papers, Harry Ault to Roger Baldwin, Mar. 10 and Aug. 29, 1922, box 18. On the raids on the *Record's* plant and charges against its management in November and December 1919, see O'Con-

throw the whole movement's energies behind a boycott grew out of a key structural shift within the Seattle labor movement after the war. Power shifted from the radical, industrial-unionist metal trades and dock unions—which placed their organizing emphasis at the point of production and were decimated by the closing of the shipyards—to the more prosperous building, teaming, and service trades, the relative conservatives. Located in local-market industries susceptible to consumer pressures, the conservatives looked favorably upon consumer organizing tactics such as the boycott.[31]

In the spring of 1920 Seattle's unions launched a major boycott campaign against the Bon Marche, with constant leaflets, daily articles in the *Record* vilifying the store, and resolutions from trade union bodies throughout the city eschewing all shopping there.[32] Labor's propaganda stressed the store's effrontery in discharging building trades unionists, as well as the prominence of the Bon Marche's owners among Seattle's open-shop leaders. A second type of attack alerted unionists to the store's ill treatment of its female clerks, noting that it paid low wages, forced workers to labor in "foul-smelling basements," and denied them the opportunity to sit down. The *Union Record* brought the campaign to its height (or perhaps we should say depth) with the headline "WIDOW MAIMED IN BON MARCHE IS IMPROVING"; a forty-five-year-old clerk had fallen down an elevator shaft and the Bon Marche was being "secretive" about her condition.[33]

The effectiveness of any boycott is extremely hard to measure, but judging by employers' protests, as well as the labor movement's claims, the boycott was at least partially damaging; by fall, the employers had backed off in their open-shop drive and adopted a more conciliatory approach to labor.[34]

nell, "Seattle *Union Record*," 95–122; *Seattle Times*, Apr. 7, 1920; *SUR*, Nov. 14, 1919–February 1920; Apr. 24, 1920.

[31] This analysis is based on an extended examination of the fates of the various sectors of the Seattle labor movement after the war; see Frank, "At the Point of Consumption," chap. 3. Sources include the *Union Record*, spy reports in the Beck Papers, Central Labor Council minutes and record books, and correspondence in the Ault and Litchman collections. See Thompson, "Development and Comparison," for general statistics.

[32] In Beck Papers: Agent 17, Mar. 18, 1920, Box 2, folder 4; June 3, 1920, folder 7; Agent 106, Mar. 10 and 31, 1920, box 1, folder 22; Apr. 11, 1920, folder 24 (leaflet attached to report); *SUR*, March and April 1920; Minutes of the Executive Board, Mar. 10, 1920, CLC; in University of Washington Manuscripts Collection: Minutes, Local 202, International Typographers' Union, Mar. 28, Apr. 25, 1920, in Records of Local 99, International Typographers' Union, box 16; Fine Book, Local 131, United Brotherhood of Carpenters and Joiners of America, in Records of Local 131, box 3; report of Agent 172, Mar. 31, 1920, box 1, folder 6, in Roy John Kinnear Papers.

[33] *SUR*, Mar. 17, 27, 31; Apr. 1, 2, 3, 21; May 18, 1920; Apr. 16, 1920.

[34] For labor's claims, see ibid., Apr. 1, 2, 17, 1920; Agent 106, Apr. 19, 1920, in Beck Papers, box 1, folder 24. For evidence that employers acknowledged the boycott's effective-

Seattle's labor leaders explicitly designed their boycott campaign in ways they thought would best enlist working-class women in the cause. They were aware that if their boycott were to be successful, it had to have the full support of the female family members of Seattle trade unionists and of female unionists. To get that support the Central Labor Council's leaders first deliberately narrowed their boycott target. Charles Doyle, Labor Council secretary, argued that "it would be impossible to convince the people not to patronize any of the large department stores for the women will buy in these stores. But it is a very easy matter to convince them not to patronize any one store in particular." Second, they stressed the issue of high prices. As Doyle put it, "This publicity will be the greatest aid in our campaign because the women knowing that if a store is liable to overcharge them they will stay away from it." Finally, the boycott promoters deliberately stressed the *Union Record* as the main vehicle for disseminating boycott propaganda because they believed it was the best means to reach women.[35]

Even the partial effectiveness of the boycott suggests that large numbers of working-class women did support the labor council's boycott. Yet no organized mass movement of women ever came forward to back the boycott. A few women activists, the stalwarts of the Women's Card and Label League (on which more later), did plan one "mass meeting" in support of the boycott, which only a handful attended, and they sent a letter to the city's locals requesting pledges not to shop at the Bon Marche.[36] But I think it is safe to assume that this was the full extent of women's involvement, since the *Union Record* would have reported, in fact exaggerated, any further women's activism.

How do we explain this lack of organized support?[37] It is intriguing to speculate. First, the Bon Marche boycott led to the layoff of large numbers of clerks, most of them women, in a time of rising unemployment. Historians usually refer to boycotts as "safer" than strikes because they entail no sacrifices of jobs or wages, but boycotts injure the unorganized workers at the boycotted firm. Seattle's largely male Retail Clerks' Union

---

ness, see Associated Industries of Seattle, *Revolution, Wholesale Strikes, Boycotts,* n.d. [1920], in Litchman Papers, and its *Bulletin,* no. 5., n.d. [1920], in Seattle Public Library; *Square Deal* (newsletter of Associated Industries), Aug. 14, Sept. 11 and 18, 1920; *Weekly Bulletin No. 1, Associated Industries of Seattle,* leaflet in Washington State Federation of Labor Records, box 6, folder 37, University of Washington Manuscripts Collection.

[35] Agent 106, Mar. 29 and 12, 1920, in Beck Papers box 1, folders 23 and 22.

[36] *SUR,* May 20, Aug. 5, 6, 7, 1920; Agent 17, May 13 and 22, 1920, in Beck Papers, box 2, folders 6 and 7.

[37] If we look at the structural position of organized wage-earning women in Seattle, it would at first appear that they would be quite disposed to support boycotts and consumer organizing—organized women worked almost exclusively in the service sector and in local-market consumer industries: Washington Bureau of Labor, *Twelfth Biennial Report,* 33–34.

did not protest the Bon Marche layoffs. After a lackluster drive to organize female department store clerks the year before, they had given up on
organizing women workers, and preferred to use the boycott to force employers to recognize their union.[38]

More important, Seattle's women activists, members of both trade
unions and the families of male trade unionists, were committed to a
quite different campaign in the same period as the Bon Marche boycott.
This was the state campaign for a minimum wage for women. Women
activists were traveling weekly to Olympia, the state capital, to testify
and lobby at hearings. With limited energies, the women, I think, saw
protective legislation as more in working-class women's interest than
support of a boycott of a local store.[39]

Historians have repeatedly spoken of the boycott as not just safer, but
cheaper.[40] But cheaper for whom? From a woman's point of view the
boycott exacted a price. A given boycott could be effective, after all, only
if the targeted commodity or service was widely purchased, and thus was
desirable to women shoppers. Evidence repeatedly suggests that prolabor shopping—whether at co-ops, of union-labeled goods, or at ap-
proved stores—was expensive.[41] Yet working-class women were
responsible for keeping a narrow budget under control. Moreover, a host
of other concerns, such as fashion, advertising allures, ethnic loyalties,
and convenience, could all have militated against women's enthusiastic
support of a trade union boycott.[42]

[38]In Beck Papers, box 1: Agent 106, May 10 and 12, 1919, folder 2; May 13, 14, 15, 16,
folder 3; June 4, 6, 9, folder 6; June 26, folder 8; Aug. 20 and 25, folder 13; Oct. 11 and
13, folder 15; Nov. 8, folder 17; Dec. 13 and 17, folder 19; Jan. 24, 26, 27, 1920, folder
20; Agent 17, Oct. 27, 1919, folder 30; Nov. 16, folder 31; Jan. 8, 1920, folder 1; also
William Short to Homer T. Bone, Sept. 25, 1925, box 36, Washington State Federation of
Labor Records.
[39]Minutes, CLC, Feb. 28; Mar. 10 and 17; Apr. 21; May 5, 12, 26, 1920. On the minimum wage in Washington State, see Joseph F. Tripp, "Toward an Efficient and Moral
Society: Washington State Minimum Wage Law, 1913–1925," *Pacific Northwest Quarterly,* 67 (July 1976), 97–112, and "Progressive Labor Laws in Washington State, 1900–
1925" (Ph.D. diss., University of Washington, 1973). For an excellent discussion of
women's relation to protective legislation nationwide, see Kessler-Harris, *Out to Work,*
chap. 7, esp. 204.
[40]Wolman, *Boycott in American Trade Unions,* 123–24; Norman Ware, *The Labor
Movement in the United States, 1860–1895* (New York: D. Appleton, 1929), 334; Laidler,
Boycotts and the Labor Struggle, 58; Scobey, "Boycotting the Politics Factory," 298. James
Duncan, secretary of the CLC, argued on Apr. 23, 1920, that the boycott "will be just as
effective as a strike and it would not cost the workers anything": Agent 106, Apr. 23,
1920, in Beck Papers, box 1, folder 24.
[41]See, e.g., Minutes, CLC, Nov. 5 and 19, 1919; *Co-operator,* February 1921, 4; *Washington State Labor News,* Mar. 29, 1929.
[42]Spedden, *Trade Union Label,* argues that women were notoriously unsupportive of
union-label shopping; evidence from Seattle supports this contention; see, e.g., *Musicland*
(newsletter of Local 76, American Federation of Musicians, in possession of Local 76,
Seattle), Aug. 1, 1923; *Washington State Labor News,* Oct. 12, 1928 (hereafter *WSLN*).

At root, the decision to boycott the Bon Marche grew out of the priorities and concerns of the male-controlled Central Labor Council. All of the council's officers and all the members of its governing bodies, with one exception, were male. These male leaders of the council presented their decision to their womenfolk as a fait accompli. Their conscious efforts to shape the boycott campaign to enlist women's support came after the decision was made. The men, in other words, wanted women's support for their own agenda, but did not want to share with women the power to set that agenda.

A revealing glimpse into the leadership's attitude toward women in their movement can be found in a story Max Eastman told of a conversation he overheard while visiting Seattle:

> At a meeting of the famous strike committee of the "Seattle Revolution," [i.e., the general strike] I heard some of the men who lead the left wing of the American Federation of Labor talk about their wives.
>
> "I want to ask the brothers here," said one of them, "if any of them think that, aside from what he might have done, his wife would have held out for another day even if we could have won our demands?"
>
> "Naw!" was the answer. "Ask 'em what the women are good for anyway!" was another, which brought a derisive laugh, and settled the matter finally for a good many of those present.[43]

This was the group of men who a year later faced the task of persuading the female members of their families to boycott the Bon Marche. The tables were turned: now the men needed the women. Just as with the cooperative movement, women held the key to the boycott's success, and this time their men knew it. The boycott would be won or lost, in part, in conversations at 100,000 Seattle working-class dinner tables. Unfortunately, what went on in those conversations we will never really know. We can only note women's lack of organizational fervor for the boycott campaign.

The Union Label

Seattle's labor movement emerged from the depression of 1921–22 with its conservative wing firmly in control and with a new relation to consumer organizing. At the top of the conservatives' new agenda lay promotion of the union label. Fed up with politics, uninterested in confrontational tactics such as the strike, and less enamored than before of the boycott, the men turned full attention in 1924 and 1925 to promo-

[43]Max Eastman, "Feminism," editorial in *Liberator,* 2 (April 1919), 7.

tion of the label and shop card. Their efforts began with meetings of a new House and Shop Card Council of men from consumer trades to coordinate label work.[44] By 1925 those efforts had been codified and expanded into the Seattle Trade Union Promotional League (TUPL), the Central Labor Council's major organizing offensive of mid-decade. Over the course of the next two years the TUPL organized a variety of pep-rally style activities, including neighborhood meetings, exhibits at fairs, and, by 1928, radio shows, all designed as much to prove to the city's employing class how complacent and friendly organized labor had become as to exhort union members to observe union precepts when they spent their money.[45]

The men's turn to label promotion, though, marked a fundamental change in the gender dynamics of consumer organizing in 1920s Seattle. For almost two decades cross-trade label work had been staked out as a unique province for women in the movement, through a citywide organization known as the Women's Card and Label League. During its heyday from 1915 to 1919 the Label League integrated promotion of the label and shop card with strike support work, fund raising, and advocacy of women wage earners. League members engaged in political activism on a host of issues, including capital punishment, suffrage, and health care for indigent women. They functioned largely independently of the male movement, and were not unwilling to clash with the men over such issues as the funding of a special organizer for women workers and, after the war, the right of married women to work for pay.[46]

After 1921, however, the Label League's membership and its organizing agenda both shrank dramatically. Its activities narrowed sharply to more purely label-support work, interspersed only rarely with political activity and even that only on behalf of officially sanctioned state labor federation campaigns. Its members dwindled from the hundreds before

---

[44]Minutes, CLC, Apr. 25, 22, and May 27, 1925.

[45]See *WSLN* throughout the mid- and late 1920s, esp. Aug. 14 and Nov. 6, 1925; May 7 and 14, Sept. 19, Nov. 26, 1926; Feb. 25, Apr. 22, Sept. 30, Nov. 4, 1927; Feb. 10 and 17, 1928; CLC, Apr. 29 and May 13, 1925; Washington State Federation of Labor, *Official Yearbook of Organized Labor, 1925* and *1927* (Seattle, 1925, 1927), 23, 31 respectively; Report of the Executive Council to the 25th Convention, Washington State Federation of Labor Records, box 60.

[46]Washington State Federation of Labor, *Proceedings of the Annual Convention* (Olympia, 1907–1929): 1913, 63; 1915, 109; 1917, 53; 1919, 68, 109; *SURW*, Mar. 8 and May 3, 1919; *SUR*, Jan. 6; Feb. 15, 22; Mar. 17, 20, 31; Apr. 2, 14, 22; May 7, 10, 16, 17, 19, 20, 23, 31; June 5, 10, 16, 19, 24; July 5, 9; Nov. 20; Dec. 3, 18, 1919; Jan. 7 and 29, Apr. 21, June 2, 1920; Minutes, CLC, Jan. 29, Feb. 12 and 26, Mar. 19, Apr. 2 and 23, June 18, Nov. 19, 1919; Jan. 28; Mar. 17, 24, 31; Apr. 7, May 12, June 2, Aug. 4, 1920; Apr. 20, May 18 and 25, June 22, July 27, Aug. 17, Sept. 7 and 14, Oct. 5 and 12, Nov. 9 and 23, Dec. 7, 1921. On the prewar league see Kathryn Oberdeck, "From Wives, Sweethearts, and Female Relatives to Sisterhood: The Seattle Women's Label Leagues and *Seattle Union Record* Women's Pages, 1905–1918," unpublished paper, Yale University, 1984.

the war to only a handful.[47] Equally important, the league largely abandoned its commitment to wage-earning women and subordinated itself to the male movement. The league's slogan for 1923, for example, was "What can we do for you?"[48]

The exact reasons for this shift are, again, difficult to explain completely. But three mutually reinforcing developments would have together contributed to the league's decline. First, the league's personnel itself changed, from women active in the cooperative movement and allied—usually through marriage—to the left-center, socialist sector of the labor movement to the wives of prominent business-unionist conservatives.[49] Second, the overall contraction of the Seattle labor movement's political vision and level of activism after 1921 must have carried the label league down in its wake.[50]

Finally, and perhaps most important, after 1925 the men's new Trade Union Promotional League largely supplanted the very raison d'être of the Label League. In effect, it professionalized label promotion, shifting responsibility for it from rank-and-file female volunteers to a paid male staff. The league's professionalization was part of a larger shift toward professionalism in the post-1922 labor movement, as union officers glorified their own positions and discouraged rank-and-file militance. Male leaders had always participated in label and shop card promotion. The difference was that now they lacked interest in other tactics, such as the strike and political action, preferring more class-harmonious label promotion. The women did not, apparently, protest this usurpation—perhaps because the Card and Label League members were themselves the

[47]To assess relative levels of activism, see *SUR*, Apr. 28, June 10 and 19, 1919; Minutes, CLC, July 5, Aug. 2, 1922; Jan. 3 and 17, May 2, Sept. 19, Oct. 17, 1923; May 5, June 4 and 29, Aug. 13, Oct. 8, Nov. 12, 1924; Feb. 4, Mar. 18, Apr. 1, 1925; *Co-operator*, August 1920, 6; *WSLN*, Sept. 19, 1924; Feb. 6, May 29, 1925.
[48]Minutes, CLC Apr. 18, 1923. On the notion of service, see also *WSLN*, July 10, Dec. 5, 1924; Sept. 18, Oct. 9, 1925; July 8, Sept. 2, 1927; Dec. 28, 1928; Mary Friermood to Local 1289, Mar. 29, 1923, in Records of Local 1289, United Brotherhood of Carpenters and Joiners, University of Washington Manuscripts Collection, box 3, folder 4. On the post-1921 Label League see regular reports in CLC and *WSLN* throughout the decade; in addition, see Minutes, Carpenters' Local 131, Apr. 3, June 19, Sept. 11, 1923; Jan. 29, 1924; Minutes, Typographers' Local 202, May 28, 1922; Nov. 29, 1925; Nov. 28, 1926; and Minutes, Seattle Building Trades Council, Aug. 3, 1923, in Records of Local 1289, box 1, folder 1; *Musicland*, May 15, 1923; Mar. 1, 1924; Dec. 24, 1927; Gertrude Millson to Harry Call, June 12, 1927, in Washington State Federation of Labor Records, box 4, folder 21; Union Record Purchasing Service to "Dear Folks," Mar. 28, 1923, in Records of Local 1289, box 2, folder 31.
[49]For members and officers of the league, see *Musicland*, May 15, 1923; *SUR*, June 19, 1919; *SURW*, July 5, 1919; Minutes, CLC, July 7, 1920; Roll Books, CLC, in Records of the King County Central Labor Council, box 10; *WSLN*, June 20, Sept. 26, Dec. 5, 1924; Jan. 9, Mar. 20, Sept. 18, Nov. 6, 1925; May 7, Oct. 8, 1926; Dec. 9, 1927; Jan. 11; Mar. 2, 9, 23; Apr. 13; Aug. 31, 1928.
[50]See Frank, "At the Point of Consumption," for the decline of the labor movement after 1919; also Dembo, "Washington State Labor Movement."

wives of the men in the leadership who effected the changes. By the time of the TUPL's formation in 1925, these wives had defined their own role so completely in terms of service that to object to the men's redefinition of their place would have been unthinkable. They may also have shared their husbands' belief that professionalization was in the best interests of the movement. More practically, the Label League's numbers were so reduced by 1925 that they were in no position to shoulder the rather mighty burden of label promotion themselves.

By 1925 and 1926 the wives' activism had retreated to the only remaining sphere, the social. A form of women's activism dating from the late nineteenth century, the ladies' auxiliary, flourished anew. In the years between 1924 and 1928 new and reinvigorated auxiliaries to Seattle's trade union locals proliferated. Yet they symbolized the final atomization of women's (as well as men's) activism. While in the Label League wives had joined hands with the wives of members of many trades, carved out an economically vital role for themselves in the labor movement, and at times integrated housewives' concerns with those of wage-earning women, in the auxiliaries the women served (quite literally) only their husbands. The auxiliaries' main activity was organizing card parties for wives to enjoy while their husbands attended union meetings, after which couples retired happily together to enjoy "socials" complete with skits, songs, and refreshments.[51]

In general, label promotion and the rise of ladies' auxiliaries accompanied a general turning inward of the labor movement in the late 1920s. As the leaders turned smiling faces to the employers, they turned their backs on the unorganized. Worse, they turned scowling, critical faces to their own members, demanding strict observance of union label shopping, excoriating those who increasingly failed to attend meetings, and enforcing both with elaborate fines.

Yet these same leaders constantly complained of the apathy with which rank-and-file union members greeted their exhortations to observe the union label. Scattered reports did on rare occasions thank unionists for increasing the demand for a given product;[52] but despite the best efforts of the TUPL, union members largely failed to shop union. The garment workers, the laundry workers, the butchers and cigarmakers all complained, for example, of the lack of support for their label and shop-card campaigns—blaming other unionists, rather than employers, for their

[51]Minutes, CLC, Apr. 22, 1925; Minutes, Seattle Building Trades Council, Nov. 9, 1928, box 13, folder 3; *WSLN*, Nov. 28, 1924; Jan. 2, Apr. 24, Aug. 14, Sept. 4, 1925; Dec. 17, 1926; Mar. 4, Apr. 26, May 27, 1927; Mar. 16 and 23, Apr. 6, May 11, June 15 and 29, Aug. 3, 10, 31, 1928.
[52]E.g., Minutes, CLC, Aug. 31, 1921; May 6, 1925.

plight.[53] The TUPL's organizer Robert Harlin acknowledged that "one of the greatest problems that the trade union movement has to meet is the indifference of members of the movement to demanding the union label, the union card." The Women's Card and Label League noted the same week that "the local movement is extremely lax in the matter of demanding the label."[54]

All pro-label camps agreed that women's support for the union label was, once again, indispensable. The TUPL's label guide argued in 1925, for example, "The American housewife is the purchasing agent of the home. It is her privilege and duty to spend the wages earned by her husband in the fields of union endeavor, and to withhold her patronage from unfriendly institutions." Seattle's typographers similarly requested "that union men educate their wives to ask for [the] union label." The musicians echoed, "Talk it over with the wife."[55]

Female family members of unionists clearly resisted their menfolk's request that they look for the union label, button, and card. "Even good union men find it hard to get their wives interested in asking for union made goods," one man wrote to the *Union Record*'s advice column in 1920. Union men's wives were "blind to all but the size of the paycheck," an activist woman lamented in 1928. This appears to have been the case nationwide: in his 1910 study of the union label, Ernest Spedden reported that the boot and shoe workers', broommakers', and butchers' internationals all decried women's lack of interest in buying union.[56]

Men were apathetic, too; but given women's position as their families' assigned shoppers, their lack of interest would have appeared especially striking—and threatening to the success of the tactic. Moreover, if loyalist male buyers represented only a fraction of trade union members, loyal wives would have been an even smaller subset—yet the decisive one. How do we explain women's special apathy? We can note, again, that union label products, like goods and services from establishments displaying the union shop card, were more expensive, and thus to observe the label would have been to exacerbate working-class women's struggle to keep within a limited budget. Women's assigned *job* within the working-class family was to stretch the family budget, all the while satisfying finicky family members. Pro-union shopping, insofar as it re-

[53]Central Labor Council of Seattle and Vicinity to All Local Unions of Seattle and Vicinity, Feb. 8, 1923, in Records of Local 1289, box 2, folder 18; CLC, Sept. 7, 1921; June 6 and Oct. 10, 1923; May 14, June 11, Aug. 13, 1924; Agent 106, May 16, 1919, in Beck Papers, box 1, folder 3; *Musicland*, Sept. 1, 1923; Mar. 1, 1924; Dec. 10, 1928; *WSLN*, Oct. 16 and 23, Nov. 20, 1925; Feb. 5, Sept. 3, 1926; June 29, 1928.
[54]Quotes: *WSLN*, June 26 and Sept. 11, 1925. See also *SUR*, Nov. 4 and Dec. 4, 1920; *WSLN*, Sept. 3, 1926.
[55]*WSLN*, Jan. 25, 1925; Minutes, CLC, Oct. 10, 1923; *Musicland*, Apr. 4, 1924. See also CLC, Jan. 31, 1922.
[56]*SUR*, Nov. 20, 1920; *WSLN*, Dec. 7, 1928; Spedden, *Trade Union Label*, 69–75.

stricted women's shopping choices, directly affected women's work in the home—negatively. What appeared to be women's lack of commitment to trade unionism underscored, rather, trade unionism's failure to understand the nature of women's work in the home. Debates within the Seattle movement as to the causes of women's apathy also concluded that women's indifference to the label reflected a larger critical stance toward the trade union movement in general. The council's label committee concluded its 1928 report, for example, with the story of "one unionist" who "up to the present . . . had not patronized the label, as his wife did all the shopping and his belonging to a union had always been a bone of contention in the family."[57]

Male unionists developed an entire genre of advice on how to win one's wife over to label shopping. The editor of the musicians' newsletter, for example, recounted how he ultimately convinced his wife (after seven years of trying) by pointing out to her the hordes of union members who patronized the scab Danz theaters; she had realized the hypocrisy involved, and joined a boycott campaign. These discussions indicate that union men exercised by no means complete control over their wives, who held independent opinions and were not necessarily easily persuaded by their men. Listen, for example, to the alternately pleading and commanding tone of the editor's advice to his brothers: "Don't say you can't. They're human and they're reasonable. . . . Make them see it—show 'em." His choice of words suggests that women weren't really all that "reasonable" and that "showing them" could be quite a task. One article in 1926 by the patternmakers' William Bailey, TUPL secretary, implicitly acknowledged, moreover, the effect feminism might have had on working-class women's compliance with their husbands' demands: "Union men must be alive to the changing conditions and exigencies of the times, the woman he helped more than any other group to throw off the shackles that bound her for centuries must be enlisted with him, economically and politically, for since she will no longer be denied, she must be abided and counselled with."[58]

As a tactic, then, the union label functioned better in theory than in practice. It gave the leadership a framework for a nonconfrontational relationship with local employers but didn't necessarily generate enthusiasm among the rank and file. It proscribed a tidy, subservient role for women in the labor movement—but women didn't necessarily want that role.

[57]*WSLN*, Oct. 12, 1928.

[58]*Musicland*, Aug. 1, 1923; *WSLN*, Sept. 3, 1926. For more on intrafamilial tension over men's union membership, see also *SUR*, Jan. 28 and Feb. 1, 1921 (letter to editor and reply); May 20 and June 10, 1919; *WSLN*, Dec. 7, 1928, and Mar. 8, 1929.

The organizational activities of Seattle workers in the 1920s don't sort out, then, in any simple pattern by gender. While many workers at the time ideologically demarcated consumption as female, production as male, in truth neither sphere of activism stayed within such boundaries. To begin with, many of the trade unionists who labored "at the point of production" were female—approximately 10 percent of organized workers in 1920. Nor, after the shipyard's demise, did most Seattle workers, organized or not, even labor in production. The vast majority worked in transportation, construction, or the service sector. Moreover, it was male workers, in these local-market sectors of the economy, who chose to politicize consumption, not the women of their class, wage earners or not. Working-class women greeted with indifference men's calls for politicized consumption in service to relations at the paid workplace. Some wives of the most highly visible men did adhere to their assigned place in the movement and attempt to steer women's shopping choices in favor of the movement. Yet, more often, women chose either social and educational pursuits or those that expanded the rights of wage-earning women. "The labor woman fights at the point of consumption," while it accurately identified women's unique responsibilities as workers in the home, reflected, ultimately, more wishful thinking than an accurate description of women's precise role in the movement. Moreover, it both denied the significant presence of organized women wage earners and legitimated their exclusion from power within the movement.

Adding consumer organizing to our picture of the labor movement nonetheless reveals a new and complexly nuanced world of working-class women's activism. Activities "at the point of consumption" were only rarely feminist, as often politically conservative as radical, and explicitly subordinate to a male-defined movement. At times they reinforced traditional gender roles with a modern concept of separate spheres for men and women, of production and consumption. Yet in consumer organizing activities Seattle's working-class women also defined goals and structures for the labor movement often quite different from their men's. Women active in the cooperatives preferred charity, socializing, and education, and had their own ideas about branch locations; trade unionists' wives preferred lobbying for minimum-wage legislation to boycotting a popular store; and women supporters of the union label flourished best when they were allowed an autonomous sphere.

Seattle's story paints a picture, in other words, of constant internal struggle and negotiation over the priorities of the labor movement. Women and men struggled together—though from quite unequal positions—over the exact organizational mix of consumer and producer activities that working-class families would undertake under the broad aegis of trade unionism. The basic form and strategies of the labor movement, in sum, were constantly contested.

The question, ultimately, was one of the balance of power. Men and women each sought to further their own visions of what the class movement should be. Seattle's example shows—and this is key—that consumer organizing activities changed the balance of power in the labor movement. Because women carried primary responsibility for shopping, once men had decided to place emphasis on a consumer tactic, they *needed* women's support in ways they did not for tactics based at the point of production. They just couldn't impose a boycott, call for unionized shopping, or build a network of consumer cooperatives without women's (preferably enthusiastic) support.

It is clear that women negotiated the meaning of their class movement from a fundamental disadvantage: the very form of trade unionism, and thus the very question of consumer organizing within the trade union movement, was, of course, defined at root by relations at the paid workplace.[59] The movement's basic premises began with a primarily male perspective on work and gender relations—albeit modified by women's ever-increasing participation in the labor force. Both the union label and the boycott offered to politicize relations of consumption, but *in service to* power relations between employer and employee at the waged workplace. The cooperative movement, by contrast, did offer to restructure consumption in tandem with production—though, we can note, without in any way challenging the division of labor in the home. With the passing of the radicalism of the immediate postwar years, however, the impulse to restructure either sphere dissipated. Imaginative solutions evaporated; accommodation was labor's watchword. And with that contraction of organized labor's vision and tactical creativity came a contraction of the space within which working-class women could, possibly, transform many forms of labor.

Seattle's story provides one key to the mystery of organized labor's rightward turn in the 1920s throughout the United States and to its relative lack of power vis-à-vis capital, despite economic recovery. As the power of the city's radical unions and unionists receded, the conservative

[59]Susan Levine, in *Labor's True Woman*, chap. 6, argues that the Knights of Labor allowed for much greater participation by women than did their successor, the AFL, because the Knights' movement structurally and theoretically allowed for the integration of both women's waged labor and their domestic roles into a larger class-based movement. Barbara Taylor's *Eve and the New Jerusalem: Socialism and Feminism in the Nineteenth Century* (New York: Pantheon, 1983) shows how the Marxist model for class struggle supplanted utopian socialism's alternative model—more open to feminist concerns—in the 1830s and 1840s. Joan Scott, in "On Language, Gender, and Working-Class History," *International Labor and Working-Class History,* 31 (Spring 1987), 1–13, similarly shows how the Chartists codified male definitions of class and the class struggle; see also responses in the same issue by Bryan D. Palmer, Anson Rabinbach, and Christine Stansell.

business unionists enamored of consumer organizing came to the fore. They placed consumer organizing at the top of labor's tactical agenda, but did so without a willingness to question fundamentally the gender relations within their movement. Yet such questioning was necessary if consumer tactics were to succeed. Without a willingness to share power with women, without a willingness to ask how women might choose to politicize consumption, and without an equal commitment to women's concerns at the waged workplace as well, consumer organizing could only partially succeed—because women would simply exercise their own form of workers' control as unwaged workers in the home, and shop according to their own lights. Organized labor thus met the newly consolidated power of employers in the 1920s with a fatal flaw at its strategic center.

CHAPTER TWELVE

Paths of Unionization: Community, Bureaucracy, and Gender in the Minneapolis Labor Movement of the 1930s

Elizabeth Faue

When Mary Heaton Vorse wrote *Labor's New Millions* in 1938, she was both witness to and advocate of a new unionism that did "not stop at the formal lodge meeting. It [saw] the union as a way of life which [involved] the entire community."[1] Central to this community-based labor movement was the participation of women as both workers and wives. Yet, in the decades that followed, the union movement of which Vorse was an eloquent spokeswoman had disappeared from the scene. Community unionism had been replaced by a vast array of institutions, bureaucrats, and rules that seemed to obscure and suppress, rather than illuminate and express, grass-roots militancy and leadership. Even as it precipitated a decline in the autonomy of local unions, the shift toward a more bureaucratic, workplace-oriented unionism reinforced women's marginality in the labor movement. Labor unions that benefited from the tremendous growth in local activism and in the central involvement of women now reasserted familiar claims of gender and authority.

From the origin of working-class politics in popular protest to the emergence of contemporary bureaucratic unions, workers have chosen the terrain of struggle on which to build a labor movement. They have shifted emphasis toward and away from the community; they have incorporated state strategies and excluded them; they have striven to focus energies in the narrow terrain of craft identity and to broaden them to include all members of the productive class. The roles of women and men have also varied in these configurations of labor. At times workers' definition of labor solidarity required women's inclusion on an equal ba-

I thank Ava Baron, Angel Kwolek-Folland, Sara Evans, Ruth Milkman, and Bonnie Smith for their help in redefining and shaping the arguments here.
[1] Mary Heaton Vorse, *Labor's New Millions* (New York: Farrar & Rinehart, 1938), 234.

sis with men, both as workers and as the wives of workers; at other times solidarity was seen as incompatible with gender and ethnic competition.

The relationship between gender and unionism took new forms in the 1930s. In the community-based, grass-roots labor militancy that prevailed through 1937, both men and women played major roles. Further, the labor movement embraced an egalitarian rhetoric that was gender neutral in its implications. Despite the masculinist tone of press, poster, and prose within the labor movement, it was understood that women as well as men were vital to the movement's survival. By the late 1930s, the base of the labor movement had shifted from the community to the workplace. Concomitant with this shift was the marginalization of women within labor unions.[2]

The Minneapolis labor movement of the 1930s provides a case study of these changes. Characterized by a communal vision, local labor activists linked the struggles of truckers, garment workers, ironworkers, and the unemployed in community-level tactics that unified workers across craft and industrial lines. Both women and men were involved in mobilizing workers through union, political, and auxiliary organizations. A central characteristic of these campaigns was the activism and leadership of women in local-level struggles—an activism that did not, however, percolate to the national level.

With the advent of a more bureaucratic unionism, the level and quality of worker participation in the labor movement changed dramatically. As conflict and competition intensified between the AFL and the CIO, unions centralized authority and rigorously repressed factionalism and dissent at the local level. Attempts to create alternative union structures were perceived as threats to the norms of union governance. While men were brought into the union bureaucracy through new channels of promotion, the role of women workers in local union leadership declined much as it had done at the national level. As the decade of the 1930s drew to a close, women's auxiliaries and community organizations waned in importance and in numbers, and grass-roots activists lost the battle for a democratic labor movement.

As a process that marginalized women and finally excluded them from union leadership, bureaucratization was not gender-neutral. The ways in which an organization or a social movement rationalizes procedures, creates and enforces rules, and makes legitimate channels of authority and communication build on societal assumptions about manhood and womanhood. In evaluating both men and women by ostensibly gender-neutral

[2]Elizabeth Faue, "The 'Dynamo of Change': Gender and Solidarity in the American Labour Movement, 1935–1939," *Gender and History,* 1 (Summer 1989), 192–212, and *Community of Suffering and Struggle: Women, Men, and the Labor Movement in Minneapolis, 1915–1945* (Chapel Hill: University of North Carolina Press, 1991).

but in fact deeply gendered and male standards of leadership and achievement, bureaucratic labor unions helped to recreate and reinforce gender inequalities in their organizational structures.[3]

Union Bureaucracy and Gender

The emergence of large-scale union bureaucracies in the twentieth century has been the subject of much historical debate.[4] These studies outline the underlying process of cooptation, legitimacy, and consent which created unprecedented power for the labor movement. At issue is the relationship between two very different forms of organizing, one diffuse and stretching beyond the boundaries of the workplace, the other centralized and exclusionary. While fixing organizational forms at its center, however, the literature has been impoverished by the failure to examine gender ideology and the roles and relations of men and women. Centralized bureaucracy and community organizing differ not just in their focus but in the way they are gendered. How the structure of power within the labor movement became gendered and how this process reflected and transformed gender roles are crucial to our understanding of the ways in which labor unions became bureaucratic structures.

The community-based unionism that emerged in the 1930s drew upon the configurations of gender and class embedded in local solidarities; it embraced familial and fraternal sanctions of activism for both men and women and legitimated struggle that was expressive of and rooted in the claims of community. It proceeded to unionize workers by recruiting through local networks and institutions and through the culture of solidarity that develops during protest.[5] Championing the brotherly solidarity of men, it gave new and collective meaning to formerly individual

---

[3]Jeff Hearn and P. Wendy Parkin, "Gender and Organizations: A Selective Review and a Critique of a Neglected Area," *Organization Studies,* 4 (1983), 219–42.

[4]E.g., C. Wright Mills, *The New Men of Power: America's Labor Leaders* (New York: Harcourt Brace Jovanovich, 1948); Joel Seidman, "Democracy in Labor Unions," *Journal of Political Economy,* 61 (June 1953), 220–31; Seymour Martin Lipset, *Political Man: The Social Bases of Politics* (New York: Doubleday, 1960), 387–436; Lloyd Ulman, *The Rise of the National Union* (Cambridge: Harvard University Press, 1955); Nelson Lichtenstein, *Labor's War at Home: The CIO during World War II* (Cambridge: Cambridge University Press, 1982); Ronald Schatz, *The Electrical Workers: A History of Labor at General Electric and Westinghouse* (Urbana: University of Illinois Press, 1983); John Schacht, *The Making of Telephone Unionism, 1920–1947* (New Brunswick, N.J.: Rutgers University Press, 1985); Steve Fraser, "From the 'New Unionism' to the New Deal," *Labor History,* 25 (Summer 1984), 405–30; Sanford Jacoby, *Employing Bureaucracy: Managers, Unions, and the Transformation of Work in American Industry, 1900–1945* (New York: Columbia University Press, 1985), 207–74.

[5]Rick Fantasia, *Cultures of Solidarity: Consciousness, Action, and Contemporary American Workers* (Berkeley: University of California Press, 1988).

violence, aggression, and struggle which in that context defined manhood for the working class. Celebrating a political role for women, it built on their social activism in both neighborhood and workplace. Women had a clear, aggressive role that was legitimized in the context of community and family.

In these ways a community-based labor movement reshaped the role of labor leader and downplayed the importance of ethnic, skill, and gender differences. On a structural level, marginalized workers, women in particular, were less disadvantaged in the community arena, where formal rules were kept to a minimum. In the garment unions, for example, women were militant shop-floor leaders and officers at the local level.[6] In the Hotel and Restaurant Employees' union, women were disproportionately represented on committees and among officers at the national level. Their national strength was rooted in their visible activism on local and state culinary boards.[7] Finally, through cultural activities, even more than in formal organizational campaigns, unions reconciled labor militancy with femaleness and sisterhood even as they remained expressive of brotherly solidarity.[8]

The development of bureaucratic organization in the labor movement required that leaders control the political skill, information, and means of communication necessary to consolidate power and stabilize the organization.[9] The routinized process of union democracy made the same assumptions as political democracy: that one have a knowledge of the rules, be skilled at coalition building at both local and national levels, possess the ideal characteristics of a leader, and be relatively unconstrained in participation in public life. Unequal levels of education, skills, and resources among men and women restricted women's access to leadership, and contradictory demands of work and family limited their participation.

[6]For an analysis of the causes of male domination within the ILGWU, see Alice Kessler-Harris, "Problems of Coalition-Building: Women and Trade Unions in the 1920s," in *Women, Work, and Protest: A Century of U.S. Women's Labor History,* ed. Ruth Milkman, 110–38 (Boston: Routledge & Kegan Paul, 1985).

[7]Dorothy Sue Cobble, "Sisters in the Craft: Waitresses and Their Unions in the Twentieth Century" (Ph.D. diss., Stanford University, 1986), 468–525; see also her essay in this volume.

[8]The most dramatic example may be seen in the Women's Trade Union League. See Nancy Schrom Dye, *As Equals and as Sisters: Feminism and Unionism in the Women's Trade Union League of New York* (Columbia: University of Missouri Press, 1979); Susan Wong, "From Soul to Strawberries: The ILGWU and Workers' Education, 1914–1950," in *Sisterhood and Solidarity: Workers' Education for Women, 1914–1984,* ed. J. Kornbluh and M. Frederickson, 38–74 (Philadelphia: Temple University Press, 1984); Colette Hyman, "Labor Organizing and Female Institution-Building: The Chicago Women's Trade Union League, 1904–24," in Milkman, *Women, Work, and Protest,* 22–41.

[9]H. J. Gerth and C. W. Mills, eds., *From Max Weber: Essays in Sociology* (New York: Oxford University Press, 1946), 196–244; Robert Michels, *Political Parties* (Glencoe, Ill.: Free Press, 1949); Lipset, *Political Man,* 389–93.

Further, labor bureaucracies, as the formal voices of tradition in the labor movement, both reflected and constructed gendered expectations of leadership. A labor leader was expected to demonstrate the manly attributes required to confront employers and to exhibit brotherly camaraderie with fellow workers.[10] These characteristics demonstrate the cultural encoding of any political behavior. As one organizing handbook had it, the goal of any union was to win the workers over and to defeat the employer. "The term 'strike' means to hit," the pamphlet explained, and violent struggle was a legitimate way for men to effect change.[11] Thus, in acting militantly and sometimes violently to achieve collective goals, men were not acting improperly. But because violence was proscribed for women in the constricted public sphere of bureaucracy, women's militancy could not be sanctioned.

Moreover, in situations in which the women workers were young, inexperienced in unionism, or reticent, unions posited a male leader as a necessary antidote. In a union's published example of a meeting based on *Robert's Rules of Order,* the serious, older, and experienced male union leader sets straight the enthusiastic but misguided and often cranky women members.[12] In the garment trades the tension was palpable between men, who dominated positions of skill and leadership, and the "young, pretty, inexperienced girls" who were "NRA babies" in the union movement. "The problem of raising the new locals is as difficult as raising children," wrote Meyer Perlstein, a regional director for the International Ladies Garment Workers' Union (ILGWU). Workers, especially women, needed to be "nursed carefully." They suffered from "infantile disorders," such as gossip and jealousy. Perlstein and other union officials agreed that women workers needed to break their individualistic habits. Only if they were "whipped into shape" could they become "trained and loyal members of our great family, the ILGWU."[13]

[10]These expectations are implicit in the model of shop-floor manliness described in David Montgomery, "Workers' Control of Machines Production in the Nineteenth Century," in his *Workers' Control in America* (New York: Cambridge University Press, 1979), 9–32.

[11]International Ladies' Garment Workers' Union (ILGWU), *Handbook of Trade Union Methods* (New York, 1937), 38. Compare Jeff Hearn's statement that "the whole conceptualization and understanding of the proletariat is male; the model of [class] war waged by the army of laborers led by vanguards and militants with the support of the rank and file. Many words and concepts of potential cooperation and intimacy have been appropriated by particular macho, 'socialist' rhetoric—'solidarity,' 'brotherhood,' 'strength' is forever between vigorous, 'manly' 'brothers,' no soft, gentle ones": *The Gender of Oppression: Men, Masculinity, and the Critique of Marxism* (London: Croom Helm, 1988), 76.

[12]ILGWU, *How to Conduct a Union Meeting* (New York, 1934).

[13]Meyer Perlstein, "The Human Side," *Justice,* July 1, 1938; Finkelstein to Dubinsky, Sept. 2, 1936, © ILGWU, in David Dubinsky Papers, box 75, folder 4B, ILGWU Records, Labor-Management Documentation Center, New York State School of Industrial and Labor Relations, Cornell University (hereafter NYSSILR). Kessler-Harris, in "Problems of

The ILGWU went to great pains to explain how women could be brought into the union and how the union hall could provide an atmosphere more conducive to women's participation; but it recognized the resentment of men toward the "damned skirts" who dared to "invade the sacred halls of masculinity." Bringing women into the union should not mean that men would be "forced to submit to an atmosphere of rose-tinted femininity." Though a woman organizer for the union "might help to overcome the girls' reluctance to join or to go on the picket line," a "personable man in a predominantly feminine group adds a certain piquancy to the situation."[14]

Within the bureaucratic unionism of the 1930s, activism for men and women was re-formed. Democratic processes defined new and appropriate routines of action, solidarity, and dissent. Taken out of the context of community, women's activism was delegitimized at the same time that normative rules of order and due process translated men's activism and rerouted male aggressive behavior into bureaucratic struggles for dominance. Bureaucratization redefined the very meaning of the political and the public. No longer were the boundaries between workplace and community permeable; the private domain of community existed separate and apart from the public domain of the union. Disagreement and dissent thus took on the aura of private and illegitimate disputes. As the bearers of the private, women were perceived as the most troublesome of unionists, workers who could not understand the rules of collective action and who severely undermined the capacity of leaders to lead.[15]

Organizing the Garment Trade

The ILGWU was one voice of community-based unionism in Minneapolis during the 1930s. Garment workers were the largest group of unorganized women industrial workers in Minneapolis. The labor force of nearly 5,000 was over 75 percent female. Women held a disproportionate number of unskilled and semiskilled jobs, as they did in such industries nationally. Although men held skilled and supervisory positions, women predominated in the skilled positions of cutter and presser

---

Coalition-Building," makes some similar points about earlier factional battles in the ILGWU in which women bore the brunt of the attacks. Factionalism, as the expression of private grievances and disagreements, was defined in many unionists' minds as a feminine characteristic.

[14]ILGWU, *Handbook of Trade Union Methods*, 25–26. See also Elizabeth Faue, "Public Soldiers, Solitary Warriors: Labor, Sex, and Solidarity on the American Left, 1929–1945," paper presented at the annual meeting of the Organization of American Historians, St. Louis, Mo., Apr. 8, 1989.

[15]Perlstein, "Human Side."

regionally.[16] As in other areas, the garment industry was subject to seasonal and fluctuating employment, a fact intensified by the economic crisis. These factors undermined attempts at organization during most of the early twentieth century. From the shop campaigns of the ILGWU to the strike origins of the Hosiery Workers' Union and the orchestrated negotiations of the Textile Workers Union, unionization proceeded along various paths to bureaucratization.

Before the 1930s only sporadic attempts had been made to organize the regional garment industry. Labor activists tried to establish unions in garment and textile plants during World War I, and there were a number of short-lived strikes in the 1920s. Labor leaders came to little agreement, if any, on how to organize this vital sector. The United Garment Workers (UGW) unionized shops in workingmen's clothing through union label campaigns, but the effort went no further. As jurisdictional disputes obstructed unionization, garment unions competed with one another for members.

While economic crisis framed the lives of women in the garment industry, the passage of the National Industrial Recovery Act (NIRA) provided the first opportunity to change the conditions of women's work in the trade. Under the legal sanctions of section 7 (a), workers began to organize in the small but growing cotton and silk dress industry. Despite the ambiguity of its provisions, the NIRA became a powerful tool in the hands of labor organizers. They sought out women who would be willing to testify that their shops violated the NRA's code minimums for wages and hours. Code enforcement soon took the central place in the circulars and pamphlets of organizing campaigns.[17]

In the dress shops of St. Paul, women reacted to the new opportunity. Groups of shop workers banded together and asked the state labor federation for aid in unionizing the industry. They wrote to David Dubinsky, head of the newly burgeoning ILGWU, requesting an organizer and admission to the union.[18] In the fall of 1934 Dubinsky hired Sander Genis of the Amalgamated Clothing Workers to organize part-time in the difficult Minneapolis shops. Genis had firsthand experience organizing in the open-shop city of Minneapolis. An immigrant from Russia, Genis worked in the coat trade in St. Paul before World War I and organized the first local of the Amalgamated in the area. From that time on, Genis devoted himself to union work. His leadership in the 1929 strike of gar-

[16]"New Dress Pacts Discussed by Twin Cities," *Justice*, Feb. 15, 1938; "Acute Labor Shortage in Three Markets," *Justice*, June 15, 1939.
[17]Affidavits of Jennie Storelie, Sarah Presant, and ten others, Oct. 27, 1934, and *To the Workers in the Ladies' Garment Industry*, pamphlet, 1934, both in Dubinsky Papers, box 75, folder 5B.
[18]George Lawson to Dubinsky, Mar. 28, 1934, in Dubinsky Papers, box 75, folder 5B; "The Union in the Twin Cities," *Justice*, May 1, 1937.

ment workers proved his familiarity with the terrain of antiunion employers, deferential workers, and a hostile police force.[19]

Genis set out to "preach the gospel of unity and unionism" to the garment workers of Minneapolis. He hired Myrtle Harris, an experienced organizer, to assist him in the shops, As "a good loyal union person," Harris had been shop steward and financial secretary of UGW Local 27 for ten years. Her involvement in organizing for the Central Labor Union led to work in the Truckers' auxiliary and to the ILGWU job.[20]

From their base in St. Paul dress shops, ILGWU members worked to organize their co-workers in Minneapolis, with Harris and Genis leading the effort. Harris stood outside dress shops when they opened for work in the morning and again when the women left for home. She contacted other women workers by making calls and visiting them in their homes.[21] While Genis worked the office end, Harris and other women who volunteered were responsible for face-to-face contact, the routine process of recruiting workers on the shop floor and in the community. Acutely aware of the obstacles facing the union drive, especially the threat of employer retaliation, they worked to subvert employer sabotage and build worker confidence.

Development of social and educational programs were essential to community organization. The ILGWU's initial drives in Minneapolis involved organization of dress shops with as few as twenty-five workers. Because of the small size of garment shops and their ability to flee union constraints by relocating, along with employers' paternalism and the isolation and poverty of garment workers, the union's success was uneven. Less than a year after workers organized the first locals, the Twin City Joint Board hired an educational director. Aided by the Minneapolis Labor School, the ILGWU organized classes in parliamentary law, public speaking, labor history, and labor journalism. Later, a dance troupe, glee club, and dramatics program developed.[22]

[19]Sander Genis, interviews, Nov. 6, 1974, and Mar. 16, 1977, in Minnesota Historical Society (MHS); Dubinsky to Genis, Apr. 19, 1935, in Dubinsky Papers, box 75, folder 5A; Hearing before Minnesota Industrial Commission, Division of Mediation and Arbitration, Sept. 10, 1929, in Garment Workers file, box 11, Arthur and Marian LeSueur papers, MHS.
[20]Genis interview, Nov. 6, 1974, 3, 36; "Flashes from North, West, and South," *Justice*, Feb. 1, 1935; Genis to Dubinsky, Aug. 15, 1935, © ILGWU, in Dubinsky Papers, box 75, folder 5A; Myrtle Harris, interviewed by James Dooley, July 9, 1975, in MHS, 1–2.
[21]Harris interview, 7.
[22]The Minneapolis Labor School was started in 1934 through the Central Labor Union of Minneapolis. During the better part of the decade, the school benefited from WPA workers' education project instructors, among them the writer Meridel LeSueur. In 1941, after the WPA stopped funding the program, local AFL affiliates continued their support. See Minneapolis Union Education Center, Directing Committee, *Workers' Education* (Minneapolis, 1938); "Labor School Records Four Years of Achievement," *Minneapolis Labor Review* (hereafter *MLR*), Sept. 21, 1938, and press release, Mar. 3, 1941, in Press file,

The ILGWU educational program was designed to develop skills in a broad base of the membership. Giving workers knowledge of their history, communication skills, and familiarity with union procedure was one way to overcome the split between organizer and organized. The enrollment figures are sketchy, ranging from 30 to 100 students per term, but impressionistic evidence suggests that women were the target audience. The union was over 75 percent female, and news reports listed women who attended the classes. Rarely if ever are men depicted. Similarly the curriculum between 1935 and 1938 was ostensibly gender-neutral, but in seeking to give members skills in public speaking, parliamentary procedure, and organizing techniques, it laid the basis for a broader distribution of leadership and activism, especially on gender grounds. Many women workers lacked skill in speaking and debate; union classes such as these made possible their participation.[23]

The attempt to wed education with organization in the ILGWU was expressed by Betty Hoff, a teacher in the labor school: "The union is more than just an organization to protect your job and working conditions. Your union provides an educational and recreational life." In the first few years, the Twin Cities Joint Board also published the *Twin City Guardian,* a newsletter that first appeared in 1937. The members felt strongly that *The Guardian* ought to express the opinions and conditions prevailing in [their] own industry before anything else."[24] Union newsletters, workers' theater, and programs that expressed the value of unionism for workers both individually and collectively were vital to the success of the community-building efforts of the local ILGWU.

The Gendering of Craft Unionism

The Strutwear strike of 1935–36 dramatically illustrates the permeability of the boundaries between shop floor and community in the 1930s. For many workers and activities, the Strutwear campaign represented a coming of age for the Minneapolis labor movement. As in the

---

Central Labor Union of Minneapolis and Hennepin County, Records, MHS (hereafter CLU Papers). On the Educational Department's history, see Wong, "From Soul to Strawberries."

[23] See the pamphlets *Handbook of Trade Union Methods* and *How to Conduct a Union Meeting.*

[24] Betty Hoff, "Education and Recreation," *Guardian,* 1 (1937); "Dorothy Rock Gets ILGWU Appointment," *MLR,* Nov. 29, 1935; "Amalgamated and ILGW Progress," ibid., Dec. 27, 1935; "From Far and Near," *Justice,* Jan. 1, 1936; Dorothy Rock, "Flashes from the Field," *Justice,* Feb. 16, 1936; "ILGW Opens Worker Classes," *MLR,* Nov. 6, 1936; "News and Views," *Justice,* Dec. 1, 1936; *Justice,* Feb. 15, 1937, notes *Guardian.* See Harry Rufer's comment to Leah Schneider, Mar. 11, 1937, © ILGWU, in Chicago Joint Board of the ILGWU, box 13, folder 3, ILGWU Records.

truckers' strike of 1934, the forces of community were both vital and visible in the struggle.[25] The culture of solidarity created by the strike promoted interunion cooperation, the coalition of political and workplace organizations, and the support of community and social activists. In this context, the community of union workers struggled with the legacy of narrow trade unionism and its privileging of men craftworkers over women and young men on the production line. It organized the unorganized.

When workers at the Strutwear hosiery plant walked out in August 1935, they challenged one of the most viciously antiunion firms in the city. They were ill prepared for the exigencies of a strike. Supported by the American Federation of Hosiery Workers, the union of knitters had organized only skilled male workers in the industry. The majority of the plant labor force—580 women workers engaged in seaming, looping, mating, and mending socks—were not members of the local; neither were the nearly 100 "boys" who worked as toppers on the production line.[26]

Strutwear had been active since World War I in antiunion activities. In 1927 the firm locked out a small union of knitters, and in the aftermath of the strike it forced workers to sign a yellow-dog contract. Under the NRA, Strutwear established a company union to undermine organizing efforts at the plant. Peter Fagerhaugh, a union leader, recalled, "100 men in my department were told to come down stairs for a meeting. We were told to form a union." If the men did not cooperate, they were forced to leave the firm.[27] The firm enrolled only skilled workers in the union. Like the hosiery union they sought to combat, Strutwear officials thought membership in their union should be restricted to men knitters, not the production workers.

In the summer of 1935 a group of knitters visited a unionized plant in Milwaukee. On their return, they held a series of mass meetings among their co-workers, where they advertised the higher pay and better working conditions of the union plant. Three-fourths of the 200 male knitters joined the new union, Local 38 of the American Federation of Full-

[25]See Charles Rumford Walker, *American City: A Rank and File History* (New York: Farrar & Rinehart, 1937); George Dimitri Tselos, "The Minneapolis Labor Movement in the 1930s" (Ph.D. diss., University of Minnesota, 1970), 215–65; Farrell Dobbs, *Teamster Rebellion* (New York: Monad, 1972).

[26]"Strike Ranks Growing Fast at Strutwear," *Northwest Organizer*, Aug. 21, 1935. Newspaper reports estimated as many as 900 women workers in a labor force of 1,200; company figures put the estimate at 581 of approximately 845 production workers. See "Code Minima and Strutwear Company Averages," Oct. 17, 1935, Citizen Alliance of Minneapolis Records, undated and 1903–1953, roll 20, frames 148–50, MHS (hereafter CAM).

[27]"McKeown Given Ovation," *MLR*, Dec. 13, 1935; "Police, Troops Plan to Open Strutwear," *United Action*, Dec. 13, 1935; "Organizer Shows Up Strutwear Company as Union Smasher," *United Action*, Mar. 27, 1936.

Fashioned Hosiery Workers (AFFFHW). But after a dispute over union recognition, managers dismissed eight workers for union activity. The leaders called a strike.[28]

Few workers crossed the picket line the first day. Most amazing, production workers refused to report for work. The knitters who called the strike had made no provision for the participation of the operatives, but their recruitment was essential to the success of the strike. In the earlier strike, failure to recruit them had caused the union's defeat, as it had in the Robitshek-Schneider garment strike in 1933.[29] A profile of Strutwear workers showed a labor force divided largely along gender and skill lines, with only the intermediary job category of topper open to both men and women. Moreover, skill lines masked inequality among workers. Knitters started at a wage nearly double that of production-line workers; and while even an experienced woman on the line could get only a few dollars above the NRA code minimum, knitters on average earned twice as much as women and boys training as toppers. Also, the company had a practice of hiring learners below the code minimum (for $6 to $8 a week) and firing them at the end of training.[30]

A strike that began with the grievances of skilled workers eventually had to address the poor pay and working conditions of operatives, both men and women. After the shop committee called the strike, union organizers began to contact them; most operatives knew about the strike from co-workers or public rumor. On the day of the strike, the divisions in the labor force seemed to make little difference. Production workers held the line; and knowing that they needed the support of all departments, union leaders urged them to attend union meetings after the strike began and actively sought their participation.[31]

The union went beyond the shop door, into the neighborhoods where workers lived. When the company tried to open the plant on the fourth day, 3,000 workers and union supporters formed a massive picket line. Police clubbed several strikers, driving them from the pavement. Afterward picketers followed the fifty knitters who stayed with the company from the factory to a department store, where the police escort hoped to

[28]"Swanson Booed by Strikers," *MLR*, Sept. 25, 1935; Roy Weir, organizer for Central Labor Union, to Emil Reeves, secretary, American Federation of Hosiery Workers, Aug. 7, 1931, and July 26, 1934; Weir to Alfred Hoffman, secretary, Hosiery Workers' local, Milwaukee, Apr. 20, 1934; all in Hosiery Workers file, CLU Records; complaint form 136, Strutwear, June 7, 1935, in Hosiery and Lingerie Code, box 388, Records of the 11th Regional Labor Board, Record Group 25, Administrative Records of the National Labor Relations Board, National Archives, Washington, D.C.
[29]Tselos, "Minneapolis Labor Movement," 186–88.
[30]"Code Minima and Strutwear Company Averages"; Oscar Hawkins to "Dear Folks," Aug. 29, 1935, in Oscar and Madge Hawkins Papers, box 4, MHS.
[31]"Organizer Shows Up Strutwear Company as Union Smasher," *United Action*, Mar. 27, 1936.

lose the company workers in the crowd. Pickets confronted disloyal male workers in the aisles of the store; some followed them home. Women who had returned to work, in contrast, were only approached in the store and asked to come to the union meeting.[32]

The labor protests at Strutwear built upon layers of meaning within the working-class community. As the funerals of workers had become massive demonstrations of commitment, unity, and mourning, so too did protests that mirrored other rites of passage, of death and rebirth. A funeral for the company union became one such ritual. On the fifth day of the strike, union leaders organized a large picket line. At midday hundreds of workers from the plant and the community formed a funeral procession for the company union. They circled the plant with the casket several times and finally held funeral rites in a vacant lot across the street. Evoking the ties among family, community, and workplace, they buried the old union and made way for the new.[33]

Over the eight months of the strike, the labor community in Minneapolis supported the Strutwear workers. Unionists organized dances for strike relief, staffed a strike commissary, and donated to the strike fund. In the course of the strike, workers at the plant were joined by members of a broad range of labor and political organizations. Emphasizing labor unity, organizations of the unemployed, the Hotel and Restaurant Workers, and the Amalgamated Clothing Workers came to walk the picket line, and at one time nearly a thousand workers could be called upon to support the strike. The Women's League against the High Cost of Living organized a boycott of Strutwear goods, and the Farm Holiday Association sent in truckloads of food for the strikers from rural communities.[34]

[32]"Strike Ranks Growing Fast at Strutwear," "Knitters Practically All Members of Union," *MLR*, Aug. 23, 1935. See also Farrell Dobbs, *Teamster Power* (New York: Monad, 1973), 91–93.
[33]"Strike Ranks Growing Fast at Strutwear," *Northwest Organizer*, Aug. 21, 1935; "Strutwear Mills Stay Closed Two Weeks," *United Action*, Sept. 2, 1935.
[34]"Enthusiasm at Strutwear Is Victory Sign," *MLR*, Sept. 20, 1935; "Strutwear Blocks Arbitration," ibid., Oct. 11, 1935; "CLU Prepares to Picket Strutwear," ibid., Nov. 15, 1935; "Prepare to Mass Picket at Strutwear," ibid., Nov. 22, 1935; "Employers Attempt Strutwear Opening," *Northwest Organizer*, Nov. 20, 1935; "Strutwear Situation Stirs CLU," *United Action*, Feb. 14, 1926. "Union Officials Tell Strutwear Facts," *MLR*, Aug. 30, 1935; "Police, Troops to Open Strutwear," *United Action*, Dec. 13, 1935; "Strikers Will Take Decision of Mayor's Group," *MLR*, Dec. 13, 1935; "Strutwear Strikers Get Three Tons of Food," *Northwest Organizer*, Nov. 13, 1935; "Congress May Probe Strutwear," *MLR*, Dec. 20, 1935. "Miller Strike Enters 9th Week," *Strutwear Worker*, March 1941, mentions the role of Ole Fagerhaugh of the Miscellaneous Workers' Local 665, the brothers of the strike leader Peter Fagerhaugh. For the role of the communists in the strike, see Carl Ross, "Labor Radicalism in the 1930s," paper presented at the annual meeting of the Minnesota Historical Society, Minneapolis, 27, 1985. Also handbill, "Make Strutwear a Union Shop," Young Communist League [1935], in Strikes, Local, Strutwear file, CAM; *United Action*, Sept. 16, 1935.

The success of the prolonged strike marked a turning point for women workers at the plant. Craft unionism, a strategy that marginalized and excluded both men and women operatives and sanctioned the poor conditions of their labor, was at least temporarily in retreat. In April 1936 Strutwear agreed to most of the strikers' demands, and the strike was won. The eight-month protest had created an opportunity for the union to enlarge and broaden its scope. At the conclusion of the strike, membership had grown to more than 700, including nearly 500 women. The Hosiery Workers' Union now rushed to recruit women. By the end of the following year, Strutwear workers signed for a closed shop. New contracts brought both higher wages and hope for greater occupational mobility within the plant.[35]

For many women who sought an active role in the union movement, neither union membership nor its benefits were sufficient to meet all of their needs. Their solution was to form auxiliaries, organizations that directed the efforts of working women and workers' wives. As the history of the Minneapolis truckers' auxiliary and the Flint Women's Emergency Brigade demonstrates, women's role in strikes proved to be crucial.[36] These organizations continued to play a political role in the labor movement by serving as a base of social support and an arena of activism for women workers.

Women workers at Strutwear organized a hosiery workers' auxiliary in May 1938. At an AFFFHW convention Wanda Pilot, the only woman organizer of the federation, suggested auxiliaries as arenas for women's activism. Sixteen women delegates had intended to form their own division of the union; but because the constitution did not permit a separate organization, they formed an auxiliary. Membership was open to union members and to the wives and daughters of members. Though it focused on social events, it expanded to organize classes in labor history and economics.[37]

[35]"Strutwear Plant Reopens," *Northwest Organizer*, Apr. 8, 1936; "Hosiery Union Moves into Strutwear as Strike Ends," *United Action*, Apr. 10, 1935; "Details Strutwear Settlement," *MLR*, Apr. 10, 1936; "Strutwear Not Strutting Like It Used To," *MLR*, Aug. 30, 1935; "Bosses Try to Smash Strutwear Strike," *United Action*, Sept. 12, 1935; "Strike Record," Local Strikes file, CAM; "750 Strutwear Employees Sign for Closed Shop," *Northwest Organizer*, May 6, 1937; "Hosiery Workers Sign Strutwear," *MLR*, May 7, 1937.
[36]Reports on the Emergency Brigade are reprinted in *Rebel Pen: Selected Writings of Mary Heaton Vorse*, ed. Dee Garrison, 175–200 (New York: Monthly Review Press, 1985). On the women's auxiliary in Minneapolis, see Marjorie Penn Lasky, " 'Where I was a Person': The Ladies' Auxiliary in the Minneapolis Truckers' Strike of 1934," in Milkman, *Women, Work and Protest*, 181–205.
[37]"Women's Auxiliary," *Strutwear Worker*, October 1938. In October 1938 the auxiliary had a membership of fifty. Its officers were President Marion Carlson, Vice President Laura Mitchell, Secretary Phyllis Mize, Treasurer Hazel Falldin, Trustees Vera Palmquist, Dorothy Hill, and Hazel Cummings. Alice Kessler-Harris has argued that men and women unionists

The coming of the union to Strutwear had reshaped not only the relation of women to unionism in the plant but also the relation of unionism to workers generally. James Tibbetts, chair of the Strutwear shop committee, understood that men in the Strutwear union, as a minority of the labor force, feared that women were going to take over the union. Competition between men and women over jobs could soon follow. Tibbetts argued that "in shops like ours where the majority of members are women, men are always fearful that the women will try to take control of the union. This fear is not justified. . . . Women are usually willing to fill the role that nature put them in, that of being the supposedly weaker sex." The auxiliary could make a necessary and important contribution to the union. Recent studies of the auto industry, he claimed, showed that "a woman on the picket line is worth two men." But in effect, Tibbetts still envisioned the auxiliary's role as supporting the union: "When shops are organized and picket lines seem a remote dream, [ladies' auxiliaries] have a different part to play. Their job is to spread the gospel of unionism into channels that otherwise wouldn't be penetrated." By support, the shop chair meant union consumerism and social organization. Finally, Tibbetts argued that auxiliaries could help women, who lacked a collective spirit and who traditionally were not good union members, to learn unionism.[38] The mutuality of the women who had supported a narrowly conceived craft union strike in 1935 had been forgotten.

Both the auxiliary and the women members of the Strutwear union helped to create a vital union culture. They organized diamondball and bowling teams in almost every department. They planned social events—dances, annual picnics, Christmas parties—to bring the members together and raise funds for the local. The union newspaper, *Strutwear Worker,* enabled union members to keep track of union events and meetings, reported the events of workers' lives from marriages and births to deaths and promotions, and included articles on political events and labor history.[39] Both men and women unionists increasingly saw the community's needs for information and education as within the purview of unions.

---

had different goals for unions; in effect, women sought "community, idealism, and spirit" while male trade union leaders wanted "unity, discipline, faithfulness." See "Problems of Coalition-Building," 129.
[38]"Women's Auxiliary," *Strutwear Worker,* October 1938; "Ladies' Auxiliary," ibid., November 1938.
[39]"Trade Union Sports Council Conference Held," *Strutwear Worker,* April 1938 (a committee included Alrose Andryski of the Hosiery Workers); "Girls' Diamondball Teams," ibid., April 1938; "Girls' Bowling Averages," ibid., November 1938; "Scenes from Branch 38's 3rd Annual Picnic," ibid., October 1938; "Join the Ladies' Auxiliary," ibid., December 1938; "The Trade Union Woman," ibid., February 1939.

The Decline of Community-Based Unionism

The high tide of community-based unionism in Minneapolis was reached during the Strutwear strike. Cooperation of the local labor establishment with national unions, political groups, and community activists underscored the importance of local activism for defeating the open shop and organizing the unorganized. In 1937, however, as rivalry between the AFL and the CIO heightened, national unions increasingly began to intervene in the affairs of locals. The recession that year made organizing workers difficult. The National Labor Relations Board's prohibition of sympathy strikes and secondary boycotts defused local union solidarity by denying legitimacy, and jurisdictional battles between unions further undermined the cooperation that was the basis of community unionism.[40]

The consequences for unions—and for their men and women members—were severe. Rank-and-file members of all unions were increasingly isolated from decision making. In the garment and textile unions, where the conflict between men and women members and leaders traditionally had been strong, women lost the fragile gains of the early 1930s. Sexual inequality in labor leadership reasserted itself as national networks, dominated by men with ties to the union movement, replaced local gender-integrated ones at the local level.[41] General Drivers' 574, the union that led the drive to make Minneapolis a union town, was increasingly besieged with directives and interference from the international union. With these losses, the promise of an egalitarian, broad-based union movement faded.[42]

In its initial campaigns in the Twin Cities, the ILGWU leadership remained largely local, relying on the skills of union veterans from the Twin Cities. By 1936, when the national union began to establish its control over the regional market, the ILGWU replaced Genis with two temporary organizers. These appointments were symbolic of changes in ILGWU policies by which the national office asserted control over local officers.[43]

In the spring of 1936 Loretta DuFour and members of the ILGWU were organizing workers at Boulevard Frocks, the fifth-largest cotton dress shop in the United States, employing from 400 to 600 workers. Origi-

[40]Christopher L. Tomlins, *The State and the Unions: Labor Relations, Law, and the Organized Labor Movement in America, 1880–1960* (New York: Cambridge University Press, 1985), 103–96.

[41]Barry Leighton and Barry Wellman, "Networks, Neighborhoods, and Communities: Approaches to the Study of the Community Question," *Urban Affairs Quarterly,* 14 (March 1979), 363–90, discuss the creation of communities through a variety of network structures.

[42]See Farrell Dobbs, *Teamster Politics* (New York: Monad, 1975).

[43]E.g., Michael Finkelstein to Dubinsky, Nov. 30, 1938, and Dubinsky to Finkelstein, Dec. 3, 1938, in Dubinsky Papers, box 16, folder 2A.

nally organizers tried to use NRA code violations as an organizing tactic. Boulevard managers, however, won a vote of confidence from the workers by claiming that they voluntarily accepted the code minimum. With the abolition of the National Recovery Administration in 1935, organizers urged workers to turn to the union to protect recent wage gains and improvements in conditions. Only through collective bargaining could workers "retain in this industry the privileges and security established by the NRA."[44]

Despite slow progress at Boulevard, Sander Genis felt that the groundwork had been laid for a generous contract with the firm. At the same time, Genis slowly withdrew from ILGWU activities and concentrated on his own union, the Amalgamated Clothing Workers. Conflicts with the ILGWU at both local and national levels were at the root of his choice. As a man familiar with the local circumstances and supported by the membership, Genis repeatedly asserted the primacy of community concerns. Cooperation was necessary to unionize the industry in the Twin Cities; expelling unemployed workers would only weaken the local union. In most cases, he was overruled by the national office. At one point Genis responded angrily to requests for regular dues payments to the international; work in the cities was scarce and many members were unemployed. Infighting between the ILGWU and the Amalgamated Clothing Workers was yet another cause for discontent.[45]

The business agents who followed Genis were more attuned to the needs of the national office. The first of these agents, George Glass, told Dubinsky that he had found "a very poor dues-paying institute" in the Twin Cities and he hoped to set it right. Contact negotiations were similarly mishandled. Glass infuriated the ILGWU organizers by agreeing to a clause making machine operators responsible for the mistakes made by the pressers, unjustly penalizing women workers to the advantage of a group of better-paid men. Resentment began to build. As Genis later reported, "a few mistakes like these and all the good girls will leave the union." Another organizer replaced Glass only months later. He and Genis continued negotiations with Boulevard Frocks to finalize the agreement. The union asked for terms that the ILGWU regional director, Meyer Perlstein, thought unrealistic. Eventually Perlstein took over the contract negotiations himself, convinced that Boulevard Frocks could become "a model union shop in the cotton dress industry naturally if properly handled." He gave no credit to local organizers, nor did he pay attention to local discontent with three successive business agents. Rather, the signing of the union contract, which brought few benefits to the workers at

[44]Genis to Dubinsky, Dec. 12, 1934, and "Attention Boulevard Frocks Workers," leaflet, enclosed in Meyer Perlstein to Dubinsky, Apr. 4, 1936, © ILGWU, both in Dubinsky Papers, box 75, folder 4B.
[45]Genis to Perlstein, Feb. 13, 1936, in Dubinsky Papers, box 75, folder 4B.

Boulevard Frocks, was portrayed as a victory for the union's efficient bureaucracy.[46]

Genis angrily predicted that the contract would make trouble for the local labor movement, and it did arouse the resentment of workers and local labor organizers. Given the recent Strutwear victory, the agreement was perceived as weak not just by garment workers but by the local labor establishment. The Boulevard Frocks contract and the personal enmity between Perlstein and Genis were recurring themes in union campaigns. They also opened the door for the ILGWU and the Amalgamated to raid each other. With the understanding that at least the leader would be placed in the union, union officers at a cloak factory tried to swing the workers to the ILGWU. Disloyalty prompted their dismissal. At the same time, Genis was accused of targeting some shops, including the large Munsingwear company, in an effort to keep them away from Perlstein's union. Serious criticisms of the Boulevard agreement led the truckers' union, General Drivers' Local 544, to try to organize those workers who were left out of the contract.[47] Members whose wives worked at the Boulevard factory provided entrée for organizers; the wives' own lack of loyalty to the ILGWU underlined the local resentment toward the international's interference.

While unionists fought for the joint board's autonomy by rejecting one organizer, the New York office intervened by appointing Michael Finkelstein at the end of 1936, but not without complaint; local ILGWU members wanted one of their own appointed.[48] The appointment coincided with other problems at the local level. Continued economic crisis, culminating in the recession of 1937, kept alive fears of unemployment, making union recruitment difficult. Reaction to the new business agent was tainted by resentment over concessions to the crisis and the weak contracts that resulted.[49]

[46]George Glass, St. Louis Joint Board, to Dubinsky, May 9, 1936; Genis to Perlstein, Mar. 4, 1936; Perlstein to Dubinsky (telegram), Apr. 17, 1936; Genis to Dubinsky, Apr. 29, 1936, © ILGWU, all in Dubinsky Papers, box 75, folder 4B. On signing, see "A Company Group Becomes a Real Union," *Justice,* July 15, 1936; "350 Join Union in Boulevard Shop," *United Action,* May 1, 1936; "Boulevard Frocks Signs with Union," *MLR,* May 1, 1936; "Boulevard Frocks, Minneapolis Shop Sings Union Pact," *Justice,* May 1, 1936.

[47]In Dubinsky Papers, Box 75, folder 4B: Genis to Morris Bialis [April 1936?]; Finkelstein to Dubinsky, Sept. 18, 1936; Genis to Dubinsky, n.d.; Harry Rufer to Dubinsky, June 24, 1936; folder 4A: Meyer Lewis, AFL, to Dubinsky, Mar. 16, 1935; Finkelstein to Dubinsky, Mar. 30, 1937; Dubinsky to Finkelstein, Apr. 2, 1937; Finkelstein to Dubinsky, Apr. 8, 1937.

[48]On several occasions workers sent letters to Dubinsky asking that Finkelstein be replaced. Finkelstein always responded that the workers were "troublemakers," but persistent complaints suggest that there was some basis for the discontent.

[49]Genis to Dubinsky, Apr. 29, 1936, in Dubinsky Papers, box 75, folder 4B; "1000 Affiliate to TWOC in Vote at Munsingwear," *Northwest Organizer,* May 6, 1937; "TWOC Continues in Munsingwear," *Northwest Organizer,* May 13, 1937.

Changes in local union leadership came at the same time the Twin Cities Joint Board was gearing up for an organizing drive at Munsingwear. Munsingwear, a major hosiery and undergarments firm, was one of the largest employers in Minneapolis, with nearly 2,000 workers. Despite the early depression of the textile and garment industries, the company began to rehire substantial numbers of workers in 1932, and it seems to have made profits during most of the Depression years.[50]

Like Strutwear Knitting, Munsingwear had a long history of company paternalism and antiunion activity. Munsingwear officers were prominent members of the Citizens' Alliance, the local employers' association, and they had played a role in the Strutwear strike by agreeing to subcontract some work for the company. To fight unions within the company, it established a company union with the NRA. Further, its management played a key role in the regional labor board of the NRA, where some of its officers were able to circumvent independent actions by the company union.[51]

Munsingwear had long been a target of the ILGWU local leadership. After signing Boulevard Frocks in 1936, they began to make contacts with workers at Munsingwear. In November 1936 Underwear and Lingerie Workers Local 265 of the ILGWU received a charter. Sam Schatz was appointed special organizer. Many women were also involved in the Munsingwear drive, including the educational director, Leah Schneider. By March 1937 officers had been elected and thirty people signed up with the promise of more. At the ILGWU convention that year, 200 members were reported.[52]

On the strength of membership growth, Meyer Perlstein sent a letter to the Munsingwear management stating that the "time is ripe for a collective bargaining agreement. Our union is eager to avoid any interruption of production and cessation of work."[53] Despite Perlstein's optimism, the ILGWU campaign was not successful. It simply could not attract enough members to call for an election. After nine months of organizing, union members had managed to sign only a small fraction of a 1,200-member labor force.

[50]"Two of City's Industries to Give 600 Jobs," *Minneapolis Times,* Jan. 1, 1932; Munsingwear annual reports in Minnesota Historical Society, Minneapolis.

[51]Munsingwear Corporation, *Program of the Employment Relationship between Management and Employees of the Munsingwear Corporation* (Minneapolis, 1935), in Industrial Relations file, CAM; Tselos, "Labor Movement in Minneapolis," 183, 189.

[52]"Stenographic Report of the Special Meeting of the Unity Committee of the Central Labor Union on Friday, May 7, 1937, re Munsingwear," in box 24, Garment Workers folder, CLU Papers; Leah Schneider to Rufer, Mar. 3, 1937, in Chicago Joint Board Papers, box 13, folder 3, NYSSILR; ILGWU, *Report of the Proceedings of the 23rd Convention* (New York, 1937), 215.

[53]Perlstein to Munsingwear Corp., Apr. 24, 1937, © ILGWU, in Dubinsky Papers, box 169, folder 1B.

At this time Munsingwear management began negotiating with the Textile Workers' Organizing Committee [TWOC-CIO]. In two mass meetings the workers voted to sign with the Textile Workers' Union and to approve a contract that appears to have gained some wage increases and union recognition for Munsingwear workers.[54] The effort was headed by the new local CIO committee, including the regional director, Sander Genis. He played a central role in persuading workers to join the Textile Worker' Local 66, CIO. The company had been negotiating with TWOC in Chicago, and its reception of union overtures may have encouraged the workers.

Distrust of the ILGWU also played a hand in the organization. A local labor unity meeting demonstrated that memories of the Boulevard Frocks contract remained intact. Despite the ILGWU's advocacy of direct appeal to the workers, "without the help of firm, foreladies, or shop facilities," and the creation of a militant membership, they did not convince the Munsingwear workers. With the signing of the contract, the Munsingwear Employees' Association dissolved, and the ILGWU members were forced to resign from their union (or, it was alleged, from the company).[55]

The failure of the ILGWU to organize Munsingwear was rooted in trends toward a more corporate, industrial unionism that stabilized the labor force and provided a higher standard of living for semiskilled workers. At the same time, the Munsingwear campaign demonstrated the choices workers had between the two models of unionism in the 1930s— the ILGWU, dominated now by nationally appointed officers, and the new CIO union, whose claims were stronger and more immediate because of the participation of a familiar community organizer. Though the company union had been outwardly controlled by management, Munsingwear workers trusted its union officers enough to sign with the CIO.

After the failure of organizing at Munsingwear, there was a noticeable change in the local ILGWU. The business agent and regional director increasingly set the priorities of the union, first and foremost by controlling union meetings. Issues raised in the midst of organizational drives had more to do with employers' demands for wage concessions than with improving working conditions.[56] The nationally appointed director and

[54]Contract and contact card, dated May 21, 1937, photocopy, courtesy of Keir Jorgenson, Research Director, Amalgamated Clothing and Textile Workers' Union.

[55]Perlstein to Dubinsky, Apr. 27, 1937; Charles H. Green to Dubinsky, June 16, 1937, © ILGWU, both in Dubinsky Papers, box 169, folder 1B; "1000 Affiliate to TWOC in Vote at Munsingwear," *Northwest Organizer*, May 6, 1937; Unity Committee, "Stenographic Report, re Munsingwear," CLU Papers.

[56]This was certainly the case with Cartwright Dress, with which the ILGWU negotiated a work-sharing agreement between its shops in Minneapolis and Cleveland. In the end the company went broke.

business agent were concerned largely with contract supervision and industrywide cooperation with management. The needs of the workers as women, as union members, and as workers were downplayed in the struggle to maintain a regional garment industry against national competition. In effect, the national union advised the women to accommodate the employer and proved intolerant of individual dissent. While many workers still experienced some improvement in hours and wages in union shops, the union became a required part of the job, a prerequisite for employment, not a refuge from the demands of management. Moreover, decisions to strike or stay in the shops were directed by the board, the business agent, and the regional director. Complaints against the nationally appointed business agent were dismissed as the work of troublemakers.[57]

At a time when women were the front line for union solidarity, labor education offered not public speaking and labor history but courses in nursing and nutrition. Overall, the ILGWU's educational program backed away from concerns about building community among workers and union democracy into a more instrumental form of union education. Union classes increasingly focused on the training of union officials and time-and-motion study. Taking three classes in union procedure was now a requirement for new union members. In this brief orientation, between thirty and sixty workers were to be introduced to the ILGWU's structure and procedure and its history. These classes promised to turn "card carrying workers into real union members," but they were a poor substitute for the earlier full-term classes in parliamentary law, labor history, and public speaking. More important, the educational program put new emphasis on training union officers, not members.[58]

Classes on time-and-motion study, piecework, and industrial engineering were set up in conjunction with local employers. While none of these programs were gender-specific in their design, they were taught chiefly by men with the object of reinforcing the role of the specialist, officer, and expert in labor relations. In one instance the foreladies, class instructors, and production managers who met as a committee to set prices on

[57]Members of shop to Dubinsky, May 25, 1939; Perlstein to Dubinsky, June 10, 1939; Finkelstein to Dubinsky, June 6, 1939; Complaints file, all in Dubinsky Papers, box 20, folder 2G. The Finkelstein letter is a lengthy denial of accusations made by members, whom he assumes worked in the Jane Arden Shop, which went on strike.
[58]"Educational Activities," *Justice*, Apr. 1, 1942, 13; clippings file, Minneapolis Labor School, CLU Papers; "Twin Cities to Study Earnings," *Justice*, Nov. 1, 1937; "St. Louis, Kansas City, and Twin Cities Stage Union Classes in Service," ibid., Feb. 1, 1939; "Starting Right," ibid., Sept. 1, 1939; "Minneapolis and Kansas City to Start Time Study Classes," ibid., Nov. 15, 1939; "Compulsory Training," ibid., May 1, 1940; "Arrange Training Institutes for Shop Chairmen, Officers," ibid., Sept. 15, 1940; "They Learn about the ILGWU and Pass It On," ibid., Feb. 15, 1943.

piecework were joined by students in the industrial problems and time-and-motion study classes. With the purpose of "developing methods of improving relations and eliminating shortcomings that affect earnings and interfere with shop efficiency," students were expected to cooperate and even emulate industrial engineers. Workers such as Stefannia Petra, a dressmaker, were chosen to supervise time-and-motion study in their own factories and sent off to various cities for training.[59] Because women were disadvantaged in that realm, their training did not bring workers such as Petra into the national leadership. Finally, during the war, both ILGWU and Minneapolis Labor School classes increasingly incorporated domestic courses into their curriculum.

By the end of the decade, national initiatives had restructured the ILGWU local joint board. The cutters' local, which had been predominantly female from its inception, now had men as officers, and these officers participated in the leadership of the joint board. It became, in effect, the men's local. The number of men in the leadership was disproportionate to their membership generally. Though the staff of the ILGWU local board remained largely female, the decision-making power rested with the business agent and the regional director, whose ties to the international were stronger than any local solidarities and who were members of the male leadership of the national ILGWU.

Finally, the dominance of men within the union movement—the product of closure and of the process by which bureaucracies reproduce themselves—had an impact on the local market. Finkelstein kept in constant contact with the national board and the Chicago Joint Board. Through them he recruited skilled male workers as cutters for local jobs. Elsewhere this move would not be remarkable, but Minneapolis was one of the few markets in the country where large numbers of women were employed as cutters. Bringing in men from the national market helped to establish a base for men on the ILGWU Joint Board, a place effectively maintained through the cutters' local.[60]

The declining fortunes of the ILGWU at the local level did not immediately reflect those of other CIO unions in the city. The continued growth and vitality of the union at Strutwear Hosiery is a case in point. In the aftermath of the strike, the Hosiery Workers' union developed a full cultural program. Unionization also provided many women with upward mobility in the firm. In 1939, for instance, women entered the previously all-male ranks of the knitters, a fact that received scant notice in the

[59]"Industry Meetings Set for All Trades in Several Cities," *Justice*, Dec. 1, 1939; "Boulevard Frocks Worker Off to Kansas City for Training," ibid., Feb. 1, 1940.
[60]E.g., Finkelstein to Morris Bialis, manager of Chicago Joint Board, Mar. 25, 1940, and May 26, 1941, in Chicago Joint Board Papers, box 13, folder 3; *Justice*, May 15, 1940, on the prevalence of women cutters.

union newsletter. Several women also served on the shop committee, even outnumbering men in a ratio that reflected the female dominance of the labor force.[61]

Despite their numerical superiority, women workers at Strutwear did not participate equally in the union leadership. There were no women officers of the union; women were noticeably absent from the contract negotiating committee.[62] The auxiliary disbanded in 1939. Given the different needs and conditions of men's and women's work at the firm, a difference paralleled in a fairly rigid division of labor along skill lines, the lack of women's participation in negotiating union contracts seriously undermined their ability to receive equal treatment from the union. It also suggests that despite women's role in establishing and building the labor union at Strutwear, they continued to be marginalized in the local itself. The fate of women workers at Strutwear reveals that women's place in the union—conditioned by its creation under a walkout of skilled workers—did not change.

Conclusion

The 1930s witnessed an upsurge of labor militancy and organization that became a turning point in the history of the U.S. working class. Rooted in a dynamic sense of community, unionism went beyond the boundaries of the workplace to encompass both craft and industrial workers; men and women; immigrants, ethnics, and native-born white and black workers. The inclusive rhetoric of community became a powerful force in giving sanction to configurations of labor organization and protest in which men and women played equal parts.

When the industrial unions in the late 1930s adopted new forms of industrial relations that emphasized national authority over local autonomy, stability over militancy, they alienated many of the rank-and-file members who were the heart of the drive to "organize the unorganized." Centralization and union support for the war changed the nature of both men's women's labor activism as unions closed down possibilities for grass-roots leadership and direction of union affairs. This bureaucratic transformation regendered the labor movement by limiting the scope and meaning of protest and organization in which women had been involved; it also redirected the activism of men into bureaucratic channels of communication, action, and authority.

[61]"Shop Committee," *Strutwear Worker,* October 1938.
[62]"Officers Nominated by Branch #38 Saturday," *Strutwear Worker,* November 1938; "Branch 38 Votes to Extend Contract," ibid., April 1939; "Final Results of Election," ibid., January 1941. During the 1935–36 strike, Dorothy Trombley was secretary of the union and was important enough to be named in the injunction suit against the local.

The movement away from community issues, organizations, and control toward a more corporate, workplace-oriented unionism took place in an atmosphere of increasing political antagonisms and continued economic crisis. Community-based unions had made possible the rise of labor in Minneapolis, but divisiveness in the distribution of union power and resources at the local level undermined their strength. By the late 1930s, unionists at both the local and national levels came to believe that highly centralized, bureaucratic national unions could give locals the stability they needed. What they neglected to see was how this choice altered the nature of unionism and the relationship of women workers to the movement.

Steve Fraser has argued that the bureaucratic trajectory of the union movement in the 1930s absorbed and usurped democratic rhetoric and thus made dissent illegitimate within the union structure.[63] Demands for special treatment of women in the context of an ostensibly gender-neutral union democracy were also delegitimized. For women unionists, the informal assumptions of democracy—that leaders/representatives have certain characteristics that fit the social role of the male—made union participation not merely difficult but culturally and personally risky.

Women in the Minneapolis labor movement of the 1930s experienced the contradictions of being in a social movement that welcomed them with the egalitarian language of labor but wanted to limit the meaning of that language. In the case of the ILGWU, women workers were members of an industrial organization that was predominantly female at both the local and national levels but was controlled and directed by the traditions of male craft union leadership. The shift over the decade from local autonomy to national control demonstrates the erosion of female power in a local arena where union initiative and leadership had come from women. For those women in the Strutwear Hosiery Workers' Union, the process was one of exclusion. They composed the substantial majority of members, but the union's origins among skilled workers gave them outsider status. Even militancy on the picket line and majority control of the shop committee did not alter that legacy.

It is important to remember that a substantial portion of union growth and recruitment in the 1930s took place in such organizations as the ILGWU and the Hosiery Workers, which were hybrid organizations.[64] Created in an era of craft unionism, they were forced by the nature of their mass-production industries to become semi-industrial unions. Historically these unions accommodated the majority of workers who were

---

[63]Steve Fraser, "Industrial Democracy in the 1980s," *Socialist Review,* 72 (November–December 1983), 102.

[64]See Christopher Tomlins, "AFL Unions in the 1930s," *Journal of American History,* 65 (1979), 1021–42.

unskilled or semiskilled and who came from diverse ethnic and racial backgrounds. Despite their extension of membership to these workers, the unions continued to make distinctions between skill levels and to privilege skilled workers.

Unlike the industrial union leaders of another era, the labor leadership in the 1930s had no alternative vision for the movement. Faced with the recruitment of hundreds and thousands of unskilled and semiskilled operatives, unions chose the path of least resistance—incorporating new workers into the membership but creating few opportunities for their input into union organization. End runs around the bureaucratic structure, such as the use of female auxiliaries to involve women operatives, appeared to threaten union structure from this frame of reference. Organized outside the union constitution, the frail attempts at democratic participation were undermined by rhetoric that declared them subversive of true union democracy. Lacking legitimacy, these organizational strategies died, even as they represented genuine attempts at adjusting the labor movement to accommodate new workers.

CHAPTER THIRTEEN

The Faces of Gender: Sex Segregation and Work Relations at Philco, 1928–1938

Patricia Cooper

Esther Davis stood with the others and watched the man behind the counter, who was screening applicants for jobs at Philco, the nation's leading radio manufacturer and Philadelphia's largest single employer. He sometimes spoke to the applicant, but frequently he just looked up, shook his head, and said no—no interview and no chance for a job at the plant. Now it was her turn. "We might be interested in hiring you," he said gruffly, "but you can't work here with all that makeup on. Go upstairs and wash it off." She paused. She was not wearing any makeup, but she needed the job, so she complied without a word. She climbed the concrete steps to the dispensary and explained to the nurse what had happened. Then she washed her face. When she finished, she and the nurse walked back down to the counter for inspection. The personnel man looked annoyed. "I thought I told you to wash your face." After she explained and the nurse confirmed that she had done so, he hired her as a wirer.[1]

Davis's experience is suggestive of some of the ways gender shaped work and work relations at Philco during the Depression. She was living with her parents in 1932 and needed a job to help support them. Although she had trained for a clerical job, she had gone to the Philco plant when she heard a rumor that the company was hiring because she had been unable to secure anything else. The personnel man had been trying to humiliate her, she believed, and make her feel inferior, something she was already feeling because factory work was, in her view, a

My warm thanks go to Mary Blewett, Michael Blim, Dorothy Sue Cobble, Carole Turbin, Gilbert Ware, and especially Ava Baron for reading and commenting on drafts of this essay.

[1]Esther Davis interview, Jan. 18, 1988. The name is a pseudonym and the interview is untaped at the interviewee's request. Identifying information is available from the author.

step down socially. The personnel man's order expressed his power over her, power derived from his class position and gender. Her physical appearance may have been important: rumor had it that pretty women had a better chance of getting a job. Finally, her sex determined what she would do at Philco—all jobs were tagged as either men's or women's in an occupational structure that was sex-segregated and sex-typed. Davis did not particularly think of herself in terms of these gendered categories. Her primary concern was getting a job and making some money.

Recent research has emphasized several aspects of the relationship between gender and work. Some scholars have explored the nature and development of occupational segregation and the forces that sustained it even in periods when logic might dictate its disruption, as during wartime.[2] Others have examined language to explore the ways in which men and women understood the meanings of masculinity and femininity, how these meanings shifted and were contested over time, and how they were central to labor struggles.[3] A few scholars have pointed out the pitfalls of conceptualizing gender in terms of separate spheres or dichotomous contrasts between men and women.[4] They have argued that it is

[2]Ruth Milkman, *Gender at Work: The Dynamics of Job Segregation by Sex during World War II* (Urbana: University of Illinois Press, 1987). See also Dorothy Sue Cobble, "'Practical Women': Waitress Unionists and the Controversies over Gender Roles in the Food Service Industry," *Labor History*, 29 (Winter 1988), 5–31, and her essay in this volume for a perspective on ways in which women workers participated in shaping the occupational structure; Susan E. Hirsch, "Rethinking the Sexual Division of Labor: Pullman Repair Shops, 1900–1969," *Radical History Review*, 35 (1986), 26–48; and Ava Baron, "Contested Terrain Revisited: Technology and Gender Definitions of Work in the Printing Industry, 1850–1920," in *Women, Work, and Technology: Transformations*, ed. Barbara Wright, 58–83 (Ann Arbor: University of Michigan Press, 1987). In general, scholars have used the concept of gender to refer to the socially constructed meanings of physical sexual differences (although recent research has noted that physical differences are also socially constructed). See Joan Acker, "Class, Gender, and the Relations of Distribution," *Signs*, 13 (Spring 1988), 477; Gisela Bock, "Women's History and Gender History: Aspects of an International Debate," *Gender and History*, 1 (Spring 1989), 10; Julia Epstein, "Either/ Or—Neither/Both: Sexual Ambiguity and the Ideology of Gender," *Genders*, 7 (Spring 1990), 99–142. My own thoughts on gender have been most affected by these scholars along with Ava Baron, Alice Kessler-Harris, Joan Scott, and Carole Turbin, cited below.

[3]Ava Baron, "Questions of Gender: Deskilling and Demasculinization in the U.S. Printing Industry, 1830–1915," *Gender and History*, 1 (Summer 1989), 178–99, and "Contested Terrain Revisited"; Mary Blewett, "Manhood and the Market: The Politics of Gender and Class among the Textile Workers of Fall River, Massachusetts, 1870–1880," in this volume. See also Joan Scott, "Gender: A Useful Category of Historical Analysis" and "Work Identities for Men and Women: The Politics of Work and Family in the Parisian Garment Trades in 1848," both in her *Gender and the Politics of History*, 28–50, 93–112 (New York: Columbia University Press, 1988).

[4]Alice Kessler-Harris, "Gender Ideology in Historical Reconstruction: A Case Study from the 1930s," *Gender and History*, 1 (Spring 1989), 31–49; Joan Scott, *Gender*, 39–41; Carole Turbin, "Beyond Dichotomies: Interdependence in Mid-Nineteenth-Century Working-Class Families," *Gender and History*, 1 (Autumn 1989), 293–308, and "Beyond Conventional Wisdom: Women's Wage Work, Household Economic Contribution, and Labor Activism in a Mid-Nineteenth-Century Working-Class Community," in *To Toil the Live-*

important not to confuse the prevailing gender ideology with our own analytical tools for uncovering the realities of women's lives. Too, gender may not be the primary way particular groups of men and women self-identify at any given time. While some scholars stress the variability in men's and women's experiences and outlooks, others highlight the power of gender ideologies and beliefs in sexual difference which opposed masculine and feminine to each other.

In the experiences of workers at Philco we can trace some of the interconnections in these seemingly disparate emphases in the analyses of gender and work. The structures of occupational segregation and sex typing in the plant and the assumptions embedded in them were related to other aspects of life and work at the firm.[5] Gender and class shaped workers' experiences and work relations even as their gendered identities shifted with circumstances. The patterns reveal diversity in men's and women's experiences and variations in gender meanings which existed alongside the rigid and seemingly clear-cut gender ideology reflected in the sexually segregated production process. A change in managerial policy in 1938 overturned the existing pattern of occupational segregation by placing women in what had previously been men's jobs. This move challenged the traditional meanings of masculine and feminine work contained in the sexually segregated job structure, increased the salience and significance of perceptions of gender difference, and created a measure of gender conflict.

This examination of gender at Philco during the Depression is based primarily on interviews with radio workers conducted in 1936, which are available at the Urban Archives of Temple University. The Industrial Research Department at the University of Pennsylvania in cooperation with the Works Progress Administration surveyed 686 radio workers (488 of whom worked or had worked for Philco) as part of a series of studies headed by Gladys Palmer which analyzed the changing labor market in the Philadelphia area. The issues discussed here are confined to those that appeared on the interview schedules. The Palmer interviews are supplemented by several others I conducted in 1988 and 1989.[6]

---

long Day: America's Women at Work, 1780–1980, ed. Carole Groneman and Mary Beth Norton, 47–67 (Ithaca: Cornell University Press, 1987).

[5]The focus on the workplace here is a factor of space and available evidence. My research thus far suggests that gender meanings were complicated and varied in other settings, such as the home, school, church, and neighborhood. My focus on the workplace here does not mean that it is the only place to study gender or that it is compartmentalized from these other settings. I do believe, however, that experiences in the workplace are unique and create their own opportunities for changing consciousness.

[6]The Palmer interviews have their limitations. Interviewers gathered uniform information on data coding sheets, but on the back of each sheet they added information that elaborated on some aspect of the codable data. Thus the information gathered is not the same

The Radio Industry and Philco

Commercial radio was a new industry in the 1920s, but by the end of the decade radio broadcasting and set manufacturing were booming businesses. Between 1922 and 1928 the number of radios in use jumped from 60,000 to 7.5 million, and in 1929 the value of radios produced was $412 million.[7] Although the manufacturing industry was competitive and volatile during the 1920s, by the early 1930s a few large radio makers were beginning to dominate production.[8] Philadelphia-area companies, such as Atwater Kent and the Radio Corporation of America (RCA) in Camden, played an important role in the early growth of the industry, but Philco, a successful storage battery manufacturer that switched to radio making in 1928, not only dominated the regional industry but made more radios by far than any other company in the country by the early 1930s.[9]

---

for all respondents and the statements of interviewees are filtered through the words and interests of the survey's various interviewers. Recent interviews are limited by the length of time that has elapsed, the ideas and concerns that have become important to interviewees in the intervening years, and the imposition of the author's questions and concerns on the interviewees' view of life in the plant during the 1930s. I have also used the local union's monthly publication, *The Microphone*, which has survived for the years between 1933 and 1936.

[7]W. Rupert MacLaurin, *Invention and Innovation in the Radio Industry* (New York: Arno, 1971 [1949], 88–108; Alex Groner, *The American Heritage History of American Business and Industry* (New York: American Heritage, 1972), 20, 279; Hugh Aitken, *The Continuous Wave: Technology and American Radio, 1900–1932* (Princeton: Princeton University Press, 1985), 250–479; Federal Trade Commission, *Report on the Radio Industry* (Washington, D.C.: U.S. Government Printing Office, 1923), 1–4; Retail Credit Corp., "Radio Industry," *Industry Report*, 3 (April 1928), 1–4; "1,250,000 out of 4,200,000 U.S. Radios Sold Last Year Bore the Philco Trademark," *Fortune*, February 1935, 75. See also Susan Douglas, *Inventing American Broadcasting, 1899–1922* (Baltimore: Johns Hopkins University Press, 1987).

[8]In 1923 there were 800 set manufacturers and 5,000 parts manufacturers; ten years later there were only 150 of the former and 600 of the latter. For more discussion of how this decline occurred see Patricia Cooper, "Philco, Radio Manufacturing, and the Promise of New Tech in Philadelphia in the 1930s," in *Toward a History of Urban Political Economy: Explorations in Industrial Philadelphia*, ed. Michael Frisch (Philadelphia: University of Pennsylvania Press, forthcoming); MacLaurin, *Invention and Innovation*, 88–108, 117–31; *Philadelphia Bulletin*, Feb. 15, 1953; May 1, 1958; Feb. 19, 1974; *New York Times*, Apr. 7, 1956; Aitken, *Continuous Wave*, 252–54.

[9]MacLaurin, *Invention and Innovation*, 145–46; Gladys L. Palmer and Ada M. Stoflet, *The Labor Force of the Philadelphia Radio Industry in 1936* (Philadelphia: Works Progress Administration, National Research Project, 1938), 3; "1,250,000 out of 4,200,000 U.S. Radios," *Fortune*, February 1935, 75–76; *Philadelphia Bulletin*, May 24, 1929; July 24, 1928; Feb. 6, 1930; Apr. 9, 1932; Dec. 7, 1928; Dec. 28, 1928; "Test Suit against Radio Corporation of America Charges Combination to Restrain Trade," *Commercial and Financial Chronicle*, 130 (May 17, 1930), 3440–43; Philip Scranton and Walter Licht, *Work Sites: Industrial Philadelphia, 1890–1950* (Philadelphia: Temple University Press, 1986), 219–21, 256; Pennsylvania Department of Internal Affairs, *Seventh Industrial Directory of Pennsylvania, 1930* (Harrisburg, 1931), 588; J. B. Nealey, "Radio Sets Put on Production Basis," *Iron Age*, Dec. 26, 1929, 1717–21; Retail Credit Corp., "Radio Industry," 1;

By contrast to most Philadelphia industries—typically small operations that employed only a few dozen or a few hundred workers to make high-quality specialty products by skilled production methods and were owned by local families and individual entrepreneurs—Philco used new technology, mass production, and assembly lines in a huge factory employing thousands of low-skilled workers. Ownership was still private, but over the course of the 1930s Philco increasingly resembled the large corporate enterprises that dominated the radio industry. Unlike most industries in the city, Philco enjoyed unparalleled profits and prosperity throughout much of the decade. The Depression had hit the city hard in 1930, and by April 1933 close to half of the city's workers were unemployed. There was some hope that the new radio industry would replace jobs lost in the city's various faltering enterprises.[10]

Philco's main building stood at C Street between Ontario and Tioga avenues, about five miles northeast of Independence Hall, on the edge of Kensington. Most of Philco's workers lived in this district, which had witnessed at firsthand the decline of the city's traditional industries, such as textiles, leather, and metal manufacturing. Residents were white, frequently of Irish, Scottish, or English descent, but the area had a mixture of nationalities represented, including several groups of eastern Europeans.[11]

In 1936 Philco had between six and seven thousand employees, almost all of whom were white and about half of whom were women. The company often recruited new workers through the friends and relatives of those already employed there (although some people applied without such links), and there were long chains of family members who worked in the plant, including many married couples who had met there. The average age of women surveyed in the Palmer study was twenty-four; men averaged just under thirty-three. Ninety percent of the women interviewed were thirty or younger; only 48 percent of men were that young.

"Problems in the Radio Industry," *American Economic Review*, 14 (June 1924), 520–23. For more on Philco's rise to the top and the story of RCA, see Cooper, "Philco."

[10]Scranton and Licht, *Work Sights;* Russell Weigley, ed., *Philadelphia: A 300-Year History* (New York: Norton, 1982), 482, 488; Gladys Palmer, *Philadelphia Workers in a Changing Economy* (Philadelphia: University of Pennsylvania Press, 1956). See also Federal Writers' Project, *Philadelphia: A Guide to the Nation's Birthplace* (Philadelphia, 1937). The Palmer radio study was designed to see if new industries, such as radio, could take up the slack created by the weakening of so many companies in the city.

[11]See *Franklin's Street and Business Occupancy Atlas of Philadelphia and Suburbs* (Philadelphia, 1946), maps 9, 12, 13, and "Social Base Map of Philadelphia," Works Progress Administration project, 1939, maps 6A, B and C, both in Urban Archives, Temple University (hereafter TUA). Forty to 60 percent of the area's homes were owner-occupied in 1939 and half of the homeowners had lived in their homes ten years or more. See also Caroline Golab, *Immigrant Destinations* (Philadelphia: Temple University Press, 1977), 111–56; David J. Pivar, "The Hosiery Workers and the Philadelphia Third Party Impulse, 1929–1935," *Labor History*, 5 (Winter 1964), 18–28.

Although the study indicated that the company had no rules prohibiting or limiting the employment of married women, its preference for young girls meant that the majority of women—62.2 percent—were single, while only 32.3 percent of men were unmarried in 1936. Of women, 8.1 percent were widowed or divorced; of men, 1.3 percent were. Philco also preferred workers who were better educated than the rest of the city's manufacturing labor force. Fifty-four percent of women and just under 39 percent of men in the Palmer study had more than an eighth-grade education.[12]

Gender and the Production System

The process of making radios called for some workers to make the parts and components and for others to install and assemble them on long conveyor belts that were threaded throughout the huge plant.[13] Though there was nothing inherently sex-specific about the jobs at Philco, managers from the outset divided the labor process and assigned men and women to different jobs, creating a gendered production system. Production workers were paid by the hour, and pay was connected to the job and to the sex of the person holding it: men's jobs paid higher hourly rates than women's jobs. All foremen and supervisors were men. All repairers, troubleshooters, cabinet finishers and assemblers, carpenters, machinists, toolmakers, and die setters—the most skilled, highest-paying nonsupervisory employees in the plant (17 percent of the total in 1936)—were men.[14] The majority of radio manufacturing jobs in Philadelphia and elsewhere, however, were considered to be semiskilled. Most required only about two to four weeks of training. Men's jobs included those in machine shop, paint shop, stockroom, toolroom, punch press, maintenance, cabinets, trucking, welding, testing, inspection, and final assembly. The latter three operations were the largest single categories, and the last two took place on the assembly lines. Women worked in coil winding, scraping, inspecting, cable splicing, wiring, riveting, tube testing, soldering, and assembling of components such as speakers and con-

[12]Palmer and Stoflet, *Labor Force*, 7, 13–17; material from data base generated by Walter Licht. Many thanks to Licht for letting me use his data base on radio workers and to Rob Gregg, who found a way to extract information on Philco workers alone. The printed tabulations are in my possession. Although overall women were better educated than men in the sample, no woman had more than twelve years of schooling while nine men, 2.8%, had received education beyond high school.

[13]For a more detailed description of what was involved in the production process, see Cooper, "Philco."

[14]*Microphone*, May 1934, 4; Palmer and Stofley, *Labor Force*, 63 (table 6). These figures do not include anyone who earned a salary.

densers, known as subassembly or light assembly.[15] Men performed most of the work in the machine shop and the cabinet shop, which were located in adjoining buildings. Sex segregation meant some physical separation of the sexes and women outnumbered men on the assembly line, but groups of men worked at intervals all along it and men and women worked near each other throughout the plant. (Racial segregation was occupational and physical: a small number of black men were assigned as laborers to the shipping room. Many whites did not even realize they worked there.)[16]

Gender was embedded in the production system, complete with definitions of the work that was appropriate for men and women to do. How and why these job assignments were made involved several factors. Since Philco typically paid women less than men, Philco managers might logically have placed women in as many positions as possible if they had been basing their policies purely on cutting the wage bill and maximizing profits. But Philco managers did not do that.[17] Throughout most of the 1930s, Philco had a higher proportion of male workers than comparable radio firms elsewhere. About half of Philco's production workers were men, while in the industry generally only about 30 percent of radio manufacturing jobs were held by men. Why Philco hired more men than most radio makers is not fully clear. It is possible that the pattern was established when the company was a battery maker and almost all employees were men doing heavy, dirty work, and that it continued into the radio-making period unexamined. This was a locally owned and run firm whose owners, all men, knew many of the workers personally. They may also have equated the new radio technology with masculinity.

Whereas other radio firms classed all assembly jobs together, labeled them semiskilled, and hired women to do them, Philco divided assembly jobs into two categories, final or heavy assembly, held by men only, and

[15]"Hourly Earnings in Radio Manufacturing," *Labor Information Bulletin*, 7 (1937), 7; interview with Mary Reynolds, Dec. 3, 1988, Southampton, Pa.; Palmer and Stoflet, *Labor Force*, 63 (table 6); "Hourly Earnings in Radio Manufacturing, August 1937," *Monthly Labor Review*, August 1938, 367; interview with Laura O'Reilly, June 16, 1988, by telephone, Philadelphia (at her request, I have used a pseudonym here); interview with Catherine McGill, Jan. 29, 1988, Philadelphia; interview with Edward Kiernan, Nov. 30, 1988, Philadelphia; "1,250,000 out of 4,200,000 U.S. Radios Sold," *Fortune*, February 1935, 75. Unless I note otherwise, all interviews are taped and in my possession. In the radio study as a whole, 32.5% of women worked in assembly, while only 10.2% of men did.

[16]Interviews with McGill, O'Reilly, Reynolds, and Kiernan. It was not until the 1950s that black men and later women were hired for production jobs. See file A-340, National Association for the Advancement of Colored People Papers, Library of Congress, Washington, D.C.

[17]Milkman, in *Gender at Work*, discusses similar trends in the electrical and auto industries at large. Her discussion of the electrical industry tends to focus more on the heavy-current side of the industry, which included such firms as General Electric and Westinghouse, than on the appliance side, but she has several pages on Philco which proved very helpful to me.

sub- or light assembly, held by women.[18] Testing was done by both men and women, but again the jobs were subdivided: women performed the simplest testing procedures on small pieces of equipment and men had heavier testing duties. Other jobs, such as soldering, were held by only one sex, and there was no internal differentiation or distinction within them.

According to one former worker, not only were women's jobs supposed to be lighter and less difficult, but many of them were thought to require manual dexterity, a characteristic company managers attributed to women rather than men. When hiring young women, "the company would always ask the girls especially, 'Do you play the piano, do you type?' . . . because of the dexterity in the fingers."[19] But were certain jobs described as lighter or requiring manual dexterity because women held them or were women assigned to jobs that management believed were inherently more appropriate for them? The answer is not clear. Recent interviews suggest that several men's jobs required manual dexterity and that many women's jobs were heavy and difficult. Managers may have used the distinctions of "light" and "heavy" simply as convenient justifications for job assignments. In any case, the sexual division of labor was clearly a social construction of sexual difference. It was in part related to the desire to cut wage expenses, but given the high proportion of men in the plant, it was based also on other assumptions about what men and women ought to do.

Management's conceptions of gender difference and hierarchy were also evident in the practice of permitting men to take women's jobs at "female rates" to avoid being laid off. Men could take these jobs as a survival measure, but they could not carry their higher male pay rates with them. Women did not have the option of taking male jobs at all, at any wages. In this policy Philco followed its economic self-interest. It seemed to be saying that although jobs were defined as appropriate to a particular sex and thus associated with male or female pay rates, they were not necessarily affected by the sex of the person who actually did the job.[20] Overall, the system of sexual segregation that Philco managers constructed established both a powerful set of definitions of masculine and feminine and a distinct boundary between them.

Gender and the Union

In the early years of Philco's radio production, between 1928 and 1933, the labor force ranged from one to three thousand workers, who

[18]See U.S. Women's Bureau, *Fluctuation of Employment in the Radio Industry,* Bulletin No. 83 (Washington, D.C.: U.S. Government Printing Office, 1931), 28.
[19]Interview with Harry Block, Dec. 16, 1987, Philadelphia.
[20]*Microphone,* May 1934, 4. See also Milkman, *Gender at Work,* on this issue.

were unorganized. Working conditions were onerous and exploitive, wages were low, and work was highly seasonal.[21] These conditions were altered substantially in the summer of 1933, when, Philco announced that everyone would work overtime to make up for time lost for a Fourth of July company-sponsored picnic. Within minutes a group of men in assembly, who had been discussing the idea of a union, walked off the job. The next day the conveyor belts were shut down when workers there (predominantly women) and elsewhere in the plant also left work. After another day, the entire plant was empty. Workers formed three separate independent unions (battery workers, machine shop workers, and all radio production workers) and initiated the process of affiliating with the American Federation of Labor (AFL) as independent federal locals.[22] Four days after the strike started, Philco management surprised everyone by agreeing to sign a very generous contract with the three newly formed unions. Workers won an eight-hour day and a 40-hour week, abolition of fines, no waiting for work without compensation, an increase in pay, time and a half for overtime, and full union recognition, bargaining rights, and a union shop: all new hires would have to join the appropriate union within two weeks.[23]

[21]For a description of working conditions during these years, see Cooper, "Philco"; *Microphone*, May 1934, 4; interview with Frank Markel, Dec. 9, 1988; Palmer radio study, schedules 131, 259, TUA (hereafter only schedule numbers will be cited); McGill interview; U.S. Women's Bureau, *Fluctuation of Employment*, 1, 28–33, and survey material for the study, in Record Group 86, National Archives, Washington, D.C. (hereafter RG 86); "Wages and Hours of Labor in the Manufacture of Radio Receiving Sets, Speakers, and Tubes, 1927," *Monthly Labor Review*, 27 (September 1928), 138–44, 568; *Philadelphia Bulletin*, Nov. 25, 1936; Retail Credit Corp., "Radio Industry," 3. The standard workweek was 47 hours in 1932 and early 1933, but during rush periods women often worked up to the 54-hour limit set by state law, while men were required to work 60 and 70 hours a week. The company pressured workers to work diligently and hired male "pushers" to bring more materials to the line and push everyone to keep up. All workers were subject to fines and penalties—from 15 cents to $5—for poor work or a missed operation.
[22]This was the beginning of industrial unionism in Philadelphia and of unionization in the electrical industry. The latter culminated in the formation of the United Electrical, Radio, and Machine Workers of America (UE), headed by a former Philco worker, James Carey, in 1936. Later that year the UE affiliated with what would soon become the Congress of Industrial Organizations, led by John L. Lewis. See Ronald Schatz, *The Electrical Workers: A History of Labor at General Electric and Westinghouse, 1923–60* (Urbana: University of Illinois Press, 1983); Ronald Fillipelli, "UE: The Formative Years," *Labor History*, 17 (Summer 1976), 371; copy of the 1936 contract in U.S. Department of Labor Library (hereafter USDL). Battery workers are not included in this discussion. They were soon moved out of the area altogether.
[23]Milton Derber, "Electrical Products," in *How Collective Bargaining Works: A Survey of Experience in Leading American Industries*, ed. Harry A. Millis (New York: Twentieth Century Fund, 1942); Pivar, "Hosiery Workers"; *Labor Record*, July 14 and 21, Aug. 11 and 26, 1933; Block interview; Markel interview; Schatz, *Electrical Workers*, 96; file 170–9063, Federal Mediation and Conciliation Service (FMCS), RG 280, National Archives; *Philadelphia Bulletin*, July 15 and 16, 1933; *People's Press* (UE publication for District 1), June 25, 1938, in USDL; *Microphone*, May 1934, 4. Note that the union did not win a

The contract was a major victory for the workers, but it was probably also a calculated industrywide strategy on the part of Philco managers, who thought it would help the company by affecting competition. It stipulated that no radio local affiliated with the AFL could agree to have lower wage rates than Philco and that the new union would get additional wage increases only if the National Recovery Act code, then under consideration, incorporated them or another radio company introduced them first. Philco managers believed that it was only a matter of time before unionization would sweep through the entire radio industry. With this contract the company could try to force competitors to pay the same high wage bill. In formulating this approach, Philco was beginning to behave more like its giant corporate competitors and less like a small local company, a trend that would increasingly affect its labor policies.[24]

Gender was a significant part of men's and women's relations to their union and to each other as members of it.[25] The initial and subsequent collective bargaining contracts did not challenge the gendered division of labor or the differential wage rates: they extended both and also codified and rationalized the plant's occupational classification structure.[26] The new system created job ladders within men's and women's separate job categories, so that workers moved up from one job to the next. Such rationalization addressed one of workers' long-time objections: the lack of job structure, which permitted favoritism and ignored individual seniority. The new plan would eliminate these abuses, create equitable opportunities for advancement, and permit the establishment of a seniority system.[27]

The union's definitions of equality and fairness built into this rationalized job structure seemed gender-blind. Workers agreed that favoritism and capriciousness needed to be eliminated and all workers benefited from this aspect of the contract. The new job structure was, however, gender-bound. Since women's and men's jobs were distinctly different, so were their job ladders. The range of women's jobs was much narrower and women had no way of moving up to the most skilled, highest-paying jobs at the top of the male ladder. They could not step onto it, much less climb anywhere. The result was that the possibility of occupational mo-

closed shop or full control over hiring—simply that anyone who was hired would have to join the union.

[24]Derber, "Electrical Products," 782–83. My thanks to Colin Gordon, now at the University of British Columbia and a fellow at the Hagely Museum and Library during 1989, for drawing my attention to employers' efforts to promote unionism during the 1930s.

[25]I am focusing here primarily on Local 101 of the UE, representing radio production workers.

[26]E.g., Milkman in *Gender at Work* notes that the industrial unions overall did not challenge the sexual division of labor during the Depression or during World War II.

[27]O'Reilly interview; Reynolds interview; copies of contracts, 1933 and 1936, USDL.

bility was attached to men's rather than women's jobs. Seniority lists were not officially separate, but since a woman could not move into a man's job, in effect men's seniority and women's seniority were unrelated. In addition, women who left work because of pregnancy lost seniority altogether. The union contract also stipulated that men could no longer take women's jobs at women's pay to avoid being laid off—a move that sharpened gender boundaries: men could no longer confuse their gender identity by doing women's work. Pay remained linked to jobs as defined by sex. In 1936 men's base pay rates were 60 cents an hour, women's 49 cents. The averages for 1937 were 78 cents an hour for men and 60.7 cents an hour for women.[28]

Women workers appear to have agreed with management and the union that men and women should do different things, that men's work is more valuable, and that this arrangement was natural and acceptable.[29] Several workers interviewed recently indicated, as Catherine McGill did, that she gave no thought to it because there was nothing unusual about such an arrangement and because that was not her major concern. "At that time, you were glad to have a job." Esther Davis explained that she accepted the pay differential because the jobs men and women did were different, and Laura O'Reilly did not recall noticing the structure. To them and to many other women in the plant, the contract probably looked familiar: men and women did different things.[30]

There were exceptions: Mary Reynolds, who began working at Philco in 1936, accepted sexual differences in aspects of her private life, yet she did not easily accept these differences with respect to occupational segregation. She recalled that she quickly found out that no matter how much training a woman had, she could never get one of the prime jobs in the plant—in repair work or troubleshooting. "That's where I used to get angry because I was always fighting for the better things, you know. Because the men got the best jobs." The union did not help. She could not try for a job such as troubleshooting "even if you went to school for it.

[28]U.S. Women's Bureau, *Fluctuation of Employment*, 28; interviews with O'Reilly and Davis; "Annual Earnings in Radio Manufacture, 1936," *Monthly Labor Review*, July 1939, 163–79; "Hourly Earnings in Radio Manufacturing, August, 1937," *Monthly Labor Review*, August 1938, 363–71; and "Average Hourly Earnings in the Radio Manufacturing Industry, August 1937," typescript, May 1938, n.p., in USDL. The 1937 study averaged the pay for the two largest radio makers. Philco was the nation's largest, so the actual figures for Philco may have been slightly higher. Women's Bureau investigators had noted as early as 1929 that radio assembly-line jobs offered women workers "no opportunity for progression."

[29]My conclusion is drawn from my search in district and national UE records, the Philco local's magazine, *The Microphone*, and the *UE News*. Milkman, in *Gender at Work*, shows how powerful this idea was even in the midst of the wartime emergency.

[30]Interviews with Iola Kelly, Oct. 28, 1988, Philadelphia; Edith Curry, Jan. 20, 1989, Blackwood, N.J.; Helen Francis, Jan. 6, 1989, Philadelphia; Ann Freeman, Jan. 25, 1989, Philadelphia.

They [the union] said you can't have it." Reynolds denied the relevance of sexual difference in her workplace and believed that a person who had the training and ability was entitled to the job.

In other ways, too, the operation of what by 1936 were locals of the United Electrical, Radio and Machine Workers of America (UE) reproduced the meaning of sexual difference contained within the contract and the system of production in the plant. Women were not an integral part of the radio local during the 1930s, although they made up half of its membership. Running the union seemed to be men's work: men were the leaders of the union and were usually the shop stewards, even in predominantly female departments. The male leadership set the course of union policy, determined the issues addressed in contract negotiations, and edited the union newspaper, *The Microphone*, during these years.

Although some women attended union meetings, as a group they did not do so in numbers proportional to their membership. Some may have felt that unions were rightly men's business. Others may have been offended by the masculine culture expressed in the very location of the meetings. Mary Reynolds explained that she had attended meetings briefly, "but then it got to the point I didn't like them because they had a place there for drinking right off the hall where you had the meeting." She consciously and disapprovingly viewed the union as a male organization that operated "for the men." How many women members shared this consciousness is impossible to determine. Susan M., interviewed in 1936, also felt that the union was a masculine organization. She told the interviewer, "I belong to the union, [but] I don't go to meetings much. The men do all the talkin', we don't have much say in it. . . . Why don't they have just girls' unions? I think it'd be better. I get scared to say anything when men are around." She had a sense that she was entitled to play a role in union affairs, but could not see a way to do so given the current structure and masculine character of the union. To her the answer might be a separate woman's union where she would feel freer to express her ideas.[31]

Women who tried to become more active in the local encountered problems. Laura O'Reilly had no relatives in the labor movement, but thought the idea of unions sounded right and asked her own shop steward a lot of questions about how union regulations worked. When he decided to leave the position in 1936, he urged her to take it (she felt that no one else wanted it). She did, but soon learned that she was not viewed in the same way her predecessor had been. There were only a few "lady shop stewards." They did not get needed information on time and were left out of important meetings. To her the message was clear: male shop

[31]*Microphone*, September 1934, 1–4, and June 1936, 4; schedules 213, 583, 608, 725, 754.

stewards did not "like the idea of women shop stewards. They made it very obvious." Her experience with men in her department suggests that male members associated authority with manhood. She learned, for example, that a man in her department refused to bring his grievance to her. When she asked him why, he replied that he would not have a woman fight his battles for him. From his perspective there was something unmanly about permitting a woman to handle his case. To O'Reilly the man's reluctance played right into the hands of management by undermining class solidarity. She quit the job of shop steward after only two years, disillusioned by such attitudes and the union's other shortcomings.[32]

Just as Philco defined appropriate work for men and women through the sexual division of labor, male union leaders and many members, male and female, believed it was appropriate for women to belong to the union and pay dues, but not to be active. Yet this assumption did not go unquestioned or uncontested. Susan M., Mary Reynolds, and Laura O'Reilly were probably not the only ones who were not satisfied with women's position in the union.

Male leaders sought to integrate women into the union, but primarily with respect to social activities and in keeping with a belief in sexual difference. They organized the Girls' Club and tried to encourage women's participation through notices in the *Microphone:* "Girls DON'T FAIL to take an active part in this female ONLY organization your Union is sponsoring for You." But such a notice only underscored the fact that men still controlled everything—even the formation of a club for "girls." The club disappeared by 1935 for lack of interest. Several issues of the journal featured "Our Own Beauty Shoppe: A Page for Our Girls," which focused on women's appearance—hosiery, hair styles, and body care ("the appearance of a well shaped leg can be marred by carelessness")—and such female activities as cooking. The page was an attempt to interest women in the journal, but it separated the sexes and marginalized women. It defined and isolated feminine interests and, since there was no equivalent page for men, it suggested that the whole journal was theirs while the women's page alone was for women. The separate page also soon disappeared.[33]

[32]O'Reilly noted particularly the slowness of change and the union's seeming collusion with management when it ignored evidence that bosses favored particular stewards.

[33]*Microphone*, May 1934, 8; June 1934, 8; July 1934, 11; August 1934, 12; September 1934, 13, 17; October 1934, 14; November 1934, 21; October 1935, 3. For a fuller look at some of the social activities the UE and other unions provided for Philadelphia workers during the 1930s, see Elizabeth Fones-Wolf, "Industrial Unionism and Labor Movement Culture in Depression-Era Philadelphia," *Pennsylvania Magazine of History and Biography,* January 1985, 5–26.

All of these aspects of union operation and activity extended and mirrored the sexual division of labor at Philco. Yet men's and women experiences were not always so separate. Apathy toward the union, for
example, was not the special province of women members—groups of
men felt distanced from the union and its operation. Although men were
active in the Radio Club, most male members also failed to show up for
social gatherings and for union meetings.[34]

Some men and women lacked interest in the union because they felt it
was too friendly with the company. "There's too much ball-playing," one
male member noted in 1936. "Quite a few" workers felt this way, he
explained to the interviewer, and this perception kept them from being
more active in the union.[35] Laura O'Reilly complained that many shop
stewards had all-too-friendly relationships with the foremen and won
special favors for particular work groups or ignored the grievances of
workers altogether. Mary Reynolds decided not to call the union steward
after a run-in one day with her supervisor because she feared the union
"might have taken up for the boss rather than me." She went to the department head to complain instead. Considerations of gender could be
intertwined with this sense of alienation. Reynolds, for example, noted
that she believed the union stewards were there principally to protect
male interests or those of the company. Too, although some workers
viewed the union suspiciously, others, especially those who had worked
at the company before 1933, paid particular attention to all the improvements the union had made. To these members, men and women, the
most important thing about the union was that their work lives and their
wages had dramatically changed for the better since its formation.[36]

Together these attitudes suggest that groups of men and women could
position themselves vis-à-vis the union in a variety of ways. Some women
who believed in sexual difference still felt entitled to a role in the union;

[34]*Microphone*, October 1935, 3, 6; January 1935, 8; August 1934, 14; February 1936,
24; October 1934, 21; January 1935, 13; February 1934, 1; October 1935, 2–3; November 1935, 1; February 1936, 24, for example. Men did take an interest in some of the team
sports that the union and the company organized, but these teams were sex-segregated.
Some mixed activities, such as the Philco Orchestra and the bowling teams, did become
very popular later on.

[35]Schedule 214 (see also schedule 138); Neil Hess interview, Jan. 28, 1989, Philadelphia.
Pages of the *Microphone* often sound as though its editors were speaking in behalf of employers. It was not unusual for it to print quotations from the *Philco Manual for Employees*
or to remind workers of the generous Christmas bonus that the company gave each year.
One article explained that "your job is your business!" and encouraged members to view
themselves as business executives who would have to oppose anything that "retards production." See *Microphone*, January 1934, 12; July 1934, 2, 5, 13; August 1934, 4; September 1934, 3; January 1935, 2; February 1936, 12.

[36]Praise for the union's accomplishments may be found in schedules 66, 74, 131, 134,
138, 142, 145, 158, 171, 176, 183, 186, 188, 225, 237, 259, 268, 286, 326, 588, 608,
612, 638, 710, 716, 725, 744, 1205, 1208, 1220, 1225, 1227, 1256, 1271.

others did not. Some workers who felt that the union was a problem saw that problem as a factor of the union's too-friendly relations with management, not of gender. Some women experienced their alienation from the union in terms of both gender and class at the same time. Men and women might have held certain attitudes toward the union in common while simultaneously regarding the segregated occupational structure as fair and logical. Men and women may have believed in the sexual division of labor without identifying themselves as male or female first all the time. While all of this variation can seem indeterminate, it illustrates the relative subjectivity of gender meanings which existed in the context of a rigid sexual division of labor.

Gender, Work, and Family

Although men were more likely than women to be married, many of those interviewed in 1936 connected work with the whole fabric of their lives, especially their responsibilities for their families. This was especially true during the 1930s, when every member of a working-class family could potentially make a vital contribution. Men and women could begin work with gendered expectations about their appropriate jobs and work roles as men and women, but disruptive experiences in that difficult depression decade, such as a death or unemployment in the family, could alter these gendered meanings or make them less salient.

Interviews suggest that most Philco workers came from families that expected everyone to work. Those who were not primary breadwinners were expected to help out at home.[37] Although the role of breadwinner was typically viewed as the province of men, several women interviewed in 1936 revealed that circumstances had altered their roles and their views of their responsibilities. One widow had not worked at all from 1914 to 1932, but when her husband died, one of his friends helped her get a job at Philco. Another woman quit her job with the company in 1933 to stay home, but returned two years later when she and her husband separated. Mrs. N. began working shortly after the birth of her child in July 1929, when her husband became unemployed. After several short-term jobs and several layoffs and stretches of unemployment, she secured a position at Philco in June 1936 and supported her family. A young wirer explained to the interviewer that her father had died and now her mother and sister depended on her income. A nineteen-year-old coil winder who was her family's only support impressed the interviewer

---

[37]Interviews with Markel, Kiernan, McGill, O'Reilly, Kelly, Reynolds, and Davis.

with her pride in having responsibility for so many people at such a young age. Supporting a family gave her a sense of self-esteem.[38] Women's new responsibilities for their families made the boundaries between masculine and feminine activities less obvious. These women had added new parts to their already complex identities. They still saw themselves as different from men, but the meanings of femaleness had shifted. Their gender was one of several things that formed their identities.

For some men, losing a job could reinforce their received notion of masculinity because they were somehow failing to support their families and thus to fulfill their expected gender roles properly. Some of the men interviewed revealed variations in their experiences, however. They reported having to shoulder domestic responsibilities sooner than they had expected. Several had interrupted their educations to begin work. One explained that he was the only one of five adults in his family who had a job and had no choice but to continue working. While the young female coiler mentioned earlier had gained self-esteem by supporting her family—something that most men did as a matter of course—a cabinetmaker felt burdened by the same responsibility. He foresaw the dismal future of his craft and wanted to learn radio mechanics, but he was the sole support of his family so he could not take time off to retrain. He accepted his responsibility for his family, but the interviewer noted that he "regrets the fact that he's married and can't do what he really likes."[39] There were also some men who gave no thought to family responsibility. Harry Block had worked in a variety of jobs, including several in department store warehouses. He had no interest in finding a permanent position. "I figured I was never going to get married. I was going to become the professional bum." In the summer of 1928 his plan had been to get a job at Philco if he could, work for the summer, and then perhaps head "down south."[40]

These accounts of workers' experiences during the 1930s suggest that sexual difference was something men and women knew and understood but life experience could alter their conceptions of their gender roles and blur or shift the boundaries between men's and women's responsibilities. The ideology of sexual difference might remain intact, but people's experiences and outlooks reflected a much more complicated set of relationships and meanings.

[38]See schedules 602, 621, 637, 653, 668, 688, 711, 712, 723, 724, 729, 734, 735, 736, 756, 763, 765. Turbin, "Beyond Conventional Wisdom," discusses the varieties in women's relations to work and family.

[39]Schedules 122, 123, 124, 146, 152, 181, 185, 203, 240, 275.

[40]Block later changed his mind: he married and happily took on family responsibilities. He helped to organize the UE in the plant in 1933 and went on to become a major force in the Pennsylvania labor movement.

Gender and Jobs

Philco workers, men and women, expressed a range of attitudes toward their specific jobs at Philco, their definition of the type of work that was acceptable for them, and their strategies for getting what they wanted. Many plainly told interviewers that they disliked their Philco jobs. They made this evaluation on the basis of the specific conditions of work. Both men and women in this group objected to the gang method (whereby no worker would receive a bonus until all workers in the gang reached a certain level of production), the speedup ("more work with less workers"), the pace (Philco was "production mad"), the instability of work, the fumes, the crowding, the boredom, and most especially the heat in summer.[41]

Many people interviewed in 1936 evaluated their jobs by contrasting them with something else they had done previously.[42] Some did so strictly in terms of intrinsic characteristics of the job. Others did so explicitly in terms of gender. One woman, for example, preferred her previous occupation in a hosiery mill, which she thought was "nicer for a girl."[43] Her exact reasoning is unclear, but perhaps she considered hosiery more feminine than radios, or perhaps the size of the plant or the type of machinery seemed more congenial. Some expressed their notions of appropriate work in class and gender terms, although less explicitly. Several women who had been trained as clerical workers, for example, had been forced to revise their expectations and take factory jobs because they could not find office work or because the pay was too low. Laura O'Reilly assumed she would work in an office and had gotten clerical training in high school. Her family expected that she would "look around for an office job and take an office job at any cost." But she took a factory job instead because of the money. "They were offering more per hour in Philco" when she applied in 1933, and the "circumstances in my own family just meant that I had to go out and get a job

[41]See schedules 84, 145, 158, 162, 178, 193, 222, 448, 556, 568, 585, 608, 617, 619, 626, 627, 637, 683, 747, 787, 794, 802, 1210. A longer version of this essay discusses ways in which workers attempted to deal with these problems informally. When the temperature rose into the 90s in the summer, for example, women along the conveyor belt might begin banging their irons and pliers against the belt's metal frame. The din would grow louder and louder until management agreed to shut the factory down. Thus women accepted certain notions about appropriate activities for women, but they collectively acted to assert some control over work and resist aspects of work to which they objected. See Cooper, "Philco."

[42]The Palmer study found that among women radio workers in Philadelphia interviewed, 18.5% had worked in textiles and 10.9% in clerical jobs. Among men, 24% had worked in textiles and 20.9% in metal products, machinery, or electrical goods.

[43]Schedule 645.

and I did." Her choice was not a happy one. To her, appropriate work was defined in part by the amount of training necessary to do it. Her Philco job was something "that could be taught to anybody. It wasn't a . . . specific skill, like nursing or typing or something that you would really have to take schooling for." Other young women she knew from school "took the attitude that it was below their dignity to work in a factory environment." She felt their disapproval, but she needed the money. Esther Davis explained that neither she nor her family had ever expected her to go into a factory and her family remained unhappy with her for doing so.[44]

Mary Reynolds likewise never expected to do factory work until she heard that the pay was so high. Like O'Reilly, she had expected to use her clerical skills. When she and a friend were offered jobs at Philco, the personnel man in charge had tried to discourage them from accepting because they had graduated from high school. He pointed to a group of job applicants nearby. "That's the type of people you'll be working with. They're not very nice. They're very crude and they are all uneducated people. I don't think you'd like it." The manager's comments were inaccurate and unkind, but they expressed a hierarchical class outlook that distinguished among categories of workers. Reynolds understood these intraclass distinctions, but she ignored them because she was more interested in the money than in status. She looked at her friend and announced, "Well, I'm going to try it."[45]

Some men at Philco also saw their work as inappropriate for people of their class and sex; they told interviewers that they were working for Philco only because more skilled jobs in their usual fields were unattainable. Among these were patternmakers, steamfitters, instrument makers, sign painters, auto repairmen, tool-and-die makers, and machinists.[46] Several of these men held jobs that were considered among the best at Philco, but in their view these jobs were inferior to the work for which they were trained. Workers in the cabinet shop, for example, many of whom had been born in Italy, were experienced furniture craftsmen and felt degraded by the elementary nature of their Philco jobs. Trained as part of a masculine family tradition to perform highly skilled woodworking, these men could make finely crafted furniture and considered themselves artists. At Philco they made only parts of cabinets or worked with machines rather than by hand in jobs it took only a week to master. They suffered frequent layoffs and several were unemployed at the time of the Palmer interviews. Work at Philco reflected the irrelevance of their

[44]Similar attitudes were expressed in 1936; see schedules 568 and 642.
[45]Reynolds worked for Philco for forty-two years.
[46]Schedules 60, 68, 135, 138, 140, 159, 190, 226, 235, 266, 313.

craft knowledge, a serious loss in status, financial insecurity, and attendant inability to provide for their families.[47]

Thus groups of men and women at Philco felt that their jobs were less than appropriate for them. Women who preferred clerical work viewed factory work as unfeminine and a step down. Men who were trained in other trades did not necessarily mind the factory, but they were accustomed to what they considered more demanding work that had promised them greater security. Both groups had had to give up what they perceived to be respectable positions in the midst of a depression. Both conformed, however, to a gendered conception of what was appropriate for their sex to do—neither group would have been likely to consider the occupations of the other. They expressed their feelings about work in similar terms—lost status, threatened sexual identity, and a regret that the skills they had acquired were being wasted—but accepted the idea that men and women do different kinds of things.

Some workers preferred their Philco jobs to something else. One woman had formerly been employed at the Campbell Soup Company in Camden, where the work was hard and heavy. "It's really men's work," she explained. Unlike the hosiery worker we met earlier, she found her job at Philco more suitable for a woman. The two women disagreed on the meaning of femininity, but they agreed that it was important to distinguish between masculine and feminine jobs. Their outlooks again suggest the variability in gender meanings and boundaries within the context of strong beliefs in the importance of gender differences.[48]

Other women interviewed saw Philco as a step up primarily because the working conditions there were better than those encountered elsewhere. Another former Campbell's Soup worker explained that the company had "worked us to death." Philco was the best place she had ever worked, she explained. Another woman was bitter about her jobs as a maid; she had jumped at the chance to work at Philco. Two women preferred Philco to office work because they disliked sitting at a desk all day.[49] Though both men and women expressed this sense of improvement, the comments of two workers suggest a possible difference. Mrs. S. disliked Philco, but explained that the job was "better'n relief"; as a

[47]The first packet of radio interview schedules in the Palmer materials is made up almost entirely of cabinet-makers. Schedules 9, 11, 23, 26, 100, and 232 are especially revealing. Other skilled male workers at the plant, including some skilled machinists and a diamond cutter, saw their work at Philco as a step down. See box 135, folder "Radio Workers," 23, in Palmer Papers, University of Pennsylvania. These papers are additional office files of Gladys Palmer and were uncatalogued at the time I used them. They are to be added to the TUA collection in the future.
[48]Schedule 676. See also schedules 560, 595, 676, 738.
[49]These and similar attitudes expressed by other women can be found in schedules 269, 560, 595, 628, 637, 645, 672, 676, 720, 727, 738, 750.

woman, perhaps she considered her source of support as most important. Working was preferable to taking a government handout. A male worker, by contrast, explained that he disliked the job but preferred it to being "idle." As a man, he may have been most concerned about being unproductive.[50] These are only speculations, of course, but they suggest subtle differences possible in men's and women's outlooks and interpretations of a basically identical experience—their fear of unemployment and their appreciation of their jobs. The reverse, as we have seen, was also possible. The former clerical workers and machinists who were unhappy because the skills they had acquired were being unused and because they felt their jobs were inappropriate for them had the same fears and interpretations. However, their specific experiences were different; the jobs for which they longed were sex-segregated.

Both men and women evaluated their work by means of contrasts, and at the same time their evaluations could be framed in gender and/or class terms. They compared jobs within the context of a sexually segregated hierarchy and used contrasts that reflected their beliefs about what men and women should do. Philco workers distinguished between men's and women's work, but they did so in variable ways. Many agreed that one should do only work that was appropriate for one's sex, but disagreed on what exactly that was. While many accepted the sexual division of labor within Philco as natural and acceptable, some, such as Mary Reynolds, rejected the very idea of gendered jobs at the plant. Gender meanings at Philco were not rigidly fixed, nor can gender differences be described in dichotomous terms. Certainly evidence suggests that workers generally believed in a gender hierarchy and that daily they operated in a work structure that reinforced that belief by separating men and women and privileging men, but their experiences and interpretations reveal diversity, similarity, and difference operating at once.

Many workers thought about work in terms of what they might expect in the future.[51] These were workers who anticipated being in the paid labor force for some time, so what they could expect mattered to them, especially in view of the history of their neighborhood. To one woman radio was the "coming thing," the "most prosperous business."

[50]Schedules 133, 650. See also 229 and 568. Ava Baron makes such a point in "Questions of Gender."

[51]Not all Philco workers thought about the future in the same way. Not all of the people interviewed mentioned improvement or mobility, and it is likely that some conceptualized their jobs and their lives in terms of the present. The way workers defined their goals relates in part to class, as Sue Cobble has argued in "Practical Women." The variability here suggests that other factors, such as the nature of the industry and the specific setting involved—radio was a new technology and Philco did appear to offer better jobs and avenues for advancement—also determined how workers saw themselves in relation to their work and to the future. It would be a mistake to argue that working-class people as a whole did not hope to advance.

A female coil wrapper told the interviewer in 1936 that she liked her job because the future looked bright. The interviewer commented that she "hopes to advance." Another woman, an assembler, expressed her enthusiasm for her job and the six-week training course Philco had provided. Even if the company fired her, at least now she had a trade, she explained. To Michael C., who hung doors on cabinets, the radio industry was attractive because it was "new" and "looked like a good one."[52]

The Philco workers with skilled, high-paying, steady jobs, such as repairmen, tool-and-die makers, and troubleshooters—all men—consistently and not surprisingly expressed the most optimism about the future and did so in terms of expectations about mobility within the plant. Their own experiences had revealed that they could advance and many had attained the highest, best-paid nonsalaried jobs in the plant. A few would eventually move into managerial positions.[53]

For many Philco wage workers, the instability of the work and the lack of opportunity to advance created pessimism about their futures at the company. Several women interviewed in 1936 felt discouraged. A female high school graduate lamented that her job as a radio packer offered "no advancement. . . . All the girls talk about is getting married and getting out of the shop." An inspector, trained as a bookkeeper, had turned down a more prestigious office job because her production job paid more, but she felt there was no future for her at Philco and worried about being laid off. One woman liked her work at Philco for the present, but the interviewer noted that she was "ambitious to do something better. Wants to learn office work."[54]

Although men had more chances for upward mobility than women, not all men could or did advance. Gender gave men privileges in relation to women, but it did not change their position in relation to capital. Many men with production jobs complained not only about their inability to advance but also about the lack of skill and ability needed for the work they did. These men clearly understood that to move up, they would need to leave the production line—something no woman could do. One male tester who worked on the conveyor felt that his job was an "insult to his intelligence." His was not a complaint about money. He linked his dignity to the job's use of his skill and intellect. Some had viewed radio work as acceptable particularly because it was a new, technology-based field—on the surface a very appropriate job for a man. But their actual experiences had proved that not all radio work required

[52]Schedules 561, 575, 449, 61.
[53]See schedules 77, 137, 143, 342. Philco managers during these years often had started at low-level jobs and worked their way upward within the plant. This is evident from interviews with salaried personnel and from issues of the company's magazine, *Philco News*, from 1945 to the 1950s, in the collection of Frank Markel.
[54]Schedules 618, 447, 568. See also 566 and 618.

much technical knowledge. An inspector, formerly a weaver, told the interviewer that he had gotten interested in radio "as a new and rising industry." He had bought radio sets and had tinkered with them and taken night school courses. His work at Philco, however, had proved "too monotonous" for him and he had quit to work in a radio repair shop, work that he liked much better. Few jobs on a conveyor system, explained a young male assembler, ever taught a person anything about the mechanics of radio. Any skills one learned at Philco were of little use elsewhere. The only way to advance was to get a job outside of "straight production." A skilled repairman noted the same thing from the other side. He liked his job, but told the enumerator he would quit if he ever had to work in production. A final tester explained that anyone could learn most radio production jobs in half an hour. He felt there would be no chance for him to advance at the company unless he could take a radio course and pass the examination for the troubleshooter's job.[55]

The tester's strategy of gaining additional training was one frequently cited by workers at the plant who had an interest in self-improvement, but many men and women had different expectations about training and saw different paths of potential mobility. Over and over male workers reported taking night courses at Drexel Institute of Technology or at some local vocational school in hopes of advancing. The union offered radio electronics courses for members in the evenings. The courses were not officially confined to men, but no women attended. Several interviewed expressed an interest in becoming troubleshooters; these workers who diagnosed and solved malfunctions in the sets made the largest non-supervisory wages in the plant. One troubleshooter explained that he had secured his job because he had studied engineering at North Carolina State University for a short time—as long as his money held out. Another Philco troubleshooter, Walter W., had moved from final assembly to testing to his present job, and expected to study at Drexel the following year so that he could advance still further. In a trade like radio, he explained, there was always a "chance for advancement."[56]

In contrast to men, women who saw education as the means to advance intended to use it to move out of, not up within, the plant. While men referred primarily to courses in electronics and mechanics, women

[55]Schedules 87, 152, 1256, 145, 123. See also 124, 148, 156, 229, 244, 253. In a letter to *Microphone*, October 1935, 26–27, a worker complained that some of the new hires were moving directly into the "better jobs." "What," he asked, "does a person have to be or do to be advanced?"

[56]Men's references to education are in schedules 69, 77, 79, 86, 122, 123, 124, 136, 137, 143, 191, 284, 1220, 1221. Their talk about mobility is in schedules 77, 101, 143, 145, 154, 191, 287, 1221, 1241, 1476. Of the nine men in the 1936 survey who had attended college, two had graduated.

mentioned clerical courses—typing, stenography, bookkeeping.[57] Clerical work still represented a ticket out for some women, although others, as we have seen, had given up on it and taken Philco jobs instead because of the money. Both groups agreed that clerical work was a step up, however (as did many other working-class women during the 1920s and 1930s). Thus for some women workers, the strategy for constructing respectable work was to leave the factory, whereas for many men, the approach was to change the work they did at the factory.

Additional training did not mean the same thing for all women, however. Mary Reynolds took clerical courses for years, but she apparently never intended to use this training to secure a clerical position because the pay was so low. She took the courses, she explained, "to better myself." To her, education itself was self-improvement, and her coursework enabled her to feel more respectable than she might otherwise have felt as a factory worker. It also meant that she was trained to do something else and thus preserved the possibility of choice in the future.[58]

Two of my interviews suggest how one man and one woman analyzed their respective situations and developed strategies to deal with them. From his first day on the job at Philco, Frank Markel tried to push himself up the ladder inside the firm. His reasons related to his family responsibilities, first to his parents and later as a husband and father; his desire to make more money; and his effort to get less arduous work. Competition for men's jobs in the plant was fierce. "You always had your eye open for a better job than what you had. And you would more or less move up the ladder. The pay may have been the same, but it was less strenuous. . . . As long as you bettered yourself, then you didn't have to work so hard. And believe me, everybody worked hard. That's the way it was. It was dog eat dog." Markel took night courses and eventually moved into a highly skilled, respectable, well-paid job in the test maintenance department. He also became very active in the union, in which he had become involved at the time it was organized in 1933.

Mary Reynolds went to work for the company in 1936, applying a heavy soldering iron to wires that moved past her on a conveyor belt. "It was murder. I'll never forget it." She hated the job. The bulky iron raised blisters on her hands (until she began wearing gloves to protect them) and the heat from it made the already-hot summer air unbearable. She

[57]One man (schedule 124) explained that he was studying stenography. Another (schedule 165) was hoping to become a medium through "self-instruction."
[58]As we have seen, Reynolds was unusual in many ways. By the late 1930s she was divorced, living alone, and supporting herself. She bought property in the 1940s and 1950s, and began selling household items and appliances at wholesale while still working at Philco. She was quite successful at this enterprise and continued to buy real estate while building a comfortable nest egg. She retired from Philco in the 1970s and later remarried.

worried that she could be electrocuted: when the company watered down the floors to try to lower the temperature in the summer, she and others were standing in a thin layer of water holding electric soldering irons. Like Markel, she wanted to find a job that was less arduous (and less dangerous) and asked whether there was something else she could do. "I was trying to get out of that right away," she explained. However, she never wanted assembly or wiring work—the most likely alternative jobs available for women. Her reason was simple but important, and related to her ideas about the relationship between being female and working. She had not minded taking a factory job even though she knew that many people, including the man who hired her, looked down on factory work. The appearance of her hands, however, mattered a great deal to her. "I always kept my hands nice," she explained. As a solderer she could wear gloves to protect her hands and preserve their appearance. As a wirer or assembler "you get your hands all cut up. . . . You couldn't wear gloves." Thus her desire for a job that was less arduous and safer was not enough to make her violate her sense of what was important to her as a woman—pretty hands. (Although she did not mention it, scarred hands might also provide undesirable evidence of her work in a factory.) The women who took wiring and other jobs may not have defined their femininity in the same way Reynolds did, or they may have been more willing to sacrifice it for something else they wanted more. After over two years, Reynolds was able to get an inspecting job that was less pressured and cleaner. But it was not until the wartime emergency that she got the chance to do repairs, a job that throughout the 1930s was reserved for men only.[59]

Both Markel and Reynolds wanted less arduous work; both sought upward mobility; and both wanted to "better" themselves. At the same time they situated themselves somewhat differently within the work force. Markel's concerns related to his drive to move up and to get less arduous work. By taking courses, maneuvering himself within the plant, and taking an active role in the union, he was able to fulfill his ambitions. For him respectability was linked to achieving a stable, skilled job in the plant. Reynolds wanted a job in repairs but knew that she could not get it. She also was unwilling to seek a clerical job because of the low pay. Given these limitations, she valued a job that would preserve her notion of femininity and she was willing to risk her physical safety to keep it. Her own strategy for respectability was to perform work that preserved her femininity, try to secure what had been a man's job during the war emergency, and take night courses in skills she never intended to use.

[59]Reynolds did repairs on radar, not radio.

Job Reclassification

Gender and class relations at Philco reached a significant turning point in 1937. Conceptions of gender difference embedded in the production system had been powerful, as we have seen, although aspects of life at the plant did not mirror the categorization of men and women faithfully. The production system had been taken for granted by many workers but now it became highly visible and contested. Philco management's policies shifted in the wake of increased competition: the company placed women in what had previously been men's jobs. This action disrupted those definitions of male and female which had been fossilized in the production system until now. They raised questions about the meaning of gender difference and equality and generated a measure of gender conflict.

By the late 1930s, Philco's economic position had changed considerably. In 1933 Philco managers had believed that unionization would spread throughout the industry and that they could use a union to help control competitive conditions nationwide. By 1937 and 1938, however, things looked different. The United Electrical Workers had been highly successful in some fields, but the union had not succeeded in organizing radio workers. Philco's stabilization strategy had not worked and the union was no longer needed. Indeed, it was an impediment, because such firms as RCA and Zenith were now successfully challenging Philco and rapidly claiming larger and larger market shares. Philco needed to cut costs in order to meet the competition.[60]

In their effort to solve the company's problems, Philco managers began restructuring the company to make it look more like its corporate competitors. They expanded into air conditioning and refrigerator production during 1938 by buying plants in other states. To save money, the company had started to subcontract more work in 1936, and by 1938 this had become an issue in bargaining. The company also began to insist on wage cuts. Managers adopted an additional strategy to lower labor costs—job reclassification. Gender was an integral part of this plan, which involved reclassification of some men's jobs and assigning them the lower, "female" base pay rate. Many men would lose their jobs and women would take new jobs without an increase in pay or any associated chance for real mobility. Occupational segregation would remain intact; only the boundaries between men's and women's jobs would change. The only workers who stood to gain were new female employees who might not otherwise have been hired. Reclassification would not only lower wage costs, it would also bring Philco more into line with other radio firms, which already had a much greater proportion of

[60] *Radio and Electrical Appliance Journal*, October 1938, quoted in *Organizer's Official Bulletin* (UE), Nov. 14, 1938, 2, reel 4, Harry Block Papers, Pennsylvania State University; Derber, "Electrical Products," 786–90.

women workers than Philco had. Only a few years earlier, Philco managers had subordinated economic concerns when they set up the sexual division of labor in the plant. Now, as the firm suffered an economic crisis, they decided to redefine male and female jobs so that they could employ more women and lower the wage bill.[61]

Once the rush season was over in December 1937, Philco began laying off thousands of workers—many more than usual. By February 1938 only 2,000 of the 6,000 to 7,000 workers were left in the plant. The company then made its demands for revision of the upcoming contract— lower pay rates, longer workweeks, elimination of the union shop, and reclassification of 1,500 jobs. The union refused the company's demands, and also called for a halt to subcontracting. Not surprisingly, union leaders, reflecting the union's masculine orientation, rejected reclassification and argued that the men's jobs at issue were too heavy and hard for women to do.[62] When the union refused to budge, the company shut down completely. Philco called it a strike; the UE called it a lockout.[63]

After four months, during which the UE launched a national boycott of Philco products and Philco threatened to leave the city altogether, the two sides reached an agreement—essentially a defeat for the union. Base wage rates were cut from 60 to 52 cents an hour for men and from 49 to 42 cents for women. Hours were extended from 36, as negotiated in the 1935 agreement, back to 40. The UE was recognized as the sole bargaining agent, but a union-shop clause was deleted. The union agreed to the reclassification of 1,500 men's jobs as women's jobs.[64] Although the

[61]"Philco Corp. No. 1 Radio Maker," *Barron's National Business and Financial Weekly,* Jan. 3, 1944, 7; "Philco: Fight for Life," *Iron Age,* Apr. 12, 1956; "Two Radio Deals," *Business Week,* Aug. 30, 1947, 26–27; "Radio, Refrigerators, and Radar," *Fortune,* November 1944, 114–21; "Philco: Its Greatest Growth May Lie Ahead," *Barron's,* Oct. 20, 1942, 11; typescript copy of 1938 agreement, Sept. 7, 1938, in "Final Report," Sept. 15, 1938, file 199–1747, RG 280, National Archives; minutes of radio conference, Mar. 18 and 19, 1939, Cleveland, 3–5, reel 1, Block Papers. James Carey, president of the UE, estimated that 75% of radio parts could be subcontracted.

[62]Unfortunately, the union newspapers, *People's Progress* and later the *UE News,* do not elaborate on unionists' full arguments about the difficulty of these jobs for women, so it is not possible to analyze their reasoning further.

[63]Derber, "Electrical Products," 787; minutes of District Council meetings, Oct. 7, Nov. 4, and Dec. 2, 1937; report to the General Executive Board of UEW, December 1937, 9–11, 19; "Resolution Condemning the Action of the Philadelphia Storage Battery Company and the Philco Radio and Television Corporation," June 9, 1938, all in reel 1, Block Papers. On subcontracting in general, see Edgar Weinberg, for U.S. Bureau of Labor Statistics, *Studies of Automatic Technology: A Case Study of a Company Manufacturing Electronic Equipment* (Washington, D.C.: U.S. Government Printing Office, Oct. 1955), 5–7.

[64]Derber, "Electrical Products," 787–90; "Collective Bargaining by United Electrical, Radio, and Machine Workers," *Monthly Labor Review,* July 1938, 67–77; file 199–1747, FMCS, RG 280, National Archives; *People's Press,* Apr. 23, 1938. Since the contract stipulated that no new workers could be hired until all laid-off workers were recalled, the unions had in effect a union shop. There is evidence that between 1938 and 1943 a clause was added to the UE contract which stated that "women placed on men's jobs shall receive the minimum rate of the new classification and will advance through the range when they

agreement stipulated that Philco would try to reduce the level of subcontracting, it gave managers a free hand in this area. Philco soon stepped
up the practice of contracting out certain operations to other firms.
These combined measures cut the total number of jobs and the number
of men working in the plant, and women became a majority of the
plant's employees. Employment for the rest of the decade did not rise above
4,000, because of subcontracting and a saturated consumer market.[65]
Reclassification reflected gender and class considerations and served as
an important managerial strategy to cope with the company's deteriorating position. It also made the relationship between jobs and sexual difference a public issue.

Laura O'Reilly was one of those assigned to what had been a man's
job. She had to use an air gun to tighten nuts on a metal cylinder. "Before that it was strictly a man's job." O'Reilly did not want to take the
new position, but she was afraid not to. When she got to the shop floor,
she received a chilly reception. A man in the department who was still
doing the job told her that it was "a man's job." She knew that, she
replied, but she had been told to do it and she didn't want to get fired.
He kept on needling her, however, and complaining that she was doing a
man's work.

Her presence confronted him with the masculine union's recent defeat,
Philco's superior power, and the elimination of his and his male co-
workers' jobs. It also had symbolic meaning to him as a man. Having a
woman do his job challenged one of the implicit meanings of being a
man in the plant—having a different and better-paying job than a
woman could hold. His own definition of masculinity in the context of
work had been until now clarified by contrast to the definition of femininity and the associated jobs for women. The sudden disjuncture between sex and job title created confusion and anger because he stood to
lose what he saw as respectable male work.

---

have performed the same quantity and quality of work under the same conditions as men in
such jobs." It is not clear, however, when the clause was added. It was not part of the
agreement signed in the fall of 1938, but it is possible that it was added within a year or
two. A 1952 Women's Bureau interview with Alexander N. Yovish, director of the Salary
and Wage Administration at the plant, revealed that during the war, women were paid
men's rates for doing what had been men's jobs. Yet in the early 1950s the Women's Bureau concluded that "there is no pretense of equal opportunity for men and women for job
assignments." Wage differentials by sex were still in place. See "Equal Pay Study, 1951"
RG 86. My thanks to a footnote in Milkman, *Gender at Work* (n. 17, 170), which brought
this study to my attention.

[65]Minutes of District Council meetings, Nov. 3 and Dec. 1, 1938; Mar. 2, 1939; minutes
of radio conference, Mar. 18 and 19, 1939, Cleveland, 3–5, all in reel 1, Block Papers;
"Final Report," Sept. 15, file 199–1747, RG 280, National Archives. I have no figures, but
my guess is that between 2,400 and 2,600 workers in the plant were women.

Perhaps in an effort to challenge her femininity just as he had himself been challenged, he kept on needling her, and finally thought of the one thing that might scare a woman the most—a threat to her appearance, especially her face. "Do you know that can explode and hit you in the face? That'll mutilate your face," he asserted. He resisted reclassification by asserting the importance of difference, and, as revealed by his attempt to intimidate or frighten her, by asserting his masculinity. O'Reilly recalled that she felt he was "trying to scare the dickens out of me," and he was succeeding. She was genuinely scared and worried about the danger he described. But she continued her work and got the job done because she felt she had no choice: she needed the job.

Neither the company nor the union had her needs or interests in mind, she felt. Company managers "were just waiting for somebody to hammer down on. They wanted a fall guy." Had she refused to do the work, "the company would jump on my back and say you are not doing what you're told." Her language suggests that she experienced the male unionists' reaction to her and the company's potential reaction to her in the same way: both were a kind of assault and a potential threat to her femininity. The union as an institution would not help. Later it occurred to her that "no union representative came up to give me moral support or anything." Too, she believed that had she refused to do the job, the union might have said there was nothing they could do "because you're being insubordinate." It even occurred to her that the union could be hoping for such a scenario so that it could argue that reclassification would not work because women would not do the jobs.

O'Reilly knew that given management's and the union's lack of interest in her situation, she had no choice but to do the job as best she could: "I knew this was the situation so I did my job." She had not felt proud of being able to do a man's job. It had been unpleasant and she had felt forced into an uncomfortable and frightening situation. "I wasn't proud and I wasn't happy. I wasn't anything. It was just something that had to be done to hold a job." Taking a man's job and exposing oneself to a man's danger did not feel familiar or comfortable or feminine. Her choice of words ("I wasn't anything") suggests that it may even have felt deadening and depersonalizing. No matter what she did, Laura O'Reilly stood to sustain the emotional and potentially physical injuries of class and gender.[66]

[66]Gradually jobs stabilized again, she recalled, and women who came to the department later encountered no problems, but at the beginning these gender divisions were strong and powerful. Some women, such as Mary Reynolds, managed to keep their improved jobs after the war. Most jobs, however, were still sex-segregated in the early 1950s, and my interviews suggest that the pattern continued well into the 1960s.

Reclassification now made gender difference a visible issue, and workers and managers contested its meaning in the context of jobs and pay. Philco managers sought to use reclassification to bolster their declining market position. They decided to move the boundary between men's and women's jobs while preserving the notion of sexual segregation. In doing so they implicitly acknowledged that women could do men's jobs, but that pay was determined by the sex of the person who actually held the job. In this regard the policy was a reversal of the company's preunion practice of permitting men to take women's jobs at women's pay.[67]

To preserve their jobs and protect their gender interests, men argued that sexual difference should be maintained intact because women did not have the ability to perform men's jobs. For O'Reilly and others, reclassification suddenly raised questions about the linkages among job content, pay, and the sex of the person performing the job.

Under the pattern of occupational segregation before 1938, many women had viewed the pay differential as justified: men's jobs were different and more difficult—men's work was compensated by men's pay. Now 1,500 women were doing jobs formerly reserved for men, yet they still received lower pay because of their sex. Some women objected. "I remember saying and hearing other women saying, 'Same work, same pay,'" noted Laura O'Reilly, but the company argued that women were not doing the "full job" men had done. "In reality they were," she explained, "but [women] weren't getting paid for it. . . . It made us angry, but we were helpless. What could we do? Because we were bound by the contract." The majority had agreed that it was all right to pay women less if the jobs were different, but women now did what men formerly did, and the pay should be the same.[68]

By opposing female rates on what had formerly been men's jobs, these women were rejecting the arguments both of management and of their male counterparts. They were saying that where a job was concerned, sexual difference was not relevant. Women such as O'Reilly rejected management's defense that job content had been altered somewhat, and the union's argument that women could not do the jobs. Women were doing the jobs, they were just not getting paid the previous and higher rate. By demanding men's pay, they were arguing that the actual content of the job, not the sex of the person who held it or its supposed gender characteristics, should determine compensation.[69]

[67]In both cases Philco sought to pay lower wages, but after 1938 this was the top priority.

[68]Essentially, these women were following the principle contained in management's earlier policy permitting men to take women's jobs at women's rates; that is, pay was linked to the job, not to the sex of the person who held it.

[69]The clause requiring women to receive men's pay when they took men's jobs in the future (n. 64) may have represented a victory for women in this debate or it may have been

Particular circumstances—the company's efforts to cut costs, to keep or expand its market share, and to weaken the union—had combined to heighten class conflict, and gender was an integral part of this struggle. A conception of sexual difference and hierarchy had been embedded in the production process and had on the surface the tacit approval of management and workers. Reclassification made sexual difference an explicit issue and exposed different conceptions of gender among male and female workers and managers as each group pursued its class and gender interests. It revealed the contradictory and convoluted reasoning behind the allocation of jobs by sex in the first place. Once the reasoning and assumptions had been challenged, gender conflict emerged. Men and women now understood and defined their interests differently. For at least some women, reclassification disassembled what had formerly been viewed as a natural association between jobs and pay. These women do not appear to have attacked the idea of occupational segregation altogether. Reclassification gave women a new experience by which to evaluate their situations and to position themselves vis-a-vis work and men.[70]

Conclusion

All workers were subordinated at Philco. The working conditions, the unbearable heat, the seasonality and layoffs, the monotony of the jobs, and the company's efforts to weaken or destroy the union all testified to their exploitation.[71] Philco managers also constructed a rigid system of occupational segregation that expressed a belief in dichotomous, hierarchical sexual differences. These same assumptions were reflected in aspects of union operation and structure. This conception of gender difference had power because of management's class position to impose it and also because most, although not all, men and women workers accepted its basic premise that men and women do different things. Beliefs in gender differences combined with other concerns and identities (such as family roles and responsibilities, worries about the quality of one's work life and the integrity of the union, and plans for the future) to create a measure of fluidity in workers' outlooks and experiences. Spe-

---

a victory for men, if they thought that such a clause would make it less likely that women would be substituted for men. Evidence is not clear, but I believe the clause was added around 1943, when Philco converted to war production.

[70]It should be noted that there probably were men and women who did not pay much attention even to this issue.

[71]Their interpretations and understandings of their class position are part of a longer story.

cific gender meanings could also vary. Most men and women seem to have taken sexual difference for granted and accepted the sexual division of labor at the plant, yet they might not necessarily have agreed on where the appropriate boundary between them was.

The events of 1937 and 1938 unglued the plant's occupational structure and exposed the fact that the location of the boundary between men's and women's jobs had been arbitrary. The notion of sexual difference now became salient and contested. Philco management wanted to adjust the boundary between men's and women's work for its own benefit; men and women, each intent on protecting their jobs and getting more pay, disagreed over the importance of sex in the allocation of jobs. Once a particular set of gender meanings was undermined and men and women identified different interests allied to particular meanings, gender conflict emerged.

The faces of gender were many at Philco. They were sculpted by the system of occupational segregation and workers' varied experiences at the plant and elsewhere. The visages of gender dimmed and sharpened over the course of daily life within the plant, but became the focus of attention in the midst of reclassification. An analysis of gender at Philco suggests the complex interconnections of occupational segregation, dichotomous beliefs about men and women, and the actual unities and variations in men's and women's ideas, experiences, and interests.

CHAPTER FOURTEEN

Time out of Mind: The UAW's Response to Female Labor Laws and Mandatory Overtime in the 1960s

Nancy Gabin

In April 1970 the United Auto Workers (UAW) broke with nearly fifty years of consensus within the labor movement and endorsed the Equal Rights Amendment (ERA). One month later, UAW vice president Olga Madar told the Senate Subcommittee on the ERA that the auto union favored "equal treatment for men and women" and sought the removal of "all legal impediments to the equal treatment of Americans, regardless of sex." Although scholars have noted the UAW's maverick move, they have overlooked the significance of this action. How did the UAW, a union in a male-dominated industry and with a membership largely male, come to play such a crucial role in the modern women's rights movement? To what extent did the UAW's public stance on the ERA reflect or depend on the views of union members of either sex? How did the UAW come to endorse not simply the principle of gender equality but a particular vision of gender equality, one that demanded that women and men be treated as alike rather than as different?[1]

An early version of this essay was delivered at the Seventh Berkshire Conference on the History of Women, Wellesley College, June 21, 1987. I thank fellow panelists Margaret Rose and Carol Groneman for their helpful comments and suggestions. I also thank Ava Baron and the anonymous reviewers of this volume for their criticism as well as their encouragement.

[1] UAW, *Proceedings, Twenty-second Constitutional Convention*, April 1970, 280; Catharine Stimpson, ed., *Women and the "Equal Rights" Amendment: Senate Subcommittee Hearings on the Constitutional Amendment, 91st Congress* (New York: R. R. Bowker, 1972), 210. Most studies of the women's movement in the 1960s and 1970s do mention the role of UAW activists in the formation of the National Organization for Women (NOW) or refer to the union's early endorsement of the ERA, but none of these works pursues the question of unions' or union women's participation in the movement. See Myra Ferree and Beth Hess, *Controversy and Coalition: The New Feminist Movement* (Boston: Twayne, 1985); Jo Freeman, *The Politics of Women's Liberation* (New York: Longman, 1975); Cynthia Harrison, *On Account of Sex: The Politics of Women's Issues, 1945–1968*

Neither fixed nor static, the UAW's perspective on gender equality in the workplace shifted in the years following its formation in 1935. But although the union formally endorsed equal treatment as a strategy for achieving gender equality in the workplace as early as the late 1940s it was not until the 1960s that policy was fully made practice. High employment and passage of Title VII of the 1964 Civil Rights Act raised women's expectations and subverted the authority of a sexual division of labor that assumed women's inferiority to men. These trends coalesced around the issues of compulsory overtime, which increased in the 1960s, and state laws limiting the number of hours women might work. Overtime had different meanings and implications for the men and women in the auto industry. Women, who represented 14 percent of the UAW's membership in the 1960s, shared men's distaste for compulsory overtime, especially if their often heavy domestic responsibilities conflicted with the obligation to work additional hours. But in states with laws limiting the number of hours women could be employed, women often were exempt from overtime requirements. Rather than see this exemption as a status to be enjoyed, increasing numbers of women came to regard it as an obstacle to larger paychecks, better jobs, and, ultimately, gender equality. As complaints about the assignment of overtime hours surfaced, the UAW Women's Department mobilized and gave vent to female discontent at the local level. Placing the overtime issue in the context of its twenty-year fight against sexually discriminatory employment practices, the department incorporated it into a critique of all state female labor laws which then became the basis for the UAW's litigative and legislative campaign to undermine women's hours and weight-lifting laws and to assert the superseding power of Title VII of the 1964 Civil Rights Act.[2]

Examination of the different responses among women and men in the UAW to the issue of protective labor legislation generally and hours limitation laws specifically offers a historical context for contemporary debate over strategies to obtain gender equality in the workplace. As conflict over pregnancy disability leaves, comparable worth, and the Sears

---

(Berkeley: University of California Press, 1987); Judith Hole and Ellen Levine, *Rebirth of Feminism* (New York: Quadrangle, 1971). The few treatments of women in unions and the contemporary feminist movement usually begin with the formation of the Coalition of Labor Union Women in 1974. For an exception, see Diane Balser, *Sisterhood and Solidarity: Feminism and Labor in Modern Times* (Boston: South End Press, 1987), 87–216.

[2]Bureau of Labor Statistics, *Employment and Earnings, United States, 1909–75*, Bulletin no. 1312–10 (Washington, D.C.: U.S. Government Printing Office, 1976), 299. In 1964 forty states and the District of Columbia had laws specifying maximum daily or weekly hours for women only in one or more occupations or industries. There was much diversity among the states in the character and scope of this coverage. For a detailed summary of women's hours laws, see U.S. Women's Bureau, *1969 Handbook on Women Workers*, Bulletin no. 294 (Washington, D.C.: U.S. Government Printing Office, 1969), 270–73.

case indicate, feminists are torn between demanding either special treatment for women in the work force or equal treatment with men. Women in the UAW wrestled with the same dilemma, but did not find either approach absolutely satisfying. Although the UAW was one of the first unions to break with the past and endorse a policy of sex-blind treatment for women in the workplace, it had not yet fully abandoned other commitments to gender difference and gender hierarchy. The UAW's response to compulsory overtime, a feature of employment in which men and women had an interest, demonstrates the limits of its perspective on gender equality and its impact on all workers regardless of sex.[3]

The UAW's shifting perspective on gender equality is best understood in the context of a series of attacks on the sexual division of labor dating back to the union's origins in the 1930s. A high degree of occupational segregation by sex historically characterized the structure and organization of work in the auto industry. Women were employed principally in the upholstery departments of auto body and assembly plants and in the manufacture of small parts and accessories. Although there was a certain degree of similarity between women's jobs and some men's jobs, few recognized or admitted it, and the first collective bargaining agreements between auto producers and the UAW simply codified the pervasive practice of sexual differentiation. World War II disturbed the UAW's equanimity with regard to the sexual division of labor. The massive influx of women into the plants made ambiguous the once-rigid boundaries between men's and women's work and provided the resources for a challenge to sexually discriminatory employment practices. Collective action in the interest of gender equity took place during the period of reconversion to peacetime production at the end of World War II, when, to protest wholesale dismissals, women unionists challenged the validity of sex-based job classifications and seniority lists. Although too few changes occurred in time to enable most women to retain their wartime jobs, the idea that industrial unionism was incompatible with any distinctions among workers on the basis of

[3]For discussion of the dilemma of defining gender equality in the workplace, see Ava Baron, "Feminist Legal Strategies: The Powers of Difference," in *Analyzing Gender: A Handbook of Social Science Research*, ed. Beth Hess and Myra Marx Ferree, 474–503 (Newbury Park, Calif.: Sage, 1987); Alice Kessler-Harris, "The Just Price, the Free Market, and the Value of Women," *Feminist Studies*, 14 (Summer 1988), 235–50; Ruth Milkman, "Women's History and the Sears Case," *Feminist Studies*, 12 (Summer 1986), 375–400; and Joan W. Scott, "The Sears Case," in *Gender and the Politics of History* (New York: Columbia University Press, 1988), 167–77. On the origins of labor's support for protective legislation and opposition to the ERA, see Nancy Cott, *The Grounding of Modern Feminism* (New Haven: Yale University Press, 1987), 115–42; Alice Kessler-Harris, *Out to Work: A History of Wage-Earning Women in the United States* (New York: Oxford University Press, 1982), 180–214; and Susan Lehrer, *Origins of Protective Labor Legislation for Women, 1905–1925* (Albany: SUNY Press, 1987), 141–84.

sex survived and was embodied in the UAW's official opposition after World War II to the inclusion in contracts of sex-based wage rates, job classifications, and seniority lists.[4]

Despite the UAW's rhetorical opposition to gender discrimination, however, several factors limited progress in the immediate postwar period. Employers opposed any union-initiated transformation of the structure and organization of work, especially one that would deprive them of a rationale for a two-tier wage system. Male union leaders also were inconsistent in advancing the principle of gender equality by seeking to erase distinctions between women and men. Men at all levels of the UAW generally continued to think about the organization of work in auto plants in terms of gender hierarchy, regarding the elimination of sex-based wage scales or job classifications as a threat to (higher) male standards. The UAW successfully pressed for some changes in the late 1940s and early 1950s, particularly with regard to discrimination against married women and unequal pay for equal work, but the sexual division of labor remained largely intact.

Established in 1944, the UAW Women's Department was the principal proponent of abolishing sexually discriminatory employment practices. The department's reinstatement after the war demonstrated that the UAW to a certain extent no longer deserved the sobriquet "no woman's land." Women carved out space for themselves during and after World War II, establishing at least a presence for themselves at the international level and making themselves even more visible at the local level as stewards and shop committee representatives. The department and its supporters in various local and regional union women's committees, however, were never sanguine about the prospects for thoroughgoing change in the status of women in the auto industry, and they were disheartened to find themselves engaged in the 1950s in another defensive battle to save women's jobs. The combination of intraindustry trends—automation, decentralization, corporate mergers—and a series of economic recessions exacerbated the persistent problem of irregular employment for auto workers in these years. Men and women suffered, but, depending on local circumstances, women were made especially vulnerable in times of layoffs and job dislocations by the still widespread existence of sex-based seniority lists and job classifications. Restricted to an already small number of jobs, women found themselves on the street while men with lesser seniority remained on or even were newly hired for jobs that women were capable of performing. Women seemed

[4]Nancy Gabin, " 'They Have Placed a Penalty on Womanhood': The Protest Actions of Women Auto Workers in Detroit-Area UAW Locals during Reconversion, 1945–1947," *Feminist Studies*, 8 (Summer 1982), 369–78.

to have become, in the words of one observer, the "shock absorbers" for the problem of layoffs in the auto industry.[5]

As developments in the auto industry reduced the number of so-called women's jobs in the mid- to late 1950s, the issue of women's place in auto plants was raised anew and sparked a second wave of challenges to the sexual division of labor. State laws regulating the employment of women appeared to the Women's Department to intensify rather than alleviate women's plight because they reinforced occupational segregation by sex. The opposition of the department to protective legislation reflected its growing concern about the power of the idea of gender difference to limit women's opportunities in the auto industry. According to Lillian Hatcher, assistant director of the Women's Department in those years, the office and its supporters began to question the benefits of female labor laws after World War II, when states reimposed restrictions on the employment of women which had been suspended for the duration of the war. As employers, citing protective laws, dismissed wartime female employees and replaced them with men with lesser seniority, Hatcher and others concluded that "to say that she wanted to be classified forever as a female worker was hurting the working woman . . . because there were many jobs that were tagged male occupations that women could perform as well as any other person." Female labor laws, Hatcher explains, were regarded as "negat[ing] opportunity for women to move up into better paying jobs and to receive equal pay for equal work." Concern in the 1950s about the vulnerability of women to job dislocations reinforced the Women's Department's negative view of female labor laws. Caroline Davis, director of the UAW Women's Department from 1948 until her retirement in the early 1970s, voiced frustration with the legal obstacles to gender equality in her report to the 1957 UAW convention. Hailing the elimination of sexually discriminatory features from many collective bargaining agreements, Davis pointed to state laws that undermined the UAW's efforts. A law limiting the number of hours a woman could be employed or the number of pounds women could lift might appear "liberal toward working women," Davis explained, but "is in reality often used by unscrupulous employers to discriminate against women." Such laws, she maintained, "are being used effectively when employers are seeking ways to prevent women from being upgraded, hired or retained on their jobs."[6]

[5]Robert A. Zaban, "Internal Union Frictions Created by a Job Security Issue: A Case Study of a UAW Internal Dispute Involving Seniority Division by Sex" (master's thesis, Purdue University, 1964), 106. On the late 1940s and 1950s, see Nancy Gabin, *Feminism in the Labor Movement: Women and the United Auto Workers, 1935–1975* (Ithaca: Cornell University Press, 1990), 143–87.

[6]Interview with Lillian Hatcher, in "The Twentieth-Century Trade Union Woman: Vehicle for Social Change," Oral History Project, Institute of Labor and Industrial Relations,

As local unionists confronted the problem of unemployment in the auto industry and the circumscribed sphere for women, many came to concur with the perspective and vision of the Women's Department. Reconsidering their commitment to the sexual division of labor and the principle of gender hierarchy on which it was based, an increasing number of men as well as women endorsed equal treatment as a strategy for improving the position of women in the auto labor force. Several factors facilitated this trend. For one, certain developments steadily invalidated the assumptions on which gender hierarchy generally and protective labor laws for women specifically were based. The greater use of hoists and conveyer belts, for example, had made auto jobs less physically demanding. The increasing presence of married women in the auto labor force and elsewhere also subverted notions about woman's proper place and relation to wage labor; 68 percent of all female auto workers in 1960 were married. Too, in contrast to the period of demobilization and reconversion after World War II, in the 1950s, women employed in auto plants could not be regarded as temporary interlopers whose claims to their jobs had limited legitimacy. Their status as workers and union members commanded attention that World War II defense workers never enjoyed. Signifying the shift in attitude within the UAW, several local unions pressed for modification or elimination of separate seniority lists, departmental or occupational group seniority agreements, and sex-based job classifications to afford women workers access to a greater number and variety of jobs. The UAW also made a single seniority list a central demand in its 1955 negotiations with General Motors. In these ways, auto unionists of both sexes demonstrated their greater commitment to gender equality and sex-blind treatment in the workplace.[7]

The UAW did not, however, make a concerted and thoroughgoing effort to secure equity for women in the mid- to late 1950s. Not everyone who sympathized with the plight of women endorsed equal treatment as a strategy for improving the position of women in the auto labor force. The pervasiveness and extent of occupational segregation by sex made such women and men circumspect in their analyses and commitments. Fearing that women would lose even their limited place without the protection afforded by state laws and sex-based job classifications and seniority lists, some believed it was better for the UAW to defend and consolidate women's sphere than to erase its already constricted boundaries. In contrast to the Women's Department, which regarded any asser-

University of Michigan, 83; Women's Bureau Report, *President's Report to the Sixteenth Constitutional Convention, UAW, April 7–12, 1957,* 181D.

[7]For more detailed discussion of these efforts, see Gabin, *Feminism in the Labor Movement,* 176–80.

tion of gender difference as an unacceptable affirmation of gender inequality, these proponents rejected sex-blind treatment as detrimental to women. And by no means did a majority or even a sizable minority of auto unionists reevaluate their views on occupational segregation by sex and the marginal status of women in the UAW. In a period of unstable employment, many men worried about their own job security, rejecting any claims made by women for "male" jobs and denying the comparability of men's and women's work. The concerns of those who endorsed the idea of gender equality but worried about the negative impact on women of sex-blind treatment tended to reinforce or make credible the views of men who still essentially believed in the separate and unequal status of women.[8]

In the absence of a consensus about the meaning of gender equality, the UAW did little more in the 1950s than pledge to fulfill the democratic promise of industrial unionism and challenge sex discrimination. Confusion over goals and purposes did allow the UAW Women's Department to play a maverick role in the 1950s. Auto union women, for example, were among those attending the National Manpower Council meetings in the mid-1950s who contended that "the existence of differential legislation provides employers with a justification for hiring men for work which women have in fact done or could undertake." But conflict over the ERA had long polarized the women's movement and organized labor steadfastly refused to consider that protective laws might discriminate against women. The Women's Department, therefore, tolerated the inconsistency of simultaneously denouncing the ERA as "a pernicious and anti-social piece of legislation which will perpetuate exploitation and discrimination" while seeking at least to debate the issue of protective legislation within and without the union.[9]

In the 1960s high employment and the potential power of Title VII of the 1964 Civil Rights Act altered the context for the struggle to expand women's access to auto jobs and provided the basis for a unified UAW assault on state laws regulating the employment of women. Title VII, the equal employment opportunity section of the law, prohibits discrimination based on sex as well as race, color, religion, and national origin in all terms and conditions or privileges of employment. The Women's Department was hopeful that Title VII would mean the death of protective labor legislation. Shortly after the law became effective, Caroline Davis asked the Equal Employment Opportunity Commission (EEOC),

[8]For discussion of these debates and tensions within the UAW in this period, see ibid., 181–87.
[9]National Manpower Council, *Womanpower* (New York: Columbia University Press, 1957), 336; UAW brief on the ERA, n.d. (1946), 12, in UAW Research Department Collection, box 11, folder 14, Walter P. Reuther Library, Archives of Labor and Urban Affairs (ALUA), Wayne State University.

the investigatory and conciliatory agency for Title VII complaints, to issue, "a policy saying that state laws affecting women cannot be used as a justification for discrimination against women." Women's hopes for prompt change were soon deflated. In a set of guidelines issued in November 1965, the commission skirted the question whether the Civil Rights Act conflicted with state laws and essentially declared the federal law subordinate to state law, ruling that "the Commission will not find any unlawful employment practice where an employer's refusal to hire women for certain work is based on a state law which precludes the employment for such work, provided that the employer is acting in good faith and that the law in question is reasonably adapted to protect rather than to subject them to discrimination." In April 1966 the EEOC modified its position somewhat by allowing charges that state laws were discriminatory but warned that it would not rule on the merits of such cases.[10]

Advocates of gender equality in the UAW and like-minded organizations picked up the gauntlet laid down by the EEOC. While unions such as the International Union of Electrical Workers (IUE) pressed for judicial and administrative recognition of the applicability of comparable worth under federal antidiscriminatory statutes, the UAW Women's Department sought ways to confirm the irrelevance and illegality of state laws that applied only to women workers.[11] Caroline Davis did not have to look too long or too far for evidence that female labor laws disadvantaged women in auto plants. At the local level, a combination of factors produced growing discontent with what many people regarded as obstacles to equal opportunity for women. Employment in such basic industries as autos increased steadily after the early 1960s, but industrial expansion did not benefit women as much as men. Auto manufacturers hired men for new jobs, denied women transfers to new or better-paying jobs, and denied women overtime hours and premium pay. Women's relative sense of deprivation was intensified by the greater legitimacy accorded the idea of equal employment opportunity by passage of the Equal Pay Act and the Civil Rights Act. Female labor laws were seen as the source of these inequities. By mobilizing and giving vent to these concerns, the Women's Department enhanced the status within the UAW of

[10]Text of statement by Stephen Schlossberg to EEOC at public hearings, May 2, 1967, in Walter P. Reuther Collection, box 118, folder 12, ALUA; EEOC guidelines, Nov. 22, 1965, quoted in Freeman, *Politics of Women's Liberation*, 186; text of Davis speech, Aug. 19–20, 1965, in Women's Department–Lillian Hatcher Collection, box 2, folder 4, ALUA. In its April 1966 policy statement, the EEOC did promise to advise women of the time limits for filing a lawsuit challenging the statutes and reserved the right to participate in a suit as *amicus curiae*.

[11]For union action in regard to comparable worth, see Winn Newman and Jeanne M. Vonhof, " 'Separate but Equal'—Job Segregation and Pay Equity in the Wake of *Gunther*," *University of Illinois Law Review*, 1981, 269–331.

its own goals and purposes and laid the foundation for an assault on state laws regulating the employment of women.

Although their applicability remained in doubt, the Equal Pay Act and Title VII did offer women workers in the auto industry and elsewhere a means of contesting discrimination and occupational segregation by sex after 1963. When employers cited state weight-lifting laws as the reason for denying women recalls, transfers, and promotions, the passed-over women cited the standard of gender equality implicit in these federal statutes. For example, when approximately 150 women employed as assemblers in the electronics division of Goodyear Aerospace in Akron, Ohio, were laid off in August 1966, management cited that state's weight-lifting law in refusing to allow the women to exercise seniority and displace lower-seniority men on other jobs. Although the job to which the women sought transfer did not require constant lifting of parts of excessive weight, the company maintained that even the potential for abuse precluded their placement in it. Local 856 officers and the women in turn emphasized the greater importance of providing female workers with equal opportunity for employment and questioned the validity of the state law.[12] A similar situation developed at the Apex Machine and Tool Company in Dayton, Ohio, when a woman requested transfer to a job as a turret lathe operator, to which her seniority entitled her and which paid a minimum of $2.66 per hour. The company allowed her to transfer only into hand mill operation, a female-dominated classification that paid a maximum of $2.55 per hour, because turret lathe operators occasionally lifted stock weighing more than twenty-five pounds and sometimes sharpened and dressed tools with emery or carborundum wheels, actions that were forbidden by state laws for female employees. Concerned by the way in which female labor laws contradicted standards of equality embedded both in the collective bargaining agreement and in federal law, Local 1040 appealed the woman's grievance to arbitration.[13]

Complaints about the adverse consequences of state laws restricting the number of hours that women could be employed also increased in this period. To meet the growing demands of the Defense Department, American consumers, and corporate planners in the 1960s, plant managers in the auto and aerospace industries increased production by regularly scheduling overtime hours for blue collar workers. Average weekly overtime hours for production workers in the auto industry, for example, increased from 2.6 in 1960 to 6.2 in 1965; between 1961 and 1970, the

[12]Grievance A-4877, Sept. 6, 1966; W. H. Smith to Caroline Davis, Oct. 27, 1966; Hatcher report of meeting of Local 856, Nov. 29, 1966; Smith to Hatcher, Dec. 9, 1966; all in Women's Department–Hatcher Collection, box 8, folder 13.

[13]Arbitrator's decision in case no. 213 A-7, Sept. 30, 1965, and Davis to Irving Bluestone, Nov. 17, 1965, both in Reuther Collection, box 172, folder 13. The arbitrator denied the local's appeal, citing the state law regulating the employment of women.

figure did not fall below 3.2 hours. As the scheduling of overtime for plant workers became both more pervasive and more persistent in the mid-1960s, more and more women confronted the negative consequences of legal restrictions on the number of hours they could work in a day or a week. The most frequent complaint was not merely that male co-workers had the opportunity for additional income but that the men were receiving premium pay for the extra hours. Women employed as inspectors at the Ternstedt plant in Elyria, Ohio, complained that whenever management scheduled overtime, male inspectors received three hours' pay for the extra two hours of work, but because state law forbade the employment of women for more than eight hours a day, they did not have the opportunity for the overtime duty and the premium pay. "Over a period of time this could amount to considerable earnings to female employees," Renilda Dougherty pointed out. "This practice has been continuing for the past month," she added, "on an average of two or three times a week." Women denied overtime at GM's Fisher Body plant in St. Louis filed grievances contending that the collective bargaining agreement forbade such discrimination on the basis of sex and that Title VII superseded a Missouri law restricting women workers to a nine-hour day.[14]

While the relative deprivation of take-home pay was reasonable cause for complaint, there were even more onerous consequences of hours-limitation laws. Women employed at a GM plant in Michigan, for example, were laid off because management temporarily required daily overtime in the department in which they worked and state law forbade the employment of women in excess of nine hours a day. A less obvious and more insidious result was the denial to women of transfer and promotional opportunities on the grounds that the jobs occasionally entailed overtime. In 1965 four women working on spring assembly in the cushion department, one of the mere handful of jobs to which women were assigned at the Fisher Body plant in Pontiac, Michigan, sought transfer on the basis of their seniority to better-paying jobs in the all-male paint department. When management ignored the women's transfer applications and instead hired new male employees without seniority for that classification in the paint department, the women filed grievances. In the grievance hearing Local 596 admitted that management had not violated

[14]Bureau of Labor Statistics, *Employment and Earnings, United States, 1909–1975*, Bulletin no. 1312–10 (Washington, D.C.: U.S. Government Printing Office, 1975), 304; John Fenlon, "Patterns in Overtime Hours and Premium Pay," *Monthly Labor Review*, 92 (October 1969), 42–46; James R. Wetzel, "Long Hours and Premium Pay," *Monthly Labor Review*, 88 (September 1965), 1083–88; EEOC Charge of Discrimination Form, May 3, 1968, in Reuther Collection, box 119, folder 10; Roy Hartzell to Stephen Schlossberg, July 31, 1966, in Women's Department–Hatcher Collection, box 2, folder 5; EEOC charges, in Reuther Collection, box 172, folder 15; Bernard Ashe to Davis, May 9, 1969, in Women's Department–Hatcher Collection, box 3, folder 6.

the contract, which forbade discrimination on the basis of sex only insofar as intradepartmental, not interdepartmental, transfers were concerned. Local officers also acknowledged management's reminder that when women's upholstery jobs were moved from the cushion department to another plant in the mid-1950s, the union had agreed not to allow the women to transfer to other departments in the plant. But, the local contended, Title VII now superseded past agreements and practices, and women's right to transfer ought to be respected. After management rejected the grievance, the women filed a complaint with the EEOC which investigated the charges in January 1966. Confronted with the fact that only one woman had been newly hired since 1958 and that not one black woman was currently employed in the plant, GM maintained that state laws were the basis for denying women access to all-male departments either as transfers or as new hires. GM admitted that women could perform some jobs within those departments without violating laws that regulated weight-lifting, hours per week, and workplace safety, but their inability to work overtime contravened managerial prerogatives in organizing production.[15]

Women who contested female labor laws did not always enjoy the support of their fellow union members. After Local 101 negotiated the elimination of separate seniority lists for women and men employed at the Standard Screw Company to comply with Title VII, management laid off women while retaining men with lesser seniority on jobs that women could perform. Plant management denied the grievance filed by the local in behalf of the women, citing Ohio's weight-lifting law as justification for its refusal to recall the laid-off female employees. Infuriated by both the indifference of male local officers to their dilemma as well as the smug attitude of their employer, the women demonstrated outside the plant. The demonstration, the chairman of the local bargaining committee complained to Caroline Davis, "was embarrassing to both management and the union."[16] Six women laid off by another Ohio company

[15]Marge Liddy to Hatcher, Nov. 30, 1965; minutes of Appeal Committee hearing, Dec. 16, 1965; Richard Graham, "EEOC Decision in Liddy et al. v. Fisher Body," Feb. 2, 1966, all in Reuther Collection, box 102, folder 12; Hatcher to Davis, Apr. 12, 1966, in Women's Department–Hatcher Collection, box 2, folder 5. The EEOC found reasonable cause to believe that GM did discriminate on the basis of sex in matters of hiring and promotion and that GM was "—perhaps unintentionally—maintaining a wage rate differential structure based on sex by refusing to open lines of progression to women so as to qualify for higher rates of pay." The aggrieved women had sought transfer in part because wage rates in the cushion department were the lowest in the plant. The IUE used a similar line of reasoning in its landmark case against Westinghouse. See Newman and Vonhof, " 'Separate but Equal' "; and Ruth G. Blumrosen, "Wage Discrimination, Job Segregation, and Title VII of the Civil Rights Act of 1964," *University of Michigan Journal of Law Reform*, 12 (Spring 1979), 397–502.

[16]Ray Webber to Davis, Oct. 19, 1966; Bernard Ashe to Dorothy Haener, Dec. 1, 1966; Haener to Mike Friedman, June 19, 1967; Ashe to John Fillion, July 14, 1967, all in Reuther Collection, box 172, folder 17.

protested when they were forced to accept jobs paying less than those in a higher classification to which their seniority entitled them but which management claimed required frequent lifting of weights in excess of twenty-five pounds. The women complained that there were jobs within the classification which did not require frequent lifting of heavy weights and that their seniority rights were being violated. Local officers, however, delayed processing the women's grievances in deference to the concerns of men with less seniority who would have to take lower-paid jobs and to the complaints of other men with equal or greater seniority who believed that they would have to take less desirable jobs in the classification, such as those entailing some lifting, to accommodate the women. To counter the women's assertion of their rights to equal opportunity, the men wrapped up the self-interested basis for their opposition in the ideological slogan that "women's place was in the home" rather than at work. Eventually an international representative from the Region 2A office negotiated with the company to allow women to perform seven of seventy-one jobs in the classification which did not require the lifting and moving of parts exceeding twenty-five pounds in weight. Men working in the area remained hostile, an indication of the extent to which any serious challenge to occupational segregation by sex could potentially intensify gender conflict on shop floors and in union offices alike. Even the international representative was miffed, reporting that he had received "quite a bit of criticism from male employees for 'sticking my nose in the matter.' "[17]

Some women who protested the treatment accorded them were vindicated in the grievance procedure. Sometimes the overtime hours or weight-lifting requirements did not exceed state limits. A few persistent union representatives and receptive employers also negotiated settlements that enabled women to work in compliance with state law. Women in one auto parts plant in Ohio, for example, were unable to work the two daily overtime hours required of fellow male employees on the weekday shift because Ohio mandated an eight-hour day for female employees. The law, however, did allow a six-day week, so the union convinced management that women could work an eight-hour shift on Sunday to share the available overtime. In other instances, state labor officials waived laws if in the judgment of all concerned the terms and conditions of employment were not too excessive. It is difficult, if not impossible, to determine how many grievances involving female labor laws were thus resolved to the advantage of women workers. We also cannot know how many more women might have benefited if employers and union representatives had been more supportive of women's interests and flexible

[17]William Garnes to Ray Ross, June 9, 1965, in Reuther Collection, box 252, folder 26.

and creative in organizing work. The nature and number of complaints about unresolved grievances which appear in the records of local unions, UAW departments, and union officers suggest that women experienced frustration more often than satisfaction at this level in their pursuit of equal employment opportunity.[18]

Appealing a grievance to arbitration, however, offered no greater likelihood of redress for women. Before 1965, arbitrators asserted either the propriety of employers in complying with state laws or the subordination of collective bargaining agreements to state laws with which they were in conflict. After Title VII of the Civil Rights Act became effective in July 1965, arbitrators either ruled that sex was a bona fide occupational qualification for jobs that occasionally required overtime or weight-lifting in excess of state regulations, thus supporting employers' defense of hiring and placement practices, or simply claimed that they had no power to resolve conflicts between state and federal law. Despite their dim prospects, more and more women pressed union officers to challenge management and insist on equal access to jobs regardless of hours or weight-lifting limitations. Local union officials who were sensitive to women's concerns and even those who were not but who worried about union liability for discrimination came to see the grievance procedure as a dead end and wondered what avenue to follow in pursuit of gender equity. Local 780 officers, for example, protested when a woman accused them of collaborating with management to deny her grievance demanding an overtime assignment. They were sympathetic to women's plight, they explained, but felt that the grievance procedure was pointless because Ohio law superseded collective bargaining agreements. "It is our opinion that the state law is not permitting the women to work overtime," the local president maintained, "and we feel that the women in specific occupations and those in this department could work the ten hours without creating a hardship." "We definitely are in a bind on this problem," he commented.[19]

The increased agitation at the local level on the issue of female labor laws served the purposes of the Women's Department in several ways. First, the general expansion of employment in the auto industry as well as the more frequent scheduling of overtime in the plants provided a timely platform on which to launch a challenge to protective labor legislation for women. Second, the greater grass-roots discontent helped legitimize the department's twenty-year-old call for union action against the

[18]Davis to Leonard Woodcock, May 20, 1958, in Leonard Woodcock Collection, box 25, folder 7, ALUA; Hartzell to Schlossberg, July 31, 1966, in Women's Department–Hatcher Collection, box 2, folder 5; Haener to Davis, Oct. 25, 1968, in Reuther Collection, box 172, folder 20.

[19]Schlossberg statement to EEOC, May 2, 1967, in Reuther Collection, box 118, folder 12; Ira Ison to William Hodges, Oct. 28, 1968, in ibid., box 119, folder 10.

laws. International leaders understood the power of the new federal laws finally to eliminate such blatantly discriminatory contract features as separate seniority lists, sex-based job classifications, and sex-differentiated wage scales. Within months of the effective date of the Civil Rights Act, for example, the International Executive Board (IEB) discussed the implications of Title VII for the treatment of women in the seniority provisions of collective bargaining agreements and agreed that each international representative who was responsible for servicing local unions would be obligated to review those provisions and "promptly" initiate efforts to "negotiate corrections" if violations of the law were found. Many top union leaders, however, seemed unaware of or insensitive to the problem of protective labor legislation insofar as it concerned workers in plants under their jurisdiction. Caroline Davis complained to Irving Bluestone, Reuther's administrative assistant, in November 1965 that Ray Ross, the director of Region 2A, "didn't approve of us doing anything about the state laws. He believes they protect women and that's that. I did my best to enlighten him over the phone," Davis reported, "but the most I could get out of him was that 'of course he didn't want to see discrimination practiced against any one, male or female.' " By the fall of 1966, however, local discontent in regard to Title VII and female labor laws had become so widespread that it reached the offices of the regional directors and department chiefs who together occupied the majority of seats on the IEB. The sheer number of complaints had overwhelmed local union officers, compelling international leaders to confront and devise policies and strategies for dealing with the obstacles posed by state laws regulating the employment of women.[20]

Many shared the view of Stephen Schlossberg, a UAW attorney, who believed that grievance and arbitration procedures were "fruitless" because managements inevitably claimed that they were bound not to employ women in violation of state laws. The EEOC complaint process was not much more satisfying. On the one hand, its procedural deadlines were not synchronized with those of the union grievance procedure; women could and did fall through the cracks. On the other hand, although the EEOC might find evidence of discrimination, it would not overrule state laws in this period. Warning that there were no "guarantees of success," Schlossberg nevertheless urged the UAW to take the EEOC at its word and seek a test case "to litigate all the way to the Supreme Court" if necessary. "Lose or win," Schlossberg asserted, the UAW should "clear the air." A second method advanced was to seek

---

[20]Reuther to Officers and IEB Members, Jan. 21, 1966, in Reuther Collection, box 79, folder 3; Davis to Bluestone, Nov. 17, 1965, in ibid., box 172, folder 13; Tony Connole to Bluestone, Nov. 11, 1966; Bluestone to Schlossberg, Dec. 5, 1966; and Bluestone to Connole, Dec. 12, 1966, in ibid., box 81, folder 15.

the amendment or repeal of the objectionable state codes, those "undesirable relics of a past era." Both approaches received the endorsement of a majority of IEB members. Most immediately, in 1967, the Women's Department participated in campaigns in two states containing large concentrations of female auto unionists to amend hours laws so that women might work overtime; the department also lobbied for repeal of Michigan's hour limitation law. Ten years earlier, Caroline Davis had been chastised by international officers for stating to women in an Ohio local union that the UAW ought to seek amendment of that state's restrictive hours limitation law. The contrast with the same leaders' sanction of political activism after 1966 indicates the importance of local pressure in legitimizing the agenda of the Women's Department.[21]

The Women's Department's litigative and legislative efforts to challenge protective labor laws for women and to assert the power of Title VII placed its leaders in the vanguard of the renascent feminist movement. Department leaders and their supporters in the local and regional women's committees had endorsed sex-blind treatment as a strategy for achieving equality in the workplace for many years. Their rejection of the idea that gender differences required different treatment for women and men in society generally and in the labor market specifically coincided with the emerging view of nonunion people such as Betty Friedan that sex roles were not immutable and that the sameness of women and men should serve as the basis of sexual equality. It is not surprising, therefore, that Caroline Davis and Dorothy Haener were founders of NOW and that the UAW provided clerical services for the new organization. But UAW feminists at the same time placed themselves at odds with organized labor. The AFL-CIO was a leading antagonist of ERA forces, and its unwavering commitment to both female labor laws and the principle of protection implicit in the legislation caused problems for those in the labor movement who were questioning the necessity, utility, and wisdom of such coverage. Women unionists, for example, were scourged for joining an attack on protective labor legislation during the June 1966 meeting of the various state commissions on the status of women because they "created the impression that labor is either divided or no longer concerned about these labor standards." Out of loyalty to the labor movement and in recognition of the lack of consensus even within the UAW, the union withdrew from NOW in 1968. But the conflict inside the house of labor could not be resolved to the

[21]Schlossberg to Bluestone, Dec. 9, 1966, in Reuther Collection, box 81, folder 15; UAW, *President's Report to the Twenty-first Constitutional Convention, May 4–10, 1968*, pt. 2, 155–56; Davis to Woodcock, May 20, 1958, in Woodcock Collection, box 25, folder 7.

satisfaction of such union feminists as Davis and Haener, and open revolt was inevitable.[22]

The challenge to protective legislation for women workers was the principal strategy adopted by the UAW in the 1960s for securing equality of opportunity for women workers. The Equal Pay Act and Title VII made the elimination of blatant forms of sex discrimination from contracts not only easier but legally imperative. The October 1967 amendment of President Johnson's Executive Order 11246 to require federal contractors not to discriminate on the basis of sex and to undertake affirmative action programs to rectify the effects of past discrimination was another long-sought means of securing equality.[23] But more subtle forms of discrimination persisted. Departmental or occupational group seniority arrangements, for example, could be discriminatory in effect if not in intent by denying women equal access to employment. Occupational segregation by sex also masked wage disparities between male and female auto workers. These were difficult problems and the obstacles to solving them loomed large. On the one hand, narrow judicial and administrative interpretations of federal antidiscriminatory statutes were inadequate for a thoroughgoing attack on the sexual division of labor in the auto industry. But on the other hand, there was much evidence that men still regarded women as threats to wage standards and competitors for jobs. Since the prospects of securing the active support of the male majority for an extensive revision of woman's place in the industry were dim, the Women's Department focused its energy and resources on removing the impediments to equal opportunity posed by female labor laws. In a real sense, it seemed easier to press for change in the political arena outside the UAW than to mobilize enough enthusiasm and action within the organization to eliminate gender inequality in the labor market.

It is ironic that in deciding to take the path of least resistance, the Women's Department stumbled into a hornet's nest of controversy. The challenge to hours limitation laws was the most nettlesome issue. By seeking for women access to overtime hours and pay, those who advocated repeal of state statutes regulating the employment of women ap-

[22]Harrison, On Account of Sex, 37, 199–200, 205; Olya Margolin to Andrew Biemiller, quoted in ibid., 195; Leila Rupp and Verta Taylor, Survival in the Doldrums: The American Women's Rights Movement, 1945 to the 1960s (New York: Oxford University Press, 1987), 144–53. The UAW disaffiliated from the AFL-CIO in 1968 on account of differences over foreign policy, civil rights, organization drives, and other union and political issues. Although I have not found any direct evidence to support such an argument, it is possible that this action freed the UAW from any obligation to oppose the ERA and contributed to its endorsement of the amendment in 1970. See John Barnard, Walter Reuther and the Rise of the Auto Workers (Boston: Little, Brown, 1983), 177–98.

[23]Harrison, On Account of Sex, 198, 201–2; Freeman, Politics of Women's Liberation, 191.

peared to be working at cross-purposes with those in the UAW who demanded relief from mandatory overtime. The seemingly contradictory aims of the two forces within the UAW gave rise to debate principally among women over feminism and unionism. The most important and interesting critics of repeal believed that sex discrimination was wrong and that UAW ought to press for its elimination. Their challenge demonstrates the persistent divisions among UAW women over the meaning of gender equality.

The most concerted effort to challenge the drive for repeal of hours limitation laws was made by women of UAW Local 3. The local, which represented production workers at Chrysler's huge auto works in Hamtramck, Michigan, had a history of militancy on behalf of gender equality. The most notable instance occurred in the late 1950s, when, in response to the elimination of jobs held by eight hundred women, the local successfully pressed for the integration of women into traditionally male jobs. Some years later the local women's committee castigated Dodge Main management for denying women jobs in violation of Title VII and vowed to use union, state, and federal resources to "assert the rights of women as first-class human beings." The same women who mobilized collective actions to demand equal opportunity for women in hiring, however, so vehemently disagreed with the effort to repeal Michigan's hours limitation law that they joined forces with others in the state to lobby against repeal, filing a lawsuit for an injunction to stay implementation of a decision by the Michigan legislature to suspend the hours limitation statute.[24]

Local 3 women opposed repeal partly on feminist grounds and partly on class grounds. Women in unorganized occupations, they asserted, needed the protection against harsh working conditions which the state law provided. They also underscored the difficult situation in which even UAW women who were self-supporting heads of households with small children or invalid husbands would find themselves if they were compelled to work in excess of their regularly scheduled shifts. Local 3 women also argued, however, that the hours limitation law for women offered "a small measure of protection against inhuman work schedules," and that it should be retained only until legislation was passed that made overtime voluntary or until a voluntary overtime provision was incorporated into collective bargaining agreements. Repeal the hours law for women but overlook the need for a voluntary overtime provision, they warned, and all workers would be "left to the mercy of unscrupulous employers," who would demand more labor from their

[24]"Local 3 Women's Committee Protest Discrimination in Hiring of Women," *UAW Women's Department Special Bulletin*, January–February 1966, 5; Haener to Davis, Sept. 4, 1968, in Reuther Collection, box 172, folder 19; *Detroit News*, Dec. 28, 1968.

employees while laying off others or refusing to hire new, job-hungry workers to assume the increased production load. "How can we hope to see an end to compulsory overtime for all workers," asked Edith Fox of Local 3, "if we now favor repeal? How can we hope to realize our goal of a 30 hour week at 40 hours pay, when we insist on repeal of the 54 hour limit in exchange for no limits—resulting in possibly 10 or 12 hour days, six to seven day weeks?" The Women's Department, Local 3 activists charged, was playing a dangerous and destructive game, because repeal of the women's hours law would undermine rather than enhance efforts to achieve a voluntary overtime act and thus benefit employers at the expense of workers. The implication was that by condemning women to brutal working conditions, advocates of repeal were betraying not only feminism but unionism and class solidarity as well.[25]

Others in the UAW came forward to criticize the position taken by the Women's Department and by extension the international union. Emily Rosdolsky, an international staff member, indicated her distress about the campaign for repeal in a letter to Walter Reuther. Claiming that the poorest and most exploited working women would be the most affected by repeal, Rosdolsky noted that "the traditional concerns of the labor movement in this country and other countries for protecting women from excessively long hours of work is still valid," and warned that "it would be harmful to the image of the UAW if it seemingly ignores the interest of these working women to pursue what it believes to be in the interest of its own members." Rosdolsky echoed the concern of Local 3 women about the lack of legislative or contractual protection against compulsory overtime for all workers regardless of sex and urged Reuther not to advocate "the repeal of a law which shields at least women against such shocking work practices." Like the Local 3 group, Rosdolsky argued from a feminist position grounded in a working-class perspective. "Even though we would all prefer it if men enjoyed the same protection," she concluded, the principle of gender equality advanced by repeal would be cold comfort to a woman forced to work against her will for sixty or seventy hours a week.[26]

Supporters of the repeal effort were quick to poke holes in such arguments. Responsibility for the lack of voluntary overtime legislation and contract clauses, they noted, lay not with the UAW, which called for them, but with the state legislators and private employers who opposed them. A feminist with a working-class perspective, moreover, could support repeal. "Nothing is more disturbing," Dorothy Haener of the

[25]*Dodge Main News*, Nov. 23, 1968; Feb. 28, 1969; Dec. 6, 1969; and Mar. 7, 1970; "Attention: Women Members of Local 3," flyer, n.d. (February 1969), in Mildred Jeffrey Collection, box 42, folder 5, ALUA.
[26]Emily Rosdolsky to Reuther, Mar. 3, 1969, in Reuther Collection, box 119, folder 11.

Women's Department said in reference to Rosdolsky and the Local 3 Women's Committee, "than their ability to drip tears of blood . . . to retain protective laws for the overworked, overburdened, underpaid women while, without any indignation, they tacitly accept and ignore the refusal of employers to hire them on $3.50 an hour jobs using these same laws as justification." The critics of repeal, however, had raised an important question about the consequences of one strategy for achieving equality in the workplace. Advocates of sex-blind treatment had never adopted an extremist stance. *How to Be Equal Though Different— Working Women Today* read the title of a 1963 Women's Department pamphlet. Laws that "really are protective," stated Stephen Schlossberg in 1967, "need to be preserved." Legislation mandating separate restrooms, job modifications for pregnant workers, and maternity leaves were acceptable because they were based "on biological facts not stereotypes," he explained. But because these issues conflicted with the view that women and men were equal as human beings, they had been muted in the pursuit of gender equality and the elimination of female labor laws. The Local 3 women's committee and Emily Rosdolsky, however, forced opponents of female labor laws to confront such inconsistencies and to reassert their positions.[27]

In response to this challenge, advocates of repeal offered arguments and strategies that promoted class and gender interests simultaneously. The very existence of hours limitation laws for women only, they contended, divided workers and precluded solidarity. Moreover, Ann Lefebvre of Local 148 noted, employers and politicians tricked male workers into endorsing female labor laws as a defense of conventional gender ideology but then used the same laws to justify excessive compulsory overtime. "Who," she asked rhetorically, "is discriminated against? We the women with protective laws, or you, the men that make the laws and are penalized [if you] won't work ten hours a day, seven days a week?" Others argued for the extension of hours limitation laws to men as an expedient solution to the problem. "I don't believe that state laws should be used to discriminate against women," asserted Marlea Stefanski at the 1968 convention. "I don't think they should use the working hour sections to deprive us of income." But, she added, "I don't think they should work you guys to death, either. So if one segment of this society is going to be governed by the number of hours that they can work, I think this should apply to all workers." Frances Rogers of Ford Local 600 criticized men "who will work until the sweat just comes right off of them and they are just about ready to bleed" for undermining union

[27]Haener to Reuther, Apr. 18, 1969, in Reuther Collection, box 173, folder 2; Bluestone to Haener, June 18, 1963, in ibid., box 172, folder 12; Schlossberg statement in box 118, folder 12.

action against excessive overtime. Although she preferred to see the hours limitation law for women repealed in the interest of gender equality and individual freedom, Rogers said she also would accept an extension of the law to men as an alternative way of addressing the problem of mandatory overtime without reinforcing occupational segregation by sex. "This way we can see that we [all] are benefiting and none of us should have to work these long backbreaking hours."[28]

As UAW women indicated in their arguments, the matter of hours of employment was an issue not just for women but for all union members. The response of men to the problem of compulsory overtime also indicates the potential of the hours issue to subvert the customarily marginal status of women's concerns. Some men criticized mandatory overtime because it prevented all auto workers from fulfilling domestic responsibilities, an argument reminiscent of the one originally made for legal protection of working women. The 1967 collective bargaining convention, for example, resolved that "the end purpose of industrial and economic activity" was "to lift the human family to new heights of economic well-being and to enhance the quality of human life," and condemned employers who regarded workers as "tools of production, to be . . . pushed about at management whim as if they belonged to the corporations and had no separate and prior life of their own." The resolution also contended that "for many of our members, compulsory, excessive overtime is a great personal inconvenience which keeps them from their families and prevents their taking care of matters of personal or family concern."[29]

Male auto unionists, however, never integrated the debate over female labor laws with the debate over excessive and compulsory overtime. Women themselves made such connections in the course of their own discussions, and the text of the Women in the UAW resolution adopted during the 1970 convention asserted that the UAW should "make every effort to have maximum hours of work . . . extended to all workers by legislation on the federal and state level." But a different resolution stating the union's legislative goals and also adopted by the delegates contained no reference to extending to men the protection of maximum hours laws. Not even men who believed that protective labor laws discriminated against women suggested that both sexes would benefit from hours limitation laws. Immediately after Frances Rogers called for the extension to men of hours limitation laws during discussion of the Women in the UAW resolution at the 1968 convention, for example, Doug Griffith of Local 148 declared that such legislation for women "vi-

[28]UAW, *Proceedings, Special UAW Collective Bargaining Convention, April 20–22, 1967,* 103; UAW *Twenty-first Constitutional Convention, May 4–10, 1968,* 130–32.
[29]UAW, *1967 Special Convention Proceedings,* 90.

olates the rights of our women workers" and asked the convention "to go on record in support of equal rights for women on this point of overtime, that women should have the same choice of overtime that our male workers do."[30]

The solutions proposed by union men to the problem of excessive, compulsory overtime also tended to reinforce the marginal status of women in the UAW. The principal strategy advocated was, as Ray Ashby of Local 659 put it, to "make overtime so expensive to management that they themselves will turn it down for us." Specifically, this meant seeking an increase in the legal penalty for overtime from the standard time and a half to double or triple time and negotiating a substantial increase in wage rates. These solutions, while not intrinsically gendered in meaning or implication, sustained the position of those men who, in commenting on the issues raised by excessive hours and mandatory overtime, mourned the passing of the traditional "family wage" and desired its return. One male delegate at the 1967 collective bargaining convention implored union leaders to negotiate a wage increase that would enable men to resist the lure of overtime pay and restore the standard of the family wage. "I remember back in the '30s," he began,

> when the Bureau of Labor Statistics used to print the income of the average American worker. It was the average American worker. It was the individual worker. It was the family head. Today they don't do that anymore. They print the income of the family unit. The old man is working, the old lady is working. Maybe the old man is working overtime. We have forgotten what it is . . . to live on a 40 hour pay.

The delegate clearly understood the "average American worker" and "the family head" to be male. To emphasize the inadequacy of a (male) wage to support a family, he offered the example of "a young fellow that is working 40 hours, he hasn't got a wife that is working, he isn't working any overtime . . . [and] he isn't moonlighting." That man "can't make ends meet." "Now, how can we honestly tell people they should give up their overtime," the delegate contended, "when they can't live on a 40 hour week?" "The fat is there on the corporations," he concluded. "They got it. It is up to us to get out there and get it. And if we don't, shame on us." Although the absence of the 170,000 women then employed in the auto industry from this man's gendered vision of the moral purpose of unionism is especially glaring, the invisibility of women in the language and perspective of male auto unionists was not unusual. During the same convention discussion, Local 980 delegate Robert Richardson

[30]UAW, *1968 Convention Proceedings*, 132; UAW, *1970 Convention Proceedings*, 278.

condemned excessive, compulsory overtime, explaining that "children of
the workers in the shop are disturbed . . . because they do not see their
fathers enough." To be sure, not all male auto unionists in the 1960s still
shared the once pervasive assumption that auto workers were ipso facto
male. Nor did all men who commented on the problem of excessive,
compulsory overtime justify the necessity of higher pay in terms of a defense of the family wage. But neither did anyone during the course of
these discussions counter formulations that rested on a view of women as
reproducers of the labor force, dependent upon men, and secondary
wage earners.[31]

The trend of administrative and judicial interpretations of the relation
of Title VII to state laws rendered moot much of the debate over hours
limitation laws. In August 1969 the EEOC announced that state laws
restricting employment opportunities for women conflicted with Title
VII. Confirming this statement of policy, the Michigan attorney general
in January 1970 ruled specifically that Title VII superseded the still-
contested state statute limiting the number of hours women could be employed. At its biannual convention several months later, the UAW became
the first union in the nation to endorse the ERA. Although the Women's
Department may have appeared to Local 3 activists and Emily Rosdolsky
to have had the international leadership in its hip pocket, Caroline
Davis and Dorothy Haener knew better. Certainly the position on gender
equality that they had advanced since the late 1940s gained adherents in
the 1960s and was firmly embedded in UAW policy by the 1970s. But
the discrepancy between policy and practice remained. Mindful of the
UAW's rhetorical commitment to advance the principle of gender equality, Paul Schrade, director of the union's California region, criticized
what he deemed the too tepid response of GM Department director
Leonard Woodcock to the EEOC's statement in August 1969 regarding
female labor laws. "After many years of struggle," Schrade began, Woodcock "recognizes the problems, yet, suggests only that . . . we *may* want
to file selective cases. . . . Shouldn't we have a more positive position and
strategy from the IEB to break into this area of discrimination against
women?" Asked how UAW leaders responded to the Women's Department's attack on protective labor laws for women, Dorothy Haener admitted that when the union "got publicity because you're far out in front
and so forth and liberal, they liked that, but when this really started
hitting close to home, they tended not to be all that happy with it. . . .
The leadership has never been terribly happy with having these concepts
implemented," Haener added, "especially when it hits them personally."
Undertones of bitterness, frustration, and betrayal color Haener's corre-

[31]UAW, *1967 Special Convention Proceedings*, 99, 65, 87–88.

spondence and memoranda from this period, confirming the retrospective observations about the marginality of the Women's Department which she made in a 1977 interview. Such comments suggest the extent to which the IEB's endorsement of the Women's Department's quest to abolish female labor laws was a matter of convenience rather than an expression of shared concern about the sexual division of labor and woman's place in the plants. The department's decision to seek elimination of state laws did, after all, take the heat off UAW leaders to challenge gender hierarchy and inequality in the workplace more aggressively and to acknowledge that responsibility for these problems lay with the union as much as with employers or government.[32]

The UAW's endorsement of the ERA and the amendment's implicit definition of gender equality was a bittersweet victory not only for the Women's Department and its allies but for women auto workers in general. The UAW in fact made almost no progress toward the goal of voluntary overtime after state laws restricting the number of hours women could be employed were found to be in conflict with Title VII. In this respect, the critics of the Women's Department who had argued that the union's renunciation of the principle of protection embodied in female labor laws contradicted its call for legislation making overtime voluntary for all employees proved both astute and prescient. It is particularly ironic that the Women's Department and union feminists began calling for a national child-care policy only after women workers complained that the persistent scheduling of mandatory overtime wreaked havoc with individual child-care arrangements. In evaluating the UAW's response to the problem of excessive, mandatory overtime, we must not lose sight of the fact that many workers wanted overtime and resisted attempts to eliminate or even curtail it. But the lassitude of UAW leaders in regard to the matter also indicates that ideas about gender and gender equality shape a variety of union policies and affect workers of both sexes. Having decided that gender equality meant that women should be treated like men, UAW leaders did not consider that men could be treated like women and receive legal protection from excessive overtime.[33]

The UAW's response to female labor laws and mandatory overtime rules indicates the complex nature of women's relation to unions.

[32]Freeman, *Politics of Women's Liberation*, 187; Woodcock to All GM Local Unions, Aug. 28, 1969, in Reuther Collection, box 217, folder 10; "Women Hail Jobs Ruling," *Solidarity*, October 1969, 15; Woodcock to GM Locals in Michigan, Mar. 19, 1970, in Woodcock Collection, box 12, folder 9; Schrade to Reuther, Sept. 18, 1969, in Reuther Collection, box 217, folder 10; interview with Dorothy Haener, 64, in "Twentieth-Century Trade Union Woman"; Haener to Reuther, Apr. 18, 1969, in Reuther Collection, box 173, folder 2; Haener to Davis, Sept. 4, 1968, in Reuther Collection, box 172, folder 19.
[33]William Serrin, *The Company and the Union* (New York: Vintage, 1974), 328, 334–37.

Scholars have tended to ascribe the subordinate status of women within organized labor to patriarchy.[34] Patriarchy, however, is a too dichotomous and ahistorical explanation. It cannot account for divisions among women, for instances of men's actions in their class as well as their gender interests, or for change over time. The circumstances and consequences of the UAW's endorsement of equal treatment for women and men in the workplace also demonstrate the significance of gender analysis for labor history, a field that in many respects is as guilty of marginalizing women as are the unions from which they were excluded or to which they belonged.[35] The shifts in union definitions of gender equality, the complex ways these meanings shaped union policies, and the varied effects of these policies on male and female workers suggest the importance of moving beyond standard approaches to women and unions to see gender as a process integral to the history of labor and its institutions.

[34]For an influential example of this approach, see Heidi Hartmann, "Capitalism, Patriarchy and Job Segregation by Sex," *Signs*, 1 (Spring 1976); 137–69.

[35]Joan W. Scott offers an important critique of labor history in "On Language, Gender, and Working-Class History," in *Gender and the Politics of History*, 53–67 (New York: Columbia University Press, 1988).

Contributors

AVA BARON, professor of sociology, Rider College, has written on gender and work in printing, sewing, and the legal profession, and on labor legislation and women's work. Research for her book in progress, "Men's Work and the Woman Question: Work and Gender in the Printing Industry, 1830–1920," has been supported by fellowships from the National Endowment for the Humanities and the Bunting Institute of Radcliffe College.

MARY H. BLEWETT is professor of history at the University of Lowell. She is the author of *Men, Women, and Work: Class, Gender, and Protest in the New England Shoe Industry, 1780–1910* (University of Illinois Press, 1988), which was awarded the Herbert G. Gutman Prize in Social History, the New England Historical Association Book Award, and the Joan Kelly Prize; and *The Last Generation: Work and Life in the Textile Mills of Lowell, Massachusetts* (University of Massachusetts Press, 1990), winner of the Harvey A. Kantor Award of the Oral History Association.

EILEEN BORIS is associate professor of history at Howard University. She is author of *Art and Labor: Ruskin, Morris, and the Craftsman Ideal in America* (Temple University Press, 1986) and co-editor of *Homework: Historical and Contemporary Perspectives on Paid Labor at Home* (University of Illinois Press, 1989) and of *Major Problems in the History of American Workers* (D. C. Heath, 1991). She received fellowships from the Woodrow Wilson Center and the Museum of American History, Smithsonian Institution, to complete her book "In Defense of Motherhood: The Politics of Industrial Homework in the U.S., 1880s–1980s."

DOROTHY SUE COBBLE is assistant professor at the Institute of Management and Labor Relations, Rutgers University. Before receiving her Ph.D.

from Stanford University in 1986, she spent six years as department chair of the Labor Studies Program, City College of San Francisco. She is the author of *Dishing It Out: Waitresses and Their Unions in the Twentieth Century* (University of Illinois Press, 1991)

PATRICIA COOPER is associate professor of history at Drexel University. She is author of *Once a Cigar Maker: Men, Women, and Work Culture in American Cigar Factories, 1900–1919* (University of Illinois Press, 1987) and is currently working on a study of labor and industry in Philadelphia between 1930 and 1955.

ILEEN A. DEVAULT is assistant professor of labor history at the School of Industrial and Labor Relations, Cornell University. She is author of *Sons and Daughters of Labor: Class and Clerical Work in Turn-of-the-Century Pittsburgh* (Cornell University Press, 1990). She is working on a study of strikes that involved both women and men during the early years of the American Federation of Labor.

ELIZABETH FAUE teaches labor and women's history at Wayne State University. From 1988 to 1990 she was Susan B. Anthony Post-Doctoral Fellow in Women's Studies at the University of Rochester. She is the author of *Community of Suffering and Struggle: Women, Men and the Labor Movement in Minneapolis, 1915–1945* (University of North Carolina Press, 1991). She is working on a study of gender, labor, and political culture from 1880 to 1920.

DANA FRANK is assistant professor of American studies at the University of California, Santa Cruz. She is completing a book on the Seattle labor movement and the politics of consumption, 1919–1929, to be published by Cambridge University Press.

NANCY GABIN is associate professor of history at Purdue University, where she teaches women's history and labor history. She is the author of *Feminism in the Labor Movement: Women and the United Auto Workers, 1935–1975* (Cornell University Press, 1990).

JACQUELYN DOWD HALL is director of the Southern Oral History Program and Julia Cherry Spruill Professor of History at the University of North Carolina at Chapel Hill. She is the author of *Revolt against Chivalry: Jessie Daniel Ames and the Women's Campaign against Lynching* (Columbia University Press, 1979) and the co-author of *Like a Family: The Making of a Southern Cotton Mill World* (University of North Carolina Press, 1987).

NANCY HEWITT is associate professor of history at the University of South Florida. Her publications include *Women's Activism and Social Change: Rochester, New York, 1822–1872* (Cornell University Press, 1984) and *Women, Families, and Communities: Readings in American History* (Scott, Foresman/Harper Collins, 1990). She was a founding editor of *Gender & History* and is currently completing a study of Anglo, Black, and Latin working women in Tampa, Florida, 1885–1945.

DOLORES JANIEWSKI, author of *Sisterhood Denied: Race, Gender, and Class in the New South Community* (Temple University Press, 1985), teaches U.S. history at Victoria University of Wellington, New Zealand. She is currently researching gender and race in North Carolina politics, 1865–1930, and also working on the same issues in settler societies.

ANGEL KWOLEK-FOLLAND is assistant professor of history at the University of Kansas. She is writing a book, "The Gender of Business: Men and Women in the Office, 1870–1930," which links the development of corporate organization to ideas about gender.

Index

Working-class culture: and ethnic diversity, 3, 7; and gender, 6–7; and women,
22–23
Working-class feminism, 241, 257
Working-class history: and labor history,
2; production/consumption in, 15.
See also Labor history; New labor
history

Work process. *See* Labor process
Work relations, 169, 174–75, 320. *See
also* Class relations
World War I, 159, 162, 173, 256,
302, 305
World War II, 90, 245; and auto workers, 217, 353–54, 356; and food service
work, 226, 228, 232, 239–40

Library of Congress Cataloging-in-Publication Data

Work engendered : toward a new history of American labor / edited by Ava Baron.
    p.   cm.
    Includes index.
    ISBN 0–8014–2256–6 (cloth : alk. paper).—ISBN 0–8014–9543–1 (paper : alk. paper)
    1. Sexual division of labor—United States—History.   2. Sex discrimination in employ-
ment—United States—History.   3. Sex role in the work environment—United States—History.   I. Baron, Ava.
HD6060.65.U5W67 1991
306.3'615'0973—dc20   91–2281